I0058520

DOS 4.5

File and Volume
Disk Management System

Walland Philip Vrbancic, Jr.

lulu

Copyright © 2022 January 1
Walland Philip Vrbancic, Jr.

All rights reserved.

No part of this publication may be reproduced,
stored in a retrieval system,
or transmitted, in any form or by any means,
electronic, mechanical, photocopying, recording, or otherwise,
without the prior written permission of the author.

DOS 4.5 File and Volume Disk Management System
and this Publication are the
Confidential and Proprietary Intellectual Properties
of
Walland Philip Vrbancic, Jr.

ISBN 978-0-578-38584-6

I am proud to dedicate this Book on the
DOS 4.5 File and Volume Disk Management System
and all of my previous achievements
to my loving Parents Walland and Melba
who continuously nourished my intellectual curiosities
with games, toys, books, education, and unconditional love.

I am truly fortunate for all of the love and support
I have always received from my sister Marile.

I am also grateful to my partner
Carlton D. Wong
who delightfully pretends to understand
what the Hell I am talking about!

Excellence is never an accident!
It is always the result of high intention, sincere effort, and intelligent execution;
it represents the wise choice of many alternatives;
choice, not chance, determines one's destiny.

~~~ Aristotle ~~~

If I have seen further than others it is because I have stood on the shoulders of giants.

~~~ Isaac Newton ~~~

Disclaimer of All Liability

Do not use the DOS 4.5 File and Volume Disk Management System software or this Book for any mission-critical applications or for any purpose in which a software error or a software failure could cause you financial or material loss. The DOS 4.5 File and Volume Disk Management System software and this Book are designed to enhance your Apple][computing experience, but they may contain design flaws that could inhibit the proper operation of your computer or they may result in the loss of recorded data on any storage device connected to your computer. You assume all risks associated with the operation of your computer and the potential loss of your recorded data when using the DOS 4.5 File and Volume Disk Management System software or this Book. If these terms are not acceptable to you, please do not use the DOS 4.5 File and Volume Disk Management System software or this Book.

Walland Philip Vrbancic, Jr., the administrator of www.applecored.net, makes no warranties either expressed or implied with respect to the DOS 4.5 File and Volume Disk Management System software or with respect to this Book, its quality, performance, or fitness for any particular purpose. Any risk of incidental or consequential damages resulting from the use of the DOS 4.5 File and Volume Disk Management System software or the use of information contained in this Book shall be assumed by you, the User. In no event shall Walland Philip Vrbancic, Jr., or www.applecored.net be liable for any direct, indirect, incidental, or consequential damages resulting from any defect, deficiency, or neglect in the DOS 4.5 File and Volume Disk Management System software or in this Book.

While all possible attempts have been made to ensure that the information contained within this publication is complete and accurate, the author shall have no liability or responsibility for any errors or omissions, or for any damages or the loss of recorded data resulting from the use of the information, circuit diagrams, and example software programs contained herein. The author reserves the right to implement any changes and/or any improvements to the DOS 4.5 File and Volume Disk Management System software or to the contents of this publication at any time and without any prior notice to you, the User, or to the general Apple][community.

Apple and all Apple hardware and software brand names are the trademarks of Apple Computer, Inc., registered in the United States of America and in other countries.
All other brand names and trademarks are the property of their respective owners.

Preface

When Brian Wiser and Bill Martens discovered my original DOS 4.1 software and documentation at www.applecored.net in 2017, they immediately contacted me and wanted Apple Pugetsound Program Library Exchange (*Call-A.P.P.L.E.*) to publish my DOS 4.1 Manual. Ha! If only this would have happened back in 1982. That's when my co-worker, Randy at Rockwell, and I were actively reading many publications featuring Apple software and hardware, and *Call-A.P.P.L.E.* was one of our favorite publications. Needless to say, to be published by any of those early computer journals would have been crazy exciting at that time, and it would have certainly been a cherished memory for a lifetime. I actually was very close to completing all of the capabilities I wanted in DOS 4.1 when I agreed to have *Call-A.P.P.L.E.* publish the DOS 4.1 Manual for Build 45. I also provided *Call-A.P.P.L.E.* with demo diskette images for both DOS 4.1L and DOS 4.1H. A month or so after Build 45 was published and available for purchase, I completed DOS 4.1 with Build 46. Only the DOS 4.1 Build 46 software and documentation in PDF form are available at www.applecored.net.

I remember telling Wiser and Martens that I wanted both versions of DOS 4.1 to provide the user with virtually the same computing experience, albeit the HELP command is found only in DOS 4.1H. This desire proved to be somewhat troublesome in that I was limited in memory for DOS 4.1L, whereas I had ample memory for DOS 4.1H. Actually, it was the unused memory in DOS 4.1H that was the impetus to introduce the HELP command in the first place. At the onset of our negotiations, I warned Wiser and Martens that I could not stop creating more functionality in DOS 4.1, but they were rather insistent on publishing the DOS 4.1 Manual for the Apple][community in its current stage of development. In 2021 I had the opportunity to republish the DOS 4.1 Manual as a book in the format that I originally intended. This publication is Build 46.

My next area of exploration for an Apple DOS was an attempt to port DOS 4.1H to Auxiliary memory. I was absolutely successful, I might add, but I could not successfully design an interface between *Lisa* (my most favorite 65C02 assembler) and this new DOS I created to reside in Auxiliary memory. Over the course of several months of significant effort, I could not realize a viable solution that would be elegant, save memory, and provide the roadmap for interfacing other utilities and tools to this unique DOS. But this effort was certainly not wasted! I documented what I had learned about Main and Auxiliary memory management and I moved forward to other areas of exploration.

I had already decided to use DOS 4.1H as my initial model for DOS 4.3. Yes, DOS 4.3 does retain the "H" designation for "High" memory. However, I did not want to develop a companion "Low" memory DOS version in parallel, so I did **not** develop a DOS 4.3L. I simply refer to this new DOS as DOS 4.3. The question then became, can *Lisa* be ported to and function in Auxiliary memory? The answer to that question turns out to be a resounding "*Yes!*" With DOS 4.3 in the memory of the Language Card partition in Main memory and *Lisa* in the memory of the Language Card partition in Auxiliary memory, the user has access to virtually all of Main memory below `0xBE00` for source code, object code, and the complete symbol list. I saw this exciting configuration as the path to many new and potential possibilities.

Now, if I can relocate *Lisa* to Auxiliary memory, what about doing the same for *Big Mac*? I have to say that that challenge was a bit uneventful because relocating *Big Mac* to the memory of the Language Card partition in Auxiliary memory was even easier to accomplish. My main focus in *Big Mac* was to align *Sourceror* and *Big Mac* in terms of their *SWEET16* sourcing and assembling capabilities, though I do not believe *Big Mac* has ever been able to assemble all of its own *SWEET16* opcodes. This task turned out to be an extraordinarily massive undertaking since I wanted *Sourceror* and *Big Mac* to disassemble/assemble my personal version of the *SWEET16* opcodes. I realized that *Big Mac* could not even assemble its own unique *SWEET16* `EVAL` opcode because the `EVAL` opcode did not even exist. This tells me that Mr. Bredon probably could not even use *Big Mac* to assemble his own *Big Mac* source code unless he possibly hardcoded these undefined opcodes as `byt` statements. I have to confess that there still remain two *SWEET16* branches in my disassembled (and verified) *Big Mac* source code that are absolutely wrong, and I do not know their solution to this day. They occur at memory addresses `0xD2C1` and `0xD2DF`. Furthermore, I have yet to discover how to force their execution in order to analyze the resulting behavior in *Big Mac*. I suspect these particular code sequences may be part of `MACRO` handling, something I have had no reason to use. After all is said and done, *Big Mac* and DOS 4.3 complemented each other beautifully.

While moving past DOS 4.3 to begin the development of the DOS 4.5 File and Volume Disk Management System, I discovered even more layers of File Manager functionality that I could code so much more effectively. DOS 4.3 certainly contains all the necessary solutions to properly close files and flush volumes when the DOS `CLOSE` command is issued from within an Applesoft program. Yet, the code resolutions found in DOS 4.3 still do not exhaust my list of all the additional capabilities I wanted in my final release of an Apple][DOS. All of the capabilities contained in DOS 4.5 are detailed in Section I.2.

I know the user will discover many, if not all of the fascinating developments I have included in the DOS 4.5 File and Volume Disk Management System. The user will be left wondering how he or she was able to accomplished anything useful in a timely fashion without having had those developments in any other version of a previous Apple][Disk Operating System. I would take that as my greatest compliment.

Enjoy the ride!

Table of Contents

This page intentionally left blank.

List of Figures

List of Tables

DOS 4.5 File and Volume Disk Management System

I. Designing Another New DOS

This publication describes the process and the products I created when I decided to design and program another enhanced Disk Operating System (DOS) for my Apple //e. Wherever I am able, I have included schematic diagrams, code samples, equations, figures, tables, and representative screen shots to help explain what I have created and many of the reasons why I did so. As in my previous designs of an Apple][DOS, i.e. DOS 4.1 and DOS 4.3, this has been an incredible journey for me. With DOS 4.5 I have again re-imagined that time when I mostly lived, breathed, and worked on Apple][computers, hardware, and software development continuously for a good period of my life many, many years ago.

1. Introduction

I have been an avid Apple][computer enthusiast, hobbyist, and professional software programmer since 1983 when I became the proud owner of an Apple][+ computer. Besides the Apple][+ computer, my initial system included an Apple][Language Card, an Apple Disk][Drive with a Disk][Interface Card, an Amdek color monitor, and an Epson MX100 printer with a Grappler+ Printer Interface card. During those early years I designed and built my own Apple][peripheral slot cards, I made electrical and hardware modifications to my Apple][+ motherboard and keyboard, and I wrote a substantial number of software programs initially using Applesoft BASIC (Applesoft hereafter) and then a few months later, I wrote software in 6502 assembly language. I soon acquired a Videx UltraTerm video display card and a Microsoft Z80 Softcard. With the Z80 Softcard I was able to write complex Fortran programs that analyzed tomographic reconstructions of the human spinal column. A year or so later I added the Southern California Research Group quikLoader and PROmGRAMER cards to my system, a Johnathon Freeman Designs (JFD) Parallel Printer Buffer, and an Axlon RAM Disk 320 with its interface card.

I used C language in my professional programming career for the design and development of ultra-high-speed data collection systems for tactical radar and sensor development. Now that I am retired from the aerospace industry, I have always wanted to dig into, tear apart, and learn the intricacies of the last available version of DOS 3.3 for the Apple][series of computers. I thought the last DOS 3.3 version was published on August 25, 1980. Then I recently came across another DOS 3.3 version published years later on January 1, 1983. That later DOS contains even more patches for the DOS APPEND command and for Apple //e initialization. What I learned from the 1980 publication flabbergasted me: the software is exciting in its originality and concept vis-à-vis it was released just after the publication of Integer BASIC. However, I found the software to be somewhat juvenile in its structure and in its implementation. Apparently, very little attention was given to software design and review. It appeared to me that Apple made a strong push to release *something or anything* to consumers and vendors in order to begin marketing software products on diskettes and hardware products to read and write those diskettes. And history does reveal that Apple Computer did outsource DOS and contracted for it to be delivered within thirty-five days for $13,000 in April, 1978. Paul Laughton at Shepardson Microsystems wrote Apple's initial disk operating system using Hollerith cards, a card reader/writer, and a minicomputer.

Now that I have the time and the continuing curiosity to delve into Apple][DOS, I have the unique opportunity to create my own version of DOS that contains the power and the flexibility I always thought DOS ought to and could have. I call this version of Apple][DOS, the DOS 4.5 File and Volume Disk Management System, and it requires an Apple][that contains memory in the Language Card partition for its complete operation. This publication describes my fifth build of DOS 4.5. What a ride I have been on! Why? To see what I could do for this brilliant machine and its equally magnificent architecture! I hope that you find my journey into DOS 4.5 as fascinating as I found developing it.

2. Overview of the Improvements and Enhancements in DOS 4.5

I know there are a great many ProDOS users in the global Apple][community, but I never became at all interested in ProDOS. The work I did at Hughes Aircraft in the mid 1980's consisted of using assembly language for programming an operating system executive and hardware interface driver routines on Gould SEL 2780, 6780, and 9780 mainframe computers. These computers hosted a proprietary operating system that allowed our team to simulate the hardware of a Radar Digital Processor (RDP) traveling above the earth's surface in virtually real time. In order to accomplish that goal and simulate real time navigation, the computer's file system was essentially flat: every software developer had their own directory, and these user directories contained no subdirectories. I was very comfortable with the idea of a flat file system as it was very much like Apple's DOS 3.3. I was simply not comfortable with a slew of subdirectories exemplified by Apple's ProDOS. My thought was always "How does one recall the path to follow in order to find anything?" With the advent of the Macintosh computer and later when I became familiar with the UNIX file system, my subdirectory fears vanished and I cannot imagine a modern computer file system without subdirectories. However, I still remain passionate about Apple][DOS and I leave ProDOS to those who are comfortable with that operating system architecture. Though what I have seen of ProDOS recently, I believe it could definitely use a facelift, seriously. I also believe that ProDOS is far better suited on a machine with a 16-bit microprocessor much like that found in the Apple //GS.

I am sure many are curious and want to know what is new and different in DOS 4.5, and what makes this version of the DOS File and Volume Disk Management System so special. Looking back over my previous publications of DOS 4.1 and DOS 4.3, I realized that I should have included this enhancement information with every version and for each software build, if only for historical reasons. Like, which version and build did I solve the Track 0x00 utilization quest? Which version and build did I start labeling volumes? Which version and build did I solve the Disk Full logic error? Taken all together, I have done an incredible amount of research, writing, and software development to reach the level of perfection that is contained in DOS 4.5 with Build 5. And, to say the least, I have done an incredible amount of unit testing for each and every logical function under normal and abnormal (i.e. error) conditions. However small the list of improvements and enhancements unique to DOS 4.5 may seem, I have spent countless hours developing and testing those improvements and enhancements alone and in concert with the overall DOS 4.5 command repertoire and its system functional capabilities.

Module	Description of Improvement or Enhancement
CMD1	Move CMDINDX to keyboard variables and clear keyboard variables before, not after parsing a new DOS command. No need to range check SV and USER parameters.
CMD2	Modified TS to read sector data into caller's specified buffer. Added ENTRMON routine that calls INITPTRS before entering RAM Monitor. Removed COPYVALS after moving CD to File Manager with CDHNDLR. Moved DOADRINC to CMD2.
CMD3	Rewrote GREP so that it no longer requires a character string marker for a multiple-word character string search, and less code was required (Aha! Moment)
CMD4	FMDRVR now copies VALSPHAS to FMPHASE, CONFIG is set to default if R keyword is included, PHASE is set to default if R keyword is included, MAXFILES is set to default if R keyword is included, SAVALRD writes CONFIG, PHASE, and MAXFILES values into the Value Read Buffer if DOS is in the RUN mode, SV writes its value into the Value Read Buffer if DOS is in the RUN mode (Aha! Moment), CD uses File Manager to read VTOC for CONFIG value, PRTSDV now prints volume lock status.
MNGR1	External File Manager entry uses FILALC/NOFILALC values to set KEYWORD1 for file allocation control, now FMTBLJMP uses memory placement of File Manager routines to selectively copy FM Context Block SDV values to FMWORK since Byte Offset and Range Length are overloaded values in FMWORK.
MNGR2	TOUCH only copies VALSCNFG to DOSCONFG if R keyword is included to save the DOS configuration, DELETE handler rewritten and its logic reordered, CATALOG handler does not show build information if DOSVRSN < 0x33 or DOSBUILD = 0, FREESECT now clears SECBTMAP before calling RORBITMP, not after. Added CDHNDLR.
MNGR3	ALLOCSEC modified to perform up to 4 scans of the VTOC bitmap, ALLOCNTR moved to CMDVALS.
DATA1	Moved CMDUSER before CMDHELP, set KWRANGEH for drive to 81.
BUFR1	Moved CMDINDX after MONVAL in keyword variables and put ALLOCNTR after CMDLNIDX where CMDINDX was, removed TRKNUMBR from FMWORK, set VALRDBUF to 8 bytes. File buffer is now 0x0245 bytes in size. Added 7-byte SCRCHTBL table (Aha! Moment) and adjusted SPAREBUF size.
BUFR2	Removed WATRKNUM in WORKAREA (parallel variable to TRKNUMBR).
RWTS1	If slot number index to SCRCHTBL is zero, RWTS scratchpad RAM locations for track and phase are cleared for drives 1 and 2, and calls BLDNIBL when RWTS is called the first time for that slot number (Aha! Moment). BLDNIBL dynamically builds RDNIBL and WRNIBL tables in same page with NBUF2.
RWTS2	PHASE value better managed and DISKFMT now initially formats track 0x00, reduces SYNCNT, then formats entire volume starting with track 0x00.
MNGEXVAL	Modified this function to return the Y-reg incremented twice when reading/writing 16-bit values and once when read/writing 8-bit values found in the CMDVALS and FMWORK Data structures. Removed access to the INITVALS Data structure.
MNGEXUSR	Removed the call to CLRVALS from this function. The call to CLRVALS is now properly made by DOSINIT just prior to the COLDSTRT entry point.
HELP	Any key press other than ESC, RTN, or arrow keys select the display of the DOS 4.5 Management screen.
USER	The USER handler now resides in Main memory, its call to the USER address returns to Main memory, and finally USER re-enables RAM memory in the Language Card partition to complete its processing.

Table I.2.1. Major Improvements and Enhancements to DOS 4.5

DOS 4.5 is designed to reside either in Main memory or in the memory of the Language Card partition. The version of DOS 4.5 that resides fully in Main memory is DOS 4.5L, and its executable code begins at 0x9F00, its variables and data buffers begin at 0x9A8A, and its two file buffers begin at 0x9600 where HIMEM is set, the very same memory location as in DOS 3.3. In comparison, DOS 4.1 sets HIMEM to 0x9625 when MAXFILES is set to three file buffers. Thus, the additional code that comprises DOS 4.5L is essentially the size of one file buffer. Unlike DOS 3.3 or DOS 4.1L, DOS 4.5L is a single, continuous object code image that is 0x2100 bytes in size. On the other hand, the version of DOS 4.5 that resides in the memory of the Language Card partition is DOS 4.5H, and it occupies both banks of memory from `0xD000` to `0xDFFF` and the remaining memory of the partition from `0xE000` to `0xF7FF`. The Apple][user has complete freedom to use all of Main memory below `0xBE00` where `HIMEM` is set.

The foundation for DOS 4.5 is DOS 4.3H which includes the `HELP` command. In order to better appreciate all of the improvements and the enhancements I have added to DOS 4.5, I have tabulated those changes according to each software module as shown in Table I.2.1. Please realize that nothing in DOS 4.3 was removed in order to provide the code space required by all of these improvements and enhancements in DOS 4.5. I simply spent a sizable amount of time and effort re-working certain modules to yield the same or better functionality in far less code space. I can truthfully say that I experienced several Aha! Moments that certainly assisted in making these improvements and enhancements to DOS 4.5 possible.

3. DOS 4.5 Software Development Strategies

Let's begin with some software design and development strategies. In order to design reliable and powerful software for a particular machine or platform, one must understand the complete architecture of that machine. I believe this design approach is fully applicable even to the Apple][computer: either code or data occupies fixed addressable memory where some defined memory locations are reserved for the stack, text, graphics, control, and peripheral slot cards. Code is further restricted in the Apple][by the rather limited 6502-microprocessor Instruction Set. My obvious goal strategy is to design software in such a way as to create the most functionality using the least amount of code and data space. I believe this methodology yields the greatest range of code effectiveness.

I highly recommend obtaining and referring to a number of reference publications for the Apple][hardware. I have used the Apple][*Reference Manual*, the Apple //e *Reference Manual*, the Apple //e *Technical Reference Manual*, the Apple][*The DOS Manual* Disk Operating System, *Beneath Apple DOS* by Don Worth and Pieter Lechner, *Understanding the Apple][* by Jim Sather, and *What's Where in the APPLE A Complete Guide to the Apple Computer* by William F. Luebbert to obtain much of my understanding in how the Apple][hardware functions. I have also referred to the *APPLESOFT][* manual to obtain my understanding of Apple's Applesoft programming language. It is an absolutely required reference manual to have in order to learn that BASIC programming language. These references provides the reader a fairly complete understanding of the architecture of the Apple][computer as well as how to create software programs using the Applesoft language. No reference manual is perfect and people do make mistakes, however these manuals contain very few errors.

In order to study how other people have approached the hardware architecture of the Apple][in creating their software applications, it is necessary to obtain their source code or generated source code from their object code, the code that actually executes from within the Apple][memory. Rarely have I ever found published source code. Glen Bredon designed *Sourceror* as a subsidiary tool to his assembler *Big Mac* that creates *Big Mac* source code files from assembly language object code files. *Big Mac* can also save source code as text files so that *Big Mac* source code can be migrated to other assemblers like *Lisa*.

For my assembly language programming I use Gerard Putter's application Virtual][, Version 9.3, to create my software applications, and that is the platform I use to perform my initial, though simulated software testing. Once I am satisfied with a software program or utility operating within the Virtual][

environment, I transfer the volume image containing that software program or utility to an Enhanced Apple //e. I have found some discrepancies between Virtual][and my Enhanced Apple //e particularly when I am enabling memory in the Language Card partition: two successive *writes* to memory address 0xC083 does **not** write enable Bank 2 in the Language Card partition in my Enhanced Apple //e as it does in Virtual][. Two successive *reads* of memory address 0xC083 function the same in both my Enhanced Apple //e and in Virtual][to enable Bank 2 memory. I have brought this to the attention of Mr. Putter. Also, Main memory is not initialized at power-up in quite the same way in my Enhanced Apple //e as it is in Virtual][. I believe DOS 3.3 always assumes that an Apple][powers up with all bytes in page-zero memory set to 0xFF. Virtual][also makes this same assumption. I know I have been caught unaware that all bytes in Auxiliary page-zero memory are not always set to 0xFF at power-up. Therefore, I have included a call to SETNORM during Boot Stage 2 to ensure that page-zero memory location 0x32 is, indeed, set to 0xFF. I have used AUXMOVE to manually *stash* some ProDOS code in Auxiliary memory from within Virtual][. The code disappears (becomes overwritten) when I then boot into DOS 4.5. This does not happen in the Enhanced Apple //e: the ProDOS code or any stashed code can still be safely found in Auxiliary memory even after a DOS reboot. Always, always, always make final tests using **real** hardware.

Memory Page	Description	Description
0x00	Page-zero variables, pointers, routines, and special addressing modes	
0x01	Stack for the 6502-microprocessor	
0x02	INPUT buffer, Applesoft interpretation buffer	
0x03	User buffer, DOS vectors and routines	
0x04-0x07	Text or LORES graphics Page 1	
0x08-0x0B	Applesoft program start, Text or LORES graphics Page 2, or available for software	
0x0C-0x1F	Available for software	
0x20-0x3F	HIRES graphics Page 1, or available for software	
0x40-0x5F	HIRES graphics Page 2, or available for software	
0x60-0xBF	Available for software	
0xC0	System Soft Switches	
0xC1-0xC7	Peripheral-card ROM memory for slots 1-7, or CX ROM	
0xC8-0xCF	Peripheral-card expansion ROM memory for slots 1-7, or CX ROM	
0xD0-0xDF	Bank 2, ROM Applesoft Interpreter routines	Bank 1
0xE0-0xF7	ROM Applesoft Interpreter routines	
0xF8-0xFF	ROM Monitor routines	

Table I.3.1. Apple][Memory Utilization

Before beginning any discussion of a complicated subject like a file and volume disk management system for the Apple][, it is usually easier to understand such a system if each component of that system is shown as part of a Big Picture. That Big Picture is shown in the following three tables, Tables I.3.1, I.3.2, and I.3.3. Though certainly not to any particular scale, Table I.3.1 shows how memory is utilized in the Apple][and where the basic Apple][system hardware and software components can be found in

Main memory and in the memory of the Language Card partition which is shown in the more shaded bottom lines in each of these three tables. The basic components shown in Table I.3.1 are the 6502-microprocessor memory requirements, the DOS vectors and routines, text and LORES graphic pages, HIRES graphic pages, system Soft Switches, peripheral-card and CX ROM memory, where the ROM Applesoft interpreter is found, and where the ROM Monitor resides. If any of the components shown in Table I.3.1 are unfamiliar, it would be to your advantage now to locate and study one or more of the above referenced publications to refresh and increase your understanding of that component. Even the Apple][*Reference Manual* that came with my Apple][+ computer contains invaluable information applicable to the entire family of Apple][computers. I even own a few *SAMS* Publications that have provided me with enhanced understanding of many of the components shown in Table I.3.1.

Memory Page	Description	Description
0x00-0x03	System, 6502-microprocessor memory utilization	
0x04-0x07	Text Page 1	
0x08-0x95	Available for software	
0x96-0x99	DOS 4.5L HIMEM, DOS 4.5L file buffers	
0x9A-0x9E	DOS 4.5L working variables, workarea buffer, VTOC and catalog buffers, nibble buffers	
0x9F-0xBE	DOS 4.5L Command and File Manager, RWTS, and all other software routines	
0xBF	DOS 4.5L bootstrap routines	
0xC0	System Soft Switches	
0xC1-0xCF	Peripheral-card ROM memory for slots, CX ROM	
0xD0-0xDF	Bank 2 ROM routines	Bank 1
0xE0-0xF7	ROM routines	
0xF8-0xFF	ROM Monitor routines	

Table I.3.2. Apple][Memory Utilization with DOS 4.5L Installed

Memory Page	Description	Description
0x00-0x03	System, 6502-microprocessor memory utilization	
0x04-0x07	Text Page 1	
0x08-0xBD	Available for software	
0xBE-0xBF	DOS 4.5H HIMEM, DOS 4.5H Language Card partition software interface, DOS 4.5H bootstrap routines	
0xC0	System Soft Switches	
0xC1-0xCF	Peripheral-card ROM memory for slots, CX ROM	
0xD0-0xDF	RAM Bank 2, DOS 4.5H Command and File Managers	RAM Bank 1, DOS RWTS
0xE0-0xE6	RAM DOS 4.5H Command and File Managers	
0xE7-0xEC	RAM DOS 4.5H working variables and workarea buffer	
0xED-0xF7	RAM DOS 4.5H file buffers	
0xF8-0xFF	RAM Monitor routines	

Table I.3.3. Apple][Memory Utilization with DOS 4.5H Installed

Table I.3.2 is similar to Table I.3.1 except that the 6502-microprocessor and ROM components have been diminished from view in lieu of showing visually where DOS 4.5L and its components are placed in memory. DOS 4.5L is typically configured to have two file buffers, and those buffers begin at 0x9600 and end at 0x9A89 in memory. From 0x9A8A to 0x9EFF is where the working variables and workarea buffer, the VTOC and catalog buffers, and the nibble buffers, the write translate, and the read translate tables are defined. The DOS 4.5L software routines reside in the continuous span of memory from 0x9F00 to 0xBFFF.

Table I.3.3 is also similar to Table I.3.1 and it, like Table I.3.2, shows visually where DOS 4.5H and its components are placed in memory. In order to manage the DOS 4.5H routines located in the memory of both banks in the Language Card partition, a set of software interface routines that control the utilization of memory in the Language Card partition is located in Page 0xBE. Page 0xBF contains the DOS bootstrap routines which are similar in nature to those same routines found in DOS 4.5L.

The following sections discuss the utilization of Apple][memory in great detail. It may be helpful to occasionally refer to Tables I.3.1 to I.3.3 in order to fully understand how that memory utilization relates to the entire hardware and software management of the Apple][computer by either version of the DOS 4.5 File and Volume Disk Management System. The Apple][computer is truly a brilliantly designed machine and it has an equally magnificent architecture. I hope you find my presentation of the Apple][computer vis-à-vis DOS 4.5 interesting, enlightening, and useful in view of your own hardware and software experiences with this delightful machine.

4. Page-Zero Utilization

The Instruction Set for the 6502-microprocessor (as well as the 65C02-microprocessor) includes certain microprocessor instructions that utilize variables located in the first 256 bytes, or page, of addressable memory, that is, locations 0x0000 to 0x00FF. I designate this area of memory to be *page-zero*.

When Steve Wozniak designed the Apple ROM Monitor (a collection of low-level software routines), he allocated a number of page-zero locations for its variables and pointers. Similarly, Applesoft, DOS, and virtually all other assembly language programs use page-zero locations in order to utilize those specific instructions. The 6502-microprocessor contains an accumulator called the A-register and two index registers called the X-register and the Y-register. Page-zero instructions using these registers include load and store instructions, indexed load and store instructions, indexed indirect addressing instructions using the X-register, and indirect indexed addressing instructions using the Y-register. Page-zero wraparound occurs with indexed and indexed indirect addressing instructions using the X-register and indexed addressing instructions of the X-register using the Y-register, but page-zero wraparound does **not** occur with indirect indexed addressing instructions using the Y-register. Yes, initially, addressing modes can certainly be a little bit confusing.

When developing a new assembly language program, it is critical to select page-zero locations that do not conflict with the Apple ROM Monitor, Applesoft, or DOS depending on whether those ROM applications and the applications that reside in the memory of the Language Card partition are important to the new program. Knowing which page-zero locations are used by or critical to ROM and resident applications can greatly simplify the selection of unused or available page-zero locations. Because DOS 3.3 supports Integer BASIC, a few page-zero locations are used to process that file type. DOS 4.5 also uses those same page-zero locations for processing the Applesoft CHAIN command, for example, and many other DOS command enhancements. There are definitely obvious page-zero locations that cannot be used except for how they were intended, like the horizontal and vertical cursor locations CH and CV, respectively. Then, there are less obvious, rather dubious page-zero locations from 0x00 to 0x1F that are used by some Applesoft commands. These page-zero locations are fair game for new programs that do not use the Applesoft interpreter or Steve Wozniak's *SWEET16* interpreter. Figure I.4.1 shows all of the used and the unused page-zero locations, and the Key defines those applications that use those particular locations according to my references and the best of my ability to decipher the ROM routines that make use of page-zero memory. The shaded areas in Figure I.4.1 are unused page-zero locations that are most likely not used by the Apple //e Monitor or Applesoft, so they are more than likely the better page-zero locations to select. Table I.4.1 summarizes all of the available page-zero locations that are not utilized by the ROM routines and by DOS 4.5 shown in Figure I.4.1. Keep in mind that indirect indexed addressing mode instructions using the Y-register **do** require a page-zero byte-pair, so it is even more critical that neither address byte is clobbered by software external to a new assembly language program.

0x	0	1	2	3	4	5	6	7	8	9	A	B	C	D	E	F
00	1234	134	34	34	34	4					4	4	4	4	4	4
10	4	4	4	4	4	4	4	4	4	4	4	4	4	24	2	3
20	134	134	134	134	1346	134	1456	1456	1346	1346	13456	13456	1456	1456	123456	123456
30	14	12	134	1246	123	1236	136	136	136	136	123	123	12345	12345	123456	123456
40	156	156	1236	1236	1236	1	1	1	1	1	56	56	6	6	13	13
50	346	346	4	4	4	4	24	24	24	24	46	6	6	6	4	4
60	4	4	4	4	4	4	4	46	46	46	46	46	46	346	346	346
70	346	4	4	346	346	4	46	4	4	4	4	4	4	4	4	4
80	4	4	4	4	4	4	4	4	4	4	4	4	4	4	4	4
90	4	4	4	4	34	34	4	4	4	4	4	34	34	4	4	4
A0	4	4	4	4	4	4	4	4	4	4	4	4	4	4	4	46
B0	46	4	4	4	4	4	4	4	4	4	4	4	4	4	4	4
C0	4	4	4	4	4	4	4	4	4	4	4	4	4			
D0	4	4	4	4	4	4	46		46	6	4	4	4	4	4	4
E0	4	4	4		4	4	4	4	34	34	4					
F0	4	4	4	14	14	4	4	4	4	4						34

Figure I.4.1. Page-Zero Memory Utilization

Key

1 – used by the ROM Monitor
2 – used by the Mini Assembler
3 – used by the Apple //e CX ROM

4 – used by Applesoft
5 – used by RWTS
6 – used by DOS 4.5

Start	End	Description
0x06	0x09	4 bytes free
0xCE	0xCF	2 bytes free
0xD7	0xD7	1 byte free
0xE3	0xE3	1 byte free
0xEB	0xEF	5 bytes free
0xFA	0xFE	5 bytes free

Table I.4.1. Available Page-Zero Locations Summary

Tables I.4.2 and I.4.3 list all of the page-zero locations utilized by DOS 4.5 and defined in the DOS 4.5 source code file INCL.L. There are certainly common page-zero locations that all software routines can use as temporary variables and pointers. The 6502-microprocessor is not time-shared and there is no context switching between routines, so if a routine uses some common page-zero locations, that routine should complete all calculations and processing using those locations and not expect to find those same results sometime later. Examples of common page-zero locations would be A1L/A1H at 0x3C/0x3D, A2L/A2H at 0x3E/0x3F, A3L/A3H at 0x40/0x41, A4L/A4H at 0x42/0x43, OPRND at 0x44 and 0x45, and the first three bytes of DSCTMP at 0x9D:0x9F. As is shown in Tables I.4.2 and I.4.3, all of these page-zero locations are defined in the DOS 4.5 file INCL.L. Using these page-zero locations to move or copy data would be safe and not interfere with the ROM Monitor or Applesoft processing. Actually, several ROM Monitor routines require that some of these page-zero locations just mentioned contain your data before using those routines. The ROM Monitor routine MOVE at 0xFE2C is one such example that uses A1L/A1H and A2L/A2H to move data in memory. It is really up to the user to confirm and verify that the selected page-zero memory locations do not interfere with other routines external to and required by any new software developed by a user.

Address	Parameter	Description
0x24	CH	horizontal cursor location
0x25	CV	vertical cursor location
0x26	BUFRADRZ	ROM firmware boot data field buffer address
0x26	TEMPZ	RWTS temporary 8-bit variable
0x27	TEMP2Z	RWTS temporary 8-bit variable
0x28	BASEZ	text screen line address
0x2A	ASPTRSAV	DOS CHAIN array descriptor addresses
0x2A	CURTRKZ	RWTS requested track
0x2B	SLOT16Z	boot slot * 16
0x2C	DRVFLAG	RWTS data-changing drive flag
0x2C	ADRDATMK	RWTS address/data mark
0x2C	ADRFIELD	RWTS sector address field array
0x2D	SECFNDZ	RWTS sector address field sector found
0x2E	TRKFNDZ	RWTS sector address field track found
0x2F	VOLFNDZ	RWTS sector address field volume found

Table I.4.2. Page-Zero Utilization in DOS 4.5 – Part 1

Address	Parameter	Description
0x32	INVFLG	text screen inverse/normal flag
0x33	PROMPT	text screen prompt character
0x34	PHASE	RWTS requested phase number
0x35	PAGECNT	boot/initialization DOS image page count
0x35	SAVXYREG	save X-reg or Y-reg 8-bit variable
0x35	SYNCNT	RWTS synchronization byte count
0x36	CSWL	output device handler address
0x38	KSWL	input device handler address
0x3C	ROMTEMPZ	ROM firmware boot temporary 8-bit variable
0x3C	MOTORTIM	RWTS motor on-time 16-bit count
0x3C	A1	general purpose temporary 16-bit variable
0x3D	ROMSECTR	ROM firmware boot requested sector
0x3E	BUFADR2Z	RWTS data field buffer address
0x3E	ODDBITSZ	RWTS temporary 8-bit variable
0x3E	A2	general purpose temporary 16-bit variable
0x3F	SECTORZ	RWTS address field sector
0x40	ROMDATA	ROM firmware boot address field track found
0x40	FILEBUFZ	file context block parameter buffer address
0x40	TRACKZ	RWTS address field track
0x41	ROMTRACK	ROM firmware boot requested track
0x41	VOLUMEZ	RWTS address field volume
0x42	A4	general purpose temporary 16-bit variable
0x42	BUFADRZ	general purpose sector data buffer address
0x44	DIRINDX	VTOC and TSL data index
0x4A	IOBADR	RWTS IOCB buffer address
0x4C	DOSPTR	DOS general purpose pointer address
0x50	LINNUM	Applesoft line number 16-bit variable
0x5A	DOSTEMP1	DOS general purpose 8-bit variable
0x5B	DOSTEMP2	DOS general purpose 8-bit variable
0x5C	DOSBUFR	DOS general purpose 16-bit variable/address
0x67	ASPGMST	Applesoft program start address
0x69	ASVARS	Applesoft simple variables pointer
0x6B	ASARYS	Applesoft array pointer
0x6D	ARYEND	Applesoft end of array pointer
0x6F	ASSTRS	Applesoft end of character string storage pointer
0x73	ASHIMEM	Applesoft HIMEM address
0x76	ASRUN	Applesoft RUN flag
0x9D	DSCTMP	Applesoft temporary character string descriptor data
0xAF	ASPEND	Applesoft end of program address
0xD6	PROTECT	Applesoft program write-protect 8-bit flag
0xD8	ASONERR	Applesoft ONERR 8-bit error flag
0xD9	RKEYWORD	DOS R keyword 8-bit variable

Table I.4.3. Page-Zero Utilization in DOS 4.5 – Part 2

5. DOS 4.5 VTOC Structure

How I remember agonizing over how best to implement date and time stamping of disk volumes and their files! Preferably, I only wanted to update a date and time stamp when either the Volume Table Of Contents (VTOC) of a disk volume or a file in a disk volume has changed. I also wanted to date and time stamp a disk volume or disk image when that volume or image is first created or initialized. However, creating or updating a date and time stamp is only half of the task: the date and time stamp needs to be displayed in an appropriate format for an appropriate reason. So, when the contents of a volume's Catalog directory is displayed, the file's date and time stamp needs to be displayed along with its filename, its file type, and its file size. Since the VTOC is basically the heart of the disk volume, I believe it is best to begin the VTOC discussion starting with the DOS 3.3 implementation of the VTOC and show its organization and content.

0x	0	1	2	3	4	5	6	7	8	9	A	B	C	D	E	F
00	00	11	0F	33	03	00	FE	00	00	00	00	00	00	00	00	00
10	00	00	00	00	00	00	00	00	00	00	00	00	00	00	00	00
20	00	00	00	00	00	00	00	7A	00	00	00	00	00	00	00	00
30	12	01	00	00	23	10	00	01	00	00	00	00	00	00	00	00
40	00	00	00	00	FF	FF	00	00	FF	FF	00	00	FF	FF	00	00
50	FF	FF	00	00	FF	FF	00	00	FF	FF	00	00	FF	FF	00	00
60	FF	FF	00	00	FF	FF	00	00	FF	FF	00	00	FF	FF	00	00
70	FF	FF	00	00	FF	FF	00	00	FF	FF	00	00	00	00	00	00
80	3F	FF	00	00	FF	FF	00	00	FF	FF	00	00	FF	FF	00	00
90	FF	FF	00	00	FF	FF	00	00	FF	FF	00	00	FF	FF	00	00
A0	FF	FF	00	00	FF	FF	00	00	FF	FF	00	00	FF	FF	00	00
B0	FF	FF	00	00	FF	FF	00	00	FF	FF	00	00	FF	FF	00	00
C0	FF	FF	00	00	00	00	00	00	00	00	00	00	00	00	00	00
D0	00	00	00	00	00	00	00	00	00	00	00	00	00	00	00	00
E0	00	00	00	00	00	00	00	00	00	00	00	00	00	00	00	00
F0	00	00	00	00	00	00	00	00	00	00	00	00	00	00	00	00

Figure I.5.1. Disk Volume VTOC in DOS 3.3

The DOS 3.3 VTOC is defined to be located on track 0x11 and it includes all of sector 0x00 for its use, though it could be located in any sector on any track. The volume Catalog sectors may be any group of sectors on any track, but typically they are defined to be located on track 0x11 as well, and they are selected to be the remaining sectors of that same track just above the VTOC sector for optimal access. Figure I.5.1 shows the VTOC for a typical DOS 3.3 volume and Table I.5.1 defines each entry in the DOS 3.3 VTOC. All entries in this VTOC are essentially static in the sense that these entries are not variable or subject to change: the number of volume Catalog sectors are always fifteen, the number of volume tracks is always thirty-five, and the number of sectors in a track is always sixteen. The remaining entries are used by DOS 3.3 routines to access volume resources in order to write or update current or new files to the volume.

11

Byte	Name	Value	Description
0x00	VTOCSB	0x00	VTOC Structure Block
0x01	FRSTTRK	0x11	Track number of first catalog sector
0x02	FRSTSEC	0x0F	Sector number of first catalog sector (default = 0x0F)
0x03	DOSRLS1	0x33	DOS release number 1 used to initialize this volume
0x04	DOSRLS2	0x03	DOS release number 2 used to initialize this volume
0x05	DOSRLS3	0x00	DOS release number 3 used to initialize this volume
0x06	DISKVOL	0xFE	Volume number assigned to this volume (default = 0xFE)
0x07–0x26	~	0x00	32 bytes not used
0x27	NUMTSENT	0x7A	Maximum number of T/S pairs in one TSL sector
0x28–0x2F	~	0x00	8 bytes not used
0x30	NXTTOALC	0x11	Last Track used to allocate a sector for data or for a TSL
0x31	ALLCDIR	0x01	Direction of Track Allocation (0x01 or 0xFF)
0x32–0x33	~	0x00	2 bytes not used
0x34	NUMTRKS	0x23	Number of tracks in this volume (always set to 0x23)
0x35	NUMSECS	0x10	Number of sectors per track in this volume (always set to 0x10)
0x36–0x37	BYTPRSEC	0x100	Number of bytes per sector (256) (Lo/Hi byte order)
0x38–0x3B	BITMAP	0x0000 0000	Bitmap of free sectors for track 0 (init to 0x0000 0000)
0x3C–0x43	: : :	0x0000 0000	Bitmap of free sectors for tracks 1-2 (init to 0x0000 0000)
0x44–0x7B	: : :	0xFFFF 0000	Bitmap of free sectors for tracks 3-16 (init to 0xFFFF 0000)
0x7C–0x7F	: : :	0x0000 0000	Bitmap of VTOC and Catalog sectors for track 17 (0x0000 0000)
0x80–0xC3	: : :	0xFFFF 0000	Bitmap of free sectors for tracks 18-34 (init to 0xFFFF 0000)
0xC4–0xFF		0x0000 0000	reserved for tracks 35-49 (init to 0x0000 0000)

Table I.5.1. VTOC Structure Block Definition in DOS 3.3

0x	0	1	2	3	4	5	6	7	8	9	A	B	C	D	E	F
00	00	11	05	45	05	C8	00	C4				Volume Name				
10						(24 characters)										
20	Date & Time Volume created						04	7A	LibNum		Date & Time VTOC last changed					
30	11	01	00	00	24	10	00	01	FF	FF	00	00	FF	FF	00	00
40	FF	FF	00	00	FF	FF	00	00	FF	FF	00	00	FF	FF	00	00
50	FF	FF	00	00	FF	FF	00	00	FF	FF	00	00	FF	FF	00	00
60	FF	FF	00	00	FF	FF	00	00	FF	FF	00	00	FF	FF	00	00
70	FF	FF	00	00	FF	FF	00	00	FF	FF	00	00	FF	C0	00	00
80	FF	FF	00	00	FF	FF	00	00	FF	FF	00	00	FF	FF	00	00
90	FF	FF	00	00	FF	FF	00	00	FF	FF	00	00	FF	FF	00	00
A0	FF	FF	00	00	FF	FF	00	00	FF	FF	00	00	FF	FF	00	00
B0	FF	FF	00	00	FF	FF	00	00	FF	FF	00	00	FF	FF	00	00
C0	FF	FF	00	00	FF	FF	00	00	00	00	00	00	00	00	00	00
D0	00	00	00	00	00	00	00	00	00	00	00	00	00	00	00	00
E0	00	00	00	00	00	00	00	00	00	00	00	00	00	00	00	00
F0	00	00	00	00	00	00	00	00	00	00	00	00	00	00	00	00

Figure I.5.2. Data Disk Volume VTOC in DOS 4.5

It is quite obvious from Figure I.5.1 and Table I.5.1 that the DOS 3.3 VTOC contains a fair amount of unimagined resource space. Truly, did Apple leave the DOS 3.3 VTOC so barren hoping that others may find a usefulness in some of its unused resource space? I believe DOS 4.5 fully answers that question! The DOS 4.5 VTOC is defined to be located on track 0x11 and it includes all of sector 0x00 for its use, though it could be located in any sector on any track. The volume Catalog sectors may be any group of sectors on any track, but typically they are defined to be located on track 0x11 as well, and they are usually the lower sectors of that same track just above the VTOC sector for optimal access. Figure I.5.2 shows the VTOC for a *Data* volume that uses five sectors for its volume Catalog. A volume that does not contain a DOS 4.5 boot image is defined as volume type D for DATA volume. A volume that **does** contain a DOS 4.5 boot image on its boot tracks is defined as volume type B for BOOT volume. Table I.5.2 defines each entry in the DOS 4.5 VTOC, Table I.5.3 defines the free sector bitmap for each initialized track having sixteen sectors, Table I.5.4 defines the free sector bitmap for each initialized track having thirty-two sectors, and Table I.5.5 defines the bytes of the six-byte date and time stamp in the order those bytes are stored in the VTOC or Catalog sectors. There is more information in Section I.6 about the free sector bitmap definition as it is utilized throughout DOS 4.5. The fundamental structure of the DOS 4.5 VTOC and Catalog sectors is the same for both DOS 4.5L and for DOS 4.5H.

Byte	Name	Value	Description
0x00	VTOCSB	0x00	VTOC Structure Block
0x01	FRSTTRK	0x11	Track number of first catalog sector
0x02	FRSTSEC	0x05	Sector number of first catalog sector (default = 0x05)
0x03	DOSVRSN	0x45	DOS version number used to initialize this volume
0x04	DOSBUILD	0x05	DOS build number used to initialize this volume
0x05	DOSRAM	0xC8	DOS RAM location used to initialize this volume (H)
0x06	DISKVOL	0x00	Volume number assigned to this volume (default = 0x00)
0x07	DISKTYPE	0xC4	Volume Type (B or D) for BOOT or DATA volume
0x08-0x1F	DISKNAME	~	Volume Name (24 ASCII characters), right filled with 0xA0
0x20-0x25	INITIME	~	Date and Time when volume was created/initialized
0x26	VTOCPHAS	0x04	Number of Half-Phases per track (1-16)
0x27	NUMTSENT	0x7A	Maximum number of T/S pairs in one TSL sector
0x28-0x29	DISKSUBJ	~	Volume Library (subject) (0x0000-0xFFFF) (Lo/Hi)
0x2A-0x2F	VTOCTIME	~	Date and Time VTOC was initialized or last changed
0x30	NXTTOALC	0x11	Last Track used to allocate a sector for data or for a TSL
0x31	ALLOCDIR	0x01	Direction of Track Allocation (0x01 or 0xFF)
0x32	DOSCONFG	0x00	DOS Configuration value (0x00-0xFF)
0x33	DISKLOCK	0x00	Disk Lock flag (0x00 for unlock and 0x80 for lock)
0x34	NUMTRKS	0x24	Number of tracks in this volume (maximum is 50)
0x35	NUMSECS	0x10	Number of sectors per track (16 or 32) in this volume
0x36-0x37	BYTPRSEC	0x100	Number of bytes per sector (256) (Lo/Hi byte order)
0x38-0x3B	BITMAP	~	Bitmap of free sectors for track 0
0x3C-0x7B	:::	~	Bitmap of free sectors for tracks 1-16
0x7C-0x7F	:::	~	Bitmap of free sectors for track 17 (VTOC and Catalog)
0x80-0xC7	:::	~	Bitmap of free sectors for tracks 18-35 (or NUMTRKS-1)
0xC8-0xFF		0x00	reserved for additional tracks (36-49 in this example)

Table I.5.2. VTOC Structure Block Definition in DOS 4.5

Byte	Sectors	Sector Order	Initial Value
0	0F–08	FEDCBA98	0xFF
1	07–00	76543210	0xFF
2	1F–18	FEDCBA98	0x00
3	17–10	76543210	0x00

Table I.5.3. Free Sector Bitmap for Each Track Having 16 Sectors

Byte	Sectors	Sector Order	Initial Value
0	0F–08	FEDCBA98	0xFF
1	07–00	76543210	0xFF
2	1F–18	FEDCBA98	0xFF
3	17–10	76543210	0xFF

Table I.5.4. Free Sector Bitmap for Each Track Having 32 Sectors

Byte	Value Range	Value
0	0x00 — 0x59	second
1	0x00 — 0x59	minute
2	0x00 — 0x23	hour
3	0x00 — 0x99	year
4	0x01 — 0x31	day
5	0x01 — 0x12	month

Table I.5.5. Date and Time Definition in Variable Order in DOS 4.5

Nearly all of the entries in the DOS 4.5 VTOC are essentially dynamic in the sense that these entries are variable and can easily be changed for different VTOC configurations. As in DOS 3.3, many of the VTOC entries are used by DOS 4.5 routines to access volume resources in order to write or update current or new files to the volume. It is quite obvious from Figure I.5.2 and Table I.5.2 that the DOS 4.5 VTOC contains a critical usage for all of the unimagined resource space that exists in the DOS 3.3 VTOC. Truly, DOS 4.5 has created great usefulness for each and every byte in the VTOC for each and every DOS 4.5 disk volume or disk image!

As shown in Tables I.3.2 and I.3.3, a simplified view of the contents of DOS includes the Command Manager, the File Manager, RWTS, and an assortment of all other software routines that comprise DOS 4.5. In DOS 3.3 much code and valuable data space is dedicated to the manipulation of Volume number beginning in the Command Manager, through the File Manager, and on to RWTS, and then back through the File Manager after RWTS processing. Since most positional parameters such as Volume, Address, and Length are initialized to zero by the Command Manager when a DOS 4.5 command is parsed, the default VOLVAL for the Volume number keyword is always going to be zero. DOS 4.5 passes Volume number through the File Manager to RWTS unchanged. Therefore, the default Volume number that is displayed by DOS 4.5 is `000` and not `254` (i.e. `0xFE`) as it is by DOS 3.3. The Volume number at byte `0x06` in the `VTOC` sector is the **official** Volume number assigned to that volume in DOS 4.5, **not** the volume number `RWTS` finds encoded in the Address Field header for a volume sector on any diskette track. Disk images that are in file format do not contain an encoded Address Field header for its data sectors, so there is absolutely no means to extract a volume number from this file data except from byte `0x06` of the `VTOC` sector. I will show throughout this book that `VOLVAL` plays a critical role in many file systems external to DOS 4.5. Along with Drive number, Track number, and Sector Number, Volume number is a required component in all `DVTS` calculations for Logical Block Address conversions for file systems that utilize block number rather than sector number.

Bytes `0x01` and `0x02` of the `VTOC` as shown in Figure I.5.2 are the track and sector numbers, respectively, that point to the first Catalog sector. As in DOS 3.3, DOS 4.5 uses byte `0x03` of the `VTOC` for the DOS Version Number, but unlike DOS 3.3, DOS 4.5 uses the unused byte at byte `0x04` for the DOS Build Number. Byte `0x05` is used to designate that H (i.e. `0xC8`) DOS RAM was the memory in which DOS 4.5H occupied when it creates or initializes a disk volume. Alternatively, byte `0x05` designates that L (i.e. `0xCC`) DOS RAM was the memory in which DOS 4.5L occupied when it creates or initializes a disk volume. DOS RAM does not have any further use in DOS 4.5 except to remind the user that DOS 4.5L resides in Main memory whereas DOS 4.5H resides in the memory of the Language Card partition. Byte `0x07` is used to specify the Disk Volume Type, either B (i.e. `0xC2`) or D (i.e. `0xC4`) that shows whether or not the volume contains a boot image. Bytes `0x08` through `0x1F` are used for the 24-character Disk Volume Name or Disk Title and bytes `0x20` through `0x25` are used for the Disk Volume Date and Time stamp when the volume was created or initialized. Bytes `0x2A` through `0x2F` are used for the `VTOC` Date and Time stamp, and this time stamp is updated whenever DOS 4.5 changes anything in the `VTOC` for any reason. Byte `0x26` is the Phase number and bytes `0x28` and `0x29` are used to assign a 16-bit (Lo/Hi byte order) Disk Library value to the volume. Byte `0x32` is used to store the system `CONFIG` value and byte `0x33` is used to store the Disk Lock value for that volume. All other `VTOC` variables are still at their original, DOS 3.3 location. The number of Bytes per Sector found at bytes `0x36` and `0x37` is retained but it has no further internal or external use in DOS 4.5: all data manipulations are performed at the sector level where a sector is defined to contain 256 bytes of data.

6. The VTOC Bitmap Definition

The free sector bitmap of a volume is located in the `VTOC` of a volume starting at byte `0x38` as shown in Figure I.5.2. Four bytes are reserved for each of the tracks in a volume whose bits determine whether a sector on that track is utilized or not utilized for a Catalog sector, a Track/Sector List (TSL) sector, or a data sector. There are two routines where DOS 3.3 **uses** `NUMSECS` (i.e. byte `0x35`) as shown in Table I.5.1, the `VTOC` variable equal to the number of sectors comprising a track: `ALLOCSEC` and `RORBITMP`. `ALLOCSEC` is a routine that finds, allocates, and reserves a disk track that contains an available sector. It uses the `VTOC` bitmap to locate and reserve this identified track. `RORBITMP` is a routine used by `FREESECT` that sets or clears the assigned bit for a sector within the 4-byte bitmap of its track as shown in Table I.5.3. The ramifications of limiting these routines to the value found in `NUMSECS` causes the definition of the bit assigned to sector `0x00` to be different in 16-sector and 32-sector tracks. In DOS 3.3 sector `0x00` is assigned to the first bit (the LSB, or bit 0) in the **second** byte of the 4-byte bitmap for its track when `NUMSECS` is equal to sixteen as shown in Table I.5.3. However, when `NUMSECS` is equal to thirty-two, sector `0x00` is assigned to the first bit in the **fourth** byte of the

4-byte bitmap of its track as shown in Table I.6.1. Furthermore, *FID* has always assumed that NUMSECS is equal to sixteen and has always rotated the bitmap of a track accordingly. *FID*, as published by Apple, cannot copy files onto a volume that contains 32-sector tracks because it does not rotate the bitmap properly for 32-sector tracks in DOS 3.3!

Byte	Sector	Bitmap
0	1F–18	FEDCBA98
1	17–10	76543210
2	0F–08	FEDCBA98
3	07–00	76543210

Table I.6.1. Free Sector Bitmap for Each Track Having 32 Sectors in DOS 3.3

Here is a confounded situation where the VTOC, presumably designed by Apple, is not fully supported even by Apple designed utilities. I wonder if Apple thought as early as 1979 when it published *FID* that there would never be a device that would support 32-sector tracks? Were 32-sector tracks merely a placeholder in the VTOC? Did Apple give up on DOS 3.3 in preference to ProDOS earlier than anyone suspected? As an aside, I have never been convinced that the family of Apple][computers was necessarily the compatible platform for the hierarchal directory structures created in ProDOS. I am even less convinced now. I maintain that ProDOS performs better on a platform that utilizes, at a minimum, a 16-bit microprocessor.

ALLOCSEC and RORBITMP manipulate the free sector bitmap for each track as shown in Table I.5.3 consistently in DOS 4.5 without regard to the value found in NUMSECS: 32-sector tracks is always implied even when a volume contains 16-sector tracks. DOS 4.5 only interacts with the VTOC bitmap by means of the variable NEXTSECR XOR'd (that is, exclusively OR'd) with the value of 0x10 in the routines ALLOCSEC and FREESECT. In other words, the bitmap is manipulated as if it looks like what is shown in Table I.6.1, but the bitmap appears in the VTOC as if it looks like what is shown in Table I.5.3. Whether a volume contains 16-sector or 32-sector tracks does not matter to the DOS 4.5 routines that utilize these bitmap values. When the bitmap is manipulated, that is, rotated consistently in this fashion, sector 0x00 is always assigned to the first bit in the **second** byte of the four-byte bitmap of its track as shown in Table I.5.3.

For volumes having 16-sector tracks, the 4-byte bitmap of each track having all sixteen sectors available in this volume would be set to FF FF 00 00. For volumes having 32-sector tracks, the 4-byte bitmap of each track having all thirty-two sectors available in this volume would be set to FF FF FF FF. When the 4-byte bitmap of a track is not rotated consistently for 16-sector and 32-sector volumes, it puts an unnecessary burden on the DOS INIT command handler to determine exactly which bit is assigned to sector 0x00 and which bit is assigned to sector 0x10. Utilizing and rotating the 4-byte bitmap of a track consistently puts no further throughput burden onto DOS 4.5. I have also incorporated the necessary bitmap utilization changes into my modified version of *FID* that models how DOS 4.5 defines the 4-byte bitmap of a track and how the bitmap must be correctly manipulated. As to be expected, DOS 4.5 and my modified version of *FID* can fully read, copy, and write to a DOS 3.3 volume that has 16-sector tracks, or to any other volume for that matter, without exception, even to a DOS 4.5 volume, whether that volume has 16-sector or 32-sector tracks.

One of the most interesting aspects of the RORBITMP routine is that it plays a critical role in undeleting a file. Not only does RORBITMP reserve or unreserve a sector for file use, its intended purpose, but it can equally be used to preserve a sector in a file when that file is undeleted. I pay humble respects to my professor of Boolean Algebra for teaching me the power of the XOR instruction. I believe it is one of the most powerful instructions in the 6502-microprocessor command repertoire, for it certainly is most powerful when it is used in the RORBITMP routine. In normal processing the Carry flag is used to allocate a sector when the flag is **clear** or to deallocate a sector when the Carry flag is **set**. Identifying the intended sector to be allocated or deallocated and either clearing or setting its respective bit in the cache copy of the track's 4-byte bitmap completes the first step of normal processing in RORBITMP. The next step is to update the 4-byte bitmap of the track that contains this sector in the actual VTOC data buffer. The RORBITMP routine simply OR's its cache copy with the actual 4-byte bitmap of the track. I cannot recall the source of the inspiration, but after the cache and actual bytes have been OR'd, and if the URMFLAG is **set** signaling that the file is to be undeleted, that sum is then XOR'd with the cache bytes: simple, elegant, and powerful! With just eight additional bytes of code, not only are the data sectors of a file, but all of its TSL sectors are fully preserved in the VTOC and the file is restored in the Catalog.

Whenever one analyzes a mathematical function, the end-points of that function present the most difficulty, and perhaps the most interest. In a similar fashion the routine ALLOCSEC presents some difficulty in processing sectors to allocate if NXTTOALC (next to allocate) happens to equal either the first track (track 0x00) or the last track (track NUMTRKS-1) of the operational range for that VTOC. Furthermore, track 0x00 needs to be processed as track 0x40 as will be explained in Section I.7. DOS 4.5 initially assigns the value of 0x11 (the Catalog track) to NXTTOALC and the value of 0x01 (i.e. forward) to ALLOCDIR (allocate direction). Once ALLOCSEC searches forward in increasing track number for free sectors in the VTOC bitmap and NXTTOALC reaches the last track, NXTTOALC is reassigned the value of 0x11 and ALLOCDIR is reassigned the value of 0xFF (i.e. backward). So, whenever NXTTOALC becomes either the first track or the last track initially, an extra count is decremented from ALLOCNTR (allocate loop counter) which basically counts for nothing. DOS 3.3 utilized the flag variable ALLCFLG for its two-state counter which was sufficient because DOS 3.3 was not required to process track 0x00 as a possible data track. Therefore, to ensure that the entire VTOC bitmap is searched for free sectors in DOS 4.5, and to include the processing of the first track or the last track if they happen to be the initial search track, four half-passes through the VTOC bitmap are counted. When ALLOCNTR is decremented to zero and a free sector has not been yet identified, the error message Volume Full can be correctly issued.

7. The DOS 4.5 Catalog

The first volume Catalog sector for DOS 4.5 is shown in Figure I.7.1. Bytes 0x01 and 0x02 of each Catalog sector point to the next Catalog sector as they do in the VTOC sector. The last Catalog sector, typically sector 0x01 on track 0x11, contains zero for these two bytes. A DOS 4.5 Catalog sector may define up to a maximum of seven file entries as they do in DOS 3.3. Table I.7.1 shows the content for each file entry. This table defines the first two bytes of a Catalog entry for a file to be the values of the track and the sector that point to the TSL for that file. The TSL lists all of the track/sector byte pairs for each and every data sector that comprises the data contents for that file.

0x	0	1	2	3	4	5	6	7	8	9	A	B	C	D	E	F
00	–	11	04									Trk 1	Sec 1	Type 1	Name 1->	–
10	–	–	–	–	–	–	–	–	–	–	–	–	–	–	–	–
20	–	–	–	–	–	Name <-1	Time 1->	–	Time <-1	Date 1->	–	Date <-1	LenL 1	LenH 1	Trk 2	Sec 2
30	Type 2	Name 2->	–	–	–	–	–	–	–	–	–	–	–	–	–	–
40	–	–	–	–	–	–	–	–	Name <-2	Time 2->	–	Time <-2	Date 2->	–	Date <-2	LenL 2
50	LenH 2	Trk 3	Sec 3	Type 3	Name 3->	–	–	–	–	–	–	–	–	–	–	–
60	–	–	–	–	–	–	–	–	–	–	–	Name <-3	Time 3->	–	Time <-3	Date 3->
70	–	Date <-3	LenL 3	LenH 3	Trk 4	Sec 4	Type 4	Name 4->	–	–	–	–	–	–	–	–
80	–	–	–	–	–	–	–	–	–	–	–	–	–	–	Name <-4	Time 4->
90	–	Time <-4	Date 4->	–	Date <-4	LenL 4	LenH 4	Trk 5	Sec 5	Type 5	Name 5->	–	–	–	–	–
A0	–	–	–	–	–	–	–	–	–	–	–	–	–	–	–	–
B0	–	Name <-5	Time 5->	–	Time <-5	Date 5->	–	Date <-5	LenL 5	LenH 5	Trk 6	Sec 6	Type 6	Name 6->	–	–
C0	–	–	–	–	–	–	–	–	–	–	–	–	–	–	–	–
D0	–	–	–	–	Name <-6	Time 6->	–	Time <-6	Date 6->	–	Date <-6	LenL 6	LenH 6	Trk 7	Sec 7	Type 7
E0	Name 7->	–	–	–	–	–	–	–	–	–	–	–	–	–	–	–
F0	–	–	–	–	–	–	–	Name <-7	Time 7->	–	Time <-7	Date 7->	–	Date <-7	LenL 7	LenH 7

Figure I.7.1. First Volume Catalog Sector in DOS 4.5

Item	Offset	Length	Format	Description
Track	0x00	0x01	%DZTT TTTT	'D'elete bit, track 'Z'ero bit, TSL 'T'rack bits
Sector	0x01	0x01	%000S SSSS	TSL 'S'ector bits
Type	0x02	0x01	%LTTT TTTT	'L'ock bit, 'T'ype bits
Name	0x03	0x18	upper ASCII	24-character ASCII filename
Time	0x1B	0x03	0xSS MM HH	'S'econds byte, 'M'inute byte, 'H'our byte
Date	0x1E	0x03	0xYY DD MM	'Y'ear byte, 'D'ay byte, 'M'onth byte
Size	0x21	0x02	0xLL HH	2-byte file size in sectors, 'L'ow/'H'igh byte order

Table I.7.1. Volume Catalog Entry in DOS 4.5

File	Track*	Sector	Type**	Name	Time	Date	Size
1	0x0B	0x0C	0x0D	0x0E–0x25	0x26–0x28	0x29–0x2B	0x2C–0x2D
2	0x2E	0x2F	0x30	0x31–0x48	0x49–0x4B	0x4C–0x4E	0x4F–0x50
3	0x51	0x52	0x53	0x54–0x6B	0x6C–0x6E	0x6F–0x71	0x72–0x73
4	0x74	0x75	0x76	0x77–0x8E	0x8F–0x91	0x92–0x94	0x95–0x96
5	0x97	0x98	0x99	0x9A–0xB1	0xB2–0xB4	0xB5–0xB7	0xB8–0xB9
6	0xBA	0xBB	0xBC	0xBD–0xD4	0xD5–0xD7	0xD8–0xDA	0xDB–0xDC
7	0xDD	0xDE	0xDF	0xE0–0xF7	0xF8–0xFA	0xFB–0xFD	0xFE–0xFF

* If the MSB is **set** the file's Name shown is **Deleted**　　** If the MSB is **set** the file's Name shown is **Locked**

Table I.7.2. Catalog Sector Data Offsets for File Entries in DOS 4.5

File Type	Catalog	Description
00	T	Text file
~~01~~	I	Integer BASIC file (not supported in DOS 4.5)
02	A	Applesoft file
04	B	Binary file
~~08~~	S	S type file (not supported in DOS 4.5)
~~10~~	R	Relocatable object file (not supported in DOS 4.5)
20	A	A type file (processed as an Applesoft file)
40	L	L (*Lisa*) type file (formally B type)
80	*	File lock bit

Table I.7.3. File Type Byte Description in DOS 4.5

The third byte of a Catalog entry for a file defines the Type parameter assigned to that file, and that byte is followed by the 24-character upper ASCII filename given to that file. The 3-byte time and 3-byte date stamp when the file was created or last modified follow the filename, and those bytes conform to the Date and Time definition shown in Table I.5.5. The last two bytes of a Catalog entry for a file defines the size of the data content for that file in sectors including all of its TSL sectors in low/high byte order. Table I.7.2 lists the volume Catalog data locations for each of the seven files in a Catalog sector. Table

I.7.3 lists all of the possible file type codes that DOS 4.5 can correctly process, the ASCII representation that is used in the DOS 4.5 volume Catalog for each file type, and a brief description of each file type. DOS 4.5 does not know how to process Integer BASIC files, S Type files, and Relocatable object files. There is absolutely no software support for these three file type codes in DOS 4.5. Perhaps someone could quite easily utilize the memory space for the DOS 4.5H HELP command in order to correctly process the I, S, and R file Type codes. First, a suitable definition for the S and R file Type codes is necessary to begin such a project. I have no idea whether the HELP command memory space can even support a project like this. I am positive a dedicated and passionate engineer can and will find the means for this project.

File Type 0x40 is used by DOS 4.5 to process *Lisa* files natively (DOS 3.3 refers to these as B type files). DOS 4.5 processes an A type (i.e. 0x20) file simply as an Applesoft file. In DOS 4.5 a file is marked *deleted* when the most significant bit (i.e. MSB, or bit 7) of the track number that is used to point to its TSL sector is **set**, that is, in bytes 0x0B, 0x2E, 0x51, 0x74, 0x97, 0xBA, or 0xDD from Table I.7.2. DOS 4.5 stipulates that there is always less than 64 tracks (i.e. 0x3F or less) that comprise a volume, so that bit 6 of the track number that is used to point to its TSL is also certainly available, and this bit, as in track 0x40, can be used to signify track 0x00. Using bit 6 to represent physical track 0x00 allows all of the File Manager logic testing for *last track/sector pair* in a TSL to remain virtually unchanged. This representation for track 0x00 also allows track 0x00 to be used for any file data like any other data track. I have updated my version of *FID* to include this representation for track 0x00 and how a deleted file is determined and identified in the volume Catalog.

If an attempt is made to load (i.e. LOAD or BLOAD) a nonexistent file into memory when the volume Catalog is full, DOS 3.3 erroneously prints the DISK FULL error message rather than the correct error message FILE NOT FOUND. If an attempt is made to save (i.e. SAVE or BSAVE) a file when the volume Catalog is full (i.e. all Catalog sectors are fully utilized), DOS 3.3 again erroneously prints the DISK FULL error message even when there are sufficient sectors available in the volume for the data content of the file. Even though this situation is rarely encountered where the volume Catalog is full, having DOS issue the wrong or inappropriate error message could lead one to make a false conclusion.

DOS 4.5 provides a default volume Catalog consisting of five sectors that can define up to thirty-five files. However, the volume Catalog may be made as small as one sector or as large as fifteen sectors by using the B keyword with the DOS INIT command. If the volume Catalog consists of one or two sectors, the volume Catalog will only support seven or fourteen files, respectively, and an erroneous DISK FULL error message can have significant consequences in this instance. I identified and rewrote the flawed DOS 3.3 routines when I designed DOS 4.3, so DOS 4.5 also prints the correct error message File Not Found when a file truly does not exist in a volume Catalog regardless whether the Catalog is full or not full. DOS 4.5 also prints the error message Catalog Full when attempting to save a file to a volume whose Catalog truly does not contain an available file entry regardless whether there are sufficient sectors available in the volume for the data content of the file.

At the heart of every file is its Track/Sector List. This list of track/sector pair entries is contained in the sector that every Catalog entry for a file points to, that is, its TSL. If a file exceeds 122 (i.e. 0x7A) sectors of data (see NUMTSENT from Table I.5.2), the TSL sector has provisions to define another TSL sector in order to provide additional track/sector pair entries. And, for every increment of 0x7A data sectors, DOS 4.5 will create another TSL sector for that file and increase the sector resource count for that file by one.

0x	0	1	2	3	4	5	6	7	8	9	A	B	C	D	E	F
00	00	Next	TSL			Offset							T/S	01	T/S	02
10	T/S	03	T/S	04												
20																
30																
40																
50																
60																
70																
80																
90																
A0																
B0																
C0																
D0																
E0																
F0															T/S	7A

Figure I.7.2. TSL Sector Structure in DOS 4.5

Byte	Name	Value	Description
0x00	TSLSB	0x00	unused, start of TSL structure block
0x01	TSTRKOFF	0x00	Track to next TSL; 0x00 if no more TSL sectors
0x02	TSSECOFF	0x00	Sector to next TSL; 0x00 if no more TSL sectors
0x03–0x04		0x00	unused
0x05–0x06	TSRECOFF	0x00	TSL record offset (RELSLAST in FMWORK); 0x00/0x00 first TSL
0x07–0x0B		0x00	unused
0x0C–0x0D	TSLTSOFF	~	T/S for data sector 0x01; at least one entry is required
0x0E–0x0F		~	T/S for data sector 0x02; 0x00/0x00 if at end
0x10–0x11		~	T/S for data sector 0x03; 0x00/0x00 if at end
0x12–0xFD		~	T/S for data sectors 0x04–0x79
0xFE–0xFF		~	T/S for data sector 0x7A

Table I.7.4. TSL Structure Block Definition in DOS 4.5

Figure I.7.2 shows a typical TSL sector and Table I.7.4 defines each entry in the TSL sector. Bytes 0x01/0x02, or Next TSL point to the next TSL sector if it exists, otherwise these bytes are set to 0x00/0x00. Offset at bytes 0x05/0x06 is equal to 0x00/0x00 for the first TSL sector, and Offset increases by 0x007A for each succeeding TSL sector in Lo/Hi byte order. The track/sector list begins with its first pair entry at bytes 0x0C/0x0D, and all files have at least one entry pair. Regardless whether the TSL contains additional track/sector entry pairs from previous file saves or file modifications, DOS only loads into memory the number of bytes specified by an Applesoft or a Binary file. The DOS TLOAD command for a TEXT file, on the other hand, reads into memory **all** data sectors listed in the TSL irrespective of the actual size of the file in bytes which is demarcated by a NULL byte (i.e. `0x00`). If the next track value in a track/sector entry pair is equal to `0x00`, no further track/sector entry pairs are read into memory. The `TSL` also concludes when the `DIRINDX` index pointer becomes `zero` and when `TSTRKOFF` is `zero`. I believe byte pairs `0x08/0x09` or `0x09/0x0A` could have been utilized for the value of the `L` keyword instead of requiring the `L` keyword to `OPEN` a random-access Data file as shown in Table III.6.1 and Figure III.6.1. At least that is how I would have designed the first `TSL` of a random-access Data file. I still have not figured out the benefit of assigning `0x0C` to `TSLTSOFF` and `0x7A` to `NUMTSENT` when there is room for `0x7B` or `0x7C` track/sector entry pairs.

8. Booting DOS 4.5 Into Memory

DOS 4.5L occupies the first two tracks, tracks `0x00` and `0x01`, and one additional sector on track `0x02` of a volume, whether the volume has sixteen or thirty-two sectors per track. DOS 4.5H also occupies the first two tracks, tracks `0x00` and `0x01`, and an additional ten sectors on track `0x02` of a volume, whether the volume has sixteen or thirty-two sectors per track. The remaining sectors on track `0x02` for either version of DOS are made available in the `VTOC` by the initialization handler. When a DOS 4.5 volume boots, the Disk][Interface Card firmware loads the bootstrap code from sector `0x00` on track `0x00` into memory address `0x0800-0x08FF`. This starts the Boot Stage 0 process and the X-register always contains the value of the slot number of the Interface Card times sixteen. The first byte of this bootstrap code must equal `0x01` for the boot process to continue and to read another sector into memory. Therefore, the Boot Stage 0 instructions actually begin at memory address `0x0801` in order to initialize the Boot Stage 1 software that is already in memory now. Bytes `0x08FE` and `0x08FF` are known as `BOOTADR` and `BOOTPGS`, respectively, as shown in Table I.8.1. These two bytes direct the Boot Stage 1 software to read sectors `0x06` to `0x00` into memory address `0xB900` to `0xBFFF` for DOS 4.5L, or sectors `0x0F` to `0x02` into Bank 1 memory address `0xD000` to `0xDDFF` and sectors `0x01` and `0x00` into memory address `0xBE00` to `0xBFFF` for DOS 4.5H.

Address	Variable	DOS 4.5L		DOS 4.5H	
		Instruction	Value	Instruction	Value
0xBFF0	BLDVRSN	BYT VERSION	0x45	BYT VERSION	0x45
0xBFF1	BLDNMBR	BYT BUILD	0x05	BYT BUILD	0x05
0xBFF2	MNGDISK	ADR MNGEXDSK	0xBDF0	ADR EXMNGDSK	0xBE4D
0xBFF4	MNGVALS	ADR MNGEXVAL	0xBE1E	ADR EXMNGVAL	0xBE53
0xBFF6	MNGUSER	ADR MNGEXUSR	0xBE42	ADR EXMNGUSR	0xBE59
0xBFF8	INITDOS	ADR DOSINIT	0xBF47	ADR DOSINIT	0xBF58
0xBFFA	INITVAL	ADR INITVALS	0xBEE2	ADR INITVALS	0xBEE2
0xBFFC	BCFGNDX	BYT BOOTCFG	0xE5	BYT BOOTCFG	0xE5
0xBFFD	NBUF1PG	HBY NBUF1	0x9D	HBY NBUF1	0xDE
0xBFFE	BOOTADR	HBY RWTSTART	0xB9	HBY RWTSTART	0xD0
0xBFFF	BOOTPGS	HBY BOOTEND-RWTSTART	0x06	HBY HELPEND-XFERSTRT	0x0F

Table I.8.1. Boot and Data Management Structure Definition in DOS 4.5

Offset	Variable	Size	DOS 4.5L	DOS 4.5H	Description
0x00	DNUM	0x01	0x01	0x01	RWTS drive number
0x01	VOLEXPT	0x01	0x00	0x00	RWTS volume expected
0x02	TNUM	0x01	0x02	0x02	RWTS initial track number
0x03	SNUM	0x01	0x00	0x09	RWTS initial sector number
0x04	DCTADR	0x02	0x0000	0x0000	DCT address (unused)
0x06	USRBUF	0x02	0x9F00	0xF000	RWTS initial start address
0x08	CFGPHASE	0x01	0x04	0x04	RWTS half-phases per track
0x09	CFGBCNT	0x01	0x00	0x00	RWTS bytes to read (256)
0x0A	CFGCCODE	0x01	0x01	0x01	RWTS command code to read

Table I.8.2. Boot Configuration Data Structure in DOS 4.5

```
      :              :            :
BF89            186    ; Used by Boot Stage 2 and INIT command.
BF89            187    ;
BF89 BD E5 BF   188    RWPAGES1 lda  BOOTCFG,X
BF8C 9D C4 BF   189             sta  DNUM,X
BF8F            190    ;
BF8F E8         191             inx
BF90            192    ;
BF90 88         193             dey
BF91 D0 F6      194             bne  RWPAGES1
BF93            195    ;
BF93 A2 1A      196             ldx  /DOSEND-DOSTART
BF95            197    ;
BF95 86 35      198    RWPAGES2 stx  PAGECNT
BF97            199    ;
BF97 20 BB BE   200    ^1       jsr  RAM1ON
BF9A            201    ;
BF9A 20 7A D2   202             jsr  INTRWTS
BF9D B0 E4      203             bcs  RWERROR
BF9F            204    ;
BF9F CE C7 BF   205             dec  SNUM
BFA2 10 08      206    ;        bpl  >2
BFA4            207    ;
BFA4 CE C6 BF   208             dec  TNUM
BFA7            209    ;
BFA7 A9 0F      210             lda  #15
BFA9 8D C7 BF   211             sta  SNUM
BFAC            212    ;
BFAC EE CB BF   213    ^2       inc  USRBUF+1
BFAF D0 05      214             bne  >3
BFB1            215    ;
BFB1 A9 E0      216             lda  /PAGEE0
BFB3 8D CB BF   217             sta  USRBUF+1
BFB6            218    ;
BFB6 C6 35      219    ^3       dec  PAGECNT
BFB8 D0 DD      220             bne  <1
BFBA            221    ;
BFBA 60         222             rts
      :              :            :
```

Figure I.8.1. RWPAGES Routine in DOS 4.5H

23

Track	Sector	Address	Code	Track	Sector	Address	Code
0x00	0x00	0xBF00	BOOT	0x01	0x00	0xAF00	MNGR
0x00	0x01	0xBE00	XFER	0x01	0x01	0xAE00	MNGR
0x00	0x02	0xBD00	RWTS	0x01	0x02	0xAD00	MNGR
0x00	0x03	0xBC00	RWTS	0x01	0x03	0xAC00	MNGR
0x00	0x04	0xBB00	RWTS	0x01	0x04	0xAB00	CMD
0x00	0x05	0xBA00	RWTS	0x01	0x05	0xAA00	CMD
0x00	0x06	0xB900	RWTS	0x01	0x06	0xA900	CMD
0x00	0x07	0xB800	DATA	0x01	0x07	0xA800	CMD
0x00	0x08	0xB700	DATA	0x01	0x08	0xA700	CMD
0x00	0x09	0xB600	DATA	0x01	0x09	0xA600	CMD
0x00	0x0A	0xB500	DATA	0x01	0x0A	0xA500	CMD
0x00	0x0B	0xB400	MNGR	0x01	0x0B	0xA400	CMD
0x00	0x0C	0xB300	MNGR	0x01	0x0C	0xA300	CMD
0x00	0x0D	0xB200	MNGR	0x01	0x0D	0xA200	CMD
0x00	0x0E	0xB100	MNGR	0x01	0x0E	0xA100	CMD
0x00	0x0F	0xB000	MNGR	0x01	0x0F	0xA000	CMD
				0x02	0x00	0x9F00	CMD

Table I.8.3. Disk Track/Sector Mapping to Memory Address in DOS 4.5L

Track	Sector	Address	Code	Track	Sector	Address	Code
0x00	0x00	0xBF00	BOOT	0x01	0x05	0xE400	MNGR
0x00	0x01	0xBE00	XFER	0x01	0x06	0xE300	MNGR
0x00	0x02	*0xDD00	HELP	0x01	0x07	0xE200	MNGR
0x00	0x03	*0xDC00	HELP	0x01	0x08	0xE100	MNGR
0x00	0x04	*0xDB00	HELP	0x01	0x09	0xE000	MNGR
0x00	0x05	*0xDA00	HELP	0x01	0x0A	0xDF00	MNGR
0x00	0x06	*0xD900	HELP	0x01	0x0B	0xDE00	MNGR
0x00	0x07	*0xD800	HELP	0x01	0x0C	0xDD00	MNGR
0x00	0x08	*0xD700	HELP	0x01	0x0D	0xDC00	MNGR
0x00	0x09	*0xD600	INRF	0x01	0x0E	0xDB00	CMD
0x00	0x0A	*0xD500	INRF	0x01	0x0F	0xDA00	CMD
0x00	0x0B	*0xD400	RWTS	0x02	0x00	0xD900	CMD
0x00	0x0C	*0xD300	RWTS	0x02	0x01	0xD800	CMD
0x00	0x0D	*0xD200	RWTS	0x02	0x02	0xD700	CMD
0x00	0x0E	*0xD100	RWTS	0x02	0x03	0xD600	CMD
0x00	0x0F	*0xD000	RWTS	0x02	0x04	0xD500	CMD
0x01	0x00	0xE900	DATA	0x02	0x05	0xD400	CMD
0x01	0x01	0xE800	DATA	0x02	0x06	0xD300	CMD
0x01	0x02	0xE700	DATA	0x02	0x07	0xD200	CMD
0x01	0x03	0xE600	DATA	0x02	0x08	0xD100	CMD
0x01	0x04	0xE500	SPCL	0x02	0x09	0xD000	CMD

Table I.8.4. Disk Track/Sector Mapping to Memory Address in DOS 4.5H

A 16-byte sector interleave table is available to the Boot Stage 1 software and to the RWTS routine whose Input/Output Context Block (IOCB) structure is now in memory page 0xBF. Transfer of control passes to the Boot Stage 2 software which is also in memory page 0xBF, and that software can now use RWTS located in Main memory for DOS 4.5L and in Bank 1 of the Language Card partition for DOS 4.5H in order to access any sector on any track in the volume. The initial RWTS IOCB values are copied from a BOOTCFG structure in memory page 0xBF. These values are used by the RWPAGES routine which is called by Boot Stage 2 software to read the remaining twenty-six sectors into memory in ascending order of memory pages. For DOS 4.5L, those twenty-six sectors begin with sector 0x00 on track 0x02 and end with sector 0x07 on track 0x00. For DOS 4.5H, those twenty-six sectors begin with sector 0x09 on track 0x02 and end with sector 0x00 on track 0x01. The DOS 4.5 BOOTCFG table is shown in Table I.8.2 and the DOS 4.5H RWPAGES routine is shown in Figure I.8.1. When all of DOS 4.5 is in memory, ROM initialization is performed, the main video and character set is selected, XMODE is initialized, and the CSWL and KSWL interface pointers are initialized, a search is made for a clock card, and DOS is cold-started and is now ready to execute the DOS CMDVAL command, a topic that is discussed further in Section I.9. As an aside, the DOS INIT command also uses the RWPAGES routine to write DOS onto a newly initialized volume in the same order DOS was booted and its pages read into memory. The complete volume track/sector mapping to memory address is shown in Table I.8.3 for DOS 4.5L and in Table I.8.4 for DOS 4.5H.

The INTRWTS entry point shown in line #202 in Figure I.8.1 for the call to RWTS simply loads the Y- and A-registers with the address of TBLTYPE, the internal structure for the RWTS IOCB shown later in Table I.10.1, before it *falls into* the DORWTS routine. According to Table I.8.2, the initial start address USRBUF for DOS 4.5H is 0xF000. The first sixteen sectors that are read fill memory block 0xF0, and when that occurs, RWPAGES2 changes the MSB address to 0xE0 as shown in line #216 in Figure I.8.1. The last ten sectors that are read fill memory block 0xE0-0xE9. Later, but before DOS COLDSTRT is initiated, the contents of memory block 0xF0 must be moved to memory block 0xD0 in Bank 2. It is not possible for RWTS, located in memory block 0xD0 of Bank 1, to read disk sectors directly into memory block 0xD0 of Bank 2. Therefore, memory block 0xF0 serves as an intermediate block of memory for Boot Stage 2 and for the DOS 4.5H INIT handler. That is, memory block 0xD0 is first copied to memory block 0xF0 before DOS 4.5H can be written to disk tracks 0x00 to 0x02 using RWPAGES. In DOS 4.5H, DORWTS always exits with Bank 2 of the Language Card partition in focus.

The file image of DOS 4.5 and how that image maps to memory is shown in Table 1.8.5 for DOS 4.5L and in Table I.8.6 for DOS 4.5H. These tables correlate file offset to memory address, and they provide the basic function of the code that is found there, such as DOS Command routine handlers (CMD), DOS File Manager routine handlers (MNGR and SPCL), Data buffers, tables, and variables (DATA), DOS Read/Write Track/Sector routines (RWTS), and the Boot Stage 0, 1, and 2 routines (XFER and BOOT). The asterisk before those entries in Tables 1.8.4 and 1.8.6 indicate that those routines or structures reside in Bank 1 of the Language Card partition for DOS 4.5H. The DOS 4.5H CMD and MNGR routines and the DATA structures all reside in Bank 2 of the Language Card partition. Once DOS 4.5 is in memory and has initialized, other Input/Output (I/O) disks or disk-emulating devices can easily attach their slot card handler address to DOS 4.5. Table I.8.1 shows where the RWTS disk management routine MNGDISK is located in DOS 4.5 (i.e. 0xBFF2) in order to set or restore a DISKADRS table entry. To attach a slot card handler, simply make an indirect call to MNGDISK with the slot number in the X-register, the address of the slot card handler in the Y- and A-registers in Lo/Hi byte order, and **set** the Carry flag. Alternatively, the X-register may contain the slot-times-sixteen value. The registers are returned unchanged. RWTS transfers control to the correct slot card handler for the requested I/O based entirely on the slot-times-sixteen value found in the IOCB.

Offset	Address	Code	Offset	Address	Code
0x0000	0x9F00	CMD	0x1000	0xAF00	MNGR
0x0100	0xA000	CMD	0x1100	0xB000	MNGR
0x0200	0xA100	CMD	0x1200	0xB100	MNGR
0x0300	0xA200	CMD	0x1300	0xB200	MNGR
0x0400	0xA300	CMD	0x1400	0xB300	MNGR
0x0500	0xA400	CMD	0x1500	0xB400	MNGR
0x0600	0xA500	CMD	0x1600	0xB500	DATA
0x0700	0xA600	CMD	0x1700	0xB600	DATA
0x0800	0xA700	CMD	0x1800	0xB700	DATA
0x0900	0xA800	CMD	0x1900	0xB800	DATA
0x0A00	0xA900	CMD	0x1A00	0xB900	RWTS
0x0B00	0xAA00	CMD	0x1B00	0xBA00	RWTS
0x0C00	0xAB00	CMD	0x1C00	0xBB00	RWTS
0x0D00	0xAC00	MNGR	0x1D00	0xBC00	RWTS
0x0E00	0xAD00	MNGR	0x1E00	0xBD00	RWTS
0x0F00	0xAE00	MNGR	0x1F00	0xBE00	XFER
			0x2000	0xBF00	BOOT

Table I.8.5. File Image Mapping to Memory Address in DOS 4.5L

Offset	Address	Code	Offset	Address	Code
0x0000	0xD000	CMD	0x1500	0xE500	SPCL
0x0100	0xD100	CMD	0x1600	0xE600	DATA
0x0200	0xD200	CMD	0x1700	0xE700	DATA
0x0300	0xD300	CMD	0x1800	0xE800	DATA
0x0400	0xD400	CMD	0x1900	0xE900	DATA
0x0500	0xD500	CMD	0x1A00	*0xD000	RWTS
0x0600	0xD600	CMD	0x1B00	*0xD100	RWTS
0x0700	0xD700	CMD	0x1C00	*0xD200	RWTS
0x0800	0xD800	CMD	0x1D00	*0xD300	RWTS
0x0900	0xD900	CMD	0x1E00	*0xD400	RWTS
0x0A00	0xDA00	CMD	0x1F00	*0xD500	INRF
0x0B00	0xDB00	CMD	0x2000	*0xD600	INRF
0x0C00	0xDC00	MNGR	0x2100	*0xD700	HELP
0x0D00	0xDD00	MNGR	0x2200	*0xD800	HELP
0x0E00	0xDE00	MNGR	0x2300	*0xD900	HELP
0x0F00	0xDF00	MNGR	0x2400	*0xDA00	HELP
0x1000	0xE000	MNGR	0x2500	*0xDB00	HELP
0x1100	0xE100	MNGR	0x2600	*0xDC00	HELP
0x1200	0xE200	MNGR	0x2700	*0xDD00	HELP
0x1300	0xE300	MNGR	0x2800	0xBE00	XFER
0x1400	0xE400	MNGR	0x2900	0xBF00	BOOT

Table I.8.6. File Image Mapping to Memory Address in DOS 4.5H

```
:                 :        :
BFF2              7    MNGDISK   equ $BFF2
C020              8    RDENTRY   equ $C020          ; $C720
C900              9    RDPAGECX  equ $C900          ; $C7
C901             10    RDSLOT    equ $C901          ; $07
:                 :        :
0940             24    ; Attach handler address.
0940 AE 01 C9    25            ldx RDSLOT
0943 A0 20       26            ldy #RDENTRY
0945 AD 00 C9    27            lda RDPAGECX
0948 38          28            sec
0949 20 90 09    29            jsr GETDISK
:                 :        :
0990 6C F2 BF    45    GETDISK   jmp (MNGDISK)
:                 :        :
```

Figure I.8.2. Attaching a Disk][Interface Card Handler in DOS 4.5

```
:                 :        :
0000              7    ZERO      equ $00
0000              8    ;
BFF2              9    MNGDISK   equ $BFF2
C020             10    RDENTRY   equ $C020          ; $C720
C900             11    RDPAGECX  equ $C900          ; $C7
C901             12    RDSLOT    equ $C901          ; $07
:                 :        :
0940             24    ; Request handler address.
0940 AE 01 C9    25            ldx RDSLOT
0943 A9 00       26            lda #ZERO
0945 38          27            sec
0946 20 90 09    28            jsr GETDISK
:                 :        :
0960             39    ; Detach a handler.
0960 AE 01 C9    40            ldx RDSLOT
0963 18          41            clc
0964 20 90 09    42            jsr GETDISK
:                 :        :
0990 6C F2 BF    65    GETDISK   jmp (MNGDISK)
:                 :        :
```

Figure I.8.3. Requesting and Detaching a Slot Card Handler in DOS 4.5

Figure I.8.2 shows an example assembly language routine that attaches the RAM Disk handler to DOS 4.5. The handler's low byte address value is that of the routine RDENTRY, its high byte address is its CX page (i.e. 0xC7 for slot 7) and that value is found in RDPAGECX, and its slot number is found in RDSLOT. Figure I.8.3 shows an example assembly language routine that calls MNGDISK that requests the address of the handler assigned to a particular slot into the Y- and A-registers because it initializes the A-register to zero and sets the Carry flag. Then the routine calls MNGDISK again with the Carry flag clear in order to disconnect that handler from DOS 4.5. Unlike DOS 4.1, it is not necessary to know where the DISKADRS table is located in memory, its structure, nor how to index it. MNGDISK takes care of all that protocol which had to be done entirely by the DOS 4.1 user. MNGDISK always returns the Carry flag clear as long as the X-register contains a valid slot number or a valid slot-times-sixteen number.

27

Having DOS 4.5 saved to disk as a file image can be very useful. For example, the DOS image could be read from a quikLoader and placed into memory according to Table I.8.5 or Table I.8.6 depending upon which version of DOS is read into memory. Getting DOS 4.5 started is as easy as using an indirect `JMP`, such as `JMP (INITDOS)`. Refer to Table I.8.1 for the address of the variable `INITDOS`. DOS 4.5 initializes, transfers control to Applesoft, and then Applesoft prints a carriage return (i.e. `0x8D`) in order to initiate the execution of the first DOS command found in `CMDVAL`. Typically, that command will `RUN` the `HELLO` file. If, on the other hand, you do not wish to lose control of DOS to Applesoft after DOS initialization, there is a very unique DOS 4.5 command that can be used to transfer control to your program after Applesoft initialization. The DOS 4.5 `USER` command has been designed to have a number of very powerful capabilities. One of its capabilities is initiated when the `USER` command is used to replace the `RUN` command in `CMDVAL` such that the `USER` command is executed rather than the `RUN` command after Applesoft initialization. Whatever instructions that are at the address that is put into `USERADR` is executed rather than the `HELLO` file. Figure I.8.4 shows an example assembly language program that calls `MNGUSER` to manage the initialization of DOS 4.5 by initializing `CMDVAL` with the `USER` command and `USERADR` with the address that is currently in the Y- and A-registers. In Figure I.8.4 that address is for the `SPCLCODE` routine at line 43. Once DOS 4.5 has initialized and Applesoft is no longer in control, `MNGUSER` can be called again within `SPCLCODE` in order to restore the default values for `CMDVAL` and `USERADR`. This essentially restores DOS 4.5 to its default or initial state for CMDVAL/USERADR: simply call `MNGUSER` with the `Carry` flag **clear**.

```
:              :        :
03D0           9  DOSWARM   equ $3D0
BFF6          10  MNGUSER   equ $BFF6
BFF8          11  INITDOS   equ $BFF8
:              :        :
0900 38       20            sec
0901 A0 80    21            ldy #SPCLCODE
0903 A9 09    22            lda /SPCLCODE
0905 20 B0 09 23            jsr SETUSER
0908 6C F8 BF 24            jmp (INITDOS)
:              :        :
0980 18       43  SPCLCODE  clc
0981 20 F6 BF 44            jsr SETUSER
0984 4C D0 03 45            jmp DOSWARM
:              :        :
09B0 6C F6 BF 59  SETUSER   jmp (MNGUSER)
:              :        :
```

Figure I.8.4. Using MNGUSER to Manage DOS 4.5

Another powerful capability of the DOS 4.5 `USER` command is initiated when the `USER` command is configured with the address of a specific routine or function. When `USER` is entered on the Apple Command Line followed by the `RETURN` character, that user specific routine or function is immediately entered and executed. Many historical software developers utilized the *Ampersand Handler*, or the `USERAHAND` routine in very much the same way. The utility Program Global Editor is an excellent example where the ampersand is used to bring that program into focus in order for the user to edit and modify an Applesoft program. Even DOS 4.5 is initially configured to utilize the `USERAHAND` routine in order to enter the REPEATCD routine that calls the DOS REPEAT function in order to repeat the last DOS command that was processed by the DOS DOCMD routine. Unlike the ampersand handler, however, the DOS USER command is a real DOS command and it carries with it all of the attributes and authorities of a real DOS command. The original DOS 3.3 version of the *Big Mac* assembler modified the DOS Command Table like the one shown in Table III.0.2 in order to utilize the resources of the INIT command for a new ASSEM command. After exiting *Big Mac*, if the user entered the ASSEM command onto the Apple Command Line followed by the RETURN character, *Big Mac* was immediately brought back into focus, and the user could continue using the assembler to modify and/or develop additional assembly code. This feature was designed to provide the user with an easy and very elegant method to develop assembly code, test the code outside of the assembler, and then re-enter the assembler to continue assembly code development. By design, DOS 4.5 does not provide a means to access the DOS Command Table in order to modify or utilize the resources of any of its commands. However, the USER command may be utilized to provide the identical capabilities of the DOS 3.3 ASSEM command. Figure I.8.5 shows precisely how the DOS 4.5 *Big Mac* loader utilizes MNGUSER to connect the USER command to the re-entry address of *Big Mac*. The *Big Mac* loader is the task that manages Auxiliary memory and places the *Big Mac* executable code at the required address in the Language Card partition of Auxiliary memory. After the user has exited *Big Mac*, if the user enters USER on the Apple Command Line followed by the RETURN character, *Big Mac* is immediately brought back into focus.

```
    :              :          :
  BC70             9   REENTRY  equ $BC70
  BFF6            10   MNGUSER  equ $BFF6
    :              :
  097A A0 70      208           ldy #REENTRY
  097C A9 BC      209           lda /REENTRY
  097E 38         210           sec
  097F 20 A7 09   211           jsr SETUSER
    :              :          :
  09A7 6C F6 BF        SETUSER  jmp (MNGUSER)
    :              :          :
```

Figure I.8.5. Using MNGUSER in LOADMAC

The DOS 4.5 Boot and Data Management Structure shown in Table I.8.1 contains a wealth of other values and vectors not yet discussed. Ever since the publication of the DOS 4.1 Manual and during the development of the DOS 4.5 software, I thought there should be a far more convenient procedure in order to obtain the current DOS Version and Build information. One could parse the version and build values from the character string supplied by the RDCLKVSN function shown later in Table I.9.3, for example. But it is far more convenient to obtain these values directly, and BLDVRSN and BLDNMBR at 0xBFF0 and 0xBFF1, respectively, provide this information. MNGVALS, similar in function to MNGDISK, no longer provides an interface to access or change the INITVALS Data structure variables in DOS 4.5. This is fully discussed in Section I.12.

The address found at INITVAL shown in Table I.8.1 is used to read or change the variables in the INITVALS Data structure shown in Table I.8.7. One should reference the variables in this data structure indirectly and, therefore, more generally using the address found at INITVAL and the offsets shown in Table I.8.7. Because the INITVALS Data structure resides in Main memory at the same address for both DOS 4.5L and DOS 4.5H, the variables in this data structure are somewhat easier to access in order to read and change directly than those variables found in `CMDVALS`, particularly for DOS 4.5H. The example assembly language routine shown in Figure I.8.6 copies the address found at `INITVAL` to a page-zero pointer. The Y-register is used to hold the desired offset found in Table I.8.7. The example routine first reads the value of `RESETADR`, saves it to `RESETSAV`, then changes it to another address. Table I.8.1 contains the offset `BCFGNDX` for the `BOOTCFG` Data structure shown in Table I.8.2. This data structure may be accessed indirectly similar to the `INITVALS` Data structure knowing that this structure resides within page `0xBF`. A page-zero pointer to access this structure is shown in Figure I.8.7. The CFFA firmware I developed is one example that dynamically modifies the `DNUM` and `VOLEXPT` variables. Drive and volume numbers are critical parameters to the CFFA boot process, and being able to change those variables makes it possible for the CFFA to boot any of the volumes on any of its drives.

Address	Offset	Variable	Size	Description
0xBEE2	0x00	WARMADR	0x02	ROM soft entry handler address
0xBEE4	0x02	COLDADR	0x02	ROM hard entry handler address
0xBEE6	0x04	ERRORADR	0x02	ROM error handler address
0xBEE8	0x06	RESETADR	0x02	ROM set/reset handler address
0xBEEA	0x08	USERADR	0x02	USERCMD handler address
0xBEEC	0x0A	CMDVAL	0x01	DOS first-time cold-start command
0xBEED	0x0B	NMAXVAL	0x01	MAXFILES at initialization
0xBEEE	0x0C	YEARVAL	0x01	Year value for Thunderclock card
0xBEEF	0x0D	FIRSTCAT	0x01	First catalog sector (reference variable)
0xBEF0	0x0E	LASTRACK	0x01	Number of tracks in volume (reference variable)
0xBEF1	0x0F	SECVAL	0x01	First catalog sector (working variable)
0xBEF2	0x10	ENDTRK	0x01	Number of tracks in volume (working variable)
0xBEF3	0x11	SUBJCT	0x02	Volume Library value (subject number)
0xBEF5	0x13	TRKVAL	0x01	Catalog track number
0xBEF6	0x14	VRSN	0x01	DOS Version number
0xBEF7	0x15	BLD	0x01	DOS Build number
0xBEF8	0x16	RAMTYP	0x01	DOS RAM type
0xBEF9	0x17	VALSPHAS	0x01	Half-phases per track
0xBEFA	0x18	TSPARS	0x01	Number of T/S pairs per sector
0xBEFB	0x19	ALCTRK	0x01	Sector to allocate next
0xBEFC	0x1A	ALCDIR	0x01	Sector allocation direction
0xBEFD	0x1B	VALSCNFG	0x01	DOS Configuration byte
0xBEFE	0x1C	ENDSEC	0x01	Number of sectors per track
0xBEFF	0x1D	SECSIZ	0x01	(Bytes per sector) / 256

Table I.8.7. INITVALS Data Structure Definition in DOS 4.5

Table I.8.1 also contains the most significant byte of the memory address for `NBUF1`. `NBUF1` is 256 bytes of memory on a page boundary that is used by the DOS 4.5 `RWTS` routines. This buffer resides in Main memory for DOS 4.5L and in Bank 1 of the Language Card partition for DOS 4.5H. This most significant address byte was included in order to provide easy access to a temporary page of memory as long as the RWTS routines are not invoked, which would obviously overwrite the contents of this particular buffer. The firmware I developed for the Rana disk drive makes excellent use of the NBUF1PG address byte. The CFFA firmware I developed also uses this buffer to temporarily save either the lower half or the upper half of a 512-byte data block.

```
    :           :           :
  00EE          4  PTR       epz $EE
    :           :           :
  0006          13 RESETOFF  equ $06
  008D          14 RETURN    equ $8D
    :           :           :
  BFFA          20 INITVAL   equ $BFFA
    :           :           :
  0940          26 ; Setup pointer.
  0940 AD FA BF 27           lda INITVAL
  0943 85 EE    28           sta PTR
  0945 AD FB BF 29           lda INITVAL+1
  0948 85 EF    30           sta PTR+1
  094A          31 ;
  094A          32 ; Get current entry and save.
  094A A0 06    33           ldy #RESETOFF
  094C B1 EE    34           lda (PTR),Y
  094E 8D 90 09 35           sta RESETSAV
  0951 C8       36           iny
  0952 B1 EE    37           lda (PTR),Y
  0954 8D 91 09 38           sta RESETSAV+1
  0957          39 ;
  0957          40 ; Change entry.
  0957 A9 09    41           lda /MYRESET
  0959 91 EE    42           sta (PTR),Y
  095B 88       43           dey
  095C A9 80    44           lda #MYRESET
  095E 91 EE    45           sta (PTR),Y
    :           :           :
  0980          50 ; My RESET handler location.
  0980 A9 8D    51 MYRESET   lda #RETURN
    :           :           :
  0990 00 00    66 RESETSAV  hex 0000
    :           :           :
```

Figure I.8.6. Accessing and Changing INITVALS in DOS 4.5

I found it was absolutely necessary to add two additional variables to the INITVALS Data structure that is found in DOS 4.1 as shown in Table I.8.7. These two variables are FIRSTCAT and LASTRACK at offsets 0x0D and 0x0E, respectively. At first glance these two variables look exactly like SECVAL and ENDTRK which are part of the VTOCVALS substructure. The VTOCVALS substructure is the darker shaded area shown in Table I.8.7. In the DOS 4.5 source code FIRSTCAT and SECVAL are set to the same value as are LASTRACK and ENDTRK. SECVAL and ENDTRK are working variables in that their values can be changed by the Command Manager or changed by an external File Manager user in order to modify the File Manager Context Block appropriately. FIRSTCAT and LASTRACK are reference variables in that their values are transferred to SECVAL and ENDTRK, respectively, when the Command

Manager determines that the values it finds in the A keyword or in the B keyword are out of range. Now, the user can set FIRSTCAT and LASTRACK to any default value without having to reassemble DOS 4.5.

```
   :            :        :
00EE            4  PTR        epz $EE
   :            :        :
0000           11  DNUMOFF    equ $00
   :            :        :
BFFC           16  BCFGNDX    equ $BFFC
   :            :        :
0940           24  ; Setup pointer.
0940 AD FC BF  25         lda BCFGNDX
0943 85 EE     26         sta PTR
0945 A9 BF     27         lda /BCFGNDX
0947 85 EF     28         sta PTR+1
0949           29  ;
0949           30  ; Change DNUM.
0949 A0 00     31         ldy #DNUMOFF
094B 85 12     32         lda #$12
094D 91 EE     33         sta (PTR),Y
094F           34  ;
094F           35  ; Change VOLEXPT.
094F C8        36         iny
0950 85 A7     37         lda #$A7
0952 91 EE     38         sta (PTR),Y
   :            :        :
```

Figure I.8.7. Changing the Boot Configuration Data Structure in DOS 4.5

9. DOS 4.5 Memory Initialization

DOS 4.5 memory initialization is a very complex procedure, and it begins even before the Disk][Interface Card firmware reads sector 0x00 on track 0x00 into memory. The Interface Card firmware must generate a RDNIBLBT table from 0x36C to 0x3D5 in order for the firmware to process the 342 *disk* bytes it reads that generate a sector of 256 *memory* bytes. This process is called *6 and 2* decoding or Data Field Decoding, and this subject is thoroughly discussed in many publications on Apple DOS 3.3. Figure I.9.1 shows a snippet of firmware that generates the RDNIBLBT table. The firmware reads the first 0x56 disk bytes to memory address 0x0300 which corresponds to an NBUF2-like buffer. Because the firmware saves the next 256 disk bytes to an address that is on a page boundary, a corresponding NBUF1-like buffer is not required. The post-nibblize routine uses the disk bytes to generate the memory bytes at the same address. Once the Boot Stage 0 bootstrap code is in memory at address 0x0800, RWTS and all of its support routines must be read into memory by the Disk][firmware in order to have all of the necessary software routines in memory for Boot Stage 2 so that RWTS can move the read/write disk head and access the rest of DOS on other disk tracks.

```
   :             :             :
C019 98          57           tya
C01A 9D 56 03    58           sta RDNIBLBT-$16,X
   :             :             :
```

Figure I.9.1. Generating RDNIBLBT in Disk][Firmware

Slot	DRV0TRK	DRV1TRK	DRV0PHAS	DRV1PHAS
1	0x0479	0x04F9	0x0679	0x06F9
2	0x047A	0x04FA	0x067A	0x06FA
3	0x047B	0x04FB	0x067B	0x06FB
4	0x047C	0x04FC	0x067C	0x06FC
5	0x047D	0x04FD	0x067D	0x06FD
6	0x047E	0x04FE	0x067E	0x06FE
7	0x047F	0x04FF	0x067F	0x06FF

Table I.9.1. RWTS Scratchpad RAM Locations in DOS 4.5

Boot Stage 2 begins by calling the CLRVALS routine primarily in order to initialize the seven byte Scratchpad Table called SCRCHTBL to zero. CLRVALS also initializes the CMDVALS Data structure and the File Manager FMWORK Data structure to zero. SCRCHTBL is used to determine if RWTS has been called previously on behalf of the slot that is currently being used to boot DOS into memory. If this is the very first call to RWTS for that slot, the Scratchpad Table entry for that slot is decremented and the drive and phase scratchpad RAM locations for both Drive 1 and Drive 2 for that slot are initialized to zero reflecting the current position of the read/write disk head onto track 0x00. Table I.9.1 shows the addresses for all of the RWTS scratchpad RAM locations available for both disk drives. It is at these RAM locations where the current track position of the read/write disk head is maintained in half-phase values for each drive on each slot that is utilized for a Disk][or Disk][-like drive. Similarly, the spacing between tracks in half-phase values is maintained for each drive on each slot as well. The firmware I designed for a RanaSystems EliteThree disk drive simply expands Table I.9.1 to accommodate four disk drives. DOS 4.5 is unique among all previous disk operating systems to always initialize its RWTS scratchpad RAM locations when RWTS accesses a disk drive for the first time on each and every slot.

Boot Stage 2 utilizes the RWTS IOCB in order to stipulate what sector on which track to read for a page of data and where that data is placed into memory. Before any of that logic can take place, RWTS must establish where the read/write disk head is currently positioned. The ROM firmware has already utilized a low-level, though effective disk head recalibration routine that initially assumes the disk head is located on track forty (i.e. 0x28), and repositions the disk head onto track 0x00. From the IOCB, the DOS 4.5 RWTS extracts the slot-times-sixteen number, divides that number by sixteen, and generates an index value which happens to also be the slot number. In this redesigned RWTS a Scratchpad Table called SCRCHTBL is used in combination with the calculated index value (or slot number) to determine if RWTS has been called previously on behalf of that slot. Since this is currently the case, the appropriate scratchpad RAM locations for the slot that is booting as shown in Figure I.9.1 is initialized to zero which happens to correspond to the current track position of the read/write disk head, that is, at track 0x00. Boot Stage 2 proceeds to read into memory the remaining twenty-six data sectors of DOS

4.5 and branches to the COLDSTRT entry point in order to bypass the DOSINIT entry point whose only function is to call the CLRVALS routine. Calling CLRVALS at this time would not be desirable because it would remove the critical information currently in SCRCHTBL and, therefore, the information in the scratchpad RAM locations for the slot that was just used to read into memory the remaining data sectors of DOS.

DOS 3.3, DOS 4.1, and even ProDOS load a Read Translate table (RDNIBL) and a Write Translate table (WRNIBL) into memory along with its DOS image when DOS is booted. The RDNIBL table is 0x6A bytes in size and the WRNIBL table is 0x40 bytes in size. As alluded to above, the companion buffer to NBUF1, whose address is listed in Table I.8.1, is NBUF2, whose size is 0x56 bytes. When NBUF1 and NBUF2 are filled with data, 342 *disk* bytes have been read. It is rather interesting and fortunate that when taken together, NBUF2, RDNIBL, and WRNIBL all fit within one 256-byte page. One could utilize the firmware to output its data to the RDNIBL address instead of to RDNIBLBT at 0x36C after the firmware boot of Boot Stage 1 and before Boot Stage 2, but that still leaves having to read in the WRNIBL table. I was fascinated to discover (yes, certainly, a very serious Aha! Moment indeed) that I could programmatically generate both tables at the same time. In other words, I could save having to read in 0xAA bytes of data at the expense of 0x25 bytes of code, thus saving over one-half page of disk space that could be used for other DOS functionality. The DOS 4.5 code snippet to generate both the RDNIBL and the WRNIBL tables is shown in Figure I.9.2. The BLDNIBL routine incorporates only six additional bytes to generate 0x40 bytes of essential data, and the routine directly follows scratchpad RAM initialization. Therefore, before RWTS is called the first time, the RDNIBL table is manufactured.

```
    :                 :              :
D2CA  8A             825            txa
D2CB  09 80          826            ora  #$80
D2CD  99 56 DF       827            sta  WRNIBL,Y
D2D0                 828        ;
D2D0  98             829            tya
D2D1  9D 80 DF       830            sta  RDNIBL-$16,X
    :                 :              :
```

Figure I.9.2. Generating RDNIBL and WRNIBL in DOS 4.5

Table I.9.2 shows the sequence of steps that are used by both DOS 4.5L and DOS 4.5H to boot and read their DOS image into memory. It should be no surprise that both versions of DOS utilize virtually the same sequence of steps except for having to call two additional routines in DOS 4.5H, HRAM2DOS and COPYROM. Also, Bank 1 of the Language Card partition must be enabled before DOS 4.5H can call CLRVALS. Because DOS 4.5H copies the ROM Monitor into its RAM memory of the Language Card partition, it uses this fact to reinitialize and call the Monitor initialization routines, and when ROM Applesoft verification fails, the Apple][is forced into the Monitor at 0xFF65, albeit it is actually the RAM Monitor that is invoked. This is the purpose for GOTOMON in DOS 4.5H when the user wishes to inspect code in Bank 2 of the Language Card partition by calling 0xBE00, or when the user wishes to inspect code in Bank 1 of the Language Card partition by calling 0xBE08.

One of the hardware design limitations in having two banks of memory in the Language Card partition, Bank 1 and Bank 2, at the same address, 0xD000, is that it is not possible to execute code in one bank and read or write data in the other bank concurrently, that is, at the same time. Once DOS 4.5H RWTS is located in Bank 1 memory after Boot Stage 1 has finished, Boot Stage 2 reads the remaining twenty-six pages into memory in two sections: sixteen pages to 0xF0-0xFF and ten pages to 0xE0-0xE9. Those sixteen pages in 0xF0-0xFF need to be moved to 0xD0-0xDF in Bank 2. The ten pages at 0xE0-0xE9 are already where they need to be. This is how DOS 4.5H reads data using one bank and then writes data into the other bank. Once DOS 4.5H is properly placed in memory, DOSINIT can begin.

Function	DOS 4.5L	DOS 4.5H
Boot Stage 0	Prepare STAG1MOD, BUFRADRZ+1	Prepare STAG1MOD, BUFRADRZ+1
Boot Stage 1	Read in RWTS code	Select Bank 1 in the Language Card partition, read in RWTS code, XFER routines
Boot Stage 2	Call CLRVALS to initialize CMDVALS and FMWORK Data structures to zero, Init IOCB, call RWTS to read in rest of DOS code, branch to COLDSTRT	Call CLRVALS to initialize CMDVALS and FMWORK Data structures to zero, Init IOCB, call RWTS to read in rest of DOS code, call HRAM2DOS to move DOS down in memory, branch to COLDSTRT
DOSINIT	Call CLRVALS to initialize CMDVALS and FMWORK Data structures to zero	Select Bank 1 of the Language Card partition, call CLRVALS to initialize CMDVALS and FMWORK Data structures to zero
COLDSTRT	Select ROM WP Bank 2	Select ROM WE Bank 2
Monitor Init/ GOTOMON	Init stack pointer, XMODE, VID80OFF, ALTCHOFF, SETNORM, INIT, SETVID, SETKBD	Init stack pointer, XMODE, VID80OFF, ALTCHOFF, SETNORM, INIT, SETVID, SETKBD
Applesoft Verification	Verify ROM Applesoft, fall into Monitor if test fails	Verify ROM Applesoft, fall into Monitor if test fails
Copy ROM Monitor and Addresses	Not applicable in this version	Call COPYROM to copy ROM Monitor to RAM, call COPYDOS to copy DOSWARM and DOSCOLD addresses to RAM
Find Clock	Call FINDCLK to locate clock card, type	Call FINDCLK to locate clock card, type
Cold-start Init	Init SLOTVAL, DRVAL, VOLVAL	Init SLOTVAL, DRVAL, VOLVAL
Begin Cold-start	Set C-flag, jump to COLDSTR2	Set C-flag, jump to COLDSTR2

Table I.9.2. Boot Sequence Steps in DOS 4.5

Monitor initialization has slightly changed as Apple introduced new platforms such as the Apple //e and the Apple //c. Now, Monitor initialization includes initializing the variable XMODE to 0xFF for proper CX ROM space functionality and to access the variables VID80OFF and ALTCHOFF in order to select the 40-column display mode and to engage the display of the main video character set. I have added a call to SETNORM to ensure that there is *normal* screen character display (**not** inverse or **not** blinking) along with the usual calls to INIT, SETVID, and SETKBD. I do not believe the order that these Monitor routines are called actually matters at all. With the ROM Monitor now in focus, DOS 4.5 can verify the presence or absence of ROM Applesoft. DOS 4.5 does not continue its initialization progress if it does not find a JMP instruction (i.e. 0x4C) at the BASCLD address of 0xE000.

DOS 4.5H copies the entire Monitor that is in ROM from 0xF800 to 0xFFFF to the same address in the RAM of the Language Card partition. Obviously, having the Monitor in RAM saves DOS 4.5H having to manage memory using Soft Switches in order to gain access to common Monitor routines. Unlike the Monitor routines in ROM, however, the Monitor routines in RAM can be modified, so DOS

4.5H copies the `DOSWARM` and `DOSCOLD` addresses shown in Table I.9.3 to the Monitor in RAM where `0xFEB0` is the cold-start location and `0xFEB3` is the warm-start location for Applesoft. DOS 4.5 can now begin its search for a clock card in one of the peripheral slots. Section I.13 is devoted entirely to clock card access in DOS 4.5. At this time DOS 4.5 prepares for cold-start initialization by initializing the Command Manager with the slot, drive, and volume variables from the `RWTS IOCB` that were just utilized to boot DOS.

Address	Variable	DOS 4.5L	DOS 4.5H	Description
0x3D0	DOSWARM	jmp WARMSTRT	jmp EXTWARM	DOS warm-start jmp
0x3D3	DOSCOLD	jmp COLDSTRT		DOS cold-start jmp
0x3D6	CALLFM	jmp FMHNDLR	jmp EXTFM	File Manager jmp
0x3D9	CALLRWTS	jmp DORWTS	jmp EXTRWTS	RWTS handler jmp
0x3DC 0x3DE	GETFMCB	ldy #FMVALS lda /FMVALS		Puts File Manager Input/Output Context Block address into #Y/A registers
0x3E1	RDCLKVSN	adr DOCLKVSN	adr EXCLKVSN	address in #Y/A, Clock clc, Version sec
0x3E3 0x3E5	GETIOCB	ldy #TBLTYPE lda /TBLTYPE		Puts RWTS I/O Input/Output Context Block address into #Y/A registers
0x3E8	PRTERADR	adr DOPRTERR	adr EXTPRERR	Prints error message for error # in X-reg
0x3EA	HOOKDOS	jmp INITPTRS	jmp EXTPTRS	DOS reconnect jmp
0x3ED	XFERADR	adr *-*		Used for the Apple //e DOXFER routine
0x3EF	AUTOBRK	jmp OLDBRK		ROM break handler jmp
0x3F2	AUTORSET	adr WARMSTRT	adr EXTWARM	ROM auto-reset routine address
0x3F4	PWRSTATE	byt 0xA5^(0x3F3)		Power up byte
0x3F5	USRAHAND	jmp REPEATCD	jmp EXTRPEAT	& handler jmp
0x3F8	USRYHAND	jmp AUXMOVE		Ctrl-Y handler jmp to 0xC311
0x3FB	NMASKIRQ	jmp MON		Non-maskable IRQ jmp to 0xFF65
0x3FE	MASKIRQ	adr MON		Maskable IRQ routine address at 0xFF65

Table I.9.3. Page 0x03 Interface Routines and Vectors in DOS 4.5

Software developers of my favorite utilities like *ADT*, *Big Mac*, *FID*, *Lisa*, *PGE*, *GPLE*, and *Sourceror*, made use of the DOS 3.3 Initial Address table located at `0x9D00` to `0x9D0F`, `0x9D56` to `0x9D83`, and, unfortunately, direct entry points to many other internal DOS 3.3 variables and routines. One can directly modify the values in the DOS 4.5 `INITVALS` table shown in Table I.8.7 to tailor a DOS boot image specific to one's needs. That is, `CMDVAL` specifies the `HELLO` file command (i.e. `0x06` for `RUN`, `0x14` for `EXEC`, and `0x34` for `BRUN`), `NMAXVAL` specifies what the initial `MAXFILES` value is set to, and `YEARVAL` specifies the current year in order to support the Thunderclock card which lacks a year register. `SECVAL` defines how many sectors are used for the volume Catalog, `ENDTRK` specifies how many tracks are used to initialize the volume, and `ENDSEC` specifies whether a track has sixteen or thirty-two sectors. In order to support hardware that provides forty tracks per volume, simply change `ENDTRK` to forty (i.e. `0x28`). If hardware supports thirty-two sectors per track, change `ENDSEC` to thirty-two (i.e. `0x20`). Modify some or all of these parameters directly in memory or use the `INIT` keywords and initialize another disk volume with an appropriate `HELLO` file. Either a Boot or a Data volume is created having a volume Catalog that is structured according to the values you select.

```
 :                     :      :
03E1                   5      RDCLKVSN  equ  $3E1
 :                     :      :
0900  A0 43            13               ldy  #VSNBUFR
0902  A9 09            14               lda  /VSNBUFR
0904  38               15               sec
0905  20 40 09         16               jsr  READVSN
 :                     :      :
0920  60               20               rts
 :                     :      :
0940  6C E1 03         40     READVSN   jmp  (RDCLKVSN)
0943  00 00 00         41     VSNBUFR   dfs  20,0
 :                     :      :
```

Figure I.9.3. Reading the DOS Version in DOS 4.5

```
 :                     :      :
03E1                   5      RDCLKVSN  equ  $3E1
 :                     :      :
0900  A0 43            13               ldy  #CLKBUFR
0902  A9 09            14               lda  /CLKBUFR
0904  18               15               clr
0905  20 40 09         16               jsr  READCLK
 :                     :      :
0920  60               20               rts
 :                     :      :
0940  6C E1 03         40     READCLK   jmp  (RDCLKVSN)
0943  00 00 00         41     CLKBUFR   dfs  6,0
 :                     :      :
```

Figure I.9.4. Reading the Date and Time in DOS 4.5

When DOS 4.5 performs a cold-start it sets MAXFILES equal to NMAXVAL, it initializes the file buffers, it makes EXEC inactive, and it copies the contents of Table I.9.3 into memory beginning at memory address 0x3D0. It is in this interface structure where the important entry addresses and vectors are found for DOS routines, such as RWTS and the File Manager. This structure is essentially the same as that found in DOS 3.3 in order to maintain compatibility with virtually all previous software, but with some important additions. I have added "read DOS version" or "read clock routine" (i.e. RDCLKVSN) at memory address 0x3E1, the "error printing routine" (i.e. PRTERROR) at memory address 0x3E8, and the Apple //e "DOXFER routine" (i.e. XFERADR) at memory address 0x3ED. The RDCLKVSN and PRTERROR routines can be accessed using an indirect JMP instruction such as JMP (RDCLKVSN). The two routines GETFMCB and GETIOCB are changed somewhat in DOS 4.5 from their DOS 3.3 implementation, but they return the same information. That is, the address of the RWTS IOCB in the Y- and A-registers, and similarly, the address of the File Manager Context Block in the Y- and A-registers in Lo/Hi byte order. These two context blocks are shown in Tables I.10.1 and I.11.1, respectively. The routine RDCLKVSN copies the version of DOS that is currently in memory which is a 20-byte upper ASCII character string (i.e. DOS 4.5.05H 01/01/22), into a buffer whose address is in the Y- and A-registers when the Carry flag is **set**. The routine RDCLKVSN reads the current date and time into a 6-byte buffer as shown in Table I.5.5 whose address is in the Y- and A-registers when the Carry flag is **clear**. The routine PRTERROR prints the error messages as shown in Table I.11.7 whose index error number is in the X-register. Example code segments to read the current DOS version into a 20-byte buffer and the current date and time into a 6-byte buffer are shown in Figures I.9.3 and I.9.4, respectively. Figure I.9.5 shows how *Big Mac* prints all of its File Manager error codes.

```
  :              :           :
0044           18    A5L      epz $44
0045           19    A5H      epz $45
  :              :           :
03D6           27    CALLFM   equ $3D6
03DC           28    GETFMCB  equ $3DC
03E8           29    PRERRADR equ $3E8
  :              :           :
D0B0 6C E8 03  101   PRTERROR jmp (PRERRADR)
  :              :           :
D12D 20 DC 03  131            jsr GETFMCB
D130 84 44     132            sty A5L
D132 85 45     133            sta A5H
  :              :           :
E58A A2 01     316            ldx #1
E58C 20 D6 03  317            jsr CALLFM
E58F 90 40     318            bcc HE5D1
E591 A0 0A     319            ldy #10
E593 B1 44     320            lda (A5L),Y
E595 AA        321            tax
  :              :           :
E5BC 8A        361            txa
E5BD 48        362            pha
  :              :           :
E5C1 E8        366            inx
E5C2 20 B0 D0  367            jsr PRTERROR
E5C5 68        368            pla
E5C6 AA        369            tax
E5C7 20 B0 D0  370            jsr PRTERROR
E5CA 20 8E FD  371            jsr CROUT
  :              :           :
E5D1 A2 0E     394   HE5D1    ldx #$0E
  :              :           :
FD8E A9 8D     586   CROUT    lda #$8D
  :              :           :
```

Figure I.9.5. Printing a File Manager Error in Big Mac

It is worthwhile to note that the DOS 4.5 RWTS only supports Disk][-type hardware since there was no other device manufactured that was substantially different. The Device Characteristics Table (DCT) was originally designed so that RWTS could support an array of disk devices each having different stepper motor phases per track that might have supported half-tracking or even different motor on-time requirements. I saw no need for DOS 4.5 to support something that simply does not, nor will ever exist. I am aware that the RanaSystems EliteThree is a dual-headed disk drive with the ability to access eighty half-tracks on both sides of a double-sided, double-density diskette. Of course, the DCT for the Rana is different, but the Rana uses its own interface handler with its own PHASEON/PHASEOFF tables for its stepper motor operation, and its own number of stepper motor phases to accomplish its half-tracking capabilities. I even developed my own firmware for the Rana that formats a diskette with forty tracks on both sides of the diskette, with the first sixteen sectors on side one and the next sixteen sectors on side two, effectively creating a volume where each track contains thirty-two sectors. I was absolutely successful and, by design, the firmware attached to the DOS 4.5 RWTS DISKADRS table. I was able to obtain double-sided, double-density 5.25-inch floppy diskettes from www.floppydisk.com. As a word of caution, double-sided, double-density 5.25-inch floppy diskettes are manufactured with an inner reinforcement ring. Significantly better performance is achieved using those diskettes whether half-tracking is employed or not. In summary, DOS 4.5 does not utilize a DCT, and it ignores any DCT address found in any RWTS IOCB for a Disk][or for any other Disk][-like drive.

10. The DOS 4.5 RWTS Interface

The DOS 4.5 RWTS interface is very straightforward and simple to use. When a call is made to GETIOCB as shown in Table I.9.3, the Y- and A-registers point to the RWTS IOCB as shown in Table I.10.1. Any other address space may be used for an RWTS IOCB as well. Once the IOCB has been initialized, a call to CALLRWTS with the address of an IOCB, or the address of the IOCB within DOS, in the Y- and A-registers begins RWTS processing. The RWTS handler pushes the current processor status onto the stack, disables interrupts, and saves the Y- and A-registers to the IOB zero-page address at 0x4A/0x4B.

Offset	Name	Size	Description
0x00	TBLTYPE	0x01	IOCB structure block
0x01	SNUM16	0x01	Slot * 16
0x02	DNUM	0x01	Drive number
0x03	VOLEXPT	0x01	Volume number expected; 0x00 for any
0x04	TNUM	0x01	Track number
0x05	SNUM	0x01	Sector number
0x06	DCTADR	0x02	Address of Device Characteristics Table
0x08	USRBUF	0x02	Data buffer address
0x0A	IOCBPHAS	0x01	Half-phases per track
0x0B	BYTCNT	0x01	Bytes to read/write; 0x00 means 256 bytes
0x0C	CMDCODE	0x01	Command
0x0D	ERRCODE	0x01	Return error code
0x0E	VOLFND	0x01	Return volume found
0x0F	SLOTFND	0x01	Return slot found
0x10	DRVFND	0x01	Return drive found

Table I.10.1. RWTS Input/Output Context Block Definition in DOS 4.5

The official volume number for any DOS 4.5 volume is DISKVOL as shown in Table I.5.2, and not the value that is encoded in the address field that prefaces each data field on a diskette. In DOS 4.5 the encoded volume number is saved to the VOLFND variable in the IOCB as shown in Table I.10.1. Disk devices like the RAM Disk 320 or the CFFA do not require an address field to preface each sector or block that contains its data. Thus, the encoded volume number can only be ascertained from Disk][-like devices and the encoded volume number simply does **not** exist in other non-Disk][-type devices. In order for DOS 4.5 to determine volume number mismatch for **all** disk devices it must rely solely on the value found in DISKVOL. Because DISKVOL is external to RWTS, volume number mismatch can only be determined external to RWTS. Therefore, the determination of volume number mismatch cannot be required of other disk devices and their established firmware algorithms. When RWTS returns to the File Manager with the Carry flag **clear**, DOS 4.5 copies IOCBPHAS to VALSPHAS and then checks for volume number mismatch. If the requested volume number VOLEXPT is zero, no further processing is required and a return is made to the caller of RWTS. If VOLEXPT is not zero, then its value is compared to DISKVOL, and if they are the same no further processing is required and a return is made to the caller of RWTS. If VOLEXPT and DISKVOL are not the same, the RWVOLERR error code is immediately submitted to the RWTS error conversion code and the appropriate error number is reported to the File Manager. When the File Manager receives this error code, it displays the Volume Number Mismatch error message, it restores the stack pointer from STKSAVE, and the File Manager exits in order to allow DOS 4.5 to continue its normal processing. Because the VTOC is the very first structure that is read from a volume when DOS begins processing I/O commands, DISKVOL becomes available "just in time" before it is compared to VOLEXPT from the IOCB. All further volume number checks will succeed while DOS continues processing the requested I/O command because the VTOC will not be read again until the next DOS I/O command is issued.

After the Y- and A-registers have been saved to the IOB address at 0x4A/0x4B, the RWTS handler extracts the supplied buffer address USRBUF from the IOCB and saves the address to BUFADR2Z and BUFADR2Z+1 at zero-page addresses 0x3E/0x3F. The handler also extracts the SNUM16 value, saves it to SLOTFND in the IOCB, divides it by sixteen, checks the Scratchpad table SCRCHTBL for first-time slot use, and calculates the low-order address byte for DISKJMP based on that original SNUM16 value. The RWTS handler then indirectly jumps to the routine whose address is located in the Disk Address table DISKADRS for the specified slot number. The assembler initializes all seven DISKADRS table entries to the address of RWTSENT so that it makes no difference into which slot or slots a Disk][or Disk][-like interface card may have been inserted.

The MOVEHD routine handles the placement of the read/write disk head and masks all track values it encounters with TRKMASK (i.e. 0x3F) in order to remove the value of TRKZERO (i.e. 0x40) if it happens to be used. When RWTS completes its processing, it saves its results into the supplied IOCB for DRVFND, VOLFND, and ERRCODE. The RWTS handler restores the original processor status and either **clear** or **set** the Carry flag based on the return status from the RWTS. If interrupts were initially enabled before the call to the RWTS handler, interrupts are re-enabled when the RWTS handler exits. Table I.10.2 shows the four command codes that are valid RWTS commands and Table I.10.3 shows all of the seven possible error codes that RWTS can generate. I have added the RWSYNERR error code for IOCBPHAS range checking errors and for errors found in the RAM Disk, Rana, and Sider firmware that perform their own range checking of their IOCB variables. The error code RWVOLERR is used at the conclusion of and external to RWTS when a check for volume mismatch is made and if the check fails. Once again, DOS 4.5 does not check for volume number mismatch with the volume number that is encoded in the Address Field of a diskette. The astute reader will assuredly notice that I have utilized the spare byte in the RWTS IOCB for the IOCBPHAS variable. Furthermore, I have used the spare byte in the File Manager Input/Output Context Block for FMPHASE as shown later in Table I.11.1. Both variables, when encountered during their specific routine utilization, are range checked and copied to VALSPHAS as shown in Table I.8.7. The value entered with the DOS PHASE command is also copied to VALSPHAS. VALSPHAS is the key variable that is used to multiply the target track number in order to obtain the number of half-phases to which the read/write disk head needs to be moved by MOVEHD before any input/output data can occur.

Command	Value	Description
RWTSSEEK	0x00	Seek to track/sector command code
RWTSREAD	0x01	Read track/sector command code
RWTSWRIT	0x02	Write track/sector command code
RWTSFRMT	0x04	Format volume command code

Table I.10.2. RWTS Command Codes

Error	Value	Description
RWNOERR	0x00	RWTS No error
RWINITER	0x08	RWTS Initialization error
RWPROTER	0x10	RWTS Write protect error
RWVOLERR	0x20	RWTS Volume number error
RWSYNERR	0x30	RWTS Syntax error (out of range)
RWDRVERR	0x40	RWTS Drive error
RWREADER	0x80	RWTS Read error (obsolete)

Table I.10.3. RWTS Error Codes

All physical tracks on a *normal* DOS diskette are separated by four half-phases, the equivalent of rotating the cam of the stepper motor 180 degrees as I prefer to imagine its operation. The stepper motor is used to move the read/write disk head along the radius of the diskette towards or away from the center of the diskette. A simplified representation of the read/write disk head mechanics in the Disk][is shown in Figure I.10.1. The read/write disk head is connected to the Carriage Rod and that rod travels along the radius of the diskette as the Cam Table is rotated by the Stepper Motor. The Cam Rider is also attached to the Carriage Rod and it essentially *rides* the Cam Channel. As the Cam Table rotates, the Cam Rider follows the Cam Channel, thereby pulling or pushing the Carriage Rod towards or away from the center of the diskette. The Stepper Motor can be made to rotate both clockwise and counter-clockwise in order to move the read/write disk head from track 0x00 to track 0x23, and then back to track 0x00.

About one year after the Disk][drive was first introduced in June, 1978, the Cam Table and supporting hardware were slightly modified in order to access thirty-six tracks rather than thirty-five tracks. For one reason or another this information never found its way into the general Apple user community.

The motor used to rotate the Cam Table in the Disk][is a general purpose 4-phase, 12-volt DC stepper motor. Each electromagnet or phase coil inside the stepper motor can be energized individually or in pairs, as well as de-energized, in such a way as to cause the Cam Table to rotate. The illustration shown in Figure I.10.2 gives the location of the first twelve half-phases as well as the location where tracks 0x00, 0x01, 0x02, and 0x03 would occur along the Cam Channel as the Cam Table is rotated clockwise or counter-clockwise. These tracks conform to the normal spacing of four half-phases like the tracks found on a DOS Master diskette. On the other hand, the Rana Elite has the ability to space tracks as close as two half-phases because the gap length of its read/write disk head is smaller than the gap length of the read/write disk head found in the Disk][. Actually, the gap length of the read/write disk head in the Disk][is somewhat equal to the size of three half-phases. Manufacturing read/write disk heads with this specification helps to minimize cross-talk between adjacent tracks that are spaced four or more half-phases apart.

In order to move the read/write disk head from track `0x00` to track `0x23`, the stepper motor needs to rotate through a span of 140 half-phases, that is, 35 * 4 half-phases. The span of tracks is always the number of possible tracks minus one. If tracks are separated by only three half-phases, it is conceivable that a diskette could possibly support up to forty-seven and maybe even forty-eight tracks. Figure I.10.3 shows the same location of those first twelve half-phases as shown in Figure I.10.2, only now the tracks are spaced every three half-phases. Of course, this is merely an illustration until it can actually be demonstrated. There are a number of parameters to consider when designing software to actuate the stepper motor in the Disk][, or in any other similar disk drive. These parameters may include present track location of the read/write disk head, direction of movement, distance of movement, desired acceleration, desired deceleration, desired velocity, induced vibration, and controlled damping. The routine that moves the read/write disk head on behalf of `RWTS` may consider all of these parameters in order to consistently place the read/write disk head at the correct location or track as efficiently as possible without regard to direction of movement, distance, and the generation of any induced angular momentum. In other words, the read/write disk head must be totally stopped and it must be held at the correct location consistently before any input or any output of data can occur with any reliability.

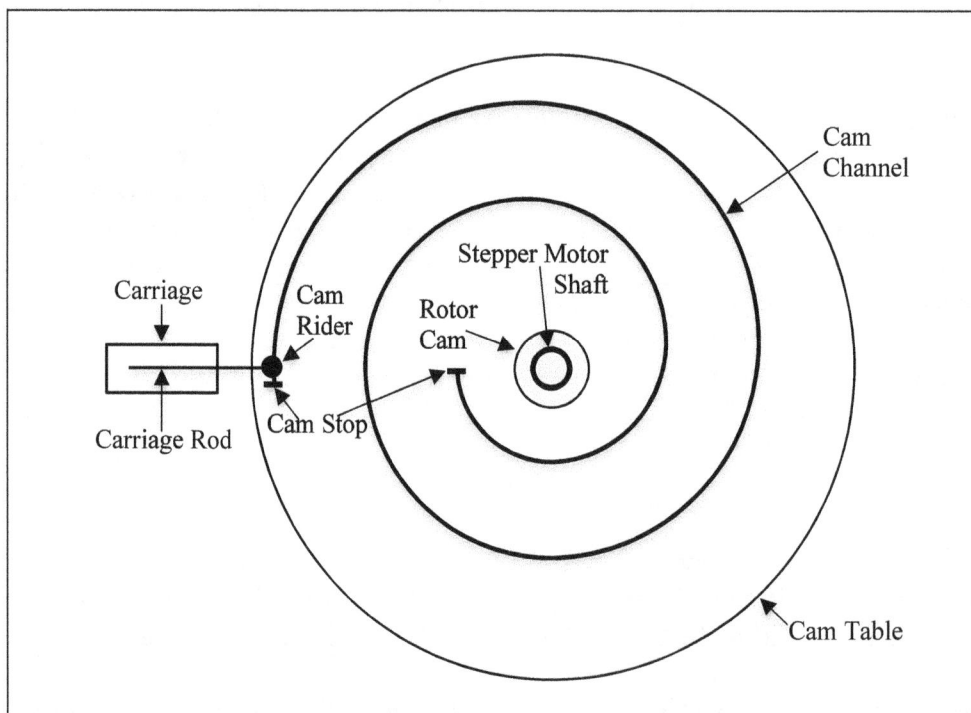

Figure I.10.1. Disk][Carriage and Cam Table

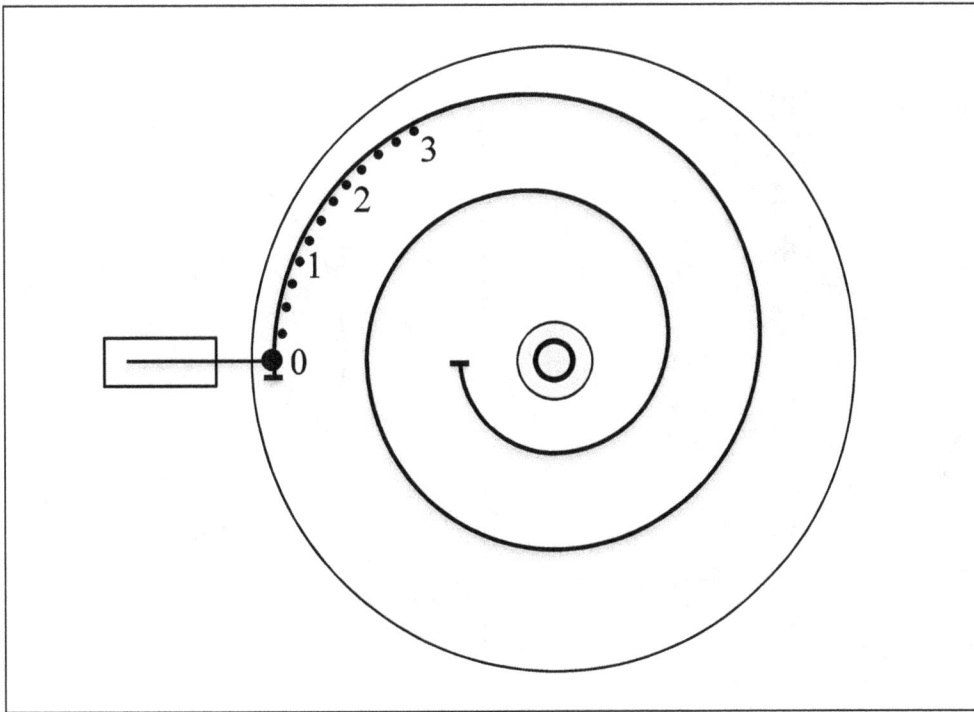

Figure I.10.2. Four Half-Phase Track Separation

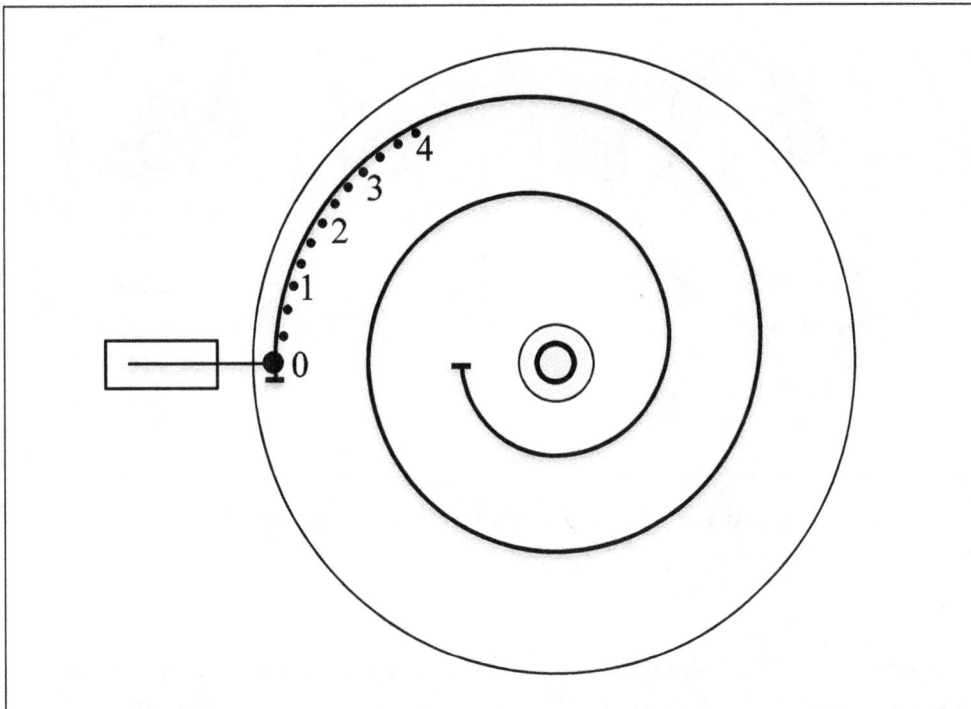

Figure I.10.3. Three Half-Phase Track Separation

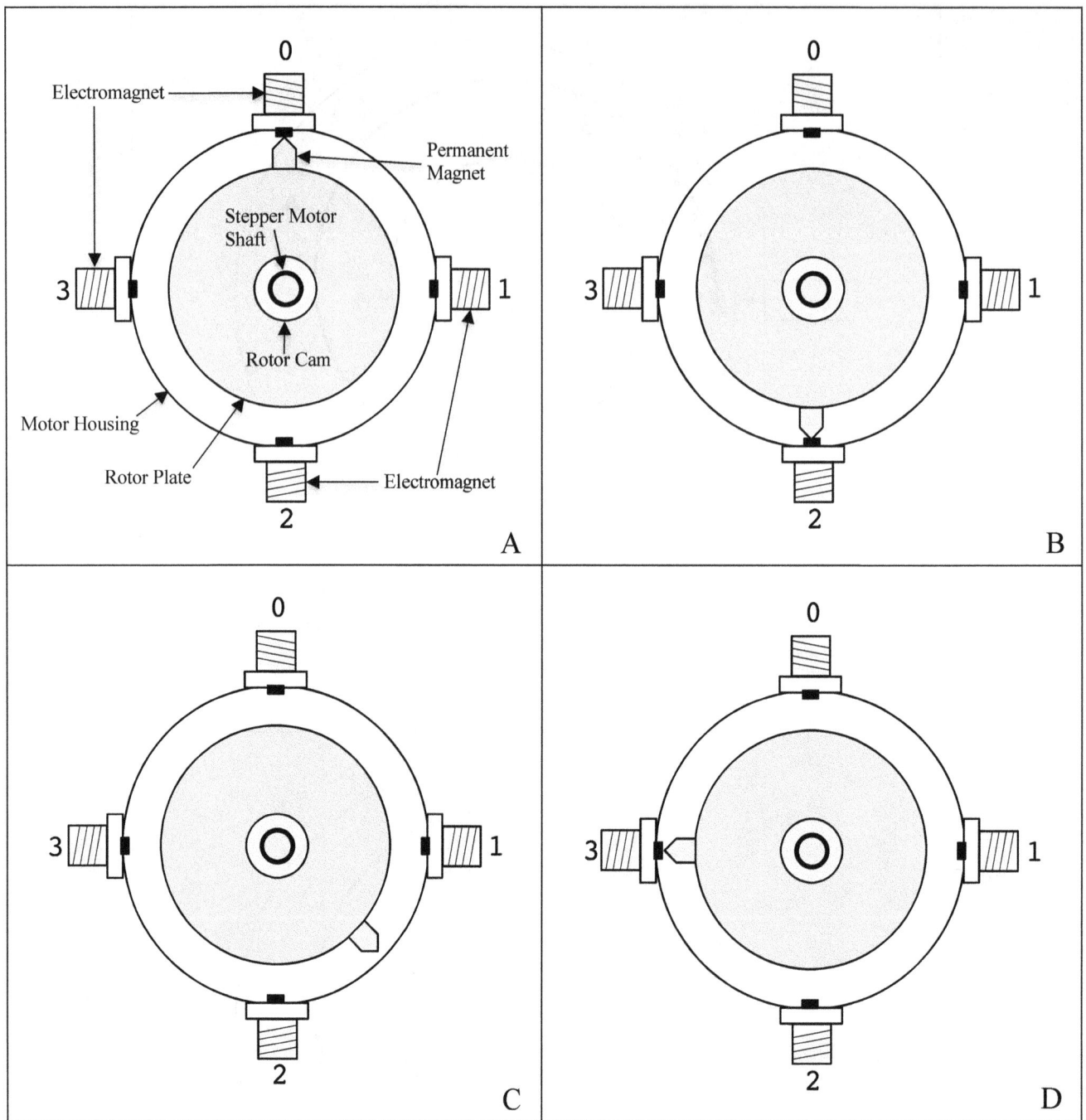

Figure I.10.4. Inside View of a Stepper Motor

For the sake of simplicity, I like to imagine the mechanical operation of a stepper motor as that represented by the illustrations shown in Figure I.10.4. The main functional components of this Disk][stepper motor are labeled in Figure I.10.4A. The permanent magnet that is attached to the Rotor Plate is attracted to each one of the four electromagnetics or phase coils as each coil is energized in succession. By design, the stepper motor is always at Phase 0 when the Cam Rider hits the outer Cam Stop, the location of track 0x00. Figure I.10.4B shows the Rotor Cam positioned clockwise at Phase Coil 2, effectively positioning the read/write disk head precisely over track 0x01 as shown in Figure I.10.2 where each track is separated by four half-phases. Essentially, the rotation of the Rotor Plate from one electromagnet to the next electromagnet amounts to one full phase or two half-phases. Every rotation of four half-phases moves the read/write disk head to the next or previous adjacent track. Figure I.10.4C shows the Rotor Cam positioned at three half-phases clockwise from Phase 0. This would position the read/write disk head precisely over track `0x01` as shown in Figure I.10.3 where each track is separated by three half-phases. Figure I.10.4D shows the Rotor Cam positioned clockwise at Phase Coil 3 which would position the read/write disk head precisely over track `0x02`, again for tracks separated by three half-phases.

The MOVEHD routine in DOS 4.1 is similar to the routine found in DOS 3.3 in that both routines move the read/write disk head to and from the even numbered phase coils 0 and 2. The odd numbered phase coils 1 and 3 simply assist in turning the Cam Table as smoothly as possible. Both routines use an acceleration and deceleration algorithm that reaches maximum velocity after moving the read/write disk head through eight phases. That is, the current track and the target track are first doubled so that a computation is made every time the current track counter in incremented, and that would occur as every new phase is selected, thus, either a specific coil is energized or a specific coil is deenergized. The time to leave a specific coil energized or deenergized is determined by an entry from either an ONTBL or an OFFTBL of eight values in each table. One can just as easily view the distance between two adjacent tracks as equal to four half-phases rather than equal to two phases as in DOS 3.3 or in DOS 4.1. Since I claim that the individual half-phase is attainable, it is the more general expression, and Occam's Razor would favor the *half-phase* as the preferred designation.

The MOVEHD routine found in DOS 4.5 is radically different from the routine found in DOS 4.1 in that a computation must be made every half-phase, and the time a coil is energized or deenergized is determined by an entry from a single ONOFFTBL table of twelve values. This table also provides the MOVEHD routine with an acceleration and deceleration component that reaches maximum velocity after moving the read/write disk head through twelve half-phases. The resulting movement of the Cam Table is smooth and efficient. Once the read/write disk head is located at its destination, the Cam Table is held in place for nearly twenty-six milliseconds to ensure all vibration transients and torque due to its angular momentum has been buffered and absorbed by the enclosure. The last coil or coils can then be deenergized to assure that the read/write disk head is held precisely over the requested track. The Carriage Rod and Carriage are designed to inhibit any further movement of the read/write disk head once the coil or coils have been deenergized. Some disk manufactures employ a tension band that can be adjusted to restrict movement of the Carriage Rod, but obviously not enough restriction that cannot be overcome by the strong startup torque of the stepper motor.

The direction of Cam Table movement in the DOS 4.5 MOVEHD routine determines the values for the NEXTON and NEXTOFF variables. One or the other variable is used every time the current track counter is incremented or decremented and a new computation is made: either NEXTON is subtracted from or NEXTOFF is added to the track counter. When the read/write disk head has reached its final destination and held in place, and if the Permanent Magnet is at rest between two coils as shown in Figure I.10.4C, the coils are deenergized in a specific order. It does not matter whether the Cam Table is turned clockwise or counterclockwise: these two coils are always deenergized in the same order. Doing this minimizes any possible skewing of the read/write disk head relative to absolute track location. Understand that it is not physically possible to deenergize two coils of the same stepper motor at precisely the same moment in time. Furthermore, there is no dependence on which microprocessor instructions are used to deenergize two coils at the same time: an absolute addressing instruction is no faster and induces no less skew than any indexed addressing instruction regardless whether the X- or the Y-register(s) are used.

Managing disk phase in RWTS is an exceedingly complex process particularly when copying files from diskette volumes that have been initialized with different phase values. Beginning with the initial boot for a volume, the start location of the read/write disk head for drive 1 is forced to be track 0x00 by the Disk][Interface Card firmware and the start location is set to be track 0x00 for both drive 1 and drive 2 in the Scratchpad table when RWTS is called for the first time. The unique design of DOS 4.5 RWTS initializes the DRV0TRK and DRV1TRK variables as well as the DRV0PHAS and DRV1PHAS variables to zero at the beginning of Boot Stage 2. DRV0TRK and DRV1TRK use the base addresses 0x0478 and 0x04F8, respectively, and DRV0PHAS and DRV1PHAS use the base addresses 0x0678 and 0x06F8, respectively. Of course, the slot number for the Disk][is used as an index from these base addresses. As an aside, the Rana uses 0x0578 and 0x05F8 as the base addresses for DRV2TRK and DRV3TRK, respectively, and 0x0778 and 0x07F8 for DRV2PHAS and DRV3PHAS, respectively.

In RWTS processing just prior to extracting the requested IOCB command, if the phase value saved at DRV0PHAS or DRV1PHAS (depending on drive number) is zero, it is set to DFLTPHAS, or four, and a page-zero PHASE variable is set to either the saved phase value or DFLTPHAS. Next, the IOCB phase value is extracted and if it is zero, it is replaced by PHASE, and then range checked not to exceed PHASMAX, or sixteen. The IOCB phase value is again compared to PHASE, and if the values differ, the read/write disk head is moved to track 0x00 using the previously saved phase value (i.e. PHASE), and then moved to the requested track using the new IOCB phase value which is then saved to the scratchpad. If the PHASE and IOCB phase values do not differ, the read/write disk head is simply moved to the requested track using the PHASE value. If the phase value changed, all further access to that drive now utilizes the new phase value. The additional logic to manage disk phase when the phase value does not change is still within the window established by the required number of 40-microsecond auto-synchronization bytes between an address field and its data field. Establishing a new phase value for a Disk][or a Disk][-like drive occurs once, so the impact to a disk copying session is only slightly minimal. This re-phasing process happens so fast, so smoothly, most users would probably never even notice its implementation.

The illustration shown in Figure I.10.3 suggests that a Disk][in pristine working order can conceivably access up to and possibly forty-eight tracks on a double-sided double-density diskette using a half-phase value of three. The DOS 4.5 INIT command can certainly initialize a diskette with that format flawlessly. And *FID*, after being modified to request Phase number like it requests Volume number, can be used to copy files from a phase-four diskette to a phase-three diskette. The new phase-three diskette boots effortlessly because the DOS 4.5 INIT handler copies the VALSPHAS value to CFGPHASE before creating the new DOS image. CFGPHASE is copied to IOCBPHAS at the beginning of Boot Stage 2. I have even created bootable diskettes initialized with VALSPHAS set to five and six. A phase-five diskette can only access at most twenty-nine tracks (i.e. 1 + 140 / 5) and a phase-six diskette can only access at most twenty-four tracks. Why would one desire this capability? First and foremost an odd-phased initialized diskette would be very difficult to copy and probably thwart a number of diskette copy applications. Because PHASE is a DOS command in DOS 4.5, its value can be changed at any given moment while a *special* diskette is booting and loading its first application. Actually, the Application Loader could *adjust* phase to ensure its copy-protection routines are well protected and difficult to access while it is loading the primary application. I have no doubt that John K. Morris can perfectly copy any DOS 4.5 phased diskette using his Applesauce floppy drive controller. And that is perfectly fine with me.

The software routines within RWTS to read and write the Address Field header data and the Data Field sector data of a Disk][diskette were all originally designed by Steve Wozniak. The critical timing these routines employ are entirely dependent on how Wozniak designed the companion Disk][Interface Card hardware, including its logic gate timing, its functional component requirements, and its data format restrictions. It has even been reported that Wozniak went so far as to modify the innovative design of his original interface card layout in order to reduce the number of feed-through holes from three to two. The most comprehensive discussions I have found on RWTS and the Disk][Interface Card can be found in *Beneath Apple DOS* and *Beneath Apple ProDOS*, both books by Don Worth and Pieter Lechner and *Understanding the Apple II* and *Understanding the Apple IIe*, both books by Jim Sather. I believe Sather's books are incredibly detailed because Sather uses tables, diagrams, and schematic drawings to explain the operation of the Apple][series of computers, and the Worth/Lechner books provide the reader with a number of excellent example programs that demonstrate how to use RWTS in software programs. But, in my opinion, even these references as well as others in my library do not adequately demonstrate how the Disk][Interface Card and its unique ROM manages to read and write Disk][information on a floppy diskette. That is, not until I took my own, personal, deep dive into exploring how the logic circuits of the Disk][Interface Card interact with the data contents of its 256-byte sequencer ROM did I fully appreciate, understand, and marvel at Wozniak's brilliant hardware design. I found the clearest schematic drawing of the Disk][Interface Card in the *Apple][The DOS Manual*. That reference book even provides the schematic drawing of the Disk][analog board.

The Disk][Interface Card contains the P5 ROM, or 256-byte bootstrap Boot Stage 0 firmware, an 8-bit shift/storage data register, the 256-byte P6 8-bit logic state sequencer ROM, and an 8-bit addressable latch, or command decoder. The schematic drawing of the Disk][Interface Card shows that the 8-bit *index byte* used to address the P6 sequencer ROM is composed of two bits from the command decoder, a negative pulse data bit from the Disk][analog board, a write protect bit which is the QA output, or MSB from the shift/storage data register, and four bits from the 8-bit data byte previously read from the same P6 ROM. The connections to the bits of this index byte is shown pictorially in Figure I.10.5. The two bits from the command decoder, named Q6 and Q7, provide the only means to control the logic state sequencer using RWTS software. Table I.10.4 shows the definition of the sixteen peripheral-card I/O memory bytes that are dedicated to the Disk][Interface Card as switches, Q1 to Q7. The value of **n** in 0xC0n0, for example, equals the slot number of the Disk][Interface Card plus eight. Furthermore, the Disk][Interface Card circuitry and P6 ROM sequencing is specifically designed such that any reference to the Disk][peripheral-card I/O memory **must** only utilize indexed addressing instructions. Typically, the X-register is primarily used for this indexing, and this register contains the slot number of the Disk][Interface Card times sixteen. For a Disk][Interface Card residing in slot 6, the address 0xC0E0 would be referenced when using the indexed addressing instruction $C080,X when the X-register is equal to 0x60. System RESET forces all eight switches into the OFF, or zero state.

One of the very first tasks the RWTS software performs when it begins its processing is to enable READ mode with the Disk][Interface Card regardless whether the call to RWTS will read or write disk data. Using Table I.10.4 as reference and shown in Table I.10.5, switches Q6 and Q7 must be both turned OFF in order to enable READ sequencing. This is shown in Figure I.10.6 taken from the DOS 4.5H RWTS software. Once the Disk][Interface Card has configured its mode to READ, it is now safe for RWTS to select Drive using switch Q5 and to enable the drive motor that rotates the diskette using switch Q4. The read/write disk head may now be safely positioned over the requested track using switches Q0 through Q3 in a controlled and precise sequence whose algorithm utilizes the requested phase in DOS 4.5. If the call to RWTS is to read a sector of disk data, Figure I.10.7 shows a code example taken from the DOS 4.5H software that reads a disk byte. As is shown later in this discussion, the MSB of a disk byte is not used as a data bit, but as a flag bit indicating that valid disk data is available to be read from the shift and storage data register. Once a disk byte has been read, the logic state sequencer immediately commands the shift register to clear, it commands the register to input a 1 bit and shift the register bits left, it commands the register to input a data pulse bit sent from the Disk][analog board that has been held for eight microseconds, and finally it shifts the register bits left again. Subsequent data pulse bits are input into the shift and storage data register and the register bits are shifted left every four microseconds which is equivalent to eight sequences of the logic state sequencer. The shift and storage data register and a 74LS174 latch (having six D-type flip-flops) that contain the D4 through D7 data bits from the previous P6 ROM data byte are clocked by *Q3* falling which has a frequency of 2 MHz that is synchronized to the 6502 (or 65C02) PHASE 0 clock.

A7	A6	A5	A4	A3	A2	A1	A0
Sequence Bit 3	Sequence Bit 2	Sequence Bit 0	Data Pulse	Q7	Q6	QA	Sequence Bit 1

Figure I.10.5. Index Byte Format for the P6 ROM

Switch	OFF Function	ON Function
Q0	$C080,X – PHASE 0 OFF	$C081,X – PHASE 0 ON
Q1	$C082,X – PHASE 1 OFF	$C083,X – PHASE 1 ON
Q2	$C084,X – PHASE 2 OFF	$C085,X – PHASE 2 ON
Q3	$C086,X – PHASE 3 OFF	$C087,X – PHASE 3 ON
Q4	$C088,X – drives OFF	$C089,X – selected drive ON
Q5	$C08A,X – select drive 1	$C08B,X – select drive 2
Q6	$C08C,X – read data or SHIFT while writing	$C08D,X – read write protect state or LOAD data while writing
Q7	$C08E,X – enable READ mode	$C08F,X – enable WRITE mode

Table I.10.4. Disk][Peripheral-card I/O Memory Definition

Q6		Q7		Sequencer Function
$C08C,X	SHIFT	$C08E,X	READ	Enable READ sequencing
$C08D,X	LOAD	$C08E,X	READ	Check state of write protect switch and initialize the logic state sequencer before writing
$C08C,X	SHIFT	$C08F,X	WRITE	Shift data register after eight sequencer clocks while writing
$C08D,X	LOAD	$C08F,X	WRITE	Load data register after eight sequencer clocks while writing

Table I.10.5. Selectable Logic State Sequencer Function

If the call to RWTS is to write a sector of disk data, RWTS must manipulate the Disk][Interface Card switches in a prescribed manner in order to synchronize with what RWTS is about to write with what RWTS has previously written. In other words, RWTS has just read an Address Field header that contains the same values for the requested track, sector, and volume numbers, and it can now begin writing new sector data over the previous sector data. Once the new 40-microsecond auto-synchronization bytes and

the new 32-microsecond prolog bytes, sector data bytes, and epilog bytes have been written, the Disk][
Interface Card must immediately set its mode to READ as shown in Figure I.10.6, otherwise the next
series of auto-synchronization bytes and the next Address Field header data will be destroyed. The
Worth/Lechner books are excellent resources to fully understand diskette, track, and sector formatting.

```
   :                :          :
  D081            142    ; Return to read mode.
  D081            143    ;          ;
  D081 BD 8E C0   144    SETREAD   lda DATAIN,X    ; enable sequencer to READ
  D084 BD 8C C0   145              lda STROBE,X    ; enable sequencer to SHIFT
   :                :          :
```

Figure I.10.6. Setting the Disk][Interface Card to READ Mode

```
   :                :          :
  D123            320    ; Now read nibbles into NBUF1.
  D123            321    ;
  D123 BC 8C C0   322    ^8        ldy STROBE,X    ; read data register latch
  D126 10 FB      323              bpl <8          ; loop until MSB is set
   :                :          :
```

Figure I.10.7. Accessing the Disk][Interface Card to READ a Disk Byte

```
   :                :          :
  D011            34     WRITSCTR sec              ; set C-flag if write protect
  D012            35     ;
  D012 BD 8D C0   36               lda LATCH,X     ; enable sequencer latch
  D015 BD 8E C0   37               lda DATAIN,X    ; read sequencer latch
  D018            38     ;
  D018 30 67      39               bmi SETREAD     ; exit; C-flag and READ set
   :                :          :
```

Figure I.10.8. Accessing the Disk][Interface Card to Sense Write Protect

In order to sense the state of the current Disk][write protection switch and to initialize the mode of the
logic state sequencer before its mode can be set to WRITE, Q6 must be turned ON like in the code taken
from the DOS 4.5H software as shown in Figure I.10.8. Auto-synchronization can be achieved
according to Worth/Lechner with a maximum of five auto-synchronization bytes written as
0b1111111100.

DOS 4.5 utilizes the same routine for the Address Field and the Data Field header data to write the auto-
synchronization bytes and the three prolog bytes where only the third prolog byte differs. Six auto-
synchronization bytes are written before every Data Field header in DOS 4.5 whereas 128 auto-
synchronization bytes are written before the sector 0x00 Address Field header and a minimum of eight
to a maximum of thirty-two auto-synchronization bytes are written before all other Address Field
headers. This is certainly a very conservative design, but this design ensures that the data gaps created

by the initial auto-synchronization bytes are wide enough to allow for the processing of Address Field header data values before a decision is made to configure the mode for the Disk][Interface Card to WRITE. Re-written auto-synchronization bytes, prolog header bytes, and its following sector disk data bytes can never be placed precisely over the original auto-synchronization, prolog, and disk data bytes when the track was first initialized. This is particularly problematic when diskettes are read and written by a variety of different Disk][drives that may have different rotational speeds. However, the initial auto-synchronization byte gaps before and after sectors of disk data are sufficiently large enough when combined to allow for some decision making variations and/or variations in disk drive rotational velocity that may occur in other versions of DOS and disk drives, respectively. The routine that actually sets the mode for the Disk][Interface Card to WRITE and writes the prescribed number of auto-synchronization bytes held in the Y-register is shown in Figure I.10.9. This routine turns Q7 ON and selectively turns Q6 OFF and ON depending on how the routine must control the logic state sequencer. The software loop creates 40-microsecond auto-synchronization disk bytes: simply add up the instruction cycles shown in parenthesis.

```
  :              :          :
D0B6 85 34      204   WRITSYNC sta ADRDATMK    ; save third prolog byte
D0B8            205   ;
D0B8 A9 FF      206        lda #SYNCMARK       ; get SYNCMARK value
D0BA            207   ;
D0BA 9D 8F C0   208        sta DATAOUT,X       ; enable sequencer to WRITE
D0BD 1D 8C C0   209        ora STROBE,X        ; enable sequencer to SHIFT
D0C0            210   ;
D0C0 48         211        pha                 ; waste 3 cycles (3)
D0C1 68         212        pla                 ; waste 4 cycles (4)
D0C2            213   ;
D0C2 20 76 D2   214   ^1   jsr WAIT24          ; waste 24 cycles (24)
D0C5            215   ;
D0C5 9D 8D C0   216        sta LATCH,X         ; LOAD sequencer data latch (5)
D0C8 1D 8C C0   217        ora STROBE,X        ; enable sequencer to SHIFT (4)
D0CB            218   ;
D0CB EA         219        nop                 ; waste 2 cycles (2)
D0CC            220   ;
D0CC 88         221        dey                 ; decrement auto-sync count (2)
D0CD D0 F3      222        bne <1              ; branch if not done (3|2)
D0CF            223   ;
D0CF            224   ;
D0CF            225   ; Write address/data marks 0xD5, 0xAA, ADRDATMK to disk
  :              :          :
```

Figure I.10.9. Accessing the Disk][Interface Card to Write Auto-Sync Bytes

Once the 40-microsecond auto-synchronization disk bytes and the 32-microsecond Data Field prolog bytes have been written, the Data Field data disk bytes can now be written. Knowing that the RTS instruction, issued before the LDX instruction on line #58 in Figure I.10.10, takes 6 cycles, the time from when the third prolog byte 0xAD is written to the time the last nibble in NBUF2 is written on line #77 take exactly thirty-two microseconds when all these instructions are combined. From that point on, the software loop to write each of the remaining nibbles in NBUF2 take exactly thirty-two microseconds. The same routine in DOS 3.3 first begins with writing the last nibble in NBUF2 in thirty-six microseconds. In READ mode the logic state sequencer simply disregards the extra four microseconds that is attached to this first data disk byte. Extra attachments of anything other than four or eight microseconds is not tolerated by the logic state sequencer and synchronization to data disk bytes will be lost until the next series of auto-synchronization bytes are encountered. The DOS 3.3 routine is further penalized for accessing NBUF2 with the instruction at line #69 that crosses a page-boundary, i.e. EOR NBUF2-1,Y, because the Y-register is indexed 56:01 and not 55:00 as in DOS 4.5. In order to compensate for this five-cycle instruction, the instruction at line #74 must access a page-zero copy of SNUM16 that is put into TEMP2Z. In terms of the overall cost to the DOS 4.5 software routine to confine **all** of the prolog bytes and **all** of the data disk bytes to exactly thirty-two microseconds amounts to a single, additional program byte. Obviously, I considered the cost to be insignificant compared to the more significant **goal** to maintain overall timing precision when writing all header and all data disk bytes in the DOS 4.5 WRITSCTR algorithm.

```
  :                 :          :
  D026              54    ; Checksum is cleared by writing the last byte of NBUF2.
  D026              55    ; Apple originally published this routine using a 36 usec
  D026              56    ; byte for this value.  I have changed this logic.
  D026              57    ;
  D026 AE 55 DF     58            ldx NBUF2+NBUF2SIZ-1 ; last nibble of NBUF2 (4)
  D029              59    ;
  D029 A0 55        60            ldy #NBUF2SIZ-1   ; point Y-reg to last byte (2)
  D02B D0 07        61            bne >2            ; always taken (3)
  D02D              62    ;
  D02D              63    ;
  D02D              64    ; Get next 6-bit nibble and XOR with current nibble to
  D02D              65    ; form index into the write translate table.
  D02D              66    ;
  D02D B9 01 DF     67   ^1      lda NBUF2+1,Y     ; get next NBUF2 nibble (4)
  D030              68    ;
  D030 59 00 DF     69            eor NBUF2,Y       ; XOR with current nibble (4)
  D033 AA           70            tax               ; make it an index (2)
  D034              71    ;
  D034 BD 56 DF     72   ^2      lda WRNIBL,X      ; get disk byte (4)
  D037              73    ;
  D037 AE C3 BF     74            ldx SNUM16        ; recall slot*16 (4)
  D03A              75    ;
  D03A 9D 8D C0     76            sta LATCH,X       ; LOAD sequencer latch (5)
  D03D BD 8C C0     77            lda STROBE,X      ; enable sequencer to SHIFT (4)
  D040              78    ;
  D040 88           79            dey               ; point to next NBUF2 nibble (2)
  D041 10 EA        80            bpl <1            ; branch if not done (3|2)
  :                 :          :
```

Figure I.10.10. Accessing the Disk][Interface Card to Write Disk Bytes

Sather explains in his books how to dump the contents of the P6 sequencer ROM using a very cleaver procedure, by simply exchanging the P6 ROM with the P5 ROM. Using another Disk][Interface Card in another slot, the contents of the P6 ROM can be saved to a diskette as a Binary file. Close inspection of the schematic drawing for the Disk][Interface Card shows that address lines A5 and A7 are swapped as well as reverse ordering the D4 to D7 data lines that are connected to the P5 ROM socket. Wozniak certainly had his work cut out for him in order to write the Boot Stage 0 firmware, swap the address lines A5 and A7, and reverse the order of the D4 to D7 data bits of the binary object code before the P5 ROM could be manufactured. So, whatever data that comprises the dump of the P6 ROM using Sather's method must take these schematic drawing observations into consideration if that data is to be displayed in any meaningful manner. The 8-bit logic state sequencer index byte shown pictorially in Figure I.10.5 must be redrawn with the bit connections to address lines A5 and A7 swapped as shown in Figure I.10.11 where the A5 and A7 address lines are presented with a darker shade.

A7	A6	A5	A4	A3	A2	A1	A0
Sequence Bit 0	Sequence Bit 2	Sequence Bit 3	Data Pulse	Q7	Q6	QA	Sequence Bit 1

Figure I.10.11. Adjusted Index Byte Format for the P6 ROM

A7	A6	A5	A4	A3	A2	A1	A0
Q7	Data Pulse	Q6	QA	Sequence Bit 3	Sequence Bit 2	Sequence Bit 1	Sequence Bit 0

Figure I.10.12. Functional Index Byte Format for the P6 ROM

Knowing that this sequencer index byte contains eight bits, it can reference a full 256 bytes of data. One can then picture this ROM data as an array of sixteen different logic states where each state can have up to sixteen difference sequences. In order to utilize the adjusted index byte shown in Figure I.10.11 as a more functional index byte, a transformation of its bit contents are required to the order shown in Figure I.10.12. This transformation can easily be accomplished in software in order to display the data of the P6 ROM as it is used functionally by the Disk][Interface Card circuitry. The required transformation for the contents of the address bits shown Figure I.10.11 to the order shown in Figure I.10.12 in 0:7 bit order would be 1, 4, 5, 7, 6, 3, 2, 0. That is, Bit 0 content in Figure I.10.11 becomes Bit 1 content in Figure I.10.12, Bit 1 content in Figure I.10.11 becomes Bit 4 content in Figure I.10.12, and Bit 7 content in Figure I.10.11 becomes Bit 0 content in Figure I.10.12. And that is precisely the order of the bit connections to address bits shown in Figure I.10.12. Once the address bits have been transformed, the data from the P6 ROM can be presented separately as READ and WRITE data tables observing that address Bit 7 is Q7 in Figure I.10.12 which selects READ or WRITE mode for the Disk][Interface Card.

Wozniak defined the lower four bits of the P6 ROM data as control bits that control the shift/storage data register and the upper four bits as the next sequence number for the logic state sequencer, though those upper four bits (i.e. D4 to D7) still need to be reverse ordered before the ROM data can be functionally displayed. Control Bits 0 and 1 control S1 and S0, respectively, Bit 2 controls SL, and Bit 3 controls CLR for the shift/storage data register. A simple truth table can be constructed using these bit controls and their functions, and labels can be assigned to specific groups of bits in their OFF/ON state as they appear in the ROM data. Table I.10.6 shows all of the labels for the distinct commands/functions used in the ROM data to control the shift/storage data register. Similar to the transformation of the address bits for the sequencer index byte, the upper four bits of the ROM data must be transformed in reverse order so that the ROM data can be displayed and shown to make functional sense. Sather wrote a comprehensive Applesoft program which he listed in his books that he used to display the P6 ROM data he obtained when he swapped the P5 and P6 ROMs. As he did in generating the Address Bit Swap

Table for address bit transformation for Figure I.10.11 to Figure I.10.12, he generated a Data Bit Swap Table to transform the sixteen possible values obtained from four bits that are reverse ordered. This data order is 0, 8, 4, 12, 2, 10, 6, 14, 1, 9, 5, 13, 3, 11, 7, and 15 for the data bit transformation of ROM nibble data. For example, data nibble `0b0001` would be reverse ordered to `0b1000` and `0b1011` to `0b1101`. Ordering the swap table entries in `0:15` data order from left to right does indeed transform 1 to 8 and 11 to 13 in this example.

Data Bit				CODE	Command Name and Data Register Operation	Data Register	
3	2	1	0				
CLR	SL	S0	S1			Before	After
0	0	0	0	0x0	CLR, clear data register	abcdefgh	00000000
1	0	0	0	0x8	NOP, no operation	abcdefgh	abcdefgh
1	0	0	1	0x9	SL0, shift left bringing in Data Bit 2 which is a 0	abcdefgh	bcdefgh0
1	1	0	1	0xD	SL1, shift left bringing in Data Bit 2 which is a 1	abcdefgh	bcdefgh1
1	0	1	0	0xA	SR, shift right, WRITE PROTECT bit is 0 shift right, WRITE PROTECT bit is 1	abcdefgh abcdefgh	0abcdefg 1abcdefg
1	0	1	1	0xB	LD, load data register from the data bus	abcdefgh	stuvwxyz

Table I.10.6. Shift/Storage Data Register Control Commands

```
                    ROM Read Index

Seq   0      1      2      3      4      5      6      7
      ----   ----   ----   ----   ----   ----   ----   ----
0   00:18  02:18  04:0A  06:0A  10:18  12:18  14:0A  16:0A
1   80:2D  82:38  84:0A  86:0A  90:2D  92:38  94:0A  96:0A
2   01:D8  03:08  05:0A  07:0A  11:38  13:28  15:0A  17:0A
3   81:D8  83:48  85:0A  87:0A  91:48  93:48  95:0A  97:0A
4   40:D8  42:D8  44:0A  46:0A  50:58  52:58  54:0A  56:0A
5   C0:D8  C2:D8  C4:0A  C6:0A  D0:68  D2:68  D4:0A  D6:0A
6   41:D8  43:D8  45:0A  47:0A  51:78  53:78  55:0A  57:0A
7   C1:D8  C3:D8  C5:0A  C7:0A  D1:88  D3:88  D5:0A  D7:0A
8   20:D8  22:D8  24:0A  26:0A  30:98  32:98  34:0A  36:0A
9   A0:D8  A2:D8  A4:0A  A6:0A  B0:29  B2:A8  B4:0A  B6:0A
A   21:CD  23:D8  25:0A  27:0A  31:BD  33:B8  35:0A  37:0A
B   A1:D9  A3:D8  A5:0A  A7:0A  B1:59  B3:C8  B5:0A  B7:0A
C   60:D9  62:D8  64:0A  66:0A  70:D9  72:A0  74:0A  76:0A
D   E0:D8  E2:E8  E4:0A  E6:0A  F0:08  F2:E8  F4:0A  F6:0A
E   61:FD  63:F8  65:0A  67:0A  71:FD  73:F8  75:0A  77:0A
F   E1:DD  E3:E0  E5:0A  E7:0A  F1:4D  F3:E0  F5:0A  F7:0A
```

Figure I.10.13. Functional ROM Read Index

```
                              ROM Read Data
    *---------------SHIFT---------------*---------------LOAD---------------*
    *------QA'------*------QA------*------QA'------*------QA------*
Seq *--RP--*-NO RP--*--RP--*-NO RP--*--RP--*-NO RP--*--RP--*-NO RP--*
    ------  ------  ------  ------  ------  ------  ------  ------
0   18-NOP  18-NOP  18-NOP  18-NOP  0A-SR   0A-SR   0A-SR   0A-SR
1   2D-SL1  2D-SL1  38-NOP  38-NOP  0A-SR   0A-SR   0A-SR   0A-SR
2   D8-NOP  38-NOP  08-NOP  28-NOP  0A-SR   0A-SR   0A-SR   0A-SR
3   D8-NOP  48-NOP  48-NOP  48-NOP  0A-SR   0A-SR   0A-SR   0A-SR
4   D8-NOP  58-NOP  D8-NOP  58-NOP  0A-SR   0A-SR   0A-SR   0A-SR
5   D8-NOP  68-NOP  D8-NOP  68-NOP  0A-SR   0A-SR   0A-SR   0A-SR
6   D8-NOP  78-NOP  D8-NOP  78-NOP  0A-SR   0A-SR   0A-SR   0A-SR
7   D8-NOP  88-NOP  D8-NOP  88-NOP  0A-SR   0A-SR   0A-SR   0A-SR
8   D8-NOP  98-NOP  D8-NOP  98-NOP  0A-SR   0A-SR   0A-SR   0A-SR
9   D8-NOP  29-SL0  D8-NOP  A8-NOP  0A-SR   0A-SR   0A-SR   0A-SR
A   CD-SL1  BD-SL1  D8-NOP  B8-NOP  0A-SR   0A-SR   0A-SR   0A-SR
B   D9-SL0  59-SL0  D8-NOP  C8-NOP  0A-SR   0A-SR   0A-SR   0A-SR
C   D8-NOP  D9-SL0  D8-NOP  A0-CLR  0A-SR   0A-SR   0A-SR   0A-SR
D   D8-NOP  08-NOP  E8-NOP  E8-NOP  0A-SR   0A-SR   0A-SR   0A-SR
E   FD-SL1  FD-SL1  F8-NOP  F8-NOP  0A-SR   0A-SR   0A-SR   0A-SR
F   DD-SL1  4D-SL1  E0-CLR  E0-CLR  0A-SR   0A-SR   0A-SR   0A-SR
```

Figure I.10.14. Functional ROM Read Data

In order for me to fully understand what Sather was doing in his LOGIC STATE SEQUENCER ROM Applesoft program, I added some additional Applesoft statements in order to create additional, intermediate listings of indices that were used to index through the ROM data. By convention, the ordering of bits in an index pointer value is typically performed from least significant bit (LSB) to most significant bit (MSB) from right to left, and that would also be the logical ordering of data from right to left. However, Sather chose to order his ROM data output display from left to right, which may have been driven by how more easily Applesoft indices are incremented and/or how more easily it is to write successive numerical data to the computer screen, that is, from left to right. Sather does describe the

Data Pulse as an inverted, or *negative pulse* such that Read Pulse, or RP for a column header means 0 and NO RP means 1. Also, QA′ means 0 and QA means 1. I found these format definitions to be rather odd, but nevertheless, I retained these format definitions. Furthermore, Sather thought it would be easier for the reader to understand the display of READ ROM data if the LOAD portion is separated from the SHIFT portion (i.e. according to the value of Q6) and when QA′ is separated from QA. Figure I.10.13 shows the index number along with its P6 ROM read data where the order of columns shown (i.e. 0:7) is unaltered and ordered by Data Pulse, Q6, and QA as shown in Figure I.10.12. Figure I.10.14 shows the same P6 ROM read data along with its command that is found in the upper four bits of that data where the order of columns is now Q6, QA, and Data Pulse. The column order in Figure I.10.14 has been transformed from the order shown in Figure I.10.13 using 0, 4, 1, 5, 2, 6, 3, 7 bit order.

When Q7, or Bit 7 in Figure I.10.12 is set, WRITE mode is selected for the Disk][Interface Card. Figure I.10.15 shows the index number along with the P6 ROM write data where the order of columns shown (i.e. 8:F) is unaltered and ordered by Data Pulse, Q6, and QA. Figure I.10.16 shows the same P6 ROM write data along with its command that is found in the upper four bits of that data where the order of columns remains unaltered. Whether a Data Pulse is present or not, according to Figure I.10.16 the write sequences and their order are the same. In other words, the Data Pulse does not affect the logic state sequencer when it is configured in WRITE mode.

```
                    ROM Write Index
Seq   8      9      A      B      C      D      E      F
---  -----  -----  -----  -----  -----  -----  -----  -----
0    08:18  0A:18  0C:18  0E:18  18:18  1A:18  1C:18  1E:18
1    88:28  8A:28  8C:28  8E:28  98:28  9A:28  9C:28  9E:28
2    09:39  0B:39  0D:3B  0F:3B  19:39  1B:39  1D:3B  1F:3B
3    89:48  8B:48  8D:48  8F:48  99:48  9B:48  9D:48  9F:48
4    48:58  4A:58  4C:58  4E:58  58:58  5A:58  5C:58  5E:58
5    C8:68  CA:68  CC:68  CE:68  D8:68  DA:68  DC:68  DE:68
6    49:78  4B:78  4D:78  4F:78  59:78  5B:78  5D:78  5F:78
7    C9:08  CB:88  CD:08  CF:88  D9:08  DB:88  DD:08  DF:88
8    28:98  2A:98  2C:98  2E:98  38:98  3A:98  3C:98  3E:98
9    A8:A8  AA:A8  AC:A8  AE:A8  B8:A8  BA:A8  BC:A8  BE:A8
A    29:B9  2B:B9  2D:BB  2F:BB  39:B9  3B:B9  3D:BB  3F:BB
B    A9:C8  AB:C8  AD:C8  AF:C8  B9:C8  BB:C8  BD:C8  BF:C8
C    68:D8  6A:D8  6C:D8  6E:D8  78:D8  7A:D8  7C:D8  7E:D8
D    E8:E8  EA:E8  EC:E8  EE:E8  F8:E8  FA:E8  FC:E8  FE:E8
E    69:F8  6B:F8  6D:F8  6F:F8  79:F8  7B:F8  7D:F8  7F:F8
F    E9:88  EB:88  ED:88  EF:08  F9:88  FB:08  FD:88  FF:08
```

Figure I.10.15. Functional ROM Write Index

```
                            ROM Write Data
   *-----------READ PULSE-----------*-----------NO READ PULSE----------*
   *-----SHIFT------*-----LOAD-------*------SHIFT------*------LOAD------*
Seq *--QA'--*---QA--*---QA'---*---QA--*---QA'--*--QA---*--QA'--*---QA--*
   ----    ----    ----     ----    ----    ----    ----    ----
0   18-NOP  18-NOP  18-NOP   18-NOP  18-NOP  18-NOP  18-NOP  18-NOP
1   28-NOP  28-NOP  28-NOP   28-NOP  28-NOP  28-NOP  28-NOP  28-NOP
2   39-SL0  39-SL0  3B-LD    3B-LD   39-SL0  39-SL0  3B-LD   3B-LD
3   48-NOP  48-NOP  48-NOP   48-NOP  48-NOP  48-NOP  48-NOP  48-NOP
4   58-NOP  58-NOP  58-NOP   58-NOP  58-NOP  58-NOP  58-NOP  58-NOP
5   68-NOP  68-NOP  68-NOP   68-NOP  68-NOP  68-NOP  68-NOP  68-NOP
6   78-NOP  78-NOP  78-NOP   78-NOP  78-NOP  78-NOP  78-NOP  78-NOP
7   88-NOP  88-NOP  88-NOP   88-NOP  88-NOP  88-NOP  88-NOP  88-NOP
8   98-NOP  98-NOP  98-NOP   98-NOP  98-NOP  98-NOP  98-NOP  98-NOP
9   A8-NOP  A8-NOP  A8-NOP   A8-NOP  A8-NOP  A8-NOP  A8-NOP  A8-NOP
A   B9-SL0  B9-SL0  BB-LD    BB-LD   B9-SL0  B9-SL0  BB-LD   BB-LD
B   C8-NOP  C8-NOP  C8-NOP   C8-NOP  C8-NOP  C8-NOP  C8-NOP  C8-NOP
C   D8-NOP  D8-NOP  D8-NOP   D8-NOP  D8-NOP  D8-NOP  D8-NOP  D8-NOP
D   E8-NOP  E8-NOP  E8-NOP   E8-NOP  E8-NOP  E8-NOP  E8-NOP  E8-NOP
E   F8-NOP  F8-NOP  F8-NOP   F8-NOP  F8-NOP  F8-NOP  F8-NOP  F8-NOP
F   88-NOP  08-NOP  88-NOP   08-NOP  88-NOP  08-NOP  88-NOP  08-NOP
```

Figure I.10.16. Functional ROM Write Data

The code snippet shown in Figure I.10.8 that senses the state of the write protect switch is the only way software can initialize the sequence number of the logic state sequencer and set the sequencer to Sequence 0 while it is in READ mode. This is shown quite clearly in Figure I.10.14 in the right four columns where the upper four bits are set to zero and the command is set to SR. As soon as the data byte SYNCMARK, i.e. 0xFF, is stored to 0xC08F,X in line #208 of Figure I.10.9, the logic state sequencer begins to execute the NOP command shown at the top of column three (or column seven) of Figure I.10.16 since the instruction at line #36 in Figure I.10.8 sets Q6 to one (or LOAD) and QA has already been determined to be zero, or not write protected, and the state of the Data Pulse does not matter. The logic state sequence progresses to Sequence 1, executes another NOP instruction, and progresses to Sequence 2. Because 0xC08F,X is an indexed absolute addressing instruction, its data will now be available on the data bus by the time the logic state sequencer reaches Sequence 2. At

Sequence 2, the shift/storage data register executes the LD command which commands it to load whatever happens to be on the data bus at that moment in time into its data register, which is 0xFF. If an absolute addressing instruction such as 0xC0EF had been used in line #208, its data would have been available only at Sequence 0 and never at Sequence 2, and, therefore, totally unavailable to the shift/storage data register. The 0xC08F,X instruction is the only valid addressing mode permitted by the logic state sequencer, and it requires five 6502 (or 65C02) cycles which ends with Sequence 9.

The instruction at line #209 in Figure I.10.9 sets Q6 to zero (or SHIFT), so the next logic state sequencer command at Sequence 10 (i.e. 0x0A) is an SL0 command regardless whether QA (the current MSB of the data being written) is zero or one and regardless whether the Read Pulse is zero or one. The shift/storage data register is shifted left while a zero is loaded into its QH, or LSB bit. Whether the active sequencing is occurring in column 1 or 2 or in column 5 or 6 at this time, sequencing continues to Sequence 15 and either transitions to Sequence 0 or to Sequence 8. In either case an SL0 command is issued to the shift/storage data register every four microseconds until new data is latched into the shift/storage data register as shown on line #76 in Figure I.10.10. When a new data disk byte is latched to 0xC08D,X three microseconds after the last SL0 command was issued for the last bit of the previous data disk byte, Q6 is set to one, an LD command is issued two microseconds later to the shift/storage data register, and after ten sequences, a 0xC08C,X program instruction must be issued setting Q6 to zero in order to begin another series of SL0 commands issued every four microseconds in order to write that new data disk byte to the Disk][analog board one bit at a time.

If you have been conscientiously following this discussion and you now believe you have a better understanding of how Wozniak designed the Disk][Interface Card to operate in symbiosis with the RWTS read and write Address Field header, Data Field header, and Data Field data sector software, you should be completely amazed and overwhelmed by his virtuosity. At least, that is my take-away after investing the time and the patience to undertake this deep dive into the deconstruction of the contents of the P6 ROM, the digital circuits of the Disk][Interface Card, and the specificity of the RWTS low level I/O routines. Only someone having very great skill at conceptualizing the flow of data and the simultaneous operation of many, many binary switches and gates could have conceived of the simplicity inherent in the design of the Disk][Interface Card and its operational software. To experience such cleverness could only be the result of massive intellectual curiosity in order to conceive of a computing device whose sole purpose is to accurately read and write data to and from a magnetic data storage medium. I simply cannot imagine the thrill and the glory Wozniak experienced when his intellectual conceptualization of this device became a reality. Like Tesla who designed the induction motor as an intellectual conceptualization, this innate ability that is observed in Wozniak is rare and very uncommon. His genius has truly benefited all of mankind in one way or another to bring more information more easily to more people at any given time in history.

0x Offset:	00	01	02	03	04	05	06	07	08	09	0A	0B	0C	0D	0E	0F	10	11
Command	**Op-code**	**Sub-code**	**Record Length Record Number Filename Address**		**Volume**	**Drive**	**Slot**	**File Type**	**Filename Address One Data Byte Byte Range Address**		**Return Status**	**Phase**	**Workarea Buffer Address**		**T/S List Buffer Address**		**Date Sector Buffer Address**	
NO OPERATION	0x00				V	D	S				Return Status	Phase Value	Workarea Buffer Address					
OPEN	0x01		Record Length or 0x0000		V	D	S	File Type	Filename Address						T/S List Buffer Address			
CLOSE	0x02																Data Sector Buffer Address	
READ	0x03	See Table I.11.4	Record Number		Byte Offset		Range Length		One Data Byte or Byte Range Address									
WRITE	0x04																	
DELETE	0x05				V	D	S		Filename Address									
CATALOG	0x06	RKEY-WORD			V	D	S											
LOCK	0x07				V	D	S		Filename Address						T/S List Buffer Address			
UNLOCK	0x08				V	D	S											
RENAME	0x09		New Filename Address		V	D	S											
POSITION	0x0A		Record Number		Byte Offset													
INIT	0x0B	Boot Type	Volume Title Address		V	D	S	SEC32 Flag	Filename Address									
VERIFY	0x0C				V	D	S								T/S List Buffer Address		Data Sector Buffer Address	
URM	0x0D				V	D	S											
TOUCH	0x0E	RKEY-WORD			V	D	S											
TS	0x0F		Track Value	Sector Value	V	D	S										Data Sector Buffer Address	
WTS	0x10	Sector Index			V	D	S	Data Byte										
CD	0x11	RKEY-WORD			V	D	S											

Figure I.11.1. File Manager Command Parameter List in DOS 4.5

11. The DOS 4.5 File Manager Interface

The DOS 4.5 File Manager interface is not as straightforward as the RWTS interface, and it is more difficult to use. One look at the File Manager Command Parameter List shown in Figure I.11.1 and another look at the File Manager Input/Output Context Block shown in Table I.11.1 demonstrates how convoluted the File Manager interface is. Essentially, the Context Block is totally command driven and it is intended to be used with that in mind. So many of the Context Block entries are overloaded and the entry definitions and their usage strictly depends on the command in question. Figure I.11.1 also shows all the buffers that are needed or required by each of the File Manager commands. Table I.11.2 shows all eighteen command codes that are available to the File Manager in DOS 4.5. The first thirteen command codes are the same as in DOS 3.3 in order to maintain compatibility with all previous software that utilizes the external File Manager interface. The last five command codes are new in DOS 4.5.

Offset	Name	Size	Description
0x00	FMOPCOD	0x01	File Manager opcode
0x01	SUBCODE	0x01	File Manager subcode
0x02	RECNUM or FN2ADR	0x02 0x02	Record number or length Secondary filename address
0x04	BYTOFFSET or VOLUME	0x02 0x01	Byte offset (two bytes) Volume number (one byte)
0x05	DRIVE	0x01	Drive number
0x06	BYTRANGE or SLOT	0x02 0x01	Range length (two bytes) Slot number (one byte)
0x07	FILETYPE	0x01	File type, SEC32 Flag, or Data byte
0x08	DATADR or FNADR or DATBYTE	0x02 0x02 0x01	Data byte address (two bytes) Primary filename address (two bytes) Data byte (one byte)
0x0A	RTNCODE	0x01	Return code
0x0B	FMPHASE	0x01	Half-phases per track
0x0C	WBADR	0x02	Workarea buffer address
0x0E	TSLTSADR	0x02	Track/sector list buffer address
0x10	DATASADR	0x02	Data buffer address

Table I.11.1. File Manager Input/Output Context Block Definition

The command codes that are new in DOS 4.5 include FMURMCD, FMTCHCD, FMTSCD, FMWTSCD, and FMCDCD. The FMURMCD command code can be used to undelete a file that has been previously deleted from the volume Catalog by the FMDELECD command code. **There is no harm in undeleting a file that already exists in the volume Catalog**. The FMTCHCD command code can be used to update the timestamp of a file. Processing a file with the FMTCHCD command code does **not** update the VTOC timestamp since nothing is changed in the VTOC, including the bitmap. If the SUBCODE is set, the VALSCNFG value is copied to DOSCONFG and the VTOC is written back to the volume. The FMTSCD command code can be used to read the desired volume sector into a specified data buffer, DATASADR, where it can be processed for display. Similarly, the FMWTSCD command code can be used to read the desired volume sector into a specified data buffer, DATASADR, where one selected byte can be changed, and the result written back to the same volume sector. The FMCDCD command code can be used to set the Slot, Drive, and Volume variables without having to process a disk file. If the SUBCODE is set, the VTOC is read in order to obtain the DOSCONFG value so that it can be copied to VALSCNFG. The File Manager has the capability to gracefully handle any volume access error or any I/O processing error.

Command	Value	Handler	Description
FMNOERR	0x00	NOERHNDL	File Manager No Operation code
FMOPENCD	0x01	OPNHNDLR	File Manager OPEN code
FMCLOSCD	0x02	CLSHNDLR	File Manager CLOSE code
FMREADCD	0x03	RDHNDLR	File Manager READ code
FMWRITCD	0x04	WRHNDLR	File Manager WRITE code
FMDELECD	0x05	DELHNDLR	File Manager DELETE code
FMCATACD	0x06	CATHNDLR	File Manager CATALOG code
FMLOCKCD	0x07	LCKHNDLR	File Manager LOCK code
FMUNLKCD	0x08	UNLKHNDL	File Manager UNLOCK code
FMRENMCD	0x09	RNMHNDLR	File Manager RENAME code
FMPOSICD	0x0A	POSHNDLR	File Manager POSITION code
FMINITCD	0x0B	INITHNDL	File Manager INIT code (modified)
FMVERICD	0x0C	VFYHNDLR	File Manager VERIFY code
FMURMCD	0x0D	URMHNDLR	File Manager URM code
FMTCHCD	0x0E	TCHHNDLR	File Manager TOUCH code
FMTSCD	0x0F	TSHNDLR	File Manager TS code
FMWTSCD	0x10	WTSHNDLR	File Manager WTS code
FMCDCD	0x11	CDHNDLR	File Manager CD code

Table I.11.2. File Manager Command Codes

Command	Value	Description
FMNOOPSC	0x00	File Manager No Operation subcode
FMRW01SC	0x01	File Manager Read/Write 1-byte subcode
FMRWNBSC	0x02	File Manager Read/Write Range subcode
FMPOS1SC	0x03	File Manager Position and Read/Write 1-byte subcode
FMPOSRSC	0x04	File Manager Position and Read/Write Range subcode

Table I.11.3. File Manager Read and Write Command Subcodes

Some File Manager commands require a subcode to specify how the command is to be used. Table I.11.3 lists the five subcodes, one of which must be used with the READ and WRITE command codes FMREADCD and FMWRITCD, respectively. Table I.11.4 shows the other parameters that are required when using one of the five subcodes. For example, to read or write a range of bytes the SUBCODE at offset 0x01 must be set to 0x02 and the Range Size and Range Address of the data must be entered into offsets 0x06/0x07 and 0x08/0x09 of the Context Block, respectively. Using the FMREADCD and `FMWRITCD` commands may appear difficult at first, but once the Context Block is configured these two commands can be quite powerful. I added a subcode to the `FMCATACD` command code in order to optionally display what the `R` keyword provides to the Command Manager. Simply save a non-zero value to the `SUBCODE` in the File Manager Context Block if that additional `CATALOG` information is desired. The `FMINITCD` command code uses the `SUBCODE` for the Boot Type information. The `FMWTSCD` command code uses the `SUBCODE` for its Sector Index parameter. The Sector Index is where the data byte (located at offset `0x07` in the context block) is placed in the `DATASADR` buffer.

SUBCODE	File Manager Command Parameter List				Description
0x01	0x02/0x03	0x04/0x05	0x06/0x07	0x08/0x09	
0x00					No operation
0x01				Byte Data	R/W 1-byte
0x02			Range Size	Range Address	R/W Range
0x03	Record Number	Byte Offset		Byte Data	Position, R/W 1 byte
0x04	Record Number	Byte Offset	Range Size	Range Address	Position, R/W Range

Table I.11.4. File Manager SUBCODE Utilization

Boot Type	DOS Installed	Description
0x00	No	Data Disk D, all of track 0x00 can be used for data
0x06	Yes	Boot Disk B, RUN; value 0x06 put into CMDVAL
0x10	Yes	Boot Disk B, CLOSE; value 0x10 put into CMDVAL
0x14	Yes	Boot Disk B, EXEC; value 0x14 put into CMDVAL
0x34	Yes	Boot Disk B, BRUN; value 0x34 put into CMDVAL
0xN, 0x00≤N≤0x62	Yes	Boot Disk B, any valid even value within the DOS command table can be utilized for CMDVAL

Table I.11.5. File Manager FMINITCD Boot Type for SUBCODE

The File Manager Context Block entries for the `FMURMCD` command code are used in the same way as they are used for the `FMDELECD` command code where bytes `0x08`/`0x09` contain the address of the filename to be undeleted. The sectors listed in the `TSL` sector(s) of a file as well as all of its `TSL` sectors are marked as used in the `VTOC` free sector bitmap. It is always prudent to undelete a deleted file before subsequent files can use those sectors made available when the file was deleted. A volume can be rendered unusable if a data sector should ever be interpreted as a `TSL` sector.

The File Manager Context Block entries for the `FMINITCD` command code have been substantially modified from its DOS 3.3 version. Before the `FMINITCD` command code is even processed, the Command Manager initializes the Context Block to `zero` except for the `FMOPCOD` and `SUBCODE` fields. The Command Manager initializes the `SUBCODE` to one of the example values shown in Table I.11.5 for Boot Type. In order to create a fully bootable DOS B type volume, the `SUBCODE` must contain a non-zero value, the signal to the `INIT` handler to write DOS to the volume. If the `INIT` handler finds a zero value in the SUBCODE, a DOS D type volume is created that does not contain a DOS. A D type volume does not boot, but all of track 0x00 is available for data. The Command Manager initializes bytes 0x02/0x03 with the address of the Volume Title SFNAME (FN2ADR), and it updates the SECVAL, ENDTRK, and SUBJCT values in the VTOCVALS substructure directly. The File Manager initializes bytes 0x08/0x09 of the Context Block with the address of FNAME (FNADR).

Offset	Name	Size	Normal Range	Description
0x00	SECVAL	0x01	0x01–0x0F	number of sectors in volume Catalog
0x01	ENDTRK	0x01	0x12–0x30	number of tracks in volume
0x02	SUBJCT	0x02	0x0000–0xFFFF	volume library (subject) value

Table I.11.6. File Manager VTOCVALS Substructure Initialization Data

```
    :           :        :
1300            395   FMVALS:
1300 0B         396   FMOPCOD   byt FMINITCD
1301 06         397   SUBCODE   byt BOOTYPE
1302 2A 13      398   FN2ADR    adr VTITLE
1304            399   ;
1304 00         400   VOLUME    hex 00
1305 01         401   DRIVE     hex 01
1306 06         402   SLOT      hex 06
1307 00         403   FILETYPE  hex 00
1308            404   ;
1308 12 13      405   FNADR     adr FNAME
130A 00         406   RTNCODE   hex 00
130B 00         407   FMPHASE   hex 00
130C            408   ;
130C 42 13      409   WBADR     adr WORKAREA
130E 00 00      410   TSLTSADR  hex 0000
1310 00 00      411   DATASADR  hex 0000
1312            412   ;
1312 E8 E5 EC   413   FNAME     asc "hello"
1315 EC EF
1317            414             dfs FNLEN-5,SPACE
132A            415   ;
132A D4 E5 F3   416   VTITLE    asc "Test Disk"
     F4 A0 C4
     E9 F3 EB
1342            417             dfs FNLEN-9,SPACE
1342            418   ;
1342            419   WORKAREA:
1342 05         420   SECVAL    hex 05
1343 23         421   ENDTRK    hex 23
1344 34 12      422   SUBJCT    hex 3412
1346            423             dfs FMWALEN-4,ZERO
    :           :        :
```

Figure I.11.2. Using the File Manager Context Block for the INIT Command

When the `INIT` handler begins its processing, it knows whether it is processing on behalf of an external user or on behalf of the Command Manager by checking the MSB of the value found in `KEYWORD1`. If an external user is calling the File Manager, the `INIT` handler uses the buffer `BUFADRZ` (`0x42/0x43`) that has already been initialized by `FILEMNGR` with the address of the file's `WORKAREA` buffer in order to copy the first four bytes of data to the `VTOCVALS` substructure as shown in Table I.11.6. The `INIT` handler then begins its generic processing for both an external user and the Command Manager. If the value of the `SEC32` Flag at offset `0x07` (i.e. `FILETYPE`) is negative, a volume is initialized with thirty-two sectors per track, otherwise the volume is initialized with sixteen sectors per track. The handler uses the address at offset `0x02/0x03` to copy a 24-character upper ASCII Volume Title to the `VTOC` and uses the address at offset `0x08/0x09` to copy a 24-character upper ASCII filename to `FNAME`. The volume is timestamped and the `VTOC` bitmap is created.

In the ideal situation the File Manager knows nothing about the Command Manager and the values it parses from the command line keywords. All the information the File Manager requires for processing its commands **must** come from its Context Block and from its `WORKAREA` buffer. And this is particularly true for `INIT` handler processing. For internal File Manager `INIT` processing the `WBADR` address at Context Block offsets `0x0C/0x0D` and its `WORKAREA` data are not used. However, for external users of the File Manager, `WBADR` must contain an address of a 37-byte `WORKAREA` buffer that includes and begins with a 4-byte `VTOCVALS` substructure containing the values for `SECVAL`, `ENDTRK`, and `SUBJCT` (in Lo/Hi byte order) as shown previously in Table I.11.6. Recall that `SECVAL` defines how many sectors are used for the volume Catalog, `ENDTRK` specifies the number of tracks in the volume, and `SUBJCT` is the two-byte Volume Library value. The 4-byte `VTOCVALS` substructure, the address for `FNAME`, the address for Volume Title, the Boot Type, and the `SEC32` Flag provide the same information the Command Manager obtains when it parses the `A`, `B`, `L`, and `R` keywords for the DOS `INIT` command. Figure I.11.2 shows an Assembly Language listing of a File Manager Context Block where bytes `0x0C/0x0D` contain the address of a `WORKAREA` buffer, and the `VTOCVALS` substructure is defined at the beginning of the `WORKAREA` buffer. This protocol is different than in previous releases of DOS 4.1 and DOS 4.3, but it is a substantially superior protocol. As shown in Figures I.11.1 and I.11.2, the `TSLTSADR` and `DATASADR` addresses for these buffers are not required by the `FMINITCD` command code.

Understand that the File Manager uses only its **own** Context Block that resides within DOS memory on page `0xBF`. `GETFMCB` can be called to obtain the address of that Context Block so that its individual fields can be modified. *FID* maintains its own **copy** of the 18-byte Context Block, modifies it as needed, and then copies it back in its entirety into DOS address space before calling `CALLFM`. Upon return from the File Manager, *FID* copies the entire Context Block again into its own address space before looking at the return code value `RTNCODE`. The File Manager Context Block resides in the boot area of DOS 4.5H, the address space that is **not** within the memory of the Language Card partition, so the use of Soft Switches is unnecessary to read and to rewrite this Context Block.

Table I.11.7 shows all of the possible error codes that can be reported by DOS 4.5, and the source or sources of those error codes: Command Manager (CMD), File Manager (FM), or RWTS. In DOS 4.5 the File Manager uses a table lookup algorithm to translate an `RWTS` error code into a File Manager error code that can be reported by DOS. The actual value of the `RWTS` error code is shown in parenthesis. An `RWTS` Initialization Error message `Volume Format Error` was added to the Error and Display Message Text table as well as the `Catalog Full` and the `Volume Locked` error messages.

Error #	CMD	FM	RWTS	Error Message Text
0	√	√	√	Ring bell and print two <rtn>
1	√			Clock Not Found
2	√	√		Range Error
3			√ (0x08)	Volume Format Error
4	√		√ (0x10)	Volume Write Protected
5	√	√		End of Data
6		√		File Not Found
7		√ (0x20)		Volume Number Mismatch
8			√ (0x40)	I/O Error
9		√		Volume Full
10		√		File Locked
11	√		√ (0x30)	Syntax Error
12	√			No Buffers Available
13	√			File Type Mismatch
14	√			Program Too Large
15	√			Not Direct Command
16		√		Catalog Full
17		√		Volume Locked

Table I.11.7. Error Messages and Sources in DOS 4.5

It is always the responsibility of the user to utilize the RWTS I/O Context Block and the File Manager Context Block rationally and with great care. When a context block value is used and that value is not within its normal range, unpredictable results should be expected. By design, the Command Manager always supplies rational values for these context blocks that are within their normal operational range. But the external user carries the full burden in selecting context block values that will provide the intended results. For example, if SECVAL is initialized to 0x00 or to any value greater than 0x0F, and the File Manager Context Block OPCODE is set to the FMINITCD command code, the VTOC in the target volume will never become initialized and DOS 4.5 will likely hang. Table I.11.6 shows that setting SECVAL to zero or to a value greater than 0x0F is not within its normal range and there may very well be unexpected results.

A File Manager Context Block that is initialized by the external File Manager user to implement the DOS URM command is shown in Figure I.11.3. According to Figure I.11.1 and Table I.11.2 the Context Block uses the FMURMCD command code 0x0D, an address for a 24-character upper ASCII filename, and addresses for the WORKAREA and TSBUFFER buffers. Like most File Manager commands, this Context Block also requires values for Volume number, Drive number, and Slot number. The specified filename is the name of the file that is to be undeleted from the specified volume Catalog, that is, from the volume Catalog found at Slot s and Drive d having a Volume number v. If the filename is found in that volume Catalog, its entry is restored and the Data sectors in the TSL(s) of the file as well as all of the TSL sectors are marked as used in the VTOC free sector bitmap. For all intents and purposes the file is restored in the volume Catalog as if it had never been previously deleted and its original timestamp is not altered, modified, or updated because the Catalog entry for the file and the contents of the file have not changed. However, the timestamp of the VTOC in the volume is updated to the present date and time because the free sector bitmap content of the VTOC has obviously changed.

```
   :                :              :
1300              395   FMVALS:
1300 0D           396   FMOPCOD  byt FMURMCD
1301 00           397   SUBCODE  byt 00
1302 00 00        398   FN2ADR   hex 0000
1304              399   ;
1304 00           400   VOLUME   hex 00
1305 02           401   DRIVE    hex 02
1306 06           402   SLOT     hex 06
1307 00           403   FILETYPE hex 00
1308              404   ;
1308 12 13        405   FNADR    adr FNAME
130A 00           406   RTNCODE  hex 00
130B 00           407   FMPHASE  hex 00
130C              408   ;
130C 2A 13        409   WBADR    adr WORKAREA
130E 4F 13        410   TSLTSADR adr TSBUFFER
1310 00 00        411   DATASADR hex 0000
1312              412   ;
1312 E8 E5 EC     413   FNAME    asc "urm file"
1315 EC EF
1317              414            dfs FNLEN-8,SPACE
132A              415   ;
132A              416   WORKAREA dfs $25,ZERO
134F              417   TSBUFFER dfs $100,ZERO
   :                :              :
```

Figure I.11.3. Using the File Manager Context Block for the URM Command

```
   :                :              :
1300              395   FMVALS:
1300 0E           396   FMOPCOD  byt FMTCHCD
1301 00           397   SUBCODE  byt RKEYWORD
1302 00 00        398   FN2ADR   hex 0000
1304              399   ;
1304 00           400   VOLUME   hex 00
1305 02           401   DRIVE    hex 02
1306 06           402   SLOT     hex 06
1307 00           403   FILETYPE hex 00
1308              404   ;
1308 12 13        405   FNADR    adr FNAME
130A 00           406   RTNCODE  hex 00
130B 00           407   FMPHASE  hex 00
130C              408   ;
130C 2A 13        409   WBADR    adr WORKAREA
130E 4F 13        410   TSLTSADR adr TSBUFFER
1310 00 00        411   DATASADR hex 0000
1312              412   ;
1312 E8 E5 EC     413   FNAME    asc "touch file"
1315 EC EF
1317              414            dfs FNLEN-10,SPACE
132A              415   ;
132A              416   WORKAREA dfs $25,ZERO
134F              417   TSBUFFER dfs $100,ZERO
   :                :              :
```

Figure I.11.4. Using the File Manager Context Block for the TOUCH Command

Similarly, an external File Manager user who wants to implement the DOS TOUCH command would initialize the File Manager Context Block like that shown in Figure I.11.4. According to Figure I.11.1 and Table I.11.2 the Context Block uses the FMTCHCD command code 0x0E, a SUBCODE value for the R keyword function, an address for a 24-character upper ASCII filename, and addresses for the WORKAREA and TSBUFFER buffers as well as values for Slot, Drive, and Volume. If a valid filename has been supplied for the specified volume Catalog found at Slot s and Drive d having a Volume number v, the File Manager updates the timestamp of the file to the present date and time. If the filename contains a SPACE character (i.e. 0xA0) for its first character at a minimum, the timestamp of the volume is updated to the present date and time. Only in this instance is the specified R keyword considered. That is, if a valid filename has been supplied, any R keyword that might also have been supplied is simply ignored. Otherwise, if the SUBCODE contains a non-zero value, VALSCNFG is copied to DOSCONFG before the timestamp of the volume is updated to the present date and time, and the modified VTOC is saved back to its volume.

An external File Manager user can implement the DOS TS command using a File Manager Context Block that is initialized as shown in Figure I.11.5. According to Figure I.11.1 and Table I.11.2, the Context Block uses the FMTSCD command code 0x0F, and the Track and Sector parameters are saved to offsets 0x02 and 0x03, respectively, as well as values for the Slot, Drive, and Volume, and the Context Block can be copied back in its entirety into DOS address space before calling CALLFM. The File Manager reads the specified sector into the data buffer specified by the user at DATASADR. As in URM and TOUCH command processing, the WORKAREA buffer is a buffer used by the File Manager for the variables it uses throughout its processing.

```
   :              :           :
 1300          395   FMVALS:
 1300 0F       396   FMOPCOD   byt FMTSCD
 1301 00       397   SUBCODE   hex 00
 1302          398   FN2ADR:
 1302 11       399   FMTSTRK   hex TRCKVAL
 1303 00       400   FMTSSEC   hex SECRVAL
 1304          401   ;
 1304 00       402   VOLUME    hex 00
 1305 02       403   DRIVE     hex 02
 1306 06       404   SLOT      hex 06
 1307 00       405   FILETYPE  hex 00
 1308          406   ;
 1308 12 13    407   FNADR     hex 0000
 130A 00       408   RTNCODE   hex 00
 130B 00       409   FMPHASE   hex 00
 130C          410   ;
 130C 12 13    411   WBADR     adr WORKAREA
 130E 00 00    412   TSLTSADR  hex 0000
 1310 37 13    413   DATASADR  adr DATABUFR
 1312          414   ;
 1312          415   WORKAREA  dfs $25,ZERO
 1337          416   DATABUFR  dfs $100,ZERO
   :              :           :
```

Figure I.11.5. Using the File Manager Context Block for the TS Command

```
:                    :              :
1300                 395    FMVALS:
1300 10              396    FMOPCOD   byt FMWTSCD
1301 00              397    SUBCODE   byt SECRNDX
1302                 398    FN2ADR:
1302 11              399    FMTSTRK   hex TRCKVAL
1303 00              400    FMTSSEC   hex SECRVAL
1304                 401    ;
1304 00              402    VOLUME    hex 00
1305 02              403    DRIVE     hex 02
1306 06              404    SLOT      hex 06
1307 00              405    FILETYPE  byt SECRBYT
1308                 406    ;
1308 12 13           407    FNADR     hex 0000
130A 00              408    RTNCODE   hex 00
130B 00              409    FMPHASE   hex 00
130C                 410    ;
130C 12 13           411    WBADR     adr WORKAREA
130E 00 00           412    TSLTSADR  hex 0000
1310 37 13           413    DATASADR  adr DATABUFR
1312                 414    ;
1312                 415    WORKAREA  dfs $25,ZERO
1337                 416    DATABUFR  dfs $100,ZERO
:                    :              :
```

Figure I.11.6. Using the File Manager Context Block for the WTS Command

```
:                    :              :
1300                 395    FMVALS:
1300 11              396    FMOPCOD   byt FMCDCD
1301 00              397    SUBCODE   byt RKEYWORD
1302 00 00           398    FN2ADR    hex 0000
1304                 399    ;
1304 00              400    VOLUME    hex 00
1305 02              401    DRIVE     hex 02
1306 06              402    SLOT      hex 06
1307 00              403    FILETYPE  hex 00
1308                 404    ;
1308 00 00           405    FNADR     hex 0000
130A 00              406    RTNCODE   hex 00
130B 00              407    FMPHASE   hex 00
130C                 408    ;
130C 12 13           409    WBADR     adr WORKAREA
130E 00 00           410    TSLTSADR  hex 0000
1310 00 00           411    DATASADR  hex 0000
1312                 412    ;
1312                 413    WORKAREA  dfs $25,ZERO
:                    :              :
```

Figure I.11.7. Using the File Manager Context Block for the CD Command

The DOS WTS command can be implemented by an external File Manager user by using a File Manager Context Block as shown in Figure I.11.6. According to Figure I.11.1 and Table I.11.2, the Context Block uses the FMWTSCD command code 0x10 and the Track and Sector parameters are similarly saved to offsets 0x02 and 0x03, respectively, a Sector Index is saved to offset 0x01, the SUBCODE, and the

Data Byte value is saved to offset `0x07`, the `FILETYPE`, as well as values for the Slot, Drive, and Volume. In other words, whatever data is supplied for `FILETYPE` is copied to the specified sector at the offset found in `SUBCODE`. The File Manager uses the specified data buffer address found in `DATASADR` to read the specified sector data, make the data byte change at the specified offset, and then write that modified sector data back to the same volume.

Finally, an external File Manager user who wants to implement the DOS `CD` command would initialize the File Manager Context Block like that shown in Figure I.11.7. According to Figure I.11.1 and Table I.11.2 the Context Block uses the `FMCDCD` command code `0x11` and it requires a `SUBCODE` value for the `R` keyword function as well as values for the Slot, Drive, and Volume. The File Manager uses the supplied values for Slot, Drive, and Volume to change those parameters currently in memory for any subsequent volume access. The `CD` command does **not** return the Slot, Drive, and Volume parameter values currently in memory if they are initialized to zero in the Context Block and, therefore, not provided. If the `SUBCODE` contains a non-zero value, the `VTOC` of the specified volume is read and its `DOSCONFG` value is copied to `VALSCNFG`.

To what extent does an external user of `RWTS` or of the File Manager expect in *hand holding* vis-à-vis the values the user selects for any of the entries in either Context Block? That is the question I have grappled with in trying to decide whether I should try and *fix* incoherent values for a user, refuse to continue processing with those values, or simply allow the processing to continue with those values knowing full well that something within DOS will undoubtedly fail. There is only so much code space and *hand holding* can be very expensive code depending upon its depth and dimension. **DOS 4.5 is designed to provide its intended results when its Context Blocks contain rational values that are within their normal operational range.** That is all a user can and should expect! If a user is intent on breaking `RWTS` or the File Manager, nothing will stand in way of the user, and any *hand holding* would be a total waste of code space and the effort to implement any such features to any depth or dimension.

It is always a good policy to test and experiment on diskette volumes that are clearly identified as `Test Disk #NNN` when testing a new program whether that program is written in Applesoft, assembly language, Fortran, or even Pascal. Even an `EXEC` file should be tested first on volumes that are exclusively used for experimentation. No one is immune to mistakes, but carelessly and irrationally using either one of these Context Blocks will surely cause very unwanted results, perhaps even the complete loss or destruction of critical data. Therefore, I say again, it is always the responsibility of the user to utilize both of these Context Blocks rationally and with very great care.

12. DOS 4.5 Data Structures

The Data Structures, or areas of memory where data is found within the DOS 3.3 code space, are spread out among the various functional managers. That is, those variables used by the Command Manager are generally found following the Command Manager. Those variables used by the File Manager are mostly found following the File Manager as well. The `RWTS IOCB` is found somewhere in the middle of all of the `RWTS` routines. I thought DOS 4.5 should have far better organization of its various collections of variables and data structures, and, therefore, reduce the number of addresses required to indirectly access any single variable or data structure if that is what is desired by the user. The `CMDVALS` Data Structure in DOS 4.5 is shown in Table I.12.1. Figure I.12.1 shows an example assembly language routine that can access and change the `DRVAL` variable highlighted in Table I.12.1.

Offset	Name	Size	Description
0x00	CURSTATE	0x01	0x00 = warm-start state 0x01 = READ state 0x02 = VALUE state 0x80 = cold-start state
0x01	CSWSTATE	0x01	CSWL intercept state number
0x02	CMDLNIDX	0x01	Apple Command Line offset
0x03	ALLOCNTR	0x01	VTOC scan allocation counter
0x04	KEYWORD1	0x01	First keyword table byte
0x05	KEYWORD2	0x01	Second keyword table byte
0x06	ASAVE	0x01	A-register save
0x07	XSAVE	0x01	X-register save
0x08	YSAVE	0x01	Y-register save
0x09	SSAVE	0x01	S-register save
0x0A	BUFRADR	0x02	Current file buffer address
0x0C	EXECBUFR	0x02	EXEC file buffer address
0x0E	CSWLSAV	0x02	True CSWL handler address
0x10	KSWLSAV	0x02	True KSWL handler address
0x12	MAXFILES	0x01	MAXFILES value
0x13	MONFLAGS	0x01	0x10 = Output 0x20 = Input 0x40 = Command
0x14	DIRTS	0x02	Catalog track and sector values
0x16	TSSAV	0x02	TS and WTS track and sector values
0x18	FRESPC	0x02	Last catalog free space value
0x1A	FILELAST	0x02	File end address
0x1C	FILESTRT	0x02	File start address
0x1E	FILELEN	0x02	File length in bytes
0x20	CLKSLOT	0x01	Clock slot
0x21	CLKINDEX	0x01	Clock data index
0x22	CLKTIME	0x06	See Table I.5.5 for variable order
0x28	SLOTVAL	0x02	S keyword, slot value
0x2A	DRVAL	0x02	D keyword, drive value
0x2C	VOLVAL	0x02	V keyword, volume value
0x2E	ADRVAL	0x02	A keyword, address value
0x30	LENVAL	0x02	L keyword, length value
0x32	RECVAL	0x02	R keyword, record value
0x34	BYTVAL	0x02	B keyword, byte value
0x36	LOADLEN	0x02	LOAD and BLOAD length
0x38	MONVAL	0x01	MON/NOMON value
0x39	CMDINDX	0x01	Index of last command * 2
0x3A	STKSAVE	0x01	Stack pointer save
0x3B	URMFLAG	0x01	Undelete flag

Table I.12.1. CMDVALS Data Structure Definition in DOS 4.5

```
  :                      :                  :
 002A                   19   DRVALOFF  equ $2A
 BFF4                   20   MNGVALS   equ $BFF4
  :                      :                  :
 094A                   32   ; Get the DRVAL value.
 094A 18                33             clc              ; read
 094B A0 2A             33             ldy #DRVALOFF
 094D 20 91 09          35             jsr MNGVAL
 0950 8E 90 09          36             sta DRIVE
 0952                   37   ;
 0952                   38   ; Change the DRVAL value.
 0952 38                39             sec              ; write
 0953 A0 2A             40             ldy #DRVALOFF
 0955 AD 90 09          41             lda DRIVE
 0958 20 91 09          42             jsr MNGVAL
  :                      :                  :
 0990                   65   DRIVE     hex 00
 0991 B8                66   MNGVAL    clv              ; set 8-bit access
 0992 6C F4 BF          67             jmp (MNGVALS)
  :                      :                  :
```

Figure I.12.1. Accessing and Changing 8-Bit CMDVALS in DOS 4.5

The CMDVALS Data structure and the File Manager FMWORK Data structure reside after the two pages of memory that are required to contain the working VTOC and Catalog buffers in DOS 4.5H. The CMDVALS and FMWORK Data structures require nearly a half page of memory. The five File Manager file buffers follow the FMWORK Data structure. The physical layout of these structures and buffers is quite the opposite in DOS 4.5L where two File Manager file buffers are followed by the CMDVALS and FMWORK Data structures, which are then followed by two pages of memory that are required to contain the VTOC and Catalog buffers. Quite a few software tools such as *Big Mac* and *Lisa* require access to several internal variables from the CMDVALS Data structure. *Big Mac* requires the internal values of DRVAL and LOADLEN, and it needs the pointer addresses to what DOS considers to be the true CSWL and KSWL interface handlers. *Lisa* also requires the internal values of DRVAL and LOADLEN. There is no telling how many other software utilities and programs that exist in many other software libraries which require specific values from these DOS internal data structures in order to complete their processing functions. DOS 4.5L and DOS 4.5H provide **easy** and **identical** access protocols to any variable within the CMDVALS and the FMWORK Data structures shown in Tables I.12.1 and I.12.2, respectively. Even though these variables are either in Main memory or in Bank 2 of the Language Card partition, the MNGVALS routine shown in Table I.8.1 can be used to access or change any of these values without regard to the version of DOS.

DOS 4.5 must always have at least one File Manager File buffer allocated, which is all that *Lisa* actually requires and uses, surprisingly. Even to implement the DOS CATALOG command requires one free file buffer. However, reducing the number of file buffers in DOS 4.5H using the DOS MAXFILES command does not provide the user with any additional program memory as it actually does in DOS 3.3 or in DOS 4.5L. Table I.12.3 shows the contents of a file buffer which is 581 (i.e. 0x245) bytes in size where one memory page (or 256 bytes) is used for the data buffer DATABUFR, one memory page is used for the track/sector list buffer TSBUFFER, thirty-seven bytes is used for the working variables buffer WORKAREA, twenty-four bytes is used for the filename buffer FILNAMBF, and eight bytes is used for the WORKAREA, TSBUFFER, DATABUFR, and NXTFNADR addresses. NXTFNADR contains the address of FILNAMBF for the next (but not necessarily following) file buffer, which functions like a single-direction linked-list. If the address in NXTFNADR is 0x0000, there are no more linked-list file buffers and the error message No Buffers Available is displayed when DOS 4.5 is unable to locate an unused File buffer.

I have changed the order and the size of some of the variables in the workarea buffer shown in Tables I.12.2 and I.12.3 from the order and size in which they are found in DOS 3.3. I have removed TRKNUMBR from FMWORK and its complementary variable WATRKNUM from the WORKAREA of a file buffer since that variable is unused by the File Manager. As long as the Workarea definition is consistent in both data buffers there will be no processing problems. I made those changes to variable order and size so that I could reduce the number of routines necessary to copy certain variables to and from the Workarea buffer of a file and its complementary version of the Workarea buffer in the File Manager. I provided *FID* with the same changes to its layout of the Workarea buffer as well.

Offset	Name	Size	Description
0x3C	FRTSTRK	0x01	First T/S track
0x3D	FRTSSEC	0x01	First T/S sector
0x3E	CURTSTRK	0x01	Current T/S track
0x3F	CURTSSEC	0x01	Current T/S sector
0x40	CURDATRK	0x01	Current data track
0x41	CURDASEC	0x01	Current data sector
0x42	DSKFLAGS	0x01	0x00 = No pending activity 0x02 = VTOC/Catalog has changed 0x40 = DATA buffer has changed 0x80 = T/S buffer has changed
0x43	DIRSECIX	0x01	Directory sector index
0x44	DIRBYTIX	0x01	Directory byte index
0x45	SECPERTS	0x01	T/S entries in a sector
0x46	FILEBYTE	0x01	Current file byte
0x47	RELSFRST	0x02	Relative sector to first sector
0x49	RELSLAST	0x02	Relative sector to last sector
0x4B	RELSLRD	0x02	Relative sector to just read sector
0x4D	FILEPOSN	0x02	Current file position
0x4F	OPNRCLEN	0x02	File open record length
0x51	RECNUMBR	0x02	Current record number
0x53	BYTEOFFS	0x02	Current byte offset
0x55	SECCNT	0x02	Sector count
0x57	CURTRACK	0x01	Current track
0x58	NEXTSECR	0x01	Next sector
0x59	SECBTMAP	0x04	Sector bitmap
0x5D	FYPTE	0x01	File Type (^0x80 = locked)
0x5E	SLOT16	0x01	Slot number times 16
0x5F	DRVNUMBR	0x01	Drive number
0x60	VOLNUMBR	0x01	Volume number

Table I.12.2. File Manager FMWORK Data Structure Definition in DOS 4.5

Offset	Name	Size	Description
		Data and Track/Sector Buffers	
0x000	DATABUFR	0x100	I/O data buffer
0x100	TSBUFFER	0x100	T/S buffer
		WORKAREA – File Manager Workarea Variables	
0x200	TSFRSTTS	0x02	T/S of first T/S List for file
0x202	TSCURRTS	0x02	T/S of current T/S List for file
0x204	TSCURDAT	0x02	T/S of current data sector
0x206	WAFLAGS	0x01	0x00 = No pending activity 0x02 = VTOC has changed 0x40 = DATA buffer has changed 0x80 = T/S buffer has changed
0x207	SECATOFF	0x01	Sector offset into catalog
0x208	BYCATOFF	0x01	Byte offset into catalog
0x209	MAXTSECR	0x01	Maximum entries in one T/S list
0x20A	BYSECOFF	0x01	Current sector byte offset
0x20B	SECFRSTS	0x02	Offset of first sector in current T/S List
0x20D	SECLASTS	0x02	Offset of last sector in current T/S List
0x20F	SECLSTRD	0x02	Relative sector number last read
0x211	SECRPOST	0x02	Current relative position in sector
0x213	RECDLNGH	0x02	Fixed record length
0x215	RECURNUM	0x02	Current record number
0x217	BYRECOFF	0x02	Byte offset into current record
0x219	SECFILEN	0x02	Length of file in sectors
0x21B	CURALOTR	0x01	Current track that is allocated
0x21C	SECALOTR	0x01	Next sector to allocate in track
0x21D	SECFRETR	0x04	Bitmap of free sectors in CURALOTR
0x221	WAFILTYP	0x01	File Type (^0x80 = locked)
0x222	WASLTNUM	0x01	Slot number times 16
0x223	WADRVNUM	0x01	Drive number
0x224	WAVOLNUM	0x01	Volume number
		Filename Buffer	
0x225	FILNAMBF	0x18	Upper ASCII filename
		Addresses of Buffer Locations	
0x23D	WABUFADR	0x02	Address of WORKAREA
0x23F	TSBUFADR	0x02	Address of TSBUFFER
0x241	DABUFADR	0x02	Address of DATABUFR
0x243	NXTFNADR	0x02	Address of next FILNAMBF

Table I.12.3. File Manager File Buffer Definition in DOS 4.5

The MNGVALS routine shown in Table I.8.1 was designed for DOS 4.3 to access the contents of the CMDVALS and FMWORK Data structures as well as the contents of the INITVALS Data structure shown in Table I.8.7. To have MNGVALS also access the contents of the INITVALS Data structure is actually an unnecessary redundancy. There is an excellent and perfectly valid procedure to access the contents of the INITVALS Data structure as shown in Figure I.8.6. It has already been noted that one should reference the variables in the INITVALS Data structure indirectly and, therefore, more generally using the address found at INITVAL and the offsets shown in Table I.8.7. Because the INITVALS Data structure resides in Main memory at the same address for DOS 4.5L and for DOS 4.5H, the variables in this data structure are somewhat easier to access in order to directly read and change than to read and change those variables found in CMDVALS, particularly in DOS 4.5H. In DOS 4.5H the CMDVALS and FMWORK Data structures reside in Bank 2 of the Language Card partition.

I have modified the MNGVALS routine in DOS 4.5 to only access the CMDVALS and FMWORK Data structures. The routine uses the V-flag to read/write 8-bit values when the flag is **clear** and the routine uses the V-flag to read/write 16-bit values when the flag is **set**. Figure I.12.2 shows another assembly language example routine that is used in *Lisa* to obtain the value of LOADLEN (highlighted in Table I.12.1), a 16-bit value, that is added to the address of BUFR to obtain the address where the data segment ends that was just read into memory from a volume. MNGVALS always returns the requested LSB value in the X-register and the next MSB value in the A-register. As shown in Figure I.12.1, MNGVALS reads or writes an 8-bit value using only the A-register. As long as the index value in the Y-register is less than CVALSLEN (which is equal to 0x61), MNGVALS always returns the Carry flag **clear**. The Y-register is incremented each time a data byte is read or written from the CMDVALS or from the FMWORK Data structures, thus simplifying the user code when a range of data is read or written from these structures. Therefore, when the V-flag is **set**, the Y-register is incremented twice.

```
    :           :       :
0002           3    BUFR     epz  $02
    :           :       :
000E           9    LDLENNDX equ  $36
BFF4          10    MNGVALS  equ  $BFF4
    :           :       :
0917 18       32             clc                     ; read
0918 A0 36    33             ldy  #LDLENNDX
091A 20 91 09 34             jsr  MNGVAL
091D 48       35             pha
091E 8A       36             txa
091F 65 02    37             adc  BUFR
0921 85 02    38             sta  BUFR
0923 68       39             pla
0924 65 03    40             adc  BUFR+1
0926 85 03    41             sta  BUFR+1
    :           :       :
0991 2C 94 09 66    MNGVAL   bit  SETVFLAG    ; set 16-bit access
0994 6C F4 BF 67    SETVFLAG jmp  (MNGVALS)
    :           :       :
```

Figure I.12.2. Reading a 16-Bit LOADLEN Value in Lisa

13. DOS 4.5 Clock Access

I applaud the individual (rarely, if at all, do teams of individuals do anything significant as I have observed) who designed the concept of using signature and classification bytes in firmware in order to assist in the identification of a peripheral slot card. All clock cards made for the Apple][conform to the convention in using a `PHP` instruction for the first signature byte, an `SEI` instruction for the second signature byte, and either a `0x03` or a `0x07` for the card's classification byte which is the last byte in its peripheral-card ROM firmware. DOS 4.5 follows this convention to determine if a peripheral slot contains a clock card, and DOS 4.5 starts looking for a clock card in slot 7 and stops looking after slot 1 if a clock card has not been found. When the `FINDCLK` search routine does find a clock card, `FINDCLK` calls the `READCLK` routine to issue a *Clock Colon Command*. This commands the clock card to generate its most generic date and time data output, i.e. `mo/dd hh:mi:ss` or `mo/dd/yy hh:mi:ss`. In this data `mo` is month, `dd` is day, `yy` is year, `hh` is hour, `mi` is minute, and `ss` is second. Some clock card firmware generates the Day number of the week `w` before the Month data, and some firmware might include a period after the Seconds' data followed by a three-digit millisecond suffix.

Clock cards from different manufactures may differ in the number of space characters (i.e. `0xA0`) that are used at the beginning of the data their clock card generates. In order to increase the efficiency of the `READCLK` routine, the `FINDCLK` search routine parses the generic clock data output and determines an index value where the month data actually begins. The clock card I designed and built as well as the TimeMaster clock card both model their generic data output after the Thunderclock card. These two clock cards produce a Year value whereas the Thunderclock card does not. (Why the Thunderclock card became the de facto standard is beyond my comprehension. Maybe it was the first clock card marketed for the Apple][computer? So, what! Maybe it was well integrated into ProDOS. Again, so what! Not including a Year value in its generic clock data output is just wrong, and infinitely shortsighted.)

Clock Card	Index Value	Generic Character String
Thunderclock card	0	`mo/dd hh;mi;ss`
possible design clock card	1	`mo/dd/yy hh:mi:ss`
possible design clock card	2	`x mo/dd/yy hh:mi:ss`
Vrbancic Clock card	3	`"w mo/dd/yy hh:mi:ss`
TimeMaster Clock card	3	`"w mo/dd/yy hh:mi:ss`
possible design clock card	4	`xxx mo/dd/yy hh:mi:ss`
possible design clock card	5	`xxxx mo/dd/yy hh:mi:ss`

Table I.13.1. Supported Clock Cards in DOS 4.5

As I stated above, in order for DOS 4.5 to efficiently process clock data generated by a Clock card, an index to where the Month data actually begins is determined by `FINDCLK` as there can be either nothing before the Month data or there can be a single space before the Month data. It does not matter what precedes that space and it does not matter what separators are used between the date and the time values. The following separators can be used in clock data: " ", "/", ":", and even ";". Table I.13.1 lists all of the clock cards I have tested with DOS 4.5, the generic clock data the card generates when it issues a *Clock Colon Command* where **x** can be any data, and the index that the `FINDCLK` routine generates for that character string. The `READCLK` routine uses that index to begin extracting the date and time values, and substituting in `YEARVAL` (see Table I.8.7) if it is parsing Thunderclock data. `READCLK` assumes that the date and time data contains a Year value if it is not parsing Thunderclock data.

Years ago when I first started investigating a process or a procedure to read a clock card within the software I had started to develop for a new DOS, I found that it was not a very easy task. Developing an Applesoft program to read the generic date and time clock data was frightfully simple. Figure I.13.1 shows a programmatically generated listing of such an Applesoft program. When the program is executed, the resulting output might be something like 01/01 08;28;48.000, for example, because this generic data was generated by a simulated Thunderclock card within the Virtual][program. Accomplishing this same task in assembly language takes far more work. Figure I.13.2 illustrates one solution in how this can be done using assembly language. Both programs yield the same results. However, the real task began more than nine years ago when I wanted to incorporate this general read clock logic into my first attempt to create a new version of DOS.

```
10   D$ = CHR$( 4 )
20   S = 4
30   PRINT D$; "PR#"; S
     PRINT D$; "IN#"; S
40   INPUT ":"; A$
50   PRINT D$; "PR#0"
     PRINT D$; "IN#0"
60   PRINT
     PRINT A$
```

Figure I.13.1. Reading Generic Clock Data Using Applesoft

```
:                 :             :
0906 A9 04        50            lda #4
0908 20 95 FE     51            jsr OUTPORT
090B A9 04        52            lda #4
090D 20 8B FE     53            jsr INPORT
0910              54   ;
0910 A9 BA        55            lda #COLON
0912              56   ;
0912 20 39 09     57   ^1       jsr RDCHAR
0915 C9 8D        58            cmp #RETURN
0917 D0 F9        59            bne <1
0919              60   ;
0919 A9 00        61            lda #ZERO
091B 20 95 FE     62            jsr OUTPORT
091E A9 00        63            lda #ZERO
0920 20 8B FE     64            jsr INPORT
0923              65   ;
0923 A0 00        66            ldy #ZERO
0925 B9 00 02     67   ^2       lda INPUT,Y
0928 20 ED FD     68            jsr COUT
092B C8           69            iny
092C C9 8D        70            cmp #RETURN
092E D0 F5        71            bne <2
:                 :             :
0939 6C 38 00     85   RDCHAR   jmp (KSWL)
:                 :             :
```

Figure I.13.2. Reading Generic Clock Data Using Assembly Language

```
  :               :           :
E5E9            101  ; Save the CSWL and KSWL on the stack
E5E9            102  ;
E5E9 A2 03      103          ldx #3
E5EB            104  ;
E5EB B5 36      105  ^1       lda CSWL,X
E5ED 48         106          pha
E5EE            107  ;
E5EE CA         108          dex
E5EF 10 FA      109          bpl <1
  :               :           :
E600            128  ; Restore the CSWL and KSWL from the stack
E600            129  ;
E600 A2 FC      130          ldx #!-4
E602            131  ;
E602 68         132  ^3       pla
E603 95 3A      133          sta CSWL+4,X
E605            134  ;
E605 E8         135          inx
E606 30 FA      136          bmi <3
  :               :           :
```

Figure I.13.3. Page-zero Wraparound in Read Clock Algorithm

When this read clock logic is inserted into DOS software, the primary issue centers around the modified content of the CSWL and KSWL interface pointers that are used to read the clock card and the restoration of these pointers. The READCLK routine must be able to support the boot process, all internal read clock processes, and the external read clock process. The initial content of these two interface pointers is not always the same before these processes are invoked. To what values to restore these two pointers was the primary question, and the two choices between the available LOADPTRS or INITPTRS routines could not be used reliably. Another concerning issue was the available code space that would be needed in order to connect to the clock card, to detach from the clock card, to restore the CSWL and KSWL interface pointers, and to determine the most economical way to extract and store the clock data. Previously presented, Table I.5.5 shows that the order that the clock data is extracted and stored is in reverse order to how the data appears in the generic clock data output. The rationale for this observation is that when a data extraction loop register is decremented rather than incremented, and that register is also used to save the processed data within that logic loop, a single two-byte compare instruction is not required to terminate the data extraction loop, and two bytes of code space is saved. It is an infinitesimal savings to be sure when the clock data is read and processed in this fashion, but there is another two-byte compare instruction savings every time that same clock data is displayed or copied. Note that the rules for indexed addressing mode are different for page-zero and for absolute page wraparound which prove to be quite useful as shown in Figure I.13.3.

The READCLK routine combines both digits for each of the six pairs of date and time numbers using the Binary-Coded Decimal (BCD) format. There are many excellent reasons and advantages for doing so, and the first advantage is the ease at which the values can be displayed using the various hexadecimal printing routines available in the Monitor. Secondly, the 6502-microprocessor as well as the 65C02-microprocessor can perform BCD arithmetic natively after the processor has been set to decimal mode by executing the SED instruction. Two BCD time buffers can be directly added or subtracted to obtain total time or elapsed time with very little effort. The microprocessor should be returned to hexadecimal mode by executing the CLD instruction after completing any BCD arithmetic. READCLK simply takes the first digit, multiplies it by sixteen using four `ASL` instructions, and saves that value to a temporary page-zero location. Then it takes the second digit and masks out the upper four bits using `0x0F`, and `OR`s that value with the previously saved value. The newly formed BCD number can be saved to any six-byte buffer for date and time including `VTOC` initialization, `VTOC` update, file creation or update, current date and time display, and the request for current date and time from a user external to DOS 4.5.

In designing a `READCLK` routine, its requirements must save the pointers it receives for the intended target buffer, check a flag status to verify that there is an available clock card, save the current `CSWL` and `KSWL` interface pointers, connect the `CSWL` and `KSWL` interface pointers to the clock card, issue the *Clock Colon Command* and read the generated generic clock data that is automatically saved to the `INPUT` buffer, restore the `CSWL` and `KSWL` interface pointers, and finally extract the date and time data located in the `INPUT` buffer and save this generated data in BCD format into the buffer whose pointers were initially provided. As I remarked earlier about developing a process or procedure to read a clock card within DOS, I noted that it was not a very easy task. Every requirement must be satisfied and there can be no shortcuts. Either the `CSWL` and `KSWL` interface pointers can be saved and restored from a memory location or from the stack. The stack is the more economical choice. And, it is better to save the pointers by decrementing a positive register and restoring the pointers by incrementing a negative register. This concept is illustrated nicely in Figure I.13.3. In order to extract the date and time from the generic clock data, the X-register is initialized to the index that was determined by the `FINDCLK` search routine when it parsed the clock data output to determine the value for the index where the month data actually begins. The Y-register must always be initialized to five in order to point to the last value in the clock data buffer where the first BCD value is saved. While the X-register is incremented as the generic clock data is processed, the Y-register is decremented as the generated BCD values are saved.

The `FINDCLK` routine is `0x44` bytes in size in DOS 4.5, and it executes only when DOS 4.5 boots or when DOS 4.5 is cold-started. The `READCLK` routine is `0x56` bytes in size in DOS 4.5, and it executes whenever the date and time is requested, which can be quite often actually, particularly in programs that create and/or modify a large number of data files. As previously mentioned, date and time values are required in DOS 4.5 for `VTOC` initialization, `VTOC` update, all file creation or update, the display of the current date and time, and the transfer of the current date and time values to a buffer for a user external to DOS 4.5. Knowing how important date and time is to DOS 4.5, particularly how important it is to the resources of the volume and to the resources of all of the files on that volume, one wonders why a more concerted effort was not undertaken early in the 1980's in order to integrate date and time into the next following version of DOS that would be issued after DOS 3.3, say DOS 3.4, but before ProDOS was released. Certainly, there were clock cards available early enough for this integration to occur in a post-DOS 3.3 release. Whether the intuition of the Apple corporation was truly insightful may be a matter of opinion, but with the release of ProDOS came a rather steep learning curve. This ProDOS learning curve included understanding how to organize one's files as system files, as executable program files, as data files, or as a myriad of other file types within a multiple-level hierarchical directory structure. At least the clock card gave users of ProDOS a very clear understanding of all of the advantages for having date and time as an additional resource in the definition of ProDOS volumes, directories, and files. It should be by now apparent that date and time is certainly a very welcomed and nearly indispensable resource in the definition of DOS 4.5 volumes and files.

14. DOS 4.5 Error Processing

When a Binary program is executing its instructions such that Applesoft is **not** in the RUN mode, or when Applesoft is executing its instructions such that it is in the RUN mode and the ASONERR (page-zero 0xD8) flag has its MSB **clear**, the first step in DOS 4.5 error processing is to beep the speaker and print the error message text as shown in Table I.11.7. Applesoft is defined to be in the RUN mode when ASRUN (page-zero 0x76) is **not** equal to 0xFF **and** PROMPT (page-zero 0x33) is **not** equal to the] character. Conversely, Applesoft is defined to be **not** in the RUN mode when ASRUN equals 0xFF **or** when PROMPT equals the] character. If Applesoft is in the RUN mode and the MSB of ASONERR is **set**, the selected error message is not printed and DOS exits indirectly into Applesoft at ROM address 0xD865 by means of ERRORADR. If an error message is printed, however, the next step in error processing is started where DOS restores its keyboard and video intercepts and it exits indirectly into Applesoft at ROM address 0xD43C by means of WARMADR. See Table I.8.7 for the locations and offsets of WARMADR, COLDADR, ERRORADR, and RESETADR in the INITVALS Data structure.

Applesoft programs can use the ONERR GOTO *<line number>* command to handle their own DOS error processing in order to prevent instantaneous program termination. Assembly language programs need to do a bit more work: store 0xFF to ASONERR, 0x00 to ASRUN and PROMPT, and replace the address stored at ERRORADR with the address of your own error handler. DOS 4.5 loads the X-register with the appropriate DOS error number as shown in Table I.11.7 before exiting indirectly to ERRORADR (or WARMADR for that matter if Applesoft is **not** in the RUN mode). As shown previously in Table I.9.3, calling PRTERADR using an indirect JMP instruction with the appropriate DOS error number stored in the X-register prints the corresponding DOS error message text without beeping the speaker and without printing a carriage return after the error message text. *Big Mac*, for example, utilizes PRTERADR for printing all DOS errors it encounters as shown previously in the assembly language routine of Figure I.9.5. In that code example, *Big Mac* loads the X-register with **zero** before the first call to PRTERROR in order to beep the speaker and print two carriage returns. Then, *Big Mac* loads the X-register with the actual error number, calls PRTERROR, and ends the routine by printing a final carriage return at line #371. There is absolutely no need to duplicate the PRTERROR routine into the *Big Mac* source code because the Page 0x03 vector for PRTERADR is so conveniently located at memory address 0x3E8.

Section I.6 introduced the error message Volume Full in terms of the status of the VTOC bitmap in the ALLOCSEC routine and Section I.7 introduced the error message Catalog Full in terms of the value of DIRINDX from the LCDIRENT routine. ALLOCSEC allocates a disk sector for a TSL sector or for a data sector for a file and LCDIRENT locates a filename in the volume Catalog. DIRINDX assumes one of the seven possible values for Track offset as shown in Table I.7.2. When DIRINDX becomes **zero** when calculating the offset for the next catalog entry and the last catalog sector has been reached (typically sector 0x01) and there are no deleted file entries to utilize, the volume Catalog is truly full. Both of these error conditions were reported as a DISK FULL error in DOS 3.3. Not that DOS 3.3 was seriously wrong in combining both error conditions into a single error message, I simply believe the user is far better off knowing what actually triggered the error condition. DOS 4.5 accurately provides meaningful error messages whenever error conditions do develop.

Both the Video Intercept routine and the Keyboard Intercept routine in the Command Manager save the contents of the registers and the current stack pointer into the CMDVALS Data structure before those routines continue with their processing. The File Manager also saves the current stack pointer into its own variable in the CMDVALS Data structure before it continues with any of its processing. However, the supporting routines in both of these managers in DOS 3.3 strive to maintain the integrity of the stack pointer throughout their processing even though the stack pointer is eventually restored once the processing completes in either manager. Many, many unnecessary instructions such as PLA are utilized in order to maintain stack pointer integrity. For example, extra code and variables are utilized to save a register value in order to avoid using the stack in case an error condition develops. Even when error conditions do occur, great effort is made in order to maintain the integrity of the stack pointer. Why?

Why bother saving the stack pointer in the first place if it isn't going to be seriously utilized when processing is complete? Error conditions in DOS 3.3 as well as error conditions in DOS 4.5 are always terminal conditions. There is simply no reason to continue any further processing when an error condition occurs because whatever intermediate results that have been obtained thus far are probably wrong anyway. If Applesoft does not handle the DOS error it created, the DOS 4.5 Command Manager prints the error message text and performs a DOS warm-start which initializes the stack pointer anyway. Otherwise, the Command Manager restores its control over the CSWL and KSWL pointers, restores the stack pointer, and finally restores the registers in order to exit normally. Whether or not the File Manager encounter any error conditions, it saves the content of the A-register to RTNCODE, it saves the File Manager workarea to the workarea of the file that was just processed, and it restores the stack pointer with the error status in the Carry flag. If the Carry flag is **set**, the caller uses the value in RTNCODE to print the relevant error message. This is how both managers avoid stack overflow or underflow with or without error conditions in DOS 4.5. There is absolutely no need to maintain stack pointer integrity during Command Manager or File Manager processing.

15. DOS 4.5 Chain Command

DOS 4.5 includes a real CHAIN command in its command repertoire that is designed specifically for Applesoft programs. Having a native CHAIN command is far more convenient than having to include an assembly language utility on each and every volume for those Applesoft programs requiring this capability. However, several careful considerations should be made when designing Applesoft programs that chain to each other.

The purpose of the DOS CHAIN command is to move two areas of data variables where they reside in memory for the *Start* program to where they need to reside in memory for the *Chained* program. These two areas of data variables include the Simple Variables and the Array Variables, or SAVs for short. Figure I.15.1 shows a typical Start Applesoft program residing in memory. In that figure Free Space exists because the Start Program, its SAVs, and its Character String Pool memory area do not exceed the value stored in HIMEM at page-zero 0x73/0x74 minus 0x0801, the memory address where the Start program begins. The Start program must never chain to another program whose size exceeds its available Free Space.

Applesoft uses a large number of byte-pairs in page-zero memory locations for its use. Many of these memory locations are to store addresses in low/high byte order that can easily be used as pointers in memory management routines. DOS always loads an Applesoft program into memory at address 0x0801, which is the value found in PRGTAB at page-zero 0x67/0x68. The DOS LOAD command knows the file size of the program in bytes before it actually loads the content of the file into memory because it reads the first data sector of the file and examines the first two bytes of that data sector where the size of the program is found. Using the size of the program, DOS can calculate the end address of the program, and save that information in PRGEND at page-zero 0xAF/0xB0. Initially, DOS sets

VARTAB to PRGEND and Applesoft sets ARYTAB and STREND to PRGEND and sets FRETOP to HIMEM. The DOS MAXFILES command must **not** be used to change HIMEM in DOS 4.5H because the address in HIMEM is fixed to 0xBE00. On the other hand, the DOS MAXFILES command **can** be used to change HIMEM in DOS 4.5L. Thus, from Table III.1.2, all Applesoft programs written for DOS 4.5H should consider **setting** CONFIG Bit 3 in order to disable the DOS MAXFILES command, or not use the DOS MAXFILES command with that version of DOS.

Pointer Addresses	Start Program	Smaller Program	Problematic Program	Bigger Program
	0x0000	0x0000	0x0000	0x0000
PRGTAB — 0x67/0x68	0x0801	0x0801	0x0801	0x0801
	Start Applesoft Program	Small Chained Applesoft Program	Problematic Chained Applesoft Program	
PRGEND — 0xAF/0xB0 VARTAB — 0x69/0x6A	Simple Variables			Big Chained Applesoft Program
ARYTAB — 0x6B/0x6C	Array Variables			
STREND — 0x6D/0x6E				
	Free Space			
FRETOP — 0x6F/0x70	Character String Pool			
HIMEM — 0x73/0x74				
	0xFFFF	0xFFFF	0xFFFF	0xFFFF

Figure I.15.1. Example Applesoft Program Layout in Memory

When the Applesoft program starts to execute its instructions, the program begins to create simple variables that include real variables, integer variables, and character string variables. These variables reside in the Simple Variables area of memory as simple descriptors starting in VARTAB at page-zero 0x69/0x6A. The definition of the descriptors for the variables that comprise the content of the Simple Variables is shown in Table I.15.1. As more and more Simple Variable descriptors are added, the Array Variables area is pushed higher and higher **up** in memory reducing the size of Free Space. Simple variable descriptors are always seven bytes in size, and depending upon the variable type, some of the descriptor bytes may not even be used. Table I.15.1 shows that real numbers require all seven bytes for the variable name, the exponent, and its 4-byte mantissa. Integer numbers require only four bytes for the variable name and its value in **high/low** byte order, leaving the remaining three bytes initialized to zero. Finally, simple character string variables require five bytes for the variable name, the length of the character string in bytes, and the memory address in **low/high** byte order where the character string resides, leaving the remaining two bytes initialized to zero. Obviously, a simple character string variable cannot contain more than 255 ASCII characters since only a single byte is used to define the number of characters in the simple character string variable. Applesoft programs should never define a character string variable to contain more than 255 ASCII characters.

The definition of the descriptors for Applesoft Array Variables is shown in Table I.15.2. As seen in Figure I.15.1 the Array Variables area of memory begins in ARYTAB at page-zero 0x6B/0x6C and ends in STREND at page-zero 0x6D/0x6E. This area of memory contains single and multi-dimensioned Array Variable descriptors for arrays of real numbers, arrays of integer numbers, and arrays of character string variables. Table I.15.2 shows example variable descriptors having two dimensions. Successive array element dimension sizes **precede** each other with the first-dimension size (**high/low** byte order) always coming **last**. The Array Variable descriptor grows in size as the number of dimensions increase in value. The nominal size of an Array Variable descriptor is seven bytes for a single dimension array. The descriptor increases in size by two additional bytes for each added dimension. Therefore, the dimension value found in Byte 5 of the Array Variable descriptor becomes a critical piece of information that is used to calculate where the array elements begin and end relative to the address of the beginning of their Array Variable descriptor. The maximum number of dimensions for an Array Variable descriptor is 255 since its dimension variable is limited to a single byte.

Bytes 3 and 4 of the current Array Variable descriptor give the offset in bytes to the beginning of the next, if any, Array Variable descriptor relative to the address of where the current Array Variable descriptor is found in memory. The array elements belonging to the current Array Variable descriptor begin immediately after the descriptor whose size can easily be calculated knowing the value in Byte 5, that is, 5 + (value in Byte 5)*2. The definition of each array element for each type of Array Variable descriptor is shown in Table I.15.3. These array element definitions are essentially the same as the definitions for the respective Simple Variable descriptors without including the name of the array variable. The name for all array elements is the same, and this name is found in its Array Variable descriptor. The array element for arrays of real numbers is five bytes in size that contains the exponent and its 4-byte mantissa. The array element for arrays of integer numbers is two bytes in size that holds its value in **high/low** byte order. The array element for arrays of character string variables is three bytes in size that holds the character string length in bytes and the memory address in **low/high** byte order where the ASCII data of the character string resides. Obviously, the character string elements of a character string array do not all have to contain the same number of ASCII characters and a character string element cannot contain more than 255 ASCII characters since only a single byte is used to define the number of ASCII characters in that character string. Applesoft programs should never define a character string to contain more than 255 ASCII characters.

Variable Type	Byte Definitions						
	Byte 1	**Byte 2**	**Byte 3**	**Byte 4**	**Byte 5**	**Byte 6**	**Byte 7**
Real Number	name1 +ASCII 65	name2 +ASCII 66	Exponent	Mantissa Byte 1	Mantissa Byte 2	Mantissa Byte 3	Mantissa Byte 4
Integer Number	name1 -ASCII 195	name2 -ASCII 196	High Value	Low Value	0	0	0
Simple Character String	name1 +ASCII 69	name2 -ASCII 198	String Length	Low Address	High Address	0	0

Table I.15.1. Simple Variable Descriptor Definitions in Applesoft

Variable Type	Byte Definitions								
	Byte 1	**Byte 2**	**Byte 3**	**Byte 4**	**Byte 5**	**Byte 6**	**Byte 7**	**Byte 8**	**Byte 9**
Real Array	name1 +ASCII 65	name2 +ASCII 66	Low Byte Offset	High Byte Offset	Number of Dimensions K	Size of Kth Dim High Byte	Size of Kth Dim Low Byte	Size of K-1 Dim High Byte	Size of K-1 Dim Low Byte
Integer Array	name1 -ASCII 195	name2 -ASCII 196	Low Byte Offset	High Byte Offset	Number of Dimensions K	Size of Kth Dim High Byte	Size of Kth Dim Low Byte	Size of K-1 Dim High Byte	Size of K-1 Dim Low Byte
Character String Array	name1 +ASCII 69	name2 -ASCII 198	Low Byte Offset	High Byte Offset	Number of Dimensions K	Size of Kth Dim High Byte	Size of Kth Dim Low Byte	Size of K-1 Dim High Byte	Size of K-1 Dim Low Byte

Table I.15.2. Array Variable Descriptor Definitions in Applesoft

Element Type	Byte Definitions				
	Byte 1	**Byte 2**	**Byte 3**	**Byte 4**	**Byte 5**
Real Number Element	Exponent	Mantissa Byte 1	Mantissa Byte 2	Mantissa Byte 3	Mantissa Byte 4
Integer Number Element	High Value	Low Value			
Character String Element	String Length	Low Address	High Address		

Table I.15.3. Single Array Element Descriptor Definitions in Applesoft

Many times, an Applesoft program contains the text of some character string variable. As long as there is no text operation on that character string variable such as A$ = A$ + B$, for example, the text pointer address found in the Simple Variable or in the Array Variable descriptor element points to the actual character string text within the memory contents of the Applesoft program. In this case the character string can never be available to a Chained program. In order for a simple character string variable or a character string element to be available to a Chained program, the actual character string text of that character string variable must be relocated into the Character String Pool memory area. A simple way to force this character string relocation is to perform some menial text operation on that character string variable, such as A$ = A$ + " ". This simple operation does nothing to character string A$ except to cause the actual text of A$ to be copied from within the contents of the Applesoft program into the contents of the Character String Pool memory area.

The purpose of the DOS CHAIN command is to move the SAVs of the Start program to the end of the Chained program, and to update PRGEND, VARTAB, and ARYTAB with their new addresses so that the Chained program may access those variables and character string variables of the Start program. Because of some required Applesoft calls, even FRETOP needs to be reinitialized. When the Chained program is smaller than the Start program or when the Chained program is larger than the Start program plus the size of the SAVs area, there is no problem in copying the SAVs directly to their new location. However, if the end of the Chained program occurs somewhere within the SAVs area of the Start program, there will be disaster if the SAVs are copied directly. Due to how the Monitor memory move routine is implemented, if the SAVs area of memory is copied in this particular situation, the move routine begins to overwrite the same area of memory it is attempting to copy. And this will certainly lead to disaster for the Chained program because some of the variable descriptors of the Start program is overwritten and, therefore, destroyed. If the SAVs area is copied in reverse order (high memory to low memory) to the end of this problematic Chained program, disaster will also occur when that algorithm is used to copy the SAVs area for a Chained program that is smaller than the Start program. The CHAIN routine can either refuse to perform the chain operation and signal an error message in those situations, or it can utilize another algorithm to copy the SAVs.

Another algorithm is to copy the SAVs to the address in STREND for the Start program and set PRGEND and VARTAB to that address as long as there is enough memory in Free Space. PRGEND does not necessarily have to be exactly the address where the Chained program ends in memory, technically at its triple-nulls. In fact, an Applesoft program may include attached assembly language subroutines that follow the Applesoft triple-null ending giving the program a different physical length and different physical end address. The DOS SAVE command uses PRGTAB and PRGEND to calculate the number of Applesoft program and assembly language program bytes to save, and not necessarily use the address where the triple-nulls occur in memory minus 0x0801 for only the Applesoft program. However, this option does potentially waste a good deal of memory if the SAVs area is large in size, even if there is adequate Free Space.

A better algorithm would be to always copy the SAVs up in memory to FRETOP and then copy them again down in memory to the new PRGEND. Unfortunately, the first memory copy would require a negatively-indexed memory move algorithm (the pointers are decremented, not incremented), which is not for the faint-of-heart due to its difficulty and complexity. Also, a negatively-indexed memory move algorithm requires more CPU instructions than a simple positively-indexed memory move algorithm. The second memory copy would require a straight-forward positively-indexed memory move algorithm like the one found in the Monitor ROM. Fortunately, there is enough code space in DOS 4.5 to implement this far superior and correct chain algorithm. The user can utilize the DOS 4.5 CHAIN command to their heart's content and rest assured that CHAIN always places the SAVs fully intact precisely where the Chained program ends with the single caveat already mentioned: the Start program must never chain to a Chained program whose size exceeds the available Free Space.

If the R keyword is **not** used with the CHAIN command, CHAIN calls the Applesoft ROM routine GARBAG at memory address 0xE484 before it moves the Simple Variable and Array Variable descriptors to their new location at the end of the Chained program. The GARBAG routine utilizes an algorithm similar in concept to a basic bubble sort algorithm to remove all unreferenced character string data from the Character String Pool memory area, thus compacting the Character String Pool contents before CHAIN relocates the SAVs in memory. The processing time for GARBAG to extract all of the little bits and pieces of unreferenced character strings and string characters is proportional to the square of the number of character strings in use. That is, if there are one hundred active character strings it will take four times longer to process those character strings than if there is only fifty active character strings.

Many Garbage Collection algorithms have been previously published that accomplish the same results as GARBAG in far less time, but there can be a number of caveats when using some of these algorithms. For instance, normal Applesoft programs save all character string data in lower ASCII, that is, with the MSB of each character string byte cleared. Furthermore, normal Applesoft programs never allow more than one character string descriptor to point to the same exact copy of that character string data in memory. Multiple character string descriptors and character string elements may each point to identical character string data, but those sets of character string data must reside at different memory locations. Some Garbage Collection algorithms depend upon these constraints. If either constraint is not true, a catastrophe will happen during the course of subsequent Applesoft processing! Of course, if the character string data of an Applesoft program is normal, there will be no subsequent problems. Only if assembly language programs, appendages to the Applesoft program, or other code segments perform exotic manipulations to the character string descriptors or to the Character String Pool content, these constraints might be violated. The Applesoft Garbage Collector is discussed in detail in Section II.4.

If an efficient Garbage Collection routine is available, the user should invoke that routine before using the DOS CHAIN command, and utilize the R keyword to bypass calling GARBAG from within the chain processing. There is always the dilemma in finding that balance between either making the Applesoft Start program and its Chained programs smaller in order to accommodate an external and complex assembly language Garbage Collection routine, or enlarging the Applesoft Start program and its Chained programs and strategically placing many Applesoft FRE(aexpr) commands throughout the programs. The FRE(aexpr) command calls GARBAG which processes the Character String Pool content more efficiently if there are fewer inactive character strings or little unreferenced character string data bytes. Again, there is always the dilemma in finding that balance for the best strategy in ensuring that memory is utilized as efficiently as possible.

16. ProDOS Disk I/O Algorithm

I have no idea whether Apple or Axlon, the manufacture of the RAM Disk 320, developed the fast disk read algorithm. As described in section V.11, the RAM Disk initialization software can transfer the contents of an entire 35-track diskette to one of the RAM Disk drives in only seven seconds, the time to make thirty-five revolutions, one revolution for each track of a Disk][volume. The Axlon software locates track 0x00 on the Disk][volume, clears a sixteen byte *sector read* table, and reads the first sector address header it encounters. It does not matter which sector address header the routine finds first. The software notes the sector number from the header information and proceeds to read the sector data that follows the sector address header putting the first eighty-six bytes it reads into a buffer called NBUF2 as shown in Table I.16.1. These eighty-six bytes contain the lower two bits for each of the next three groups of data bytes that are about to be read. The first group of data bytes is comprised of another eighty-six bytes, where each byte is OR'd with its lower two bits obtained from a `BITNIBL` table indexed by the respective byte from `NBUF2`, and stored directly into the designated RAM Disk sector. The second group of data bytes is comprised of the next eighty-six bytes of data that follow, similarly processed with the respective index byte from `NBUF2`, and stored in the designated RAM Disk sector. The last eighty-four bytes of data that follow are similarly processed and stored in the designated RAM Disk sector, now totaling `0x100` data bytes. The final byte read, or byte 343, is the checksum byte. If the checksum calculation is `zero` then no read error is flagged and the *sector read* table is updated with this sector number marked as read. Once the *sector read* table is complete the Axlon software moves the Disk][read/write disk head to the next volume track, clears the *sector read* table, and processes that track. The Axlon software is finished when it has read and processed track `0x22`.

Routine, Table, or Buffer	DOS 4.5		ProDOS	
	Bytes	Cycles	Bytes	Cycles
PRENIBL	36	10557	172	6331
POSTNIBL	23	9524	n/a	
READSCTR	84	11207	206	11248
WRITSCTR	128	11419	222	11420
RDNIBL	106		106	
WRTNIBL	64		n/a	
BITNIBL	n/a		256	
NBUF1	256		n/a	
NBUF2	86		86	
Total	783	42707	1048	28999

Table I.16.1. Comparison of DOS 4.5 and ProDOS RWTS

The ProDOS version of the fast disk read algorithm is essentially the same as the Axlon version except that ProDOS incorporates the contents of the `WRTNIBL` table into the unused portion of the ProDOS `BITNIBL` table. Since only three of every four bytes are needed for processing using the data in `NBUF2`, it made sense to utilize the unused fourth byte for the `WRTNIBL` table. Axlon did not provide a fast disk write algorithm so there was no need to incorporate a `WRTNIBL` table in the Axlon `BITNIBL` table. Closer inspection of the two algorithms indicates to me that the Axlon version is a little cleaner programmatically. Perhaps Axlon obtained the ProDOS version and tweaked it some? If I had seen the ProDOS version initially I probably would have made the same modifications Axlon did. I cannot imagine the reverse taking place where Apple obtained the Axlon version and purposefully sabotaged it. I could be wrong. Whatever the case, the algorithm is clever and it works well, and there is no need for a `POSTNIBL` routine when using either algorithm. However, the `READSCTR` routine that implements the ProDOS fast disk read algorithm is nearly twice the size of the DOS 4.5 `READSCTR` and `POSTNIBL` routines combined, that is, 206 bytes versus a sum of 107 bytes, respectively. The ProDOS `READSCTR` routine also takes a few more startup processing cycles than the DOS 4.5 `READSCTR` routine. ProDOS requires the `BITNIBL` table for its data processing and DOS 4.5 requires the `NBUF1` buffer for its data processing. The ProDOS `BITNIBL` table and the DOS 4.5 `NBUF1` buffer are the same size, but the `BITNIBL` table also includes the `WRTNIBL` table, a table that is a standalone table in

DOS 4.5. To read and process a DOS 4.5 sector takes 20,731 cycles, or 20.73 milliseconds. ProDOS takes 11.25 milliseconds to read and process a sector. In order for ProDOS to read a block of data it must read two sectors sequentially.

The processing time for the ProDOS version of its fast disk write algorithm is essentially the same as the DOS 4.5 write algorithm, and this is to be expected. Both algorithms must write at least five 40-microsecond auto-synchronization bytes, three 32-microsecond prologue bytes, 343 32-microsecond data bytes and checksum, three 32-microsecond epilogue bytes, and a final 32-microsecond synchronization byte. However, their algorithm sizes are substantially different and that is because NBUF1 lies on a page boundary for DOS 4.5 and the user data buffer may or may not lie on a page boundary for ProDOS. ProDOS must prenibblize its buffer data in the same way and for the same reason that DOS 4.5 prenibblizes its buffer data. However, ProDOS must modify its WRITSCTR code *on the fly*, or dynamically because it does not utilize a page bounded intermediary NBUF1 buffer. ProDOS must determine whether the data buffer that is in focus lies on a page boundary, and if not, then which pages contain what portion of the data buffer. There is one exception the ProDOS algorithm must also handle, and that is when the data buffer falls off of a page boundary by just one byte. The ProDOS fast disk write algorithm requires 394 bytes for its PRENIBL and WRITSCTR routines, and it gets its WRITNIBL table for free. On the other hand, DOS 4.5 requires a mere 164 bytes for its PRENIBL and WRITSCTR routines, but it requires a WRITNIBL table, for a total of 228 bytes which is still about 58% the size of the ProDOS memory requirements. To process and write a DOS 4.5 sector takes 21,976 cycles, or 21.98 milliseconds. ProDOS takes 17,751 cycles to process and write a sector, or 17.75 milliseconds. In order for ProDOS to write a block of data it must write two sectors sequentially.

I have been referring to the data in Table I.16.1 that I collected for the information in the above sizing and timing comparisons. Overall, the amount of software, table data, and buffer space required by DOS 4.5 to read and write a sector of data to and from a diskette totals 783 bytes. ProDOS requires 1048 bytes, a difference of 265 bytes, or an additional page of memory plus nine bytes. This difference in code/data amounts to a 25% increase in the memory requirements by ProDOS. The time to read and write a sector of data takes 42.71 milliseconds for DOS 4.5 and 29.00 milliseconds for ProDOS. The ProDOS algorithms are 32% faster than the DOS 4.5 algorithms overall. With these results it is obvious that the extensive use of table data and of self-modifying code alone cannot account for the visible and extraordinary differences the two operating systems demonstrate when reading and writing files.

ProDOS achieves its significant speed difference by employing a sector interleaving (or skewing) such that only two revolutions are required to read all eight data blocks on a track, similar to the technique Apple Fortran and Apple Pascal use for reading their data diskettes. The sectors are arranged such that there is one sector between each of the sectors that comprise a block, and there is one sector between each successive block. Data blocks are read and written in ascending block number (i.e. 2 ascending skew) in ProDOS and sectors are read and written in descending sector number (i.e. 2 descending skew) in DOS 4.5. DOS 4.5 employs a sector interleaving such that it is physically possible to read all sixteen sectors on a track in two revolutions, but typically three revolutions are more realistic. For a more complete discussion on sector interleaving refer to Worth's and Lechner's *Beneath Apple DOS*, *Beneath Apple ProDOS*, and *Bag of Tricks*. These references provide the reader with a thorough understanding of this rather complicated subject.

17. Using DOS 4.5 Commands

I have enhanced many of the original DOS 3.3 commands primarily using the R keyword as a command modifier or switch since this keyword has very limited usage in the original DOS command repertoire other than in the commands EXEC, POSITION, and the Random-Access Data file commands READ and WRITE. All DOS 4.5 commands and their arguments may be entered in lowercase and/or in uppercase on the Apple Command Line, in EXEC files, and in Applesoft and assembly language executable files. Filenames may be entered in a mixture of lowercase and uppercase ASCII, and the filenames are treated as case sensitive. For example, the filenames HELLO and Hello are treated as two different files. In order to make full use of lowercase and uppercase in DOS 4.5, an Apple //e or similar is preferred. DOS 4.5 does function quite nicely on an Apple][or an Apple][+ if it has a character generator ROM (for example, the Dan Paymar *Lowercase Adaptor Interface PROM*) that can display the complete lowercase and uppercase Latin character set. DOS 4.5 does print error messages in mixed case. The enhanced Apple //e ROM also supports lowercase and/or uppercase entry for Applesoft commands. In my opinion, however, this ROM continues to retain at least two substantial deficiencies: there is no native DELETE key utilization and the HLIN drawing algorithm is hopelessly flawed.

There is no consistency in DOS 3.3 in whether to print one or two carriage returns after DOS completes its processing for a DOS command when that command is entered on the Apple Command Line. Certainly, it would be a mistake to print any additional carriage returns after DOS completes its processing for a DOS command when that command is issued from within an Applesoft program or during the processing of an EXEC file. DOS 4.5 does print **one** carriage return after DOS completes its processing for a DOS command when that command is entered on the Apple Command Line. This policy is to ensure that there is at least one blank line between all DOS commands entered on the Apple Command Line. Having this blank line helps to keep each DOS command and its output data as legible as possible on the display screen. Of course, DOS 4.5 does not print any additional carriage returns after DOS completes its processing for a DOS command when that command is issued from within an executing Applesoft program or during the processing of an EXEC file. However, DOS commands that are issued from within assembly language programs using COUT will appear with the additional carriage return. One way to prevent DOS 4.5 from printing that additional carriage return is to store zero for the variables ASRUN (page-zero 0x76) and PROMPT (page-zero 0x33). When DOS 4.5 checks these variables after DOS completes its processing for a DOS command, it will appear to DOS that Applesoft is in the RUN mode, and therefore, DOS will not print the additional carriage return.

Both DOS 3.3 and DOS 4.5 save files to a volume Catalog using the TSL resources of the file if the file already exists in the volume Catalog. For example, if the file TEMP already exists and its TSL sector contains eight track/sector entries, those same entries are used to save TEMP again whether TEMP is smaller or larger than its initial size. If TEMP is larger, the File Manager simply requests additional data sectors and adds them to the TSL sector of the file. If TEMP is edited and the file now uses only three data sectors, the first three track/sector entries in the TSL sector are used to save the new content of the file and the remaining TSL entries in that TSL sector go unused. In other words, the last five TSL entries in this example remain allocated to the file and, therefore, these data sectors are unavailable for use by any other file. This inherent resource wastefulness in DOS 3.3 and in DOS 4.5 is perpetuated by programs like *FID*. *FID* uses the File Manager to copy files in total, and it assumes that all track/sector entries in a TSL sector of a file belong to and are utilized by that file. But DOS 4.5 introduces a new strategy called *File Delete/File Save*. The DOS commands BSAVE, LSAVE, SAVE, and TSAVE can now utilize the B keyword to implement the *File Delete/File Save* strategy. This strategy first deletes the file from the volume Catalog and then saves the file to the same volume and Catalog in order to ensure that the TSL sectors of the file contain only those track/sector entries that are actually required and utilized by that file.

II. Apple][ROM Modifications

I presented all of my modifications to the Apple CX and D0:F0 ROM space in the DOS 4.1 Manual and in my book *DOS 4.1 Disk Operating System Second Edition*. These modifications include my corrected HLIN Drawing Algorithm, the Delete Key Utilization, the Apple //e 80-Column Text Card, the Apple //e ROM Monitor, and the Apple Character Generator ROM. The DOS 4.1 Manual is available for download at www.applecored.net as a PDF. The DOS 4.1 *Second Edition* includes Build 46 (the last build) and it can be purchased from Lulu.com. If anyone is interested in exploring the benefits of the modifications I made to the Apple][ROM that I presented in both of these publications, those ROM images are available for download at www.applecored.net. The ROM images are located in the ROM2e folder which can be found in the DOS 4.5 Source Code TAR file.

The topics I have included in this section are important in DOS 4.5 and they are particularly important to me. I have edited all of these topics with DOS 4.5 specifically in mind.

In my version of the Apple //e firmware (or ROM) source code, I use the variable HLINMOD for a conditional assembly directive that is used to optionally assemble the original, though hopelessly flawed ROM code or assemble the modified, corrected ROM code. The generated object code can be programmed into either a single 27128 EPROM as found in the Enhanced and Platinum Apple //e or programmed into two 2764 EPROMs for the earlier versions of the Apple //e. The modified contents of the Apple //e character generator ROM that defines each ASCII character in pixels can be programmed into a 2732 EPROM. An EPROM programmer is required in order to program new EPROMs in order to replace the Apple //e firmware ROM or ROMs (depending on the motherboard) and the character generator ROM. I have not sourced the Apple][+ Autostart ROM. I have no doubt that the contents of the Apple][+ Autostart ROM was the basis for the *Lisa* and the *Big Mac* Monitors, which I have sourced. I believe very little, if anything was changed in the Apple][+ version of the Applesoft interpreter to that found in the Apple //e firmware, except to support the CX ROM space. There are no additions or deletions to the set of Applesoft commands contained in the Apple //e firmware. All Apple //e Applesoft commands function identically to how they function in the Apple][and in the Apple][+.

1. Corrected HLIN Drawing Algorithm

I have always disliked the unsymmetrical look of a HIRES diagonal line either in the horizontal or in the vertical direction ever since acquiring my Apple][+. And this same HLIN code resides in the Apple //e ROM unchanged, which is shameful. When I was assigned the task to provide all of the icons for HomeWord Speller at Sierra On-Line, I analyzed the HLIN algorithm and found that the algorithm does not correctly calculate the delta difference of the horizontal and the vertical start to end points before drawing a line. It is easy to demonstrate this error before and after installing my ROM modifications.

There are two memory locations that require a small code adjustment. The first code adjustment is made at 0xF57A and that adjustment is shown in Figure II.1.1. In that figure ZPGD4 is the page-zero memory location 0xD4 and HF465 is a label for a routine at memory address 0xF465.

```
0xF57A:
            .if HLINMOD
            bcs  HF580              ; branch to 0xF580 if set
            asl                     ; times 2
            jsr  HF465              ; call 0xF465
HF580       clc                     ; prepare for delta, not diff
            lda  ZPGD4              ; 0xD4
            .el
            bcs  HF581              ; branch to 0xF581 if set
            asl                     ; times 2
            jsr  HF465              ; call 0xF465
            sec                     ; prepare for diff, not delta
HF581       lda  ZPGD4              ; 0xD4
            .fi
```

Figure II.1.1. First HLIN Code Adjustment

```
0xF5A5:
            .if HLINMOD
            sec                     ; prepare for diff, not delta
            .el
            clc                     ; prepare for delta, not diff
            .fi
```

Figure II.1.2. Second HLIN Code Adjustment

```
10 HOME                            300 HPLOT 100,110
20 HGR                             310 HPLOT TO 101,151
30 HCOLOR= 3                       320 HPLOT TO 139,150
40 HPLOT 10,10                     330 HPLOT TO 140,111
50 HPLOT TO 50,10                  340 HPLOT TO 100,110
60 HPLOT TO 50,50                  350 GOSUB 1000
70 HPLOT TO 10,50                  400 HPLOT 200,15
80 HPLOT TO 10,10                  410 HPLOT TO 260,10
90 GOSUB 1000                      420 HPLOT TO 265,30
100 HPLOT 100,10                   430 HPLOT TO 250,35
110 HPLOT TO 140,11                440 HPLOT TO 270,55
120 HPLOT TO 139,50                450 HPLOT TO 255,75
130 HPLOT TO 101,51                460 HPLOT TO 275,100
140 HPLOT TO 100,10                470 HPLOT TO 245,115
150 GOSUB 1000                     480 HPLOT TO 215,117
200 HPLOT 10,110                   490 HPLOT TO 200,15
210 HPLOT TO 10,150                500 GOSUB 1000
220 HPLOT TO 50,150                900 TEXT : END
230 HPLOT TO 50,110                1000 POKE - 16368,0
240 HPLOT TO 10,110                1010 WAIT - 16384,128
250 GOSUB 1000                     1020 RETURN
```

Figure II.1.3. HLIN Demonstration Program in Applesoft

The second code adjustment is made at `0xF5A5` and that is shown in Figure II.1.2. You will simply be amazed at how *lovely* and *symmetrical* diagonal lines are drawn either from left to right, from right to left, from top to bottom, or from bottom to top. And I am appalled that the old ROM code passed any sort of testing and/or code review vis-à-vis how trivial these two modification are and how elegant the results appear.

Figure II.1.3 shows a simple Applesoft program that can be used to demonstrate the visual differences between the original `HLIN` drawing algorithm and my corrected drawing algorithm. Figure II.1.4 shows what this Applesoft program visually produces when it is `RUN` on an Apple //e before the `HLIN` modifications are made to the Apple //e ROM code.

In Figure II.1.4 the two boxes on the left are square boxes and they draw perfectly no matter in which direction the lines are drawn. The two middle boxes are nearly square boxes except that the horizontal and vertical line end points differ by just one pixel. They show different anomalies depending upon in which direction the lines are drawn. That is, the upper middle box is drawn clockwise and the lower middle box is drawn counterclockwise. The shape on the right is drawn clockwise and it shows many odd corner anomalies as the direction and angle of the lines change.

Figure II.1.5 shows what this same Applesoft program produces visually when this program is `RUN` on the same Apple //e, but with the `HLIN` modifications made to the Apple //e ROM code. All corner anomalies disappear without regard to drawing direction, and when the lines are drawn diagonally, the lines are segmented equally. It is obvious from Figure II.1.5 that having the `HLIN` modifications allows one to draw any shape in any direction and its lines in any order without having to consider the possible introduction of any irregular corner anomalies and inconsistent line segmentation. They do not exist.

Obviously, the two middle boxes are for demonstration purposes only in order to visually see what precise line segmentation looks like; otherwise, these two boxes have no other practical use. The shape on the right is far more representative of a very complex figure that shows precise corner detail as well as precise line segmentation. Even double-high-resolution graphics show some degree of line roughness for diagonal lines due to line segmentation that is inherent in the relatively low pixel density of the Apple //e display. In its day, however, Apple high-resolution graphics are still totally awesome.

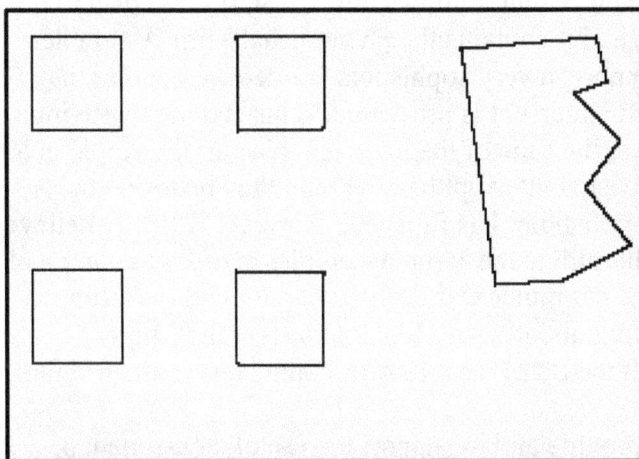

Figure II.1.4. Original ROM HLIN Routine   Figure II.1.5. Modified ROM HLIN Routine

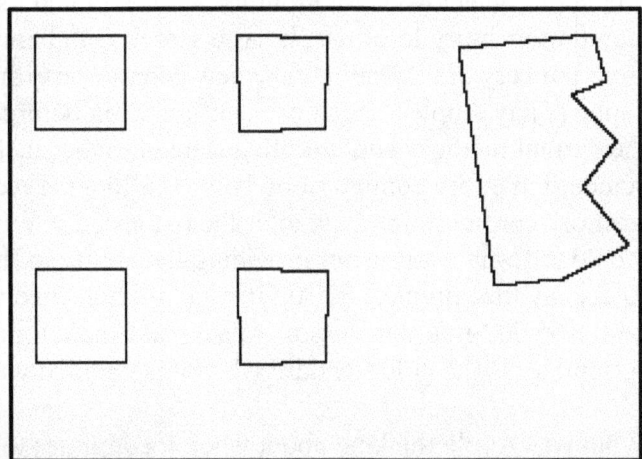

2. Soft Switches in the Apple //e

While I was working at Sierra On-Line, my parents purchased their Apple //e with the understanding that I would set up their system, teach them how to use its capabilities, fix and/or repair any software or hardware problems that might occur, and perform any regular maintenance as required. I didn't fully realize what I was getting myself into particularly when I attempted to teach my father how to use VisiCalc: his hands were quite large and his fingers were not keyboard-nimble, he had poor close-up vision, and he could not remember repetitive key-entry sequences very well. I designed his VisiCalc daily expenses spreadsheet for each month (requiring the wide paper in their Epson MX-100 printer) and wrote an Applesoft program to extract his monthly totals from his monthly data files in order to create his annual summary file containing all of his summarized data. I provided him detailed instructions on how to begin his daily VisiCalc session and how to enter his data into each row and column. When he entered wrong data, or he entered data in the wrong row and column, or he skipped instructions, he became rather agitated and blamed the computer for causing his errors. My mother would then enter the data for him to keep everyone calm. I should say that these were our typical family dynamics!

My parents purchased their Apple //e when it first became available, probably three or four years before the enhanced version was developed. I have no recall if we were even aware of an Enhanced Apple //e while I was at Sierra On-Line around 1983 and 1984. Because I was assisting another engineer in porting *ScreenWriter* to the Apple //e, I became very familiar with the 80-column text card, the routines AUXMOVE and XFER, and a whole gamut of new Soft Switches. Also, Ken Williams asked me to extract the database from *the Dic-tio-nary*, the companion spell checker to *ScreenWriter*. He wanted this massive database for his new product called HomeWord Speller, the companion spell checker to HomeWord which he had already released. HomeWord and HomeWord Speller were both developed in-house. I made multiple calls to XFER within a printer driver I developed for *the Dic-tio-nary*, its only vulnerable access location at 0x300. My special driver extracted specific partitions of the database and copied the partition to Auxiliary memory instead of to a printer. Once I took control of the computer after the data transfer, I was able to copy that database partition from Auxiliary memory to Main memory, and then into a file onto a disk. It is important to note that the XFER starting address is found at 0x3ED and 0x3EE in the Page 0x03 Interface Routines and Vectors as shown in Table I.9.3.

I believe the enhanced version of the Apple //e provides MouseText characters in place of the alternate uppercase inverse characters, and it also introduced double high-resolution graphics. Furthermore, this Apple provides lowercase input for Applesoft and its new Monitor allows lower ASCII input data to be stored in memory locations, it has a search command, and it contains the phenomenal Mini-Assembler from the very old Apple][. The new Monitor also supports a very sophisticated interrupt handler that captures any Apple //e memory configuration before the interrupt is processed. This is done by saving the current memory configuration state onto the stack at the time of the interrupt, placing the Apple in a standard memory configuration before calling the requested interrupt handler, and then restoring the memory configuration state after the requested interrupt handler has finished. However, I firmly believe Apple fell way short in not providing the ability to fully utilize the Mini-Assembler in order to enter and to display the complete 65C02 Instruction Set since the computer was designed to use and was shipped with a 65C02-microprocessor. What was Apple thinking about? Any fool knows that the Mini-Assembler is the gold standard when it is coupled with the STEP and TRACE commands in the Monitor.

What was Apple thinking about when it continues to provide and to support the use of a cassette tape recorder in order to store and retrieve programs, multi-dimensioned integer and real arrays, and shape tables? I know of no software engineer in my professional career or among my personal friends who ever used a cassette tape recorder with any Apple computer for any reason. I designed a communication protocol for a programmable keyboard by means of a wire, which was similar to the output data to a cassette tape recorder. Other than programming a keyboard using an annunciator, I have never used a cassette tape recorder with any of my Apple computers. I have never used the Applesoft LOAD, RECALL, SAVE, STORE, or SHLOAD commands in any of my Applesoft programs, nor have I seen these commands used in any professional or commercial Applesoft programs. And, I have never used the READ or WRITE commands in the Monitor at any time. Why would I use such a ridiculous and incredibly slow and error prone data archiving method when I have the Disk][, the Rana, the RAM Disk 320, the Sider, or the CFFA card to save programs and data in the form of files, visible within its media, and date and time stamped? Honestly, I derive no personal satisfaction in knowing that a user can read data into an Apple][computer from a cassette tape recorder port. I do have a few suggestions for what could replace the useless READ and WRITE commands with something rather quite spectacular.

The Apple //e Main and Auxiliary memory together total 128 KB, and each 64 KB area can be controlled by means of an MMU and an IOU device using Soft Switches. By design, the memory of a 65C02 processor within the Apple //e hardware architecture can be naturally divided into four strategic areas: page-zero and the stack, 0x200 to 0xBFFF, 0xC000 to 0xCFFF, and 0xD000 to 0xFFFF which also includes the bank-switched 0xD000 to 0xDFFF memory space. These memory areas can be individually activated from Main or Auxiliary memory resources using the appropriate Soft Switches. What is also unique to the Apple //e is that the Monitor firmware has been expanded to include additional ROM memory that is mapped to the 0xC100 to 0xCFFF address space called CX ROM. This address space is enabled or disabled using the appropriate Soft Switches. If there is a display slot card residing in Slot 3, the firmware of that card can be activated rather than using the internal 80-column text card firmware. Table II.2.1 summarizes the new memory management and video Soft Switches used to control Main and Auxiliary memory. Some data must be written to all of these Soft Switches in order to invoke their action. It does not matter what that data is because that data is not stored anywhere. Table II.2.2 summarizes the new Soft Switch status flags. It is by means of these status flags that one may determine the complete memory and video configuration of the Apple //e.

Address	Access	Name	Description	Notes
0xC000	W	STR80OFF	Disable 80-column store	1
0xC001	W	STR80ON	Enable 80-column store	1
0xC002	W	RAMRDOFF	Read enable Main RAM, 0x0200-0xBFFF	2
0xC003	W	RAMRDON	Read enable Auxiliary RAM, 0x0200-0xBFFF	2
0xC004	W	RAMWROFF	Write enable Main RAM, 0x0200-0xBFFF	2
0xC005	W	RAMWRON	Write enable Auxiliary RAM, 0x0200-0xBFFF	2
0xC006	W	CXROMOFF	Enable slot ROMs, slots 1-7, or 0xC100-0xC7FF	3
0xC007	W	CXROMON	Enable internal CX ROM, or 0xC100-0xCFFF	3
0xC008	W	AUXZPOFF	Enable Main ZP, stack, Language Card partition, Av1 BSR RAM	4
0xC009	W	AUXZPON	Enable Auxiliary ZP, stack, lang. card, Av1 BSR RAM	4
0xC00A	W	C3ROMOFF	Enable internal CX3 ROM, 0xC300-0xC3FF	
0xC00B	W	C3ROMON	Enable Slot ROM, 0xC300-0xC3FF	
0xC00C	W	VID80OFF	Disable 80-column video	
0xC00D	W	VID80ON	Enable 80-column video	
0xC00E	W	ALTCHOFF	Enable normal Apple character set	
0xC00F	W	ALTCHON	Enable alternate character set (no flash)	

Table II.2.1. New Memory Management and Video Soft Switches

Address	Access	Name	Description	MSB Clear	MSB Set	Notes
0xC000	R/R7	KEY	Read keyboard for keypress	None	Yes	
0xC010	R/R7	CLRKEY	Clear keyboard strobe, keypress	None	Yes	
0xC011	R7	RDBANK2	Which LC bank in use	BANK1	BANK2	
0xC012	R7	RDLCRAM	LC RAM or ROM read-enabled	ROM	RAM	
0xC013	R7	RDRAMRD	Main, AUX RAM read-enabled	AUX	Main	
0xC014	R7	RDRAMWR	Main, AUX RAM write-enabled	AUX	Main	
0xC015	R7	RDCXROM	Slot or internal ROM enabled	Slot	Internal	
0xC016	R7	RDAUXZP	Which ZP & LC enabled	Main	AUX	
0xC017	R7	RDC3ROM	Slot or CX ROM enabled	Slot	CX3	
0xC018	R7	RDSTR80	State of STR80 switch	Off	On	
0xC019	R7	RDVRTBLK	State of vertical blanking	Off	On	
0xC01A	R7	RDTEXT	State of TEXT switch	Graphics	Text	
0xC01B	R7	RDMIXED	Read MIXED switch	Off	On	
0xC01C	R7	RDPAGE2	State of PAGE2 switch	Main	AUX	
0xC01D	R7	RDHIRES	State of Graphics resolution	LOWRES	HIRES	
0xC01E	R7	RDALTCH	State of Alternate Character Set	Off	On	
0xC01F	R7	RDVID80	State of VID80 video	Off	On	
0xC07E	R7	RDIOUDIS	Read IOUDIS switch	On	Off	5
0xC07F	R7	RDDHIRES	Read DHIRES switch	Off	On	5

Table II.2.2. New Soft Switch Status Flags

Address	Access	Name	Description	Notes
0xC020	R	TAPEOUT	Cassette output Toggle	
0xC030	R	SPKRTOGL	Speaker output Toggle	
0xC040	R	UTILTOGL	Utility Strobe; 1 Ms. pulse Game I/O pin 5	
0xC050	R/W	TEXTOFF	Display Graphics	
0xC051	R/W	TEXTON	Display Text	
0xC052	R/W	MIXEDOFF	Full Screen graphics	6
0xC053	R/W	MIXEDON	Text with graphics	6
0xC054	R/W	PAGE1ON	Display Page 1 or Main video memory	7
0xC055	R/W	PAGE2ON	Display Page 2 or Auxiliary video memory	7
0xC056	R/W	HIRESOFF	Select low resolution Graphics	6
0xC057	R/W	HIRESON	Select high resolution Graphics	6
0xC058	R/W	ANN1OFF	Annunciator 1 off (active if IOUDIS off)	
0xC059	R/W	ANN1ON	Annunciator 1 on (active if IOUDIS off)	
0xC05A	R/W	ANN2OFF	Annunciator 2 off (active if IOUDIS off)	
0xC05B	R/W	ANN2ON	Annunciator 2 on (active if IOUDIS off)	
0xC05C	R/W	ANN3OFF	Annunciator 3 off (active if IOUDIS off)	
0xC05D	R/W	ANN3ON	Annunciator 3 on (active if IOUDIS off)	
0xC05E	R/W	ANN4OFF	Annunciator 4 off (active if IOUDIS off)	
0xC05E	R/W	DHRESON	Double HIRES on (active if IOUDIS on)	
0xC05F	R/W	ANN4ON	Annunciator 4 on (active if IOUDIS off)	
0xC05F	R/W	DHRESOFF	Double HIRES off (active if IOUDIS on)	

Table II.2.3. Original Input/Output Control Soft Switches, Part 1

Address	Access	Name	Description	Notes
0xC060	R	TAPEIN	Cassette input	8
0xC061	R	PB1IN	Push Button 1 input	8
0xC062	R	PB2IN	Push Button 2 input	8
0xC063	R	PB3IN	Push Button 3 input	8
0xC064	R	GC1IN	Game Controller 1 input	9
0xC065	R	GC2IN	Game Controller 2 input	9
0xC066	R	GC3IN	Game Controller 3 input	9
0xC067	R	GC4IN	Game Controller 4 input	9
0xC070	R	GCTOGL	Game Controller Strobe; resets GC1-GC4	
0xC073	W	BANKSEL	RamWorks Bank Select; 64 KB bank select	
0xC07E	W	IOUDISON	Disable annunciators, enable double HIRES	
0xC07F	W	IOUDISOFF	Enable annunciators, disable double HIRES	

Table II.2.4. Original Input/Output Control Soft Switches, Part 2

For completeness I have included Tables II.2.3, II.2.4, II.2.5, and II.2.6 showing the original Input/Output, memory management, and Disk][control Soft Switches. In all cases the names of each Soft Switch are those that I use within the *Lisa* assembler because *Lisa* has an eight-character limitation for labels. Figure II.2.1 contains all notes referenced by Tables II.2.1 to II.2.6.

Address	Access	Name	Description	Notes
0xC080	R	RAM2WP	Select Bank 2; write protect RAM	
0xC081	R | RR	ROM2WE	Deselect Bank 2; enable ROM | write enable RAM	
0xC082	R	ROM2WP	Deselect Bank 2; enable ROM; write protect RAM	
0xC083	R | RR	RAM2WE	Select Bank 2 | write enable RAM	
0xC084			See 0xC080	
0xC085			See 0xC081	
0xC086			See 0xC082	
0xC087			See 0xC083	
0xC088	R	RAM1WP	Select Bank 1; write protect RAM	
0xC089	R | RR	ROM1WE	Deselect Bank 1; enable ROM | write enable RAM	
0xC08A	R	ROM1WP	Deselect Bank 1; enable ROM; write protect RAM	
0xC08B	R | RR	RAM1WE	Select Bank 1 | write enable RAM	
0xC08C			See 0xC088	
0xC08D			See 0xC089	
0xC08E			See 0xC08A	
0xC08F			See 0xC08B	

Table II.2.5. Original Memory Management Soft Switches

Address	Access	Name	Description	Notes
0xC080	R	PHAS0OFF	Turn stepper motor phase 1 off	
0xC081	R	PHAS0ON	Turn stepper motor phase 1 on	
0xC082	R	PHAS1OFF	Turn stepper motor phase 2 off	
0xC083	R	PHAS1ON	Turn stepper motor phase 2 on	
0xC084	R	PHAS2OFF	Turn stepper motor phase 3 off	
0xC085	R	PHAS2ON	Turn stepper motor phase 3 on	
0xC086	R	PHAS3OFF	Turn stepper motor phase 4 off	
0xC087	R	PHAS3ON	Turn stepper motor phase 4 on	
0xC088	R	MOTOROFF	Turn motor off	
0xC089	R	MOTORON	Turn motor on	
0xC08A	R	DRV0EN	Select Drive 1	
0xC08B	R	DRV1EN	Select Drive 2	
0xC08C	R	STROBE	Read data or shift while writing	
0xC08D	R/W	LATCH	Sense write protect or load data while writing	
0xC08E	R	DATAIN	Prepare latch for input	10
0xC08F	W	DATAOUT	Prepare latch for output	11

Table II.2.6. Original Disk][Control Soft Switches

1) If STR80OFF, then access PAGE1/PAGE2 and use RAMRD and RAMWR; if STR80ON, then access Main or Auxiliary display page (0x400) using PAGE2.
2) If 80STORE is ON these switches do not affect video memory.
3) If INTCXROM is ON, then switch SLOTC3ROM is available; otherwise Main ROM is accessed.
4) Use bank enable and write protect switches to control 0xD000-0xFFFF.
5) Triggers paddle timer and resets VBLINT.
6) This mode is only effective when TEXT switch is OFF.
7) This switch changes function when 80STORE is ON.
8) Data is on MSB only.
9) Read 0xC070 first, then count until MSB is zero.
10) DATAIN with STROBE for Read and DATAIN with LATCH for Sense Write Protect.
11) DATAOUT with STROBE for Write and DATAOUT with LATCH for Load Write Latch.

Figure II.2.1. Notes for Tables II.2.1 to II.2.6

Table II.2.7 shows the Soft Switches that are used to control the *Zip Chip* if it is used in place of the 65C02 processor. The *Zip Chip* includes a 65C02 processor along with cache memory and a cache memory controller in order to execute processor instructions and to manage memory data faster. Table II.2.8 shows the Soft Switches that are used to control the CFFA and Table II.2.9 shows the Soft Switches that are used to control the quikLoader. Table II.2.10 shows the Soft Switches that are used to control the Sider, RAM Disk 320, RAM Card, and Rana drives. Typically, the X-register contains the slot number in which the interface card or device resides times sixteen, and this register is used in combination with the addresses shown in Tables II.2.8, II.2.9, and II.2.10. Or, if speed is critical and the address space where the device driver is writable, the slot number of the device times sixteen can be added to the base addresses shown in these tables except in the case for the Disk][where indexed, absolute addressing instructions must always be used.

In addition to what is shown in Table II.2.10, the Rana Elite Controller card also uses the original Disk][control Soft Switches as shown in Table II.2.6. The Rana Elite Controller card uses a complicated algorithm where some of the PHASEON and PHASEOFF control Soft Switches are used to select its upper or lower playback/recording head and the 0xC800/0xC801 memory addresses are used to select a pair of drives, either drives 1 and 2 or drives 3 and 4.

Address	Access	Name	Description
0xC05A	W	ZIPCTRL	4 writes of 0x5A unlocks *Zip Chip*; 0xA5 locks *Zip Chip*
0xC05B	W	ZIPSTATS	Any byte written enables *Zip Chip*
0xC05B	R	ZIPSTATS	Bits 0 and 1 is RAM size: 0–8K, 1–16K, 2–32K, 3–64K; bit 3 for memory delay: 0 = fast mode (no delay), 1 = sync mode (delay); bit 4 is ZIP enable: 0 = enabled, 1 = disabled; bit 5 is paddle speed: 0 = fast, 1 = normal; bit 6 is cache update: 0 = no, 1 = yes; bit 7 is clock pulse every 1.0035 milliseconds
0xC05C	R/W	ZIPSLOTS	read/write speaker/slot 0 = fast, 1 = normal. Bit 0 = speaker, bits 1 to 7 for slots 1 to 7
0xC05D	W	ZIPSPEED	Write speed: bit 2 = clk2/3, bit 3 = clk3/4, bit 4 = clk4/5, bit 5 = clk5/6, bit 6 = clk/2, bit 7 = clk/4
0xC05E	W	ZIPDELAY	Bit 7: 0 = enable delay, 1 = disable and reset delay
0xC05E	R	ZIPDELAY	0 = OFF; 1 = ON: bit 0 = ROMRD, bit 1 = RAMBNK, bit 2 = PAGE2, bit 3 = HIRES, bit 4 = 80STORE, bit 5 = MWR, bit 6 = MRD, bit 7 = ALTZP
0xC05F	W	ZIPCACHE	Bit 6 for paddle delay: 0 = disable, 1 = enable; bit 7 for Language Card partition cache: 0 = enable, 1 = disable

Table II.2.7. Zip Chip Control Soft Switches

Address	Access	Name	Description
0xC080	R/W	ATADATAH	Read or write high data byte register
0xC081	R	SETCSMSK	Disable pre-fetch register
0xC082	R	CLRCSMSK	Enable pre-fetch register
0xC086	R	ATASTAT2	Read alternate status register
0xC086	W	ATADEVCT	Write device control register
0xC088	R/W	ATADATAL	Read or write low data byte register
0xC089	R	ATAERROR	Read error register
0xC08A	W	ATASECCT	Write sector count register
0xC08B	W	ATASECTR	Write LBA3 (07:00) address register
0xC08C	W	ATACYLNL	Write LBA2 (15:08) address register
0xC08D	W	ATACYLNH	Write LBA1 (23:16) address register
0xC08E	W	ATAHEAD	Write LBA0 (27:24) address register and drive/head config
0xC08F	W	ATACMD	Write command register
0xC08F	R	ATASTAT	Read primary status register

Table II.2.8. CFFA Control Soft Switches

Address	Access	Name	Description
0xC080	W	QLSELC0	Select Banks 0 or 1, ON/OFF, USR, EPROM number
0xC081	W	QLSELC1	Select Banks 2 or 3, ON/OFF, USR, EPROM number
0xC082	W	QLSELC2	Select Banks 4 or 5, ON/OFF, USR, EPROM number
0xC083	W	QLSELC3	Select Banks 6 or 7, ON/OFF, USR, EPROM number

Table II.2.9. quikLoader Control Soft Switches

Address	Access	Name	Description
0xC080	R	SDINPUT	Sider read status
0xC080	W	SDINPUT	Write drive number, DCB data, input data
0xC081	R	SDOUTPUT	Sider read output data
0xC081	W	SDOUTPUT	Write start, flush, and stop commands
0xC080	W	RDSECTR	RAM Disk sector number
0xC081	W	RDTRACK	RAM Disk track number
0xC084	W	RAMCARD	RAM Card ON/OFF, track*2, sector/8
0xC800	W	ROMCODE1	Select Rana drive pairs 1 and 2
0xC801	W	ROMCODE2	Select Rana drive pairs 3 and 4

Table II.2.10. Sider, RAM Disk, RAM Card, and Rana Control Soft Switches

Even though the Apple //e has additional ROM memory in the CX ROM (0xC100 to 0xCFFF) address space, the original STEP and TRACE entry points are still disabled and cannot be used in conjunction with the enabled Mini-Assembler command (the ! command). And, this ROM also contains a silly SEARCH command (the S command). In my opinion the SEARCH command is extremely limited for it can find at most two consecutive bytes in low/high byte order. And, I am still annoyed that the cassette tape recorder READ and WRITE commands are retained in the Apple //e ROM. What disturbs me the most is that the Monitor cannot even display the additional opcodes that are part of the 65C02 Instruction Set that pertains to the specific 65C02-microprocessor that is supplied in and used by the Apple //e. As an aside, the 65C02 Instruction Set was expanded even further in the Rockwell and WDC versions of that processor to include the BBR, BBS, RMB, and SMB mnemonics adding thirty-two additional opcodes. However, these opcodes are not available in the Apple //e supplied 65C02-microprocessor.

In summary, it makes no sense to me to provide a computer to a user that utilizes a particular microprocessor and its firmware cannot even display the complete set of mnemonics for that microprocessor. What I would have done is to recommend to Apple to retire the READ and WRITE commands in the Monitor and reintroduce the Monitor STEP and TRACE commands, and to provide a more useful Monitor command in addition to the SEARCH command if there was sufficient code space for such a command. And, of course, the Monitor must be able to display all of its useable 65C02 mnemonics. Will retiring the READ and WRITE commands in the Monitor provide enough code space for all of my suggestions? Can the new lower ASCII data input routine in the Monitor be further enhanced? Let's find out. The Monitor software begins at 0xF800. The CX ROM support routines along with the 80-column support routines are found in ROM memory from 0xC100 to 0xCFFF.

3. SWEET16 Metaprocessor

The *SWEET16* Metaprocessor is a "pseudo microprocessor" implemented in 6502 assembly language. Originally conceived and written by Steve "Woz" Wozniak, *SWEET16* and Integer BASIC were included in the ROM firmware of the early Apple II computers. *SWEET16* is a really smart and useful extension to a 6502 based computer and it can be ported to other 6502 based systems to provide useful 16-bit functionality. It can be thought of as a virtual machine that gives the 6502 programmer a 16-bit extension to the 8-bit microprocessor. *SWEET16* utilizes sixteen 16-bit registers/pointers at the beginning of page-zero and it provides new opcodes that use those registers or pointers. Although *SWEET16* instructions are not as fast as native 6502 instructions, *SWEET16* can reduce the code size of programs and ease some programming difficulties.

Steve Wozniak wrote "While writing Apple BASIC for the 6502-microprocessor, I repeatedly encountered a variant of Murphy's Law. Briefly stated, any routine operating on 16-bit data will require at least twice the code that it should. Programs making extensive use of 16-bit pointers such as compilers, editors, and assemblers are included in this category. In my case, even the addition of a few double-byte instructions to the 6502's Instruction Set would have only slightly alleviated the problem. What I really needed was a hybrid of the MOS Technology 6502 and RCA 1800 architectures: a powerful 8-bit data handler complemented by an easy to use processor with an abundance of 16-bit registers and excellent pointer capability. My solution was to implement a non-existent 16-bit "metaprocessor" in software, interpreter style, which I call *SWEET16*. *SWEET16* is based around sixteen 16-bit registers called R0 to R15, which are actually implemented as thirty-two memory locations. R0 doubles as the *SWEET16* Accumulator (ACC), R15 as the Program Counter (PC), and R14 as the Status Register. R13 holds compare instruction results and R12 is the Subroutine Return stack pointer if *SWEET16* subroutines are used. All other *SWEET16* registers are at the user's unrestricted disposal.

"*SWEET16* instructions fall into register and non-register categories. The register instructions specify one of the sixteen registers to be used as either a data element or as a pointer to data in memory, depending on the specific instruction. For example, the instruction INR R5 uses R5 as a data register and ST @R7 uses R7 as a pointer register to data in memory. Except for the SET instruction, register instructions require one byte. The non-register instructions are primarily 6502 style branch operations with the second byte specifying a +/- 127-byte displacement relative to the address of the following instruction. If a Prior Register (PR) operation result meets a specified branch condition, the displacement is added to the *SWEET16* Program Counter, thus effecting a branch. *SWEET16* is intended as an enhancement package to the 6502 processor, not as a standalone processor. A 6502 program switches to *SWEET16* mode with a subroutine call, and subsequent code is interpreted as *SWEET16* instructions. The non-register instruction RTN returns the user program to the 6502's direct execution mode after restoring the A, X, Y, P, and S internal registers. Even though most opcodes are only one byte long, *SWEET16* runs approximately ten times slower than equivalent 6502 code, so it should be employed only when code is at a premium or execution is not. As an example of its usefulness, I have estimated that about 1K byte could be weeded out of my 5K byte Apple][BASIC interpreter with no observable performance degradation by selectively applying *SWEET16*."

SWEET16 was probably the least used and least understood seed in the original Apple][. In exactly the same sense that the Integer and Applesoft BASICs are languages, *SWEET16* is a language, too. Compared to the BASICs, however, *SWEET16* would be classified as a lower level language with a strong likeness to conventional 6502 assembly language. Obviously, to use *SWEET16*, you must learn the language. And according to "Woz", "The opcode list is short and uncomplicated." *SWEET16* was ROM based in every early Apple][and it resided in memory from `0xF689` to `0xF7FC`. It uses the `SAVE` and the `RESTORE` routines in the Monitor of the Apple in order to preserve the 6502 registers during its use, allowing *SWEET16* to be used as a subroutine. Table II.3.1 lists the *SWEET16* registers and the function of these registers. The complete *SWEET16* Instruction Set is shown in Tables II.3.2 and II.3.3. These tables list each opcode, its mnemonic, and a brief description of the opcode and what the opcode does. Table II.3.2 lists the non-register opcodes and Table II.3.3 lists the register opcodes.

Glen Bredon utilized *SWEET16* extensively in his *Big Mac* software by incorporating the *SWEET16* interpreter within the *Big Mac* source code since the interpreter did not exist in the Apple][+ or in the Apple //e ROMs. Mr. Bredon re-coded the `NUL` (not shown) and `BNM1` opcodes to provide other functionality specific to his needs in *Big Mac*. He also did not use the `R12` register as a Return from Subroutine stack pointer and he did not use the `R14` register for the `PR` and Status functions. Rather than using a stack pointer at all, he simply saved the Return from Subroutine address at page-zero `0xDA`/`0xDB` and the `PR` and Status at page-zero `0xFF`.

Register	Description
R0	*SWEET16* Accumulator (`ACC`)
R1–R11	*SWEET16* user registers
R12	*SWEET16* subroutine return Stack Pointer (`SP`)
R13	*SWEET16* compare instruction results
R14	*SWEET16* Status Register (`PR` & `Carry` flag)
R15	*SWEET16* Program Counter (`PC`)

Table II.3.1. SWEET16 Register Descriptions

Opcode	Mnemonic	Opcode Description
0x00	RTN	Return to 6502 mode to process native 6502 instructions
0x01	BR rel	Branch always to PC+rel+2→PC
0x02	BNC rel	Branch if prior operation left carry clear to PC+rel+2→PC
0x03	BC rel	Branch if prior operation left carry set to PC+rel+2→PC
0x04	BP rel	Branch if Prior Register is positive to PC+rel+2→PC
0x05	BM rel	Branch if Prior Register is negative to PC+rel+2→PC
0x06	BZ rel	Branch if Prior Register is zero to PC+rel+2→PC
0x07	BNZ rel	Branch if Prior Register is not zero to PC+rel+2→PC
0x08	BM1 rel	Branch if Prior Register is minus one to PC+rel+2→PC
0x09	BNM1 rel	Branch if Prior Register is not minus one to PC+rel+2→PC
0x0A	SOUT chr	Send character chr to COUT (originally the BK opcode)
0x0B	RS	Return from Subroutine, and POPD @SP→PC, SP=SP-2
0x0C	BS rel	Branch to Subroutine, and PC→STD @SP, SP=SP+2, PC+rel+2→PC
0x0D	RSNS	Return from Subroutine without stack, and SP→PC (originally unassigned opcode)
0x0E	BSNS rel	Branch to Subroutine without stack, and PC→SP, PC+rel+2→PC (originally unassigned opcode)
0x0F	SJMP adr	Jump to 16-bit address adr and adr-1→PC (originally unassigned opcode)

Table II.3.2. SWEET16 Non-Register Opcodes

Opcode	Mnemonic	Opcode Description
0x1n	SET Rn,val	Load Rn with 16-bit value val
0x2n	LD Rn	Load ACC from Rn, PR=n
0x3n	ST Rn	Store ACC into Rn, PR=n
0x4n	LD @Rn	Load LO ACC indirectly using Rn, HO ACC=0, Rn=Rn+1, PR=0
0x5n	ST @Rn	Store LO ACC indirectly using Rn, Rn=Rn+1, PR=0
0x6n	LDD @Rn	Load ACC indirectly using Rn, Rn=Rn+2, PR=0
0x7n	STD @Rn	Store ACC indirectly using Rn, Rn=Rn+2, PR=0
0x8n	POP @Rn	Rn=Rn-1, load LO ACC indirectly using Rn, HO ACC=0, PR=0
0x9n	STP @Rn	Rn=Rn-1, store LO ACC indirectly using Rn, PR=0
0xAn	ADD Rn	ACC = ACC + Rn, status = carry, PR=0
0xBn	SUB Rn	ACC = ACC – Rn, status = carry, PR=0
0xCn	POPD @Rn	Rn=Rn-2, load ACC indirectly using Rn, PR=0
0xDn	CPR Rn	R13 = ACC – Rn, status = carry, PR=13
0xEn	INR Rn	Rn = Rn + 1, PR=n
0xFn	DCR Rn	Rn = Rn – 1, PR=n

Table II.3.3. SWEET16 Register Opcodes

I am simply astounded at how easy it is to utilize the *SWEET16* instructions for any task that processes large sets of data, like an assembler. In fact, the early versions of the S-C (Sander-Cederlof) Assembler II used *SWEET16* in several locations within its code. The TED/ASM assembler and all of its descendants, including the DOS Tool Kit, TED II+, Merlin, and many others, used *SWEET16* heavily. Several of the programs in the Apple Programmer's Aid ROM used *SWEET16* particularly for the Integer BASIC Renumber/Append programs.

As Tables II.3.2 and II.3.3 show, the *SWEET16* opcode list is short and uncomplicated. Except for relative branch displacements, hand assembly is trivial. All register opcodes are formed by combining two hexadecimal digits, one for the opcode and one to specify a register. For example, opcodes 0x15 and 0x45 both specify register R5 while opcodes 0x23, 0x27, and 0x2B are all LD Rn instructions. Most register instructions are assigned in complementary pairs to facilitate remembering them. Thus, LD Rn and ST Rn are opcodes 0x2n and 0x3n, while LD @Rn and ST @Rn are opcodes 0x4n and 0x5n, respectively.

Opcodes 0x00 through 0x0F are assigned to the sixteen Non-Register Opcodes and opcodes 0x1n through 0xFn are assigned to the fifteen Register Opcodes. Except for the RTN (0x00), SOUT (0x0A), RS (0x0B), RSNS (0x0D), and SJMP (0x0F) opcodes, the non-register opcodes are basic 6502 style branches. The second byte of a branch instruction contains a +/- 127-byte displacement value (in two's complement form) relative to the address of the instruction immediately following the branch. The RTN opcode (0x00) calls the RESTORE routine in the Monitor in order to restore the 6502 registers and return to 6502 mode using the *SWEET16* program counter. The SOUT opcode (0x0A) sends its second byte to COUT at ROM address 0xFDED. Before the BS/RS opcodes can be used, R12 must be initialized with the address of a stack buffer that is used for the return-from-subroutine 16-bit addresses. The stack buffer must be of sufficient size to hold n-levels of subroutine calls, or n-number of 16-bit addresses. Of course, the SJMP opcode, like the SET opcode, takes its second and third byte to form a 16-bit address, or a 16-bit value in the case of the SET opcode.

If a specified branch condition is met when using the PR instruction result, the displacement is added to the Program Counter effecting a branch. Except for the BR (BRanch always), the BS (Branch to a Subroutine), and the BSNS (Branch to a Subroutine using No Stack) opcodes, the branch opcodes are assigned in complementary pairs like the register opcodes, thus rendering them easily remembered for hand coding. For example, Branch if Plus and Branch if Minus are opcodes 0x04 and 0x05 while Branch if Zero and Branch if Not Zero are opcodes 0x06 and 0x07, respectively.

The original *SWEET16* software left the last three non-register opcodes unassigned, where any of them could be used as a NUL opcode, and the BK opcode (BreaK, 0x0A) simply executed a 6502 BRK instruction. The PR and the Carry flag were both combined in the high order (HO) byte of R14. I chose to separate the PR and Carry flag into separate bytes of the R14 register in order to reduce the code size and number of execution cycles for all of the non-register operations. Doing this allowed the inclusion of more code to process four additional opcodes within the limited, single memory page area that must contain all of the *SWEET16* routines. Those added routines send character to COUT, Branch to Subroutine using No Stack, Return from Subroutine using No Stack, and JuMP to address. Incidentally, one can jump to an address using other *SWEET16* opcodes, but it requires using two of them (SET and ST), and the address must already be decremented by one, or decremented using a third opcode, DCR. The new instruction, SJMP ADR, loads the *SWEET16* Program Counter directly with ADR-1.

My implementation of *SWEET16* saves the register number (PR) of the register receiving the value or change in value into the low order (LO) byte of R14 when a register opcode is processed. If the register opcode is ADD, SUB, or CPR, I save the state of the Carry flag in bit 0 of the HO byte of R14. The reasons for doing this were quite compelling. Originally, the LO byte of R14 is not utilized by the *SWEET16* interpreter, so it is available to the user. Personally, I found that that unused byte is virtually useless. So, if there is a way to transform that byte into a more useful function, I am more inclined to adopt that strategy. Each time a non-register opcode is encountered, the original code uses nine cycles in five bytes for part of the setup code, and ten additional bytes are used for five of the branch instructions. My implementation requires only eight cycles in five bytes for the setup code, and no additional bytes for the same five branch instructions. This does not seem like very much of a savings; that is, one cycle for every invocation of a non-register opcode, but in data processing loops that execute many hundreds or thousands of times, a single cycle in savings does add up. However, Mr. Bredon chose to use sixteen cycles in seven bytes for the same capability.

The SET command is another example where a few cycles can be saved just by using a different strategy. The original code uses thirteen cycles in ten bytes to increment the *SWEET16* Program Counter by two, not including its RTS instruction. My implementation requires only eleven cycles in ten bytes every time the SET command is utilized. Mr. Bredon requires thirty-five cycles in seven bytes for the same functionality. To me, that seems like a lot of overhead just to save three bytes of code. This simply exemplifies the observable fact that when code is made extremely compact, the price paid is usually slower execution time.

As stated above the original image of *SWEET16* was located in ROM from 0xF689 to 0xF7FC, so it was 372 bytes in size, though the last three bytes of the 0xF7 page were set to 0xFF. My implementation of *SWEET16* is exactly 400 bytes in size, though it includes four additional, and very useful opcodes in my opinion. I believe having the *SWEET16* Metaprocessor located in the Apple //e CX ROM space rather than the RESET diagnostic routines certainly makes far more sense to me. And, there is more than sufficient room for the *SWEET16* interpreter to reside there only if there is sufficient room for a calling and a return location in the 0xF0 Monitor firmware. I believe a suitable ROM entry point for *SWEET16* is at `0xFA72`. And, the *SWEET16* return address can follow at `0xFA78`. The DOS 4.1 Manual provides the details for why I chose those Monitor ROM addresses for *SWEET16*. My Apple //e ROM images include my implementation of *SWEET16*.

4. Applesoft Garbage Collector

The Applesoft Garbage Collector routine `GARBAG` is located in ROM from `0xE484` to `0xE597`, and that routine moves all currently active character string variables up in Character String Pool memory as far as possible. There are several Applesoft routines like the Applesoft command `FRE( aexpr )` in ROM that rely on the garbage collector to consolidate the contents of the Character String Pool memory when there is not enough Free Space memory as shown in Figure I.15.1 to perform the next requested character string variable manipulation. When certain conditions are met while these Applesoft ROM routines process character string data, `GARBAG` is called. Depending upon how many character string variables are active, the processing time for `GARBAG` is proportional to the square of the number of active character strings currently in use. This processing time may be a few seconds if there are less than fifty active character strings, or many minutes if there are hundreds of active character strings. It may even appear as if the Applesoft program has literally stopped, or hanged for no apparent reason. In Section I.15 it was even suggested that strategically placing multiple Applesoft `FRE( aexpr )` statements throughout an Applesoft program may help to alleviate many processing delays.

Many years ago, Cornelis Bongers of Erasmus University in Rotterdam, Netherlands, published a brilliant Garbage Collector algorithm for Applesoft character strings in *Micro*, August, 1982. According to an article in *Apple Assembly Line*, March, 1984, the speed of his program was incredible when compared to the `GARBAG` algorithm in ROM. And the processing time for his algorithm was directly proportional to the number of active character strings, rather than to the number of active character strings squared. The only problem with his algorithm was that the magazine that published it owned the algorithm. Worse yet, the algorithm was tied to a program called Ampersoft, marketed by Microsparc, then publishers of *Nibble* magazine. It was reported that a license to use Bongers' algorithm was very expensive at that time.

Recall that Table I.15.1 shows the definition of a simple character string variable descriptor as it is found in the Simple Variables memory area and Table I.15.2 shows the definition of a character string array variable descriptor as it is found in the Array Variables memory area. After analyzing these two tables, Bongers introduced the idea of *marking* active character strings that are located in the Character String Pool memory area: he set the third byte in the character string data to its upper ASCII value and swapped in the address of the character string descriptor in place of the first two bytes of the character string data. Also, during this first pass through the Simple Variables and Array Variables memory area he saved those first two bytes of the character string data safely in the address field of its descriptor or character string element. The address previously in the address field would be changed anyway after all the character strings are moved up in memory to their final destination. The second pass through the Character String Pool memory area moved all active character strings up in memory as far as possible, it retrieved the first two characters from storage in its descriptor or character string element, and it updated the address field to the new memory location for that string.

Bongers' algorithm is most efficient when the active character strings are a least three bytes in length, so one- and two-character strings require different handling. On the first pass through the Simple Variables and Array Variables memory area, the first byte of character string data pointed to by these *short* descriptors is stored in the character string length byte of its descriptor. If the character string length is two, the second data byte is stored in the low address byte of its descriptor. For single byte character strings the low address byte is flagged with an `0xFF` value. The high address byte in all *short* descriptors is flagged with an `0xFF` value since no character string can have an address greater than `0xFF00`. If *short* character strings are found during the first pass, a flag is set and a third pass returns them to the Character String Pool memory with their descriptors updated to their new memory location. *Short* character strings do slow down Bongers' algorithm a little. However, the processing time is still directly proportional to the number of active character strings, and not to the number of active character strings squared. Tables II.4.1 and II.4.2 illustrate Bongers' algorithm during the first pass.

ADL/ADH Descriptor Before Pass 1							⇒	ADL/ADH Descriptor After Pass 1						
+AS	−AS	1	LSB	MSB	0	0		+AS	−AS	41	FF	FF	0	0

LSB/MSB Memory Before Pass 1							⇒	LSB/MSB Memory After Pass 1						
41								41						

ADL/ADH Descriptor Before Pass 1							⇒	ADL/ADH Descriptor After Pass 1						
+AS	−AS	2	LSB	MSB	0	0		+AS	−AS	41	42	FF	0	0

LSB/MSB Memory Before Pass 1							⇒	LSB/MSB Memory After Pass 1						
41	42							41	42					

ADL/ADH Descriptor Before Pass 1							⇒	ADL/ADH Descriptor After Pass 1						
+AS	−AS	LEN	LSB	MSB	0	0		+AS	−AS	LEN	41	42	0	0

LSB/MSB Memory Before Pass 1							⇒	LSB/MSB Memory After Pass 1						
41	42	43	44	45	46	47		ADL	ADH	C3	44	45	46	47

Table II.4.1. Simple Variable Descriptor Processing in Bongers' Pass 1

Pass two in Bongers' algorithm uses only the information in the Character String Pool memory to move all currently active character string variables up in Character String Pool memory as far as possible. This is accomplished by initializing a pool pointer and a character string pointer to `HIMEM` and searching down to `FRETOP` for any upper ASCII bytes. Once an upper ASCII byte is found, its character string descriptor is located at the memory location two bytes prior to the upper ASCII byte. That character string descriptor contains the length of the character string and the first two ASCII characters of the character string. Those two characters may be safely moved back to the character string data and the upper ASCII byte changed to a lower ASCII byte. The character string length can now be subtracted from the current character string pointer address, the new character string address can be copied to the second and third bytes in its character string descriptor, and the character string data can be copied to its new Character String Pool memory address. However, the character string must be copied from its last character to its first character in order to prevent possibly overwriting part of the character string if the character string is copied from its first character to its last character. Once the pool pointer reaches the original address in FRETOP, the current character string pointer address becomes the new address in FRETOP if the *short* descriptors flag is clear.

ADL/ADH Element Before Pass 1			⇒	ADL/ADH Element After Pass 1		
1	LSB	MSB		41	FF	FF

LSB/MSB Memory Before Pass 1			⇒	LSB/MSB Memory After Pass 1		
41				41		

ADL/ADH Element Before Pass 1			⇒	ADL/ADH Element After Pass 1		
2	LSB	MSB		41	42	FF

LSB/MSB Memory Before Pass 1			⇒	LSB/MSB Memory After Pass 1		
41	42			41	42	

ADL/ADH Element Before Pass 1			⇒	ADL/ADH Element After Pass 1		
LEN	LSB	MSB		LEN	41	42

LSB/MSB Memory Before Pass 1							⇒	LSB/MSB Memory After Pass 1						
41	42	43	44	45	46	47		ADL	ADH	C3	44	45	46	47

Table II.4.2. Array Variable Element Processing in Bongers' Pass 1

If the *short* descriptors flag is set then a third pass must be made through the Simple Variables and Array Variables memory area. A memory pointer is initialized to VARTAB and the 0xFF byte is searched for in either the fifth byte of a Simple Variable descriptor or the third byte of an Array Variable element. If there is an 0xFF byte in the prior byte then the descriptor is for a single byte character string, otherwise the descriptor is for a two byte character string. The current character string pointer is adjusted for one or two characters, the character string data is copied from its descriptor to the Character String Pool memory area, and the character string pointer address is copied to its character string descriptor. Once the memory pointer reaches STREND, the current character string pointer address becomes the new address in FRETOP.

It must be emphasized that Bongers' algorithm depends upon two important caveats: normal Applesoft programs save all character string data in **lower** ASCII, i.e. with the MSB of each character byte cleared, and normal Applesoft programs never allow more than one character string descriptor to point to the same exact copy of that character string data in memory. If a user should program something like A$ = CHR$(193), Bongers' algorithm will **fail**. If an assembly language program should modify two character string descriptors to point to the same character string data in the Character String Pool memory area, Bongers' algorithm will **fail**. Therefore, reasonable care must be given when creating Applesoft programs and/or assembly language programs that take the above caveats seriously in order to exact the stupendous benefit in using a garbage collector routine that is based on Bongers' algorithm. Armed with only these limited details of Bongers' algorithm that I just presented, my analysis of those details, and my complete understanding of Tables I.15.1, I.15.2, and I.15.3 as well as Tables II.4.1 and

II.4.2, my attempt to recreate Bongers' algorithm resulted in an assembly language program that was 0x200 bytes in size. This necessitated creating a suitable Applesoft test program that would verify the accuracy of my algorithm and confirm to me that no character string was altered in length, modified in content, or destroyed during processing. My ultimate goal would be to replace GARBAG in ROM with my version of Bongers' algorithm. GARBAG occupies 0x113 bytes of ROM memory and there is 0x70 bytes of memory available in the CX ROM space from 0xC600 to 0xC66F (0xC670 is where I put the *SWEET16* program code). If the CX ROM space is used then CX ROM memory management must also be incorporated in the routine. When all totaled, my garbage routine must fit within 0x183 bytes if it is to be located in ROM. On the other hand, my garbage routine, after some adjustment, could be attached to an Applesoft program and simply called prior to issuing the DOS CHAIN command providing that the R keyword is utilized with CHAIN. At least that would mitigate having to call GARBAG in this particular instance. Periodically, the Applesoft program could check the remaining Free Space and call its attached garbage routine based on reasonable criteria. There is still much indeterminacy whether a particular character string manipulation will trigger a call to GARBAG during Applesoft processing. If that should happen Applesoft processing could come to a grinding halt until the Character String Pool data is processed without regard to the attached garbage routine. There is no flag available indicating when Applesoft intends to call GARBAG and there is no flag to turn OFF GARBAG.

In order to compact an assembly language routine certain decisions must be made that, hopefully, do not cause the introduction of more processor cycles than absolutely necessary. Example strategies would be to limit subroutine calls in the inner-most loops and to limit the pushing and popping of variables onto the stack. Sometimes simply reorganizing the order of a number of processing loops can greatly simplify the code and eliminate having to re-initialize registers. Keeping a variable's MSB address in a register when addresses need to be compared can often help simplify and accelerate the code as well. I have no doubt that Mr. Bongers could have condensed my initial attempt in programming his algorithm down from 0x200 bytes to 0x183 bytes (where six of those 0x70 bytes are required for CX ROM memory management). My initial attempt to condense my garbage routine could not meet the goal of 0x183 bytes unless I removed the flag that signaled whether a third pass was necessary, and so the routine always made a third pass. Many times, it is helpful to just take a break from a difficult programming task like this one, and work on something else for a while. Thus, when I returned to my garbage routine, I took a fresh look and I found several additional strategies that could condense the code even further, and allow the reintroduction of the third pass flag. Hurray! I was able to fit one segment of the routine into the 0x70 bytes located in CX ROM space and the other segment into the 0x113 bytes where GARBAG normally resides. All that was left to do was the testing, the timing, and the verification of the routine after it was installed in the ROM (actually, in an EPROM to be precise).

As mentioned earlier, a verification test must prove that no character string is altered in length, modified in content, or destroyed by the garbage collector algorithm. The test results of the new algorithm must be **identical** to the results obtained using the GARBAG algorithm. And since there is a DOS 4.5 DATE command available, each pass through the character string array variables can be easily time stamped. The Applesoft test created three two-dimension character string arrays where both dimensions are set to twenty-six. Each character string element is initialized with a single character that was *forced* into the Character String Pool memory. On each successive pass another character is added to each element within the dimension that is being processed, from one to twenty-six. This causes the utilization of memory to grow larger on each successive pass. Before each pass, I noted the size of Free Space. If Free Space is less than 15,000 bytes, I issued the Applesoft FRE(aexpr) command forcing the garbage collector to process the Character String Pool content. I obtained identical memory results for each and every pass in my Applesoft test program whether I used the original GARBAG routine in ROM or my new garbage routine in ROM. The timing results for my test program are shown in Table II.4.3.

Time is shown in minutes and seconds. The three columns of timings to the right of **Pass Number** summarize the results obtained from the original GARBAG routine. The time each pass begins is shown in the first of the three columns starting at time 00:00. If the Free Space fell below 15,000 bytes another timestamp is recorded after I made another call to FRE(aexpr). This timestamp is shown in the middle of the three columns. The delta time the routine required for its processing is shown in the third of the three columns. The right three columns of timings contain the same information for my new garbage collector routine starting at time 00:00.

Pass Number	Original Garbage Collector			New Garbage Collector		
	Time	<15000	Delta	Time	<15000	Delta
0	00:00			00:00		
1	00:02			00:02		
2	00:05			00:05		
3	00:09			00:09		
4	00:14			00:14		
5	00:21			00:20		
6	00:28			00:28		
7	00:37			00:36		
8	00:47	01:26	00:39	00:46	00:47	00:01
9	02:37			00:58		
10	02:49	04:55	02:06	01:10	01:12	00:02
11	05:11			01:25		
12	05:25	07:57	02:32	01:39	01:41	00:02
13	08:13	11:08	02:55	01:56	01:58	00:02
14	11:29	14:31	03:02	02:15	02:16	00:01
15	14:59	18:12	03:13	02:34	02:36	00:02
16	18:36	21:59	03:23	02:55	02:56	00:01
17	22:27	26:00	03:33	03:17	03:19	00:02
18	30:27	34:14	03:47	03:42	03:43	00:01
	34:40			03:43		

Table II.4.3. Garbage Collector Comparison and Verification Timing Results (Minutes)

My implementation of Bongers' algorithm shows how amazing this routine actually is. Table II.4.3 shows only a small peek into the capacity of this routine. When I changed the Free Space parameter from 15,000 to 5,000 bytes, the Applesoft program calling the original GARBAG routine could not complete, even after an hour, and I simply terminated the program. The Applesoft program using my new garbage collector routine completed in 06:54 minutes, and twenty-four of the twenty-six possible passes finished before I finally terminated that program due to my silly impatience. Table II.4.3 shows that only the first eighteen of the twenty-six possible passes finished before insufficient memory remained when calling the original GARBAG routine. After every pass a verification routine is called that simply confirms that the contents of all arrays still contain the ASCII data that is expected to be there, and that no other data is present, and that no data is added or missing. Therefore, this verification test routine confirms and verifies that no character string is altered in length, modified in content, or destroyed by both the original GARBAG routine and by my new garbage collector routine. I give total credit to Cornelis Bongers for creating the original concept of this brilliant Garbage Collector algorithm. I would be fascinated to know if my implementation is anything like Mr. Bongers' implementation of his algorithm and how much code space he required versus how much code space I require to implement this algorithm. Someone may someday tell me the answer to these questions.

5. Building a New Apple //e ROM

The DOS 4.1 Manual includes an in-depth analysis of the Apple //e ROM including the CX ROM space and the Apple //e 80-column text card. That Manual explains and shows where some of the 0xF0 ROM routines are incorrectly coded using example code segments. The analysis begins with the BASCALC routine and my Delete Key handler in order to provide sufficient memory space for the new 65C02 16-byte FMT2 table and its data content. The GETFMT routine is also presented along with the TBLC and TBLL tables, as well as the MNEML and MNEMR tables which grew to be 0xA6 bytes larger in size. STEP and TRACE are introduced along with GETNSP to where these routines must now reside. Also, an enhancement to the SEARCH routine is presented along with a new Monitor routine called ZAPMEM that can initialize a range of memory to any single value. These enhancements require changes to the LOOKASC routine that now offers both lower ASCII **and** upper ASCII data input support. Part of the RESET handler is moved to the CX ROM space in order to create additional memory space in the 0xF0 ROM for the entry and exit code that manages the CX ROM memory for the *SWEET16* metaprocessor. Even the NXTCHR and OLDRST routines are discussed.

In the DOS 4.1 Manual I explain why the Applesoft LOAD, RECALL, SAVE, STORE, and SHLOAD commands are useless without the cassette tape TAPEOUT and TAPEIN routines, which I removed from the 0xC5 ROM in favor of the STEP and TRACE routines. Instead of replacing the calls to the TAPEOUT and TAPEIN routines with a call to IORTS at 0xFF58, for example, I replaced the addresses to these Applesoft commands with that of IORTS. This frees a total of 0xAE bytes for other processing and/or other Applesoft commands. The entry addresses for Applesoft commands are located from 0xD000 to 0xD0CF, and the ASCII text for Applesoft commands is located from 0xD0D0 to 0xD25F. Table II.5.1 shows the available ROM memory and its location when the Applesoft LOAD, RECALL, SAVE, STORE, and SHLOAD commands are disabled and effectively removed from Applesoft processing. As I said in that Manual, I have no doubt that I will innovate a terrific use for these ROM memory spaces in the next development cycle. Unfortunately, that innovation has yet to take place. Someone is bound to create a terrific new Applesoft command or commands and use this valuable ROM memory to implement those new Applesoft commands.

Start	End	Length	Applesoft Commands
0xD8B0	0xD900	0x51	LOAD and SAVE
0xF39F	0xF3D7	0x39	STORE and RECALL
0xF775	0xF786	0x12	SHLOAD
0xF7D5	0xF7E6	0x12	GETARYPT

Table II.5.1. Disabled Applesoft Commands

Table II.5.2 shows the migration, removal, and insertion of various routines and tables of data that transform the stock Apple //e ROM and CX ROM address space into a new and more powerful Apple //e ROM in my most humble opinion. I call this new Apple //e ROM ROM2E.SW16GC.5 because Build 5 contains the *SWEET16* metaprocessor, the STEP and TRACE routines, the display and logic for all 65C02 mnemonics, the Delete Key handler, and the incredible Garbage Collector based on the algorithm developed by Cornelis Bongers. What this ROM does not contain are the Apple //e diagnostic routines DIAGS, the cassette tape recorder routines TAPEOUT and TAPEIN, and all those routines dependent on the TAPEOUT and TAPEIN routines.

The ROM2E.SW16GC.5 ROM image has no provisions to read from or to write to an external cassette tape recorder. The TAPEOUT Soft Switch at 0xC020 as shown in Table II.2.3 and the TAPEIN Soft Switch at 0xC060 as shown in Table II.2.4 can certainly be used for other crafty external devices. Both of the cassette tape recorder external ports are unique in that they can be used to read and to write a stream of electrically buffered digital data. TAPEOUT is the electrically buffered output of a 74LS74 D-type flip flop. There is no way to know whether the output signal is high or low at any given moment when the 0xC020 Soft Switch is read. This behavior is more like the SPKRTOGL Soft Switch at 0xC030 than any of the four annunciators whose output follow address bit A0. TAPEIN is a capacitor filtered and electrically buffered input whose signal is amplified by a 741 op amp. This op amp requires a minimum input threshold voltage to create an ON state for data bit D0, otherwise data bit D0 is OFF. The value for data bit D0 is obtained by reading the 0xC060 Soft Switch. This behavior is totally unlike the four paddle inputs that are Resistor/Capacitor (R/C) filtered and connected to a 558 quad timer device whose output is capable of sinking up to 100 mA of current.

I have been using the ROM2E.SW16GC.5 ROM image for at least two years with Virtual][as well as having this image programmed into EPROM for an early Apple //e, for an Enhanced Apple //e, and for a Platinum Apple //e. In all instances the ROM image has been totally stable. All Applesoft routines that rely on the TAPEOUT and TAPEIN routines simply return immediately and without error to the caller.

I have no doubt that the individuals or the engineering teams of individuals who designed the Apple //e ROM firmware, and subsequently the Enhanced Apple //e ROM firmware, were given a momentous task. That task was to preserve sixteen *classic* ROM entry points and to introduce a few new Monitor routines in order to support 40-column and 80-column screen displays. This ROM also must support most all previously written software for the Apple][and the Apple][+. Obviously, one can no longer expect to enter any of the previous Monitor code that was *within* these *classic* entry points and expect reliable results. For example, the entry points for SETKBD, INPORT, SETVID, and OUTPORT are at their *classic* entry points, but the code within these entry points that implement the modifications to the configuration of the Apple][computer has changed: it is **not** safe to jump into any of the code within these *classic* entry points. It must be understood and accepted that the location for some of the data tables in this new Apple //e Monitor is not sacrosanct, and that these tables have been moved to other ROM locations. I believe it is fair to say that ROM memory is very, very precious. And, I believe that the Apple engineers did a remarkable job in building a quality Apple //e 80-column text card and firmware product that performs its task simply and elegantly. Before starting a unique and complex software development project, have a copy of ROM source code at hand in order to use that resource wisely.

ROM2E		ROM2E.SW16GC.5		Description
Start	**End**	**Start**	**End**	
0xC1B6	0xC1BD	0xC1B6	0xC1BC	add BASCALC support
0xC204	0xC209	0xC203	0xC207	modify VTAB support; saves Y-reg in BASL
0xC230	0xC230	0xC22E	0xC22E	add CLD before address calculation
0xC298	0xC29F	0xC297	0xC2A4	change DELETE (0xFF) to LARROW (0x88)
0xC2B0	0xC2ED	0xC2B5	0xC2EA	modify RESET support, remove DIAGS support
0xC2F2	0xC2FD	0xCE15	0xCE1E	move XRDKEYX routine near INVERT
0xC600	0xC66F	0xC600	0xC66F	remove DIAGS, add Bongers' algorithm Part 2
0xC670	0xC7FF	0xC670	0xC7FF	remove DIAGS, add *SWEET16*
0xC849	0xC84B	0xC849	0xC84B	add jump to CONTKEY
0xC9A4	0xC9A9	0xC2EF	0xC2F4	move KBDOUT
0xCA71	0xCA88	0xC5E7	0xC5FE	form mnemonic table index; put TBLC and TBLL
0xCC90	0xCC95	0xC9A4	0xC9A9	move XFF, put CONTKEY here
0xCE14	0xCE1E	0xCE15	0xCE1E	remove duplicate UPRCASE, put KRDKEYX here
0xCF16	0xCF16	0xCF16	0xCF18	fix logic for X-register
0xCF37	0xCF39	0xCF39	0xCF39	change 3 unused bytes to 1 unused bytes
0xD034	0xD035	0xD034	0xD035	use IORTS for SHLOAD address
0xD04E	0xD04F	0xD04E	0xD04F	use IORTS for RECALL address
0xD050	0xD051	0xD050	0xD051	use IORTS for STORE address
0xD06C	0xD06D	0xD06C	0xD06D	use IORTS for LOAD address
0xD06E	0xD06F	0xD06E	0xD06F	use IORTS for SAVE address
0xD8B0	0xD8C8	0xD8B0	0xD8C8	remove SAVE code; empty (0x19 bytes)
0xD8C9	0xD8EF	0xD8C9	0xD8EF	remove LOAD code; empty (0x27 bytes)
0xD8F0	0xD900	0xD8F0	0xD900	remove SAVE, LOAD code; empty (0x11 bytes)
0xE484	0xE596	0xE484	0xE596	replace GARBAG with Bongers' algorithm Part 1
0xF39F	0xF3BB	0xF39F	0xB3BB	remove STORE code; empty (0x1D bytes)
0xF3BC	0xF3D7	0xF3BC	0xF3D7	remove RECALL code; empty (0x1C bytes)
0xF57A	0xF582	0xF57A	0xF582	add HLINMOD
0xF5A5	0xF5A5	0xF5A5	0xF5A5	add HLINMOD
0xF775	0xF786	0xF775	0xF786	remove SHLOAD code; empty (0x12 bytes)
0xF7D5	0xF7E6	0xF7D5	0xF7E6	remove STORE, RECALL code; empty (0x12 bytes)
0xF9A6	0xF9B3	0xFBC7	0xFBD6	move FMT2 table, add (zpage), (absolute,X) modes
0xF9B4	0xF9BF	0xFA30	0xFA3B	move CHAR1 and CHAR2 tables
0xF9C0	0xFA3F	0xF9A6	0xFA2F	move MNEML and MNEMR tables (0xA6 added), CXOFF/RTN
0xFA62	0xFA81	0xFA62	0xFA81	modify RESET; add SWEET16, SW16RTN
0xFB08	0xFB18	0xFB08	0xFB18	remove Apple text; put RSETINIT, move XLTBL
0xFBC1	0xFBD8	0xFBC1	0xFBD8	use BASCALC in CX ROM (Y-reg=2), add FMT2 table
0xFC5D	0xFC5F	0xFC5D	0xFC5F	unused bytes, add STEPRTN2
0xFCC9	0xFCD1	0xFCC9	0xFCD1	remove HEADR (rts); add STEPRTN
0xFEC2	0xFEC3	0xFEC2	0xFEC3	add TRACE
0xFEC4	0xFEC9	0xFA3C	0xFA3F	add STEP, move CXOFF add CXRTN
0xFECD	0xFED6	0xFECD	0xFED6	remove WRITE, add ZAPMEM
0xFEF1	0xFEF5	0xFEFD	0xFF04	move MINIASM, modify SEARCH2
0xFEFD	0xFF12	0xFEFD	0xFF0E	remove READ, add MINIASM, modify TITLE
0xFF13	0xFF1A	0xC500	0xC507	move GETNSP to CX ROM
0xFF1B	0xFF2C	0xFF18	0xFF2C	enhance LOOKASC, add "X" search command
0xFFCC	0xFFE2	0xFFCC	0xFFE2	remove "W" & "R", add "T" & "Z", "S" for STEP

Table II.5.2. Transformations to Build a New Apple //e ROM

6. Apple //e Character Generator ROM

Virtual][, Gerard Putter's MacOS application to emulate the Apple][computer, provides the capability to use a personally designed ASCII display input character set for the Apple][character display. The input character set is defined to be a character set bitmap that is either a PNG or TIFF file that must be exactly 128 pixels wide and exactly 64 pixels high. The bitmap depth must be one or eight pixels. Each character in the bitmap is defined to be within a character cell that is eight pixels by eight pixels. Because characters displayed by the Apple][are only seven pixels wide, the right most column of the character cell is ignored by Virtual][. The black pixels within a character cell comprise the background of the character; all other pixels comprise the character itself. The directory that must contain this input character set bitmap file is at *Users/<username>/Library/Application Support/Virtual][/CharacterSets*. A filename suggested by the Virtual][documentation for this bitmap file is MyCharacters.tif. An XML file named International.plist must also be located in this same directory and it defines the actual name for the input character set bitmap file. This XML file may include the name of an icon bitmap file called MyCharSetIcon.tif whose size may be up to sixteen pixels wide by eleven pixels high, and this icon bitmap is displayed in the upper left corner of the Virtual][window. The XML file may also include a keyboard translation table if that is needed as well. The XML file I created is shown in Figure II.6.1, and it includes the resources for two different input character set bitmap files.

Key	Type	Value
▼ Root	Dictionary	(2 items)
▼ My new character set	Dictionary	(3 items)
CharacterSet	String	MyNewCharacters.tif
Icon	String	MyCharSetIcon.tif
▶ KeyboardTranslation	Dictionary	(0 items)
▼ My old character set	Dictionary	(3 items)
CharacterSet	String	MyOldCharacters.tif
Icon	String	MyCharSetIcon.tif
▶ KeyboardTranslation	Dictionary	(0 items)

Figure II.6.1. International XML File

I used Xcode to easily create the XML file shown in Figure II.6.1. Any *Property List Editor* works as well. To create the TIFF bitmap files I used the MacOS *Paintbrush* application because it was available for download at no charge. I am certainly not an expert *Paintbrush* user and I had some difficulties with the application to produce what I wanted easily. Most of my difficulties occurred when I tried to save my work during incremental stages of testing. I found that if I used the Lasso tool to copy the entire bitmap area into the clipboard, I could save the contents of the clipboard into a new bitmap file of the same size, and then discard the original file. I do not know why the *save* or *save as* option failed to save my incremental work to the original file, and I do not know why I had to save my work in such a round-about way. I used the Line tool configured for a *stroke* of one in order to toggle a pixel from black to white or white to black. *Paintbrush* saves the bitmap file as a TIFF file having a Color Space of RGB, a Color Profile of Generic RGB Profile, and the Alpha Channel set to Yes. I have no idea what these specifications mean or imply, but Virtual][had no problem reading and utilizing all of the TIFF files I created in this manner.

My greatest source of irritation came when I discovered that the *Library* directory specified in the above pathname for the *CharacterSets* directory is a hidden file by default. I lost more time putting the XML and TIFF files into the wrong folder because I could not see the hidden *Library* directory in my personal Users account. Once I realized that the *Library* directory is hidden, it was extremely easy to unhide it using XQuartz or the Terminal application found in the Utilities directory, which is located in the Applications directory. Simply launch the Terminal application and enter bash on the command line. This starts the GNU *Bourne-Again SHell*. Now, when you enter the UNIX command ls -AF at */Users/<username>*, all files, including . files and hidden files (i.e. directories), are displayed. Now enter the command chflags nohidden Library and have a look at a Finder window for your personal Users account. You should now see a *Library* directory. Once you locate the XML and TIFF files properly and launch Virtual][, select *Quick settings>Character Set>My character set*. After selecting the desired character set bitmap file, be sure to save your Virtual][session when you are satisfied with its character display, and it will be selected and loaded every time Virtual][is launched.

Figure II.6.2. Character Set Bitmap TIFF File

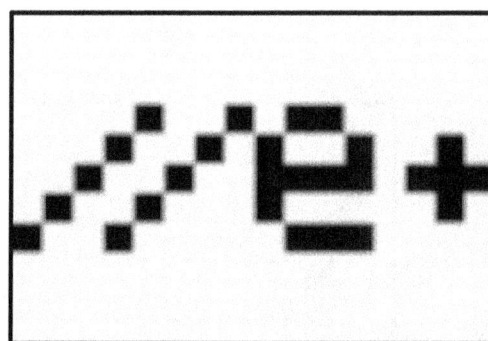

Figure II.6.3. Icon TIFF Bitmap File

Figure II.6.2 shows the inverse view of the MyNewCharacters.tif file and Figure II.6.3 shows the normal view of the MyCharSetIcon.tif file that I created for Virtual][. I used *Paintbrush* to modify a number of the ASCII characters to suit my preferences. Once I was satisfied with my input character set bitmap file, I created a simple Apple][tool using LORES graphics that allows me to create a 4 KB character ROM Binary data file. This LORES graphics tool is called *EDITROM*. The ROM file that *EDITROM* can edit must also contain the inverse characters as well as the alternate keyboard characters, but these characters are not included in Figure II.6.2. I found that it was easier to begin the editing process by reading the stock character ROM into a Binary file using the PROmGRAMER, for example. I can display the data for each character in the character ROM using *EDITROM* which also has the capability to edit any of the characters in that ROM data. Once I make all the changes to the character data, I can save the character ROM data that is currently in memory to another Binary data file and program an equivalent sized 2732 EPROM with that new ROM data. My Apple][+ and all three of my Apple //e computers use the same character ROM data or a subset of that data as shown in Figure II.6.2.

To begin a ROM editing session with *EDITROM*, a suitable filename for ROM data may be entered as shown in Figure II.6.3. Simply press RETURN if there is no new ROM data file to read. The ROM data

110

file is `0x1000` (or 4096) bytes in size and it is read into memory at memory address `0x1000`. Figure II.6.4 shows the `LORES` display of the first character entry in ROM data and four lines of Text at the bottom of the display. Line twenty-two in this display shows the location in memory where the first of eight bytes of character data begin, the value for each byte of data, and how the character is currently displayed by the Apple][hardware. There are two modes of operation used in *EDITROM*: Show Mode and Edit Mode. Show Mode simply duplicates the `LORES` character that is displayed on the left side to the right side of the screen and the data that is currently in memory at the bottom of the screen on line twenty-four.

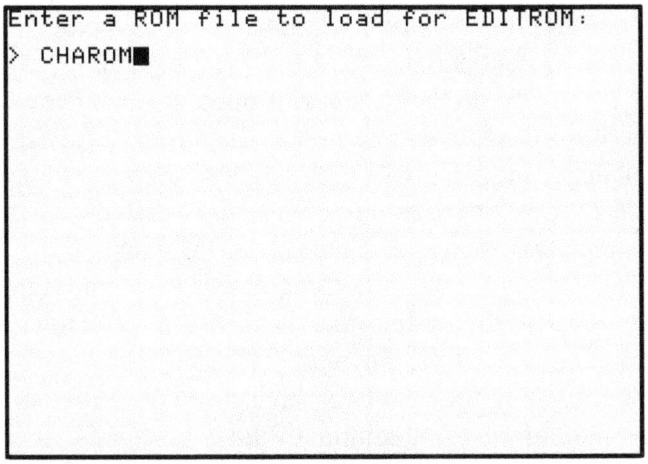

Figure II.6.3. Load ROM File for EDITROM

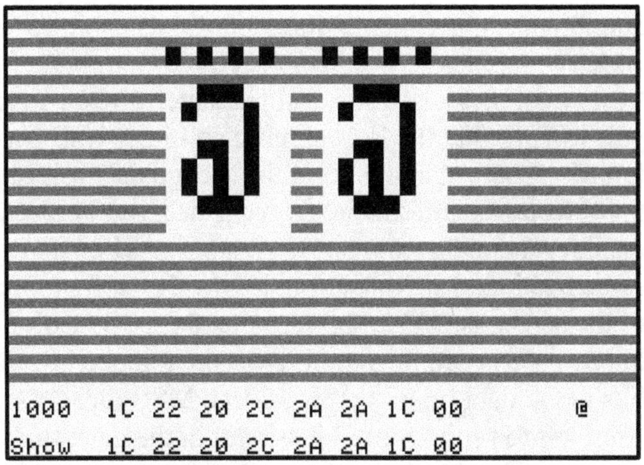

Figure II.6.4. ROM Data Show Mode

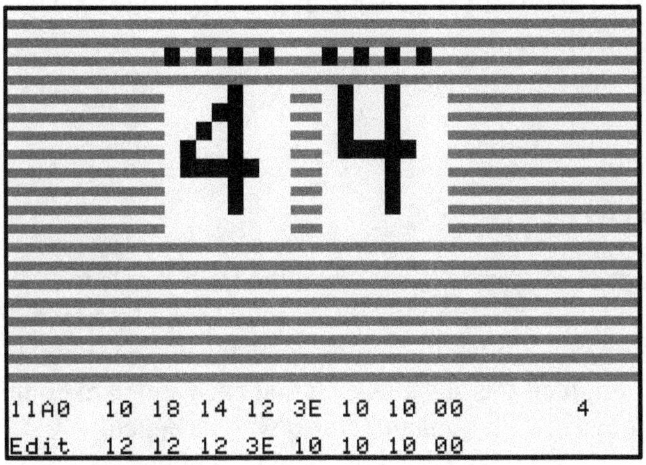

Figure II.6.5. ROM Data Edit Mode

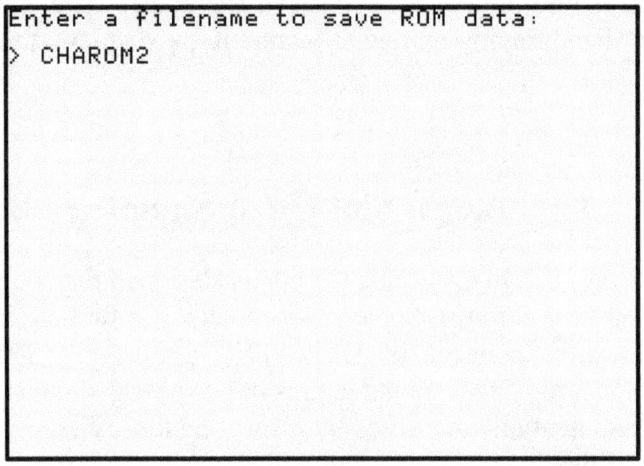

Figure II.6.6. Save ROM Data for EDITROM

There are only four commands that are used in Show Mode: `B` goes back one character, `E` enters Edit Mode, `RETURN` displays the next character, and `ESCAPE` exits the program. There are only three commands along with the arrow key movements that are used in Edit Mode: `SPACE` toggles a character pixel, `RETURN` exits Edit Mode and saves all changes, `ESCAPE` exits Edit Mode and discards all changes, and the arrow keys move the pixel cursor up/down or left/right. As shown in Figure II.6.5 Edit Mode displays the new character data on line twenty-four that corresponds to the LORES character that is displayed on the right side of the screen. Pressing RETURN will accept these changes and pressing ESCAPE will discard these changes. Once all changes have been made to the ROM data, pressing ESCAPE will exit the editor and the *EDITROM* program will ask for a filename in order to save the 4 KB of ROM data that is currently in memory as shown in Figure II.6.6. If a filename is not entered when *EDITROM* begins or when *EDITROM* exits, no file is read or saved, respectively. The DOS 4.5 DIFF command can be used to compare both the input and the output ROM files to *EDITROM* in order to ensure that the output ROM file contains the desired changes that were made to the input ROM file.

For those who are interested in understanding the correspondence with ROM data and the display of that data by the Apple][hardware, a few data samples will easily illustrate their relationship by using the HIRES graphics screen. On the Apple Command Line enter HGR and then CALL-151. Assuming MIXEDON or 0xC053 is enabled, enter 2000:1 and 2400:40 on the Monitor Command Line. Now you will see that the least significant bit, or LSB (or bit 0) of the first data sample is displayed to the far left of the screen and bit 6 of the second data sample is displayed six pixels to the right of the far left of the screen. Therefore, the Apple][hardware processes data starting from the LSB to the MSB and displays that data from left to right. The same hardware logic displays the character ROM data in the same fashion. Looking at Figure II.6.5, the first three data bytes for the edited character "4" on the right of the screen is 0x12. In this data, the LSB or bit 0 is OFF and the far left pixel is also OFF. The next bit, or bit 1 is ON, thus turning ON the top pixel of the left column of the character "4". The next two bits in the data (moving towards the MSB) are OFF, thus keeping the next two pixels also OFF moving from left to right. Since bit 4 is ON in the data, the top pixel of the right column of the character "4" is also ON. The fourth data byte, or 0x3E turns the first pixel OFF (the far left pixel) and moving to the right, turns the next five pixels ON. All of the ASCII characters from 0x20 to 0x7F are designed to keep their far left pixel OFF, thus keeping the LSB in their data set to OFF, and utilize only the next five bits in their data for the display of the character. On the other hand, many of the icon characters shown in Figure II.6.2 utilize all seven bits in their data bytes. The MSB for a character in ROM data is not utilized for any particular feature in the display of that character.

7. Peripheral Slot Card Signature Bytes

More than likely Apple Computer designed the concept of Signature Bytes when the Disk][was first introduced to the Apple][consumer. The first eight bytes of the firmware that resides in the Interface Card that connects the Disk][drive to the Apple][computer are the Signature Bytes for this peripheral slot card. Other manufactures of peripheral slot cards adopted this scheme such that each slot card could be potentially identified by inspecting those first eight bytes. Other manufactures who designed peripheral slot cards for their disk drives used the same scheme developed by Apple Computer. Manufactures of real time clock cards also used the signature byte scheme developed by ThunderClock. Similarly, signature byte schemes were developed for printer interface slot cards, serial data interface slot cards, mouse interface slot cards, and display interface slot cards to list just a few examples. Each scheme utilizes a general pattern of bytes that contains identical portions and unique portions of bytes. Table II.7.1 lists the signature bytes for a number of peripheral slot cards that I happen to own or happen to know about.

Peripheral Slot Card	Signature Bytes							
	0	1	2	3	4	5	6	7
Disk][	LDX	#$20	LDY	#$00	LDX	#$03	STX	$3C
	0xA2	0x20	0xA0	0x00	0xA2	0x03	0x86	0x3C
SCSI][	LDX	#$20	LDX	#$00	LDX	#$03	LDX	#$00
	0xA2	0x20	0xA2	0x00	0xA2	0x03	0xA2	0x00
RANA	LDX	#$20	LDY	#$00	LDX	#$03	LDX	#$3C
	0xA2	0x20	0xA0	0x00	0xA2	0x03	0xA2	0x3C
SIDER	LDA	#$20	LDA	#$00	LDA	#$03	LDA	$3C
	0xA9	0x20	0xA9	0x00	0xA9	0x03	0xA9	0x3C
RAM Disk	LDX	#$20	LDY	#$00	LDX	#$03	STY	$3C
	0xA2	0x20	0xA0	0x00	0xA2	0x03	0x84	0x3C
CFFA	LDA	#$20	LDX	#$00	LDA	#$03	LDA	#$00
	0xA9	0x20	0xA2	0x00	0xA9	0x03	0xA9	0x00
ThunderClock	PHP	SEI	PLP	BIT	$FF58		BVS	$Cs0D
	0x08	0x78	0x28	0x2C	0x58	0xFF	0x70	0x05
TimeMaster II	PHP	SEI	PLP	BIT	$FF58		BVS	$Cs0D
	0x08	0x78	0x28	0x2C	0x58	0xFF	0x70	0x05
My Clock	PHP	SEI	BIT	$CFFF		CLR	BCC	$Cs38
	0x08	0x78	0x2C	0xFF	0xCF	0x18	0x90	0x30
SuperSerial	BIT	$FF58		BVS	$Cs11	SEC	BCC	$Cs20
	0x2C	0x58	0xFF	0x70	0x0C	0x38	0x90	0x18
Grappler	CLC	BCS	$Cs3B	BCC	$Cs11	SEC	BCC	$Cs20
	0x18	0xB0	0x38	0x90	0x0C	0x38	0x90	0x18
Mouse	BIT	$FF58		BVS	$Cs20	SEC	BCC	$Cs20
	0x2C	0x58	0xFF	0x70	0x1B	0x38	0x90	0x18
80-Column	BIT	$CE43		BCS	$C317	SEC	BCC	CLC
	0x2C	0x43	0xCE	0x70	0x12	0x38	0x90	0x18

Table II.7.1. Peripheral Slot Card Signature Bytes

All of the odd signature bytes for peripheral slot cards that interface disk drives must be the same. This is done purposefully because the Autostart ROM that Apple Computer copyrighted in 1978 checks those four odd bytes during a powerup or during a restart. However, the Autostart routine was modified for the Apple //e Video Firmware, copyrighted in 1981 and in 1984. The specific firmware note for this modification is shown in Figure II.7.1. In other words, only the first three odd signature bytes are checked by the Apple //e Autostart ROM for a bootable disk drive. After analyzing the disk startup firmware that follows the first eight bytes in the Disk][Interface Card, the firmware shows that upon entry the Y-register must be set to zero, the X-register can be set to any value from 0x00 to 0x16, and the A-register may contain any value. The page-zero location 0x3C is a temporary storage location so any value may be stored there, which is done in the fourth instruction, STX $3C. The first instruction, `LDX #$20`, does nothing since the third, and critical instruction rewrites the value contained in the X-register that is used to generate the `RDNIBLBT` table.

```
Check 3 ID bytes instead of 4.  Allows devices
other than Disk II's to be bootable.
```

Figure II.7.1. Video Firmware Note for the Apple //e

Peripheral Slot Card	Signature Bytes							
	0	1	2	3	4	5	6	7
Disk][	LDX	#$20	LDY	#$00	LDX	#$03	STX	$3C
(no change)	0xA2	0x20	0xA0	0x00	0xA2	0x03	0x86	0x3C
SCSI][	LDX	#$20	LDX	#$00	LDX	#$03	LDX	#$00
(no change)	0xA2	0x20	0xA2	0x00	0xA2	0x03	0xA2	0x00
RANA	ORA	#$20	LDY	#$00	LDX	#$03	STX	$3C
	0x09	0x20	0xA0	0x00	0xA2	0x03	0x86	0x3C
SIDER	AND	#$20	LDY	#$00	LDX	#$03	STX	$3C
	0x29	0x20	0xA0	0x00	0xA2	0x03	0x86	0x3C
RAM Disk	EOR	#$20	LDY	#$00	LDX	#$03	STX	$3C
	0x49	0x20	0xA0	0x00	0xA2	0x03	0x86	0x3C
CFFA	ADC	#$20	LDY	#$00	LDX	#$03	STX	$3C
	0x69	0x20	0xA0	0x00	0xA2	0x03	0x86	0x3C
available	LDA	#$20	LDY	#$00	LDX	#$03	STX	$3C
	0xA9	0x20	0xA0	0x00	0xA2	0x03	0x86	0x3C
available	CMP	#$20	LDY	#$00	LDX	#$03	STX	$3C
	0xC9	0x20	0xA0	0x00	0xA2	0x03	0x86	0x3C
available	SBC	#$20	LDY	#$00	LDX	#$03	STX	$3C
	0xE9	0x20	0xA0	0x00	0xA2	0x03	0x86	0x3C
available	LDY	#$20	LDY	#$00	LDX	#$03	STX	$3C
	0xA0	0x20	0xA0	0x00	0xA2	0x03	0x86	0x3C
available	CPY	#$20	LDY	#$00	LDX	#$03	STX	$3C
	0xC0	0x20	0xA0	0x00	0xA2	0x03	0x86	0x3C
available	CPX	#$20	LDY	#$00	LDX	#$03	STX	$3C
	0xE0	0x20	0xA0	0x00	0xA2	0x03	0x86	0x3C

Table II.7.2. Revised Disk Drive Peripheral Slot Card Signature Bytes

Applied Engineering used the same signature bytes for their TimeMaster II clock card as those found in the ThunderClock card. Only the first two bytes are significant as well as the last, or classification byte in its firmware page. This last byte, or CLKID for the ThunderClock firmware is 0x07 and the last byte for the TimeMaster II firmware is 0x03. I also set the last byte for my clock card firmware to 0x03. It is these three bytes, the first two and the last, that DOS 4.5 checks for a valid clock card. In many cases a peripheral slot card not only must be compatible with DOS, but possibly it must be also compatible with ProDOS, CP/M, Fortran, and Pascal as well. The peripheral-card ROM memory and the peripheral-card expansion ROM memory totals only nine pages of code space. Therefore, even the signature bytes may also perform a necessary function besides being unique to the particular peripheral slot card. In some cases, the signature bytes provide multiple return entry points for input and output data control. If the peripheral slot card supports Pascal, the Pascal initialization, read, write, and status routine offsets closely follow the initial signature bytes.

Since the operation of the first signature byte instruction is not utilized in the Disk][Interface Card for data or for a logic operation, any of the other ten 6502 Immediate Addressing Mode instructions can be used as a product identifier within the Disk][signature byte scheme. Once I realized which were the important and the unimportant bytes within the signature byte data, I could design a very simple strategy to quickly identify a Disk][product device by first checking the first three odd bytes similar to the strategy used in the Apple //e Autostart ROM, and then use the first instruction byte to select the actual product or device type. Table II.7.2 lists the revised signature bytes for my collection of Disk][, Disk][-like, and disk drive peripheral devices.

This page intentionally left blank.

III. DOS 4.5 Commands

The DOS 4.5 commands comprise a set of commands that are in addition to the Applesoft ROM commands. As in Applesoft ROM commands, DOS 4.5 commands and keywords may be entered in uppercase and/or in lowercase. DOS 4.5 uses a number of data tables in order to parse a valid DOS command when that command is found in the DOS Command Name Text table. This table consists of the DCI ASCII name for each DOS command in the order of command index value that is generally used in DOS 3.3. The Command Valid Keyword table is used to determine which keywords if any are required or may be used in conjunction with each DOS command based upon command index value. Each command has a two-byte table entry, thus providing sixteen possible bit flags and one two-bit flag indicating which keywords are legal, or if a filename is expected, for example. The bit flag settings for the DOS Command Valid Keywords are defined in Table III.0.1. The legal keywords have been ordered in a more logical, hierarchical, and useful way than in the order used by DOS 3.3. Before processing a valid DOS 4.5 command, the value of the R keyword is copied to the File Manager SUBCODE variable. This allows the user of the external File Manager handler to utilize the SUBCODE in order to simulate the R keyword for the File Manager command codes FMCATACD for CATALOG, FMTCHCD for TOUCH, and FMCDCD for CD. The DOS INIT command, however, overwrites the SUBCODE variable with a BOOTYPE value for its own specific use as shown previously in Figures I.11.1 and I.11.2.

Valid Keyword bits 10 and 11 form a two-bit flag, and these two bits are mutually exclusive in that no DOS 3.3 command uses both of these bits together in any single command. I chose to identify a special non-keyword *integer value* category by setting both of these bits in the DOS CONFIG, PHASE, SV, and USER commands. This special category of *integer value* commands is easily identified and range-checked as appropriate in the DOS 4.5 Command Manager.

Bit	Bit Position	Value	Flag Bit Description
15	%1000 0000 0000 0000	0x8000	Filename legal but optional
14	%0100 0000 0000 0000	0x4000	Command has no positional operands
13	%0010 0000 0000 0000	0x2000	Filename #1 is expected
12	%0001 0000 0000 0000	0x1000	Filename #2 is expected
11	%0000 1000 0000 0000	0x0800	Slot number positional operand is expected
11&10	%0000 1100 0000 0000	0x0C00	Non-keyword *integer value* number is expected
10	%0000 0100 0000 0000	0x0400	MAXFILES value positional operand is expected
9	%0000 0010 0000 0000	0x0200	Command is only issued from within a program
8	%0000 0001 0000 0000	0x0100	Command creates a new file if file is not found in the Catalog
7	%0000 0000 1000 0000	0x0080	C, I, O keywords are legal
6	%0000 0000 0100 0000	0x0040	S keyword is legal but not necessarily expected
5	%0000 0000 0010 0000	0x0020	D keyword is legal but not necessarily expected
4	%0000 0000 0001 0000	0x0010	V keyword is legal but not necessarily expected
3	%0000 0000 0000 1000	0x0008	A keyword is legal but not necessarily expected
2	%0000 0000 0000 0100	0x0004	L keyword is legal but not necessarily expected
1	%0000 0000 0000 0010	0x0002	R keyword is legal but not necessarily expected
0	%0000 0000 0000 0001	0x0001	B keyword is legal but not necessarily expected

Table III.0.1. Command Valid Keyword Table in DOS 4.5

Command Name	Index	ASCII Text	S/W Handler	Keyword
CMDINIT	0x00	INIT	DOINIT	0x317F
CMDLOAD	0x02	LOAD	DOLOAD	0xA072
CMDSAVE	0x04	SAVE	DOSAVE	0xA173
CMDRUN	0x06	RUN	DORUN	0xA074
CMDCHAIN	0x08	CHAIN	DOCHAIN	0x2276
CMDDELET	0x0A	DELETE	DODELETE	0x2072
CMDLOCK	0x0C	LOCK	DOLOCK	0x6070
CMDUNLCK	0x0E	UNLOCK	DOUNLOCK	0x6070
CMDCLOSE	0x10	CLOSE	DOCLOSE	0x6000
CMDREAD	0x12	READ	DOREAD	0x2203
CMDEXEC	0x14	EXEC	DOEXEC	0x2073
CMDWRITE	0x16	WRITE	DOWRITE	0x2203
CMDPOSTN	0x18	POSITION	DOPSTION	0x2202
CMDOPEN	0x1A	OPEN	DOOPENTX	0x2374
CMDAPND	0x1C	APPEND	DOAPND	0x2270
CMDRENAM	0x1E	RENAME	DORENAME	0x3072
CMDCAT	0x20	CATALOG	DOCAT	0x4072
CMDMON	0x22	MON	DOMON	0x4080
CMDNOMAN	0x24	NOMON	DONOMON	0x4080
CMDPRNUM	0x26	PR#	DOPRNUM	0x4800
CMDINNUM	0x28	IN#	DOINNUM	0x4800
CMDMXFLS	0x2A	MAXFILES	DOMXFLS	0x4402
CMDDATE	0x2C	DATE	DODATE	0x4000
CMDLIST	0x2E	LIST	DOLIST	0x2077
CMDBSAVE	0x30	BSAVE	DOBSAVE	0x217F
CMDBLOAD	0x32	BLOAD	DOBLOAD	0x207A
CMDBRUN	0x34	BRUN	DOBRUN	0x2078
CMDVERFY	0x36	VERIFY	DOVERIFY	0x2072
CMDLSAVE	0x38	LSAVE	DOLSAVE	0x217F
CMDLLOAD	0x3A	LLOAD	DOLLOAD	0x207A
CMDTSAVE	0x3C	TSAVE	DOTSAVE	0x2173
CMDTLOAD	0x3E	TLOAD	DOTLOAD	0x207F
CMDDIFF	0x40	DIFF	DODIFF	0x3070
CMDGREP	0x42	GREP	DOGREP	0x3070
CMDMORE	0x44	MORE	DOLIST	0x2077
CMDCAT2	0x46	CAT	DOCAT	0x4072
CMDURM	0x48	URM	DOURM	0x2070
CMDCD	0x4A	CD	DOCD	0x4072
CMDLS	0x4C	LS	DOCAT	0x4072
CMDMV	0x4E	MV	DORENAME	0x3072
CMDRM	0x50	RM	DODELETE	0x2072
CMDSV	0x52	SV	DOSV	0x4C00
CMDTS	0x54	TS	DOTS	0x407F
CMDWTS	0x56	WTS	DOWTS	0x407F
CMDTW	0x58	TW	DOTW	0x2170
CMDPHASE	0x5A	PHASE	DOPHASE	0x4C02
CMDTOUCH	0x5C	TOUCH	DOTOUCH	0x6072
CMDCONFG	0x5E	CONFIG	DOCONFIG	0x4C02
CMDUSER	0x60	USER	DOUSER	0x4C00
CMDHELP	0x62	HELP	DOHELP	0x4000

Table III.0.2. Command Table in DOS 4.5

Table III.0.2 is a comprehensive listing of all of the DOS 4.5 commands in processing order showing the command name, its command index value, its ASCII text, its software handler, and its valid keywords. CMDHELP is only available in DOS 4.5H because there is additional room in Bank 1 of the Language Card partition where RWTS is located. This additional memory seemed like an ideal location for placing a HELP Command handler in order to provide instant syntactical usage information for all of the DOS 4.5 commands. DOS 4.5H needs an additional memory page for the interface that controls the memory of the Language Card partition, so the DOS image requires at least one sector on track 0x02 anyway. Why not use a few more sectors on track 0x02 for something quite useful like the HELP Command handler? Another DOS developer may choose to eliminate the HELP Command handler and utilize that memory and/or those volume sectors for something else entirely.

CMDUSER is designed and available to a user who needs to load DOS 4.5 into memory, initialize it, and then have DOS 4.5 return control back to the user instead of to Applesoft after Applesoft initialization. After DOS 4.5 has been copied into memory from a file, for example, all the user needs to do is to call the MNGUSER routine with the address of the routine that will take control after DOS 4.5 has initialized. MNGUSER sets or resets the address found at USERADR so that CMDUSER simply executes an indirect jump to USERADR. Previously shown, Figure I.8.4 is an example assembly language program that totally manages the initialization of DOS 4.5. DOS 4.5 can always be restored to its default state by calling MNGUSER with the Carry flag **clear**. Another excellent use for the DOS USER command was shown previously in Figure I.8.5. When that code is used to connect the USER command to the re-entry address of *Big Mac*, *Big Mac* is immediately brought back into focus when the USER command is entered on the Apple Command Line followed by the RETURN character.

DOS 4.5 uses the following four tables to parse valid keywords, ascertain a keyword's bit position, and determine if the value of a keyword is within a minimum and a maximum range: PPARMS, PARMBITS, KWRANGEL, and KWRANGEH. The content of these four tables is summarized in Table III.0.3. Unlike DOS 3.3, DOS 4.5 allows up to 81 drives in order to support CFFA Volume Manager software for a Compact Flash card having up to 8 GB of memory, allow default Volume numbers to be zero, and allow BSAVE and LSAVE to write files up to 0xFFFF bytes in size. The Bit Positions for the keywords C, I, and O are actually used to generate the MONVAL variable once the MSB of the bit position value is cleared. The other Bit Positions are added to the variable KYWRDFND as each keyword is parsed. It is no accident that the Bit Position of each keyword in Table III.0.3 is the same as it is in the lower byte of each Command Keyword as shown in Table III.0.1.

The syntax of a DOS 4.5 command begins with the command, and the command is immediately followed by one or two filenames if they are required. All keywords and their parameter values, whether they are required or optional, must follow the filename(s), or they must follow the command if there are no required filename(s), and usually a comma must delineate each keyword after its parameter value. Table III.0.4 lists all keywords, their name, and a brief description. In all of the command definitions shown throughout this section, optional keywords and their parameter values are contained in square brackets, as in [,Vv]. Commands and keywords are shown in CAPITAL letters and keyword parameter values are shown in lowercase letters for ease of explanation and **not** in how they should be used in a program or entered on the Apple Command Line. Keyword parameter values may be entered as a decimal or as a hexadecimal number; hexadecimal numbers are always prefaced by the dollar sign $ as in $1234. However, DOS 4.5 usually prints hexadecimal values prefaced with 0x as in 0x1234 unless a keyword precedes the hexadecimal number. There are times when the value of zero is shown as 0x00 for ease of explanation.

Keyword Name	Bit Position - Value	Minimum Value	Maximum Value
C	%1100 0000 - 0xC0	–	–
I	%1010 0000 - 0xA0	–	–
O	%1001 0000 - 0x90	–	–
MON/NOMON	%1000 0000 - 0x80	–	–
S	%0100 0000 - 0x40	1 (0x01)	7 (0x0007)
D	%0010 0000 - 0x20	1 (0x01)	81 (0x0051)
V	%0001 0000 - 0x10	0 (0x00)	255 (0x00FF)
A	%0000 1000 - 0x08	0 (0x00)	65535 (0xFFFF)
L	%0000 0100 - 0x04	0 (0x00)	65535 (0xFFFF)
R	%0000 0010 - 0x02	0 (0x00)	32767 (0x7FFF)
B	%0000 0001 - 0x01	0 (0x00)	32767 (0x7FFF)

Table III.0.3. Keyword Name and Range Table in DOS 4.5

Keyword	Name	Description
S	Slot	Keyword followed by slot number
D	Drive	Keyword followed by drive number
V	Volume	Keyword followed by volume number
A	Address	Keyword followed by address number
L	Length	Keyword followed by length number
R	Record	Keyword followed by record number or nothing
B	Byte	Keyword followed by byte number
C	Command	Keyword to display or not display DOS commands
I	Input	Keyword to display or not display input data
O	Output	Keyword to display or not display output data
f	filename	Must begin with "A" or greater and be 1-24 characters in length
f2	2nd filename	Must begin with "A" or greater and be 1-24 characters in length
s	slot number	Slot number of a peripheral slot card, value range 1-7
d	drive number	Initialized to 1, value range 1-81 (for CFFA use)
v	volume number	Initialized to 0, value range 0-255
a	address number	Initialized to 0, value range 0-65535
l	length number	Initialized to 0, value range 0-65535
r	record number	Initialized to 0, value range 0-32767
b	byte number	Initialized to 0, value range 0-32767
n	number	Some numerical value required by some commands

Table III.0.4. Keywords and Their Definition in DOS 4.5

In keeping with the original DOS 3.3 documentation,
DOS 4.5 commands may be grouped into six categories,
and those categories are shown on the following page.

System Commands

CONFIG	DATE	HELP	IN#
MAXFILES	MON	NOMON	PHASE
PR#	SV	USER	

File System Commands

CAT	CATALOG	CD	DELETE
DIFF	GREP	INIT	LIST
LOCK	LS	MORE	MV
RENAME	RM	TOUCH	TS
UNLOCK	URM	VERIFY	WTS

Applesoft File Commands

CHAIN	LOAD	RUN	SAVE

Binary File Commands

BLOAD	BRUN	BSAVE	LLOAD
LSAVE			

Sequential Text File Commands

APPEND	CLOSE	EXEC	OPEN
POSITION	READ	TLOAD	TSAVE
TW	WRITE		

Random-Access Data File Commands

CLOSE	OPEN	READ	WRITE

Command	Command Syntax
CONFIG	[n][,R]
DATE	
HELP	
IN#	s
MAXFILES	[n][,R]
MON	[,C][,I][,O]
NOMON	[,C][,I][,O]
PHASE	[n][,R]
PR#	s
SV	[n]
USER	[n]

Table III.1.1. System Commands in DOS 4.5

1. System Commands

The DOS 4.5 System commands consist of those commands that manage the general operation of DOS 4.5, the Input/Output data streams, the display of commands and data items, the syntactical usage of DOS commands, the conversion of decimal and hexadecimal values, the track size in half-phases, and the number of active data file buffers within DOS 4.5. The syntax of the System commands is shown in Table III.1.1. The DOS commands CONFIG, PHASE, SV and USER belong to a special non-keyword *integer value* category of commands. Either decimal or hexadecimal values that are prefaced by a dollar sign $ are used with this category of commands because there is **no** keyword associated with these commands. If only the R keyword without a parameter value is entered with the DOS commands CONFIG, MAXFILES, and PHASE, followed by a comma, that DOS command is *reset* to its default value. All of the System commands except for the HELP command are permitted to be used from within an Applesoft or a Binary program file as well as on the Apple Command Line.

```
CONFIG    [n][,R]


Example:   CONFIG
           CONFIG,R
           CONFIG 123
           CONFIG $C7
```

This command is not available in DOS 3.3 for System commands. The DOS CONFIG command provides the user with the ability to configure the operation of eight key processing elements in DOS 4.5. The DOS CONFIG command belongs to a special non-keyword *integer value* category of commands. CONFIG values may be entered directly on the Apple Command Line in either decimal or in hexadecimal whose value must be prefaced by the dollar sign $. If no value or zero is entered with the CONFIG command, its current or operational value is displayed in decimal if its value is less than ten, otherwise its value is displayed in hexadecimal on the Apple Command Line when DOS 4.5 is **not**

122

in the RUN mode. Several examples in using the DOS CONFIG command in this way are shown in Figure III.1.1. When DOS is in the RUN mode and the DOS CONFIG command is issued from within an Applesoft program, the value of CONFIG can be obtained and displayed according to the design of that program. A simple Applesoft program that displays several examples in using the DOS CONFIG command is shown in Figure III.1.2. The Value Read Buffer is used by the DOS CONFIG command handler in order to obtain its current value only when DOS is in the RUN mode.

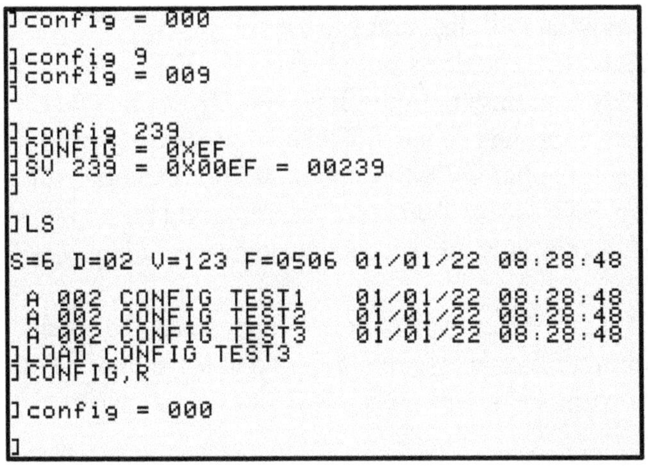

```
]config = 000

]config 9
]config = 009
]

]config 239
]CONFIG = 0XEF
]SV 239 = 0X00EF = 00239
]

]LS

S=6 D=02 V=123 F=0506 01/01/22 08:28:48

 A 002 CONFIG TEST1    01/01/22 08:28:48
 A 002 CONFIG TEST2    01/01/22 08:28:48
 A 002 CONFIG TEST3    01/01/22 08:28:48
]LOAD CONFIG TEST3
]CONFIG,R

]config = 000

]
```

Figure III.1.1. CONFIG Command Line Display

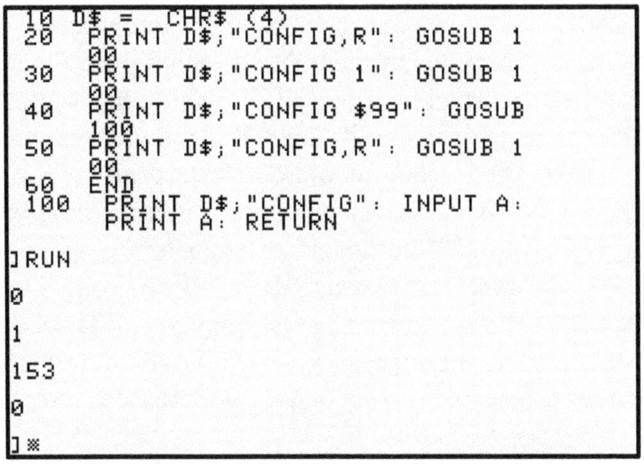

```
10 D$ =  CHR$ (4)
20  PRINT D$;"CONFIG,R": GOSUB 1
    00
30  PRINT D$;"CONFIG 1": GOSUB 1
    00
40  PRINT D$;"CONFIG $99": GOSUB
    100
50  PRINT D$;"CONFIG,R": GOSUB 1
    00
60  END
100  PRINT D$;"CONFIG": INPUT A:
     PRINT A: RETURN
]RUN
0

1

153

0

]*
```

Figure III.1.2. Set CONFIG Program Display

Bit	On	Off	Description
0	Disable	Enable	Print an extra carriage return between DOS commands
1	Disable	Enable	Verify files after a DOS SAVE, BSAVE, LSAVE, or TSAVE
2	Disable	Enable	Print PROMPT character] during EXEC processing
3	Disable	Enable	Process the DOS MAXFILES command when requested
4	Disable	Enable	Enforce all volume and file locks
5	Disable	Enable	Push DOSWARM-1 address onto the stack before DOS BRUN
6	Enable	Disable	Convert all output characters to uppercase
7	Enable	Disable	Convert all input characters to uppercase

Table III.1.2. CONFIG Command Bit Definitions

Each of the eight available bits for CONFIG control one processing element. As shown in Table III.1.2, the LSB, or Bit 0 is the first processing element bit listed. If only the R keyword without a parameter value is entered with the CONFIG command followed by a comma, all CONFIG bits are cleared to zero. All other combinations of the R keyword with a parameter value causes DOS 4.5 to issue a Syntax Error.

CONFIG Bit 0, when set or ON, eliminates the extra carriage return between command entries on the Apple Command Line.

CONFIG Bit 1, when set or ON, eliminates the automatic verification of a file after that file has been saved to a volume when using the DOS SAVE, BSAVE, LSAVE, or TSAVE commands. Enabling this bit visibly reduces the amount of time that is required to save a file to a volume, but it eliminates the verification that that file can be read into memory without error.

CONFIG Bit 2, when set or ON, eliminates printing the PROMPT character (usually]) while EXEC is processing its file. Setting this bit will not change how EXEC processes DOS commands.

CONFIG Bit 3, when set or ON, bypasses the DOS MAXFILES command when that command is requested in an Applesoft or in an assembly language program. However, if the DOS MAXFILES command is used without a value, the command functions as normal without regard to CONFIG Bit 3.

CONFIG Bit 4, when set or ON, does not enforce, but bypasses all disk and file locks.

CONFIG Bit 5, when set or ON, does not push the DOSWARM-1 address onto the stack before jumping to the BRUN start address of a file. Pushing the DOSWARM-1 address onto the stack simply ensures that DOS is reconnected to its keyboard and video intercepts after the file has finished its processing.

CONFIG Bit 6, when set or ON, converts all DOS 4.5 output characters to uppercase. For example, all DOS 4.5 error messages will appear in uppercase when Bit 6 is set. Even text printed using an Applesoft PRINT command will appear in uppercase. Essentially, everything printed to the display will appear in uppercase when CONFIG Bit 6 is set.

CONFIG Bit 7, when set or ON, converts all DOS 4.5 input filename characters to uppercase. In other words, whether the caps lock key is enabled or not, all input filenames are converted to uppercase. This makes it possible to load or save uppercase file names while the keyboard is set for lowercase when CONFIG Bit 7 is set.

It is important to understand that there is no benefit in changing the value of MAXFILES in DOS 4.5H. DOS 4.5H builds five file buffers within the memory of the Language Card partition that should not be used for any other purpose. Reducing the number of file buffers in DOS 4.5H does not provide any additional memory to programs, and HIMEM is always set to memory address 0xBE00 without regard to the number of active file buffers. HIMEM, on the other hand, **is** dependent on the number of active file buffers in DOS 4.5L.

DATE

Example: DATE

This command is not available in DOS 3.3 for System commands. The DOS DATE command displays on the screen the current date and time as shown in Figure III.1.3. DOS 4.5 supports at least three clock cards and possibly others: Thunderclock, TimeMaster, and the clock card I designed and built. The major difference in these clock cards is the index to where the date and time data begin in their respective raw data character output string each card generates. Figure III.1.3 also shows an example Applesoft program that displays the raw data character output string for a Thunderclock card residing in slot 4. The index that points to where the date and time data begin for this clock card is zero from Table I.13.1. The TimeMaster clock card and my clock card both have an index of 0x03 that points to where their date and time data begin. DOS 4.5 supports any clock card whose firmware contains the standard signature bytes, the classification byte or CLKID, and when its generic raw data character output string is examined, yields an index value from 0x00 to 0x05 to where the date and time data begin.

```
]date = 01/01/22 08:28:48
]load read clock
]list

 10  D$ =   CHR$ (4)
 20  SLOT = 4
 30   PRINT D$;"pr#";SLOT
 40   PRINT D$;"in#";SLOT
 50   INPUT ":";A$
 60   PRINT D$;"pr#0"
 70   PRINT D$;"in#0"
 80   PRINT
 90   PRINT A$
]run

01/01 08;28;48.000
]※
```

```
]DATE = 01/01/22 08:28:48
]LOAD GET CLOCK5
]LIST

 10  D$ =   CHR$ (4): GOSUB 1000
 20   VTAB 21: PRINT "Date and Tim
      e is ";DT$
 999  END
 1000  VTAB 1: HTAB 1: PRINT D$;"
       DATE":DT$ = "":DT = 1024
 1010  CH =   PEEK (DT): POKE DT,16
       0:DT$ = DT$ +   CHR$ (CH - 12
       8):DT = DT + 1: IF (DT < >
       1041) THEN  GOTO 1010
 1020  HTAB 1: RETURN

]RUN
Date and Time is 01/01/22 08:28:48
]
```

Figure III.1.3. DATE Command for Thunderclock   Figure III.1.4. Capturing DATE Data

When the DOS **DATE** command is issued from within an Applesoft program, DOS 4.5 only prints the date and time information; the equal sign is not printed as it is printed on the Apple Command Line. The program as shown in Figure III.1.4 captures the date and time information beginning at memory address 0x0400 to 0x0411 after the DOS **DATE** command is issued in the subroutine beginning at line #1000. The subroutine places the cursor at 0x0400 using the **VTAB** and **HTAB** commands, issues the DOS **DATE** command, initializes the date and time character string **DT$**, extracts each character of the date and time information from memory while it stores a space character, or 0xA0 over each data byte. When all of the date and time information has been extracted from memory, the program replaces the cursor back to 0x0400 and returns to the caller. This technique cleverly extracts the date and time information from memory while it hides, or covers up that same information. The program prints the content of the **DT$** character string in line #20. Notice that in line #1010 the character string **DT$** is constructed by adding one character at a time after first clearing the MSB for each added character using subtraction. Section I.15 thoroughly explains why normal Applesoft programs save all character string data in **lower** ASCII, that is, with the MSB of each character byte cleared. This program simply adheres to that fundamental policy in case Applesoft calls the garbage collection **GARBAG** routine.

HELP

Example: **HELP**

This command is not available in DOS 3.3 for System commands. The DOS **HELP** command was originally developed only for DOS 4.1H. I have modified that **HELP** routine logic for the benefit of DOS 4.5H. The **HELP** command provides instant syntactical usage information for all of the DOS 4.5 commands. When **HELP** is entered onto the Apple Command Line, Figure III.1.5 is displayed showing the entire DOS 4.5 command repertoire. Arrow keys must be used to navigate to the specific DOS command for which **HELP** is desired. The left/right arrow keys step through the command list either backwards or forwards, respectively. The up/down arrow keys step through a column of commands either upwards or downwards, respectively. Stepping backwards from the first command **CONFIG** navigates to the last command **WRITE**, and vice versa. Pressing the **RTN** key selects the command and displays its HELP content. Pressing the ESC key even while viewing HELP content resumes normal DOS processing. Pressing any other key displays the HELP content that shows DOS 4.5 Management vectors as shown in Figure III.1.6.

Two example displays for DOS HELP command content are shown in Figures III.1.7 and III.1.8 for the DOS INIT and LSAVE commands, respectively. It is certainly not possible with the limited memory resources of the Apple][and its limited volume space to provide any further help content than what this command already provides. The HELP command is intended to display sufficient information in how each command is used and all of the keywords associated with that command. Keywords that have been added to a DOS command are also defined. At least one example is given for each command showing how that command can be used. If more information is required, the DOS 4.5 File and Volume Disk Management System Book is always available and is always the ultimate resource for DOS 4.5 usage.

```
              System Commands
 CONFIG   DATE      IN#   MAXFILES    MON
 NOMON    PHASE     PR#      SV       USER

         File System Commands
   CAT    CATALOG    CD     DELETE    DIFF
   GREP    INIT     LIST    LOCK      LS
   MORE     MV      RENAME    RM      TOUCH
   TS     UNLOCK    URM     VERIFY    WTS

        Applesoft File Commands
  CHAIN   LOAD      RUN      SAVE

         Binary File Commands
  BLOAD   BRUN     BSAVE    LLOAD    LSAVE

     Sequential Text File Commands
 APPEND   CLOSE     EXEC     OPEN    POSITION
  READ    TLOAD    TSAVE     TW      WRITE

     Random-Access Data File Commands
  CLOSE    OPEN     READ     WRITE

            <+>   RTN   ESC
```

Figure III.1.5. HELP Command Display

```
            DOS 4.5 Management

*BE00G  -  RAM Monitor Bank 2
*BE08G  -  RAM Monitor Bank 1

0xBFF0  -  BLDVRSN  (DOS version number)
0xBFF1  -  BLDNMBR  (DOS build number)

0xBFF2  -  MNGDISK  (manage Disk Table)
0xBFF4  -  MNGVALS  (manage DOS values)
0xBFF6  -  MNGUSER  (manage DOS CMDUSER)

0xBFF8  -  INITDOS  (DOS init address)
0xBFFA  -  INITVAL  (INIT values address)

0xBFFC  -  BCFGNDX  (BOOTCFG Table offset)
0xBFFD  -  NBUF1PG  (NBUF1 MSB Page)

0xBFFE  -  BOOTADR  (address)
0xBFFF  -  BOOTPGS  (sectors)

               RTN   ESC
```

Figure III.1.6. HELP Command HELP Content

```
INIT f, f2 [,Ss][,Dd][,Vv][,An][,Bn]
           [,Ln][,R[n]]

INIT HELLO,<Title>,L$1234          (Boot)

INIT HELLO,<Title>,A40,B4,R        (Data)

INIT HELLO,<Title>,R$14            (EXEC)


A = volume tracks
B = catalog sectors|sectors/track flag
L = volume subject
R = volume type




                    RTN   ESC
```

Figure III.1.7. HELP Command INIT Content

```
LSAVE f [,Ss][,Dd][,Vv][,Aa][,B][,L1]
        [,R[1]]

LSAVE TEST

LSAVE TEST,A$1234,L$123,R

LSAVE TEST,B,R1


B  = file delete/save option
R  = show address, length
R1 = show address, length, sectors read




                    RTN   ESC
```

Figure III.1.8. HELP Command LSAVE Content

```
IN#         s
```

Example: `IN#4`

This command is available in DOS 3.3 for System commands. The DOS `IN#` command configures the
`KSWL` interface pointer to receive all subsequent data from the peripheral device residing in the specified
slot `s` instead of from the Apple keyboard. Previously, Figure III.1.3 shows an example Applesoft
program that uses the DOS `IN#` command to configure the `KSWL` interface pointer in order to
communicate with the Thunderclock card.

```
MAXFILES [n][,R]
```

Example: `MAXFILES`
           `MAXFILES,R`
           `MAXFILES 3`
           `MAXFILES $4`

This command is available in DOS 3.3 for System commands. The DOS `MAXFILES` command
specifies the number of file buffers n that can be active at any given time up to a maximum value of
nine buffers in DOS 4.5L and five buffers in DOS 4.5H. When DOS 4.5 boots, the default number of
active file buffers is configured using the `NMAXVAL` variable as shown in Table I.8.7. This default value
is set to two in the DOS 4.5L source code and to five in the DOS 4.5H source code. Each file buffer
requires 581 (or `0x245`) bytes of memory. DOS 4.5L builds its file buffers down in memory beginning
at `BUFREND` at memory address `0x9A9A` and DOS 4.5H builds its file buffers up in memory beginning
at memory address `0xECA0`. DOS 4.5H was designed this way such that setting `MAXFILES` to three
allows the installation of the MiniAssembler and its monitor at memory address `0xF500` and not
perturb any of the three active file buffers that are in memory below `0xF500`. Apple][memory is very
precious, and specifying fewer than five file buffers in DOS 4.5H does not provide any more memory
for programs in that version of DOS. `HIMEM` is always set to memory address `0xBE00` regardless how
many file buffers are configured. On the other hand, `HIMEM` is very much dependent on the number of
file buffers in DOS 4.5L, and `HIMEM` is set to `0x9600` when two file buffers are configured.

`MAXFILES` with no parameter n displays the current number of active file buffers on the Apple
Command Line as shown in Figure III.1.9 for DOS 4.5L and Figure III.1.10 for DOS 4.5H. Figure
III.1.9 shows that changing the number of file buffers in DOS 4.5L **does** change the location of `HIMEM`.
Figure III.1.10 shows that changing the number of file buffers in DOS 4.5H **does not** change the
location of `HIMEM` and it remains set to `0xBE00`. The number of file buffers can never be `zero`. Even
the `CATALOG` command requires a file buffer for the `CLOSOPEN` routine used by the File Manager.

Table III.1.3 shows the memory locations for the contents of the first five file buffers in DOS 4.5L.
When DOS 4.5L is configured with two active file buffers, the address in `HIMEM` is exactly the same as
the address in `HIMEM` for DOS 3.3 when it is configured with three active file buffers, which is
`0x9600`. Having two file buffers is certainly a far more practical choice. Table III.1.4 shows the
memory locations for the contents of all five file buffers in DOS 4.5H. There is just enough room for

the 32-byte `SECMAP` buffer at `0xEC80` to precede the DOS file buffers that end very near to the beginning of the ROM Monitor routines. As a reminder, reducing the number of file buffers in DOS 4.5H does not provide any additional memory for software programs because all of these active file buffers reside in the memory of the Language Card partition. Before the `MAXFILES` command rebuilds the file buffers so that they can be utilized, DOS 4.5 terminates any active `EXEC` file and closes all open files. If the DOS `MAXFILES` command is issued within an active `EXEC` file, the `EXEC` file is terminated and closed, and any remaining commands in the `EXEC` file are not processed.

```
]MAXFILES = 2
]PRINT PEEK(116);",";PEEK(115)
150,0
]PRINT 150*256+0
38400
]SV 38400 = 0x9600 = 38400
]MAXFILES 3
]MAXFILES = 3
]PRINT PEEK(116);",";PEEK(115)
147,187
]PRINT 147*256+187
37819
]SV 37819 = 0x93BB = 37819
]
```

```
]MAXFILES = 5
]PRINT PEEK(116);",";PEEK(115)
190,0
]PRINT 190*256+0
48640
]SV 48640 = 0xBE00 = 48640
]MAXFILES 4
]MAXFILES = 4
]PRINT PEEK(116);",";PEEK(115)
190,0
]PRINT 190*256+0
48640
]SV 48640 = 0xBE00 = 48640
]
```

Figure III.1.9. DOS 4.5L MAXFILES Command   Figure III.1.10. DOS 4.5H MAXFILES Command

File Buffer	Data Buffer	TS Buffer	Workarea	Filename
1	0x9845-0x9944	0x9945-0x9A44	0x9A45-0x9A69	0x9A6A-0x9A81
2	0x9600-0x96FF	0x9700-0x97FF	0x9800-0x9824	0x9825-0x983C
3	0x93BB-0x94BA	0x94BB-0x95BA	0x95BB-0x95DF	0x95E0-0x95F7
4	0x9176-0x9275	0x9276-0x9375	0x9376-0x939A	0x939B-0x93B2
5	0x8F31-0x9030	0x9031-0x9130	0x9131-0x9155	0x9156-0x916D

Table III.1.3. DOS 4.5L File Buffer Memory Locations

File Buffer	Data Buffer	TS Buffer	Workarea	Filename
1	0xECA0-0xED9F	0xEDA0-0xEE9F	0xEEA0-0xEEC4	0xEEC5-0xEEDC
2	0xEEE5-0xEFE4	0xEFE5-0xF0E4	0xF0E5-0xF109	0xF10A-0xF121
3	0xF12A-0xF229	0xF22A-0xF329	0xF32A-0xF34E	0xF34F-0xF366
4	0xF36F-0xF46E	0xF46F-0xF56E	0xF56F-0xF593	0xF594-0xF5AB
5	0xF5B4-0xF6B3	0xF6B4-0xF7B3	0xF7B4-0xF7D8	0xF7D9-0xF7F0

Table III.1.4. DOS 4.5H File Buffer Memory Locations

If CONFIG Bit 3 is **set** in order to disable the DOS MAXFILES command as shown in Table III.1.2, the DOS 4.5 Command Manager bypasses MAXFILES processing when the DOS MAXFILES command is encountered **with** a parameter n. The DOS MAXFILES command is **not** bypassed when the command is encountered **without** a parameter n. In this instance DOS 4.5 displays the current number of active file buffers on the Apple Command Line. Setting CONFIG Bit 3 is far easier than having to modify and edit an Applesoft program to eliminate all DOS MAXFILES commands thereby transforming the program to be far more suitable when operating in the DOS 4.5H processing environment. Even assembly language programs could benefit from setting CONFIG Bit 3 in order to bypass MAXFILES processing and unnecessarily changing the configuration of DOS to have a specific number of file buffers to process files. If only the R keyword without a parameter value is entered with the MAXFILES command followed by a comma, MAXFILES is reset to its default value of IMAXFLS **except** when CONFIG Bit 3 is set. IMAXFILS has a value of two in DOS 4.5L and a value of five in DOS 4.5H.

```
]MON C,I,O

]LIST EXECFILE
MON C,I,O
LIST TEXTFILE.TXT

]EXEC EXECFILE
]MON C,I,O
]LIST TEXTFILE.TXT
This is line 1.
This is line 2.
This is line 3.
]
]*
```

Figure III.1.11. MON Command Display

```
]NOMON C,I,O
]LIST EXECFILE2
NOMON C,I,O
LIST TEXTFILE.TXT

]EXEC EXECFILE2
]
This is line 1.
This is line 2.
This is line 3.
]

]*
```

Figure III.1.12. NOMON Command Display

MON   [,C][,I][,O]

Example: MON
            MON C,I,O

This command is available in DOS 3.3 for System commands. The DOS MON command enables the display of commands, input data, and output data to the screen. All programmatically executed DOS commands are displayed to the screen if the C keyword is included. All Input data from a volume is displayed to the screen if the I keyword is included. All Output data to a volume is displayed to the screen if the O keyword is included. Figure III.1.11 shows an example in using the DOS MON command before processing an EXEC file. First, the EXEC file EXECFILE is listed to show its contents, and then the file is processed. Each statement in EXECFILE is echoed to the screen before that statement is processed. If no keywords are included with the MON command, the CSWL and KSWL interface pointers are initialized and DOS enters the Apple Monitor at memory address 0xFF65. Entering a ctrl-C from within the Apple Monitor re-enables DOS's control over the CSWL and KSWL interface pointers.

```
NOMON      [,C][,I][,O]

Example:   NOMON
           NOMON C,I,O
```

This command is available in DOS 3.3 for System commands. The DOS NOMON command disables the display of commands, input data, and output data to the screen. All programmatically executed DOS commands are no longer displayed to the screen if the C keyword is included. All Input data from a volume is no longer displayed to the screen if the I keyword is included. All Output data to a volume is no longer displayed to the screen if the O keyword is included. Figure III.1.12 shows an example in using the DOS NOMON command before processing an EXEC file. First, the EXEC file EXECFILE2 is listed to show its contents, and then the file is processed. Now, each statement in EXECFILE2 is no longer echoed to the screen before that statement is processed. If no keywords are included with the NOMON command, the CSWL and KSWL interface pointers are initialized and DOS enters the Apple Monitor at memory address 0xFF65. Entering a ctrl-C from within the Apple Monitor re-enables DOS's control over the CSWL and KSWL interface pointers.

```
PHASE      [n][,R]

Example:   PHASE
           PHASE,R
           PHASE 4
           PHASE $A
```

This command is not available in DOS 3.3 for System commands. The DOS PHASE command provides the means to change the number of half-phases between adjacent tracks of a DOS volume when the volume is initialized. The DOS PHASE command belongs to a special non-keyword *integer value* category of commands. A PHASE value may be entered directly on the Apple Command Line in either decimal or in hexadecimal whose value must be prefaced by the dollar sign $. Once the volume is initialized with a particular phase value other than the default value of four, that phase value must be established prior to accessing that volume for any I/O data. The phase value for an Apple Master DOS diskette is equal to the default value of DFLTPHAS which is defined to be four. If only the R keyword without a parameter value is entered with the PHASE command followed by a comma, VALSPHAS as shown in Table I.8.7 is reset to the default value of DFLTPHAS. DFLTPHAS has a value of four in both DOS 4.5L and DOS 4.5H. It is quite possible to initialize a volume with multiple phase values where the software residing on this unique volume knows when to change the phase value before it accesses those particular tracks. Figure III.1.13 shows a volume that is initialized with a phase value of three so that this volume may contain forty-eight tracks within the same area that volumes having a phase value of four contain thirty-six tracks. Figure III.1.14 shows the VTOC of this same volume after the volume has been initialized with forty-eight tracks.

I spent a significant amount of time once again analyzing the algorithm that DOS 3.3 and DOS 4.1 use in order to move the Disk][read/write disk head from one track to an adjacent track and from one track to many distant tracks in either direction. This algorithm includes an acceleration and deceleration component to ensure that radial movements to and from distant tracks occur smoothly in the least amount of time. When moving the read/write disk head to distant tracks it is necessary to account for all induced momentum and mechanical reluctance in the Cam Rider and in the Carriage Rod as shown in Figure I.10.1. I literally opened a Disk][drive enclosure and marked where tracks 0, 1, 2, 3, and 4 were located along the Cam Channel on the Cam Table. After much trial and error and experimentation, I developed an algorithm to move the Cam Rider in half-phase steps perfectly and repeatably in either direction. Lastly, I added in the acceleration and deceleration components that have sufficient electromagnetic holding time to buffer any induced momentum and mechanical reluctance, and to provide smooth track-to-track movements in the least amount of time.

In order to obtain the highest signal-to-noise ratio for physical diskette recording, Apple designed the Disk][read/write disk head to be somewhat smaller than the width of a nominal, four half-phase track. Actually, Apple manufactured their read/write disk heads about the size of three half-phases. As an aside, Rana manufactured their read/write disk heads for their Rana drives slightly smaller than the size of two half-phases. A Disk][is not capable of reading and writing tracks that are spaced less than three half-phases due to the extreme crosstalk between adjacent tracks; however, it is capable of reading and writing tracks that are spaced three half-phases or more. The MOVHD algorithm I designed is capable of de-energizing two adjacent electromagnetic poles within four microseconds, and the position of the read/write disk head is maintained between those electromagnetic poles by mechanical reluctance of the Carriage Rod. The DOS PHASE command, normally set to four as its default, can be set from one to sixteen half-phases.

Virtual][is capable of storing data in the WOZ 1.0 and WOZ 2.0 disk image formats. These formats were basically an offshoot of the Applesauce project started by John K. Morris, and they duplicate the way data is stored on a physical diskette. Using Virtual][, a WOZ 2.0 volume may be initialized by DOS 4.5 using a PHASE value other than four to create unique volume images.

```
]PHASE 3

]INIT HELLO,PHASE Figure,A48,B4,L$F00B,D
2

]LS

S=6 D=02 V=000 F=0719 01/01/22 08:28:48

 A 002 HELLO             01/01/22 08:28:48

]LSR

B=4505H boot T=PHASE Figure

M=4505H P=03 L=0xF00B 01/01/22 08:28:48

S=6 D=02 V=000 F=0719 01/01/22 08:28:48

 001 0x13,0x0F HELLO

]*
```

Figure III.1.13. PHASE Command Display

```
]PHASE 3

]TS A17
0011 0445 05C8 00C2 D0C8 C1D3 C5A0 C6E9
E7F5 F2E5 A0A0 A0A0 A0A0 A0A0 A0A0 A0A0
4828 0822 0101 037A 0BF0 4828 0822 0101
1301 0000 3010 0001 0000 0000 0000 0000
FC00 0000 FFFF 0000 FFFF 0000 FFFF 0000
FFFF 0000 FFFF 0000 FFFF 0000 FFFF 0000
FFFF 0000 FFFF 0000 FFFF 0000 FFE0 0000
FFFF 0000 3FFF 0000 FFFF 0000 FFFF 0000
FFFF 0000 FFFF 0000 FFFF 0000 FFFF 0000
FFFF 0000 FFFF 0000 FFFF 0000 FFFF 0000
FFFF 0000 FFFF 0000 FFFF 0000 FFFF 0000
FFFF 0000 FFFF 0000 FFFF 0000 FFFF 0000
FFFF 0000 FFFF 0000 0000 0000 0000 0000
TS = 0x11,0x00

]*
```

Figure III.1.14. PHASE 3 VTOC Display

This command is available in DOS 3.3 for System commands. The DOS PR# command configures the CSWL interface pointer to send all subsequent data to the peripheral device residing in the specified slot s instead of to the Apple display. Previously, Figure III.1.3 shows an example Applesoft program that uses the DOS PR# command to configure the CSWL interface pointer in order to communicate with the Thunderclock card.

SV   [n]

Example: SV
            SV 1234
            SV $1234

This command is not available in DOS 3.3 for System commands. The DOS SV (i.e. Show Value) command displays on the Apple Command Line the decimal and hexadecimal values of the submitted number n. The DOS SV command belongs to a special non-keyword *integer value* category of commands. SV values may be submitted directly on the Apple Command Line in either decimal or in hexadecimal whose value must be prefaced by the dollar sign $. Figure III.1.15 shows the use of the DOS SV command. Using the DOS SV command is a convenient way to convert numbers from decimal to hexadecimal or hexadecimal to decimal without having to reach for the hexadecimal calculator.

When the DOS SV command is utilized from within an Applesoft program, the value that is processed by SV can be obtained and displayed according to the design of that program. A simple Applesoft program displaying two examples in using the DOS SV command is also shown in Figure III.1.15. The Value Read Buffer is used by the DOS SV command in order to obtain its current value when DOS is in the RUN mode.

The Print Decimal PRTDEC routine is severely flawed in DOS 3.3, and it can only convert 8-bit hexadecimal values to decimal. DOS 4.5 requires the conversion of 16-bit hexadecimal values to decimal in order to selectively print numbers having up to five zero-prefaced decimal digits. The DOS SV command is a function that is required to print up to five zero-prefaced decimal digits to the display. The algorithm I designed for the DOS 4.5 PRTDEC routine requires one additional byte for the low-order bytes in its Decimal Table DECTBLL and five additional bytes for the added high-order bytes in its Decimal Table DECTBLH.

```
]LIST

 10 D$ =  CHR$ (4)
 20  PRINT D$;"SV 123"
 30  INPUT A: PRINT "A=";A
 40 B = 12345
 50  PRINT D$;"SV ";B
 60  INPUT C: PRINT "C=";C

]RUN

A=123

C=12345

]SV $1234 = 0x1234 = 04660

]SV 1234 = 0x04D2 = 01234

]SV = 0x0000 = 00000

]SV $ffff = 0xFFFF = 65535

]
```

Figure III.1.15. SV Command Display

```
10 D$ =  CHR$ (4):A% = 1234:A =
    65535: PRINT D$;"BLOAD MNGUS
    ER,A$4000": CALL 16384
30  PRINT D$;"USER"
40  PRINT D$;"USER ",A%
50  PRINT D$;"USER $1234"
60  PRINT D$;"USER ",A

]RUN
Activating the MNGUSER program.
Content of USERADR variable:   0xD49D

Initializing CMDUSER.
Content of USERADR variable:   0x404C

Entered USER function, value = 0x0000
Entered USER function, value = 0x04D2
Entered USER function, value = 0x1234
Entered USER function, value = 0xFFFF

Exiting MNGUSER, program completed.
Content of USERADR variable:   0xD49D
]
```

Figure III.1.16. USER Command Usage

`USER [n]`

Example: `USER`
`USER 1234`
`USER $1234`

This command is not available in DOS 3.3 for System commands. The DOS `USER` command can be configured by the user to function in several different ways. The DOS `USER` command belongs to a special non-keyword *integer value* category of commands. A `USER` value may be entered directly on the Apple Command Line in either decimal or in hexadecimal whose value must be prefaced by the dollar sign `$`. The DOS `USER` command is designed to provide the user with several modes of operation. In its default configuration, when the DOS `USER` command is issued on the Apple Command Line it initializes the `CSWL` and `KSWL` interface pointers and DOS enters the Apple Monitor at memory address `0xFF65`. Entering a `ctrl-C` from within the Apple Monitor re-enables DOS's control over the `CSWL` and `KSWL` interface pointers.

After loading DOS 4.5 into memory from a file, to prevent losing control of DOS to Applesoft after DOS initialization, the user can configure the DOS `USER` command using `MNGUSER` to replace the `RUN` command in `CMDVAL` with that of `USER`. The `USER` command executes rather than the `RUN` command after Applesoft initialization. Whatever instructions that are at the address that is put into `USERADR` are executed rather than the `HELLO` file. Refer to Figure I.8.4 and its discussion explaining how to utilize `MNGUSER`. The DOS `USER` command may also be attached to an assembly language routine to process selected functions. A `USER` integer value may be entered using integer and real variables within an Applesoft program. Figure III.1.16 shows an example Applesoft program where the DOS `USER` command passes various numerical values using direct, integer, and real variables to an assembly language program designed to print those values that it receives by means of the DOS `USER` command. Creative program design possibilities are virtually infinite in how the DOS `USER` command may be utilized as a conduit between an Applesoft program and a function using assembly language.

Command	Command Syntax
CAT CATALOG LS	`[,Ss][,Dd][Vv][,R]` `[,Ss][,Dd][Vv][,R]` `[,Ss][,Dd][Vv][,R]`
CD	`[,Ss][,Dd][Vv][,R]`
DELETE RM	`f [,Ss][,Dd][,Vv][,R]` `f [,Ss][,Dd][,Vv][,R]`
DIFF	`f, f2 [,Ss][,Dd][,Vv]`
GREP	`f, f2 [,Ss][,Dd][,Vv]`
INIT	`f, f2 [,Ss][,Dd][,Vv][,An][,Bn][,Ln][,R[n]]`
LIST MORE	`f [,Ss][,Dd][,Vv][,Bb][,Ll][,R]` `f [,Ss][,Dd][,Vv][,Bb][,Ll][,R]`
LOCK	`[f] [,Ss][,Dd][,Vv]`
MV RENAME	`f, f2 [,Ss][,Dd][,Vv][,R]` `f, f2 [,Ss][,Dd][,Vv][,R]`
TOUCH	`[f] [,Ss][,Dd][,Vv][,R]`
TS	`[,Ss][,Dd][,Vv][,An][,Bn][,L][,R]`
UNLOCK	`[f] [,Ss][,Dd][,Vv]`
URM	`f [,Ss][,Dd][,Vv]`
VERIFY	`f [,Ss][,Dd][,Vv][,R1]`
WTS	`Ln, Rn [,Ss][,Dd][,Vv][,An][,Bn]`

Table III.2.1. File System Commands in DOS 4.5

2. File System Commands

The DOS 4.5 File System commands consist of those commands that manage the file system of a disk volume, manage the display of the content of a disk volume, manage the individual and pairs of files of a disk volume, and manage the display of the content of individual and pairs of files of a disk volume. The syntax of the File System commands is shown in Table III.2.1. All of the File System commands are permitted to be used from within an Applesoft or a Binary program file as well as on the Apple Command Line.

```
CAT       [,Ss][,Dd][,Vv][,R]              ; short version of CATALOG
CATALOG   [,Ss][,Dd][,Vv][,R]
LS        [,Ss][,Dd][,Vv][,R]              ; UNIX version of CATALOG


Example:  CAT D1
          CATALOG S6,D2
          LS R
```

This command is available in DOS 3.3 for File System commands. The DOS CATALOG command displays on the screen a wealth of information for the specified volume: the current slot (S=), the drive (D=), and the volume number (V=) for the volume, the remaining free space (F=) on the volume, the date and time the VTOC was last modified, and a list of all of the files in the volume. Each file is displayed with its lock/unlock status, with its file type, with its size in sectors including all TSL sectors, with the first fourteen characters of its filename, and with the date and time the file was created or last modified. Table I.7.3 lists all file types that are native to DOS 4.5. Figure III.2.1 shows an example screen display of the CATALOG and the CAT commands. Notice that the asterisk before the file type shows that the files DOS4.5 and INSTALL are locked. DOS 4.5 commands may be entered in lowercase.

If the R keyword is included with the CATALOG command, the screen displays the version and build of the DOS that created this volume (B=), the volume type (boot or data), the twenty-four ASCII character volume title (T=), the version of DOS that is currently in memory (M=), the phase value that was used to create this volume (P=), the volume library value assigned to this volume (L=), and the date and time this volume was created, followed by the information above.

Without the R keyword each file is displayed as shown in Figure III.2.1.

With the R keyword each file is displayed with its lock/unlock status, with its sequence number, with the track and sector values of its first TSL sector, and with all twenty-four ASCII characters of its filename. Figure III.2.2 shows an example screen for the LS R command. Having the track and sector values of the first TSL sector for a file is absolutely necessary in order to begin any investigation of a file, its TSL sector resources, and the location of all of its data sectors that are currently on that volume.

```
]CATALOG S6,D2

S=6 D=02 V=000 F=0488 01/01/22 08:28:48

*B 044 DOS4.5           01/01/22 08:28:48
 L 013 INSTALL.L        01/01/22 08:28:48
*B 003 INSTALL          01/01/22 08:28:48
 L 006 MOVEDOS.L        01/01/22 08:28:48

]cat

S=6 D=02 V=000 F=0488 01/01/22 08:28:48

*B 044 DOS4.5           01/01/22 08:28:48
 L 013 INSTALL.L        01/01/22 08:28:48
*B 003 INSTALL          01/01/22 08:28:48
 L 006 MOVEDOS.L        01/01/22 08:28:48

]※
```

Figure III.2.1. CATALOG and CAT Command

```
]LS R

B=4505H data T=CATALOG Figure

M=4505H P=04 L=0xF001 01/01/22 08:28:48

S=6 D=02 V=000 F=0488 01/01/22 08:28:48

*001 0x12,0x0F DOS4.5
 002 0x15,0x0F INSTALL.L
*003 0x16,0x0F INSTALL
 004 0x17,0x0F MOVEDOS.L
x005 0x18,0x0F DOS2TO1

]※
```

Figure III.2.2. LS R Command Display

```
CD          [,Ss][,Dd][,Vv][,R]

Example:    CD
            CD,R
            CD S6,D2,V3
```

This command is not available in DOS 3.3 for File System commands. The DOS CD command was originally developed for DOS 4.1 and it was expanded for DOS 4.5 in order to utilize the newly created File Manager FMCDCD (i.e. 0x11) command handler. The CD command can change the current slot, drive, and volume parameters used by the Command Manager and by the File Manager. If no keywords are used with the CD command, the current slot, drive and volume parameters are displayed on the Apple Command Line after the CD command. Figure III.2.3 shows two examples of using the CD command. When the CD command is used with keywords, the keyword values are stored in the CMDVALS Data structure. When the CD command is used without keywords, two values are displayed for volume. The first value comes from DISKVOL as shown in Table I.5.2 and the second value comes from VOLNUMBR as shown in Table I.12.2. DISKVOL is the actual volume number value that is in the VTOC and VOLNUMBR is the volume number value that is used by the File Manager. When these values differ and VOLNUMBR is not zero then the Volume Number Mismatch error message is issued.

When the R keyword is included with the CD command followed by a comma, the VTOC of the specified volume is read and its variable DOSCONFG as shown in Table I.5.2 is copied to the variable VALSCNFG as shown in Table I.8.7. Using the CD command with the R keyword in this way can restore the DOS CONFIG configuration that was used when this volume was initialized. The value of VALSCNFG can be displayed by entering the DOS CONFIG command without any arguments.

```
DELETE      f [,Ss][,Dd][,Vv][,R]
RM          f [,Ss][,Dd][,Vv][,R]                        ; UNIX version of DELETE

Example:    DELETE COPYDOS
            RM COPYDOS,R
```

This command is available in DOS 3.3 for File System commands. The DOS DELETE command removes the filename f from the volume Catalog listing of the specified volume if the filename exists by setting the most significant bit of its TSL track byte, and marking the sectors listed in the TSL sector(s) of the file and all of its TSL sectors as available. Refer to Figure I.7.1 showing a volume Catalog entry. Figure III.2.4 shows an example of a file being deleted. It is prudent to undelete a deleted file as soon as possible because the sectors listed in the TSL sector(s) of the file and all of its TSL sectors are now available in the VTOC and can be utilized by another file. A locked file cannot be deleted unless the R keyword is used to override the lock status.

When the R keyword is included with the DELETE command, the specified filename f is deleted from the volume Catalog regardless whether the file is locked or not. That is, the R keyword can be used to override the lock status of a file when a file is deleted. This capability is quite useful when a set of files must be deleted without regard to the lock status of each file and without having to determine what that lock status happens to be. Locking a file still provides a level of protection from accidental file deletion. Providing the capability of deleting a file without regard to the lock status of the file using the R keyword must not be used indiscriminately, but only when the power of the R keyword is fully understood and properly appreciated.

```
]CD S6,D2,V123
]LS
S=6 D=02 V=123 F=0518 01/01/22 08:28:48
 A 004 HELLO          01/01/22 08:28:48
]
]CD = S=6 D=02 V=123 123
]
]LS V23
Volume Number Mismatch
]cd = S=6 D=02 V=123 023
]※
```

Figure III.2.3. CD Command Display

```
]DELETE DOS1TO2
]CAT
S=6 D=02 V=000 F=0510 01/01/22 08:28:49
 B 044 DOS4.5          01/01/22 08:28:48
]
]CAT R
B=4505H data T=DELETE Figure
M=4505H P=04 L=0xF005 01/01/22 08:28:48
S=6 D=02 V=000 F=0510 01/01/22 08:28:49
 001 0x12,0x0F DOS4.5
x002 0x15,0x0F DOS1TO2
]※
```

Figure III.2.4. DELETE Command Display

DIFF   f, f2 [,Ss][,Dd][,Vv]

Example: DIFF TEST1,TEST2

This command is not available in DOS 3.3 for File System commands. The DOS DIFF command was originally developed for DOS 4.1 to compare any two files f and f2 in the specified volume up to the end of SECCNT-1 sectors for the second file, f2. The routine displays the number of bytes compared on the Apple Command Line, and the location(s) from the beginning of the files to where the two files differ and the differing bytes from each file. **The two files must reside on the same volume.** The location(s) where the files differ are the number of bytes from the beginning of each file. The first differing byte comes from the first file, or file f, and the second differing byte comes from the second file, or file f2. Displayed values are all shown in hexadecimal. Figure III.2.5 shows an example of three pairs of files that are compared using the DOS DIFF command. The first pair of files are identical and the display shows that 0x0100 bytes were compared even though the files themselves are only 0x0080 bytes in size. DIFF compares whole sectors. The second pair of files are exactly 0x1000 bytes in size but DIFF compared 0x1100 bytes. Because these are Binary files their address and length bytes occupy the first four bytes in each file, thus making the files actually 0x1004 bytes in length. Again, DIFF compares whole sectors, and the last four bytes of data in each file reside in an additional sector. These files differed at only one location. The third pair of files are 0x300 bytes in actual size and they differ at five specific locations.

```
]DIFF F1,F2 = 0x0100            ]GREP HELLO,WINDOW = 0x0500
                               0x0449
]DIFF N1,N2 = 0x1100           ]
0x0F84 = 0x00,0xFF             ]GREP VOLMGR,Images,D2 = 0x3700
]                              0x22C9
                               0x256D
]DIFF Z1,Z2 = 0x0400           0x3373
0x0084 = 0x00,0xFF             0x33E9
0x0104 = 0x00,0xFF             ]
0x0184 = 0x00,0xFF
0x0204 = 0x00,0xFF             ]grep VOLMGR,Drive Information = 0x3700
0x0284 = 0x00,0xFF             0x32A8
]                              0x32C1
                               ]
```

Figure III.2.5. DIFF Command Display   Figure III.2.6. GREP Command Display

GREP   f, f2 [,Ss][,Dd][,Vv]

Example: GREP HELLO,TEST
                 GREP HELLO,Manage Test

This command is not available in DOS 3.3 for File System commands. The DOS GREP command was originally developed for DOS 4.1 and enhanced for DOS 4.5 to search file f for the single or multiple word ASCII character string f2 in the specified volume up to the end of SECCNT-1 sectors for file f. The routine displays the number of bytes searched in file f on the Apple Command Line and the location(s) where the character string f2 is found in the file. The location(s) where f2 is found is the number of bytes from the beginning of the file to the first character of f2. Displayed values are all shown in hexadecimal. Figure III.2.6 shows an example of three searches on two files. The first search is on an Applesoft file. The second and third searches are on a Binary file. The third search uses a multiple word character string for f2. GREP searches whole sectors. Regardless how many actual bytes that are associated with the file in its last sector, the entire last sector of the file is included in the data search. GREP is case sensitive as shown in Figure III.2.6., and GREP masks out the MSB of all data read from file f so lower ASCII character 0x41 is the same as upper ASCII character 0xC1. DOS 4.5 expects the character string contained in f2 to conform to the format and length of a filename. Therefore, the first character must be an alpha character, that is, equal to or greater than an A character. Otherwise, processing of the Apple Command Line passes from DOS to Applesoft, and Applesoft parses the Apple Command Line as if it contains a GR command and issue a ?SYNTAX ERROR message. The maximum length of f2 is twenty-four characters and all characters after the first alpha character must be equal to or greater than 0xA0. In the first example in Figure III.2.6, GREP found one occurrence of WINDOW in the file HELLO. GREP found four occurrences of Images in the file VOLMGR. In the third example GREP found two occurrences of Drive Information in the same file VOLMGR.

```
INIT        f, f2 [,Ss][,Dd][,Vv][,An][,Bn][,Ln][,R[n]]
```

Example: `INIT HELLO,<title>,V123,L$101`   ; creates Volume Type B
           `INIT EXECFILE,<title>,V123,R$14`   ; creates Volume Type B
           `INIT Hello,<title>,V123,r`   ; creates Volume Type D

This command is available in DOS 3.3 for File System commands. The DOS `INIT` command initializes the specified volume with the filename `f`, and the command handler can write a DOS 4.5 image onto tracks `0x00`, `0x01`, and one additional sector onto track `0x02` for DOS 4.5L and ten additional sectors onto track `0x02` for DOS 4.5H. A Boot volume, or Volume Type B, is created with a DOS 4.5 image when the R keyword is **not** included as shown in Figure III.2.7, or the value of the R keyword is **not** equal to `zero`. All initialized volumes are titled with the required upper ASCII character string in `f2`. The parameter `v` is assigned to the volume number if the V keyword is included; otherwise, the volume is initialized with a volume number of `zero`. A Data volume, or Volume Type D, is created without a DOS 4.5 image and with an empty volume catalog when the R keyword **is** included without a parameter as shown in Figure III.2.8, or with a value of `zero`. All volume sectors are available for data storage including track `0x00` in a Data volume. The upper ASCII character string in `f2` is still used for the volume Title, but the filename `f` is simply a placeholder and it is discarded. If the R keyword is included with a nonzero value, that value is copied to `CMDVAL` and a Boot volume is initialized having a DOS 4.5 image. No Boot file is saved to that volume if Boot Type (`SUBCODE`) does not equal `0x06` (the DOS RUN command), even if there is an Applesoft file in memory. This logic is new in DOS 4.5. The user is required to copy an `EXEC` file for R$14 or a Binary file for R$34 to the volume as its `HELLO`, or `f` filename. Other possible values for the R keyword could include R$10 for `CLOSE`, R$2C for `DATE`, and R$2E for `LIST`, all obtained from Table III.0.2.

```
]INIT HELLO,Boot Disk,S6,D2,V123,L$F007      ]init hello,Data Disk,v101,l$f007,r
]                                            ]
]CAT R                                       ]cat r
B=4505H boot T=Boot Disk                     B=4505H data T=Data Disk
M=4505H P=04 L=0xF007 01/01/22 08:28:48      M=4505H P=04 L=0xF007 01/01/22 08:28:48
S=6 D=02 V=123 F=0510 01/01/22 08:28:48      S=6 D=02 V=101 F=0554 01/01/22 08:28:48
 001 0x12,0x0F HELLO                         ]*
]*
```

Figure III.2.7. INIT Command for Boot Volume   Figure III.2.8. INIT Command for Data Volume

The complete set of `INIT` initialization values is available at the address found in `INITVAL` at memory address `0xBFFA`. These initialization values can be modified directly or indirectly before invoking the DOS `INIT` command in order to tailor a DOS 4.5 volume specific to ones needs and that of the target hardware. See Table I.8.7 for a list of all of the available initialization values. If the A and B keywords are not used or they are set to `zero`, the default initialization values for ENDTRK and SECVAL come from `LASTRACK` and `FIRSTCAT`, respectively. The `A` keyword is used to specify a new ENDTRK, the *accepted* number of tracks in a DOS volume. The `B` keyword is used to specify a new SECVAL, the number of Catalog sectors from 1 to 15, and to select a new ENDSEC: 16-sector tracks if the MSB of the `B` keyword is **clear** or 32-sector tracks if the MSB is **set**. The default value is 16-sector tracks. The `L` keyword is used to specify a Library Value (or subject value) for the DOS volume if it is included, from `0x0000` to `0xFFFF`, otherwise the Library Value is set to `zero`. Once an initialization parameter has been changed, it remains equal to that value except for CMDVAL, SECVAL, ENDTRK, SUBJCT, and ENDSEC. There is no reset to *default* settings for NMAXVAL, YEARVAL, TRKVAL, VRSN, BLD, RAMTYP, VALSPHAS, TSPARS, ALCTRK, ALCDIR, VALSCNFG, and SECSIZ as shown previously in Table I.8.7. Please, use common sense when modifying these values.

The value in SECVAL determines the number of sectors the catalog contains not including the VTOC sector. The useable values for SECVAL are 0<SECVAL<16. If its value is greater than fifteen, no more than fifteen Catalog sectors are created. Table III.2.2 shows the number of available sectors for file data and TSL sectors in a volume based on Volume Type for volumes having thirty-six tracks with sixteen or thirty-two sectors per track. A few disk drives, either physical or solid state, were manufactured to access forty tracks for a volume. Set ENDTRK to `0x28` (either use `A40` or `A$28`) to provide access to all forty tracks, or set ENDTRK to `0x30` (either use `A48` or `A$30`) to access forty-eight tracks if they are available on the target device, such as the CFFA. The VTOC is designed to manage up to fifty tracks per volume as shown previously in Figure I.5.2. Table III.2.3 shows the total number of sectors in a volume having thirty-five, thirty-six, forty, or forty-eight tracks with sixteen or thirty-two sectors per track.

SECVAL	Catalog Sectors	16 Sectors/Track			32 Sectors/Track		
		4.5L	4.5H	Data	4.5L	4.5H	Data
0x01	1	541	532	574	1117	1108	1150
0x02	2	540	531	573	1116	1107	1149
0x03	3	539	530	572	1115	1106	1148
0x04	4	538	529	571	1114	1105	1147
0x05	5	537	528	570	1113	1104	1146
0x06	6	536	527	569	1112	1103	1145
0x07	7	535	526	568	1111	1102	1144
0x08	8	534	525	567	1110	1101	1143
0x09	9	533	524	566	1109	1100	1142
0x0A	10	532	523	565	1108	1099	1141
0x0B	11	531	522	564	1107	1098	1140
0x0C	12	530	521	563	1106	1097	1139
0x0D	13	529	520	562	1105	1096	1138
0x0E	14	528	519	561	1104	1095	1137
0x0F	15	527	518	560	1103	1094	1136

Table III.2.2. Available Data Sectors for 36 Tracks, 16/32 Sectors/Track

Tracks/Volume	16 Sectors/Track	32 Sectors/Track
35	560	1120
36	576	1152
40	640	1280
48	768	1536

Table III.2.3. Total Sectors in Initialized Volumes

```
]LIST EXECFILE.T

MON CIO
BLOAD FOO
NOMON CIO

]

]LIST EXECFILE.T,L6

MON CI

]LIST EXECFILE.T,B9,L7

LOAD FO

]LIST EXECFILE.T,B9,L7,R

CFC1 C4A0 C6CF CF8D

]*
```

```
]LOAD HELLO,R

A$0801,L$04E7

]LIST HELLO

E704 1308 0A00 4424 D0E7 2831 3329 C8E7
2834 2900 3B08 1400 864E 414D 2428 3230
292C 434D 4424 2832 3029 2C50 474D 2428
3230 292C 4144 5228 3230 2900 5308 1E00
973A 9631 363A BA22 546F 6F6C 7320 4D65
6E75 2200 A008 2800 874E 3A81 49D0 30C1
4EC9 313A 874E 414D 2428 4929 2C43 4D44
2428 4929 2C50 474D 2428 4929 2C41 4452
2849 293A B032 3030 3A82 3A4E 25D0 31C9
284E CB32 D0D3 284E CB32 2929 3A49 D030
00D2 0832 009E 3AB0 3230 303A B033 3030
3A9D 3AB0 3230 303A AD41 25D0 3237 C497
3ABA 4424 3B22 4341 5441 4C4F 4722 3ABA
3ABF 00ED 083C 00AD 4125 D032 31C4 49D0
49C8 31C9 4ECA 2849 CF4E C932 2900 1D09
4600 AD41 25D0 3130 C449 D049 C832 C94E
```

Figure III.2.9. LIST Text File Command   Figure III.2.10. LIST Applesoft File Command

```
LIST     f [,Ss][,Dd][,Vv][,Bb][,Ll][,R]
MORE     f [,Ss][,Dd][,Vv][,Bb][,Ll][,R]      ; UNIX version of LIST
```

Example: LIST EXECFILE
           LIST TESTFILE,B8,L10,R

This command is not available in DOS 3.3 for File System commands. The DOS LIST command was originally developed for DOS 4.1 and it displays on the screen the data contained in file f in the specified volume in ASCII if the file type is a Text file or in hexadecimal for all other file types. Table I.7.3 lists all of the file types that are native to DOS 4.5. If the R keyword is included, the data of a Text file is displayed in hexadecimal rather than in ASCII. If the B keyword is included, that number of bytes, b, into the file is skipped. If the L keyword is included, that number of bytes, l, of data is only displayed, or until the end of the file, whichever occurs first. LIST displays a complete sector of data at a time, and the LIST display can be terminated at any time by pressing the ESC key. The DOS LIST command displays the contents of a file whereas the Applesoft LIST command displays the contents of an Applesoft program as long as an Applesoft program resides in memory. Figure III.2.9 shows examples of using the DOS LIST command on a Text file while utilizing the various keywords. First, the entire file is displayed. Then, the first six bytes of the file are displayed. Then, the first nine bytes are skipped and the next seven bytes are displayed. Finally, those same seven bytes are displayed in hexadecimal. Hexadecimal data is displayed in even/odd byte-pairs from the beginning of the file, starting with byte zero. Thus, the L in the data word BLOAD is an odd byte in the file and that byte is skipped. The second O in the data word `FOO` and the carriage return character that follows are added to the displayed byte-pairs. Remember to count the carriage return character (i.e. `0x8D`) because it is an ASCII character as well. `LIST` does not skip over a `NULL` byte (i.e. `0x00`) like those found in Random Access Data files when those files are displayed in ASCII. Random Access Data files should only be displayed in hexadecimal in order to show the complete contents of the records that are contained in those type of data files. The Applesoft file `HELLO` as shown in Figure III.2.10 is first read into memory using the `R` keyword to show its length in bytes, and then the DOS `LIST` command is used to display its first 256 bytes. The first two bytes of this file show that this file has a length of `0x4E7` bytes.

```
]CAT

S=6 D=02 V=000 F=0486 01/01/22 08:28:48

 B 044 DOS4.5          01/01/22 08:28:48
 L 013 INSTALL.L       01/01/22 08:28:48
 B 003 INSTALL         01/01/22 08:28:48
 L 006 MOVEDOS.L       01/01/22 08:28:48
 B 002 DOS1TO2         01/01/22 08:28:48

]LOCK DOS4.5

]CAT

S=6 D=02 V=000 F=0486 01/01/22 08:28:48

*B 044 DOS4.5          01/01/22 08:28:49
 L 013 INSTALL.L       01/01/22 08:28:48
 B 003 INSTALL         01/01/22 08:28:48
 L 006 MOVEDOS.L       01/01/22 08:28:48
 B 002 DOS1TO2         01/01/22 08:28:48

]*
```

Figure III.2.11. LOCK File Command Display

```
]CD = S=6 D=02 V=000 000
]LOCK
]LS R
B=4505H data T=LOCK Figure
M=4505H P=04 L=0xF00A 01/01/22 08:28:48
*S6 D=02 V=000 F=0486 01/01/22 08:28:49
*001 0x1B,0x0F DOS4.5
 002 0x1E,0x0F INSTALL.L
 003 0x1F,0x0F INSTALL
 004 0x20,0x0F MOVEDOS.L
 005 0x21,0x0F DOS1TO2
]DELETE DOS1TO2
Volume Locked
]
```

Figure III.2.12. LOCK Volume Command Display

LOCK	[f] [,Ss][,Dd][,Vv]
Example:	LOCK
	LOCK TEST

This command is available in DOS 3.3 for File System commands. The DOS `LOCK` command **sets** the most significant bit of the `Type` byte of the file `f` in the specified volume as shown in Tables I.7.1 through I.7.3. A locked file cannot be deleted, renamed, or touched until it is unlocked. The lock status of a file is indicated in the volume Catalog by using an asterisk before the `Type` character of the file. The date and time stamp of the file is updated when the file `f` is locked as shown in Figure III.2.11. The date and time stamp for the `VTOC` is **not** updated when a file is locked because nothing is changed in the `VTOC`.

When the DOS `LOCK` command is used without specifying a filename and any keyword parameters in DOS 4.5, the current volume in focus is locked. The `TSL` and data buffers are flushed, the volume `DISKLOCK` byte is **set** as shown in Table I.5.2, the `VTOC` is updated with a current date and time stamp, and the updated `VTOC` is written to the volume. A locked volume may be read at any time but DOS 4.5 cannot write to the volume until the volume is unlocked. In order to specify a particular volume to be locked, precede the `LOCK` command with the DOS `CD` command and utilize its command capabilities in selecting the intended volume to be locked. Figure III.2.12 shows the same volume from Figure III.2.11

after the volume has been locked. Files may not be deleted, renamed, touched, or even saved when a volume is locked by DOS 4.5. On the other hand, files may be read into memory or displayed using the DOS LIST command even when a volume is locked. In Figure III.2.12 the DISKLOCK byte status is shown in the S=6 data with an asterisk, as in *S6. The lock asterisk for a volume is conveniently placed in the first column of the display on the line that contains the date and time stamp for the VTOC, which happens to be the same column that is used to display the lock asterisk for a file when a file is locked. The date and time stamp for the VTOC is updated since the VTOC is changed because the DISKLOCK byte is changed to the lock state (i.e. 0x80). There is **no** harm in locking a volume that is already locked, and conversely, there is **no** harm in unlocking a volume that is already unlocked.

```
RENAME    f, f2 [,Ss][,Dd][,Vv][,R]
MV        f, f2 [,Ss][,Dd][,Vv][,R]              ; UNIX version of RENAME

Example:  RENAME COPYDOS,COPYDOS.EXEC
          mv test1,test2,r
```

This command is available in DOS 3.3 for File System commands. The DOS RENAME command changes the name of the file f to f2 in the specified volume if the file f exists. The date and time stamp of the renamed file is also updated as shown in Figure III.2.13. A locked file cannot be renamed unless the R keyword is used to override the lock status of the file. A file cannot be renamed when it resides in a volume that is locked unless the volume is first unlocked or when CONFIG Bit 4 is **set** that disables all volume and file locks. The VTOC date and time stamp remains **unchanged** when a file is renamed because nothing in the VTOC is changed.

```
TOUCH     [f] [,Ss][,Dd][,Vv][,R]

Example:  TOUCH
          TOUCH,R
          TOUCH TESTFILE
```

This command is not available in DOS 3.3 for File System commands. The DOS TOUCH command updates the date and time stamp of the file f in the specified volume if the file f exists. Figure III.2.14 shows an example in using the DOS TOUCH command. TOUCH cannot update the date and time stamp of a locked file unless the R keyword is used to override the lock status of the file. The VTOC date and time stamp remains **unchanged** when the TOUCH command is used because nothing in the VTOC is changed. This command is implemented by adding the FMTCHCD (i.e. 0x0E) command code to the File Manager Command Code table as shown in Table I.11.2. When the DOS TOUCH command is used without specifying a filename, the date and time stamp of the VTOC is updated for the specified volume. If the R keyword is included with just the TOUCH command followed by a comma, the DOS 4.5 internal variable VALSCNFG as shown in Table I.8.7 is copied to the VTOC variable DOSCONFG as shown in Table I.5.2, the date and time stamp of the VTOC is updated, and the changed VTOC is saved to the specified volume. Using the DOS TOUCH command in this way saves the current DOS configuration variable DOSCONFG to the specified volume. The DOS configuration variable DOSCONFG in the VTOC of a volume cannot be updated when that volume is locked.

```
]LS

S=6 D=02 V=000 F=0488 01/01/21 08:28:48

  B 044 DOS4.5          01/01/21 08:28:48
  L 013 INSTALL.L       01/01/21 08:28:48
  B 003 INSTALL         01/01/21 08:28:48
  L 006 MOVEDOS.L       01/01/21 08:28:48
]RENAME INSTALL,put DOS 4.5

]ls

S=6 D=02 V=000 F=0488 01/01/21 08:28:48

  B 044 DOS4.5          01/01/21 08:28:48
  L 013 INSTALL.L       01/01/21 08:28:48
  B 003 put DOS 4.5     01/01/21 08:28:49
  L 006 MOVEDOS.L       01/01/21 08:28:48
]
```

Figure III.2.13. RENAME Command Display

```
]LS

S=6 D=02 V=000 F=0494 01/01/21 08:28:48

*B 044 DOS4.5          01/01/21 08:28:48
 L 013 INSTALL.L       01/01/21 08:28:48
*B 003 INSTALL         01/01/21 08:28:48
]TOUCH DOS4.5

File Locked

]TOUCH DOS4.5,R

]LS

S=6 D=02 V=000 F=0494 01/01/21 08:28:48

*B 044 DOS4.5          01/01/21 08:28:49
 L 013 INSTALL.L       01/01/21 08:28:48
*B 003 INSTALL         01/01/21 08:28:48
]*
```

Figure III.2.14. TOUCH Command Display

```
]TS A17
0011 0545 05C8 00C4 D4D3 A0C6 E9E7 F5F2
E5A0 A0A0 A0A0 A0A0 A0A0 A0A0 A0A0 A0A0
4828 0822 0101 047A 3412 4828 0822 0101
1101 0000 2310 0001 FFFF 0000 FFFF 0000
FFFF 0000 FFFF 0000 FFFF 0000 FFFF 0000
FFFF 0000 FFFF 0000 FFFF 0000 FFFF 0000
FFFF 0000 FFFF 0000 FFFF 0000 FFFF 0000
FFFF 0000 FFFF 0000 FFFF 0000 FFC0 0000
FFFF 0000 FFFF 0000 FFFF 0000 FFFF 0000
FFFF 0000 FFFF 0000 FFFF 0000 FFFF 0000
FFFF 0000 FFFF 0000 FFFF 0000 FFFF 0000
FFFF 0000 0000 0000 0000 0000 0000 0000
0000 0000 0000 0000 0000 0000 0000 0000
0000 0000 0000 0000 0000 0000 0000 0000
0000 0000 0000 0000 0000 0000 0000 0000
TS = 0x11,0x00

]*
```

Figure III.2.15. TS Command of a VTOC

```
0011 0545 05C8 00C4 D4D3 A0C6 E9E7 F5F2 E5A0 A0A0 A0A0 A0A0 A0A0 A0A0 A0A0 A0A0
4828 0822 0101 047A 3412 4828 0822 0101 1101 0000 2310 0001 FFFF 0000 FFFF 0000
FFFF 0000 FFFF 0000 FFFF 0000 FFFF 0000 FFFF 0000 FFFF 0000 FFFF 0000 FFFF 0000
FFFF 0000 FFFF 0000 FFFF 0000 FFFF 0000 FFFF 0000 FFFF 0000 FFFF 0000 FFC0 0000
FFFF 0000 FFFF 0000 FFFF 0000 FFFF 0000 FFFF 0000 FFFF 0000 FFFF 0000 FFFF 0000
FFFF 0000 FFFF 0000 FFFF 0000 FFFF 0000 FFFF 0000 FFFF 0000 FFFF 0000 FFFF 0000
FFFF 0000 0000 0000 0000 0000 0000 0000 0000 0000 0000 0000 0000 0000 0000 0000
0000 0000 0000 0000 0000 0000 0000 0000 0000 0000 0000 0000 0000 0000 0000 0000

TS = 0x11,0x00

]tsr
0000 0000 0000 0000 0000 0000 0000 0000 0000 0000 0000 0000 0000 0000 0000 0000
0000 0000 0000 0000 0000 0000 0000 0000 0000 0000 0000 0000 0000 0000 0000 0000
0000 0000 0000 0000 0000 0000 0000 0000 0000 0000 0000 0000 0000 0000 0000 0000
0000 0000 0000 0000 0000 0000 0000 0000 0000 0000 0000 0000 0000 0000 0000 0000
0000 0000 0000 0000 0000 0000 0000 0000 0000 0000 0000 0000 0000 0000 0000 0000
0000 0000 0000 0000 0000 0000 0000 0000 0000 0000 0000 0000 0000 0000 0000 0000
0000 0000 0000 0000 0000 0000 0000 0000 0000 0000 0000 0000 0000 0000 0000 0000

TS = 0x11,0x01

]
```

Figure III.2.16. TS Command in 80-Column

TS	[,Ss][,Dd][,Vv][,An][,Bn][,L][,R]
Example:	TS
	TS A$11,B7
	TS L

This command is not available in DOS 3.3 for File System commands. The DOS TS command was originally developed for DOS 4.1 and it displays on the screen the contents of the specified sector in hexadecimal of the specified track for the specified volume. The A keyword is used to specify a track value and the B keyword is used to specify a sector value, and if not included with the TS command, their values are zero. The value n for these keywords may be entered in decimal or in hexadecimal, and range checking is done against the VTOC parameters NUMTRKS (i.e. number of tracks in the volume) and NUMSECS (i.e. number of sectors in a track) of the specified volume. It is critical that a suitable DOS command, like CATALOG for example, has been previously issued to ensure that the VTOC of the specified volume has been read and is currently in memory so that NUMTRKS and NUMSECS have relevant values. If the L or R keyword is included then any A or B keyword is ignored if they happen to be included also. The R keyword takes precedence over the L keyword if both keywords are included. The L keyword displays the previous sector (i.e. to the Left, or down) and the R keyword displays the next sector (i.e. to the Right, or up). Figure III.2.15 shows a typical TS view of an initialized data disk VTOC whose volume contains no files. The sector data is displayed in hexadecimal byte pairs followed by the TS command and the requested track and sector values shown in hexadecimal. The TS command is designed to view two complete sectors of data when the 80-column display is in view as shown in Figure III.2.16. This command is implemented by adding the FMTSCD (i.e. 0x0F) command code to the File Manager Command Code table as shown in Table I.11.2.

```
]LS

S=6 D=02 V=000 F=0486 01/01/22 08:28:48

*B 044 DOS4.5              01/01/22 08:28:48
 L 013 INSTALL.L           01/01/22 08:28:48
 B 003 INSTALL             01/01/22 08:28:48
 L 006 MOVEDOS.L           01/01/22 08:28:48
 B 002 DOS1TO2             01/01/22 08:28:48

]UNLOCK DOS4.5

]LS

S=6 D=02 V=000 F=0486 01/01/22 08:28:48

 B 044 DOS4.5              01/01/22 08:28:49
 L 013 INSTALL.L           01/01/22 08:28:48
 B 003 INSTALL             01/01/22 08:28:48
 L 006 MOVEDOS.L           01/01/22 08:28:48
 B 002 DOS1TO2             01/01/22 08:28:48

]※
```

Figure III.2.17. UNLOCK File Command

```
]LSR

B=4505H data T=UNLOCK Figure 2

M=4505H P=04 L=0xF00A 01/01/22 08:28:48

*S6 D=02 V=000 F=0510 01/01/22 08:28:48

*001 0x12,0x0F DOS4.5

]UNLOCK

]LSR

B=4505H data T=UNLOCK Figure 2

M=4505H P=04 L=0xF00A 01/01/22 08:28:48

S=6 D=02 V=000 F=0510 01/01/22 08:28:49

*001 0x12,0x0F DOS4.5

]
```

Figure III.2.18. UNLOCK Volume Command

UNLOCK   [f] [,Ss][,Dd][,Vv]

Example: UNLOCK
            UNLOCK TEST

This command is available in DOS 3.3 for File System commands. The DOS UNLOCK command **clears** the most significant bit of the Type byte of the file f in the specified volume as shown in Tables I.7.1 through I.7.3. A locked file cannot be deleted, renamed, or touched until it is unlocked. The lock status of a file is indicated in the volume Catalog using an asterisk before the Type character of the file. The date and time stamp of the file is updated when the file f is unlocked as shown in Figure III.2.17. The date and time stamp for the VTOC is **not** updated when a file is unlocked because nothing is changed in the VTOC.

145

When the DOS UNLOCK command is used without specifying a filename and any keyword parameters the current volume in focus is unlocked. The TSL and data buffers are flushed, the volume DISKLOCK byte is **cleared** as shown in Table I.5.2, the VTOC is updated with a current date and time stamp, and the updated VTOC is written to the volume. A locked volume may be read at any time but DOS 4.5 cannot write to the volume until the volume is unlocked. In order to specify a particular volume to be unlocked, precede the UNLOCK command with the DOS CD command and utilize its command capabilities in selecting the intended volume to be unlocked. Figure III.2.18 shows a volume before and after the volume has been unlocked. Files may not be deleted, renamed, touched, or saved when a volume is locked by DOS 4.5. On the other hand, files may be read into memory or displayed using the DOS LIST command even when a volume is locked. In Figure III.2.18 the DISKLOCK byte status is shown in the S=6 data with an asterisk, as in *S6. The lock asterisk for a volume is conveniently placed in the first column of the display on the line that contains the date and time stamp for the VTOC, which happens to be the same column that is used to display the lock asterisk for a file when a file is locked. The date and time stamp for the VTOC is updated since the VTOC is changed because the DISKLOCK byte is changed to the unlock state (i.e. 0x00). There is **no** harm in unlocking a volume that is already unlocked, and conversely, there is **no** harm in locking a volume that is already locked.

```
]cat r
B=4505H data T=URM Figure
M=4505H P=04 L=0xF00D 01/01/21 08:28:48
S=6 D=02 V=000 F=0510 01/01/21 08:28:48
 001 0x12,0x0F DOS4.5
x002 0x15,0x0F INSTALL
]urm INSTALL
]LS
S=6 D=02 V=000 F=0507 01/01/21 08:28:49
 B 044 DOS4.5          01/01/21 08:28:48
 B 003 INSTALL         01/01/21 08:28:48
]※
```

Figure III.2.19. URM Command Display

```
]CAT
S=6 D=02 V=000 F=0507 01/01/21 08:28:48
 B 044 DOS4.5          01/01/21 08:28:48
 B 003 INSTALL         01/01/21 08:28:48
]
]VERIFY DOS4.5
]VERIFY DOS4.5,R1 = 043
]LS
S=6 D=02 V=000 F=0507 01/01/21 08:28:48
 B 044 DOS4.5          01/01/21 08:28:48
 B 003 INSTALL         01/01/21 08:28:48
]※
```

Figure III.2.20. VERIFY Command Display

URM	f [,Ss][,Dd][,Vv]
Example:	URM MOVEDOS

This command is not available in DOS 3.3 for File System commands. The DOS URM command was originally developed for DOS 4.1 and it restores the filename f to the volume Catalog of the specified volume by **clearing** the most significant bit of its TSL track byte, and marking the sectors listed in the TSL sector(s) of the file and all of its TSL sectors as used. Refer to Figure I.7.1 showing a volume Catalog entry. It is prudent to undelete a deleted file as soon as possible before the sectors listed in the TSL sector(s) of the file and any of its TSL sectors are utilized by another file. Even if a file requires multiple TSL sectors, all data sectors and all TSL sectors are restored to the file by the URM command. There is no harm in attempting to undelete a file that is already displayed in the volume Catalog.

Figure III.2.19 shows an example of a deleted file being restored using the DOS URM command. The x before the deleted filename in the first column is now removed once the file is restored and free sectors are reduced by the size in sectors of the restored file. This command is implemented by adding the FMURMCD (i.e. 0x0D) command code to the File Manager Command Code table as shown in Table I.11.2. The DOS 4.5 File Manager handles this command much like the FMDELECD command code. The date and time stamp for the VTOC is updated because the VTOC is changed when a file is restored. The date and time stamp for the restored file is **not** updated even when the URM command is used to restore a file that is already displayed in the volume Catalog.

```
VERIFY    f [,Ss][,Dd][,Vv][,R1]

Example:   VERIFY DOS4.1,R1
```

This command is available in DOS 3.3 for File System commands. The DOS VERIFY command reads into memory each sector listed in the TSL sector(s) of the file f in the specified volume. The read routine in RWTS simply reads each selected sector in order to verify its checksum. No data is copied to another memory location or modified, and the date and time stamp of the file is **not** changed. The TSL sectors are indirectly verified since they are read into a DOS TS buffer and are used to obtain the list of track/sector pairs that point to the data sectors that comprise the file, but they are not included in the verified sector count. Only when a non-zero R keyword is included with the DOS VERIFY command is the number of verified sectors displayed on the Apple Command Line as shown in Figure III.2.20. When a non-zero R keyword is included with the DOS SAVE, BSAVE, LSAVE, and TSAVE commands, not only is the address and length information displayed, but also the number of verified sectors displayed as well. The VTOC and the time stamp of the file remain **unchanged** when a file is verified because nothing in the VTOC or in the file is changed.

If CONFIG Bit 1 is set in order to disable file verification as shown in Table III.1.2, DOS 4.5 bypasses the automatic verification of a file after the file is saved to a volume when using the DOS SAVE, BSAVE, LSAVE, or TSAVE commands. Disabling the automatic verification of a file visibly reduces the amount of time it takes to save a file to a volume, but it eliminates the verification that the file can be read into memory without error.

```
WTS       Ln, Rn [,Ss][,Dd][,Vv][,An][,Bn]

Example:   WTS A17,L4,R3
           WTS L0,R1
```

This command is not available in DOS 3.3 for File System commands. The DOS WTS command was originally developed for DOS 4.3 and it provides the ability to modify a single byte on any sector of the specified volume. The L and R keywords are required by the DOS WTS command, and they provide the sector index and the data byte value, respectively, that is used by WTS to modify the specified sector. As in the DOS TS command, the A keyword is used to specify a track value and the B keyword is used to specify a sector value, and if not included with the WTS command, their values are zero. The value n for all four keywords may be entered in decimal or in hexadecimal. Range checking is done against the A and B keywords for the VTOC parameters NUMTRKS (i.e. number of tracks in the volume) and NUMSECS (i.e. number of sectors in a track), respectively, of the specified volume. It is critical that a suitable DOS command, like CATALOG for example, has been previously issued to ensure that the VTOC of the specified volume has been read and is currently in memory, and NUMTRKS and NUMSECS have relevant values.

Figure III.2.21 shows a Boot Stage 0 sector (sector 0x00 on track 0x00) that has been modified using WTS such that this boot image is no longer valid and the volume no longer boots because the first byte is changed from 0x01 to 0x02. Once WTS modifies the specified byte, WTS saves the sector to the specified volume and then displays the contents of the sector in hexadecimal byte pairs followed by the WTS command and its specified track and sector values. The WTS command is designed to view two complete sectors of data when the 80-column display is in view as shown in Figure III.2.22. In Figure III.2.22 the VTOC sector was first modified at byte 0xF0 with the value of 0x96. Then, the DOS WTS command was used to change byte 0xF0 again, and it restored the byte to its original value of 0x00. The DOS WTS command is implemented by adding the FMWTSCD (i.e. 0x10) command code to the File Manager Command Code table as shown in Table I.11.2.

```
]WTS A0,B0,L0,R2
02A5 2730 1078 8A4A 4A4A 4A09 C08D 3008
ADFE 0885 272C 8BC0 2C8B C0AC FF08 3011
CEFF 08D0 04A9 BE85 27B9 3408 853D 4C5C
C04C 44BF 000D 0B09 0705 0301 0E0C 0A08
0604 020F 8EC3 BF20 4DD6 A200 A00B 2090
BFA9 F020 28E6 F006 20BB BE20 4DD6 2C81
C0A2 FF9A 8EFB 048E 0CC0 8E0E C020 84FE
202F FB20 93FE 2089 FEAD 00E0 C94C D00D
20C4 BE20 DCD5 384C 07D0 2C81 C04C 65FF
BDE5 BF9D C4BF E888 D0F6 A21A 8635 20BB
BE20 71D2 B0E4 CEC7 BF10 08CE C6BF A90F
8DC7 BFEE CBBF D005 A9E0 8DCB BFC6 35D0
DD60 0160 0100 0000 0000 0000 0000 0000
0000 0000 00C0 E900 0000 00A8 E900 00A0
EEA0 EDA0 EC01 0002 0900 0000 F004 0001
4505 4DBE 53BE 59BE 58BF E2BE E5DE D00F

WTS = 0x00,0x00

]
```

Figure III.2.21. WTS Command Display

```
0011 0545 05C8 7BC2 D4E5 F3F4 A0D6 EFEC F5ED E5A0 C2EF EFF4 A0A0 A0A0 A0A0 A0A0
4828 0822 0101 047A 2301 4828 0822 0101 1D01 0000 2310 0001 0000 0000 0000 0000
0C00 0000 FFFF 0000 FFFF 0000 FFFF 0000 FFFF 0000 FFFF 0000 FFFF 0000 FFF0 0000
FFFF 0000 FFFF 0000 FFFF 0000 FFFF 0000 FFFF 0000 FFFF 0000 FFFF 0000 FFC0 0000
03FF 0000 0000 0000 0000 0000 0000 0000 0000 0000 0000 0000 0000 0000 0000 0000
3FFF 0000 03FF 0000 03FF 0000 03FF 0000 FFFF 0000 FFFF 0000 FFFF 0000 FFFF 0000
FFFF 0000 0000 0000 0000 0000 0000 0000 0000 0000 0000 0000 0000 0000 0000 0000
0000 0000 0000 0000 0000 0000 0000 0000 9600 0000 0000 0000 0000 0000 0000 0000

WTS = 0x11,0x00

]wts a17,1$f0,r
0011 0545 05C8 7BC2 D4E5 F3F4 A0D6 EFEC F5ED E5A0 C2EF EFF4 A0A0 A0A0 A0A0 A0A0
4828 0822 0101 047A 2301 4828 0822 0101 1D01 0000 2310 0001 0000 0000 0000 0000
0C00 0000 FFFF 0000 FFFF 0000 FFFF 0000 FFFF 0000 FFFF 0000 FFFF 0000 FFF0 0000
FFFF 0000 FFFF 0000 FFFF 0000 FFFF 0000 FFFF 0000 FFFF 0000 FFFF 0000 FFC0 0000
03FF 0000 0000 0000 0000 0000 0000 0000 0000 0000 0000 0000 0000 0000 0000 0000
3FFF 0000 03FF 0000 03FF 0000 FFFF 0000 FFFF 0000 FFFF 0000 FFFF 0000 FFFF 0000
FFFF 0000 0000 0000 0000 0000 0000 0000 0000 0000 0000 0000 0000 0000 0000 0000
0000 0000 0000 0000 0000 0000 0000 0000 0000 0000 0000 0000 0000 0000 0000 0000

WTS = 0x11,0x00

]
```

Figure III.2.22. WTS Command in 80-Column

Command	Command Syntax
CHAIN	f [,Ss][,Dd][,Vv][,Ll][,R]
LOAD	f [,Ss][,Dd][,Vv][,R]
RUN	f [,Ss][,Dd][,Vv][,Ll]
SAVE	f [,Ss][,Dd][,Vv][,B][,R[1]]

Table III.3.1. Applesoft File Commands in DOS 4.5

3. Applesoft File Commands

The DOS 4.5 Applesoft File commands consist of those commands that only manage Applesoft files. The syntax of the Applesoft File commands is shown in Table III.3.1. All of the Applesoft File commands except for the CHAIN command are permitted to be used from within an Applesoft or a Binary program file as well as on the Apple Command Line.

```
]load START
]list

 10 D$ =  CHR$ (4):AB = 123:CD% =
    456:EF$ = "Test Chain" + ""
 20 PRINT : PRINT "This is the S
    TART program to test CHAIN":
    PRINT
 30 PRINT "AB = ";AB;", CD% = ";
    CD%;",  EF$ = ";EF$: PRINT
 40 PRINT D$;"CHAIN PROGRAM2"

]load PROGRAM2
]list

 10  PRINT : PRINT "Now running p
     rogram PROGRAM2": PRINT
 20  PRINT "AB = ";AB;", CD% = ";
     CD%;",  EF$ = ";EF$
 30  PRINT D$;"CATALOG": PRINT

]
```

Figure III.3.1. Listing of START & PROGRAM2

```
]run START
This is the START program to test CHAIN
AB = 123, CD% = 456, EF$ = Test Chain

Now running program PROGRAM2
AB = 123, CD% = 456, EF$ = Test Chain

S=6 D=02 V=000 F=0550 01/01/22 08:28:48
 A 002 START           01/01/22 08:28:48
 A 002 PROGRAM2        01/01/22 08:28:48
]*
```

Figure III.3.2. Output of START & PROGRAM2

CHAIN   f [,Ss][,Dd][,Vv][,Ll][,R]

Example: CHAIN TESTPART2,D2

This command is not available in DOS 3.3 for Applesoft File commands. The DOS CHAIN command was originally developed for DOS 4.1 The CHAIN command can only be used from within an Applesoft program. The command will LOAD and then RUN the Applesoft program f in the specified volume in a unique way: it does not clear the value(s) of any previous Applesoft program variable(s). Therefore, the program f can utilize the data and the results from the previous program(s) and program f can provide its data and its results to any following program that is run by CHAIN. If the L keyword is included with the CHAIN command, processing begins at that line number in program f only if that line number exists, otherwise Applesoft reports an error and it terminates processing. This capability opens up a myriad of programming possibilities. If the R keyword is **not** used with the CHAIN command, the CHAIN handler calls the Applesoft ROM routine GARBAG at memory address 0xE484 before the CHAIN handler moves the Simple Variable and Array Variable descriptors to their new location found at the end of program f. Using the R keyword bypasses GARBAG and it allows the user to utilize another method or process for character string garbage collection before or after using the CHAIN command. It is critical that the program calling CHAIN to locate (i.e. cause to move) all of its simple character string variables and character string array variables that are used in the next program to the Character String Pool memory area where character string data is safely stored before using CHAIN. See Section I.15 for a more thorough discussion of the DOS CHAIN command.

Figure III.3.1 shows two Applesoft programs called START and PROGRAM2. START defines four simple variables D$, AB, CD%, and EF$. The character string variable EF$ is defined in such a way as to force Applesoft to locate it immediately into the Character String Pool memory area where character string data is safely stored. Applesoft also moves the variable D$ to the Character String Pool memory area before the variable is used with the CHAIN command. All four variables are available to program PROGRAM2 when CHAIN is used as shown in Figure III.3.2 after the program START is RUN.

Table I.15.1 shows the definition of the descriptor for simple variables that are used in Applesoft programs. The character string descriptor consists of only the first two characters of the character string name (so care must be given in naming variables), the character string length, the address in low/high byte order where that character string resides in memory, and two zero filler bytes. Character string descriptors for array variables are shown in Table I.15.2 and each character string element contains the character string length and the address in low/high byte order where that character string resides in memory. The address in the character string descriptor or in the character string element is initially the location where the actual character string data exists within the contents of the Applesoft program. Once CHAIN has replaced the current Applesoft program in memory with the next Applesoft program specified by file f, the actual character string data is overwritten and lost, and its address now becomes invalid. Therefore, caution must be exercised when using character string variables and CHAIN when the character string variables are **not** moved to the Character String Pool memory area and safely stored in that memory location for general access.

LOAD	f [,Ss][,Dd][,Vv][,R]
Example	LOAD HELLO
	LOAD HELLO,R

This command is available in DOS 3.3 for Applesoft File commands. The DOS LOAD command reads the Applesoft program file f in the specified volume into memory at address 0x0801. Applesoft program files are file Type 0x02 as shown in Table I.7.3. This command also processes A Type files (i.e. Type 0x20) as an Applesoft program similarly as in DOS 3.3. If the R keyword is included with the LOAD command, the memory load address (i.e. 0x0801) and the number of bytes loaded (i.e. 0x0494 in this example) are displayed as shown in Figure III.3.3.

RUN	f [,Ss][,Dd][,Vv][,Ll]
Example:	RUN
	RUN START

This command is available in DOS 3.3 for Applesoft File commands. The DOS RUN command reads the Applesoft program file f in the specified volume into memory at address 0x0801 and begins program execution. DOS 4.5 calls ASROMCLR at ROM memory address 0xD665 in order to initialize all Applesoft pointers that include PRGEND, VARTAB, ARYTAB, and STREND. DOS 4.5 then calls ASROMSET at ROM memory address 0xD955 in order to initialize LINNUM, clears the PROMPT and

ASONERR flags, and finally jumps to ASROMNEW at ROM memory address 0xD7D2 to begin program execution. If the L keyword is included with the RUN command, processing begins at that line number in program f only if that line number exists, otherwise Applesoft reports an error and immediately terminates processing. An example of using the RUN command was shown previously in Figure III.3.2.

```
]CATALOG
S=6 D=02 V=000 F=0506 01/01/22 08:28:48
 A 006 HELLO            01/01/22 08:28:48
]LOAD HELLO
]LOAD HELLO,R
A$0801,L$0494
]SAVE HELLO2
]SAVE HELLO2,R
A$0801,L$0494
]SAVE HELLO2,R1
A$0801,L$0494 = 005
]
```

Figure III.3.3. LOAD and SAVE Commands

```
]load HELLO
]save HELLO3
]save HELLO3,r1
A$0801,L$0494 = 005
]config 2
]config = 002
]save HELLO3,r1
A$0801,L$0494
]config,r
]config = 000
]*
```

Figure III.3.4. SAVE Commands Display

SAVE   f [,Ss][,Dd][,Vv][,B][,R[1]]

Example: SAVE HELLO2
           SAVE HELLO2,R
           SAVE HELLO2,R1

This command is available in DOS 3.3 for Applesoft File commands. The DOS SAVE command saves the Applesoft program file f to the specified volume. If the R keyword is included with the SAVE command, the save address (i.e. 0x0801) and the number of bytes saved (i.e. 0x0494 in the example) are displayed as shown previously in Figure III.3.3. If a non-zero R keyword is included, the number of verified sectors is also displayed after the number of bytes saved as shown previously in Figure III.3.3. The B keyword can be used with the SAVE command to implement the *File Delete/File Save* strategy. That is, the Applesoft program file f is deleted from the volume Catalog and then saved to the same volume in order to ensure that the TSL sectors of the file contain only those track/sector entries that are required and utilized by the file. If CONFIG Bit 1 is set the Applesoft program file is not verified after it is saved. Figure III.3.4 shows that even when a non-zero R keyword is used with the DOS SAVE command, no sectors are verified. The VALSCNFG variable as shown in Table I.8.7 can be cleared by using the R keyword with the DOS CONFIG command followed by a comma as shown in Figure III.3.4.

Command	Command Syntax
BLOAD	f [,Ss][,Dd][,Vv][,Aa][,R]
BRUN	f [,Ss][,Dd][,Vv][,Aa]
BSAVE	f [,Ss][,Dd][,Vv][,Aa][,B][,Ll][,R[1]]
LLOAD	f [,Ss][,Dd][,Vv][,Aa][,R]
LSAVE	f [,Ss][,Dd][,Vv][,Aa][,B][,Ll][,R[1]]

Table III.4.1. Binary File Commands in DOS 4.5

4. Binary File Commands

The DOS 4.5 Binary File commands consist of those commands that manage Binary data or assembly language files. The syntax of the Binary File commands is shown in Table III.4.1. All of the Binary File commands are permitted to be used from within an Applesoft or a Binary program file as well as on the Apple Command Line.

BLOAD   f [,Ss][,Dd][,Vv][,Aa][,R]

Example: BLOAD RD
            BLOAD RD,R
            BLOAD RD,A$1000,R

This command is available in DOS 3.3 for Binary File commands. The DOS BLOAD command reads the Binary file f in the specified volume into memory at address a if the A keyword is included. If the A keyword is not included, the Binary file f is read into memory at the address the file was originally saved or last saved. Binary files are file Type 0x04 as shown in Table I.7.3. If the R keyword is included with the DOS BLOAD command, the memory load address and the number of bytes read into memory are displayed as shown in Figure III.4.1.

BRUN   f [,Ss][,Dd][,Vv][,Aa]

Example: BRUN INSTALL
            BRUN INSTALL,A$1000

This command is available in DOS 3.3 for Binary File commands. The DOS BRUN command reads the Binary file f in the specified volume into memory at address a if the A keyword is included, and begins program execution at address a. If the A keyword is not included, the Binary file f is loaded into memory at the address the file was originally saved or last saved, and execution begins at that address. In DOS 4.5 the DOSWARM address is pushed onto the stack before processing an indirect jump to ADRVAL, the Binary file memory load address, to guarantee that DOS 4.5 is in control when the Binary program exits. In order to disable this unique feature of DOS 4.5, simply **set** CONFIG Bit 5 as shown in Table III.1.2 before using the DOS BRUN command. Figure III.4.2 shows an example of using the DOS BRUN command that begins processing immediately after the file has been read into memory.

```
]BLOAD RD,R
A$4000,L$1B00
]BLOAD RD,A$1000,R
A$1000,L$1B00
]BSAVE RD2
]BSAVE RD3,R
A$1000,L$1B00
]BSAVE RD4,A$4000,L$1B00,R1
A$4000,L$1B00 = 028
]DIFF RD,RD4 = 0x1C00

]
```

Figure III.4.1. BLOAD and BSAVE Commands

```
]BRUN INSTALL
Reading DOS 4.5H image into memory.

DOS 4.5H image now in memory.

Insert diskette into Slot 6, Drive 2.
Press any key to continue.

Installing DOS 4.5H.
. . . . . . . . . . . . . . . . . . . . . . . . . . . . . . . . . . . . . . . . .
. .

Installation of DOS 4.5H is complete.

]
```

Figure III.4.2. BRUN Command Display

BSAVE   f [,Ss][,Dd][,Vv][,Aa][,B][,Ll][,R[1]]

Example: BSAVE RD2
               BSAVE RD2,R
               BSAVE RD3,A$4000,L$1C00,R1

This command is available in DOS 3.3 for Binary File commands. The DOS BSAVE command saves the Binary file f to the specified volume using the memory address a and the length l in bytes if the A and L keywords are included. In DOS 4.5 these keywords are **optional**, but if they are included both values are required. If the A and L keywords are not included, the address a and the length l values of the previous BLOAD or BSAVE command are used. If the R keyword is included with the DOS BSAVE command, the memory save address and the number of bytes written to the specified volume are displayed as shown previously in Figure III.4.1. If a non-zero R keyword is included, the number of verified sectors is also displayed as shown in Figure III.4.1. If CONFIG Bit 1 is **set** the Binary file is not verified after it is saved as shown previously for the DOS SAVE command in Figure III.3.4.

Figure III.4.1 shows a byte comparison of the two files RD and RD4 using the DOS DIFF command. The DIFF command proves that both of these saved files are identical because no differences are shown. The B keyword can be used with the DOS BSAVE command to implement the *File Delete/File Save* strategy. That is, the Binary file f is deleted from the volume Catalog and then saved to the same volume in order to ensure that the TSL sectors of the file contain only those track/sector entries that are required and utilized by the file.

```
LLOAD      f [,Ss][,Dd][,Vv][,Aa][,R]
```

Example: LLOAD README.L
           LLOAD README.L,R
           LLOAD README.L,A$1000,R

This command is not available in DOS 3.3 for Binary File commands. The DOS LLOAD command was originally developed for DOS 4.1 and it reads into memory the *Lisa* Binary file f in the specified volume at memory address a if the A keyword is included. If the A keyword is not included with the DOS LLOAD command, the *Lisa* file is read into memory at the address the file was originally saved or last saved. *Lisa* files are file Type 0x40 as shown in Table I.7.3. If the R keyword is included with the DOS LLOAD command, the memory load address and the number of bytes read into memory are displayed as shown in Figure III.4.3.

```
]LLOAD README.L,R
A$3800,L$1627
]LLOAD README.L,A$1000,R
A$1000,L$1627
]LSAVE README2.L
]LSAVE README3.L,R
A$1000,L$1627
]LSAVE README4.L,A$3800,L$1627,R1
A$3800,L$1627 = 023
]DIFF README.L,README4.L = 0x1700

]
```

Figure III.4.3. LLOAD and LSAVE Commands

```
LSAVE      f [,Ss][,Dd][,Vv][,Aa][,B][,Ll][,R[1]]
```

Example: LSAVE README2.L
           LSAVE README2.L,R
           LSAVE README3.L,A$2100,L$CED,R1

This command is not available in DOS 3.3 for Binary File commands. The DOS LSAVE command was originally developed for DOS 4.1 and it saves the *Lisa* Binary file f to the specified volume using the memory address a and the length l if the A and L keywords are included. In DOS 4.5 these keywords are **optional**, but if they are included both values are required. If the A and L keywords are not included, the address a and the length l of the previous LLOAD or LSAVE command are used. If the R keyword is included with the DOS LSAVE command, the memory save address and the number of bytes saved to the specified volume are displayed as shown in Figure III.4.3. If a non-zero R keyword is included, the number of verified sectors is also displayed as shown in Figure III.4.3. If CONFIG Bit 1 is **set** the

154

Binary file is not verified after it is saved as shown previously for the DOS SAVE command in Figure III.3.4.

Figure III.4.3 shows a byte comparison of the two files README.L and README4.L using the DOS DIFF command. The DIFF command proves that both of these saved files are identical because no differences are shown. The B keyword can be used with the DOS LSAVE command to implement the *File Delete/File Save* strategy. That is, the *Lisa* Binary file f is deleted from the volume Catalog and then saved to the same volume in order to ensure that the TSL sectors of the file contain only those track/sector entries that are required and utilized by the file.

Command	Command Syntax
APPEND*	f [,Ss][,Dd][,Vv]
CLOSE	[f]
EXEC	f [,Ss][,Dd][,Vv][,Rr]
OPEN*	f [,Ss][,Dd][,Vv]
POSITION*	f [,Rr]
READ*	f [,Bb]
TLOAD	f [,Ss][,Dd][,Vv][,A][,Bb][,Ll][,R]
TSAVE	f [,Ss][,Dd][,Vv][,B][,R[1]]
TW	f [,Ss][,Dd][,Vv]
WRITE*	f [,Bb]

Table III.5.1. Sequential Text File Commands in DOS 4.5

5. Sequential Text File Commands

The DOS 4.5 Sequential Text File commands consist of those commands that manage sequential Text files. The syntax of the Sequential Text File commands is shown in Table III.5.1. All Sequential Text File commands are permitted to be used from within an Applesoft or Binary program file and those commands shown without an asterisk in Table III.5.1 are also permitted to be used on the Apple Command Line. Those commands shown **with** an asterisk are **not** permitted to be used on the Apple Command Line. Sequential Text files are comprised of sequential records of ASCII characters where a RETURN character (i.e. 0x8D) terminates each record, and a NULL character (i.e. 0x00) terminates the file. DOS 4.5 differentiates between sequential Text files and random-access Data files in how the file is opened. If the L keyword is **not** included with the DOS OPEN command, the file is treated as a sequential Text file and the DOS READ and WRITE commands **must not include** the R keyword as shown in Table III.5.1. See Table III.6.1 that shows the DOS 4.5 random-access Data file READ and WRITE commands in order to understand how those commands are syntactically different from the DOS 4.5 sequential Text file READ and WRITE commands.

Data may be read from or written to a sequential Text file immediately after the file is opened, after the file pointer has been positioned to a particular byte location, or after the file pointer has been positioned to a particular record location. If the B keyword is included with the DOS READ or WRITE command, that keyword takes precedence over any previous POSITION command. That is, even though the file pointer may be positioned at the beginning of the rth record as specified by a previous POSITION command, the B keyword, if it is included with a subsequent DOS READ or WRITE command, forces the recalculation of the file pointer location so that the pointer now points to the bth byte relative to the beginning of the file.

Many DOS commands utilize the File Manager to open a Text file, which is handled by the Common Open routine CMNOPEN. This routine initializes the File Manager workarea, checks if the RECNUM value as shown in Table I.11.1 is zero, and allocates a new file if the requested filename is not found in the volume Catalog. If RECNUM equals zero, DOS 3.3 sets the value of OPNRCLEN as shown in Table I.12.2 to 0x0001. On the other hand, when RECNUM equals zero, DOS 4.5 sets the value of OPNRCLEN equal to 0x0100. This is a far better and more logical design because Text file records are rarely, if ever one byte in size, and using 0x0100 for an initial record size is far closer to reality.

```
]LOAD STEST
]LIST

 10 D$ =   CHR$ (4):F$ = "STEST.T"
    : ONERR  GOTO 100
 20   PRINT D$;"OPEN ";F$
 30   PRINT D$;"WRITE ";F$
 40   PRINT "This is a sequential
      TEXT file."
 50   PRINT D$;"CLOSE ";F$
 100  END

]RUN

]LIST STEST.T

This is a sequential TEXT file.

]*
```

Figure III.5.1. OPEN, WRITE, and CLOSE

```
]LOAD STEST2
]LIST

 10 D$ =   CHR$ (4):F$ = "STEST.T"
    : ONERR  GOTO 100
 20   PRINT D$;"OPEN ";F$
 30   PRINT D$;"APPEND ";F$
 40   PRINT D$;"WRITE ";F$
 50   PRINT "This is an appended 1
      ine."
 60   PRINT D$;"CLOSE ";F$
 100  END

]RUN

]LIST STEST.T

This is a sequential TEXT file.
This is an appended line.

]
```

Figure III.5.2. APPEND Command Display

APPEND   f [,Ss][,Dd][,Vv]

Example: APPEND STEST.T

This command is available in DOS 3.3 for Sequential Text File commands. The DOS APPEND command opens the sequential Text file f in the specified volume if it is not already open. The APPEND command must be followed by a WRITE command for the same file f. The APPEND command reads the entire file f and then positions the file pointer at the first NULL character (i.e. 0x00) it finds in the file. All subsequent input data is written to the file beginning at that location in the file. Figure III.5.1 shows an example Applesoft program that uses the OPEN, WRITE, and CLOSE commands in order to create the sequential Text file STEST.T. Figure III.5.2 shows another example Applesoft program that is similar to the program shown in Figure III.5.1 except that this program uses the DOS APPEND command to add more information to the sequential Text file STEST.T.

The APPEND command is flawed in several locations in DOS 3.3 which requires multiple software patches in order to correct the flawed manipulation of the internal variable BYTOFFST and the File

156

Manager Context Block variable RECNUM. DOS 4.5 manipulates these variables correctly within the File Manager driver routine FMDRVR and in the Common Open routine CMNOPEN. The original DOS 3.3 Calculate Position routine CALPOSN fails to ensure that the Carry flag is clear before it manipulates its variables in order to calculate the requested file position within a sequential Text file. DOS 4.5 guarantees that the Calculate Position routine does manage the Carry flag correctly in order to manipulate all of the routine variables correctly in order to calculate the requested file position within a sequential Text file with mathematical precision.

CLOSE   [f]

Example: CLOSE
           CLOSE STEST.T

This command is available in DOS 3.3 for Sequential Text File commands. The DOS CLOSE command flushes and de-allocates the file buffer associated with the sequential Text file f, thereby closing the file from any further data input or data output. The File Manager CLOSE handler CLSHNDLR utilizes two routines, CHKBUF and CHKTSL, that test whether two specific bits are set or clear in the DSKFLAGS variable, DATAFLAG and TSLFLAG. See Table I.12.2 showing DSKFLAGS where DATAFLAG has a value of 0x40 and TSLFLAG has a value of 0x80. If either one of these two bits are **set**, either the current data buffer or the TSL buffer needs to be written to the volume currently in focus. DSKFLAGS also contains a bit reserved for CATFLAG having a value of 0x02, and if that bit is **set** the VTOC and/or Catalog buffer needs to be written to the volume currently in focus. This process is referred to as *flushing a file buffer*.

In DOS 4.5 the process of closing a file after the data and TSL buffers have been written to the volume in focus, also includes updating the file size from SECCNT and updating the time and date stamp of the file so that the Catalog buffer that includes these file updates can be written to the volume. All buffer resources allocated to the sequential Text file f are relinquished when a zero is written to the first character of FNAME that corresponds to the filename that was used in the initial DOS OPEN command.

If a filename is not supplied with the DOS CLOSE command, **all** open files regardless of their file type are closed except for an open EXEC file. If a file f is open for data input, a CLOSE command forces all of the remaining data in the data buffer of the file to be written to the file and then the file f is closed. Figures III.5.1 and III.5.2 show examples of using the DOS CLOSE command in an Applesoft program.

EXEC   f [,Ss][,Dd][,Vv][,Rr]

Example: EXEC ETEST.T
           EXEC ETEST.T,R3

This command is available in DOS 3.3 for Sequential Text File commands. The DOS EXEC command opens the file f in the specified volume with the expectation of reading either Applesoft commands or DOS 4.5 commands as if the commands have been issued from the Apple Command Line. There can be only one active `EXEC` file, but an `EXEC` file may transfer its control to another `EXEC` file. If the `R` keyword is included with the DOS `EXEC` command, the file pointer is positioned that number of ASCII records `r` from the beginning of the file. `EXEC` files are sequential Text files that are composed of sequential records that are terminated with a `RETURN` character (i.e. `0x8D`). Figure III.5.3 shows an example of an `EXEC` file and its output.

There is one obvious and undesirable feature in Figure III.5.3, and that is the presence of the `PROMPT` character `]` on nearly every line of the `EXEC` file output. I vividly remember my co-worker in 1982 asking me "Why? Why is that `PROMPT` character there in first place?" Now, I can honestly answer that question! In `EXEC` file processing DOS always prepares the Apple Command Line for the next command to be typed immediately after DOS has output the `RETURN` character after processing has completed for the previous command. Thus, DOS outputs the `PROMPT` character `]`. The `EXEC` file proceeds to *type in* the data for the next command to be processed after the `PROMPT` character. When `CONFIG` Bit 2 is **set** in order to disable the printing of the `PROMPT` character `]` during `EXEC` processing as shown in Table III.1.2, DOS 4.5 simply bypasses the routine that prints the `PROMPT` character whenever there is an active `EXEC` file. The same `EXEC` file is processed again in Figure III.5.4 with `CONFIG` Bit 2 **set** and the `PROMPT` character `]` is not printed during `EXEC` processing. There is a remarkable difference in the look of the screen output.

Also shown in Figure III.5.4 is the `R` keyword utilization for DOS `EXEC` processing where the file pointer is positioned at the first character after counting three `RETURN` characters, thus ignoring those records. All subsequent commands are issued from that point on in the `EXEC` file. That is, the first three commands in the `EXEC` file `ETEST.T` are skipped and only the date and time are printed.

If the DOS `MAXFILES` command is used in an `EXEC` file, `EXEC` command processing terminates immediately and the `EXEC` file is closed. The DOS `MAXFILES` command causes all of file buffers to be regenerated and `HIMEM` to be reset. Since the DOS `EXEC` command utilizes a file buffer, `EXEC` cannot continue processing after its file buffer has been regenerated. In both Figures III.5.3 and III.5.4 command line spacing is set to single spacing while an `EXEC` file is open. DOS 4.5 returns to double spacing between successive DOS commands when the `EXEC` file is closed unless `CONFIG` Bit 0 is **set**.

```
]LIST ETEST.T

print "This is ETEST running."
mon c
brun BTEST
date

]EXEC ETEST.T
]
This is ETEST running.

]

]
This is an example Binary program.
Clock data:  01/01/22 08:28:48
End of Binary program.

] = 01/01/22 08:28:48
]

]
```

```
]CONFIG 4

]EXEC ETEST.T

This is ETEST running.


This is an example Binary program.
Clock data:  01/01/22 08:28:48
End of Binary program.

 = 01/01/22 08:28:48

]EXEC ETEST.T,R3
 = 01/01/22 08:28:48

]CONFIG,R

]*
```

Figure III.5.3. EXEC Command Display   Figure III.5.4. No PROMPT, EXEC,Rr Display

OPEN   f [,Ss][,Dd][,Vv]

Example: OPEN STEST.T

This command is available in DOS 3.3 for Sequential Text File commands. The DOS OPEN command allocates one of an available file buffers, which is 581 (i.e. 0x245) bytes in size, for the sequential Text file f in the specified volume. This file buffer is initialized to read from or write to the beginning of file f. If this file does not exist in the specified volume, file f is created and an entry is made into the volume Catalog. If this file is already open, the file is flushed so that any remaining data in its data buffer is written to the file before the file is closed, and the specified file is again opened. Previous Figures III.5.1 and III.5.2 show examples in using the DOS OPEN command to open a sequential Text File in an Applesoft program. The L keyword must **not** be included with the DOS OPEN command when reading from or writing to a sequential Text file.

POSITION f [,Rr]

Example: POSITION STEST.T,R1

This command is available in DOS 3.3 for Sequential Text File commands. The DOS POSITION command reads the file f and counts that number of ASCII records r ahead relative to the current file pointer position. A record is a sequence of ASCII characters terminated with a RETURN character (i.e. 0x8D). Figure III.5.5 shows an example Applesoft program where the file pointer is positioned at the first character after counting one RETURN character relative to the beginning of the file STEST.T. This POSITION command directly follows a DOS OPEN command for this particular sequential Text file. Otherwise, the file pointer would be positioned that number of ASCII records r ahead relative to the current file pointer position wherever that file pointer position may currently occur within the file f.

```
]LIST STEST.T
This is a sequential TEXT file.
This is an appended line.

]LOAD STEST3
]LIST

 10 D$ =   CHR$ (4):F$ = "STEST.T"
    : ONERR  GOTO 100
 20  PRINT D$;"OPEN ";F$
 30  PRINT D$;"POSITION ";F$;",R1
    "
 40  PRINT D$;"READ ";F$
 50  INPUT A$: PRINT A$
 60  GOTO 50
 100  PRINT D$;"CLOSE ";F$: END

]RUN
This is an appended line.

]
```

```
]LIST STEST.T
This is a sequential TEXT file.
This is an appended line.

]LOAD STEST4
]LIST

 10 D$ =   CHR$ (4):F$ = "STEST.T"
    : ONERR  GOTO 100
 20  PRINT D$;"OPEN ";F$
 30  PRINT D$;"READ ";F$;",B3"
 40  INPUT A$: PRINT A$
 50  GOTO 40
 100  PRINT D$;"CLOSE ";F$: END

]RUN
s is a sequential TEXT file.
This is an appended line.

]※
```

Figure III.5.5. POSITION and READ Commands   Figure III.5.6. READ,Bb Command Display

READ   f [,Bb]

Example: READ STEST.T

This command is available in DOS 3.3 for Sequential Text File commands. The DOS READ command configures the sequential Text file buffer for file f such that all input data is read from that file. If the B keyword is included with the DOS READ command, the file pointer position is located that many actual bytes b from the beginning of the file before any data is read from the file. Figure III.5.6 shows an example Applesoft program that uses the DOS READ command to read a sequential Text file with a byte b offset. Any previous DOS POSITION command and calculated file pointer position value is ignored when the B keyword is included with the DOS READ command, and a new file pointer position is recalculated and utilized.

TLOAD   f [,Ss][,Dd][,Vv][,A][,Bb][,Ll][,R]

Example: TLOAD ETEST.T,L31
TLOAD STEST,A,R
TLOAD ETEST.T,A,B31

This command is not available in DOS 3.3 for Sequential Text File commands. The DOS TLOAD command was originally developed for DOS 4.1 and it reads into memory the sequential Text file f in the specified volume to memory address 0x0900. Memory address 0x0900 is internal to DOS 4.5 and its value is not a parameter and, therefore, its value cannot be changed. If the A keyword is included in a subsequent DOS TLOAD command, that sequential Text file f is appended to the sequential Text file(s) already in memory as long as the internal variable FILELAST+1 is not zero. If FILELAST+1 is zero (meaning a sequential Text file is not yet in memory) and the A keyword is included, the Text file f is read into memory to memory address 0x0900. If the B keyword is included with the DOS TLOAD command, that number of bytes b is skipped before reading the remaining contents of the file into memory. If the L keyword is included with the DOS TLOAD command, that number of bytes l is read into memory, or until the end of the file if that should occur first. If the R keyword is included with the DOS TLOAD command, the start address and the total number of bytes of Text data that currently resides in memory is displayed once the TLOAD command completes its processing.

In Figure III.5.7 the first thirty-one bytes of the file ETEST.T are read into memory to memory address 0x0900. The entire contents of the file STEST.T is read into memory next and appended to the previous Text data already in memory because the A keyword is included. The total Text data that now resides in memory is shown to be 0x59 (i.e. 89) bytes. Finally, the first thirty-one bytes of the file ETEST.T are skipped and the remaining contents of the file ETEST.T is appended to all of the previous Text data that is already in memory. The complete sequential Text data is written to the file TOTAL.T, and the entire file of 0x6F (i.e. 111) bytes is displayed using the DOS LIST command. It is quite apparent that a complete sequential Text file may be easily created by extracting pieces of other sequential Text files using the TLOAD command and its very powerful set of keywords.

```
]TLOAD ETEST.T,L31
]TLOAD STEST.T,A,R
A$0900,L$0059
]TLOAD ETEST.T,A,B31
]TSAVE TOTAL.T,R1
A$0900,L$006F = 001
]LIST TOTAL.T
print "This is ETEST running."
This is a sequential TEXT file.
This is an appended line.
mon c
brun BTEST
date

]
```

```
]LIST TEST.T
PRINT "This is TEST.T running."
PRINT "Ready to run BTEST."
BRUN BTEST

]TW TEST.T
>DATE
>
]LIST TEST.T
PRINT "This is TEST.T running."
PRINT "Ready to run BTEST."
BRUN BTEST
DATE

]※
```

Figure III.5.7. TLOAD and TSAVE Commands   Figure III.5.8. TW Command Display

---

TSAVE   f [,Ss][,Dd][,Vv][,B][,R[1]]

Example: TSAVE TOTAL.T,R
           TSAVE TOTAL2.T,R1

This command is not available in DOS 3.3 for Sequential Text File commands. The DOS TSAVE command was originally developed for DOS 4.1 and it saves the sequential Text data currently in memory to the file f in the specified volume. The start address and total number of bytes of Text data currently in memory is internal to DOS 4.5 and uses the variables FILESTRT and FILELEN in the CMDVALS Data structure as shown in Table I.12.1. If the R keyword is included with the DOS TSAVE command, the start address and total number of bytes of sequential Text data currently in memory is displayed as shown in Figure III.5.7 once the TSAVE command completes its processing. If a non-zero R keyword is included with the DOS TSAVE command, the number of verified sectors is also displayed. If CONFIG Bit 1 is **set** the Text file f is not verified after it is saved. The B keyword can be used with the DOS TSAVE command to implement the *File Delete/File Save* strategy. That is, the Text file f is deleted from the volume Catalog and then saved to the same volume in order to ensure that the TSL sectors of the file contain only those track/sector entries that are required and utilized by the file.

TW   f [,Ss][,Dd][,Vv]

Example: TW ETEST

This command is not available in DOS 3.3 for Sequential Text File commands. The DOS TW command was originally developed for DOS 4.1 and it records all keystrokes typed on the Apple Command Line after the PROMPT character > into the data buffer of the sequential Text file f in the specified volume. If the file does not exist in the specified volume, the file f is created, otherwise the file is always opened in APPEND mode and all keystrokes typed are saved directly into the data buffer of the file. The file is flushed and closed when the ESC key (i.e. 0x9B) is typed. That is, when the ESC key is typed all

161

buffered data is flushed and written to the file f, and then the file is closed. No line editing is provided and **all** keystrokes, including arrow keystrokes (like the left arrow keystroke for quasi editing), are captured and recorded to the file as well. The DOS TW (i.e. Text Write) command provides a very convenient and expeditious way to create or to append an EXEC file or any other sequential Text file as the example shows in Figure III.5.8.

> WRITE   f [,Bb]
>
> Example: WRITE STEST.TXT

This command is available in DOS 3.3 for Sequential Text File commands. The DOS WRITE command configures the sequential Text file buffer for file f such that all output data is written to that file. If the B keyword is included with the DOS WRITE command, the file pointer position is located that many actual bytes b from the beginning of the file before any data is written to the file. Any previous data that existed in file f is overwritten starting at the bth byte from the beginning of the file. Any previous DOS POSITION command and calculated file pointer position value are ignored when the B keyword is included with the DOS WRITE command, and a new file pointer position is recalculated using the value of the B keyword. Previous Figures III.5.1 and III.5.2 show examples of using the sequential Text file WRITE command in an Applesoft program.

Command	Command Syntax
CLOSE	[f]
OPEN*	f, Ll [,Ss][,Dd][,Vv]
READ*	f, Rr [,Bb]
WRITE*	f, Rr [,Bb]

Table III.6.1. Random-Access Data File Commands in DOS 4.5

6. Random-Access Data File Commands

The DOS 4.5 Random-Access Data File commands consist of those commands that manage random-access Data files. The syntax of the Random-Access Data File commands is shown in Table III.6.1. All Random-Access Data File commands are permitted to be used from within an Applesoft or Binary program file and those commands shown without an asterisk are also permitted to be used on the Apple Command Line. Those commands shown **with** an asterisk are **not** permitted to be used on the Apple Command Line. Random-access Data files are composed of records that have a specified size, or length in bytes. A record may be comprised of Text fields, numerical data fields, unallocated bytes, or a combination of all three, and a record can be as small as one byte or as large as 32767 bytes (i.e. 0x7FFF) in size. The record size is established by the OPEN command using the required L keyword where the record size in bytes is determined by the l value. Only two bytes are provided in order to contain the l value in the variable RECDLNGH that is located in the workarea of the file as shown in

Table I.12.3. A Text field is any number of sequential ASCII characters that are terminated with a RETURN character (i.e. 0x8D). A numerical data field may be any number of digits, either integer values or floating point values in decimal, hexadecimal, or expressed in scientific notation as in the case of real and imaginary numbers. All fields including any unallocated bytes must reside within the specified record size. All records comprising a file f are not required to contain the same number or order of fields; but all records within file f must be the same size. **Only those records that contain any data whatsoever will actually exist within file f.** All other records are created whenever any data is generated or supplied for those records. DOS 4.5 allows the r value of the R keyword to be specified up to 65535, thus permitting up to 65536 records in a single file f. There is no mathematical or logical reason for this limitation; maximum number of records in DOS 3.3 is set to 32767, and again, there is no mathematical or logical reason for this limitation. However, only two bytes are provided in order to contain the r value in the variable RECURNUM that is located in the workarea of the file as shown in Table I.12.3.

DOS 4.5 differentiates sequential Text files and random-access Data files in how the file is opened. If the L keyword is **included** with the OPEN command, the file is treated as a random-access Data file and the READ and WRITE commands **must use** the R keyword as shown in Table III.6.1. See Table III.5.1 that shows the DOS 4.5 sequential Text file READ and WRITE commands in order to understand how those commands are syntactically different from the DOS 4.5 random-access Data file READ and WRITE commands. Applesoft programs that access a random-access Data file must open this file with the same record size l using the L keyword. Otherwise, computations for locating a specific record will result in obtaining unpredictable data and quite likely will become disastrous to the program as the file is processed. DOS 3.3 could have provided the value for l in the first TSL for a random-access Data file. There certainly is enough room for that value in that structure, particularly at bytes 0x08 and 0x09.

Data sectors are created as necessary and their track/sector pairs are added to a respective TSL sector when a random-access Data File record is supplied with any amount of data. The file pointer value is calculated based on record size l and the supplied record number r. Using the file pointer value, the necessary TSL index is determined, and if there is no track/sector entry for the respective data sector, a data sector is obtained from the volume Catalog and an entry is made in the TSL sector for that data sector. Any numerical remainder from the TSL index calculation plus any b index value that may be included with the READ or WRITE command determines the byte offset within the data sector where the supplied data is written for the specified record. If the complete record requires additional sectors to contain the supplied data, those sectors are obtained from the volume Catalog and their track/sector pairs are added to the respective TSL sector.

CLOSE　　　[f]

Example:　　CLOSE RTEST.T

This command is available in DOS 3.3 for Random-Access Data File commands. The DOS CLOSE command flushes and de-allocates the file buffer that is associated with the random-access Data file f, thereby closing the file from any further data input or data output. The File Manager CLOSE handler CLSHNDLR utilizes two routines, CHKBUF and CHKTSL, that test whether two specific bits are set or clear in the DSKFLAGS variable, DATAFLAG and TSLFLAG. See Table I.12.2 showing DSKFLAGS where DATAFLAG has a value of 0x40 and TSLFLAG has a value of 0x80. If either one of these two bits are **set**, either the current data buffer or the `TSL` buffer needs to be written to the volume currently in focus. `DSKFLAGS` also contains a bit reserved for `CATFLAG` having a value of `0x02`, and if that bit is **set** the `VTOC` and/or Catalog buffer needs to be written to the volume currently in focus. This process is referred to as *flushing a file buffer*.

In DOS 4.5 the process of closing a file after the data and `TSL` buffers have been written to the volume in focus, also includes updating the file size from `SECCNT` and updating the time and date stamp of the file so that the Catalog buffer that includes these file updates can be written to the volume. All buffer resources allocated to the random-access Data file `f` are relinquished when a `zero` is written to the first character of `FNAME` that corresponds to the filename that was used in the initial DOS `OPEN` command.

If a filename is not supplied with the DOS `CLOSE` command, **all** open files regardless of their file type are closed except for an open `EXEC` file. If a file `f` is open for data input, a `CLOSE` command forces all of the remaining data that is in its file buffer to be written to the file and then the file `f` is closed. Figure III.6.1 shows an example of using the DOS `CLOSE` command in an Applesoft program.

```
]LOAD RTEST
]LIST

 10 D$ =   CHR$ (4):F$ = "RTEST.T"
    :L = 32: ONERR  GOTO 60
 20  PRINT D$;"OPEN ";F$;", L";L
 30  PRINT D$;"WRITE ";F$;", R3"
 35  PRINT "This is Record 3."
 40  PRINT D$;"WRITE ";F$;", R2,
     B6"
 45  PRINT "This is Record 2."
 50  PRINT D$;"WRITE ";F$;", R1,
     B12"
 55  PRINT "This is Record 1."
 60  PRINT D$;"CLOSE ";F$: END
]RUN

]
```

Figure III.6.1. OPEN, WRITE, and CLOSE

```
]LIST RTEST.T,R
0000 0000 0000 0000 0000 0000 0000 0000
0000 0000 0000 0000 0000 0000 0000 0000
0000 0000 0000 0000 0000 0000 D4E8 E9F3
A0E9 F3A0 D2E5 E3EF F2E4 A0B1 AE8D 0000
0000 0000 0000 D4E8 E9F3 A0E9 F3A0 D2E5
E3EF F2E4 A0B2 AE8D 0000 0000 0000 0000
D4E8 E9F3 A0E9 F3A0 D2E5 E3EF F2E4 A0B3
AE8D 0000 0000 0000 0000 0000 0000 0000
0000 0000 0000 0000 0000 0000 0000 0000
0000 0000 0000 0000 0000 0000 0000 0000
0000 0000 0000 0000 0000 0000 0000 0000
0000 0000 0000 0000 0000 0000 0000 0000
0000 0000 0000 0000 0000 0000 0000 0000
0000 0000 0000 0000 0000 0000 0000 0000

]
```

Figure III.6.2. Contents of RTEST.T Display

OPEN   f, Ll [,Ss][,Dd][,Vv]

Example: OPEN RTEST.T, L32

This command is available in DOS 3.3 for Random-Access Data File commands. The DOS `OPEN` command allocates one of an available file buffers, which is 581 (i.e. `0x245`) bytes in size, for the random-access Data file `f` in the specified volume, and sets the record length to the number of bytes `l` specified by the required `L` keyword. This file buffer is initialized to read from or write to the beginning of file `f`. If this file does not exist in the specified volume, file `f` is created and an entry is made into the volume Catalog. If this file is already open, the file is flushed so that any remaining data in its file buffer is written to the volume before the file is closed, and the specified file is again opened. Figures III.6.1 and III.6.3 show examples in using the DOS `OPEN` command to open a random-access Data File

164

in an Applesoft program. The L keyword **must** be included with the DOS OPEN command when
reading data from or writing data to a random-access Data file.

READ   f, Rr [,Bb]

Example: READ RTEST.T,R1,B12

This command is available in DOS 3.3 for Random-Access Data File commands. The DOS READ
command configures the random-access Data file buffer for file f such that all input data is read from
that file. Data is read from the specified Record r, one field at a time. If the R keyword is **not** included
with the DOS READ command, no error is generated within DOS and the file pointer is simply
positioned at the beginning of file f. DOS 4.5 does not check for the presence or absence of the R
keyword; it simply utilizes its value if it is provided. However, even though the R keyword is initialized
to zero before any DOS command is parsed, the practice of not including the R keyword with the DOS
READ command for a random-access Data file is strongly **not** advised. If the B keyword is included
along with the DOS READ command, the file pointer position is calculated that many bytes b from the
beginning of the specified Record r before any data is read from the file at that file pointer position.
Note that this usage of the B keyword is very different in random-access Data files from its usage in
sequential Text files.

```
]LOAD RTEST2

]LIST

10 D$ =   CHR$ (4):F$ = "RTEST.T"
   :L = 32: ONERR  GOTO 60
20 PRINT D$;"OPEN ";F$;", L";L
30 PRINT D$;"READ ";F$;", R2, B
   6": INPUT D2$
40 PRINT D$;"READ ";F$;", R3": INPUT
   D3$
50 PRINT D$;"READ ";F$;", R1, B
   12": INPUT D1$
60 PRINT D$;"CLOSE ";F$
70 PRINT : PRINT D1$: PRINT D2$
   : PRINT D3$: END

]RUN

This is Record 1.
This is Record 2.
This is Record 3.
]
```

Figure III.6.3. READ Command

Figure III.6.2 shows a hexadecimal listing of the contents of RTEST.T using the DOS LIST command
that includes the R keyword. The R keyword for the DOS LIST command selects hexadecimal data
output rather than ASCII data output for a Text **Type** file. It is easy to see that each record is thirty-two
bytes in size and that Record 0 ranges from byte 0x00 to byte 0x1F in Figure III.6.2. There is no data
in Record 0, the first record in the file; there is data in Record 1 that begins at offset byte 0x0C (see line
50 in Figure III.6.3); there is data in Record 2 that begins at offset byte 0x06 (see line 30 in Figure
III.6.3); there is data in Record 3 that begins at offset byte 0x00 (see line 40 in Figure III.6.3). Figure

III.6.3 shows an example Applesoft program that uses the DOS READ command for a random-access Data file. The data file records may be specified and the data file record data may be read from the random-access data file in any order, hence the descriptive term *random-access* data file. Figure III.6.3 also shows the results of running the RTEST2 Applesoft program.

> WRITE   f, Rr [,Bb]
>
> Example: WRITE RTEST.T,R1,B12

This command is available in DOS 3.3 for Random-Access Data File commands. The DOS WRITE command configures the random-access Data file buffer for file f such that all output data is written to that file. Data is written to the specified Record r, one field at a time. If the R keyword is **not** included with the DOS WRITE command, no error is generated within DOS and the file pointer is simply positioned at the beginning of file f. DOS 4.5 does not check for the presence or absence of the R keyword; it simply utilizes its value if it is provided. However, even though the R keyword is initialized to zero before any DOS command is parsed, the practice of not including the R keyword with the DOS WRITE command for a random-access Data file is strongly **not** advised. If the B keyword is included along with the DOS WRITE command, the file pointer position is calculated to be that many bytes b from the beginning of the specified Record r before any data is written to the file at that file pointer position. Note that this usage of the B keyword is very different in random-access Data files from its usage in sequential Text files. Previously, Figure III.6.1 shows an example in using the DOS WRITE command for a random-access data file in an Applesoft program. The file records may be specified and the data file record data may be written to the random-access data file in any order, hence the descriptive term *random-access* data file.

```
]LOAD CREATE
]LIST

 100 D$ =  CHR$ (4)
 200 F$ = "BIGFILE"
 300 L = 467
 400  PRINT D$;"OPEN ";F$;",L";L
 500 R = 32767
 600  PRINT D$;"WRITE";F$;",R";R
 700  PRINT "RECORD ";R
 800  PRINT D$;"CLOSE ";F$: END

]RUN

]LS

S=6 D=02 V=000 F=0061 01/01/22 08:28:49

 A 002 CREATE           01/01/22 08:28:48
 T 491 BIGFILE          01/01/22 08:28:49

]※
```

Figure III.6.4. Random-Access Data File CREATE

166

Random-Access Data File Design Considerations

Denis Molony, a citizen of Australia and the author of the extraordinarily useful tool *DiskBrowser*, provided me with an excellent example of an Applesoft program that creates a random-access Data file that quickly becomes useless after a few records are written to the file. Figure III.6.4 shows Molony's Applesoft program that he saved on a volume that he initialized with DOS 3.3. I copied his Applesoft program CREATE to a volume that I initialized with DOS 4.5. His program certainly looks simple enough until you realize that this program writes to the last possible record permitted by DOS 3.3, record 32767 (i.e. 0x7FFF), or the 32768th record. Just to be clear, DOS 4.5 changes the record specification size from 32767 to 65535 (i.e. 0x7FFF to 0xFFFF), but this does not in any way alter the results of this program nor the concepts this program teaches. When DOS first creates a random-access Data file, only the first TSL sector is created as in line 400 and the value of the L keyword, 467 in this example, is saved in the workarea of the file in the RECDLNGH variable as shown in Table I.12.3 at offset 0x213. When this file is reopened sometime in the future, the file must be opened with the **same** L keyword value in order to accurately locate the desired records and the data for those records. When Molony's program writes to record 32767 in line 600, a file pointer is calculated and sufficient TSL sectors are created in order to save that particular data record to its rightful data sector and save its track/sector entry for that data sector in its rightful TSL sector.

How many TSL sectors are created in order to write data to record 32767 may seem puzzling at first, though it is easy to determine that value. Each TSL sector contains 122 (i.e. 0x7A) track/sector entries. These entries are for **sectors** of data, not for **records** of data. Each sector of data contains 256 (i.e. 0x100) bytes. Including record 0, therefore,

```
{ ( 467 bytes/record * 32768 records ) / 256 bytes/sector } /

    122 sectors/TSL = 490 TSLs
```

When the data is actually written to the file in line 700, an entry is made in the 490th TSL sector for the data sector that is created to contain the provided data. The data is not necessarily written to the first byte of the sector, but in this instance to byte 46, which comes after the end of record 32766 (the 32767th record) which is the beginning of record 32767. The entire record of 467 bytes is not written to the file but only the data that is provided in the Applesoft PRINT statement in line 700 which amounts to only twelve bytes. The byte offset into the data sector where these twelve bytes are written is the remainder from the data file pointer calculation:

```
( 467 bytes/record * 32767 records ) / 256 bytes/sector =

    59,774 sectors + 45 bytes
```

Figure III.6.4 shows that BIGFILE is 491 sectors in size, currently composed of 490 TSL sectors and one data sector. There are only sixty-one sectors free on this DOS 4.5 Data volume which originally contained 554 sectors when it was first initialized. Why has DOS created all these TSL sectors? It seems rather ludicrous, because 59,774 sectors are required to contain all of the data for all 32768 records if every 467 byte record contains some data and if all of these records are written to this file. But that would require a volume having at least 3,736 additional disk tracks. At the very least, DOS has created the minimum number of required linked-list `TSL` sectors in order to write record number 32767. It is rather obvious that the file `BIGFILE` is not at all suitable to contain all of the data that the Applesoft program `CREATE` intended. Therefore, it is critical that random-access Data files are properly sized to the volumes in which they are stored.

Family Roots by Stephen C. Vorenberg and marketed by Quinsept, Inc., utilizes sequential Text files and random-access Data files for its *Family Roots* data base. Each Data volume contains a minimum of three files: `CONTROL`, `NAMELIST`, and `FAMILY`. The random-access Data file `NAMELIST` uses twenty-six sectors. The sequential Text file `CONTROL` uses two sectors, and it contains the `Start` and `End` record numbers that exist within the random-access Data file `FAMILY` whose records have been pre-initialized using a 256-byte empty buffer. The `CONTROL` file also contains the size of the `FAMILY` file records, and a few other operating parameters, so that the file `FAMILY` is always opened with the correct value 1 for the L keyword. Essentially, each `FAMILY` file contains 224 records and each record is configured to be two sectors in size so that a maximum of 512 bytes can be utilized for each record. The equations required to verify whether there is sufficient disk space for this random-access Data file when all of its records are completely filled with data can be expressed as follows:

```
( 224 records * 512 bytes/record ) / 256 bytes/sector = 448 sectors

448 sectors / 122 sectors/TSL = 4 TSLs
```

Since *Family Roots* utilizes the DOS 3.3 disk operating system, tracks `0x00`, `0x01`, and `0x02` are not available for data (they are reserved for DOS 3.3), and the `VTOC` and Catalog sectors combined require another sixteen sectors. This leaves 496 sectors for data in a volume having thirty-five tracks. Using the above results, each Data volume for *Family Roots* requires 26 + 2 + 448 + 4 = 480 sectors. Therefore, at least sixteen sectors should be left available in each Data volume that could be used for any additional files. A few Data volumes did contain one or two additional files: `LASTID` and `DATE`. These files were only two sectors each in size and they appeared transitory. Vorenberg sized his data files such that 96.8% of each Data volume is utilized giving the program *Family Roots* a little margin of safety.

The Molony and Vorenberg Data volume examples demonstrate how important it is to consider whether a single Data volume can provide sufficient room to store the contents of a particular random-access Data file, or whether several volumes would be required to store all of the generated data when using multiple random-access Data files. Performing the file sizing analysis upfront certainly saves much grief later on when and if a random-access Data file should exceed its storage media capacity. Certainly, a random-access Data file cannot grow endlessly and it must have boundaries built into its design and capacity.

Given R for the number of records, L for the size or length of each record in bytes, and S for the number of available sectors where each sector contains 256 bytes, the random-access Data file sizing equations incorporating `TSL` sector overhead can be expressed as follows:

```
S = ( R * L * 123 ) / ( 256 * 122 ) sectors      (always round up)

R = ( S * 256 * 122 ) / ( L * 123 ) records       (always round down)

L = ( S * 256 * 122 ) / ( R * 123 ) bytes         (always round down)
```

Inserting Vorenberg's parameters in these equations where `R = 224` and `L = 512`:

```
S = ( 224 * 512 * 123 ) / ( 256 * 122 ) = 451.67 => 452 sectors
```

This is precisely the same value obtained above: 448 data sectors + 4 `TSL` sectors = 452 sectors.

For Molony's example program, the required number of sectors for his random-access Data file is:

```
S = ( 32768 * 467 * 123 ) / ( 256 * 122 ) => 60,266 sectors
```

A single 35-track volume is hardly the appropriate media for this random-access Data file.

Now, assuming Molony's Data file can be spread over several 36-track volumes each providing 570 sectors when using DOS 4.5, the number of records on each volume would be:

```
R = ( 570 * 256 * 122 ) / ( 467 * 123 ) => 309 records  (round down)
```


And, the number of volumes required would be:

```
32768 records / 309 records/volume => 106 volumes          (round up)
```


A database of this magnitude would require quite a substantial programing effort, but easily managed on the CFFA that is initialized first using the *VOLMGR* and DOS 4.5. Vorenberg strongly recommended using the Sider with *Family Roots* and that is precisely the hard drive my mother utilized with *Family Roots* in order to digitize our family tree which happens to be rather extensive in size. My mother was able to obtain family history and documentation on individuals where some in our family tree arrived in America on the *Mayflower*. My parents traveled through parts of Scotland and Ireland searching for any records my mother could find for her great-great-great-grandparents. She was able to create an amazing data base for our family tree.

This page intentionally left blank.

IV. DOS 4.5 Assembly Language Routines

DOS 4.5 provides unapparelled support for assembly language routines that need to acquire or change the value of some of the operational variables used throughout the DOS software routines and functional handlers. DOS 4.5 also provides access to interface routines and vectors that handle error reporting, obtaining the date and time, and for displaying the DOS version and build information easily. Even though the data management routines and Page `0x03` vectors have been previously discussed, I thought it would be informative to present all of these routines and vectors together, in one section, showing their address, the registers and values they use, and the processor flags that are required upon entry for these routines and the vectors that support their processing, and the registers, values, and flags that are returned to the user.

There are two basic approaches a user may call, or invoke an assembly language routine or vector: directly or indirectly. The direct approach is simply to use the `JSR` instruction. The indirect approach is to use the `JSR` instruction coupled with an indirect `JMP` instruction like `JMP(ADR)`. Figure IV.0.1 shows both approaches a user may use in order to invoke a DOS 4.5 assembly language routine or vector. Depending upon how the assembly language routine or vector is entered (i.e. by a `JMP` instruction) or how the routine or vector is specified (i.e. by an address) usually determines which approach is more favorable to use within the software of the user.

```
   :                 :          :
  03E1              10   RDCLKVSN equ $3E1
  03EA              11   HOOKDOS  equ $3EA
   :                 :          :
   :                 :          :
  1000             100   ; Direct subroutine approach.
  1000 20 EA 03    101          jsr HOOKDOS
   :                 :          :
   :                 :          :
  2000             200   ; Indirect vector approach.
  2000 A0 83       201          ldy #VSNBUFR
  2002 A9 20       202          lda /VSNBUFR
  2004 38          203          sec
  2005 20 80 20    204          jsr READVSN
   :                 :          :
   :                 :          :
  2080 6C E1 03    300   READVSN  jmp (RDCLKVSN)
  2083 00 00 00    301   VSNBUFR  dfs 20,0
   :                 :          :
```

Figure IV.0.1. Direct and Indirect Approach for a Subroutine Call

I have always viewed software development as a set of very complex strategies involving highly developed problem solving techniques. To develop such programming skills requires passion, perseverance, and practice. One cannot be expected to perform a Fiorillo Caprice overnight without expending a little passion, a little perseverance, and a little practice. Learning how to utilize and manage the memory of the Language Card partition in the Apple][machine is, in itself, very complicated, tricky, and certainly not intuitive. But when managed correctly, the memory of the Language Card partition provides great opportunities to expand one's programming skills. But those skills are still considerably simple compared to the skills required to utilize and manage Auxiliary memory. Only with passion, perseverance, and practice will the Apple][hardware completely reveal itself and yield its computational power to that competent software and hardware engineer.

1. DOSWARM Entry Address 0x3D0

Function	Address	X-reg	Y-reg	A-reg	C-flag	Description
Entry	0x03D0	–	–	–	–	Enters (WARMADR) handler
Return	0xD43C	–	–	–	–	ASROMWRM (no return to caller)

After DOS 4.5 has booted, the DOSWARM entry at memory address 0x3D0 as shown in Table I.9.3 jumps to the DOS WARMSTRT routine. In DOS 4.5L this is a direct jump. In DOS 4.5H this is a jump indirectly through the Interface page 0xBE routine EXTWARM in order to write enable Bank 2 of the Language Card partition before jumping to the WARMSTRT routine. The WARMSTRT routine sets the stack pointer to 0xFF, resets the state machine, initializes the MON flags and the keyboard and video intercepts, turns ROM memory ON in DOS 4.5H, and then exits indirectly by means of the WARMADR vector in the page 0xBE INITVALS Data structure as shown in Table I.8.7.

The assembler initially sets the WARMADR vector to memory address 0xD43C, the address of the Applesoft ASROMWRM routine. The ASROMWRM routine is entered at the Applesoft warm-start entry address in ROM that performs a partial reinitialization of Applesoft, and this routine does not return to the caller. The user is encouraged to change the address at WARMADR (i.e. 0xBEE2) in order to tailor the DOSWARM routine not to exit into the Applesoft ROM, but into a user specific routine, and then exit into the ASROMWRM routine. Use the Direct approach in order to enter the DOS WARMSTRT routine at the DOSWARM entry address 0x3D0.

2. DOSCOLD Entry Address 0x3D3

Function	Address	X-reg	Y-reg	A-reg	C-flag	Description
Entry	0x03D3	–	–	–	–	Enters (COLDADR) handler
Return	0xE000	–	–	–	–	BASCLD (no return to caller)

After DOS 4.5 has booted, the DOSCOLD entry at memory address 0x3D3 as shown in Table I.9.3 jumps to the DOS COLDSTRT routine. The COLDSTRT routine initializes the stack pointer to 0xFF, initializes XMODE, selects the main video and deselects the alternate character set, sets the video output to normal, initializes the text and graphics modes and sets the window operating parameters, initializes the CSWL and KSWL interface pointers, verifies that Applesoft is in ROM, copies the ROM Monitor to RAM in DOS 4.5H, searches for a clock card, initializes SLOTVAL, DRVAL, and VOLVAL, and then jumps to the DOS COLDSTR2 routine. The COLDSTR2 routine sets the stack pointer to 0xFF, resets the state machine, initializes the MON flags and the keyboard and video intercepts, turns ROM memory ON in DOS 4.5H, and then exits indirectly by means of the COLDADR vector in the page 0xBE INITVALS Data structure as shown in Table I.8.7.

The assembler initially sets the COLDADR vector to memory address 0xE000, the address of the Applesoft BASCLD routine. The BASCLD routine is entered at the Applesoft cold-start entry address in ROM that performs a complete reinitialization of Applesoft, and this routine does not return to the caller. The user is encouraged to change the address at COLDADR (i.e. 0xBEE4) in order to tailor the COLDSTRT routine not to exit into Applesoft ROM, but into a user specific routine, and then exit into the BASCLD routine. Use the Direct approach in order to enter the DOS COLDSTRT routine at the DOSCOLD entry address 0x3D3.

3. CALLFM Entry Address 0x3D6

Function	Address	X-reg	Y-reg	A-reg	C-flag	Description
Entry	0x03D6	File Flag	–	–	–	Enter external File Manager handler
Return	–	Error #	–	–	Status	Return to caller

After DOS 4.5 has booted, the CALLFM entry at memory address 0x3D6 as shown in Table I.9.3 jumps to the DOS FMHNDLR routine. In DOS 4.5L this is a direct jump. In DOS 4.5H this is a jump indirectly through the Interface page 0xBE routine EXTFM in order to write enable Bank 2 of the Language Card partition before jumping to the FMHNDLR routine. The FMHNDLR routine loads the FILALC flag value (i.e. 0x81) when the X-register (File Flag) is set to zero, otherwise it loads the NOFILALC flag value (i.e. 0x80) and saves that value to KEYWORD1. Both flags have their MSB **set** which tells the INIT handler INITHNDL that the call to the FMHNDLR routine was by means of the CALLFM entry and not from within DOS. All registers are saved and the CSWL and KSWL interface pointers to DOS are disconnected. Processing continues with the FILEMNGR routine.

When File Manager processing is complete, the FILEMNGR routine preserves the Carry flag and its status in the X-register and returns to the caller. For the external caller in DOS 4.5L, FMHNDLR returns to the caller by means of INITPTRS which restores the control over the CSWL and KSWL interface pointers by DOS. For the external caller in DOS 4.5H, FMHNDLR returns to Interface page 0xBE, calls INITPTRS, enables ROM memory, and then returns to the caller. From the FILEMNGR routine, if the Carry flag is **set** the X-register contains an error number, otherwise the Carry flag is **clear** and the X-register is set to zero. The File Manager uses its **own** context block to process either an internal or an external File Manager command. Use the Direct approach in order to enter the DOS FMHNDLR routine at the CALLFM entry address 0x3D6.

4. CALLRWTS Entry Address 0x3D9

Function	Address	X-reg	Y-reg	A-reg	C-flag	Description
Entry	0x03D9	–	#IOCB	/IOCB	–	Enter external RWTS handler
Return	–	–	–	Error #	Status	Return to caller

After DOS 4.5 has booted, the CALLRWTS entry at memory address 0x3D9 as shown in Table I.9.3 jumps to the DOS DORWTS routine. In DOS 4.5L this is a direct jump. In DOS 4.5H this is a jump indirectly through the Interface page 0xBE routine EXTRWTS in order to write enable Bank 1 of the Language Card partition before jumping to the DORWTS routine. The DORWTS routine disables interrupts, saves the Y- and A-registers that contain the address of the IOCB of the user to IOBADR, extracts the USRBUF address from the IOCB and saves that address to BUFADR2Z, extracts the SNUM16 slot-times-sixteen value from the IOCB and saves it to SNUM16Z and to the IOCB at SLOTFND, divides the SNUM16 value by sixteen and copies it to the X-register, and formulates the DISKJMP pointer. The Scratch Pad table SCRCHTBL, indexed using the X-register, is checked to determine whether the scratch pad RAM locations have been initialized for this slot, and if this is the first time, the BLDNIBL routine is called to generate the RDNIBL and WRNIBL nibble tables. The X-register is restored from SNUM16Z, the Y- and A-registers are restored from IOBADR, and an indirect jump is made to the requested RWTS slot handler.

When the requested RWTS slot handler processing is complete, the DORWTS routine restores the processor status and **clears** the Carry flag if the A-register contains a zero value, otherwise it **sets** the Carry flag. For the external caller in DOS 4.5L, the DOS DORWTS routine returns to the caller. For the external caller in DOS 4.5H, the DOS DORWTS routine returns to Interface page 0xBE, enables ROM memory, and then returns to the caller. RWTS can use any context block located anywhere within Main memory, even the DOS internal context block in page 0xBF as long as the Y- and A-registers contain the address of that context block. Use the Direct approach in order to enter the DOS DORWTS routine at the CALLRWTS entry address 0x3D9.

5. GETFMCB Routine at 0x3DC

Function	Address	X-reg	Y-reg	A-reg	C-flag	Description
Entry	0x03DC	–	–	–	–	Gets the FMVALS address
Return	0x03E0	–	#FMVALS	/FMVALS	–	Return to caller

After DOS 4.5 has booted, the GETFMCB routine at memory address 0x3DC as shown in Table I.9.3 loads the Y- and A-registers with the address of the File Manager Context Block FMVALS. FMVALS resides within page 0xBF immediately following the internal RWTS IOCB. The File Manager uses **only** this context block to process either an internal or an external File Manager command. *FID*, for example, maintains its own copy of the 18-byte Context Block, modifies the Context Block values as needed, and then copies the Context Block back in its entirety into DOS address space before calling the File Manager CALLFM. Upon return from the File Manager, *FID* copies the entire Context Block again into its own address space before processing the return code value RTNCODE. Use the Direct approach in order to call the GETFMCB routine at 0x3DC.

6. RDCLKVSN Vector Address at 0x3E1

Function	Address	X-reg	Y-reg	A-reg	C-flag	Description
Entry	0x03E1	–	#CLKBUF	/CLKBUF	clear	Puts date and time into a 6-byte buffer
Return	–	–	–	–	–	Return to caller
Entry	0x03E1		#VSNBUF	/VSNBUF	set	Puts DOS Version into a 20-byte buffer
Return	–					Return to caller

After DOS 4.5 has booted, the RDCLKVSN vector at memory address 0x3E1 as shown in Table I.9.3 is used to indirectly jump to the DOS DOCLKVSN routine. In DOS 4.5L this is an indirect jump directly to the DOCLKVSN routine. In DOS 4.5H this is an indirect jump through the Interface page 0xBE routine EXCLKVSN in order to write enable Bank 2 of the Language Card partition before jumping to the DOCLKVSN routine. The DOCLKVSN routine saves the address in the Y- and A-registers to DOSPTR. If the Carry flag is **clear**, DOSPTR contains the address of a 6-byte clock buffer in order to capture the current date and time values, and processing continues in the READCLK routine. If the Carry flag is **set**, DOSPTR contains the address of a 20-byte version buffer in order to capture the 20-byte DOS Version character string, and processing continues in the READVSN routine. The supplied 20-byte DOS Version character string will contain only upper ASCII characters for the string data. The DOS Version character string will not contain a termination byte nor is the string data in DCI format. Once processing has completed in either routine in DOS 4.5L, the DOCLKVSN routine returns to the caller. Once processing has completed in either routine in DOS 4.5H, the DOCLKVSN routine returns to Interface page 0xBE, enables ROM memory, and then returns to the caller. Use the Indirect approach in order to enter the DOS DOCLKVSN routine through the RDCLKVSN vector address at 0x3E1.

7. GETIOCB Routine at 0x3E3

Function	Address	X-reg	Y-reg	A-reg	C-flag	Description
Entry	0x03E3	–	–	–	–	Gets RWTS IOCB address
Return	0x03E7	–	#IOCB	/IOCB	–	Return to caller

After DOS 4.5 has booted, the GETIOCB routine at memory address 0x3E3 as shown in Table I.9.3 loads the Y- and A-registers with the address of the RWTS Input/Output Context Block TBLTYPE. TBLTYPE resides within page 0xBF immediately before the internal File Manager Context Block FMVALS. RWTS uses this context block to process either an internal or an external RWTS command. RWTS can use virtually any Main memory address space for its IOCB as long as the Y- and A-registers contain the address for that context block. Use the Direct approach in order to call the GETIOCB routine at 0x3E3.

8. PRERRADR Vector Address at 0x3E8

Function	Address	X-reg	Y-reg	A-reg	C-flag	Description
Entry	0x03E8	Error #	–	–	–	Print error message handler
Return	–	–	–	–	–	Return to caller

After DOS 4.5 has booted, the PRERRADR vector at memory address 0x3E8 as shown in Table I.9.3 is used to indirectly jump to the DOS DOPRTERR routine. In DOS 4.5L this is an indirect jump directly to the DOPRTERR routine. In DOS 4.5H this is an indirect jump through the Interface page 0xBE routine EXTPRERR in order to write enable Bank 2 of the Language Card partition, save the registers, and disconnect the CSWL and KSWL interface pointers from DOS before jumping to the DOPRTERR routine. The DOPRTERR routine range checks the error value in the X-register to be less than 0x12, and then prints the character string based on the respective error number. No carriage return is printed after printing the character string. Once processing is complete in DOS 4.5L, the DOPRTERR routine returns to the caller. Once processing is complete in DOS 4.5H, the DOPRTERR routine returns to Interface page 0xBE, restores the registers and restores the control over the DOS CSWL and KSWL interface pointers, enables ROM memory, and then returns to the caller. Use the Indirect approach in order to enter the DOS PRERRADR routine through the PRTERADR vector address at 0x3E8.

9. HOOKDOS Entry Address 0x3EA

Function	Address	X-reg	Y-reg	A-reg	C-flag	Description
Entry	0x03EA	–	–	–	–	DOS reconnect handler
Return	–	–	–	–	–	Return to caller

After DOS 4.5 has booted, the HOOKDOS entry at memory address 0x3EA as shown in Table I.9.3 jumps to the DOS INITPTRS routine. In DOS 4.5L this is a direct jump. In DOS 4.5H this is a jump indirectly through the Interface page 0xBE routine EXTPTRS in order to write enable Bank 2 of the Language Card partition before jumping to the INITPTRS routine. The INITPTRS routine restores the control over the DOS CSWL and KSWL interface pointers. Once processing is complete in DOS 4.5L, the INITPTRS routine returns to the caller. Once processing is complete in DOS 4.5H, the INITPTRS routine returns to Interface page 0xBE, enables ROM memory, and then returns to the caller. Use the Direct approach in order to enter the DOS INITPTRS routine at the HOOKDOS entry address 0x3EA.

10. XFERADR Transfer Address at 0x3ED

Function	Address	X-reg	Y-reg	A-reg	C-flag	V-flag	Description
Address	0x03ED	–	–	–	Xfer Dir	page-zero	Target program starting address
Return	–	same	same	same	–	–	Return to caller

Whether or not DOS 4.5 has booted, the transfer address XFERADR at memory address 0x3ED as shown in Table I.9.3 is utilized by the built-in ROM routine XFER at memory address 0xC314. The XFER routine uses XFERADR for an indirect jump to the starting address contained in XFERADR in order to enter the target program that exists in the alternate memory. The target program exists in either Main memory or in Auxiliary memory. XFER jumps to DOXFER at memory address 0xC3C3 in order to transfer control to a program segment in Main or in Auxiliary memory. Three parameters must be initialized before the user should attempt a jump to XFER (i.e. JMP XFER): the start address contained in XFERADR, the direction of transfer (Main memory to Auxiliary memory or Auxiliary memory to Main memory), and which page-zero/stack to use (Main memory or Auxiliary memory). The Carry flag controls the transfer direction and the Overflow flag (or V-flag) controls the page-zero/stack selection. The A-, X-, and Y-registers are maintained without change by XFER when control is transferred to the target program.

Copy the start address of the target program to XFERADR in Lo/Hi byte order. **Set** the Carry flag to transfer control from Main memory to Auxiliary memory or **clear** the Carry flag to transfer control from Auxiliary memory to Main memory. **Set** the Overflow flag to use the page-zero/stack in Auxiliary memory or **clear** the Overflow flag to use the page-zero/stack in Main memory.

The 6502 (and 65C02) Instruction Set **does** contain a native *clear Overflow flag* instruction (i.e. CLV). Unfortunately, the Instruction Set does **not** contain a native *set Overflow flag* instruction. I am not sure why this microprocessor operation is missing. Actually, I believe there is no rationale for this shortcoming. Generally, one can use the BIT IORTS statement to easily achieve setting the Overflow flag. The IORTS address is the address for the RTS instruction in the ROM Monitor at memory address 0xFF58.

The XFER routine saves the address in XFERADR onto the stack, enables the requested memory where the target program exists, restores the address that was in XFERADR from the stack, enables the requested page-zero/stack memory, and indirectly jumps to the address found in XFERADR (i.e. JMP (XFERADR)). Processor control is henceforth taken by the target program.

11. AUTOBRK Entry Address 0x3EF

Function	Address	X-reg	Y-reg	A-reg	C-flag	Description
Entry	0x03EF	–	–	–	–	Enters OLDBRK (0xFA59)
Return	0xFA59	–	–	–	–	No return to caller

After DOS 4.5 has booted, the AUTOBRK entry at memory address 0x3EF as shown in Table I.9.3 directly jumps to the Autostart ROM BRK handler OLDBRK at memory address 0xFA59. OLDBRK prints the current program counter and the contents of all processor registers, and then enters the ROM

Monitor MON at memory address 0xFF65. MON does not return to the caller. Use the Direct approach in order to enter the ROM OLDBRK routine at the AUTOBRK entry address 0x3EF.

12. AUTORSET Vector Address at 0x3F2

Function	Address	X-reg	Y-reg	A-reg	C-flag	Description
Entry	0x03F2	–	–	–	–	Enters (WARMADR) handler
Return	0xD43C	–	–	–	–	ASROMWRM (no return to caller)

After DOS 4.5 has booted, the AUTORSET vector at memory address 0x3F2 as shown in Table I.9.3 is used by the Autostart ROM to contain the vector address that is used when a ROM reset is issued. In DOS 4.5 that vector address is the address for the DOS WARMSTRT routine. The Autostart ROM makes an indirect jump to the routine whose address is contained in the AUTORSET vector. In DOS 4.5L this is an indirect jump directly to the WARMSTRT routine. In DOS 4.5H this is an indirect jump indirectly through the Interface page 0xBE routine EXTWARM in order to write enable Bank 2 of the Language Card partition before jumping to the WARMSTRT routine. The WARMSTRT routine sets the stack pointer to 0xFF, resets the state machine, initializes the MON flags and the keyboard and video intercepts, turns ROM memory ON in DOS 4.5H, and then exits indirectly by means of the WARMADR vector in the page 0xBE INITVALS Data structure as shown in Table I.8.7.

The assembler initially sets the WARMADR vector to memory address 0xD43C, the address of the Applesoft ASROMWRM routine. The ASROMWRM routine is entered at the Applesoft warm-start entry address in ROM that performs a partial reinitialization of Applesoft, and this routine does not return to the caller. The user is encouraged to change the address at WARMADR (i.e. 0xBEE2) in order to tailor the DOSWARM routine not to exit into the Applesoft ROM, but into a user specific routine, and then exit into the ASROMWRM routine. Use the Indirect approach in order to enter the DOS WARMSTRT routine through the AUTORSET vector address at 0x3F2.

13. PWRSTATE Variable Byte at 0x3F4

Function	Address	X-reg	Y-reg	A-reg	C-flag	Description
Verification	0x03F4	–	–	–	–	Power up byte

After DOS 4.5 has booted, the PWRSTATE variable at memory address 0x3F4 as shown in Table I.9.3 is used to verify whether or not the Apple][has already powered up. When pin 40 of the 6502-microprocessor (or 65C02-microprocessor) is brought low, the microprocessor is designed to indirectly jump to the address found in the RESET Vector at memory address 0xFFFC. In the Autostart ROM that address is for the RESET handler at 0xFA62. After the RESET handler has initialized the annunciators, the window specifications, the DOS CSWL and KSWL interface pointers, and XMODE, it enters the NEWMON routine at memory address 0xFA81. After ringing the bell at 0xFF3A, the NEWMON routine calculates its own PWRSTATE value and compares that calculation to the value it finds at 0x3F4. If the comparison fails then NEWMON branches to the PWRUP routine at memory address

`0xFAA6`. The `PWRUP` routine locates a disk bootable device and proceeds to execute the slot handler firmware if such firmware is found.

There is a 1-in-256 probability that this logic will fail to sense a real power up condition. The `PWRSTATE` variable at `0x3F4` may randomly equal the `PWRSTATE` value that `NEWMON` calculates when the Apple][is first turned on or when the machine is physically reset. The probability of this logic failing to detect a real reset condition is virtually inconsequential. The ROM routine `SETPWRC` at memory address `0xFB6F` calculates the power up state variable and saves it to `PWRSTATE` at `0x3F4`.

The assembler calculates `PWRSTATE` using the following statement:

> `PWRSTATE byt PWRUPBYT^(AUTORSET/PAGESIZE)`

where `PWRUPBYT` is defined to be `0xA5`, the address for the `AUTORSET` vector is at `0x3F2`, and the value of `PAGESIZE` is `0x100`.

In DOS 4.5L the `AUTORSET` vector contains the address of `WARMSTRT` which is `0x9F06`. The `PWRSTATE` variable byte would be calculated from `0xA5^0x9F`, which is computed to be `0x3A`. In DOS 4.5H the `AUTORSET` vector contains the address of `EXTWARM` which is `0xBE3E`. The `PWRSTATE` variable byte would be calculated from `0xA5^0xBE`, which is computed to be `0x1B`.

14. USRAHAND Entry Address 0x3F5

Function	Address	X-reg	Y-reg	A-reg	C-flag	Description
Entry	0x03F5	–	–	–	–	Enters REPEATCD
Return	–	–	–	–	–	No return to caller

After DOS 4.5 has booted, the `USRAHAND` entry at memory address `0x3F5` as shown in Table I.9.3 jumps to the DOS `REPEATCD` routine. In DOS 4.5L this is a direct jump. In DOS 4.5H this is a jump indirectly through the Interface page `0xBE` routine `EXTRPEAT` in order to write enable Bank 2 of the Language Card partition before jumping to the `REPEATCD` routine. The `REPEATCD` routine saves the registers, disconnects the `CSWL` and `KSWL` interface pointers from DOS, and then calls the DOS `REPEAT` function to load the Y-register with the index of the last DOS command that DOS processed.

The `USRAHAND` routine is known as the *Ampersand Handler* and it is a favorite routine vehicle for many software programs and utilities to utilize in order for its program user to easily and quickly enter any processing routine for that software. The Program Global Editor is one example of a software program that is designed to enter its main processing routine when the `AMPERSAND` character is entered on the Apple Command Line. When DOS 4.5 is first initialized, the `USERAHAND` routine is connected to the `REPEATCD` routine in order to repeat the last DOS command when the `AMPERSAND` character is entered and followed by the `RETURN` character. `USRAHAND` typically does not return to the caller. Use the Direct approach in order to enter the DOS `REPEATCD` routine at the `USRAHAND` entry address `0x3F5`.

15. USRYHAND Entry Address 0x3F8

Function	Address	X-reg	Y-reg	A-reg	C-flag	Description
Entry	0x03F8	–	–	–	Direction	Enters AUXMOVE (0xC311)
Return	–	same	same	same	–	Return to caller

After DOS 4.5 has booted, the USRYHAND routine at memory address 0x3F8 as shown in Table I.9.3 directly jumps to the AUXMOVE routine in C3SPACE memory at memory address 0xC311. AUXMOVE is a built-in ROM routine that can copy blocks of data from Main memory to Auxiliary memory or from Auxiliary memory to Main memory. Before AUXMOVE is called, three byte-pair locations in page-zero must be initialized with the starting and ending addresses of the data source and the starting address of the data destination. The Carry flag is used to select the direction of transfer.

If the Carry flag is **set**, data is moved from Main memory to Auxiliary memory and if the Carry flag is **clear** data is moved from Auxiliary memory to Main memory. Page-zero A1 at 0x3C/0x3D must contain the data source starting address, page-zero A2 at 0x3E/0x3F must contain the data source ending address, and page-zero A4 at 0x42/0x43 must contain the data destination starting address. All three page-zero byte-pair locations expect the address to be saved in Lo/Hi byte order.

USRYHAND returns to the caller with the A-, X-, and Y-registers unchanged. Use the Direct approach in order to enter the C3SPACE AUXMOVE routine at the USRYHAND entry address 0x3F8.

16. NMASKIRQ Entry Address 0x3FB

Function	Address	X-reg	Y-reg	A-reg	C-flag	Description
Entry	0x03FB	–	–	–	–	Enters MON (0xFF65)
Return	0xFF65	–	–	–	–	No return to interrupted code

After DOS 4.5 has booted, the NMASKIRQ routine at memory address 0x3FB as shown in Table I.9.3 contains a jump instruction to the address for a non-maskable IRQ handler and it directly jumps to the ROM Monitor MON at memory address 0xFF65. The address for NMIRTN, or 0x3FB, is coded in ROM at the 0xFFFA non-maskable IRQ vector. Whenever the microprocessor receives a non-maskable IRQ interrupt, the microprocessor indirectly jumps to the NMASKIRQ routine in order to handle the IRQ interrupt.

When a non-maskable IRQ interrupt handler routine first executes, it must initialize 0x3FC with the entry address in Lo/Hi byte order for the unique software routine that will handle a non-maskable IRQ interrupt. An intelligently written non-maskable IRQ interrupt handler **will** return to the instruction immediately following the instruction that was interrupted by means of the RTI instruction when the microprocessor receives a non-maskable IRQ interrupt. Use the Direct approach in order to enter a non-maskable IRQ interrupt handler at the NMASKIRQ entry address 0x3FB.

Bit	Name	If Bit is OFF	If Bit is ON	Function Address
0	RDCXROM	state is OFF	state is ON	read 0xC015
1	RDBANK2	state is OFF	either bit 1 or bit 2 is ON, the other bit is OFF	read 0xC011, Bank 1
2		state is OFF		read 0xC011, Bank 2
3	RDLCRAM	state is ROM	state is RAM	read 0xC012
4	RDRAMWR	state is OFF	state is ON	read 0xC014
5	RDRAMRD	state is OFF	state is ON	read 0xC013
6	RDPAGE2	state is OFF	state is ON	read 0xC01C
7	RDAUXZP	state is Main	state is Auxiliary	read 0xC016

Table IV.17.1. Interrupt Handler System Status Byte Definition

17. MASKIRQ Vector Address at 0x3FE

Function	Address	X-reg	Y-reg	A-reg	C-flag	Description
Entry	0x03FE	–	–	–	–	Enters (MON) (0xFF65)
Return	0xFF65	–	–	–	–	No return to interrupted code

After DOS 4.5 has booted, the MASKIRQ vector at memory address 0x3FE as shown in Table I.9.3 contains the address for the maskable IRQ handler and it is used to indirectly jump to the ROM Monitor MON at memory address 0xFF65. The address for IRQRTN, or 0xC3FA, is coded in ROM at the 0xFFFE maskable IRQ vector. Whenever the microprocessor receives a maskable IRQ interrupt, the microprocessor indirectly jumps to the IRQRTN routine in order to handle the IRQ interrupt. IRQRTN read enables the internal CX ROM space so that ROM page 0xC4 is in focus for interrupt processing.

The Apple //e interrupt handler is highly complex and it begins its processing at memory address 0xC400. This handler creates a System Status byte that is saved to page-zero 0x44. If a system function is found to be turned ON, that function is turned OFF during handler processing, and the state of the system function in captured in the System Status byte. RAM memory of the Language Card partition is always turned off. Table IV.17.1 summarizes the system function that each bit represents in the System Status byte. There are two caveats to Table IV.17.1.

1) If bit 3 is OFF, then bits 1 and 2 are both OFF.
2) If bit 3 is ON, then bit 1 **or** bit 2 is ON and the other bit is OFF.

The Main and Auxiliary memory stack pointers are both saved along with the System Status byte at page-zero 0x44. The processor status is restored and the interrupt handler jumps to the GOTOIRQ routine at memory address 0xFC74. The GOTOIRQ routine disables the CX ROM and it indirectly jumps to the address found at MASKIRQ.

When a maskable IRQ interrupt handler routine first executes, it must initialize MASKIRQ with the entry address in Lo/Hi byte order for the unique software routine that will handle a maskable IRQ interrupt. An intelligently written maskable IRQ interrupt handler **will** return to the instruction immediately following the instruction that was interrupted by means of the RTI instruction when the microprocessor receives a maskable `IRQ` interrupt. Use the Indirect approach in order to enter a maskable `IRQ` interrupt handler through the `MASKIRQ` vector address at `0x3FE`.

18. DOS 4.5H GOTOMON Notes

DOS 4.5H is fully resident in the memory of the Language Card partition in Main memory except for two pages that are located in Main memory that begin with page `0xBE`. Page `0xBE` contains the Interface page for DOS 4.5H that performs all the necessary Bank switching protocol that is necessary to put into focus the memory of the particular Bank in the Language Card partition in order to access the routine or routines that are required for the requested processing. The five file buffers that are established for DOS 4.5H utilize the memory in the Language Card partition from `0xECA0` to `0xF7F8`. This provides sufficient room for the eight pages of memory that are required to provide a copy of the ROM Monitor to reside in RAM memory in the Language Card partition at precisely the same memory location from `0xF800` to `0xFFFF`.

When either the `COLDSTRT` or `GOTOMON` routine is called, the ROM Monitor is fully copied to RAM memory in the Language Card partition before either routine looks for a clock card. Having a copy of the ROM Monitor in RAM memory in the Language Card partition provides many, many benefits to the DOS user. It allows the user to inspect, modify, copy, and move the contents of memory in either Bank of the Language Card partition using the same tools and in the same fashion as one inspects, modifies, copies, and moves the contents of Main memory. There is no need having to remember which switches are required in order to enable the memory of a particular Bank in the Language Card partition nor having to remember which switches are required to write enable memory of a particular Bank in the Language Card partition.

DOS 4.5H is so elegantly designed that the contents of memory in the Language Card partition, whether it is part of Main memory or part of Auxiliary memory, can be inspected, modified, copied, and moved easily, and with virtually no extra knowledge of which Soft Switches to employ. Another advantage of having the ROM Monitor in RAM memory of the Language Card partition is that the `DOSWARM` and `DOSCOLD` addresses can be copied to `0xFEB4` and `0xFEB1`, respectively, instead of having the Applesoft routines at `0xE003` and `0xE000`, respectively, handle a RAM warm-start or a RAM cold-start. Certainly, a seasoned assembly language programmer will celebrate the ease at which software can be developed and inspected anywhere within the memory of the Language Card partition, specifically code that is designed to be resident in Auxiliary memory. Auxiliary memory, to be sure, is unique, perhaps the most difficult memory to manage, yet available for many brilliant, unimagined uses that could create highly versatile and extraordinary tools, utilities, and games.

19. GOTOMON2 Entry Address 0xBE00

Function	Address	X-reg	Y-reg	A-reg	C-flag	Description
Entry	0xBE00	–	–	–	–	Enters RAM MON with LC Bank 2 ON
Return	–	–	–	–	–	No return to caller

Only in DOS 4.5H, the GOTOMON2 routine at memory address 0xBE00 write enables **Bank 2** in the Language Card partition and then directly jumps to the GOTOMON routine in page 0xBF. The GOTOMON routine is an integral part of the DOS cold-start initialization routine that is used when DOS 4.5H boots or when a user utilizes the INITDOS vector at 0xBFF8 in order to initialize DOS. The GOTOMON routine initializes the stack pointer to 0xFF, initializes XMODE, selects the main video and deselects the alternate character set, sets the video output to normal, initializes the text and graphics modes and sets the window operating parameters, initializes the DOS CSWL and KSWL interface pointers, purposefully fails the verification check that Applesoft is in ROM, and the GOTOMON routine is made to enter the RAM Monitor at 0xFF65.

Because RAM memory in the Language Card partition is still enabled, the GOTOMON routine deliberately fails the Applesoft ROM verification check. The verification byte at RAM memory address 0xE000 in DOS 4.5H happens to be set to 0x90, and that byte value is certainly not equal to the 0x4C value found at ROM memory address 0xE000. RAM MON is the normal entry address for the RAM Monitor and it does not return to the caller. Bank 2 in the Language Card partition remains in focus. Use the Direct approach in order to enter the DOS GOTOMON routine using the GOTOMON2 entry address 0xBE00, typically entering BE00G on the Monitor Command Line.

20. GOTOMON1 Entry Address 0xBE08

Function	Address	X-reg	Y-reg	A-reg	C-flag	Description
Entry	0xBE08	–	–	–	–	Enters RAM MON with LC Bank 1 ON
Return	–	–	–	–	–	No return to caller

Only in DOS 4.5H, the GOTOMON1 routine at memory address 0xBE08 write enables **Bank 1** in the Language Card partition and then directly jumps to the GOTOMON routine in page 0xBF. The GOTOMON routine is an integral part of the DOS cold-start initialization routine that is used when DOS 4.5H boots or when a user utilizes the INITDOS vector at 0xBFF8 in order to initialize DOS. The GOTOMON routine initializes the stack pointer to 0xFF, initializes XMODE, selects the main video and deselects the alternate character set, sets the video output to normal, initializes the text and graphics modes and sets the window operating parameters, initializes the DOS CSWL and KSWL interface pointers, purposefully fails the verification check that Applesoft is in ROM, and the GOTOMON routine is made to enter the RAM Monitor at 0xFF65.

Because RAM memory in the Language Card partition is still enabled, the GOTOMON routine deliberately fails the Applesoft ROM verification check. The verification byte at RAM memory address 0xE000 in DOS 4.5H happens to be set to 0x90, and that byte value is certainly not equal to the 0x4C value found at ROM memory address 0xE000. RAM MON is the normal entry address for the RAM Monitor and it does not return to the caller. Bank 1 in the Language Card partition remains in focus.

Use the Direct approach in order to the enter the DOS GOTOMON routine using the GOTOMON1 entry address 0xBE08, typically entering BE08G on the Monitor Command Line.

21. BLDVRSN Variable Byte at 0xBFF0

Function	Address	X-reg	Y-reg	A-reg	C-flag	Description
Identification	0xBFF0	–	–	–	–	Read or compare DOS Version number

After DOS 4.5 has booted or has been copied into memory, the BLDVRSN variable byte at memory address 0xBFF0 as shown in Table I.8.1 identifies the DOS version number of the DOS that currently resides in memory. Using this variable byte to identify the current DOS version number in memory is far more convenient than having to parse the version number from the DOS Version character string provided by indirectly calling the RDCLKVSN routine at memory address 0x3E1 and supplying the address of a 20-byte buffer. Use the Direct approach in order to read or compare the BLDVRSN variable byte at 0xBFF0 using any of the registers.

22. BLDNMBR Variable Byte at 0xBFF1

Function	Address	X-reg	Y-reg	A-reg	C-flag	Description
Identification	0xBFF1	–	–	–	–	Read or compare DOS Build number

After DOS 4.5 has booted or has been copied into memory, the BLDNMBR variable byte at memory address 0xBFF1 as shown in Table I.8.1 identifies the DOS build number of the DOS that currently resides in memory. Using this variable byte to identify the current DOS build number in memory is far more convenient than having to parse the build number from the DOS Version character string provided by indirectly calling the RDCLKVSN routine at memory address 0x3E1 and supplying the address of a 20-byte buffer. Use the Direct approach in order to read or compare the BLDNUMBR variable byte at 0xBFF1 using any of the registers.

23. MNGDISK Vector Address at 0xBFF2

Function	Address	X-reg	Y-reg	A-reg	C-flag	Description
Entry	0xBFF2	slot #	#handler	/handler	set	Attach interface card disk handler
Return	–	same	same	same	clear	Return to caller
Entry	0xBFF2	slot #	–	0x00	set	Request DISKADRS disk handler address
Return	–	same	#handler	/handler	clear	Return to caller
Entry	0xBFF2	slot #	–	–	clear	Detach interface card disk handler
Return	–	same	#RWTSENT	/RWTSENT	clear	Return to caller

After DOS 4.5 has booted or has been copied into memory, the MNGDISK vector at memory address 0xBFF2 as shown in Table I.8.1 can be used to indirectly jump to the DOS MNGEXDSK routine. In DOS 4.5L this is an indirect jump directly to the MNGEXDSK routine. In DOS 4.5H this is an indirect jump through the Interface page 0xBE routine EXMNGDSK in order to write enable Bank 1 in the Language Card partition before jumping to the MNGEXDSK routine. The MNGEXDSK routine reads, writes, or restores a DISKADRS Table entry.

To attach a peripheral interface card disk handler to RWTS and write to the DISKADRS Table, indirectly jump to the address at MNGDISK with the interface card number or the slot-times-sixteen number in the X-register, the address of the interface card disk handler in the Y- and A-registers in Lo/Hi byte order, and **set** the Carry flag. The registers will be returned unchanged and the Carry flag will be returned **clear**. RWTS transfers control to the interface card disk handler for the requested I/O based entirely on the slot-times-sixteen value found in the RWTS IOCB. Figure I.8.2 shows an example assembly language routine that attaches the RAM Disk interface card disk handler to RWTS. Figure I.8.3 shows an example assembly language routine that calls MNGDISK to request the address of the handler currently assigned to a particular slot number to be returned in the Y- and A-registers. Therefore, to read the address of an entry in the DISKADRS Table, indirectly jump to the address at MNGDISK with the interface card number or the slot-times-sixteen number in the X-register, clear the A-register to zero, and **set** the Carry flag. The X-register will be returned unchanged, the Y- and A-registers will contain the address of the current device handler, and the Carry flag will be returned **clear**. In the same example shown in Figure I.8.3, in order to detach an entry address in the DISKADRS Table, indirectly jump to the address at MNGDISK with the interface card number or the slot-times-sixteen number in the X-register and **clear** the Carry flag. The X-register will be returned unchanged and the Y- and A-registers will contain the address of RWTSENT. The designated entry in the DISKADRS Table will be replaced with the default handler address, that is, the address of the internal RWTS handler routine RWTSENT.

For all MNGDISK functions the X-register must contain a valid slot number or a valid slot-times-sixteen number. A valid slot number is any number in the range from one to seven. If MNGDISK processing determines that the X-register contains an invalid value, MNGDISK immediately returns to the caller with the Carry flag **set** before any further processing occurs. Otherwise, MNGDISK returns to the caller with the Carry flag **clear**.

Unlike DOS 4.1 it is not necessary to know where the DISKADRS Table resides within DOS 4.5 memory nor how that table is managed nor how that table is utilized. MNGDISK takes care of all the necessary protocol that had to be done manually and entirely by the DOS 4.1 user. MNGDISK always returns the Carry flag **clear** unless the X-register contains an invalid value, then MNGDISK returns the

`Carry` flag **set**. Once processing is complete in DOS 4.5L, the `MNGEXDSK` routine returns directly to the caller. Once processing is complete in DOS 4.5H, the `MNGEXDSK` routine returns to Interface page `0xBE`, enables ROM memory, and then returns directly to the caller. The X-register is returned to the user unchanged and the Y- and A-registers are returned to the user with their appropriate or requested values. Use the Indirect approach in order to enter the DOS `MNGEXDSK` routine through the `MNGDISK` vector address at `0xBFF2`.

24. MNGVALS Vector Address at 0xBFF4

Function	Address	X-reg	Y-reg	A-reg	C-flag	V-flag	Description
Entry	0xBFF4	–	<0x61	variable	set	clear	Write one CMDVALS variable
Return	–	same	++1	same	clear	clear	Return to caller
Entry	0xBFF4	–	<0x61	–	clear	clear	Read one CMDVALS variable
Return	–	same	++1	variable	clear	clear	Return to caller
Entry	0xBFF4	variable	<0x61	variable+1	set	set	Write two CMDVALS variables
Return	–	same	++2	same	clear	set	Return to caller
Entry	0xBFF4	–	<0x61	–	clear	set	Read two CMDVALS variables
Return	–	variable	++2	variable+1	clear	set	Return to caller

After DOS 4.5 has booted or has been copied into memory, the `MNGVALS` vector at memory address `0xBFF4` as shown in Table I.8.1 can be used to indirectly jump to the DOS `MNGEXVAL` routine. In DOS 4.5L this is an indirect jump directly to the `MNGEXVAL` routine. In DOS 4.5H this is an indirect jump through the Interface page `0xBE` routine `EXMNGVAL` in order to write enable Bank 1 in the Language Card partition before jumping to the `MNGEXVAL` routine. The `MNGEXVAL` routine reads or writes the `CMDVALS` Data structure variables and the File Manager Workarea structure variables as shown in Tables I.12.1 and I.12.2, respectively. In all cases the Y-register is range checked and if it is greater than or equal to `CVALSLEN` (i.e. `0x61`), `MNGVALS` returns with the `Carry` flag **set**, otherwise `MNGVALS` returns with the `Carry` flag **clear**.

In order to change or write to a single `CMDVALS` or Workarea variable, the A-register must contain the desired data, the Y-register must contain the index to the desired variable that is to be changed, the `Carry` flag must be **set**, and the `Overflow` flag (or V-flag) must be **clear**. The Y-register is returned and incremented by one. Variable indices for the `CMDVALS` Data structure variables and the File Manager Workarea structure variables are shown in Tables I.12.1 and I.12.2, respectively. In order to access and read the value of a single `CMDVALS` or Workarea variable the Y-register must contain the index for the variable that is to be read, the `Carry` flag must be **clear**, and the `Overflow` flag must be **clear**. The data for the desired variable is returned in the A-register and the Y-register is returned and incremented by one. `MNGVALS` always returns to the caller with the `Carry` flag **clear** unless the Y-register contains an invalid value. When the Y-register contains an invalid value, the `Carry` flag is returned **set**.

When the V-flag is **set**, the Y-register must contain the index to the first variable that is to be read or written and the register is range checked to be less than `CVALSLEN` (i.e. `0x61`). In this instance the `MNGEXVAL` routine reads or writes two consecutive variables from either the `CMDVALS` Data structure or from the File Manager Workarea structure. When the `Carry` flag is **set**, the two data variables that are currently in the X- and A-registers are written consecutively to the CMDVALS Data structure or to the File Manager Workarea structure. The variable in the X-register is written first. When the Carry flag is **clear**, two consecutive variables are read from the CMDVALS Data structure or from the File Manager Workarea structure and returned in the X- and A-registers. The first variable read is copied into the X-register. In both instances the Y-register is returned and incremented by two. MNGVALS returns to the caller with the Carry flag **clear** unless the Y-register contains an invalid value. When the Y-register contains an invalid value, the Carry flag is returned **set**. It is possible to read or write one byte value beyond the CMDVALS Data structure when the Y-register is set to 0x60 and the V-flag is **set**. In this case there is a SPAREVAL byte located immediately after VOLNUMBR that ensures that no important data is affected.

Figures I.12.1 and I.12.2 show example assembly language routines in how to access and change the value of any variable in the CMDVALS Data structure or in the File Manager Workarea structure using the MNGVALS vector. In all cases the Overflow flag is returned unchanged. The 6502 (and 65C02) Instruction Set **does** contain a native *clear Overflow flag* instruction (i.e. CLV). Unfortunately, the Instruction Set does **not** contain a native *set Overflow flag* instruction. I am not sure why this microprocessor operation is missing. Actually, I believe there is no rationale for this shortcoming. Generally, one can use the BIT IORTS statement to easily achieve setting the Overflow flag. The IORTS address is the address for the RTS instruction in the ROM Monitor at memory address 0xFF58. Use the Indirect approach in order to enter the DOS MNGEXVAL routine through the MNGVALS vector address at 0xBFF4.

25. MNGUSER Vector Address at 0xBFF6

Function	Address	X-reg	Y-reg	A-reg	C-flag	Description
Entry	0xBFF6	–	#USERADR	/USERADR	set	Change USERADR/CMDVAL
Return	–	#USERADR	same	same	clear	Return to caller
Entry	0xBFF6	–	–	–	clear	Restore USERADR/CMDVAL
Return	–	#CMDRUN-CMDTBL	#GOTOMON	/GOTOMON	clear	Return to caller

After DOS 4.5 has booted or has been copied into memory, the MNGUSER vector at memory address 0xBFF6 as shown in Table I.8.1 can be used to indirectly jump to the DOS MNGEXUSR routine. In DOS 4.5L this is an indirect jump directly to the MNGEXUSR routine. In DOS 4.5H this is an indirect jump through the Interface page 0xBE routine EXMNGUSR in order to write enable Bank 1 in the Language Card partition before jumping to the MNGEXUSR routine. The MNGEXUSR routine changes or restores USERADR and CMDVAL which are variables in the INITVALS Data structure as shown in Table I.8.7. In either case MNGUSER returns to the caller with the Carry flag **clear**.

In order to utilize the DOS CMDUSER command during the DOS 4.5 boot process, the Y- and A-registers must contain the address of a DOS post-initialization routine in Lo/Hi byte order and the Carry flag must be **set**. MNGEXUSR initializes the CMDVAL command variable with the value of the DOS CMDUSER command (i.e. 0x60) and copies the address of the post-initialization routine found in the Y- and A-registers to the USERADR variable. Both variables USERADR and CMDVAL are found in the INITVALS Data structure. If the Carry flag is **clear**, then MNGEXUSR restores the values of the variables USERADR and CMDVAL to their default values: USERADR contains the address of the internal DOS ENTRMON routine and CMDVAL contains the value of CMDRUN-CMDTBL which is 0x06. The ENTRMON routine prints a carriage return, initializes the DOS CSWL and KSWL interface pointers, and enters the GOTOMON routine.

A DOS post-initialization routine is extremely useful to a user who wishes to load DOS 4.5 or copy a DOS 4.5 image into memory and initialize it such that it returns control back to that user via the post-initialization routine instead of normally losing control to Applesoft. In the normal boot scenario DOS 4.5 loads the value found in CMDVAL to initiate the first DOS command, typically a RUN command of an Applesoft program whose filename is found in FNAME, the HELLO filename. If, after copying the DOS 4.5 image into memory, an indirect jump can be made to MNGUSER in order to initialize USERADR with the address of a DOS post-initialization routine, and then an indirect jump can be made to DOSINIT. DOS will find the CMDUSER value in CMDVAL and initiate the processing of that DOS command. For CMDUSER processing, DOS simply makes an indirect jump directly to the address found in USERADR. What could be easier? One of the first tasks in the DOS post-initialization routine could be an indirect jump to MNGUSER with the Carry flag **clear**. This would restore the values normally found in the USERADR and CMDVAL variables effectively restoring DOS to its unmodified state. Then, finally, that same post-initialization routine could initiate an indirect jump to DOSINIT which would clear the CMDVALS Data structure and cold-start DOS in order to begin normal HELLO file processing or any number of other initial processing options. The list of initial processing options is virtually limitless with one's imagination. Figure I.8.4 shows an example assembly language routine in how to utilize MNGUSER as a post-initialization routine.

The default address found in USERADR is for the DOS ENTRMON routine. Whenever DOS parses the Apple Command Line and finds the USER command as shown in Table III.0.2, DOS begins CMDUSER processing which is simply loading the X- and A-registers with the decimal or hexadecimal number that is used in conjunction with the USER command, if any, (i.e. USER $1234) and then making an indirect jump directly to the address found in USERADR, normally the DOS ENTRMON routine that puts the user into the ROM or RAM Monitor. The address found in USERADR can point to any piece of code that needs to execute whenever DOS parses the USER command on the Apple Command Line or from within an Applesoft or EXEC file as in the example shown in Figure III.1.16. *Big Mac*, for example, uses the USER command in order to restart the *Big Mac* program once the user has exited *Big Mac* to DOS. The DOS USER command may be utilized for any programmed command need or requirement that is invoked by DOS when DOS makes an indirect jump to MNGUSER. Use the Indirect approach in order to enter the DOS MNGEXUSR routine through the MNGUSER vector address at 0xBFF6.

26. INITDOS Vector Address at 0xBFF8

Function	Address	X-reg	Y-reg	A-reg	C-flag	Description
Entry	0xBFF8	–	–	–	–	Enters (COLDADR) handler
Return	0xE000	–	–	–	–	BASCLD (no return to caller)

After DOS 4.5 has booted or has been copied into memory, the INITDOS vector at memory address 0xBFF8 as shown in Table I.8.1 can be used to indirectly jump directly to the DOS DOSINIT routine that resides in memory page 0xBF. The DOSINIT routine calls the CLRVALS routine that clears the

CMDVALS Data structure, and then DOSINIT enters the DOS COLDSTRT routine. Refer to Section IV.2 for a complete description of the COLDSTRT routine.

When COLDSTRT processing is complete, DOS exits indirectly into Applesoft by means of the COLDADR vector in the page 0xBE INITVALS Data structure. The assembler initially sets the COLDADR vector to memory address 0xE000, the address of Applesoft BASCLD. The BASCLD routine is entered at the Applesoft cold-start entry address in ROM that performs a complete reinitialization of Applesoft, and this routine does not return to the caller. The user is encouraged to change the address at COLDADR (i.e. 0xBEE4), a variable in the INITVALS Data structure, in order to tailor the COLDSTRT routine not to exit into Applesoft ROM, but into a user specific routine, and then exit into the BASCLD routine. Figure I.8.4 shows an example assembly language routine in how to utilize INITDOS. Use the Indirect approach in order to enter the DOS DOSINIT routine through the INITDOS vector address at 0xBFF8.

27. INITVAL Vector Address at 0xBFFA

Function	Address	X-reg	Y-reg	A-reg	C-flag	Description
Address	0xBFFA	-	-	-	-	Address of INITVALS Data structure
Return	-	-	-	-	-	

After DOS 4.5 has booted or has been copied into memory, the INITVAL variable at memory address 0xBFFA as shown in Table I.8.1 contains the address of the INITVALS Data structure as shown in Table I.8.7. The INITVALS Data structure resides within page 0xBE in both DOS 4.5L and in DOS 4.5H at precisely the same address by design, so its variables can be modified directly without having to manage any Soft Switches in order to enable a particular Bank in the Language Card partition. However, accessing and changing the values of the variables in this data structure is far easier and more general as shown in the example assembly language routine in Figure I.8.6. The address in the INITVAL variable is simply copied to a page-zero pointer in Lo/Hi byte order and any or all of the variables in the INITVALS Data structure may be accessed using the offsets (or indices) for those variables as shown in Table I.8.7. The address 0xBFFA for the INITVAL variable will not change in any version of DOS 4.5, but the address it contains for the INITVALS Data structure may, indeed, change. Use the page-zero pointer approach using the address in the INITVAL variable at 0xBFFA to access any of the variables in the DOS INITVALS Data structure.

28. BCFGNDX Variable Byte at 0xBFFC

Function	Address	X-reg	Y-reg	A-reg	C-flag	Description
#Address	0xBFFC	-	-	-	-	BOOTCFG Table offset

After DOS 4.5 has booted or has been copied into memory, the BCFGNDX variable byte at memory address 0xBFFC as shown in Table I.8.1 is the page offset to the DOS 4.5 Boot Configuration Data structure BOOTCFG that always resides within memory page 0xBF as shown in Table I.8.2. This data structure may be accessed indirectly by using a page-zero pointer as shown in Figure I.8.7.

The Boot Stage 1 process can be easily monitored, and at the appropriate moment when the Boot Stage 1 process has completed, the BOOTCFG Data structure can be tailored, that is, modified specifically for the Boot Stage 2 process that is about to begin. As Figure I.8.7 shows, the variables DNUM and VOLEXPT can be dynamically modified using the CFFA drive and volume values, respectively, for the Boot Stage 2 process that is about to begin.

Boot Stage 1 sectors are directly copied into memory by the CFFA firmware. However, Boot Stage 2 is unique for each Boot volume and that Boot volume process must be tailored for its own unique DOS, that is, for the DOS that is currently booting. When the Boot Stage 2 process begins, the RWPAGES routine is now correctly configured dynamically by means of the contents of its BOOTCFG Data structure. Once DOS is loaded into memory, DOS can then initialize and properly execute its initial HELLO program.

29. NBUF1PG Address Byte at 0xBFFD

Function	Address	X-reg	Y-reg	A-reg	C-flag	Description
/Address	0xBFFD	–	–	–	–	NBUF1 MSB Address

After DOS 4.5 has booted or has been copied into memory, the NBUF1PG address byte at memory address 0xBFFD as shown in Table I.8.1 is the most significant byte of the memory address for NBUF1. NBUF1 is a buffer that is 256 bytes in size that is unique because it begins on a page boundary and this buffer is exclusively used for RWTS processing. In DOS 4.5L this buffer resides in Main memory above the file buffers, the VTOC structure block, and the Catalog structure block, but below the DOS routines. In DOS 4.5H this buffer is one of the last memory pages in Bank 1 that resides in the Language Card partition. NBUF1PG contains the most significant address byte of the NBUF1 buffer, and this address byte is included in order to provide easy access to the address of a temporary page of memory as long as RWTS processing is not invoked, which would obviously overwrite the contents of this buffer.

To utilize this page of memory, the NBUF1PG address byte needs to be copied to the MSB of a page-zero pointer, and Bank 1 in the Language Card partition would need to be write enabled in DOS 4.5H. The LSB of this page-zero pointer needs to be set to zero. Oftentimes, having access to a temporary buffer that is a full page in size that begins on a page boundary can alleviate a very difficult programming situation. This full page buffer can also be used to temporally contain a page of data that needs to be swapped for another page of data. In order to write enable NBUF1 in DOS 4.5H, the soft-switch 0xC08B must be read twice consecutively. In the *Lisa* assembler this is coded as follows:

```
BIT $C08B
BIT $C08B
```

30. BOOTADR Variable Byte at 0xBFFE

Function	Address	X-reg	Y-reg	A-reg	C-flag	Description
/Address	0xBFFE	–	–	–	–	Boot Stage 1 MSB Address

The BOOTADR variable byte at memory address 0xBFFE as shown in Table I.8.1 is configured by the assembler to equal the most significant memory address byte of the page of DOS 4.5 data that is contained in the first data sector that is read from track 0x00 during Boot Stage 1. In DOS 4.5L the data in the first sector that is read from a Boot volume is copied to page 0xB9. In DOS 4.5H the data in the first sector that is read from a Boot volume is copied to page 0xD0. Variable bytes 0xB9 and 0xD0 are the BOOTADR variable bytes for DOS 4.5. In Boot Stage 0 the BOOTADR variable byte must be copied to the page-zero MSB pointer BUFRADRZ+1 which is at page-zero address 0x27. The Disk][firmware has already set the LSB address 0x26 to zero. The BUFRADRZ+1 pointer is incremented in the Disk][firmware at 0xCnEB, where **n** is the slot number of the Disk][peripheral interface card.

DOS 4.5 is unique in that as the BUFRADRZ+1 address is incremented, the next sector number to be read is decremented during the Boot Stage 1 boot processing as shown in Tables I.8.3 and I.8.4 for DOS 4.5L and for DOS 4.5H, respectively. The DOS 3.3 Boot Stage 1 algorithm boots in a totally opposite direction in that the BUFRADRZ+1 address is decremented while the sector number is incremented. DOS 4.5 takes advantage of all of the native firmware logic found in the Disk][peripheral interface card which increments both the BUFRADRZ+1 address and the sector number. However, sector number is not utilized directly in a linear direction like the BUFRADRZ+1 address is utilized. In DOS 3.3 as well as in DOS 4.5 sector number is decremented sequentially and utilized as in index into a sector interleave table in order to accelerate the loading of volume sectors that are resident in a given track. The entire DOS 4.5 boot image is read into memory starting from the furthest sector from track 0x00 and ending with track 0x00, sector 0x00. Every file that is saved to a volume attempts to save its first TSL sector to sector 0x0F of a given track and all of the data sectors of the file are saved in a sequentially decremented order entirely for the purpose in order to accelerate the read sector or the write sector processing. ProDOS, Fortran, and Pascal utilize specific and unique sector interleave tables that are different from the sector interleave table used in DOS 3.3 and in DOS 4.5.

31. BOOTPGS Variable Byte at 0xBFFF

Function	Address	X-reg	Y-reg	A-reg	C-flag	Description
Sectors	0xBFFF	–	–	–	–	Boot Stage 1 sectors read

After DOS 4.5 has booted or has been copied into memory, the BOOTPGS variable byte at memory address 0xBFFF as shown in Table I.8.1 is configured by the assembler to equal the number of sectors that must be consecutively read from track 0x00 during the Boot Stage 1 processing. In DOS 4.5L the first sector that is read from a Boot volume on track 0x00 is sector 0x06. In DOS 4.5H the first sector that is read from a Boot volume on track 0x00 is sector 0x0F. Variable bytes 0x06 and 0x0F are the BOOTPGS variable bytes for DOS 4.5. In Boot Stage 1 the BOOTPGS variable byte serves both as a counter and as the next sector index into the sector interleave table to obtain the value of the next physical sector to read. In DOS 4.5H specifically, the BOOTPGS variable byte value is also used to determine when to change the address value in BUFRADRZ+1 from 0xDE to 0xBE. Tables I.8.3 and

I.8.4 show the relationship of track 0x00 sector value and its corresponding memory page MSB for DOS 4.5L and for DOS 4.5H boot images, respectively. In other words, DOS 4.5 always loads sector 0x01 on track 0x00 to page 0xBE and sector 0x00 on track 0x00 to page 0xBF.

DOS 4.5 is designed as a result of high intension, sincere effort, and intelligent execution.

V. DOS 4.5 Operational Environment

DOS 4.5, as in DOS 4.1 previously, provides a far more advanced operational environment for the entire genre of Apple][software design be it for tools, utilities, or games, particularly when this software makes full use of the open and documented architecture of DOS 4.5. I have developed my own software such as *Applesoft Formatter*, Binary File Installation (*BFI*), *Real Time Clock* (my own hardware, too), *Disk Window*, EPROM Operating System (*EOS*), Volume Manager for the CFFA card (*VOLMGR, BOOTVOL, BOOTDOS*), VTOC Manager (*VMGR*), *TrackScan*, and *ICON Maker*. On the other hand, I have created source files for commercial programs that include Asynchronous Data Transfer (*ADT*), *Big Mac*, PROmGRAMER, CFFA card firmware, File Developer (*FID*), Lazer's Interactive Symbolic Assembler (*Lisa*), Program Global Editor (*PGE*), Global Program Line Editor (*GPLE*), RAM Disk 320 firmware, RanaSystems EliteThree firmware, Sider firmware, and *Sourceror* to utilize the features of DOS 4.5.

Because so much time has passed since these commercial programs were first published, I did not even consider requesting permission from the respective authors of this commercial object code, to *source* their software for sadly, many of these authors may have already passed on. My intent was to learn the internal dependencies from these commercial programs on DOS 3.3. Collectively, these dependencies partially drove my initial design of DOS 4.1, and now my design of DOS 4.5, to best provide enough visibility into the DOS 4.5 processing internals and data structures these authors required. As is said, *The proof is in the pudding!* I have successfully modified all the above-mentioned commercial programming tools, utilities, and firmware to be fully DOS 4.5 compliant as if DOS 4.5 is some black box with sufficient special access points to data, and there should be no need to directly access any of the DOS 4.5 internal routines. I created these source code files for my own intellectual edification and for my own use. I am simply demonstrating and showing the effort and the time I have invested in order to modify what I consider to be valuable software programs written by other brilliant Apple][software programmers, and to still function successfully within the operational environment of DOS 4.5.

Previously, I did spend a considerable amount of time attempting to relocate DOS 4.3 to Auxiliary memory. I was absolutely successful in this exercise! However, I could not successfully interface this DOS with either *Big Mac* or *Lisa*. The interface code became unwieldy and started to consume precious code space in Main memory that became too significant. Next, I chose to leave DOS 4.3 in the Language Card partition in Main memory and relocate *Lisa* to the Language Card partition in Auxiliary memory. This proved to be far easier than I anticipated given the previous interface challenges. Now that I have developed the Auxiliary memory interface routines for *Lisa* and have amassed considerable experience working with Auxiliary memory, I attempted to relocate *Big Mac* to the Language Card partition in Auxiliary memory as well. This proved to be easier to accomplish, and the interface routines for *Big Mac* are very similar to the ones I developed for *Lisa*. Furthermore, I developed all of the remaining code in both *Sourceror* and in *Big Mac* to fully support the *SWEET16* Metaprocessor Instruction Set I presented in Section II.3.

The achievements I accomplished during the development of DOS 4.3 came easier because I had far more memory available. I found it burdensome during DOS 4.1 development having substantially less memory for DOS 4.1L than I had for DOS 4.1H. Keeping DOS 4.1L and DOS 4.1H synchronized consumed a great deal of energy. Not having to also develop a DOS 4.3L version allowed me to utilize my time far more efficiently during DOS 4.3 development. However, once I was satisfied with all of the new content and capabilities I engineered into DOS 4.5, I found that I could, with some clever rearrangement of the source code, produce a DOS 4.5L version that only cost one additional disk sector.

1. Disk Window

I have no doubt that Don Worth and Pieter Lechner inspired thousands of computer hobbyists like me with their Example Programs found in their book *Beneath Apple DOS*, for these authors certainly inspired me. The learning curve was a bit steep as I recall, diskettes were expensive at that time, and I had some preconceived underlying fears that I could possibly destroy something precious, be it hardware or software, if I casually started to tinker around with RWTS back in 1981. Patience was certainly a virtue, and when one is examining the sectors and tracks of a diskette, it was like peering through some sort of digital microscope. The idea of reading a specific sector on a diskette and being able to display that sector content was awe-inspiring. Furthermore, having a utility that could edit those data bytes and write those edits back to that same sector, or to any other sector for that matter, was totally mind blowing. *What can of worms would that capability open?* Worth's and Lechner's utility Zap did inspire me to design *Disk Window*, what I call my fancy Zap program. It is like having a digital window focused on any device, track, sector, or Logical Block Address (LBA) of my choosing.

The current version of *Disk Window* now supports the reading and writing of any valid LBA sector on a CFFA card. If a CFFA card is detected to be resident in the selected slot, LBA mode is utilized for reading and writing block data. If a Disk][interface or similar peripheral card is detected to be resident in the selected slot, track-sector mode is utilized for reading and writing sector data. Regardless which mode is utilized to read and write data, the appropriate LBA for the selected volume-track-sector is displayed according to the conversion algorithm I developed for the CFFA card. The startup screen for *Disk Window* is displayed as shown in Figure V.1.1. The four commands at the bottom of the screen are Configure, Select LBA, Select D/V, and Select T/S that utilize the respective variables at the top of the screen. The commands Forward and Backward simply increment or decrement the track/sector values if in track-sector mode or LBA values if in LBA mode. The commands Edit, Write, and Print display a respective command screen for their particular function.

Figure V.1.2 shows the display of the VTOC data for the diskette in Drive 2 of a Disk][whose peripheral interface card resides in Slot 6. The data is displayed both in hexadecimal and in ASCII, unless the ASCII data byte is a control character. The hexadecimal values from 0x00 to 0x1F and from 0x80 to 0x9F are displayed as an ASCII PERIOD character. Lower ASCII values from 0x20 to 0x7F are displayed in inverse text and upper ASCII values from 0xA0 to 0xFF are displayed in normal text. If Edit is selected the same VTOC data is displayed as shown in Figure V.1.3, and the cursor is initially placed on row 0x70 and in column 0x07. After all edits have been applied, the Write command can write the sector data to the selected sector or to any other sector (or LBA) as shown in Figure V.1.4. Note that LBA blocks are 512 bytes in size. *Page 0* refers to the first 256 bytes and *Page 1* refers to the second 256 bytes of an LBA block. Thus, CFFA sectors 0x00-0x0F reside on Page 0 and CFFA sectors 0x10-0x1F reside on Page 1. The 256-byte sector data may be saved to any available LBA, either on Page 0 or on Page 1. Page 0 is selected by pressing the 0 or L key and Page 1 is selected by pressing the 1 or H key. The data shown on the display can also be printed using the Print command as shown in Figure V.1.5. The command Configure at the bottom of Figure V.1.5 allows the user to change the configuration values like Printer Slot if desired without having to return to the main menu display as shown in Figure V.1.1. If an RWTS error should occur during *Disk Window* processing, the error is prominently printed in the center of the hexadecimal data display window as shown in Figure V.1.6. I purposefully opened the diskette door of the Disk][drive in order to cause a disk drive error before any data could be written to the diskette. According to Table I.9.4 an RWTS error having a value of 0x40 is an RWTS Drive error. The error message remains displayed until any key is pressed on the keyboard.

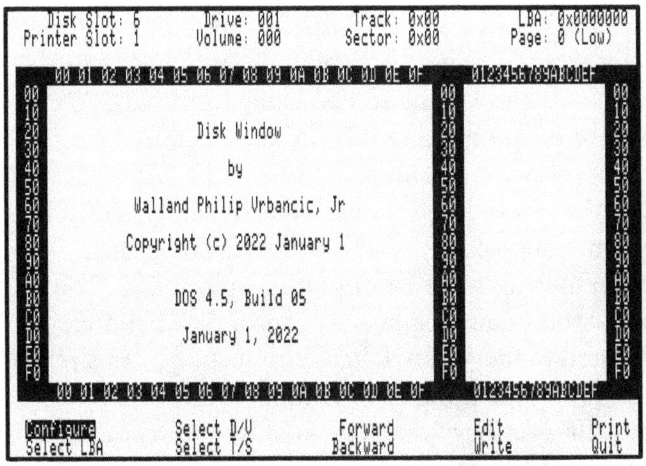

Figure V.1.1. Disk Window Startup Display

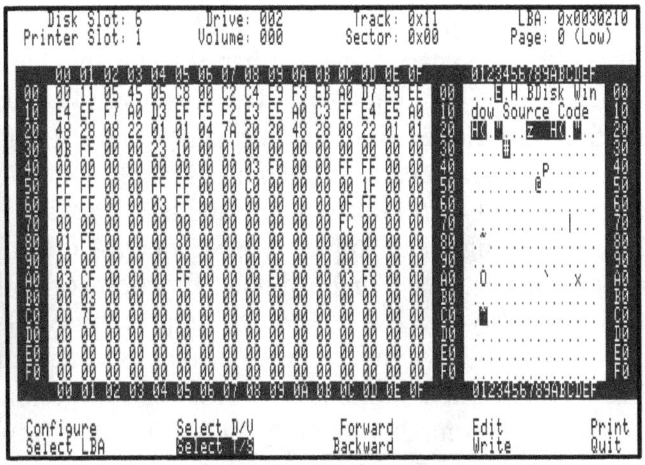

Figure V.1.2. Select T/S Mode Display

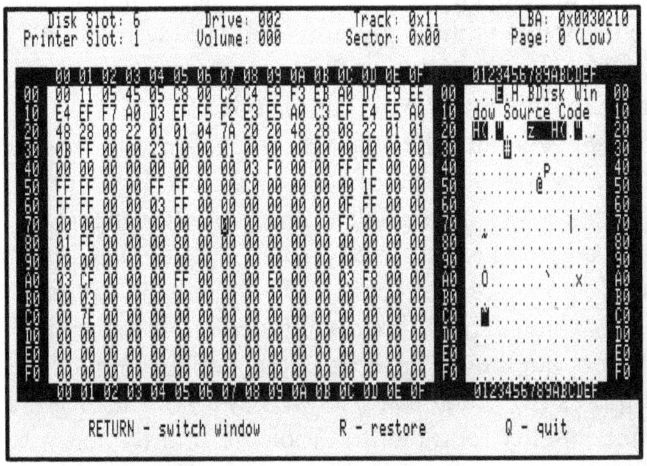

Figure V.1.3. Edit Data Display

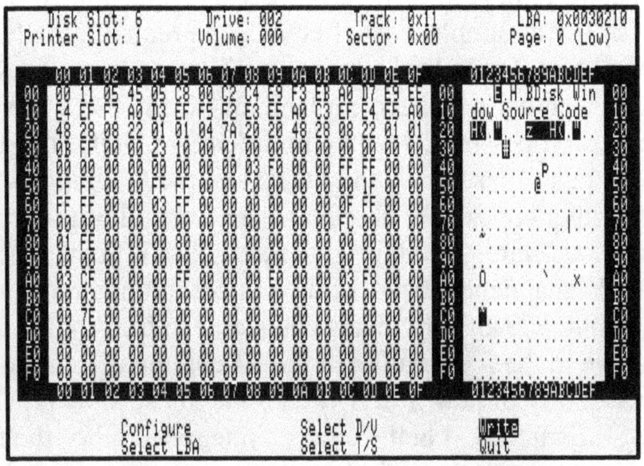

Figure V.1.4. Write Sector Data Display

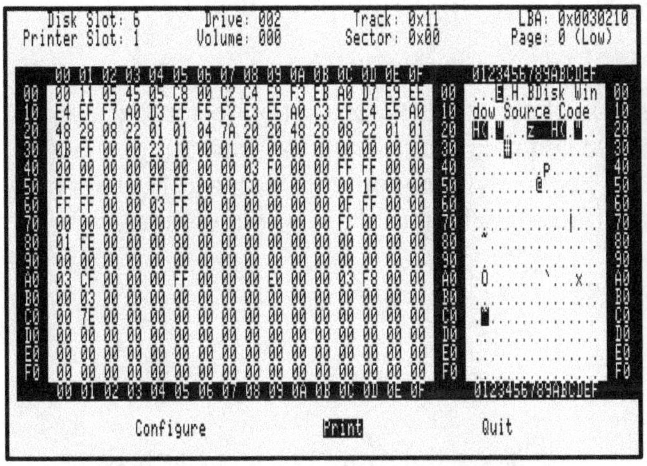

Figure V.1.5. Print Sector Data Display

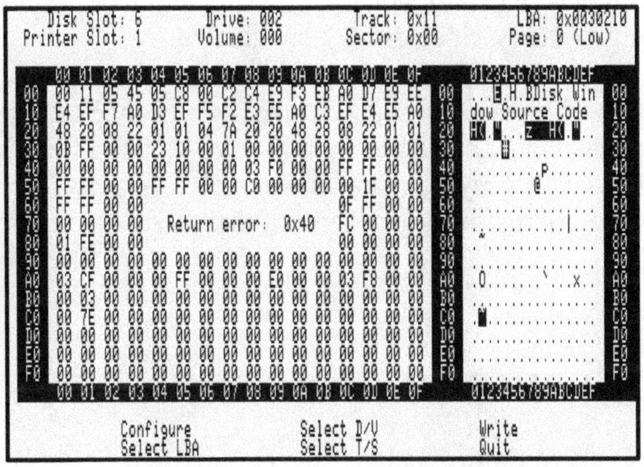

Figure V.1.6. Disk Window Error Message Display

I originally wrote *Disk Window* after I purchased the Videx UltraTerm video display card for my Apple][+. This video card has a number of beautiful character sets with inverse display for both upper and lower case ASCII characters. The cursor can be placed anywhere on the screen using a simple GOTO routine I developed since the normal CH and CV page-zero locations cannot be used especially when their values are outside of the normal Apple][+ 40-column screen locations. I believe this video display card was well worth every penny and the firmware was very well thought out. Unfortunately, when I began working on an Apple //e at Sierra On-Line, all of my 80-column screen handling code that I developed for *Disk Window* did not function correctly on the Apple //e 80-column display card. The task of modifying *Disk Window* to support the Apple //e 80-column display gave me a first-hand view of how dumbed-down the Apple //e display is when compared to the Videx UltraTerm display. As a result, I have very mixed opinions as to Apple's solution in doubling the number of column characters by doubling the computer memory and using what Apple calls Auxiliary memory, that is, a mirror image of Main memory. I also question Apple's logic in retaining its wide selection of upper case display options and very limited selection of lower case display options. Would Wozniak have designed the Apple //e display differently? I wonder if his opinion was ever solicited.

Then again, Apple did have a great responsibility when it developed the 80-column display solution so that it was simple, cost effective, and remain greatly compatible with all previous software written for the basic Apple][platform. Auxiliary memory does offer a unique solution that is easily managed by the Memory Management Unit, or MMU, that generates the address signals for the 65C02-microprocessor and by the Input/Output Unit, or IOU, that generates the address signals for the video display. These units, the MMU and the IOU, are not strictly independent of each other, but they work together cohesively in order to generate all of the required addressing signals that are used throughout the hardware. The third integrated circuit in the Apple //e is the Programmed Array Logic device, or PAL, that generates all of the critical timing and control signals for the Apple //e hardware and for any peripheral slot card that is connected to the Apple //e hardware. These three integrated circuits not only serve in the formulation of the 80-column display solution, but they also serve in the management of the vast array of new Soft Switches like those shown in Figures II.2.1 and II.2.2 as well as all of the original Soft Switches. I believe Apple integrated all of the functionality found in the Apple //e smartly and with an eye on simplicity and cohesiveness. The Videx UltraTerm as well as the Videx VideoTerm are 80-column high fidelity peripheral slot video display cards. These display cards cannot be integrated into the overall Apple //e hardware design because of their very high cost and their total disassociation from the Apple //e MMU, IOU, and PAL integrated circuits. My Videx UltraTerm video display card remains seated in Slot #3 of my Apple][+ where it provides the most beautiful, flexible, and dynamic high fidelity video display imaginable.

Disk Window is certainly a giant leap from Worth's and Lechner's utility Zap, but these authors are the giants whose shoulders I stand on in utilizing their insight and their enthusiasm for everything Apple][. I know that my efforts in creating *Disk Window* serve to genuinely compliment Worth and Lechner and to return my thanks to them for their early efforts in the history making of the Apple][computer.

2. EPROM Operating System (EOS) for SCRG quikLoader

Southern California Research Group (SCRG) developed and marketed the quikLoader as well as the PROmGRAMER, and they were must-have peripheral slot cards when they first appeared in the early 1980's. Without question, data can be loaded many, many times faster from the Disk][than data can be loaded from cassette tape. But data can be loaded many, many times faster from a quikLoader EPROM than data can be loaded from the Disk][. Literally, in a fraction of a second, DOS can be loaded into memory from a quikLoader EPROM, initialized, and begin its Apple Command Line processing.

I attended a Los Angeles computer convention where I bought the quikLoader after seeing several demonstrations in how fast data can be loaded from EPROM. Essentially, it is a very simple, though elegant peripheral interface card that can hold up to eight 2716 to 27512 EPROMs. The card contains some hardware logic that maps the selected EPROM to the 0xC100 to 0xFFFF address space.

The control and management software that SCRG provided with the quikLoader resides in the first EPROM, or EPROM 0, and this EPROM has sufficient room for a few additional programs as well. The SCRG documentation explains how to organize the contents of other programs and utilities in an EPROM and how to build a Catalog for those EPROM contents. Once an EPROM is programmed with its Catalog and software contents, and seated in the quikLoader, a selected *Primary* program is loaded into memory when pressing and holding its EPROM number followed by pressing the RESET key. The EPROM Catalog is displayed when the letter Q is pressed followed by pressing the RESET key. I built several quikLoader EPROMs using the SCRG software interface, but I found the process to be tedious and cumbersome, and I thought I might be able to design a better software interface. Once I sourced the SCRG EPROM control code, I realized their software interface could have been perhaps better thought out. But I discovered that there was absolutely no way to programmatically access any of the quikLoader EPROM contents using the current SCRG hardware unless I included a substantial portion of their EPROM control code routines within my software. Unfortunately, the EPROM control code routines are not actually published, so that made accessing the quikLoader contents even more tenuous.

Peripheral interface cards for the Apple][computer typically incorporate and utilize firmware code in its peripheral-card ROM addressing, that is, 0xCs00 to 0xCsFF where s is the slot number of the peripheral interface card. Also, when the appropriate hardware logic is included, a peripheral interface card can use its peripheral-card expansion ROM addressing, 0xC800 to 0xCFFF, for additional firmware code when the interface card is enabled. As an aside, if 0xCFFF (i.e. CLRROM) is put onto the address bus a card is required to disable its peripheral-card expansion ROM addressing. This allows another peripheral interface card, enabled by accessing its peripheral-card ROM addressing, to utilize its peripheral-card expansion ROM addressing. This protocol prevents addressing contention with other peripheral interface cards. The quikLoader hardware did not have the ability to utilize its peripheral-card ROM addressing and, therefore, it could not utilize any peripheral-card expansion ROM addressing in any of its software. This inability is simply a hardware design choice, but I viewed it as a hardware design deficiency due to the missing hardware logic.

I did find one unused 74LS08 AND gate on the quikLoader. That single AND gate allowed me to modify the quikLoader hardware logic such that it was now possible to access its peripheral-card ROM memory that was mapped to a single page of quikLoader EPROM memory. Now I had something physical I could work with, and this simple hardware logic modification allowed me to develop the EPROM Operating System, or *EOS*. In addition to this simple hardware logic modification, I added an LED to glow whenever the quikLoader was enabled and an SPDT switch to physically disable the quikLoader without having to actually remove it from its peripheral slot in the computer. The complete circuit diagram of my modified quikLoader including the switch settings for bank selection is shown in Figure V.2.1.

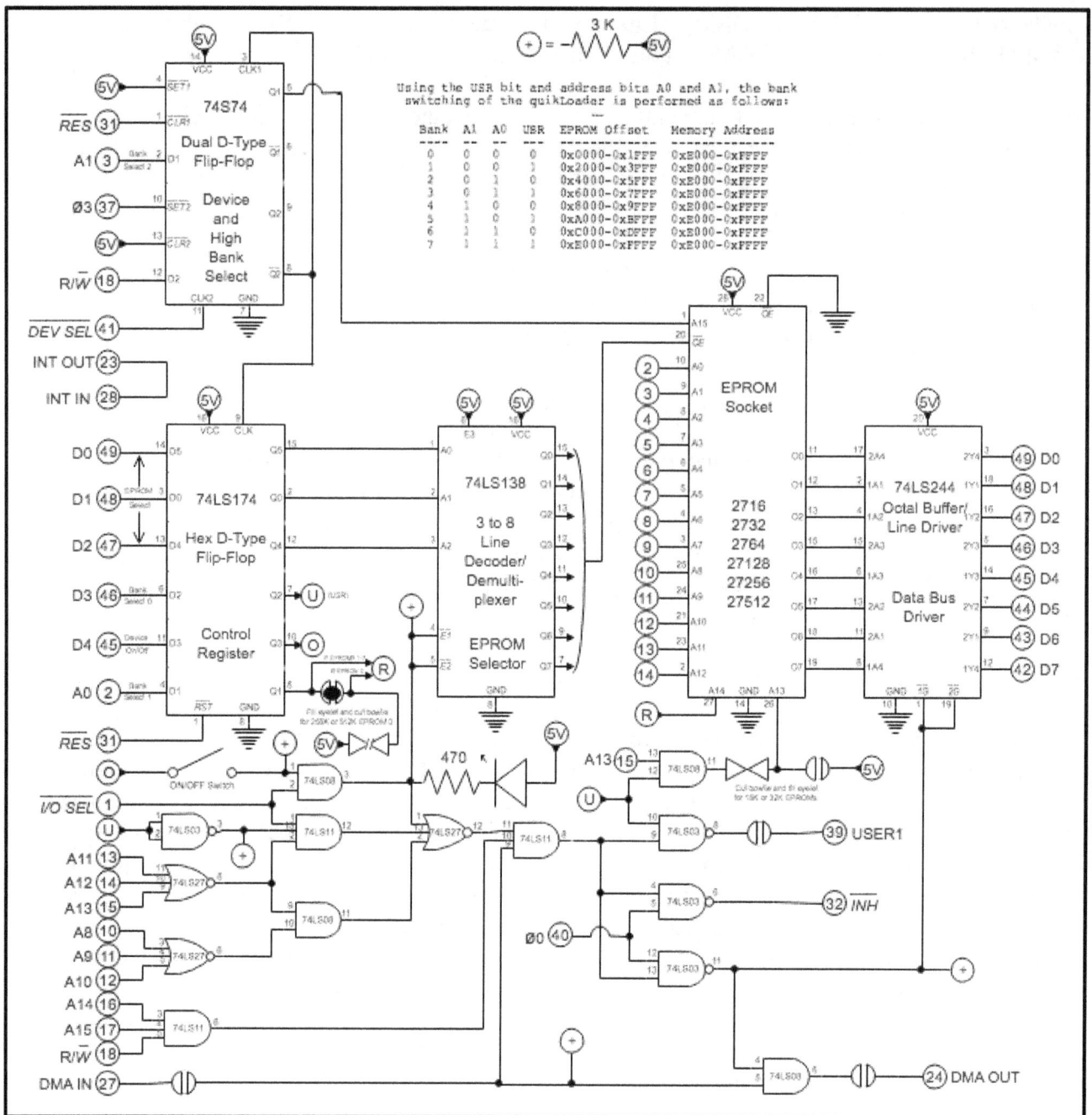

Figure V.2.1 quikLoader Schematic with Circuit Modifications

Fortunately, I had acquired the *improved* quikLoader, the model capable of addressing a 27512 EPROM. A 74LS74 dual D flip-flop was added to the original quikLoader in order to capture the state of the 6502 A1 address line when writing to the 74LS174 control register of the quikLoader, and to ever so slightly delay the 6502 φ3 clock edge for latching EPROM data. The control register data byte can be written to any of the sixteen I/O memory locations dedicated to the slot of the quikLoader, that is, 0xC0n0 through 0xC0nF, where **n** is equal to the slot number of the quikLoader plus eight. However, only the first four address locations (or their relatives) do anything different since the control register only latches the state of address line A0 while the added 74LS74 latches the state of address line A1. The state of

198

address lines A2 and A3 are not latched, and their values are not utilized. Data lines D0, D1, and D2 are latched by the control register and they select one of eight quikLoader EPROMs. Data line D3 is latched for the USR bit and data line D4 is latched to turn the quikLoader ON or OFF. If data line D4 is zero the quikLoader is turned ON. The state of data lines D5, D6, and D7 are not latched or utilized.

The SCRG documentation describes how an area of quikLoader EPROM memory at a given offset is mapped to the 0xC100 to 0xFFFF address space in the Apple][, but I found that using the first half of this address space was strange and confusing to me, and it was not very amenable to programmatic utilization. Rather, I found that I could access an entire 27512 EPROM simply by using eight 8-KByte banks, where each bank uses the upper 0xE000 to 0xFFFF address space. The described function of the USR bit was also strange and confusing to me as well as the role it was designed to perform according to the SCRG documentation. The USR bit was intended to be used as a master/slave flag when multiple quikLoaders are seated in the same computer. For the moment I have quite a few programs that I routinely use, and all those programs along with *EOS* fit comfortably into three 27512 EPROMs. I cannot imagine needing more than one quikLoader in my computer, so my vision of *EOS* became even more tailored when I limited *EOS* to manage a single quikLoader and utilize the USR bit only for bank selection. Table V.2.1 expands on the bank selection switch settings that are shown in Figure V.2.1 and the table lists the six EPROM memory sizes that the quikLoader can address, their associated memory bank(s), and the latched data values that are used by the data control registers (74LS174 and 74LS74) that are necessary for USR (D3), A0, and A1 in order to access those eight memory banks. The memory content of those eight memory banks when they are sequentially accessed is equivalent to accessing the entire memory contents of a 27512 EPROM. That is a significant achievement in itself, and it allows *EOS* to manage and load data from any sized EPROM simply and elegantly.

Bank	EPROM	EPROM Access	Memory Access	A1	A0	USR
0	2716	0x0000-0x07FF	0xF800-0xFFFF	0	0	0
0	2732	0x0000-0x0FFF	0xF000-0xFFFF	0	0	0
0	2764	0x0000-0x1FFF	0xE000-0xFFFF	0	0	0
0	27128	0x0000-0x1FFF	0xE000-0xFFFF	0	0	0
1		0x2000-0x3FFF	0xE000-0xFFFF	0	0	1
0	27256	0x0000-0x1FFF	0xE000-0xFFFF	0	0	0
1		0x2000-0x3FFF	0xE000-0xFFFF	0	0	1
2		0x4000-0x5FFF	0xE000-0xFFFF	0	1	0
3		0x6000-0x7FFF	0xE000-0xFFFF	0	1	1
0	27512	0x0000-0x1FFF	0xE000-0xFFFF	0	0	0
1		0x2000-0x3FFF	0xE000-0xFFFF	0	0	1
2		0x4000-0x5FFF	0xE000-0xFFFF	0	1	0
3		0x6000-0x7FFF	0xE000-0xFFFF	0	1	1
4		0x8000-0x9FFF	0xE000-0xFFFF	1	0	0
5		0xA000-0xBFFF	0xE000-0xFFFF	1	0	1
6		0xC000-0xDFFF	0xE000-0xFFFF	1	1	0
7		0xE000-0xFFFF	0xE000-0xFFFF	1	1	1

Table V.2.1. quikLoader Bank Switching

Offset	Name	Description
0x00	QLASEOS	Applesoft interface entry, parses command variables
0x5F	QLEXIT01	Return Unknown Command error, 0x01
0x62	QLEXIT02	Return Wrong Number of Parameters error, 0x02
0x65	QLEXIT03	Return Search Range Invalid error, 0x03
0x68	QLEXIT04	Return File Not Found error, 0x04
0x6B	QLEXIT00	Return no error, 0x00
0x9D	QLEXIT1	If ZipChip present flush cache and enable it, fall into QLEXIT2
0xC3	QLEXIT2	Turn quikLoader OFF, jump to (MEMJMP) at 0x0290
0xCB	QLUSER1	Return from DOS CMDUSER 1 command
0xCE	QLUSER2	Return from DOS CMDUSER 2 command
0xE0	QLBINEOS	Turn quikLoader ON, load QBMCODE, jump to BINEOS2 at 0xF229
0xF0	QLEOS	Turn quikLoader ON, jump to EOS at 0xE800
0xF8	QLBINTXT	ASCII text string *QLBINEOS* used to find the slot number for a quikLoader

Table V.2.2. quikLoader Firmware Entry Points

When RESET is pressed the 74LS174 and 74LS74 data control registers are cleared in order to select quikLoader EPROM 0, force EPROM Bank 0 to be mapped into Apple][memory from 0xE000 to 0xFFFF, and turn the quikLoader ON. The 6502-microprocessor automatically loads the RESET vector at 0xFFFC/0xFFFD into the program counter and it continues to fetch instructions beginning from the address stored at that location. As an aside, the NMI vector is at 0xFFFA/0xFFFB and the IRQ/BRK vector is at 0xFFFE/0xFFFF. From EPROM 0, the Bank 0 content is now in focus in the 0xE000 to 0xFFFF memory range, and these three hardware vectors all point to the start of *EOS* which begins at 0xE800. The *EOS* Catalog page resides at 0xE000 and *EOS* uses the remaining 0x16FA bytes in Bank 0 memory. Therefore, a 2764 EPROM, at a minimum, can be used for EPROM 0 in order to support *EOS*. Otherwise, some sort of bank switching would need to be utilized in order to extend *EOS* processing into another EPROM bank, an option I did not wish to employ. Table V.2.2 shows the firmware entry points for one of the seven copies of firmware that is mapped to the peripheral-card ROM memory of the quikLoader in order to support each slot simply by incorporating that single, unused 74LS08 AND gate as shown in Figure V.2.1. I am sure a *knock-off* quikLoader hardware design would be extraordinarily silly if it did not incorporate that same simple modification, including an LED and a SPDT switch at a minimum, which I added to my own quikLoader.

Fortunately, from 0xE800 to 0xFFFA there is sufficient room for *EOS* to process the 26 commands as shown in Figure V.2.2. There is even room for the EPROM Catalog function, the Applesoft interface (ASEOS), the assembly language interface (BINEOS), the ZipChip configuration software to support a ZipChip if one is present, and the software to manage Primary files. Unlike the SCRG interface, *EOS* does not capture the state of the keyboard at the moment the RESET key is pressed. Rather, *EOS* displays an EOS Main Selection Menu, and any one of the displayed options may be selected. I simply chose those programs and utilities I liked best for display as menu options. Someone else may display a different set of favorite options. The way I have organized EPROM 0 is so simple that others may simply model their EPROM 0 after mine. The remaining seven banks in EPROM 0, a 27512, contain DOS 4.5L, DOS 4.5H, *Lisa80*, *SETUP80*, and *LOADLISA80*, RAM Disk Installation, *FID*, *Set Clock*, and *ASLIST*. Table V.2.3 shows the content of my EPROM 0 along with *EOS*. All other programs reside on the other quikLoader EPROMs. *EOS* uses the power and the flexibility of BINEOS to load and to run those other programs without regard to a specific EPROM number. An EPROM Catalog display is shown in Figures V.2.3. and V.2.4, and an example Catalog File Entry Values display is shown in Figure V.2.5. Simply press numbers 0-7 to display the Catalog for that EPROM.

Bank	Offset	Memory	Size	Contents
0	0x0000	0xE000	0x0004	Synchronization bytes
0	0x0004	0xE004	0x00FC	Catalog
0	0x0100	0xE100	0x0100	Slot 1 ASEOS/BINEOS interface
0	0x0200	0xE200	0x0100	Slot 2 ASEOS/BINEOS interface
0	0x0300	0xE300	0x0100	Slot 3 ASEOS/BINEOS interface
0	0x0400	0xE400	0x0100	Slot 4 ASEOS/BINEOS interface
0	0x0500	0xE500	0x0100	Slot 5 ASEOS/BINEOS interface
0	0x0600	0xE600	0x0100	Slot 6 ASEOS/BINEOS interface
0	0x0700	0xE700	0x0100	Slot 7 ASEOS/BINEOS interface
0	0x0800	0xE800	0x17FA	*EOS* software
0	0x1FFA	0xFFFA	0x0002	NMI vector, address of *EOS*
0	0x1FFC	0xFFFC	0x0002	RESET vector, address of *EOS*
0	0x1FFE	0xFFFE	0x0002	IRQ/BRK vector, address of *EOS*
1	0x2000	0xE000	0x2100	DOS4.5L
2	0x4100	0xE100	0x2A00	DOS4.5H
3	0x6B00	0xEB00	0x2800	LISA80.1 code segment
4	0x9300	0xF300	0x1000	LISA80.2 code segment
5	0xA300	0xE300	0x05F0	LISA80.3 code segment
5	0xA8F0	0xE8F0	0x1998	*SETUP80*
6	0xC288	0xE288	0x019B	*LOADLISA80*
6	0xC423	0xE423	0x1B04	RAM Disk
6	0xDF27	0xFF27	0x1316	*FID*
7	0xF23D	0xF23D	0x064A	*Set Clock*
7	0xF887	0xF887	0x06D9	*ASLIST*
7	0xFF60	0xFF60	0x00A0	unused

Table V.2.3. quikLoader EPROM 0 Containing EOS and Programs

Value	Catalog	Description
0x01	T	Text file, NULL terminated, similar to an EXEC file
0x02	A	Applesoft file
0x04	B	Binary file or segment, Main memory
0x08	B	Binary file or segment, Bank 1 Language Card partition
0x10	B	Binary file or segment, Bank 2 Language Card partition
0x20	R	Reserved file
0x40	S	System file
0x80	P	Primary file

Table V.2.4. EOS File Types

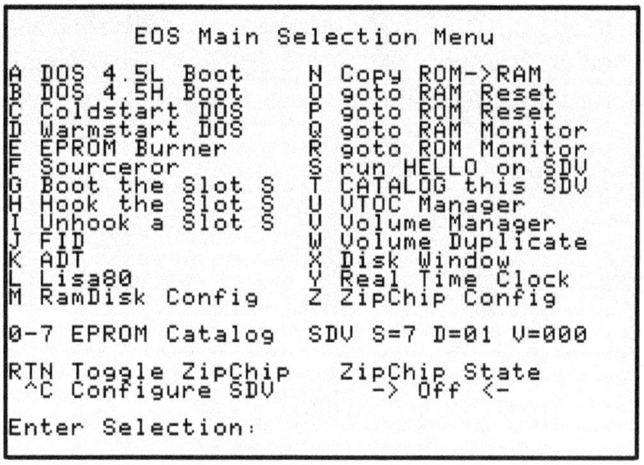

```
        EOS Main Selection Menu
A DOS 4.5L Boot       N Copy ROM->RAM
B DOS 4.5H Boot       O goto RAM Reset
C Coldstart DOS       P goto ROM Reset
D Warmstart DOS       Q goto RAM Monitor
E EPROM Burner        R goto ROM Monitor
F Sourceror           S run HELLO on SDV
G Boot the Slot S     T CATALOG this SDV
H Hook the Slot S     U VTOC Manager
I Unhook a Slot S     V Volume Manager
J FID                 W Volume Duplicate
K ADT                 X Disk Window
L Lisa80              Y Real Time Clock
M RamDisk Config      Z ZipChip Config

0-7 EPROM Catalog     SDV S=7 D=01 V=000

RTN Toggle ZipChip    ZipChip State
^C Configure SDV         -> Off <-

Enter Selection:
```

Figure V.2.2. EOS Main Selection Menu

```
quikLoader EOS - EPROM Catalog
    Slot 4              EPROM 0

  B 0x04  >RamDisk Config

  B 0x04   FID

  B 0x04   Set Clock

  B 0x04   Applesoft Formatter

  P 0x84   LOADLISA80

  B 0x04   SETUP80

  S 0x44   DOS4.5.05L

  S 0x5C   DOS4.5.05H

  RTN - File Info          (L)oad
  SPC - Next EPROM         (R)un
  0-7 - Select EPROM       (Q)uit
```

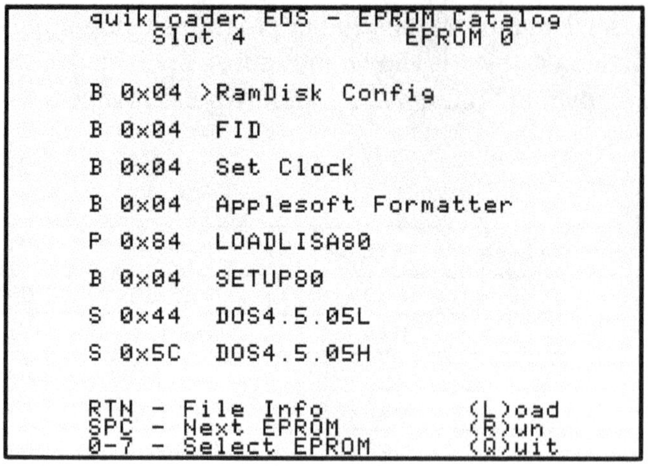

Figure V.2.3. EPROM 4 Catalog, Part 1

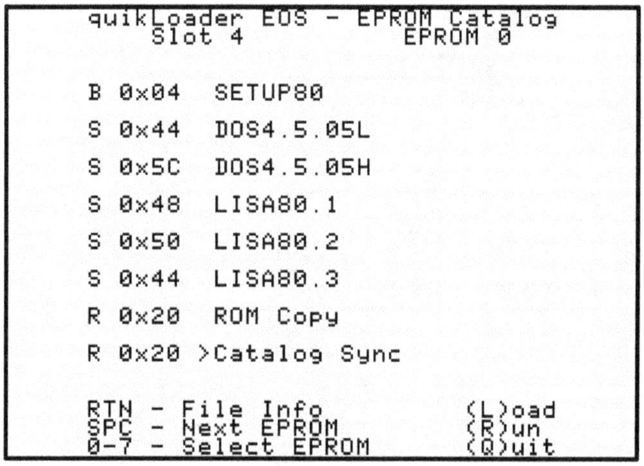

```
quikLoader EOS - EPROM Catalog
    Slot 4              EPROM 0

  B 0x04   SETUP80

  S 0x44   DOS4.5.05L

  S 0x5C   DOS4.5.05H

  S 0x48   LISA80.1

  S 0x50   LISA80.2

  S 0x44   LISA80.3

  R 0x20   ROM Copy

  R 0x20  >Catalog Sync

  RTN - File Info          (L)oad
  SPC - Next EPROM         (R)un
  0-7 - Select EPROM       (Q)uit
```

Figure V.2.4. EPROM 4 Catalog, Part 2

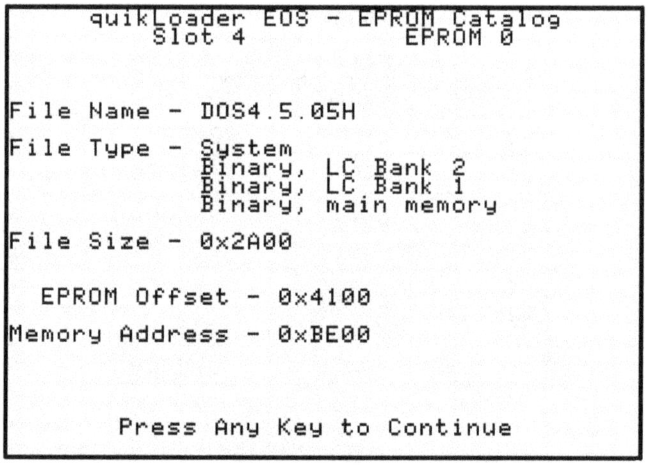

```
quikLoader EOS - EPROM Catalog
    Slot 4              EPROM 0


File Name - DOS4.5.05H
File Type - System
            Binary, LC Bank 2
            Binary, LC Bank 1
            Binary, main memory
File Size - 0x2A00

  EPROM Offset - 0x4100

Memory Address - 0xBE00



      Press Any Key to Continue
```

Figure V.2.5. EOS Catalog File Entry Values

Table V.2.4 shows the definition of the file types that are utilized in *EOS*, the ASCII character that is used to display each file type in the EPROM Catalog display, and the hexadecimal value for each file type. Notice in Figure V.2.4 that the DOS.4.5.05H entry is file **Type S** having a value of **0x5C**. This value is derived from the logical **OR** of System file, Binary file Bank **2** memory, Binary file Bank **1** memory, and Binary file Main memory because parts of DOS.4.5.05H reside in all those memory locations as shown in Figure V.2.5. Mathematically, the file **Type** for the DOS.4.5.05H entry is:

FILETYPE = 0x40 ∨ 0x10 ∨ 0x08 ∨ 0x04 = 0x5C

EOS provides Applesoft users with three commands when using the Applesoft, or **ASEOS** interface for **LOAD** file, **RUN** file, and **CATALOG**. In order to access **ASEOS** by means of Applesoft, the quikLoader control register must be initially configured to EPROM 0, Bank 0, and turned **OFF**. For example, if the quikLoader resides in slot 4, the program must **POKE 49344,16** (i.e. **POKE 0xC0C0,0x10**) in order to initially configure the quikLoader hardware before making the **CALL** to **ASEOS**. This configuration will bring *EOS* into focus when the quikLoader is turned ON. In this example CALL 50176 (i.e. CALL 0xC400) begins ASEOS processing. The CALL command must be followed by some required arguments, and there are some optional arguments that can be used as well. These arguments **must be** integer variables, integer arrays, ASCII character strings, or ASCII character string arrays where indicated. Real variables and real arrays must **never** be used in an ASEOS CALL statement because real numbers are floating point numbers and they are not supported by the ASEOS routines.

1) LOAD file. This command loads a file into memory from a quikLoader EPROM using ASEOS:

```
QL    = quikLoader slot number
OFF   = 16                               ; 0x10
DEV   = QL * 16 + 49280                   ; QL * 0x10 + 0xC080
EOS   = QL * 256 + 49152                  ; QL * 0x100 + 0xC000
C%    = 1                                 ; LOAD file command
S%    = -1                                ; set Status to ERROR
E%    = EPROM search range
F$    = Filename (1 to 24 upper ASCII characters)
[A%]  = Alternate load address (optional)

POKE DEV, OFF
CALL EOS, C%, S%, E%, F$ [, A%]
```

2) RUN file. This command loads a file into memory from a quikLoader EPROM and runs that file using ASEOS:

```
QL    = quikLoader slot number
OFF   = 16                               ; 0x10
DEV   = QL * 16 + 49280                   ; QL * 0x10 + 0xC080
EOS   = QL * 256 + 49152                  ; QL * 0x100 + 0xC000
C%    = 2                                 ; RUN file command
S%    = -1                                ; set Status to error
E%    = EPROM search range
F$    = Filename (1 to 24 upper ASCII characters)
[A%]  = Alternate load address (optional)

POKE DEV, OFF
CALL EOS, C%, S%, E%, F$ [, A%]
```

3) CATALOG files. This command reads the Catalogs of all quikLoader EPROMs into a character string array using ASEOS:

```
QL      = quikLoader slot number
OFF     = 16                             ; 0x10
M%      = Maximum number of anticipated entries
DEV     = QL * 16 + 49280                 ; QL * 0x10 + 0xC080
EOS     = QL * 256 + 49152                ; QL * 0x100 + 0xC000
C%      = 3                               ; CATALOG command
```

```
S%             = -1                                  ; set Status to error
E%             = EPROM search range
N%             = Last index used and returned (set to start index)
F$(N%)         = Filename array (1 to 24 upper ASCII characters)
[P%(0,N%)]     = Parameter Array returned (optional)

    M% = 128
    DIM  F$(M%), P%(4,M%)
    POKE DEV, OFF
    N% = 0
    CALL EOS, C%, S%, E%, N%, F$(N%) [, P%(0,N%)]
```

Returned Status values for all commands:

```
    S% = 0     no error
    S% = -1    Number of Parameters Exceeded       ; 0xFF
    S% = 1     Unknown Command
    S% = 2     Number of Parameters Invalid
    S% = 3     Search Range Invalid
    S% = 4     File Not Found
```

EPROM search range for all commands:

```
    E% = 0-7 for a single, specific quikLoader EPROM
    E% = 0-7:0-7, or ( last EPROM ) * 16 + ( start EPROM )
```

Optional Parameter Array returned for **CATALOG** command:

```
    P%(0,N%) = quikLoader EPROM number
    P%(1,N%) = file type
    P%(2,N%) = EPROM offset
    P%(3,N%) = file size in bytes
    P%(4,N%) = destination memory address
```

EOS file types were shown previously in Table V.2.4 with their value and their display designation in the EPROM Catalog function. *EOS* currently uses two Reserved type files in the *EOS* EPROM Catalog. The ROM code from 0xD000 to 0xFFFF and the four Catalog synchronization bytes are Reserved type files. Primary files are Binary files that can use the **BINEOS** interface and Primary files may be activated directly by the quikLoader EPROM Catalog function in order to load or to run System files. The quikLoader EPROM Catalog function **cannot** directly load or run System files. System files may be Text, Applesoft, or other Binary files. System files may be attached to a Primary file, or loaded or run by activating its associated Primary file either using the quikLoader EPROM Catalog function, **ASEOS**, or **BINEOS**. *EOS* is not designed to support Integer BASIC type files because DOS 4.5 does not support Integer BASIC type files. A DOS image and the software tool *Sourceror* are examples of System type files. The program that loads *Sourceror* into memory for processing is an example of a Primary file. Primary and System files that are used in *EOS* are different in function and in concept than

Primary and System files that are used in the SCRG interface. It is important that this distinction is fully understood in order to differentiate *EOS* and the SCRG interface.

A quikLoader EPROM Catalog for the files contained in that EPROM is always prefaced with four synchronization bytes, 0xC4, 0xB8, 0x90, and 0xED. The actual catalog begins at offset 0x0004 and it may contain any number of entries, where each entry is a variable size that depends on the length in bytes for its filename. An EPROM Catalog filename is a character string that uses lower ASCII characters for all of its bytes except for the last byte in the character string which is an upper ASCII character. When a character string is comprised of lower ASCII characters except for the last upper ASCII character, the *Lisa* assembler designates this character string to be in the DCI format. The Catalog is terminated with a NULL character (i.e. 0x00). An example Catalog file entry structure is shown in Table V.2.5.

Offset	Length	Variable	Description
0	1	FILETYPE	File type as defined in Table V.2.4
1	2	SRCVAL	EPROM source address (EPROM offset)
3	2	LENVAL	File length or size in bytes
5	2	DSTVAL	Destination memory address (Apple][memory address)
7	1–24	FILENAME	Filename, 1 to 24 ASCII bytes (in DCI format)

Table V.2.5. EOS Catalog File Entry Structure

```
0800        1                    ttl "QLBINEOS Utilization, QLBINEOS.L"
0800        2   ;
0800        3   ;
0800        4   ; QLBINEOS.L
0800        5   ;
002A        6   SRCPTR    epz $2A
002E        7   DSTPTR    epz $2E
0800        8   ;
0000        9   ZERO      equ $00
00FF       10   NEGONE    equ $FF
0800       11   ;
0000       12   QLON      equ $00
0010       13   QLOFF     equ $10
0800       14   ;
C080       15   QLSELC    equ $C080
0800       16   ;
C0E0       17   QLBINEOS  equ $C0E0
C0F8       18   QLBINTXT  equ $C0F8
0800       19   ;
C700       20   PAGEC7    equ $C700
E700       21   PAGEE7    equ $E700
0800       22   ;
CFFF       23   CLRROM    equ $CFFF
0800       24   ;
0800       25   ;
0800       26             org $800
0800       27             obj $800
0800       28             usr
0800       29   ;
```

```
0800 20 0C 08    30           jsr FINDQL              ; find quikLoader
0803 B0 07       31           bcs FINDERR
0805             32 ;
0805 A0 6A       33           ldy #EOSDCBL            ; address of
0807 A9 08       34           lda /EOSDCBL            ;  LOAD DCB
0809             35 ;
0809 20 5C 08    36           jsr QLBINJMP            ; LOAD the file
080C             37 ;
080C             38 ;         :::
080C             39 ;
080C             40 FINDERR:
080C             41 ;         :::
080C             42 ;
080C A0 00       43 FINDQL    ldy #PAGEC7             ; get 0xC700 slot
080E A9 C7       44           lda /PAGEC7             ;  address
0810             45 ;
0810 84 2A       46           sty SRCPTR              ; store address at
0812 85 2B       47           sta SRCPTR+1            ;  source pointer
0814             48 ;
0814 A9 E7       49           lda /PAGEE7             ; get EPROM Bank 0 address
0816             50 ;
0816 84 2E       51           sty DSTPTR              ; store address at
0818 85 2F       52           sta DSTPTR+1           ;  destination pointer
081A             53 ;
081A A9 07       54           lda #7                  ; initialize
081C 8D 5F 08    55           sta QLSLOT              ;  for slot 7
081F             56 ;
081F AD 5F 08    57 ^1        lda QLSLOT              ; get slot number
0822             58 ;
0822 0A          59           asl                     ; multiply by 16
0823 0A          60           asl
0824 0A          61           asl
0825 0A          62           asl
0826             63 ;
0826 AA          64           tax                     ; use as index
0827             65 ;
0827 A9 00       66           lda #QLON               ; turn quikLoader ON
0829 9D 80 C0    67           sta QLSELC,X
082C             68 ;
082C 2C FF CF    69           bit CLRROM              ; detach shared slot memory
082F             70 ;
082F A0 F8       71           ldy #QLBINTXT           ; point to QLBIN text
0831             72 ;
0831 B9 6A 07    73 ^2        lda QLTEXT-QLBINTXT&NEGONE,Y ; get QLBIN text
0834             74 ;
0834 D1 2A       75           cmp (SRCPTR),Y          ; compare slot memory
0836 D0 16       76           bne >3
0838             77 ;
0838 D1 2E       78           cmp (DSTPTR),Y          ; compare EPROM memory
083A D0 12       79           bne >3
083C             80 ;
083C C8          81           iny
083D D0 F2       82           bne <2
083F             83 ;
083F A9 10       84           lda #QLOFF              ; turn quikLoader OFF
0841 9D 80 C0    85           sta QLSELC,X
0844             86 ;
0844 A5 2B       87           lda SRCPTR+1            ; get slot memory address
0846 8D 61 08    88           sta QLBINADR+1          ; save to vector
0849             89 ;
0849 2C FF CF    90           bit CLRROM              ; detach shared slot memory
```

206

```
084C              91   ;
084C 18           92          clc                    ; quikLoader found
084D              93   ;
084D 60           94          rts
084E              95   ;
084E C6 2B        96   ^3      dec SRCPTR+1           ; next slot memory
0850 C6 2F        97          dec DSTPTR+1           ; next quikLoader slot
0852              98   ;
0852 CE 5F 08     99          dec QLSLOT             ; next slot number
0855 D0 C8        100         bne <1
0857              101  ;
0857 2C FF CF     102         bit CLRROM             ; detach shared slot memory
085A              103  ;
085A 38           104         sec                    ; no quikLoader found
085B              105  ;
085B 60           106         rts
085C              107  ;
085C              108  ;
085C 6C 60 08     109  QLBINJMP jmp (QLBINADR)
085F              110  ;
085F              111  QLSLOT   dfs 1,ZERO            ; quikLoader slot
0860              112  ;
0860 E0 C0        113  QLBINADR adr QLBINEOS         ; QLBINEOS vector
0862              114  ;
0862 D1 CC C2     115  QLTEXT   asc "QLBINEOS"        ; QLBIN text
0865 C9 CE C5
0868 CF D3
086A              116  ;
086A              117  ;
086A              118  EOSDCBL:
086A              119  ;
086A 01           120  DCBLCMD  hex 01                ; LOAD command
086B 70           121  DCBLEP   hex 70                ; search all EPROMs
086C 00 00        122  DCBLOAD  hex 0000              ; no alternate LOAD address
086E FF           123  DCBLSTAT hex FF                ; return status
086F 0F           124  DCBLFLEN byt FILENDL-FILNAML   ; filename length
0870 72 08        125  DCBLFADR adr FILNAML           ; filename address
0872              126  ;
0872 C1 F0 F0     127  FILNAML  asc "Apple File List"
0875 EC E5 A0
0878 C6 E9 EC
087B E5 A0 CC
087E E9 F3 F4
0881              128  FILENDL:
0881              129  ;
0881              130  ;

BSAVE QLBINEOS,A$0800,L$0081
0881              131         usr QLBINEOS
0881              132  ;
0881              133  ;
0881              134         end 000

*** End of Assembly
```

Figure V.2.6. Example Code for QLBINEOS Utilization

207

EOS provides assembly language users with three commands when using the assembly language, or BINEOS interface for LOAD file, RUN file, and CATALOG. An eight-byte Data Context Block, or DCB is used for the input variables and returned status. The structure of the DCB is command specific. Any assembly language program like Primary files can use QLBINEOS to load and to run System files. QLBINEOS is located at the 0xE0th byte in the peripheral-card ROM memory of the quikLoader as shown in Table V.2.2. For example, if the quikLoader resides in slot 4, QLBINEOS resides at memory address 0xC4E0. The code shown in Figure V.2.6 shows how to utilize the QLBINEOS interface.

LOAD file. This DCB loads a file into memory from a quikLoader EPROM using BINEOS:

```
EOSDCBL    equ *                      ; LOAD file DCB
DCBCMDL    hex 01                     ; LOAD command
DCBEPNL    hex 70                     ; search all EPROMs
DCBFALTL   hex 0000                   ; no alternate address
DCBSTATL   hex FF                     ; return status
DCBFLENL   byt FILELENL               ; filename length
DCBFADRL   adr FILENAML               ; filename address

FILENAML   asc "Applesoft File List"
FILELENL   equ *-FILENAML
```

RUN file. This DCB loads a file into memory from a quikLoader EPROM and runs that file using BINEOS:

```
EOSDCBR    equ *                      ; RUN file DCB
DCBCMDR    hex 02                     ; RUN command
DCBEPNR    hex 70                     ; search all EPROMs
DCBFALTR   hex 0000                   ; no alternate address
DCBSTATR   hex FF                     ; return status
DCBFLENR   byt FILELENR               ; filename length
DCBFADRR   adr FILENAMR               ; filename address

FILENAMR   asc "Volume Copy"
FILELENR   equ *-FILENAMR
```

CATALOG files. This DCB catalogs the quikLoader EPROMs using BINEOS:

```
EOSDCBC    equ *                      ; CATALOG EPROMs DCB
DCBCMDC    hex 03                     ; CATALOG command
DCBEPNC    hex 70                     ; CATALOG all EPROMs
DCBCALT    hex 0000                   ; not used
DCBSTATC   hex FF                     ; return status
DCBCNUM    hex 00                     ; CATALOG entries number
DCBCADR    adr CATBUFR                ; CATALOG buffer address

CATBUFR    dfs 32*n,ZERO              ; n 32-byte entries
```

The call to BINEOS returns one of the following Status values:

```
0x00 = no error
0x01 = Unknown Command error
0x02 = Filename Length Invalid error
0x03 = Search Range Invalid error
0x04 = Buffer/Filename Address error
0x05 = Requested File Not Found error
```

Offset	Length	Variable	Description
0	1	FILEPNUM	EPROM number containing this file
1	1	FILETYPE	File type
2	2	SRCVAL	EPROM source address (EPROM offset)
4	2	LENVAL	File length or size in bytes
6	2	DSTVAL	Destination memory address (Apple][memory)
8	24	FILENAME	Filename, space padded, upper ASCII

Table V.2.6. BINEOS Catalog File Entry

The quikLoader EPROM search range and file types are the same in BINEOS as they are in ASEOS. The Catalog buffer contains the number of entries which is given by DCBCNUM. A maximum of 255 entries is provided. Even if the quikLoader contains eight 27512 EPROMs, the EPROMS would each have to exceed thirty-two entries in order to exceed a total maximum value of 255 entries. There is very little likelihood that DCBCNUM would ever exceed 255 entries. Each Catalog entry is thirty-two bytes in size regardless of the exact length of the filename in bytes. The filename characters are converted to upper ASCII characters and padded with the upper ASCII SPACE character (i.e. 0xA0) to be exactly twenty-four characters in length. A BINEOS Catalog file entry is structured as shown in Table V.2.6.

EOS makes extensive use of the 6502-microprocessor stack page from 0x0110 to 0x018F for the QBMCODE consisting of the routines QLCONFIG, QLMOVE, QLJMP, QLJSR, QLRTN, and QLEXEC. When *EOS* is activated it initializes the stack pointer to 0xFF in order to ensure that these temporary stack page routines are safe while *EOS* is active. And, it is extremely unlikely that the stack pointer will ever venture into the region where these stack routines are placed because Applesoft tightly controls this pointer. The same argument can be made for software using the BINEOS interface as long as the calling software is mindful of the stack pointer location and where the QBMCODE routines reside. *EOS* also makes extensive use of the text input page from 0x0280 to 0x02EF. It is extremely unlikely that a lengthy Applesoft or DOS command is ever issued during ASEOS or BINEOS processing. However, an Applesoft user should be aware that *EOS* does use the upper half of the INPUT page. *EOS* uses the stack and input pages so that the User buffer page from 0x0300 to 0x03CF is still left available for program loaders. The original loader for *Sourceror* (a Primary file) is one example of a very short Binary program that uses 0x300 to 0x32C to load *Sourceror* (a System File) from a quikLoader EPROM to memory address 0x8900 using a LOAD DCB. The original code segment to set MAXFILES to 0x01 is unnecessary for DOS 4.5H. The possibilities are virtually endless in how *EOS* can be utilized to obtain information and data from an EPROM or from all EPROMs residing in a quikLoader.

3. VTOC Manager (VMGR)

The Volume Table of Contents (VTOC) Manager, or *VMGR*, is a utility I developed while I was designing the enhancements to the DOS 4.1 VTOC and volume Catalog. *VMGR* provides the user with the ability to display and to change the contents of the VTOC of a volume for any given slot, drive, and volume number. Figure V.3.1 displays the Option Menu for *VMGR*. Initially, the program displays the slot, drive, and volume number values currently in focus. The user can change those values using Option 1. Option 2 reads the VTOC for the selected volume and displays the VTOC contents as shown in Figure V.3.2. Option 3 displays the same VTOC contents shown in Figure V.3.2 except that the user can edit, or change that information. Great harm can easily be done to a volume, even making the volume unusable, if the VTOC information is changed inappropriately. It is critical that the user understands the effects of any change to the VTOC and to accept all consequences. Figure V.3.3 displays the VTOC contents as Edit VTOC Contents and shows the arrow -> in front of the disk name for the volume. Using the up and down arrow keys, the arrow can be positioned in front of any of the VTOC contents in order to edit that content. Simply follow the directions after selecting a VTOC item to edit.

```
┌─────────────────────────────────┐
│     Apple ][ VTOC Manager        │
│      DOS 4.5.05H 01/01/22        │
│                                  │
│                                  │
│          Option Menu             │
│                                  │
│  1 - Set Slot/Drive/Volume (6/01/000) │
│                                  │
│  2 - Show VTOC Contents          │
│                                  │
│  3 - Edit VTOC Contents          │
│                                  │
│  4 - Show Sector Bitmap Contents │
│                                  │
│  5 - Edit Sector Bitmap Contents │
│                                  │
│  6 - Quit                        │
│                                  │
│                                  │
│Select Option: ■                  │
└─────────────────────────────────┘
```

Figure V.3.1. VMGR Option Menu

```
┌─────────────────────────────────┐
│          VTOC Contents           │
│1st Cat T/S    - 0x11/0x04        │
│DOS Version    - 4.5              │
│DOS Build      - 05               │
│DOS RAM        - H (High RAM)     │
│                                  │
│Volm Number    - 0x00 (000)       │
│Volm Type      - B (Boot Disk)    │
│Volm Subject   - 0x4505 (17669)   │
│Volm DiskName  - DOS 4.5.05H Tools Master│
│Volm DateTime  - 01/01/22 08:28:48│
│VTOC DateTime  - 01/01/22 08:28:48│
│                                  │
│T/S Pairs      - 0x7A (122)       │
│Next Track     - 0x10 (16)        │
│Tk Allocation  - 0xFF (negative)  │
│Config/Lock    - 0x01/0x00 (unlocked)│
│Volume Tracks  - 0x23 (35)        │
│Track Sectors  - 0x10 (16)        │
│Track Phases   - 0x04 (04)        │
│Sector Bytes   - 0x100 (256)      │
│          Press Any Key           │
└─────────────────────────────────┘
```

Figure V.3.2. Show VTOC for Option 2

```
┌─────────────────────────────────┐
│       Edit VTOC Contents         │
│1st Cat T/S    - 0x11/0x04        │
│DOS Version    - 4.5              │
│DOS Build      - 05               │
│DOS RAM        - H (High RAM)     │
│                                  │
│Volm Number    - 0x00 (000)       │
│Volm Type      - B (Boot Disk)    │
│Volm Subject   - 0x4505 (17669)   │
│Volm DiskName ->DOS 4.5.05H Tools Master│
│Volm DateTime  - 01/01/22 08:28:48│
│VTOC DateTime  - 01/01/22 08:28:48│
│                                  │
│T/S Pairs      - 0x7A (122)       │
│Next Track     - 0x10 (16)        │
│Tk Allocation  - 0xFF (negative)  │
│Config/Lock    - 0x01/0x00 (unlocked)│
│Volume Tracks  - 0x23 (35)        │
│Track Sectors  - 0x10 (16)        │
│Track Phases   - 0x04 (04)        │
│Sector Bytes   - 0x100 (256)      │
│       Press ESC to Quit          │
└─────────────────────────────────┘
```

Figure V.3.3. Edit VTOC for Option 3

```
┌─────────────────────────────────┐
│       Edit VTOC Contents         │
│1st Cat T/S    - 0x11/0x04        │
│DOS Version    - 4.5              │
│DOS Build      - 05               │
│DOS RAM        - H (High RAM)     │
│                                  │
│Volm Number    - 0x00 (000)       │
│Volm Type      - B (Boot Disk)    │
│Volm Subject   - 0x4505 (17669)   │
│Volm DiskName  - DOS 4.5.05H Tools Master│
│Volm DateTime  - 01/01/22 08:28:48│
│VTOC DateTime  - 01/01/22 08:28:48│
│                                  │
│T/S Pairs      - 0x7A (122)       │
│Next Track     - 0x10 (16)        │
│Tk Allocation  - 0xFF (negative)  │
│Config/Lock    - 0x01/0x00 (unlocked)│
│Volume Tracks  - 0x23 (35)        │
│Track Sectors  - 0x10 (16)        │
│Track Phases   - 0x04 (04)        │
│Sector Bytes   - 0x100 (256)      │
│Save these changes (Y/N): ■       │
└─────────────────────────────────┘
```

Figure V.3.4. Save VTOC for Option 3

```
      Sector Bitmap Contents                    Edit Sector Bitmap Contents
           35 Tracks                                     35 Tracks

Trk|00001111 00001111 00001111 00001111   Trk|00001111 00001111 00001111 00001111
Num|C840C840 C840C840 C840C840 C840C840   Num|C840C840 C840C840 C840C840 C840C840
Rng|FB73FB73 FB73FB73 FB73FB73 FB73FB73   Rng|FB73FB73 FB73FB73 FB73FB73 FB73FB73
---------------------------------------   ---------------------------------------
 00|00000000 00000000 00000000 00000000    00|00000000 00000000 00000000 00000000
 04|00000000 00000000 00000000 00000000    04|00000000 00000000 00000000 00000000
 08|00000000 00000000 00000000 00000000    08|00000000 00000000 00000000 00000000
 0C|00000000 00000000 00000000 00000000    0C|00000000 00000000 00000000 00000000
 10|00000000 00000000 003E0000 00000000    10|00000000 00000000 003E0000 00000000
 14|00000000 00000000 00000000 00000000    14|00000000 00000000 00000000 00000000
 18|00000000 00000000 00000000 00000000    18|00000000 00000000 00000000 00000000
 1C|00000000 00000000 00000000 00000000    1C|00000000 00000000 00000000 00000000
 20|00000000 00000000 00000000             20|00000000 00000000 00000000



           Press Any Key                  Enter track number to edit:   0x█
```

| Figure V.3.5. Show VTOC Bitmap Option 4 | Figure V.3.6. Edit VTOC Bitmap Option 5 |

When all edits have been completed, the instruction at the bottom of the screen says to press ESC to quit. When ESC is pressed, the `Save these changes` screen is displayed as shown in Figure V.3.4. ESC may be pressed at any time to escape any function or when making any change so that that change does not become effective.

When Option 4 is selected the sector bitmap contents for the selected volume is displayed as shown in Figure V.3.5. Selecting Option 5 allows one to change or edit the sector bitmap contents for whatever reason as shown in Figure V.3.6. Great harm can easily be done to a volume, even making the volume unusable, if the VTOC information is changed inappropriately.

Each track of a DOS 4.5 volume may contain either sixteen or thirty-two sectors depending on the hardware media. The VTOC can support up to fifty tracks. Figure I.5.2 shows the complete sector bitmap that begins at byte 0x38 in the VTOC. The sector bitmap allocates four bytes, or thirty-two bits, for every track to determine if a sector in that track is available or not. If a sector is available its respective bit is set to one, or ON. If a sector is not available its respective bit is set to zero, or OFF. Table I.5.3 shows the sector order from left to right so that sectors 0x0F to 0x00 use the left two bytes followed by sectors 0x1F to 0x10 and they use the right two bytes. DOS 4.5 indirectly interacts with the VTOC bitmap by means of the variable NEXTSECR exclusively OR'd with the value of 0x10. Therefore, if a volume only supports sixteen sectors per track, the right two bytes are set to zero. In Figures V.3.5 and V.3.6 track 18 (i.e. 0x12) contains five free sectors (0x3E = 0b00111110).

4. Big Mac

I first started using *Big Mac* by Glen E. Bredon on my Apple][+ as soon as I took an interest in writing assembly language programs. Also, *Sourceror* is designed as a subsidiary tool to *Big Mac* that creates *Big Mac* source code files from assembly language object code files. *Big Mac* and *Sourceror* are also capable of assembling and sourcing *SWEET16* instructions, respectively. The main menu for *Big Mac* is shown in Figure V.4.1. This menu is another example where I have used lowercase characters to assist in making the Apple][screen text easier for me and other users to read. When I started working at

Sierra On-Line the programmers there only used *Lisa*, not *Big Mac*. However, whenever I use *Sourceror* I am still dependent on *Big Mac* in order to perform some edits on the output source files that are generated by *Sourceror*. I use the ED/ASM Option E in *Big Mac* to make the necessary edits and then save the file as a TEXT file using Option W which happens to create a Text file that is compatible with *Lisa*. *Lisa* is able to EXEC a *Big Mac* TEXT file into its assembler quickly. And this is precisely the procedure I still use today. When Option Q is selected to quit *Big Mac*, *Big Mac* connects the DOS USER command to the *Big Mac* launch routine in order to restart *Big Mac* as shown in Figure V.4.2.

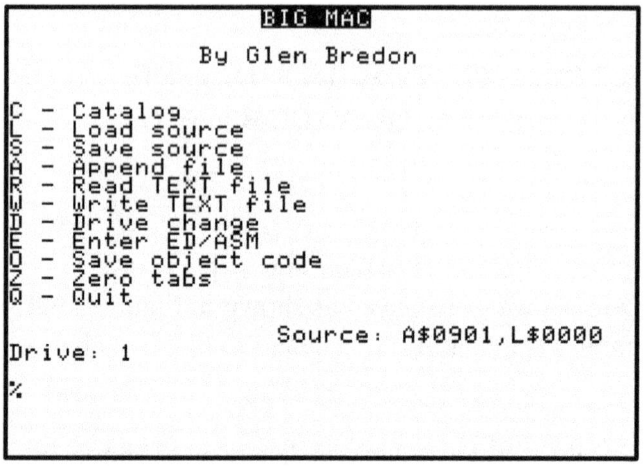

Figure V.4.1. Big Mac Main Menu    Figure V.4.2. Big Mac Exit

Big Mac made frequent use of DOS 3.3 internal variables and routines so it was not at all compatible with DOS 4.1 and, therefore, not compatible with DOS 4.5. I needed to know every instance where *Big Mac* utilized DOS 3.3 internals, and then modify those dependencies to make use of the DOS 4.5 data structure interfaces. *Big Mac* was certainly a challenge because it packaged a huge wallop of a program into the limited memory of the Language Card partition in Main memory. Creating source code for *Big Mac* that could be modified required a huge effort. It is one thing to have source code that assembles into object code which compares perfectly to the original object code. It is quite another thing to turn that source code into routines whose addresses may change as some code is modified, deleted, and added, and still assemble into a working, viable program. I did remove the ASSEM re-entry command because DOS 4.5 provides no visibility into its command tables, the command handler addresses, and the companion keyword tables for a reason. However, the new DOS 4.5 USER command is specifically designed to have many functions. One of its functions can be used to restart *Big Mac* as shown in Figure V.4.2. DOS 4.5 does provide access to structures for drive number, file start address, and file length. I am satisfied that my sourced and modified version of *Big Mac* is fully DOS 4.5 compliant and, as a utility, *Big Mac* is still providing me with a terrific interface between *Sourceror* and *Lisa*.

In order to make *Big Mac* fully DOS 4.5H compliant required me to relocate *Big Mac* to Auxiliary memory. Why? Because DOS 4.5H is designed to be resident in the Language Card partition in Main memory and *Big Mac* is designed to be resident in the Language Card partition in Main memory as well. Both cannot reside concurrently in the same Language Card partition. Auxiliary memory also contains its own Language Card partition. It seemed natural to relocate *Big Mac* to Auxiliary memory. It was definitely a challenge to understand how to master Auxiliary memory in terms of its operation and what it could provide and what it could not provide as far as resources. Certainly, to assist in Auxiliary memory utilization would be to decide which memory would handle input data (keyboard and disk) and which memory would handle output data (screen and disk). Once I established the operating rules for memory, it became very clear to me in how to build the interface between Main memory and Auxiliary memory specifically for *Big Mac*. Fortunately, I was able to leverage on lessons learned from relocating *Lisa* to Auxiliary memory. Since DOS 4.5H occupies the Language Card partition in Main memory, it was quite logical to utilize Main memory for the input and the output of all disk data. It was totally unnecessary to maintain two page-zeros particularly for the variables CH, CV, BASL, BASH, and the text window variables. So, all keyboard and screen display are handled within Auxiliary page-zero memory.

The original *Big Mac* contained its own version of the Monitor. This Monitor mostly resembled the monitor that is found in the Apple][+. In order for *Big Mac* to utilize the current Apple //e ROM Monitor, *Big Mac* simply copies the ROM Monitor into its memory space and uses the RAM Monitor for all of its functions. The interface between Main memory and Auxiliary memory is injected primarily at the COUT (i.e. 0xFDED) routine. A small handler is needed for the GETFMCB, CALLFM, HOOKDOS, PRTERROR, GOTODOS, GOTOMON, GOTOCOLD, and GOTOWARM vectors. DOS errors have to be handled uniquely by the interface in order to always re-enter *Big Mac* appropriately. The state of the Bank currently in focus in the Language Card partition must be captured in order to reconfigure Auxiliary memory for all subroutines returning to *Big Mac*. Because *Big Mac* utilizes Bank 1 memory in the Language Card partition for its symbol table and Bank 2 memory for its software routines, there is no way of knowing which Bank is in focus at any given time during *Big Mac* processing. The greater challenge was to align *Big Mac* and *Sourceror*, particularly in terms of assembling and sourcing *SWEET16* instructions.

Initially, *Big Mac* could process only some of the *SWEET16* opcodes. And, as it turned out, *Big Mac* could not even process its own unique EVAL opcode because there is no entry in any of the *Big Mac* hash tables for that opcode. To this end, I chose to update *Sourceror* and *Big Mac* so that they could both process my version of the *SWEET16* opcodes. *Sourceror* is only able to recognize 65C02 opcodes because my Apple //e Monitor can display 65C02 instructions (you must tear apart *Sourceror* to thoroughly understand what I mean by this statement). *Big Mac*, however, could not initially recognize nor process any of the new instructions in the 65C02 Instruction Set. It was fairly easy to update the Monitor support logic for *Big Mac* so it could at least parse and display those instructions. It was not so easy to give *Big Mac* the ability to assemble the new 65C02 instructions. The original tables and logic in *Big Mac* that give it its ability to parse 6502 instructions and to handle all of their addressing mode rules is exceedingly dense. The original tables are found at 0xF339 to 0xF4DD. After enhancing *Big Mac*, the tables are now found at 0xF339 to 0xF4FF. To make this enhancement possible, a number of routines and ASCII tables have to be moved elsewhere.

In order to add the STZ, TRB, and TSB hash table entries, for example, to the end of the table data starting at 0xF4EC, I have to move two ASCII tables. One table is at 0xF4E8 and the other is at 0xF4EF. I only need twelve bytes for these three new instructions, and when combined, the ASCII tables are fifteen bytes in size. I do have an 18-byte gap in the code at 0xE408 and this is where I moved those two ASCII tables. The 10-byte table left at 0xF4DE simply moves up to 0xF501. To the best of my ability I have verified that *Big Mac* can assemble all of the additional 65C02 instructions and it can increment its program counter correctly for all of the addressing modes for these additional instructions. Furthermore, the *Big Mac* Monitor support code can display all of the additional 65C02 instructions correctly with opcode, value, address, and displacement.

Mr. Bredon utilized a hashing algorithm in order to calculate a two-byte hash value for each assembly instruction he encountered as his *Big Mac* program assembled each line of source code. The hash value is used to identify a table entry that provides additional data and/or format information used to process that particular instruction. The GETHASH routine in *Big Mac* is found at 0xE740 and the routine is shown in its entirety in Figure V.4.3. The lower ASCII values of the four-character assembly instruction text is always placed starting at memory address 0x0234, and the 2-byte hash value created from that ASCII character assembly instruction text is placed in page-zero at 0xEA and 0xEB. The hash value is unique to each assembly instruction which also includes assembly directives, macro instructions, and *SWEET16* instructions.

```
   :              :          :
E740 AD 34 02    640   HE740    lda  H0234        ; get first character
E743             641   ;
E743 0A          642            asl              ; shift left
E744 0A          643            asl              ; shift left
E745 0A          644            asl              ; shift left
E746             645   ;
E746 85 EA       646            sta  H00EA        ; save to hashA
E748             647   ;
E748 AD 35 02    648            lda  H0235        ; get second character
E74B             649   ;
E74B 6A          650            ror              ; shift right
E74C 66 EB       651            ror  H00EB        ; save bit to hashB
E74E             652   ;
E74E 6A          653            ror              ; shift right
E75F 66 EB       654            ror  H00EB        ; save bit to hashB
E751             655   ;
E751 29 07       656            and  #7           ; keep lower 3 bits
E753 05 EA       657            ora  H00EA        ; add to hashA
E755 85 EA       658            sta  H00EA        ; save to hashA
E757             659   ;
E757 AD 37 02    660            lda  H0237        ; get fourth character
E75A 29 5F       661            and  #$5F         ; mask; look for SOUT
E75C             662   ;
E75C C9 44       663            cmp  #$44         ; set carry if T
E75E F0 07       664            beq  HE767        ; bypass if SOUT
E760             665   ;
E760 AD 36 02    666            lda  H0236        ; get third character
E763 49 BF       667            eor  #$BF         ; looking for @
E765 C9 FF       668            cmp  #NEGONE      ; set carry if 0x40
E767             669   ;
E767 AD 36 02    670   HE767    lda  H0236        ; get third character
E76A 29 1F       671            and  #$1F         ; keep lower 5 bits
E76C 2A          672            rol              ; shift in carry
E76D             673   ;
E76D 05 EB       674            ora  H00EB        ; add to hashB
E76F 85 EB       675            sta  H00EB        ; save to hashB
   :              :          :
```

Figure V.4.3. Big Mac Mnemonic Hashing Algorithm

Mnemonic	Table Address	Hash Value		Handler Address
		0xEA	0xEB	
]@	0xF339	0xE8	0x00	0xEFE0
EQU	0xF33D	0x2C	0x6A	0xEFE0
^^^	0xF341	0xF7	0xBC	0xF118
PMC	0xF345	0x83	0x46	0xF118
HEX	0xF349	0x41	0x70	0xEE80
DFB	0xF34D	0x21	0x84	0xEE68
DA	0xF351	0x20	0x40	0xEE42
DDB	0xF355	0x21	0x04	0xEE41
DS	0xF359	0x24	0xC0	0xF08C
LST	0xF35D	0x64	0xE8	0xEEB1
AST	0xF361	0x0C	0xE8	0xF04B
ORG	0xF365	0x7C	0x8E	0xF243
OBJ	0xF369	0xF2	0x42	0xF22A
SET	0xF36D	0x99	0x68	0xE892
SKP	0xF371	0x9A	0xE0	0xF048
PAG	0xF375	0x80	0x4E	0xF041
PAU	0xF379	0x80	0x6A	0xEB57
EXP	0xF37D	0x2E	0x20	0xEEB5
PUT	0xF381	0x85	0x68	0xF1DC
TR	0xF385	0xA4	0x80	0xEEA3
CHK	0xF389	0x1A	0x16	0xF20B
VAR	0xF38D	0xB0	0x64	0xEE35
SAV	0xF391	0x98	0x6C	0xF27B
KBD	0xF395	0x58	0x88	0xEF9E
END	0xF399	0x2B	0x88	0xF5B2

Table V.4.1. Hash Table 1 – Assembly Directives

Mnemonic	Table Address	Hash Value		Handler Address
		0xEA	0xEB	
ASC	0xF39D	0x0C	0xC6	0xEF60
DCI	0xF3A1	0x20	0xD2	0xEF5F
PLS	0xF3A5	0x33	0x26	0xEF53
INV	0xF3A9	0x4B	0x55	0xEF55

Table V.4.2. Hash Table 2 – Text Directives

Mnemonic	Table Address	Hash Value 0xEA	Hash Value 0xEB	Handler Address
\\\	0xF3AE	0xE7	0x38	0xF18F
DO	0xF3B2	0x23	0xC0	0xF101
ELS	0xF3B6	0x2B	0x26	0xF0F8
FIN	0xF3BA	0x32	0x5C	0xF18A
MAC	0xF3BE	0x68	0x46	0xF0B1
EOM	0xF3C2	0x2B	0xDA	0xF18F

Table V.4.3. Hash Table 3 – Macro Directives

The first table of hash values in *Big Mac* is found at 0xF339 and is shown in Table V.4.1, and this table contains the hash values for assembly directives. In order to create the contents of this hash table, I had to reverse engineer each 2-byte hash value in order to derive its mnemonic. I also provide the memory address where each 4-byte table entry begins. Table V.4.1 shows the mnemonic, the memory address where the entry begins, its 2-byte hash value, and the address of the software handler routine that processes that particular instruction. The next hash table is found at 0xF39D and that table is shown in Table V.4.2. This second hash table is similar in structure to Table V.4.1, and it contains the hash value for each text directive, its mnemonic, the memory address where each 4-byte table entry begins, and the address of the software handler routine that processes this particular directive. This table is terminated with a NULL character (i.e. 0x00) so that *Big Mac* can reconfigure its current indexing value and its pointers. The address bytes for each software handler in both of these tables are decremented and reversed so that they can be readily pushed onto the stack and in that order. The third hash table is shown in Table V.4.3 and this table contains the 4-byte table entries for all of the macro directives that can be used in *Big Mac*. It is structured like Table V.4.2 and it is terminated with a NULL character as well.

Table V.4.4 contains all of the single byte 65C02 and *SWEET16* instructions. This table is found at 0xF3C7 and each 3-byte table entry begins with the 2-byte hash value followed by the value of the opcode for that instruction. These instructions are the easiest to process and very little supporting code is required. It is to this table that I added the *SWEET16* RSNS instruction. All of the branch instructions for both the 65C02 Instruction Set and for the *SWEET16* opcodes are contained in Table V.4.5 which is found at 0xF428. As in Table V.4.4 each 3-byte table entry begins with the 2-byte hash value followed by the value of the opcode for that instruction. However, a branch offset, or displacement value needs to be calculated for these instructions as well. *Big Mac* must refer to its symbol table and subtract the current program counter from the address of the symbol that the branch instruction references. This calculation provides a signed two's complement value from -128 to +127, and this value is a byte displacement relative to the address of the following instruction. It is to this table that I added the *SWEET16* BSNS instruction. Tables V.4.4 and V.4.5 are both terminated with a NULL character.

Table V.4.6 contains the hash values and the opcode/register values for the single byte *SWEET16* instructions that utilize a *SWEET16* register. Several of these opcode/register value entries may appear puzzling. The first entry, for example, is actually nibblized for the LD and the LD@ instructions. The second entry is nibblized for the ST and the ST@ instructions. It does not matter whether the actual opcode is in the upper nibble or in the lower nibble of the opcode/register value for these instructions. Whenever *Big Mac* processes an instruction from Table V.4.6, it knows how to formulate the upper nibble of the *SWEET16* opcode and to logically OR this nibble with a register number in order to complete the opcode. Table V.4.6 is terminated with a NULL character.

Mnemonic	Table Address	Hash Value 0xEA	Hash Value 0xEB	Opcode
CLC	0xF3C7	0x1B	0x06	0x18
DEX	0xF3CA	0x21	0x70	0xCA
DEY	0xF3CD	0x21	0x72	0x88
INX	0xF3D0	0x4B	0xB0	0xE8
INY	0xF3D3	0x4B	0xB2	0xC8
RTS	0xF3D6	0x95	0x26	0x60
SEC	0xF3D9	0x99	0x46	0x38
TAX	0xF3DC	0xA0	0x70	0xAA
TAY	0xF3DF	0xA0	0x72	0xA8
TXA	0xF3E2	0xA6	0x02	0x8A
TYA	0xF3E5	0xA6	0x42	0x98
PHA	0xF3E8	0x82	0x02	0x48
PHP	0xF3EB	0x82	0x20	0x08
PLA	0xF3EE	0x83	0x02	0x68
PLP	0xF3F1	0x83	0x20	0x28
TSX	0xF3F4	0xA4	0xF0	0xBA
TXS	0xF3F7	0xA6	0x26	0x9A
CLD	0xF3FA	0x1B	0x08	0xD8
SED	0xF3FD	0x99	0x48	0xF8
SEI	0xF400	0x99	0x52	0x78
RTI	0xF403	0x95	0x12	0x40
CLI	0xF406	0x1B	0x12	0x58
CLV	0xF409	0x1B	0x2C	0xB8
NOP	0xF40C	0x73	0xE0	0xEA
BRK	0xF40F	0x14	0x96	0x00
PHX	0xF412	0x82	0x30	0xDA
PHY	0xF415	0x82	0x32	0x5A
PLX	0xF418	0x83	0x30	0xFA
PLY	0xF41B	0x83	0x32	0x7A
RTN	0xF41E	0x95	0x1C	0x00
RS	0xF421	0x94	0xC0	0x0B
RSNS	0xF424	0x94	0xDC	0x0D

Table V.4.4. Hash Table 4 – Single Byte Instructions

Mnemonic	Table Address	Hash Value		Opcode
		0xEA	0xEB	
BCC	0xF428	0x10	0xC6	0x90
BCS	0xF42B	0x10	0xE6	0xB0
BEQ	0xF42E	0x11	0x62	0xF0
BMI	0xF431	0x13	0x52	0x30
BNE	0xF434	0x13	0x8A	0xD0
BCC	0xF437	0x13	0x28	0x90
BCS	0xF43A	0x11	0xCA	0xB0
BPL	0xF43D	0x14	0x18	0x10
BVC	0xF440	0x15	0x86	0x50
BVS	0xF443	0x15	0xA6	0x70
BRA	0xF446	0x14	0x82	0x80
BR	0xF449	0x14	0x80	0x01
BNC	0xF44C	0x13	0x86	0x02
BC	0xF44F	0x10	0xC0	0x03
BP	0xF452	0x14	0x00	0x04
BM	0xF455	0x13	0x40	0x05
BZ	0xF458	0x16	0x80	0x06
BNZ	0xF45B	0x13	0xB4	0x07
BM1	0xF45E	0x13	0x62	0x08
BNM1	0xF461	0x13	0x9A	0x09
BS	0xF464	0x14	0xC0	0x0C
BSNS	0xF467	0x14	0xDC	0x0E

Table V.4.5. Hash Table 5 – Branch Instructions

Mnemonic	Table Address	Hash Value		Opcode/ Register
		0xEA	0xEB	
LD & LD@	0xF46B	0x61	0x00	0x24
ST & LD@	0xF46E	0x9D	0x00	0x35
LDD@	0xF471	0x61	0x08	0x06
STD@	0xF474	0x9D	0x08	0x07
POP@	0xF477	0x83	0xE0	0x08
STP@	0xF47A	0x9D	0x20	0x09
ADD	0xF47D	0x09	0x08	0xA0
SUB	0xF480	0x9D	0x44	0xB0
POPD	0xF483	0x83	0xE1	0x0C
CPR	0xF486	0x1C	0x24	0xD0
INR	0xF489	0x4B	0xA4	0xE0
DCR	0xF48C	0x20	0xE4	0xF0

Table V.4.6. Hash Table 6 – Single Byte SWEET16 Register Instructions

Mnemonic	Table Address	Hash Value 0xEA	Hash Value 0xEB	Valid Formats	Base Value for Opcode
STA	0xF490	0x9D	0x02	0x3E	0x81
STX	0xF494	0x9D	0x30	0x01	0x82
STY	0xF498	0x9D	0x32	0x04	0x80
LDA	0xF49C	0x61	0x02	0xBE	0xA1
LDX	0xF4A0	0x61	0x30	0x83	0xA2
LDY	0xF4A4	0x61	0x32	0x8C	0xA0
ADC	0xF4A8	0x09	0x06	0xBE	0x61
AND	0xF4AC	0x0B	0x88	0xBE	0x21
ASL	0xF4B0	0x0C	0xD8	0x4C	0x02
CMP	0xF4B4	0x1B	0x60	0xBE	0xC1
CPX	0xF4B8	0x1C	0x30	0x80	0xE0
CPY	0xF4BC	0x1C	0x32	0x80	0xC0
DEC	0xF4C0	0x21	0x46	0x4C	0xC2
EOR	0xF4C4	0x2B	0xE4	0xBE	0x41
INC	0xF4C8	0x4B	0x86	0x4C	0xE2
JMP	0xF4CC	0x53	0x60	0x20	0x4C
JSR	0xF4D0	0x54	0xE4	0x00	0x20
SBC	0xF4D4	0x98	0x86	0xBE	0xE1
ORA	0xF4D8	0x7C	0x82	0xBE	0x01
LSR	0xF4DC	0x64	0xE4	0x4C	0x42
BIT	0xF4E0	0x12	0x68	0x8C	0x20
ROL	0xF4E4	0x93	0xD8	0x4C	0x22
ROR	0xF4E8	0x93	0xE4	0x4C	0x62
STZ	0xF4EC	0x9D	0x34	0x0C	0x64
TRB	0xF4F0	0xA4	0x84	0x00	0x10
TSB	0xF4F4	0xA4	0xC4	0x00	0x04
SOUT	0xF4F8	0x9B	0xEA	0x80	0x0A
SJMP	0xF4FC	0x9A	0x9A	0x00	0x0F

Table V.4.7. Hash Table 7 – Multiple Addressing Mode Instructions

Bit	7	6	5	4	3	2	1	0		
Mode	IMM	ACC	(IND,X)	(IND),Y	ABS,X	ZP,X	ABS,Y	ZP,Y	ABS	ZP
Value	0x08	0x08	0x00	0x10	0x1C	0x14	0x18	0x14	0x0C	0x04

Table V.4.8. Format Byte Definition

The last table of hash values in *Big Mac* is shown in Table V.4.7 and it begins at 0xF490, and this table is terminated with a NULL character. It is the most complex table to process because it contains the entries for those 65C02 instructions that can be used in multiple addressing modes. This table also contains two *SWEET16* instructions because those instructions require special processing, also. Each 4-byte hash table entry begins with the 2-byte hash value for the instruction mnemonic followed by its valid format byte and its opcode base value byte. Depending upon how the instruction is utilized in context within the source code, the opcode base value byte is adjusted by one of the ten possible mode adjustment values with all ten values located beginning at 0xF501 (formally 0xF4DE) in the *Big Mac* source code. Those ten mode adjustment values are shown in Table V.4.8, and they are mapped to each of the ten possible addressing modes. It only takes a cursory look at the 65C02 Instruction Set to understand how Mr. Bredon was able to reconstruct the opcode values for all of the instructions in Table V.4.7 by using the opcode base value byte and adding that value to one of the ten mode adjustment value bytes based simply on how that instruction is utilized in context within the source code. The valid format byte for each table entry stipulates all of the legal addressing modes that can be utilized by that instruction. Each bit in the valid format byte is mapped to a particular addressing mode. When a bit is ON, that addressing mode is legal for that instruction. Table V.4.8 shows the mapping of the legal addressing modes to each bit in the valid format byte.

The addressing modes shown in Table V.4.8 are Immediate (IMM), Accumulator (ACC), Indirect (IND) using the X-register, Indirect (IND) using the Y-register, Absolute (ABS) using the X-register, page-zero (ZP) using the X-register, Absolute (ABS) using the Y-register, and page-zero (ZP) using the Y-register. The remaining two modes, Absolute (ABS) and page-zero (ZP), are determined at the time of processing since a register is not associated with these two modes. Also, the standalone (IND) mode, new to the 65C02 Instruction Set except for the JMP indirect instruction, must be determined by how the instruction is used in context within the source code.

The source code that I have generated for *Big Mac* program is not perfect. I have verified that two *SWEET16* branch displacements in the source code have the same value as to what exists in the original object code. I think Mr. Bredon somehow allowed two coding errors to pass his design reviews. More likely, Mr. Bredon hand-coded the two routine displacements which are close in proximity, and for one reason or another these two displacements were simply not checked or verified. The first displacement error occurs at 0xD2C0 for a BP instruction having a 0xD3 displacement. That displacement would put 0xD295 into the program counter register. There is a BZ instruction at 0xD294 and a ST instruction at 0xD296. I would choose the ST instruction as the more logical branch. The second displacement error occurs at 0xD2DE for a BNZ instruction having a 0x08 displacement. That displacement would put 0xD2E8 into the program counter register. There is a BZ instruction at 0xD2E7 and a SET instruction at 0xD2E9. I would choose the SET instruction as the more logical branch. I have not yet had an opportunity to do more than just document these errors, so I have not yet changed these displacement values. If I cannot ascertain a strategy to exercise this section of code, then I will not have any more information than I already have in order to make an educated decision as to what Mr. Bredon intended.

Another interesting anomaly in *Big Mac* occurs in the routine that begins at 0xDC60. For all intents and purposes that code looks unremarkable until 0xDC91. At that point there is a JSR instruction to 0xC9AA. Bizarre! I am aware of only one possible reason for this call. In the Apple //e CX ROM code there does exist a purposefully placed Pascal 1.0 output entry point at 0xC9AA called PXWRITE. The nearby routines in this region of code must either branch around or leave room for the PXWRITE entry point. PXWRITE loads the A-register from the variable CHAR located at 0x067B, and then it jumps to 0xC356, an address in the Slot 3 peripheral-card ROM memory, presumably to write that data to a Pascal object. Why would Mr. Bredon make such a call in *Big Mac* when *Big Mac* was originally written for the Apple][+? This Pascal interface did not even exist for the Apple][+. If Mr. Bredon did update *Big Mac* for the Apple //e, why didn't he also update his *Big Mac* Monitor to display the full 65C02 Instruction Set? So far this call to 0xC9AA is just an interesting anomaly in *Big Mac*. Perhaps Mr. Bredon modified the address for the JSR at 0xDC91 *on the fly*. I see no evidence of a label in that region of code to even suggest that such an address modification was even considered. The code could also be simply hogwash. I have yet to investigate this subject any further.

In order to display the 65C02 specific instructions in the Monitor, two format bytes need to be included in the FMT2 table. These format bytes are for the (ZP) format and for the (ABS,X) jump format. For one reason or another every monitor or MiniAsm monitor that I have studied sets the (ZP) format to 0x4B and the (ABS,X) format to 0x5A. I have no problem with the value for the (ABS,X) format. However, I strongly believe that the value for the (ZP) format can only be 0x49 and not 0x4B. This (ZP) format value becomes even more critical in order to produce the correct opcodes that are generated by the ROM based mini-assembler. Even though *Big Mac* does not have enough room nor any reason to support the code for a mini-assembler, the FMT2 table is still necessary and its values are still critical in order to properly display the complete 65C02 Instruction Set.

5. CFFA Card

The CompactFlash For Apple, or CFFA card is an Apple II peripheral interface card that is able to read from and write to a CompactFlash memory card seated in its on-board CF card socket or to an external hard drive by means of a 40-pin IDE header socket. Later enhancements of the CFFA replaced the 40-pin IDE header socket with a USB socket. This peripheral card is able to present the onboard flash storage as either a hard drive or as a stack of floppy disks when using Disk][emulation firmware. Richard Dreher of R&D Automation created the CFFA card, and the first production run was released in 2002. I purchased my CFFA card in 2006, CFFA Version 2.0, revision B. It is my understanding that the CFFA card was most likely designed to be more compatible with ProDOS. Unfortunately, I never participated in the ProDOS movement. When ProDOS was introduced my software interests had already been redirected to UNIX based high-end professional workstations manufactured by SGI (running IRIX) and SUN (running SunOS). In view of my recent development of DOS 4.1, and now DOS 4.5, I began developing my own Disk][emulation firmware specifically for the CFFA card. I simply want a means to digitally archive my hundreds (yes, many hundreds) of 5.25-inch diskettes, and the CFFA card is the ideal reservoir.

I understand, however, that Mr. Dreher has enhanced the CFFA card in many ways since my purchase in 2006. I have no idea if the hardware interface of the current version of the CFFA card resembles that of the past interface, and whether or not my firmware will even function on the current version of hardware. I strongly suspect my CFFA card firmware will function perfectly in all ways on the current hardware design if it still interfaces a CF memory card. Table V.5.1 shows the entry points of the firmware interface I developed that is mapped to the peripheral-card ROM memory for the CFFA card.

The CFFA firmware interface allows access to each of the 512-byte blocks on a CompactFlash memory card up to 8 GB in size. Each block has a Logical Block Address (LBA) that is 24-bits in size, divided among three bytes, and saved to three of the sixteen peripheral-card I/O memory locations, or registers. There are four upper address bits available in a fourth register that can extend CFFA firmware addressing to 28 bits. CFFA firmware is limited to accessing up to an 8 GB CompactFlash memory card. Even the Master Boot Record (MBR) can be read and saved. Only three processing commands are necessary to utilize the CFFA, and those processing commands are READ, WRITE, and ID. If the peripheral-card I/O locations have been changed to accept a 32-bit LBA, my CFFA firmware interface will still only address up to an 8 GB CompactFlash memory card.

Offset	Name	Description
0x00	CFBOOT	Entry point for DOS PR# command to boot selected DOS
0x10	ROMHOOK	Entry point to attach the CFFA to the DOS in memory
0x18	ROMUHOOK	Entry point to detach the CFFA from the DOS in memory
0x20	USRBOOT	Boot selected DOS image
0x30	VOLBOOT	Boot selected volume DOS image
0x3B	DISKRWTS	DOS 3.3 RWTS entry if DOS 3.3 is in memory
0x4B	CFRWTS	DOS 4.1 and DOS 4.5 RWTS entry if DOS 4.1 or if DOS 4.5 is in memory
0x5C	ROMBOOT	Disk][firmware entry point for Boot Stage 1 code at 0x0801
0x64	CFRWTS3	Convert DVTS to LBA to seek, read, write, and format CF volumes
0xF3	MODOS3	Entry point to modify DOS 3.3 during Boot Stage 2 for CFFA use
0xFE	VERSION	Version number for CF firmware (0x05)
0xFF	BUILD	Build number for CF firmware (0x05)

Table V.5.1. CFFA Card Firmware Entry Points

The complete firmware interface fits comfortably in the peripheral-card ROM memory and expansion ROM memory of the CFFA card. The peripheral-card ROM memory has the normal slot boot entry signature bytes with a CFFA unique byte at offset 0x00, my standard DOS connection ON/OFF at offsets 0x10 and 0x18, respectively, a user boot entry at offset 0x20, and a volume boot entry at offset 0x30. The user can boot one of eight versions of DOS and twenty-four LBA blocks are provided for each DOS image. The first six DOS images include DOS 3.3, DOS 4.1L, DOS 4.1H, DOS 4.3H, DOS 4.5L, and DOS 4.5H. Thus, there is room for two User Defined DOS images that may be installed, and those images are called IMAGUSR1 and IMAGUSR2. Additionally, the CFFA firmware can boot any bootable volume on any drive within the CF whether the boot tracks contain boot images for DOS 3.3, DOS 4.1, DOS 4.3, or DOS 4.5.

Card Size	Cylinders	Heads	Sectors	Total Blocks
256 MB	0x03D4	0x10	0x20	0x07A800
512 MB	0x03E1	0x10	0x3F	0x0F45F0
1 GB	0x07C2	0x10	0x3F	0x1E8BE0
2 GB	0x0F82	0x10	0x3F	0x3D0FE0
4 GB	0x1F1C	0x10	0x3F	0x7A7E40
8 GB	0x3E08	0x10	0x3F	0xF43F80

Table V.5.2. CompactFlash Card CHS Geometry

Table V.5.2 shows the sizes of available CompactFlash cards in total blocks based on their Cylinder, Head, and Sector (CHS) geometry according to CompactFlash datasheets. Knowing the geometry for a particular card allows one to convert CHS to LBA. However, it is not necessary to know or even to utilize this conversion to LBA in order to address the CFFA in LBA mode. Also, the CFFA card I own was designed and manufactured to address a CompactFlash card up to 8 GB in size and smaller. As stated above the LBA value is 24-bits in size, divided among three bytes. The READ and WRITE processing commands are the only commands that are necessary in order to read or to write any 512-byte data block in the CF card. The ID command can be used to read the IDENTIFY DEVICE block in the CF card. That block provides the serial number, model number, and its capacity in LBA addressable blocks as well as other useful information for the CompactFlash card. Table V.5.3 shows the peripheral-card I/O memory locations that are used in order to initiate a CF processing command. The value of **n** in 0xC0n0, for example, equals the slot number of the CFFA card plus eight.

Address	Name	I/O	Description
0xC0n0	ATADATAH	R/W	Used with register #8 to R/W data. Write this byte first
0xC0n1	SETCSMSK	R/W	Disable 6502 pre-fetch when writing to CF
0xC0n2	CLRCSMSK	R/W	Enable 6502 pre-fetch when reading CF
0xC0n6	ATASTAT2	R	Secondary CF status register; does not clear IRQ
0xC0n6	ATADEVCT	W	Device control register to disable IRQ
0xC0n8	ATADATAL	R/W	Used with register #0 to R/W data. Read this byte first
0xC0n9	ATAERROR	R	Processing error source when register #15 not zero
0xC0nA	ATASECCT	R/W	Number of blocks to read or write; always set to 1
0xC0nB	ATASECTR	R/W	Bits 07:00 of LBA
0xC0nC	ATACYLNL	R/W	Bits 15:08 of LBA
0xC0nD	ATACYLNH	R/W	Bits 23:16 of LBA
0xC0nE	ATAHEAD	R/W	Bits 27:24 of LBA; select LBA or CHS mode
0xC0nF	ATASTAT	R	Primary CF status register; does not clear IRQ
0xC0nF	ATACMD	W	Command register

Table V.5.3. CFFA Firmware Interface Control Registers

Parameter	Range	Description
Drive	1 - 81	in order to support up to an 8 GB CF card
Volume	0 - 255	supported by the DOS 4.5 VTOC
Track	0 — 47	supported by the DOS 4.5 VTOC
Sector	0 - 31	supported by the DOS 4.5 VTOC

Table V.5.4. CFFA Firmware DVTS Variable Range

I approached my design of the CFFA firmware interface as a way to communicate with a massive data storage device. To that end, I devised an equation to convert Drive/Volume/Track/Sector (DVTS) to LBA and an algorithm to perform the reverse conversion. There is only one unique solution for either conversion routine. Any DOS that is designed for the Apple][is limited by the variables it can control. DOS 4.5 is no exception, and the variables that are available to DOS 4.5 for the management of any collection of data and bootable volumes are Drive number, Volume number, Track number, and Sector number. The variables Volume, Track, and Sector already have predefined limitations or ranges for their values. Drive number has mostly been thought of as being two disk devices until Rana developed a peripheral interface card that supports up to four disk devices. In order to utilize the extraordinary resources of a CompactFlash card, the concept of Drive number must be re-imagined and thought of as a large bank of virtual disk devices all strapped together that can each accommodate a very large number of volumes. Being able to accommodate a large number of drive devices is an opportunity to manage an exceedingly large collection of disk volumes with very little effort. The ranges that are allowed in my CFFA firmware for the variables Drive, Volume, Track, and Sector are shown in Table V.5.4.

The equations to convert DVTS to LBA are given by:

```
   block = Sector & 0x0F
    page = Sector & 0x10
 offset1 = 0x100

     LBA = ( ( Drive-1 ) * 0x30000 ) +
           ( Volume * 0x300 ) +
           ( Track * 0x10 ) + block + offset1
```

These equations conclude that each Volume contains 0x300 LBA blocks and each Drive contains 0x30000 LBA blocks. A Volume can consist of up to a maximum of forty-eight Tracks and each Track consists of sixteen LBA blocks by definition. Since an LBA block contains 512 bytes of data, the block is partitioned by the page variable. When page is equal to zero then disk sectors 0x00 to 0x0F reside on page 0, or the lower half of the LBA block. When page is not zero then disk sectors 0x10 to 0x1F reside on page 1, or the upper half of the LBA block. I agree that forcing a Volume to be 768 LBA blocks in size (i.e. 1536 disk sectors) rather than 576 disk sectors in size having thirty-six tracks in a volume does potentially waste a lot of resource space on the CompactFlash card. DOS 4.5 has the potential to address a volume having up to fifty tracks in size, but I considered forty-eight to be the better upper limit for mathematical reasons and for ease in calculating LBA from DVTS. Because the VTOC can support thirty-two sectors per track and an LBA block contains 512 bytes, it makes sense to split an LBA block into a lower 256-byte disk sector and an upper 256-byte disk sector. The algorithm to calculate an LBA for a given DVTS using the above equations is exceedingly fast in the CFFA firmware because all of the multiplication is done by using the addition of values obtained from indexing into three lookup tables. The indexing into the three lookup tables use 4-bit nibbles derived from Volume and Drive.

Card Size	Sectors	Drives	Extra Volumes	Residue
256 MB	0x07A800	2	141	0x000
512 MB	0x0F45F0	5	22	0x2F0
1 GB	0x1E8BE0	10	46	0x0E0
2 GB	0x3D0FE0	20	90	0x0E0
4 GB	0x7A7E40	40	212	0x140
8 GB	0xF43F80	81	106	0x080

Table V.5.5. CompactFlash Card Drive/Volume Parameters

Block Start	Block End	Description
0x000000	0x000001	Not used
0x000002	0x000002	Saved Slot firmware
0x000003	0x000006	Saved ROM firmware
0x000007	0x000007	Saved Identify Device
0x000008	0x00000F	DOS descriptions (8)
0x000010	0x0000CF	DOS Images (8 24-block images)
0x0000D0	0x0000FF	Drive descriptions (room for 96)
0x000100	0x1E00FF	10 Drives each having 256 volumes
0x1E0100	0x1E8AFF	1 Drive having 46 volumes
0x1E8B00	0x1E8BDF	Not used

Table V.5.6. Block Utilization for a 1 GB CompactFlash Card

Using the values shown in Table V.5.2 for the Total Blocks in CompactFlash cards, the total number of drives and extra volumes can be determined, and they are shown in Table V.5.5. The conversion equation for DVTS to LBA stipulates that 0x30000 LBA blocks comprise one Drive and that 0x300 LBA blocks comprise one Volume. For example, a 1 GB CompactFlash card contains ten full drives and the last, or eleventh drive has room for only forty-six volumes. There is 0x0E0 unused LBA blocks after accounting for offset1 which is 0x100 LBA blocks. Table V.5.6 shows the block utilization for a 1 GB CompactFlash card.

There is sufficient room reserved for eight complete DOS images and these images follow the DOS image descriptions beginning at LBA block 0x000010. The first six DOS images are used for DOS 3.3, DOS 4.1L, DOS 4.1H, DOS 4.3H, DOS 4.5L, and DOS 4.5H. The remaining two DOS images can be used for the User Defined DOS images called IMAGUSR1 and IMAGUSR2. Each DOS image is assigned a volume number from one to eight and the image is fully contained within its twenty-four LBA blocks that are reserved for that image. Each DOS image is saved to the CompactFlash card as it exists and written to the boot tracks of a bootable DOS volume. The only difference between a booting CFFA image and a booting volume image is that a booting CFFA image has a DRIVE value set to zero whereas a booting volume image has a DRIVE value that is set to a value that is greater than zero.

As shown in Table V.5.6 the 0x30 blocks allocated for drive descriptions provide enough room for 96 descriptions and each description is 256 bytes in size. The drive description contains the drive name in the first twenty-four bytes, the date and time the drive description was created in the next six bytes, and the actual NULL-terminated drive description verbiage in the remaining 226 bytes.

The LBA and page value for a particular drive description is calculated as follows:

```
offset = 0xD0

  LBA = | ( ( Drive-1 ) / 2 ) | + offset

 page = ( Drive-1 ) - ( ( LBA - offset ) * 2 )
```

Connecting the CFFA to DOS 4.5 is trivial because DOS 4.5 contains a reserved address location for each slot that contains a peripheral interface card that is a Disk][-like I/O device that has an RWTS interface address. When the CFFA is booted with one of the installed DOS images, DOS 4.5H for example, Boot Stage 1 is monitored for BOOTPGS to become negative. Unlike DOS 3.3, Boot Stage 1 in DOS 4.5H reads sectors 0x0F to 0x00 on track 0x00 in descending order into memory from page 0xD0 to page 0xDD and from page 0xBE to page 0xBF in ascending order. After sector 0x00 is read into memory at 0xBF00, all of DOS 4.5H RWTS is now available to read into memory the remaining pages (i.e. sectors) of DOS 4.5H. Normally, a Disk][-like I/O device only boots from drive one of two possible drives (or four in the case of the Rana peripheral interface card) regardless of the volume number of the diskette. However, the CFFA must be able to boot from any of its DOS images and from any of its drives and from any of its volumes, so this puts a special burden on monitoring the Boot Stage 1 process.

In addition to the boot variable BOOTPGS common to all varieties of DOS, and the DOS 4.5 Disk Address table, there is a variable called BCFGNDX that points to a structure on page 0xBF. BCFGNDX points to the BOOTCFG table of variables that is used to initialize the RWTS IOCB by the RWPAGES routine at the beginning of Boot Stage 2. It is at this crucial juncture when Boot Stage 1 completes, but before Boot Stage 2 begins, that the BOOTCFG table must be updated with the current CF Drive and Volume that is currently booting. The CHKDRVZ routine in the CFFA firmware is called during Boot Stage 1 and during Boot Stage 2 in order to ensure that the LBA block number for the given DVTS values is correctly calculated when the value for DRIVE is set to zero. When the value for DRIVE is **not** set to zero, the values for DNUM and VOLEXPT (i.e. the DRIVE and VOLUME values in BOOTCFG) are utilized by Boot Stage 2 and pushed onto the CFRWTS interface using the RWTS IOCB so that the correct LBA is calculated from the given DVTS values. Unfortunately, the situation for a booting DOS 3.3 volume is a horrible nightmare for any firmware, and the CFFA firmware is no exception, but certainly it is not impossible to monitor and to manage the booting of DOS 3.3 correctly.

Boot Stage 1 for DOS 3.3 reads sectors 0x09 to 0x00 on track 0x00 in descending order into Apple][memory from page 0xBF to page 0xB6, also in descending order. After sector 0x00 is read into memory at page 0xB6, all of DOS 3.3 RWTS is now available to read into memory the remaining pages of DOS 3.3. Before Boot Stage 2 begins, DOS 3.3 initializes the RWTS IOCB with DNUM set to 0x01 and VOLEXPT set to zero, which allows any volume to boot in disk drive 1. These values must be patched, or overwritten in order for the CF firmware to calculate the correct LBA from the booting DVTS values. Once the routine RWPAGES has read in the remaining pages of DOS using the correct Drive and Volume values, the DOS 3.3 code must be patched yet again in order for it to function properly within the CF environment. The prime issue with DOS 3.3 is how DOS 3.3 manages (or mismanages in my opinion) Volume number. In the CF environment Volume number cannot be ascertained from the address field of a sector because there are no address fields to read from the CF blocks. Therefore, a DOS 3.3 routine such as CATHNDLR that handles the DOS CATALOG command must not presuppose any value for the booting Volume number. Similarly, the SETDFLTS routine must not initialize or change the current value for Volume number so that other DOS 3.3 commands will work properly when the V keyword is not included with a DOS 3.3 command. Furthermore, in order for DOS 3.3 to read into memory any DOS 4.5 file, the maximum filename length must be adjusted down to twenty-four bytes in length. Before any CF volume is initialized with DOS 3.3, all patches like the ones just described probably should be removed. A simple tool can do this, of course, but in order for DOS 3.3 to communicate with the CF firmware and perform volume initialization, its CALLRWTS routine must remain patched. Thus, I believe the better solution is to leave DOS 3.3 patched and totally useable in the CF environment, initialize a CF volume as desired, and overwrite the DOS image on tracks 0x00,

`0x01`, and `0x02` with whatever *pure* DOS 3.3 image you wish knowing full well that it may not boot or function properly in the `CF` environment. There may be other equally viable solutions. Table V.5.7 documents all of the patches that are applied to a DOS 3.3 image before and after Boot Stage 2 processing by the `CF` firmware.

Address	Old	New	Boot Stage 2	Description
0xB707	0x01	drive	before	update for DNUM
0xB7EB	0x00	volume	before	update of VOLEXPT
0xB748	0x84	#modos3	before	replace address of DOSSTRT with #MODOS3
0xB749	0x9D	cfpage	before	and CFPAGE at 0xB748/0xB749
0xAA66	VOLVAL	volume	after	update VOLVAL with volume
0xB7EB	VOLEXPT	volume	after	update IOCB VOLEXPT with volume
0xA0DA	0x66	0x65	after	change address from VOLVAL to KYWRDIDX
0xA95B	0x02	cfmaxdrv	after	update KWRANGE for DRIVE
0xAD9E	0xF9	0xFE	after	change address from VOLNUMBR to unused address after File Manager Work Area
0xB203	0x1E	0x18	after	change NAMESIZE value for filename length
0xB707	drive	0x01	after	restore original value
0xB748	#modos3	0x84	after	restore address of DOSSTRT at
0xB749	cfpage	0x9D	after	0xB748/0xB749

Table V.5.7. DOS 3.3 Patches for CFFA

Referring to Table V.5.7, all of the variables listed that are in lowercase reside in `CF` firmware. All of the uppercase variables reside in DOS 3.3 source code. The first four substitutions are made just after Boot Stage 1 completes and before Boot Stage 2 begins. The LSB address for the firmware entry point `MODOS3` as shown in Table V.5.1 and `CFPAGE` for the MSB address of the CFFA card firmware is used to replace the address for `DOSSTRT`, or `0x9D84`, at `0xB748/0xB749`. Once Boot Stage 2 completes, these patches force DOS 3.3 to re-enter the `CF` firmware in order to install the remaining patches and code replacements. After the patches have been made, the `CF` firmware simply jumps to the intended `DOSSTRT` address at this time. I fondly recall meeting many software engineers, particularly those at Sierra On-Line, who I refer to as *DOS 3.3 Purists. Thou shalt not modify DOS 3.3!* Only when we were able to demonstrate to Ken Williams that we were able to make DOS 3.3 smarter, faster, and safer did Williams remove the DOS 3.3 Purity Shield. Now, from my current vantage point, I see that DOS 3.3 contains a lot of really crappy code based on some very silly ideas, like how volume number is handled, and mishandled, and complimented, and substituted, and on and on and on. So, I see nothing wrong with *adjusting* DOS 3.3 here and there in order for it to function decently in the `CF` environment. Hopefully, DOS 4.5 demonstrates how simple and powerful it is to use Volume number in the `CF` environment; that is, using Volume number like any other parameter including Slot number, Drive number, Track number, and Sector number.

There are times when desperation leads to utilizing very creative and sneaky programming techniques. To be sure I was desperate in finding enough memory space to include the DOS 4.5 interface into the CFFA. I did not want to exclude the DOS 3.3 or the DOS 4.1 and DOS 4.3 interfaces, and I did not want to remove any of the informational text messages when a DOS volume is connected to or detached from the CFFA. I had already faced a similar dilemma for the DOS 4.5 HELP command where I desperately needed a little more code space. There, I used every scheme in my arsenal and still it was not enough to give me the code space I required. What saved the day was recursive programming! Recursive programming depends upon solutions to smaller instances of the same problem. In C-language recursive programming is very simple to implement and it is very much like winding up a spring. The spring continues to be *wound* until a solution end-point is reached, and then the spring is allowed to unwind transferring each *next* solution to the *previous* iteration. It was the final weapon to win the battle for more memory and code space in order to fully complete the DOS 4.5 HELP command handler. For the CFFA firmware, it was the utilization of phrases to formulate informational and error messages. Each error message contains three phrases so that the error message data can be highly compacted. Not only was I able to include the DOS 4.5 interface and retain all informational and error message texts (including the new DOS 4.5 text messages), but I succeeded in adding a new DOS image load manager and still retain fifty additional bytes that can be used for new CFFA features I have yet to imagine. Using phrases and recursive programming in these instances proved to be the right solution.

6. Volume Manager (VOLMGR)

The Volume Manager (*VOLMGR*) is a utility I developed in order to manage the CFFA firmware interface, manage the CFFA CompactFlash card utilization and identity, manage the CF Drives, manage the CF Volumes of a CF Drive, and manage the CF User DOS Images. The following figures show a few of the primary menu displays from *VOLMGR* as well as an example display of the Device Identity contents of a CompactFlash card. Additionally, the utility *BOOTDOS* can be used to boot any one of the six currently defined DOS images on the CF card and the utility *BOOTVOL* can be used to boot any one of the bootable CF volumes on any of the CF drives.

```
        CFFA Volume Manager
          DOS 4.5, Build 05
        Copyright (c) 2022 January 1
                  by
        Walland Philip Vrbancic Jr

       Use this CompactFlash For Apple
         installer and the accompanying
      software programs at your own risk.

      You are responsible for any damage or
   loss of productivity this installer or
      the accompanying software may cause.

         If you agree to these terms
        press any key to continue, or
      press ESC to exit this program now.
```

```
      CFFA Volume Manager Main Menu


   1 - Manage Firmware

   2 - Manage CompactFlash

   3 - Manage Drives

   4 - Manage Volumes

   5 - Manage Bootable DOS Images

   6 - Exit Volume Manager


   Select Option:  ■
```

Figure V.6.1. VOLMGR Product Warning Display   Figure V.6.2. VOLMGR Main Menu

When *VOLMGR* first starts it displays a warning screen as shown in Figure V.6.1. This display reminds the user that using powerful software like *VOLMGR* and its utilities can indeed cause damage to directories and file systems when this software is used carelessly. If a CFFA card is detected to reside in an Apple][peripheral card slot, the `CFFA Volume Manager Main Menu` is displayed as shown in Figure V.6.2. This menu shows that there are five main managers that comprise the *VOLMGR* utility.

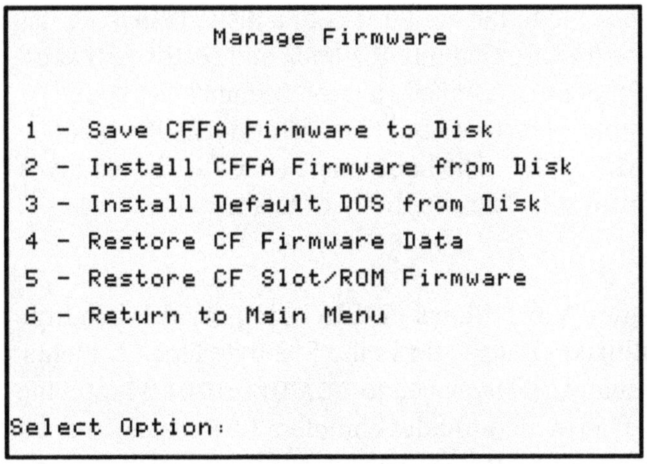

```
        Manage Firmware                    Manage CompactFlash


1 - Save CFFA Firmware to Disk     1 - Display CF Memory Utilization
2 - Install CFFA Firmware from Disk 2 - Display Identify Device Contents
3 - Install Default DOS from Disk  3 - Save Identify Device to LBA 7
4 - Restore CF Firmware Data       4 - Save Selected LBA to Disk
5 - Restore CF Slot/ROM Firmware   5 - Restore Selected LBA from Disk
6 - Return to Main Menu            6 - Clear Selected LBA Range
                                   7 - Return to Main Menu


Select Option:                     Select Option:  ■
```

Figure V.6.3. Manage Firmware Menu 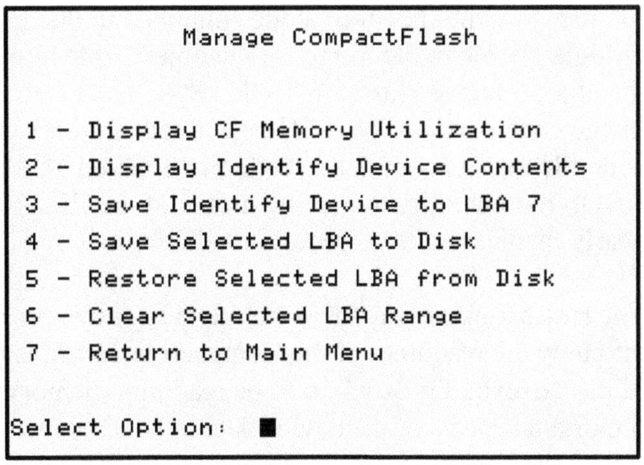   Figure V.6.4. Manage CompactFlash Menu

VOLMGR detects a previously unmodified CFFA card by inspecting the first eight firmware bytes known as the signature bytes, and it continues its processing nevertheless for this single instance of the firmware configuration. This allows the user to save the current factory supplied CFFA firmware to a file on a diskette and to install my CFFA firmware onto the CFFA card from a diskette as shown in Figure V.6.3. The `Manage Firmware` menu provides for the installation of CFFA firmware and the installation of all six default DOS images. After *VOLMGR* installs this CFFA firmware, the first eight firmware bytes, or signature bytes are changed to those listed for the CFFA card as shown in Table II.7.2. When *VOLMGR* is launched again sometime in the future, *VOLMGR* continues processing because reading the new CFFA signature bytes verifies that the CFFA card contains my CFFA firmware. Detecting any other firmware bytes will not allow *VOLMGR* to continue any further processing. *VOLMGR* also copies the CFFA Slot Firmware that is written to the peripheral-card ROM memory of the CFFA card to `LBA 0x0000002` and the CFFA ROM Firmware that is written to the peripheral-card expansion ROM memory of the CFFA card to `LBA 0x0000003-0x0000006`. This allows `VOLMGR` to restore the critical firmware data located at `0xC804-0xC83C` from `LBA 0x0000003` and to restore all of the Slot Firmware from `LBA 0x0000002`. The CompactFlash device buffers all data written to a specific `LBA` block such that it is **not** necessary to throttle the speed at which data is written to the CFFA `ATADATAL` and `ATADATAH` registers. This is **not true** for data written to the CFFA peripheral-card ROM memory or to the peripheral-card expansion ROM memory. Data written to these memory areas must be actively throttled. However, data read from these memory areas do not need to be actively throttled such that these memory areas may be read like any other peripheral card memory. A delay of at least 225 µsec must be inserted after a data byte is written and before a register or a pointer is incremented. To write a page of peripheral-card ROM memory for the CFFA peripheral interface card requires 63233 µsec rather than 3841 µsec to write the same data without a delay throttle of 225 µsec. In other words it is around 16.46 times slower to write any data to the CFFA peripheral interface card memory.

The six default DOS images must be preprocessed into their boot image code format from their object code format before the images can be installed into the CFFA in the `LBA 0x0000010-0x00000CF` block region. For example, the object code format for a DOS 4.5H Binary file is shown in Table I.8.6. This object code format is the order of object code data that the assembler generated when it assembled the source code for DOS 4.5H. When all of the *Lisa* assembler output `SEG` files are sequentially read into memory, the complete object code for DOS 4.5H is created and saved as its object code Binary file. In order to write the object code contained in this Binary file to the boot tracks of a diskette making that diskette bootable, the format of the object code must be transformed into the track and sector format of the object code as shown in Table I.8.4. The result of this format transformation becomes the boot image code for the DOS 4.5H object code in this example. The tool used to transform a DOS object code file into its boot image code file is called `INSTALL_DOS`. The boot image code file format gives a DOS its capability to boot by means of the CFFA firmware. The simplicity of this firmware makes it nearly magical in its power and its flexibility.

The `Manage CompactFlash` menu as shown in Figure V.6.4 allows *VOLMGR* to provide visibility into how the resources of the CompactFlash card is utilized. It also allows the 512-byte block contents of the `Identify Device` to be read into memory, automatically saved to `LBA 0x0000007`, and the important aspects of the device data to be displayed. This menu provides complete `LBA` management as well. The contents of any `LBA` can be saved to a diskette, any `LBA` can be restored from a diskette, and a selected range of `LBA` blocks can be cleared where all 512 bytes of a block are set to `zero`. These routines are surprisingly fast in view of the amount of `CF` data that must be accessed. Figure V.6.5 shows an example display of a 1 GB CompactFlash card that is capable of hosting ten full drives where each drive contains 256 volumes. In order not to waste the remaining resources on this card, an eleventh drive is available that contains forty-six volumes. Thus, $0x30000 * 0x0A + 0x300 * 0x2E = 0x01E8A00$. The `Identify Device` contents for this same CF card is shown in Figure V.6.6. From this information the `LBA` contents in this CF card is equal to $0x07C2 * 0x0010 * 0x003F = 0x01E8BE0$. The Serial Number is used to verify that the same `CF` card matches the same critical firmware data that is located at `0xC804-0xC83C` in the peripheral-card expansion ROM memory of the CFFA firmware. This Serial Number verification takes place whenever the CFFA firmware boots a DOS image from the DOS Partition or whenever any volume is booted from the Drive and Volume Partition. The firmware makes a call to `READID` that reads the `Identify Device` data to page `0x08`. A Serial Number mismatch between the seated `CF` card and the CFFA firmware is simply not tolerated, the `Wrong CF card` error message is issued, expansion ROM memory is deselected, and a jump is made to the ROM Monitor. When many CompactFlash cards need to be utilized in the same CFFA card, simply use *VOLMGR* to restore the CompactFlash data using the `Manage Firmware` menu in order to synchronize the CompactFlash card and the CFFA firmware.

The `Manage Drives` menu is shown in Figure V.6.7. All of the drives contained on the `CF` card that is seated in the CFFA peripheral interface card are displayed in groups of no more than sixteen when Option 1 is selected. In Option 2 each drive is displayed showing its drive number, the number of volumes contained in that drive, and the Drive Name. All drives should contain 256 volumes except for the last drive. From Figure V.6.5, forty-eight `LBA` blocks at `0x00000D0-0x00000FF` contain room for ninety-six drive descriptions. In other words, each `LBA` block in this region contains two drive descriptions, and each drive description can be displayed for viewing and each drive description can be easily changed. When Option 3 is selected in Figure V.6.7 and an available drive number is entered, a request to change the Drive Name is offered followed by a request to update the timestamp associated with this drive. The Original drive description is displayed in the upper part of the screen and the lower part of the screen provides enough room to enter a New drive description. If the `RETURN` key is entered before entering any new information for the Drive Name, the timestamp, or the New drive description, no changes are made to the original data as a safe-guard.

```
┌─────────────────────────────────────┐
│     Display CF Memory Utilization    │
│                                      │
│   CFFA slot - 5                      │
│   Card name - CF 1.0 GB Storage Media│
│   Date/Time - 01/01/22 08:28:48      │
│ LBA sectors - 0x01E8BE0 (1 GB)       │
│ Total drives - 011 + 046 extra volumes│
│ 0000000-0000001 = Not used           │
│ 0000002-0000002 = Saved Slot Firmware│
│ 0000003-0000006 = Saved ROM Firmware │
│ 0000007-0000007 = Saved Identify Device│
│ 0000008-000000F = DOS Descriptions (8)│
│ 0000010-00000CF = DOS Images (8)     │
│ 00000D0-00000FF = Drive Descriptions │
│ 0000100-01E8AFF = Drives and Volumes │
│ 01E8B00-01E8BDF = Not used           │
│                                      │
│             Press Any Key            │
└─────────────────────────────────────┘
```

Figure V.6.5. CF Memory Utilization

```
┌─────────────────────────────────────┐
│    Display Identify Device Contents  │
│                                      │
│    Cylinders - 0007C2                │
│        Heads - 000010                │
│ Sectors/Track - 00003F               │
│  Maximum LBA - 1E8BE0                │
│ Serial Number - 020805J2806R5550     │
│   Firmware - HDX 4.03                │
│      Model - SanDisk SDCFB-1024      │
│                                      │
│ Status:  Okay, press any key         │
└─────────────────────────────────────┘
```

Figure V.6.6. Device Identity Contents

```
┌─────────────────────────────────────┐
│           Manage Drives              │
│                                      │
│                                      │
│  1 - List All Drives                 │
│  2 - Display Drive Information        │
│  3 - Change Drive Information         │
│  4 - Return to Main Menu             │
│                                      │
│                                      │
│ Select Option:                       │
└─────────────────────────────────────┘
```

Figure V.6.7. Manage Drives Menu

```
┌─────────────────────────────────────┐
│           Manage Volumes             │
│                                      │
│  1 - Display Drive Volumes Catalog Size│
│  2 - Display Drive Volumes DOS       │
│  3 - Display Volume LBA Range        │
│  4 - Display Volume VTOC Information  │
│  5 - Display Sector Bitmap Information│
│  6 - Initialize a CF Volume          │
│  7 - Boot a CF Volume                │
│  8 - Return to Main Menu             │
│                                      │
│ Select Option:                       │
└─────────────────────────────────────┘
```

Figure V.6.8. Manage Volumes Menu

The Manage Volumes menu is shown in Figure V.6.8. When Option 1 is selected and an available drive number is entered, all volumes available on this selected drive are displayed showing the number of Catalog sectors that are contained in each volume. This is the most optimal way to quickly show whether a particular volume on a drive has been initialized. If a volume has been initialized, its number of Catalog sectors will be some value other than zero and not greater than fifteen. Option 2 is very similar to Option 1 in how the volume information is displayed for a selected and available drive. A DOS Table is first displayed that lists the available DOS images from 1 to 8, 0 for no DOS found, and 9 for unknown DOS found. Instead of showing the number of Catalog sectors that are contained in each volume, a value from the DOS Table is displayed for each volume. Option 3 displays the LBA ranges for the selected Drive and Volume on that drive. This information may be useful in order to calculate a particular LBA to save or to restore. Options 4 and 5 provide the same information as Options 2 and 4 in *VMGR*, respectively, that display VTOC information and Sector Bitmap information. *VOLMGR* does not provide the ability to edit the VTOC information nor the Sector Bitmap information. Those capabilities are reserved solely for *VMGR*. Option 6 may be selected to initialize a volume using many parameters for track, sector, and Catalog size. Option 7 may be selected to boot any bootable volume.

```
      Manage Bootable DOS Images

  1 - List Installed DOS Images

  2 - Select DOS Image for Boot

  3 - Show DOS Image Description

  4 - Modify DOS Image Description

  5 - Return to Main Menu




Select Option:  ■
```

```
        List Installed DOS Images

  DOS Image 1 - DOS 3.3
  DOS Image 2 - DOS 4.1L
  DOS Image 3 - DOS 4.1H
  DOS Image 4 - DOS 4.3H
  DOS Image 5 - DOS 4.5L
  DOS Image 6 - DOS 4.5H
  DOS Image 7 - DOS User1 (Blank)
  DOS Image 8 - DOS User2 (Blank)




             Press Any Key
```

Figure V.6.9. Manage DOS Images Menu   Figure V.6.10. List DOS Images Display

The Manage Bootable DOS Images menu is shown in Figure V.6.9. When Option 1 is selected, all installed DOS images are displayed as shown in Figure V.6.10. If a default or user DOS image has not yet been installed, its image number and category name is still listed but the image content is displayed as (Blank). Option 2 displays the same list of default and user DOS images as shown in Figure V.6.10 as well as the current active DOS image number and an opportunity to enter a new DOS image number for the selected DOS that will automatically boot. Options 3 and 4 utilize the same list of default and user DOS images in order to manage the DOS image descriptions. Option 3 displays the selected DOS image description if a description exists for that DOS image. From Figure V.6.5, eight LBA blocks at 0x0000008-0x000000F contain room for eight DOS image descriptions. In other words, each LBA block in this region contains one complete DOS image description, or enough room for 511 bytes of data. One byte is always reserved for the terminating NULL character in all text-entry buffers in *VOLMGR*. Each DOS image description can be displayed for viewing and each DOS image description can be easily changed. After selecting Option 4, the Original DOS image description is displayed in the upper two-thirds area of the screen and the lower one-third area of the screen provides enough room to begin entering a New DOS image description. Additional room will be made available in this area by scrolling the previously entered text upwards within this screen area. When the RETURN key is entered after entering any and all new information for the selected DOS image, an opportunity is offered to save or not to save this new DOS image description. Option 4, like all text-entry menu options in *VOLMGR*, displays the number of characters that remain available in the buffer that is reserved for completing that text-entry menu option. This remaining character count is extraordinarily useful in planning and executing a text-entry menu option so that only the most critical and most important information is included in order to use the available buffer space as efficiently as possible.

7. File Developer (FID)

File Developer (*FID*) was an original Apple][assembly language utility found on the DOS 3.3 System Master diskette that I received with my new Apple][+. I suspect it was and it still is the most widely used DOS utility of all time. Instead of writing my own file management utility for DOS 4.1, and now for DOS 4.5 having Volume number and Phase Number included as input parameters, I decided to source *FID* and add what I needed to that software. Anytime I start tearing into software that was written by someone else, I find it to be a real, sometimes rare educational experience. *FID* did not disappoint me. *FID* utilizes the RWTS and the File Manager interfaces as noted elsewhere in this book, which gave me a good insight in how the *Apple Experts* made use of those interfaces. I received the most grief from *FID*'s hardcoded insistence that track 0x00 could never be used for data storage, and that it was a track used only for booting DOS. There were only a few locations in the *FID* software where I had to insert the parameters TRKMASK (i.e. 0x3F) and TRKZERO (i.e. 0x40) so that *FID* would accommodate track 0x00 properly, as a data track, as it is accommodated properly in DOS 4.5.

```
************************************
*     Apple ][ File Developer     *
*  Version N with DOS 4.5, Build 05 *
*                                  *
*  Copyright 1979 Apple Computer Inc. *
************************************


  Choose One of the Following Options

   <1>   Copy Files
   <2>   Catalog
   <3>   Space on Disk
   <4>   Unlock Files
   <5>   Lock Files
   <6>   Delete Files
   <7>   Reset Slot, Drive, Volume
   <8>   Verify Files
   <9>   Undelete Files
   <Q>   Quit


Which Option would you like:
```

```
                Copy Files

Source Slot:    6
       Drive:   1
       Volume:
       Phase:

Target Slot:    6
       Drive:   2
       Volume:
       Phase:

File (<name>/*):   FID

Insert Volume 000 and Volume 000.

Press <ctrl-C> to return to Main Menu.
Press any other key to begin.
*
```

Figure V.7.1. FID Main Menu   Figure V.7.2. FID Copy Files

I found that the most essential task was to implant the use of Volume number into *FID* because I wanted *FID* to work with the CFFA hardware which greatly depends upon Volume number. My CFFA firmware can access up to 81 Drives (for an 8 GB CompactFlash card), where each drive can support 256 Volumes. Actually, I originally derived this dependency upon Volume number from the Sider firmware that utilizes Volume number in order to calculate the beginning sector number for the start of each DOS 3.3 volume partition on its 10 MB hard drive. And, of course, I wanted *FID* to include my new DOS URM command in order to **undelete** files because that capability exists in DOS 4.5 by means of the File Manager. *FID* also makes use of the SUBCODE field for the Catalog command in order to display the current list of files on a volume with or without listing the deleted files as well. *FID* must use the free sector bitmap in the VTOC properly, as it is used properly in DOS 4.5, and not how it is used improperly in DOS 3.3. Finally, *FID* must include the Phase number for the Source and Target volumes in order to share files between those two different volume structural formats. Phase number is like any of the other parameters that are used in either the RWTS IOCB or in the File Manager Context Block.

The main menu for *FID* that is modified for DOS 4.5 is shown in Figure V.7.1. Option 9 has been added in order to undelete a selected file. This option uses the same interface as options 4, 5, 6, and 8 that operate on a single file. The `Quit` option has been given a new entry selection, or `Q`. The first part of Option 1 is shown in Figure V.7.2 in order to display the added Volume and Phase input variables. If `RETURN` is entered for those two variables, the default value of `zero` is entered for them. Unlike the DOS 3.3 version of *FID*, the DOS 4.5 version of *FID* uses the asterisk for its *wild card* in replacing any characters in a file name. When the asterisk is used alone, then all filenames are copied in Option 1.

Because *FID* uses the File Manager in order to copy files from one volume to another, there are certain limitations that one needs to be aware of when using *FID*. Whatever sectors that are associated with a file that are specified in the `TSL` for that file are copied from the source volume to the destination volume. The File Manager has no idea whether all or some of those sectors are actually being used by that file. If a Binary file is created with the DOS command `BSAVE TEST1,A$1000,L$6000`, for example, a file having ninety-eight sectors is created, and there will be one sector allocated for the `TSL` sector and ninety-seven track/sector entries will be specified in that `TSL` sector for all of the allocated data sectors. Then, if the DOS command `BSAVE TEST1,A$1000,L$1000` is issued next, the DOS Catalog will show that ninety-eight sectors are still allocated for `TEST1`. *FID* blindly copies all ninety-seven data sectors even though only the first seventeen data sectors now contain valid data. This same situation can occur with Applesoft files as well. If the original Applesoft file utilizes forty-one sectors, then the file is edited to nearly half its size and saved, the Applesoft file will continue to utilize the forty-one track/sector entries in its `TSL` and not, say, just the first twenty-five entries unless the file is saved under a new name. There is simply no way for *FID* to know whether a file uses all or some of the entries specified in its `TSL` sector unless additional and complex logic is included in *FID* that compares `TSL` utilization and file size. If disk space is a premium then *FID* should not be used to copy files; the files should be copied manually or by another utility.

Why does DOS (any Apple][DOS for that matter) potentially waste valuable disk space when one is saving less data to a file that already exists in the volume Catalog? There are probably many reasons, some of which are valid and some are merely cosmetic and more easy to implement. I believe the most valid reason is safety. In order to guarantee that a file only uses the disk space it truly requires when that file already exists in the volume Catalog would be to first delete the existing file, create a new file with the same name, and finally save the requested data to that new file. But would this procedure be entirely safe? What if something causes an error after the file is deleted but before the new file is created, or before the requested data can be saved? Is having a DOS `URM` command enough insurance if such a situation like this should ever occur? Perhaps the requested data should be saved to a `XXTEMPXX` file first, then the original file can be safely deleted before the `XXTEMPXX` file is renamed? There may not be enough disk space to support two copies of the file, or there may not be enough file entry space in the volume Catalog for an additional filename. This procedure would also rearrange the order of files in the volume Catalog which may not be appealing to some. I believe the best alternative is to save the requested data to an existing file using the `TSL` resources of that file, and if there are more entries in the `TSL` than needed, those entries should be marked as unused (zeroed out), and the sectors returned to the `VTOC` bitmap of the volume. Of course, I would only use this algorithm for the DOS `SAVE`, `BSAVE`, `LSAVE`, and `TSAVE` commands. It would be a moderately interesting exercise to implement this algorithm, and certainly be the cause for the release of yet another DOS 4.5 build. At this moment there is not enough code space left in DOS 4.5 to even consider implementing such a complex algorithm.

At this time DOS 4.5 provides the use of the `B` keyword to implement the *File Delete/File Save* strategy for the DOS `SAVE`, `BSAVE`, `LSAVE`, and `TSAVE` commands if desired. I have found this strategy to be quite useful and it has not caused me any concerns for the safety of my files: I tend to back up my work regularly, regardless. If the *File Delete/File Save* strategy should fail, having a backup does ensure that all is not lost. However, I believe I would be more inclined to suggest the creation of a simple utility devoted to the sole task of expunging unused `TSL` entries from the `TSL` sector of a file or files, and return those sectors to the `VTOC` bitmap of the volume. Applesoft and Binary files would be the easiest to process since their size (in bytes) for those files is found at the head of its data on disk. Text files would be problematic to process, particularly if they are random-access Data files. Sequential Text files would have to be read completely, or perhaps in part in order to locate its terminating `NULL` character before any extra `TSL` entries could be safely expunged. There is no way to identify whether a Text file is a random-access Data file or a sequential Text file, though one could compile a list of possible filters or conditions. I have already stated that bytes `0x08/0x09` or `0x09/0x0A` as shown in Figure I.7.2 could have been utilized for the value of the `L` keyword instead of requiring the `L` keyword and its value to `OPEN` a Text file as a random-access Data file. That would have definitely distinguished a random-access Data file from a sequential Text file without having to know anything about how the Text file is utilized programmatically.

For the time being *FID* is perhaps the easiest utility to utilize in order to copy a set of files from one volume to another volume. *FID* is certainly not perfect in that it cannot differentiate between `TSL` track/sector entries for valid data sectors and bogus data sectors. Because *FID* can cross Volume and Phase barriers makes it exceedingly powerful in the DOS 4.5 environment. It would indeed be an interesting challenge to add the additional, somewhat complex logic to *FID*, selectable of course, that would verify `TSL` utilization for its track/sector entries in Applesoft and in Binary files at a minimum.

8. Lazer's Interactive Symbolic Assembler (Lisa)

I have to say that I have spent a considerable amount of time and energy modifying, adjusting, and fine tuning Lazer's Interactive Symbolic Assembler (*Lisa*) to my every whim and need. It truly has been a joy! First and foremost, my task was to modify *Lisa* to use the DOS 4.5 interfaces in order for *Lisa* to obtain the various pieces of information it requires for some of its special functions. Next, I wanted to eliminate the need for *Lisa* to save the first file of a multiple-file program as a `.TEMP` file before it completes its Pass 1 processing. That task required adding a new directive. I wanted the Sort algorithm that is used to sort the Symbol Table to be an integral part of *Lisa* as well as an option to print one or all of the Symbol Table Lists. I wanted to add an additional directive to define the text for the Symbol List title. I wanted `LED` (Lisa EDitor) to be an integral part of *Lisa* and always be included whenever *Lisa* was activated. I wanted an easier way to enter a DOS `PR#` command and any `ctrl-D`, or DOS command. I wanted an additional command-line command besides `A` to assemble source code that forces the `PRNTFLAG` to be `OFF` as if the `NLS` directive is the first directive in the source code. I wanted *Lisa* to obtain the date and time directly from DOS 4.5. I wanted to move *Lisa* into Auxiliary memory. I wanted to fix some of the quirkiness *Lisa* sometimes displays. And, finally, I wanted to display a *Lisa* file and I wanted to be able to fully edit *Lisa* source code in 80-column mode. While on this journey, I also found and fixed a few more coding errors in *Lisa*. Ah, have I made *Lisa* absolutely perfect? Maybe. I certainly hope so!

Unlike *Big Mac*, *Lisa* resides in both Banks of the Language Card partition in Auxiliary memory, and `LED`, written by Bob Rosen of RSQ Software Products © 1983, now occupies the Main memory address space from `0xB967` to `0xBCC9`. *Lisa* only requires one DOS buffer but it no longer needs to change

235

the number of DOS buffers in DOS 4.5. The momentous task of sourcing *Lisa* took many, many hours, not just for the conversion of the assembly language object code to source code, but the laborious task of understanding the idiosyncrasies of how Randall Hyde designs and writes software. The optimal desire is to understand the newly generated source code so that 1) it assembles and perfectly matches the original object code, and 2) it can be modified and all structures and tables and their lengths and sizes remain unaffected. Quite frequently an author may pass the address of a structure or of a data table in one or two registers, or as an index into a table of addresses or values, and initially the source code appears as if those structures or those tables of values are hardcoded. What needs to be done is to assign a variable name to the structure or data table so that if the structure or table shifts up or down in memory, the registers will always contain the correct offset or memory location of the variable name. It is necessary to find all such occurrences in order to reach that optimal state of perfectly sourced code. *Sourceror* can only do so much magic! Figure V.8.1 shows the *Lisa* startup display showing that *Lisa80* is running under DOS 4.5 in 80-column display mode. Figure V.8.2 shows the first page of the *Lisa80* source code in 80-column display mode.

```
Lazer's
Interactive
Symbolic
Assembler

LISA (c) 1983 Lazerware

LISA80 with DOS 4.5.05H

▐█
```

Figure V.8.1. Lisa80 Startup Display

```
 1        ttl "LISA80 Source Code, LISA.L"
 2        src "LISA.L"
 3 ;
 4 ;
 5 ; LISA.L
 6 ;
 7 ;
 8 ; LISA80 Source Code
 9 ;
10 ; 2022 January 1
11 ;
12 ;
13 ; DOS 4.5, Build 05
14 ;
15 ; 2022 January 1
16 ;
17 ;
18 ; Start of Source Code:  0x4000
19 ; Start of Symbol List:  0x7800
20 ;
21 ;
22 ; Copyright (c) 2022 January 1 by
```

Figure V.8.2. Lisa80 Source Code List Display

In order to make *Lisa* fully DOS 4.5 compliant required me to relocate *Lisa* to Auxiliary memory. Why? Because DOS 4.5 is resident in the Language Card partition in Main memory and *Lisa* is resident in Language Card partition in Main memory as well. Both cannot reside in the same Language Card partition concurrently. However, Auxiliary memory also contains its own Language Card partition. It seemed natural to relocate *Lisa* to Auxiliary memory. It was definitely a challenge to understand how to master Auxiliary memory in terms of its operation and what it could provide and what it could not provide in terms of resources. Certainly, to assist in its operation would be to decide which area of memory would handle input data (i.e. keyboard and disk) and which area of memory would handle output data (i.e. display, printer, and disk). Once I established the operating rules for memory it became very clear in how to build the interface between Main memory and Auxiliary memory specifically for *Lisa*. Since DOS 4.5 occupies the Language Card partition in Main memory, it was quite logical to utilize Main memory for the input and the output of all disk data. It was totally unnecessary to maintain two page-zeros particularly for the variables CH, CV, BASL, BASH, and all the other text window variables. Furthermore, DOS 4.5 must be in complete control of all input and output data for a volume. Thus, all keyboard, printer, and display data are handled within Auxiliary memory.

Lisa contains its own version of the Monitor. Previously, this Monitor mostly resembled the monitor found in the Apple][+. In order to prepare *Lisa* to make use of the Apple //e 80-column display, the Apple //e Monitor needs to be utilized, whatever version of the Monitor it is. Unfortunately, Mr. Hyde embedded a few routines within his Monitor that has no place in the Apple //e Monitor. And, so, back to the drawing board in order to squeeze out even more code space within *Lisa* in order to provide a new location for those displaced routines. In order for *Lisa* to utilize any of the various iterations of the Apple //e Monitor, *Lisa* simply copies the ROM Monitor for its RAM Monitor. The interface between Main memory and Auxiliary memory is injected primarily at the COUT (i.e. 0xFDED) and RDKEY2 (i.e. 0xFD18) routines in the RAM Monitor of *Lisa*. A small handler is needed for the HOOKDOS, DOSWARM, WRMSTRT, PRTERROR, and READCLK vectors. DOS errors have to be handled uniquely by the interface in order to re-enter *Lisa* appropriately. Finally, the state of the Bank currently in focus in the Language Card partition must be captured in order to reconfigure Auxiliary memory for all subroutines that are returning from Main memory. Because *Lisa* utilizes memory in both Banks of the Language Card partition, it is difficult to know which Bank is in focus at any given moment during *Lisa* processing. However, the greater challenge is to enhance the source code editing capabilities of *Lisa* while displaying *Lisa* source code in using the Apple //e 80-column mode.

```
SETSCRN    sta STR80ON      ; enable PAGE Soft Switches
           sta PAGE1ON      ; assume Main memory
           lda OURCH        ; get character index
           sta CH           ; save index to CH
           lsr              ; shift LSB into carry flag
           tay              ; copy |OURCH/2| to Y-reg
           bcs >1           ; branch if odd (Main memory)
           sta PAGE2ON      ; enable Auxiliary memory
^1         rts              ; return to caller
```

Figure V.8.3. Lisa80 SETSCRN Routine

```
READSRN1   sty OURCH        ; save character index
READSCRN   jsr SETSCRN      ; select screen PAGE
           lda (BASL),Y     ; read the screen character
           sta PAGE1ON      ; enable Main memory
           ldy CH           ; get original index from CH
           rts              ; return to caller
```

Figure V.8.4. Lisa80 READSCRN Routine

The page-zero variable CV for the current screen line number is used to calculate the BASL/BASH pointer. The page-zero variable CH for the current line character index is used to address an ASCII character on the screen. As easy as it is to write to the screen, reading from the screen is just as easy. Mr. Hyde utilized these variables in his source code line editing routines. The Apple //e requires twice

237

as much memory for the text buffer in order to display 80-column text. The additional buffer memory comes from Auxiliary memory such that every odd numbered screen character comes from Main memory and every even numbered screen character comes from Auxiliary memory. The variables OURCH (0x057B) and OURCV (0x05FB) are used instead for character index and line number, respectively. In order to provide the same line editing capabilities in 80-column display mode it is necessary to read and write screen characters using a different algorithm. The SETSCRN routine shown in Figure V.8.3 demonstrates one component of this complicated algorithm. The PAGE Soft Switches only function in 80-column mode when 80-Column Store, or STR80ON (0xC001) is enabled as shown in that figure. The READSCRN routine shown in Figure V.8.4 utilizes SETSCRN. The final routine SAVESCRN shown in Figure V.8.5 also utilizes SETSCRN to save the character of interest to the screen.

```
SAVESRN1    sty OURCH        ; save character index
SAVESCRN    pha              ; save character on stack
            jsr SETSCRN      ; select screen PAGE
            pla              ; retrieve character
            sta (BASL),Y     ; write the screen character
            sta PAGE1ON      ; enable Main memory
            ldy CH           ; get index from CH
            rts              ; return to caller
```

Figure V.8.5. Lisa80 SAVESCRN Routine

```
      L.I.S.A. SETUP80 Utility


Current values are:

1) Start of Source Code    - 0x4000
2) Start of Symbol List    - 0x7000
3) Start of Page 2 Source  - 0x7800
4) Start of Page 2 Symbols - 0x9000
5) End of Symbol List      - 0xB800

6) Number of Lines/Page    - 68
7) Print Title on Page     - YES
8) Lower Case Mnemonics    - YES

9) Screen Editing Definitions

Q) Quit

Enter option: █
```

```
        Screen Editing Definitions

A) Cursor up                  ^O, 0x0F
B) Cursor down                ^L, 0x0C
C) Go to start of line        ^C, 0x03
D) Go to end of line          ^D, 0x04
E) Insert character           ^I, 0x09
F) Delete character           ^R, 0x12
G) Home and Clear             ^Q, 0x11
H) Clear to end of line       ^E, 0x05
I) Clear to end of screen     ^F, 0x06
J) Insert a line              ^V, 0x16
K) Delete current line        ^N, 0x0E
L) Skip blanks character      ^S, 0x13
M) Show length of line        ^T, 0x14
N) Quit insert mode           ^A, 0x01

Enter Q to leave.

Enter option: █
```

Figure V.8.6. Lisa80 SETUP80 Utility   Figure V.8.7. Lisa80 Screen Editing Definitions

Command	Context	Description
USR	after OBJ $$	uses OBJ address to save start address for BSAVE
USR FN	at end of code	BSAVEs current code to filename; follow with another USR
USR .FN	to BLOAD file	BLOADs the filename using the current object code pointer

Table V.8.1. Lisa USR Command

238

There are certainly other routines needed to handle all of the `ctrl`-key functions that *Lisa* provides, but the above code samples are the most basic routines. Because the 80-column ROM routines already support the left and right arrow keys, I chose to replace the Cursor Left (`ctrl-J`) and the Cursor Right (`ctrl-K`) options with the `Go To Start of Line` (`ctrl-C`) and `Go To End of Line` (`ctrl-D`) options. (I liked these two cursor movement routines so much that I added them to the 40-column version of Auxiliary memory *Lisa*.) The other configuration parameters in *Lisa* may be modified using the *SETUP80* utility. *SETUP80* may be invoked simply by typing the `SE` command on the *Lisa80* command line. The *SETUP80* utility is activated from the Lisa Image volume `LISA80.Image` in disk drive 1. Figure V.8.6 shows the main `L.I.S.A. SETUP80 Utility` screen and Figure V.8.7 shows the `Screen Editing Definitions` screen.

Having DOS in the Language Card partition in Main memory provides substantially more memory for object code, source code, and the symbol list. The judicious selection of memory locations and sizes for object code, source code, and the symbol list ensures a successful assembly no matter how large or how complex a program or a set of program modules are presented to *Lisa*. The values shown in Figure V.8.6 provide 56 memory pages for object code (`0x0800` to `0x3FFF`), 56 memory pages for source code for a single program or for one module of a complex program (`0x4000` to `0x77FF`), and nearly 64 memory pages for the symbol list (`0x7800` to `0xB7CF`). Each symbol requires ten bytes, eight bytes for the symbol name and two bytes for the value of the symbol. This symbol list allocation provides enough memory for about 1600 symbols. *Lisa80* uses `0x1EF0` bytes for its symbol list of 792 symbols. On the other hand, DOS 4.5 uses `0x33F4` bytes for its symbol list of 1330 symbols. This information is found just before the symbol list is printed when the `A` command is used on the *Lisa* command line. These setup values are my recommended settings and they should be appropriate for nearly every program instance. But, of course, there are situations where a program or a program module may exceed 56 memory pages, in other words, a file that is 57 sectors in size having one `TSL`.

I wish to give all credit to Robert Heitman who I met at Sierra On-Line for creating the `USR` directive routine and the `ctrl-P` routine that I have incorporated within *Lisa* and *Lisa80*. Heitman called the original source code modules `LOADER.S` and `LINKER.S` for the `USR` and the `ctrl-P` routines, respectively. I may have adjusted them slightly for my own particular needs, but essentially their basic functionalities were all created by Heitman. The `USR` directive has a number of important uses depending upon how it is utilized in the source code and which arguments are utilized with the directive. Its syntax and usages are shown in Table V.8.1. The combination of

```
ORG $$/OBJ $$/USR/<some source code>/USR <filename>
```

is a very powerful set of directives.

The first use of the `USR` directive alone, at the top of a program after the `ORG` and `OBJ` directives, saves the current value of the object code pointer that is set by the `OBJ $$` directive, where `$$` is some hexadecimal address. After some source code has been assembled, the generated object code can be saved to a file using the `USR FN` directive, where `FN` is some filename. `USR FN` uses the object code pointer address value that is saved by the first `USR`, it calculates the length of the code segment knowing the memory location in the current object code pointer, and it constructs a DOS `BSAVE` command. The `USR .FN` (that is, *period* + `FN`) directive is also useful in order to read a Binary file into memory at the memory location in the current object code pointer. Once the Binary file is in memory, the object code pointer can be incremented using the `DFS` directive knowing the size of the included Binary file. I use the USR .FN directive in order to BLOAD into memory every Binary object file that is to be contained in an EPROM image that is used by the EPROM Operating System.

Source code for programs such as *Big Mac* or *Lisa* or DOS 4.5 cannot possibly fit in the Apple][memory along with its generated object code, its symbol list, DOS, and the assembler. Large and complex software programs need to be segmented into a number of manageable sized files and their assembled outputs saved to separate object code files that can be ultimately linked to form the complete executable program. At a minimum, *Lisa*, DOS, and some program source code must reside concurrently in memory and still have room for its generated object code and its complete symbol list. It is simply amazing what can be accomplished in such a ridiculously small amount of memory as that found in the Apple][computer when judicious values are chosen for memory configuration in *Lisa*.

The source code files that comprise DOS 3.3 are shown in Figure V.8.8. Several source code files are processed before their collective object code is saved to a Binary file. The convention used to name these object code files is to begin the filename with a SEG prefix and end the filename with a two digit number suffix generally beginning with 01. The reason will become apparent shortly. It makes no difference how many SEG files are created, remembering, of course, that for each file created an additional disk sector is required for its TSL. In the case of DOS 3.3 there are ninety-five sectors remaining in the volume, so there are plenty of sectors left to make many significant changes and additions to this source code. When all SEG files are sequentially read into memory the entire image for DOS 3.3 is created. I have the convention, if not the habit, to begin the load of an object code file at address 0x1000. Loading the first SEG file is easy, as in BLOAD SEG01,A$1000. To what address is SEG02 loaded next? If the R keyword is used with the BLOAD command, the length of SEG01 is given, and one can simply calculate the load address for SEG02, which is BLOAD SEG02 at 0x1000 + length of SEG01 and so forth. There is an easier method built into *Lisa*: a ctrl-P user function that loads a range of sequentially numbered SEG files. Thank you again, Bob Heitman! *Lisa* provides software hooks into the two 0xDF00 pages where a user can add any routine(s) of their choosing. The USR directive mentioned earlier is found at memory address 0xDF00 when Bank 2 is enabled using the BIT 0xC080 instruction. The ctrl-P user function is also found at memory address 0xDF00 when Bank 1 is enabled using the BIT 0xC088 instruction.

The ctrl-P function allows the user to enter the number of segments to be loaded into memory, the segment start number, the object code start address, and optionally a filename in order to save the composite image which is comprised of all of the object code segments. If a filename is not entered, the length of the image in bytes and its final memory address are displayed instead. Figure V.8.9 shows all of the SEG files that are created when the *EOS* source code is assembled. Those SEG files need to be linked into two 0x8000 byte files that are then used to program a 27512 EPROM. In order to perform this process most efficiently, SEG files 1 to 4 are linked into one file and SEG files 5 to 8 are linked into the second file. The ctrl-P user function is the perfect tool in order to perform this linking task.

Figure V.8.10 shows how SEG files 1 to 4 are linked into the first *EOS* image file, EOS1, and Figure V.8.11 shows how SEG files 5 to 8 are linked into the second *EOS* image file, EOS2. Notice that Lisa utilizes the B keyword to implement the *File Delete/File Save* strategy for the DOS BSAVE command. This strategy first deletes the file if it exists, returns the sector resources of the file back to the VTOC of the volume, and then saves the file using newly acquired VTOC resources. The two binary image files EOS1 and EOS2 are now ready to be programmed into an erased 27512 EPROM where EOS1 is programmed into the first half and EOS2 is programmed into the second half of the EPROM. In fact, the utility *BURNER* is conveniently located on the same volume as these two image files. This makes the process of preparing and programming an EPROM very simple, very reliable, and very accurate.

```
CATALOG

S=6 D=02 V=000 F=0095 01/01/22 08:28:48

 L 005 DOS3.3.L      01/01/22 08:28:48
 L 037 INCL.L        01/01/22 08:28:48
 L 017 DISK.L        01/01/22 08:28:48
 L 008 BUFR.L        01/01/22 08:28:48
 L 054 CMD1.L        01/01/22 08:28:48
 L 045 CMD2.L        01/01/22 08:28:48
 L 040 CMD3.L        01/01/22 08:28:48
 L 040 CMD4.L        01/01/22 08:28:48
 L 037 MNGR1A.L      01/01/22 08:28:48
 L 032 MNGR1B.L      01/01/22 08:28:48
 L 033 MNGR2A.L      01/01/22 08:28:48
 L 040 MNGR2B.L      01/01/22 08:28:48
 L 036 RWTS1.L       01/01/22 08:28:48
 L 035 RWTS2.L       01/01/22 08:28:48

!█
```

Figure V.8.8. DOS 3.3 Source Code Volume

```
!/LSR

LSR

B=4505H data T=EOS 512 Image Files

M=4505H P=04 L=0x3032 01/01/22 08:28:48

S=6 D=02 V=000 F=0013 01/01/22 08:28:48

 001 0x12,0x0F BURNER
 002 0x0E,0x0A EOS1
 003 0x14,0x0F EOS2
 004 0x20,0x0F SEG01
 005 0x0E,0x06 SEG02
 006 0x09,0x00 SEG03
 007 0x17,0x0A SEG04
 008 0x22,0x0E SEG05
 009 0x09,0x0F SEG06
 010 0x02,0x0F SEG07
 011 0x17,0x07 SEG08

!█
```

Figure V.8.9. EOS Image Segment Files

```
!

 Segments = #4

First Seg = #1

  Address = $1000

BLOAD SEG01,A$1000
BLOAD SEG02,A$3000
BLOAD SEG03,A$5100
BLOAD SEG04,A$7B00

Load end = $9000

Save file = EOS1

BSAVE EOS1,B,A$1000,L$8000

!█
```

Figure V.8.10. EOS1 Image Creation

```
!

 Segments = #4

First Seg = #5

  Address = $1000

BLOAD SEG05,A$1000
BLOAD SEG06,A$3300
BLOAD SEG07,A$5288
BLOAD SEG08,A$6F27

Load end = $9000

Save file = EOS2

BSAVE EOS2,B,A$1000,L$8000

!█
```

Figure V.8.11. EOS2 Image Creation

Lisa makes three passes through all source code files as its data input source in order to create object code files as its data output source. The first pass may be terminated using the ENZ directive, or ENd of page-Zero when all of the page-zero parameter definitions are given. Pass 2 and Pass 3 must process all included source code files. In order to return to the first, or initial source code file when an ICL, or InCLude filename directive is encountered, *Lisa* has always saved the initial source code file as an additional file named .TEMP. In this way processing can begin with a known first file for the next pass. Certainly, this method is the easiest to implement but it comes with an unfortunate price because it wastes some valuable disk space by duplicating the initial or first file. In the example above for the volume containing the DOS 3.3 source code, Figure V.8.8, there is enough disk space available for a sizeable .TEMP file having the same contents as the initial source code file, or DOS3.3.L in this example. However, many times this may not be the case where there is insufficient room for a duplicate .TEMP file.

Lisa had a few unused opcodes available, so I added the SRC directive that requires a filename in parenthesis as shown in Figure V.8.2. The complete syntax is SRC <filename>. I gave LED some additional memory at its end where I moved the .TEMP filename buffer, and that is where the SRC directive copies its filename. Naturally, if the SRC directive is not used and there is at least one use of the ICL directive, *Lisa* still creates a .TEMP file as usual. The filename specified in the SRC directive should be the filename of the file where the directive is found, but this does not necessarily have to be the case. Referring to Figure V.8.8, if the SRC directive in the DOS3.3.L file was SRC INCL.L, the file DOS3.3.L would not be processed during Pass 2 and Pass 3, thus saving some processing time, but at the expense of not including the DOS3.3.L file as part of the complete print listing, if an incomplete print listing is acceptable. Personally, I like to place the SRC directive on line 2, right after the TTL directive, in the very first file when there are several source code files comprising the program. Even if all of the source code resides in a single file, using the SRC directive does no harm.

I challenged myself to make room in *Lisa* to include the sort algorithm and the code found in the external program called SYMBOLS. If SYMBOLS is activated immediately after *Lisa* processes some source code, SYMBOLS would print the complete symbol list alphabetized, and then print the list again with the symbols ordered by their value or their address. I liked what SYMBOLS offered but not well enough to fumble around locating a copy of it, even if I did have it in EPROM, especially after processing a huge project like DOS3.3. (I never considered adding another command-line command like SY to BRUN SYMBOLS similar in how I added the SE command-line command to BRUN SETUP.) Fortunately, SYMBOLS is a little program and it did not take much effort to source its code. Now I had some idea how much room I required for SYMBOLS within *Lisa*. Of course, I could always make LED larger and rob memory from the symbol list, the source code, and the object code memory areas.

I know Randall Hyde used good sense when he developed his routines for each opcode in the Pass 2 implementation and separately in the Pass 3 implementation. Regardless of good sense, I studied those routines and found a number of ways to compact a rather large amount of this code giving me more than enough code space in order to include SYMBOLS. Now that *Lisa* was headed down this path, I thought it would be exemplary to provide a means to give the symbol list a name on the page title line. I replaced the CSP directive (it mixes a JSR instruction with a .DA directive) with the STT directive whose syntax is STT <title>. This directive copies the character string title to the buffer currently used by the TTL directive during Pass 3. If the symbol list is printed, its pages will contain the new TTL title. If this directive is not used, the symbol list pages are printed with the same title from the original TTL directive. Unfortunately, if the TTL directive should be used at the end of the source code in order to title the symbol list pages instead, the last printed page of the assembled code will contain the new symbol list title and not the original source code title. I did not care for that solution so that is the primary reason why I added the separate STT directive.

To complete this challenge required one further modification, and that was to the END directive. This directive provided the perfect location to control which of three symbol lists to print after the assembled code listing. That is, no symbol lists, unsorted symbols (new), alphabetically sorted symbols, and numerically sorted symbols. Regardless which if any listings are desired, if at least one is selected the symbol list includes the memory address where the symbol list begins, where the symbol list ends, how many bytes are used for the symbol list, and the remaining bytes in the symbol table partition. From Figure V.8.6 the absolute physical end of the symbol list is set at 0xB7C0. If there is substantial memory not used as reported by the remaining bytes in the symbol table partition, the `Start of Symbol List` in Figure V.8.6 could be adjusted to allow for larger source code files. It is always good to have visibility in how effectively *Lisa* is configured particularly when problems due to source code file size begin to generate errors during assembly. Therefore, to complete this discussion, the `END` directive now allows a three-digit binary parameter to control which of the three symbol lists to print in the order stated above. The syntax for the directive is `END nnn` where **n** can be a 0 or a 1 for `OFF` and `ON`, respectively.

I prefer to keep the default setting of the `PRNTFLAG` variable `ON` during Pass 3 in order to obtain a printed listing of the assembly, particularly when I am using Virtual][. Rarely do I use the `LST` and `NLS` directives anymore. However, when I am debugging software using real Apple][hardware along with the RAM Disk 320, leaving the `PRNTFLAG` variable `ON` greatly impacts assembly throughput, even with the ZipChip enabled and the Parallel Printer Buffer enabled. And, it is a nuisance having to insert and then delete the `NLS` directive in the source code during the debugging development phase. So, I added the `Z` command-line command to *Lisa* that functions exactly like the `A` command-line command in order to start the assembly process. Now, the `Z` command-line command sets the `PRNTFLAG` variable to `OFF` instead of to `ON` as if the `NLS` directive is the first directive that is processed.

Many times it is necessary to enter a DOS command directly onto the *Lisa* command line. In order to do so a `ctrl-D` must precede the command so that *Lisa* knows to send the command to DOS rather than parsing the command for itself. I found it cumbersome for me to enter a `ctrl-D` before each and every DOS command when I needed some information from DOS. So, I added another *Lisa* command-line command, `/`, which is so much easier for me to enter before a DOS command. For example, to display the contents of the `VTOC` sector, the following can be entered on the *Lisa* command line:

        !/TS A17

The *Lisa80 SETUP80* utility shown in Figure V.8.6 no longer provides the options to select the clock slot number and its `0xCs05` and `0xCs07` values, where **s** is the clock slot number. *Lisa* used to obtain the date and time information similarly in how DOS 4.5 obtains that information, so *Lisa* also required a value for the current year because the Thunderclock card lacks a year register. Instead of having a duplicate date and time algorithm and a duplicate `YEARVAL` variable to manage in *Lisa*, I simply removed the date and time algorithm and `YEARVAL` variable from *Lisa* and utilized the DOS 4.5 `RDCLKVSN` vector at `0x3E1`. I placed the `CLKBUFF` buffer conveniently at `0x3C8`. Now, whenever *Lisa* requires the current date and time, it requests that information from DOS 4.5. The *SETUP* utility or the *SETUP80* utility no longer configures the clock slot, its `0xCs05` and `0xCs07` values since *Lisa* no longer requires that information.

It is always an unspoken goal whenever sourcing software written by someone else to never introduce new and unwanted problems. On the other hand, there is always a very good opportunity in finding and repairing mistakes made by someone else because of the intensity in concentration that is required to understand every single line of code in context with the surrounding lines of code. I suspect there might be some mistakes still resident in *Lisa* that I have yet to uncover, but for the moment *Lisa* is rock solid stable and it is providing me with object code output files that are true to their source code input files. Whether the source code input files are necessarily perfect is quite another story.

Relocating *Lisa* to Auxiliary memory was an exhilarating experience. Much of the action of an assembler is to display the assembled code to the screen and, quite often, to the printer. The assembler code can function virtually in any memory space; the screen and printer display code cannot. Main memory and Auxiliary memory in the Apple //e can be partitioned in a variety of ways. I chose to keep the fundamental *Lisa* code in the Language Card partition in Auxiliary memory. Doing so drove the relocation design in using only two Soft Switches in order to control memory management: `AUXZPOFF` (i.e. `0xC008`) and `AUXZPON` (i.e. `0xC009`). The default Apple //e memory configuration is with `AUXZPOFF` such that Main memory is enabled with its own page-zero, stack, and Language Card partition. Using the `AUXZPON` Soft Switch, Auxiliary memory page-zero, the stack, and its Language Card partition are enabled, thus leaving the bulk of memory in Main memory still enabled (i.e. memory from `0x0800` to `0xBFFF`). In other words, whether `AUXZPOFF` or `AUXZPON` are enabled, the object code, the source code, and the symbol list are all visible to both *Lisa* and to DOS because these data areas occupy memory from `0x0800` to `0xBDFF`. This area of memory is not toggled using these two Soft Switches.

The *Lisa* loader *LOADLISA* cannot load *Lisa* from disk directly into Auxiliary memory. Either the Language Card partition in Main memory or the Language Card partition in Auxiliary memory is in focus, not both, and one memory Partition cannot be set for read and the other memory Partition be set for write. So, the *LOADLISA* loader calls on DOS to load each of the first two *Lisa* files into Main memory sequentially, starting at `0x1000`, and then the loader copies the content of each of the files from Main memory to the target memory in the Language Card partition in Auxiliary memory after setting `AUXZPON`. The third *Lisa* file contains the Main/Auxiliary control and interface routines as well as `LED`, and that file is loaded directly to `0xB810`. Hence, the `End of Symbol List`, or `SYMEND` is set to `0xB800`, or sixteen bytes before `0xB810` for safety. The DOS command `MON C,I,O` is issued, `AUXZPON` is enabled, Bank 2 of the Language Card partition in Auxiliary memory is enabled, and a jump is made to the *Lisa* `COLDSTRT` entry point at `0xE000`.

The functional relocation of *Lisa* to Auxiliary memory is only made possible by the Main/Auxiliary control and interface routines I have developed. It is this code, from `0xB810` to `0xB966` that makes this relocation functional. Some of the routines have familiar names because they are the necessary counterpart routines that toggle between `AUXZPOFF` and `AUXZPON`. The routines include `XCONSOLE`, `CONSOLE`, `HOOKDOS`, `XDOSWARM`, `XWRMSTRT`, `XCSWL`, `XKSWL`, `GETVALS`, `PUTVALS`, `READCLK`, `PUTZP`, `GETZP`, `ROMON`, and `AUXRTN`. Both DOS and *Lisa* share the Text Page from `0x400` to `0x7FF` in both Main and Auxiliary memory, but they do not share the same page-zero or stack memory. Screen coordinates are calculated by their respective Monitor routines, so keeping track of whose turn it is to update the Text Page is paramount. Similarly, it is necessary to keep track when a DOS command is issued by *Lisa* and when that command is completed by DOS. It is necessary to handle additional `CSWL` interface traffic when the printer is enabled. `KSWL` interface traffic is not as complex, but it still has to be managed. Because *Lisa* operates in both Banks of the Language Card partition in Auxiliary memory, the current Bank in focus must be read (`0xC011`), saved, and restored (`0xC080` or `0xC088`) in order for external routines to reenter *Lisa* properly. Again, relocating *Lisa* to Auxiliary memory was an exhilarating experience.

The *Lisa80* installer *INSTALL80* can be used to copy the *Lisa80* object code, the *LOADLISA80* utility, and the *SETUP80* utility to another volume. Like the *SETUP80* utility, *Lisa80* contains a built-in command to invoke this action. When the command `U` is entered on the *Lisa80* command line the *INSTALL80* utility is activated from the Lisa Image volume `LISA80.Image` in disk drive 1. The target volume receiving the *Lisa80* object code, the *LOADLISA80* utility, and the *SETUP80* utility must be in disk drive 2. Table V.8.2 lists all of the available *Lisa80* command-line commands as well as all of the available LED commands.

How does a software design engineer accomplish a task of this magnitude, of moving a software program having the complexity and the size of *Lisa* from being resident in Main memory to now being resident in Auxiliary memory? I believe the first paragraph in Section I.3 helps to answer this question.

In order to design reliable and powerful software for a particular machine or platform, one must understand the complete architecture of the machine.

Command	Usage	Description
BR	BR	Break, enter Monitor with beep from speaker
LO	LO filename	Load *Lisa* file into memory
LE	LE	Print length of source code currently in memory in HEX
SA	SA filename	Save source code currently in memory to a *Lisa* file
SE	SE	BRUN SETUP utility
AP	AP filename	Append source code currently in memory from another *Lisa* file
U	U	BRUN INSTALL utility
I	I <line number>	Insert more source code at optional <line number>
D	D start,end	Delete range of source code using line number start,end
L	L <start,end>	List range of source code at optional line number start,end
A	A	Assemble the source code currently in memory
Z	Z	Assemble the source code currently in memory, PRNTFLAG=OFF
N	N	Clear all source code from memory and begin new code
M	M start,end	Modify range of source code using line number start,end
W	W <start,end>	Write a range of source code to a TEXT file at optional line start,end
F	F string	Find all occurrences of character string in source code
FC	FC <n>	CATALOG volume or optional disk drive <n>
FT	FT token	Find all occurrences of *Lisa* token (directive) in source code
FM	FM start,end>new	Move lines of source code to a new line location
FR	FR start,end>new	Replicate lines of source code to a new line location
FP	FP <n>	Show source code Page number; select source code Page
FX	FX <#>	Check for damaged source code; optional # enables print flag
R	R <n,> filename	Read TEXT file into memory as source code; optional at line number
P	P <#>	Issue a PR# command to DOS to change CSW address
^P	^P	ctrl-P command to sequentially load SEG files into memory
^M	^M	allows a blank command line by executing a RTS instruction
/	/ command	Call HOOKDOS, issue ctrl-D, send command to DOS

Table V.8.2. Lisa80 Command-Line Commands

Start any task with a list of requirements. From those requirements decide how hardware can be or should be utilized. It is not necessary to know how to accomplish this hardware utilization for the moment, but you should be able to decide how the hardware can be or could be or should be configured.

As you develop the scope of your software design, that should drive or identify the list of software *knowns* and *unknowns* for each segment of the design. A list of *unknowns* can be very frustrating to the software engineer when that list contains unknown hardware functionality. Breaking down a single *unknown* into smaller components and pairing those components with sufficient unit testing usually yields the necessary knowledge to move forward. The task becomes an incredible mosaic of many hundreds if not thousands of bits of knowledge woven together in order to allow only a precise stream of consciousness, or flow to occur as I like to imagine a software design taking form. At this stage in the software design process, the scope of the software design should be well under control. The primary key to be gained here is derived solely from *sufficient unit testing*.

The unit testing of each design segment is incredibly important. After a design segment has been thoroughly tested and verified to provide the results as per its design, another design segment can be developed. When all design segments have been developed in this manner, the completed project only requires a simple system verification test. I have been developing tasks using this methodology for so long that it has become ingrained in how I approach each and every software design whether that design is for a simple program or for a highly complex program. This methodology assures me that the final product will conform to all established requirements.

Lisa80 is indeed a remarkable assembler and a remarkable Apple //e program. Surely, *Lisa80* is an example that contains many possibilities that can be designed into Apple //e software. Having a complete and thorough understanding of the Apple //e hardware design can only *assist* in driving the design of any software program to utilize that hardware to its fullest potential. Being able to *see* more of the source code for any project allows far easier and faster software development, and *Lisa80* certainly shows more source code in every screen. Being able to edit source code in 80-column mode can never be overstated in its significance and overall utility.

9. Program Global Editor (PGE)

When I received my Apple][+ in the early 1980's, I spent my first few months writing Applesoft programs. I was fortunate to obtain a copy of the Program Global Editor (*PGE*) written by C. A. Greathouse and Garry Reinhardt. *PGE* certainly helped to make programming Applesoft much easier especially when one has excellent tools at hand. I have to say that there is one particular difficulty when writing Applesoft programs, and that is dealing with program line numbers. So many functions depend upon program line numbers, thus making the line numbers a highly critical part of any Applesoft program. There are not many ways to partition an Applesoft program into functions and subroutines except by using program line numbers that may use large line increments from function to function, and smaller line increments within a function. Or, many REM *** statements can be used to partition an Applesoft program, but those statements consume program line numbers as well as memory, which also impacts program execution. Here is where *PGE*'s forte provided me the most assistance: its capability of quickly renumbering program line numbers within a program or within a section of a program.

PGE functionality requires the ability to modify the WARMADR and RESETADR vectors, and to obtain the values found at ADRVAL and LOADLEN within DOS. *PGE* simply modified those vectors and read the ADRVAL and LOADLEN parameters directly from within DOS 3.3 knowing the memory location for these vectors and these parameters. DOS 4.5 has these vectors and parameters, of course, and a set procedure to read and to write them. As shown in Table I.8.1 the address of INITVAL is 0xBFFA. The address contained by INITVAL points to the table of address vectors called INITVALS as shown in Table I.8.7. This is where the vectors WARMADR at offset 0x00 and RESETADR at offset 0x06 can be found. The address of the vector MNGVALS is located at 0xBFF4 as shown in Table I.8.1. Section IV.23 shows how to access or change the value of any variable within the CMDVALS Data structure using MNGVALS. According to Table I.12.1 the offset for ADRVAL is 0x2E and the offset for LOADLEN is 0x36. The representative code in Figures I.12.1 and I.12.2 to access and change any 8-bit or 16-bit variable in the CMDVALS Data structure can be used as a model to access and change the value for the variables ADRVAL and LOADLEN. Programs like *PGE* do not utilize memory in the Language Card partition for any purpose, thus a user may also safely employ those same procedures under DOS 4.5. After I adjusted the *PGE* software to locate the vectors and parameters it needs from within DOS 4.5 using the same procedures just outlined, *PGE* executes its commands flawlessly.

One of the worst designed Applesoft functions is the LIST function because of the 40-column width of the display, and program lines are truncated, multiple space characters are used between tokens and data, and there are only twenty-four text lines that make up the entire display. The LIST function in *PGE* parses the Applesoft tokens and displays them as well as the remaining ASCII program data without using any spaces whatsoever. Perhaps the screen is far more difficult to read, far more cluttered, but considering the *day and age* when *PGE* was utilized for program editing, having no screen clutter was a small sacrifice, even respected. Printer paper and ink were expensive at that time, and it was not practical to print programs a multitude number of times during their development. In those days most software engineers initially wrote out their code using paper and pencil, and typed in their programs after reviewing their code for structural logic and for the most obvious programming errors. I found that the activity of typing in a program from my written notes served as another major review process as well. So, *PGE* was very useful in displaying far more data within the available lines per screen for my review. However, the 80-column card changed all of that protocol. The Applesoft LIST function is shown in Figure V.9.1 and the *PGE* LIST function is shown in Figure V.9.2 for the beginning lines of the HELLO file on my DOS.4.5H.Tools volume. I believe all will agree that Figure V.9.1 is far more readable when displaying program code. Although, if the two displays were compared in 40-column mode the *PGE* LIST function would be for more practical in displaying the most program data.

PGE excelled in renumbering small portions, larger portions, and even entire portions of programs. Upon initialization *PGE* remaps the ampersand vector to its READY [prompt. The renumber command R requires four parameters for the start number, the end number, the increment, and the new start number. *PGE* scours the entire Applesoft program and changes every occurrence of a program line number within the given specified range to the new program line number based on the new start number and some program line number increment, say 5 or 10 or 100. To say the results were marvelous would be an understatement. As one's Applesoft programming capabilities mature, better choices for line numbers are usually made, and it becomes easier to create sections of Applesoft code that resemble a function or a subroutine. In these instances, being able to renumber a small section of code is quite powerful. Figure V.9.3 demonstrates how simple it is to renumber the beginning lines of the HELLO program shown in Figure V.9.1. This program now begins with line number 8 and the line increment is set to 4 for all lines up to line 199. The line numbers following line 199 in Figure V.9.1 are not affected except when those earlier line numbers are referenced within the later line numbers. An astute observer will notice that *PGE* only accepts uppercase ASCII commands. I have no doubt that it would be easy to modify *PGE* to accept lowercase ASCII commands as well. That same renumbered program is shown in Figure V.9.4 using the Applesoft LIST function. It appears identical to Figure V.9.1 except for its line numbers.

```
]LIST 1,199

 10  D$ =  CHR$ (13) +  CHR$ (4)
 20  DIM NAM$(20),CMD$(20),PGM$(20),ADR(20)
 30  HOME : HTAB 16: PRINT "Tools Menu"
 40  READ N: FOR I = 0 TO N - 1: READ NAM$(I),CMD$(I),PGM$(I),ADR(I): GOSUB
     200: NEXT :N% = 1 - (N / 2 =  INT (N / 2)):I = 0
 50  INVERSE : GOSUB 200: GOSUB 300: NORMAL : GOSUB 200: IF A% = 27 THEN
      HOME : PRINT D$;"CATALOG": PRINT : NEW
 60  IF A% = 21 THEN I = I + 1 - N * (I > N - 2)
 70  IF A% = 10 THEN I = I + 2 - N * (I > N - 3):I = I + N% * ((I = 0) -
     (I = 1))
 80  IF A% = 8 THEN I = I - 1 + N * (I = 0)
 90  IF A% = 11 THEN I = I - 2 + N * (I < 2):I = I + N% * ((I = N - 2) -
     (I = N - 1))
100   IF A% < > 13 THEN 50
110  PRINT D$;CMD$(I);PGM$(I);: IF ADR(I) THEN  PRINT ",A";ADR(I);
120  PRINT : END

]█
```

Figure V.9.1. Applesoft LIST Function 1

```
]&
READY
[L1,199
10 D$=CHR$(13)+CHR$(4)
20 DIMNAM$(20),CMD$(20),PGM$(20),ADR(20)
30 HOME:HTAB16:PRINT"Tools Menu"
40 READN:FORI=0TON-1:READNAM$(I),CMD$(I),PGM$(I),ADR(I):GOSUB200:NEXT:N%=1-(N/2=
INT(N/2)):I=0
50 INVERSE:GOSUB200:GOSUB300:NORMAL:GOSUB200:IFA%=27THENHOME:PRINTD$;"CATALOG":P
RINT:NEW
60 IFA%=21THENI=I+1-N*(I>N-2)
70 IFA%=10THENI=I+2-N*(I>N-3):I=I+N%*((I=0)-(I=1))
80 IFA%=8THENI=I-1+N*(I=0)
90 IFA%=11THENI=I-2+N*(I<2):I=I+N%*((I=N-2)-(I=N-1))
100 IFA%<>13THEN50
110 PRINTD$;CMD$(I);PGM$(I);:IFADR(I)THENPRINT",A";ADR(I);
120 PRINT:END
READY
[█
```

Figure V.9.2. PGE LIST Function

```
]&
READY
[R1,199,4,8

READY
[L1,199
8 D$=CHR$(13)+CHR$(4)
12 DIMNAM$(20),CMD$(20),PGM$(20),ADR(20)
16 HOME:HTAB16:PRINT"Tools Menu"
20 READN:FORI=0TON-1:READNAM$(I),CMD$(I),PGM$(I),ADR(I):GOSUB200:NEXT:N%=1-(N/2=
INT(N/2)):I=0
24 INVERSE:GOSUB200:GOSUB300:NORMAL:GOSUB200:IFA%=27THENHOME:PRINTD$;"CATALOG":P
RINT:NEW
28 IFA%=21THENI=I+1-N*(I>N-2)
32 IFA%=10THENI=I+2-N*(I>N-3):I=I+N%*((I=0)-(I=1))
36 IFA%=8THENI=I-1+N*(I=0)
40 IFA%=11THENI=I-2+N*(I<2):I=I+N%*((I=N-2)-(I=N-1))
44 IFA%<>13THEN24
48 PRINTD$;CMD$(I);PGM$(I);:IFADR(I)THENPRINT",A";ADR(I);
52 PRINT:END

READY
[█
```

Figure V.9.3. PGE RENUMBER Function

```
]LIST 1,199

  8  D$ =  CHR$ (13) +  CHR$ (4)
 12  DIM NAM$(20),CMD$(20),PGM$(20),ADR(20)
 16  HOME : HTAB 16: PRINT "Tools Menu"
 20  READ N: FOR I = 0 TO N - 1: READ NAM$(I),CMD$(I),PGM$(I),ADR(I): GOSUB
     200: NEXT :N% = 1 - (N / 2 =  INT (N / 2)):I = 0
 24  INVERSE : GOSUB 200: GOSUB 300: NORMAL : GOSUB 200: IF A% = 27 THEN
      HOME : PRINT D$;"CATALOG": PRINT : NEW
 28  IF A% = 21 THEN I = I + 1 - N * (I > N - 2)
 32  IF A% = 10 THEN I = I + 2 - N * (I > N - 3):I = I + N% * ((I = 0) -
     (I = 1))
 36  IF A% = 8 THEN I = I - 1 + N * (I = 0)
 40  IF A% = 11 THEN I = I - 2 + N * (I < 2):I = I + N% * ((I = N - 2) -
     (I = N - 1))
 44  IF A% < > 13 THEN 24
 48  PRINT D$;CMD$(I);PGM$(I);: IF ADR(I) THEN  PRINT ",A";ADR(I);
 52  PRINT : END

]█
```

Figure V.9.4. Applesoft LIST Function 2

The downside in using *PGE* occurs when *PGE* is used to renumber an Applesoft program that has one or more attached Binary programs. When the renumber function finds the triple-zero termination marker for an Applesoft program, it sets the end of program at ASPEND (0xAF/B0) to that memory address. In other words, *PGE* processing loses the address of the true end of the program and changes it to the address where the triple-zero termination marker is found regardless whether the Applesoft program has any attached Binary programs or not. This situation is not insurmountable because the Binary programs may be easily re-attached using Binary File Installation (or *BFI*) as described in Section V.16. Though it is a little inconvenient having to re-install Binary programs after *PGE* processing, it is certainly nothing compared to the overwhelming convenience of the line renumbering capability of *PGE*.

PGE activation required a small program loader to load the *PGE* program into memory and to set FRETOP (0x6F/70), HIMEM (0x74/75), and the ampersand vector at 0x3F5. The *PGE* program used the upper part of the INPUT buffer from 0x2D0 to 0x2FF. Two 256-byte buffers are used at the end of the *PGE* program as well as a number of variables at the end of a third 256-byte buffer from 0xnnE0 to 0xnnFF, where **nn** is the page number for that third buffer. I had already completed the sourcing of the *PGE* code so that it could function at any memory address. I decided to combine the *PGE* loader, the page-two variables, and the variables at the end of the third buffer into a page preceding the main *PGE* code. Now, the *PGE* system has been drastically simplified and only one file is required to be launched. *PGE* still depends upon reading and writing directly to the TEXT pages using CH and BASL. There are some *PGE* problematic functions that still do not work properly if the 80-column card in enabled. The renumber function is not one of those problematic functions.

DOS 4.5H is required by this new formulation of *PGE*. Seriously, there is not enough room in Main memory to support DOS 4.5L, *PGE*, and a large Applesoft program. An interested user can always reformulate my single file version of *PGE* to function in the Language Card partition. As of now, I have placed *PGE* at 0x8E00 and HIMEM is set at 0x8DF0. This configuration should be able to accommodate a massive Applesoft program. The two 256-byte *PGE* buffers are now located at 0xAB00 and 0xAC00. Also, *GPLE* can be placed at 0xAD00 and not overwrite the DOS 4.5H interface at 0xBE00 that controls and manages DOS 4.5 in the Language Card partition.

10. Global Program Line Editor (GPLE)

Another invaluable Applesoft program editing tool that I was fortunate enough to obtain was Global Program Line Editor (*GPLE*). Neil Konzen published *GPLE* in 1982, and I obtained version V3.4. *GPLE* uses the entire Bank 1 of the Language Card partition beginning at 0xD000, so it is obviously not compatible with DOS 4.5H in its original format. *GPLE* did not utilize any vectors or parameters within DOS 3.3 so I did not have to adjust any of my sourced code for *GPLE* whatsoever in order for it to execute at another memory location. What I like about *GPLE* is that it works very much like a global word processor specifically for Applesoft programs. It has the ability to globally search and replace any variable, word, or character with any other variable, word, or character within an Applesoft program. And *GPLE* does its work extremely fast.

The original *GPLE* loader first verifies that the Apple][computer contains at least 48 KB of memory and that there is an available Language Card partition. Then the loader write-enables Bank 1 of the Language Card partition and issues a DOS BLOAD command in order to load *GPLE* to memory address 0xD000. Finally, the *GPLE* loader copies a set of routines comprised of the ctrl-Y entry location, the ampersand entry location, and the CSWL and KSWL interface pointers to memory at 0xB6B3 to 0xB6F9, a small, unused area within DOS 3.3. These routines also control the Bank switching of the Language Card partition as well as providing the entry location for a modifiable JSR instruction used in *GPLE* processing. Of course, DOS 4.5L does not have seventy bytes free at 0xB6B3, or seventy bytes free anywhere within DOS 4.5L for these routines if *GPLE* is to reside in the Language Card partition.

I decided to combine the *GPLE* loader, the ctrl-Y and the CSWL and KSWL interface routines, and the *GPLE* program into one, drastically simplified program. Thus, only one file needs to be launched. I specifically redesigned *GPLE* to function in Main memory below 0xBE00 so that DOS 4.5H can reside in the Language Card partition. *GPLE* still depends upon reading and writing directly to the TEXT pages using CH and BASL. Therefore, some *GPLE* capabilities still do not function properly if the 80-column card in enabled. I disabled the ampersand entry location since its primary function is to initialize *GPLE*. Instead, I reserve the ampersand function entirely for *PGE*. *GPLE* provides a host of ctrl short cuts that are intended to issue certain DOS commands, calculate the size of an Applesoft program in memory, or calculate the number of free sectors in a volume. Because I only use *GPLE* to find and to replace text in Applesoft programs, I have ignored those other, special capabilities of *GPLE*. Those capabilities are primarily intended to be used within the DOS 3.3 architecture and I have not had the interest nor the desire to modify or update this particular code in *GPLE*. Figure V.10.1 shows *GPLE* after it has initialized. The `ctrl-E` function, or `EDIT`, provides access to all of the editing capabilities that are available in *GPLE*. It is this *GPLE* function that I use exclusively.

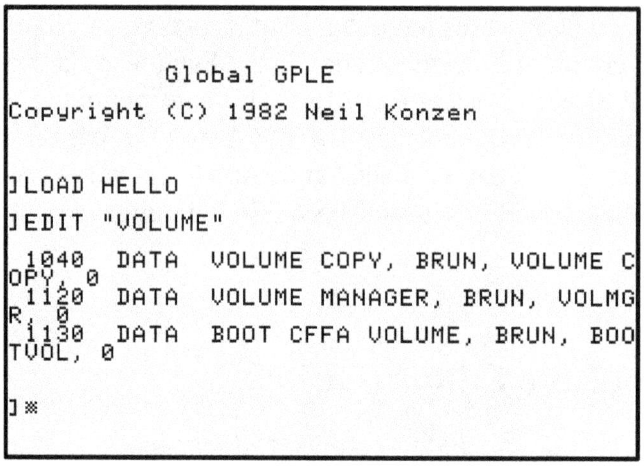

```
              Global GPLE
Copyright (C) 1982 Neil Konzen


]LOAD HELLO
]EDIT "VOLUME"

 1040  DATA   VOLUME COPY, BRUN, VOLUME C
OPY, 0
 1120  DATA   VOLUME MANAGER, BRUN, VOLMG
R, 0
 1130  DATA   BOOT CFFA VOLUME, BRUN, BOO
TVOL, 0


] ▒
```

Figure V.10.1. GPLE EDIT Function

I made a gallant attempt to modify *GPLE* so that it would perform its functions with the 80-column card enabled. I even utilized some of the routines that I had developed for *Lisa* so that *Lisa* would function with the 80-column card enabled. Even after several bouts of frustration I finally had to shelve that effort from sheer mental exhaustion. I did, however, manage to update the *GPLE* `CSWL` and `KSWL` interface routines and capture the state of the Bank currently in focus in the Language Card partition. These two vectors must restore not only the state of the Language Card partition, but they must also restore which Bank was enabled at the very moment when either vector was entered since DOS 4.5H utilizes both Banks of memory in the Language Card partition for all of its processing capabilities.

Once the current version of *GPLE* has been launched, my generic `HELLO` program on my `DOS.4.5H.Tools` volume cannot capture any `ctrl` codes in order to select which programs to launch, say *PGE*. All keystrokes are filtered through *GPLE*, and any `ctrl` character such as the arrow keys are trapped. The `HELLO` program requires that arrow key information in order to properly select any of the available programs to launch. When the user requires the services of both *GPLE* and *PGE*, the global editor *PGE* should be launched first. Once *PGE* is operational, `HELLO` can be used to launch *GPLE* so that both utilities are available and glorious Applesoft programming and editing can begin!

11. Axlon RAM Disk 320

I first became aware of the Axlon RAM Disk 320 when I was self-employed and working under contract for Sierra On-Line around 1985. Living in Oakhurst, California, was really awesome, and being able to work at home was even better. Except when thunderstorms developed in the area and electrical power was temporarily interrupted, it was heavenly to live and work in Oakhurst. Due to the propensity of thunderstorms in the California Sierra mountains, I was alert to any hardware solutions that I might find in the various Apple and computer subscriptions I maintained. Perhaps I might find an affordable solution offered in one of the many advertisements throughout those magazine subscriptions. UPS battery backups, or Uninterrupted Power Supplies were not easy to obtain and they were not very affordable at that time. But when I was in the middle of a massive software development session and I lost power to the house causing me to lose hours of work, the cost of a UPS seemed trivial. That was the time when I decided to purchase an Axlon RAM Disk. Actually, I purchased two because my best friend wanted a RAM Disk, too, after I described to him all of its features. The RAM Disk emulates two 40-track disk drives using DRAM memory, and it has its own built-in power supply and backup lead-acid battery. As long as the power outage did not last more than four hours, all of my files would be safe within the RAM Disk memory. My software development pace vastly accelerated as well because files were assembled from RAM, not from diskette. And when the RAM Disk was mated with the ZipChip, large projects could be assembled and linked in seconds rather than in many, many minutes.

Axlon provided excellent software utilities with the RAM Disk. Their RAM Disk initialization software could transfer an entire diskette to one of the RAM drives in the time it took the Disk][(revolving at 300 revolutions per minute) to make thirty-five revolutions, one revolution per track, in 35 * (60 / 300) = 7 seconds. That is impressive. From their software and from the hardware design of their peripheral interface card I truly learned the importance of reading the CLRROM address (i.e. 0xCFFF) in order to detach peripheral-card expansion ROM memory.

Whenever the 6502-microprocessor fetches an instruction in peripheral-card ROM memory, 0xCs00 to 0xCsFF, where **s** is the slot number of the peripheral interface card, the peripheral interface card typically enables its peripheral-card expansion ROM memory, 0xC800 to 0xCFFF, if the hardware is designed to do so and if it contains the memory to do so. The RAM Disk peripheral interface card was designed to enable its peripheral-card expansion ROM memory only when the card was accessed in the address range of 0xCs00 to 0xCs7F. Interesting. Software residing in the upper half of its peripheral-card ROM memory can read the CLRROM address in order to detach the expansion ROM memory without re-enabling that memory. That was indeed a very, very clever design. In fact, I made good use of that hardware design in all of my versions of RAM Disk firmware. Another interesting design of the RAM Disk peripheral interface card was its use of a static RAM chip, a 6116, for its firmware memory. The static RAM chip needs to be programmed only once when power to the computer is first turned ON, and regardless how many times the Apple][is powered OFF and back ON again, the static RAM chip retains its data because its operating power comes from the RAM Disk and not from the Apple][.

The first page of the static RAM chip is mapped to the peripheral-card ROM memory (i.e. 0xCs00 to 0xCsFF) and its 0xC8 page is mapped to the selected page of RAM Disk DRAM. The remaining seven pages of static RAM chip memory are mapped to the peripheral-card expansion ROM memory, 0xC900 to 0xCFFF. I made good use of the idea of utilizing a static RAM chip instead of an EPROM when I was testing my new firmware for the Sider Host adapter card. It was amazing how much easier it was to test different software algorithms for the Sider without having to program yet another, and another EPROM. However, I have recently replaced the RAM Disk static RAM chip with a 28C16A EEPROM. I connected Pin 18, its chip enable, to an SPDT switch in order to write-protect the EEPROM. This EEPROM needs to be programmed only once, and it retains its data until it is re-programmed at a later time. It has the conveniences of both a static RAM chip and an EPROM. This EEPROM cannot be programmed quickly like a static RAM chip, so care must be taken in developing any EEPROM programming software to contain the appropriate time delays between program bytes.

I no longer remember when and where I became an owner of a 128K RAM peripheral interface card, or RAM Card. It may have been left inside a used Apple //e that I purchased at a garage sale. Regardless, I have no idea who manufactured this RAM Card either. This RAM Card is designed to operate much like a Language Card in any peripheral slot in an Apple][+ or in an Apple //e, and it can be easily configured as one of eight Language Card partitions. Since Address Bit A02 is ignored when configuring the Language Card partition using its dedicated Soft Switches, this RAM Card utilizes Address Bit A02 in order to select a Language Card partition block. Table V.11.1 shows the memory management Soft Switches used by this RAM Card. Simply reading address 0xC084 selects RAM Card block 0, or reading address 0xC08D selects RAM Card block 5.

Address	Access	Name	Description
0xC080	R	RAM2WP	Select Bank 2; write protect RAM
0xC081	R || RR	ROM2WE	Deselect Bank 2; enable ROM || write enable RAM
0xC082	R	ROM2WP	Deselect Bank 2; enable ROM; write protect RAM
0xC083	R || RR	RAM2WE	Select Bank 2 || write enable RAM
0xC084	R	RCBLK0	Select RAM Card block 0
0xC085	R	RCBLK1	Select RAM Card block 1
0xC086	R	RCBLK2	Select RAM Card block 2
0xC087	R	RCBLK3	Select RAM Card block 3
0xC088	R	RAM1WP	Select Bank 1; write protect RAM
0xC089	R || RR	ROM1WE	Deselect Bank 1; enable ROM || write enable RAM
0xC08A	R	ROM1WP	Deselect Bank 1; enable ROM; write protect RAM
0xC08B	R || RR	RAM1WE	Select Bank 1 || write enable RAM
0xC08C	R	RCBLK4	Select RAM Card block 4
0xC08D	R	RCBLK5	Select RAM Card block 5
0xC08E	R	RCBLK6	Select RAM Card block 6
0xC08F	R	RCBLK7	Select RAM Card block 7

Table V.11.1. RAM Card Memory Configuration Soft Switches

The original hardware circuit of the RAM Card is shown in Figure V.11.1. The circuit utilizes an Intel 3242 address multiplexer and refresh counter in order to periodically refresh the sixteen dynamic RAM chips on board. This address multiplexer is designed to refresh 16K dynamic RAM chips, not 64K dynamic RAM chips like those found on this RAM card. Therefore, the RAM Card circuit derives Row Address 7 from the selected RAM Card block number. Data that is read from or written to the RAM Card is latched in the 0xD000 to 0xFFFF memory address range. Therefore, the RAM Card must pull the INH line low in order to disable the Apple][ROMs appropriately and to enable the memory of the respective Language Card partition block according to the last read configuration Soft Switch as shown in Table V.11.1. In order to utilize the RAM Card for anything useful, software must be specifically designed to access the RAM Card as eight individual Language Cards, or an interface driver must reside somewhere else in memory in order to provide RAM Card memory access. Neither of these ideas appealed to me, and I wanted to use the 128K memory of the RAM Card in a more generic fashion.

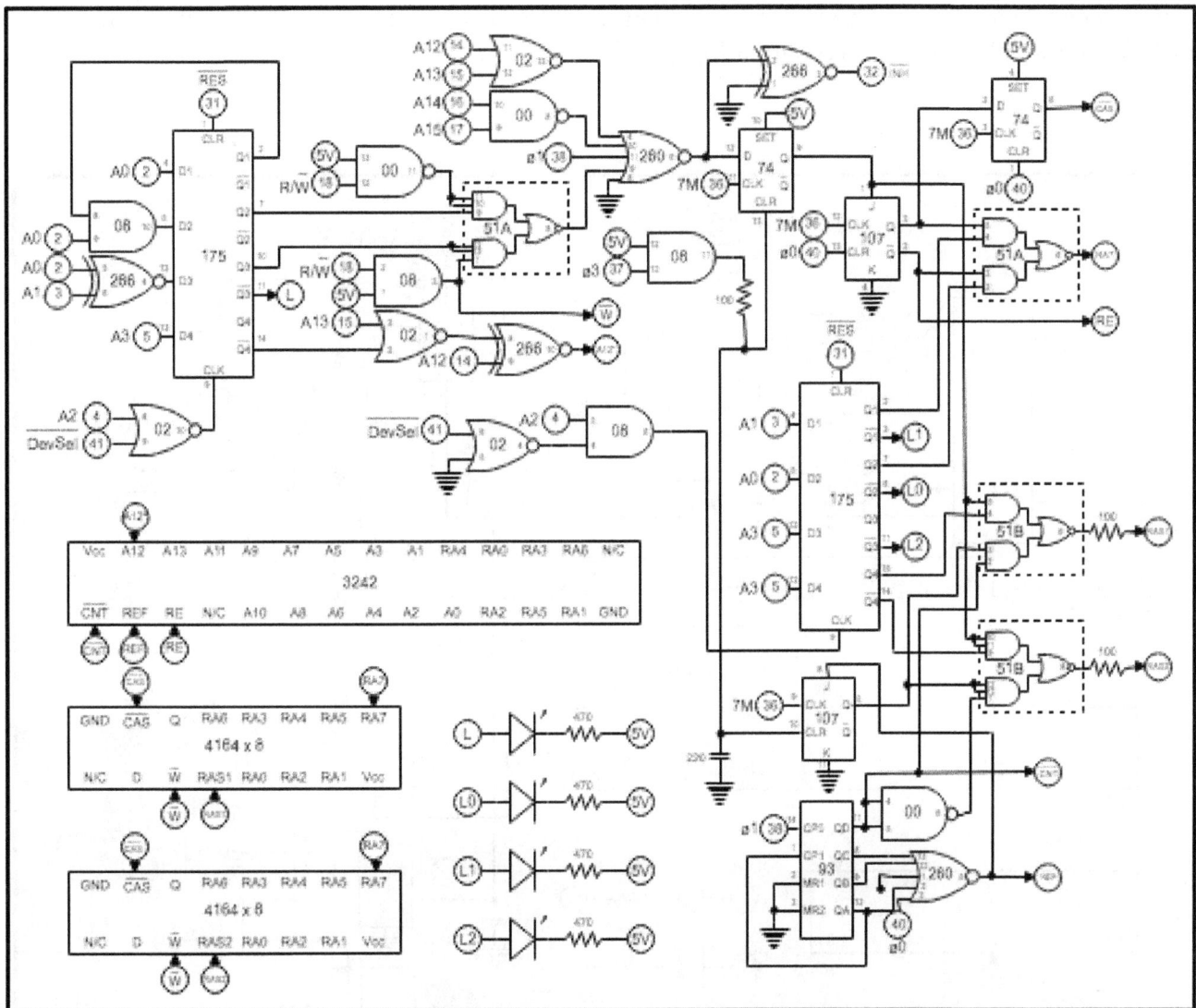

Figure V.11.1. Original RAM Card Hardware Circuit Diagram

The hardware of the RAM Disk responds only to the first two of sixteen peripheral-card I/O memory locations dedicated to the RAM Disk in order to select sector and track, so Address Bit A02 is always low. The RAM Card is designed to latch Address Bits A00, A01, and A03 when Address Bit A02 is high. Thus, the active peripheral-card I/O memory locations for the RAM Disk and for the RAM Card are mutually exclusive in selecting RAM Disk sector and track versus RAM Card block number. For example, if the RAM Disk resides in slot 7, sector number is saved to 0xC0F0 and track number is saved to 0xC0F1. If the RAM Card resides in slot 7, block number is selected by reading 0xC0F4 to 0xC0F7 or 0xC0FC to 0xC0FF. Once I understood the hardware circuit of the RAM Card vis-á-vis its software utilization, I thought perhaps the circuit could be easily re-engineered. I also had some unused space within the RAM Disk peripheral-card ROM memory and I had plenty of unused space for additional software within the RAM Disk peripheral-card expansion ROM memory. From within the RAM Disk peripheral-card ROM memory, I knew I could turn off the RAM Disk peripheral-card expansion ROM memory and use that address space to possibly access eight continuous pages of the RAM Card. Therefore, instead of accessing RAM Card data in the 0xD000 to 0xFFFF memory address range, I could access RAM Card data in the peripheral-card expansion ROM memory from `0xC800` to `0xCFFF` as one of sixty-four 8-page windows.

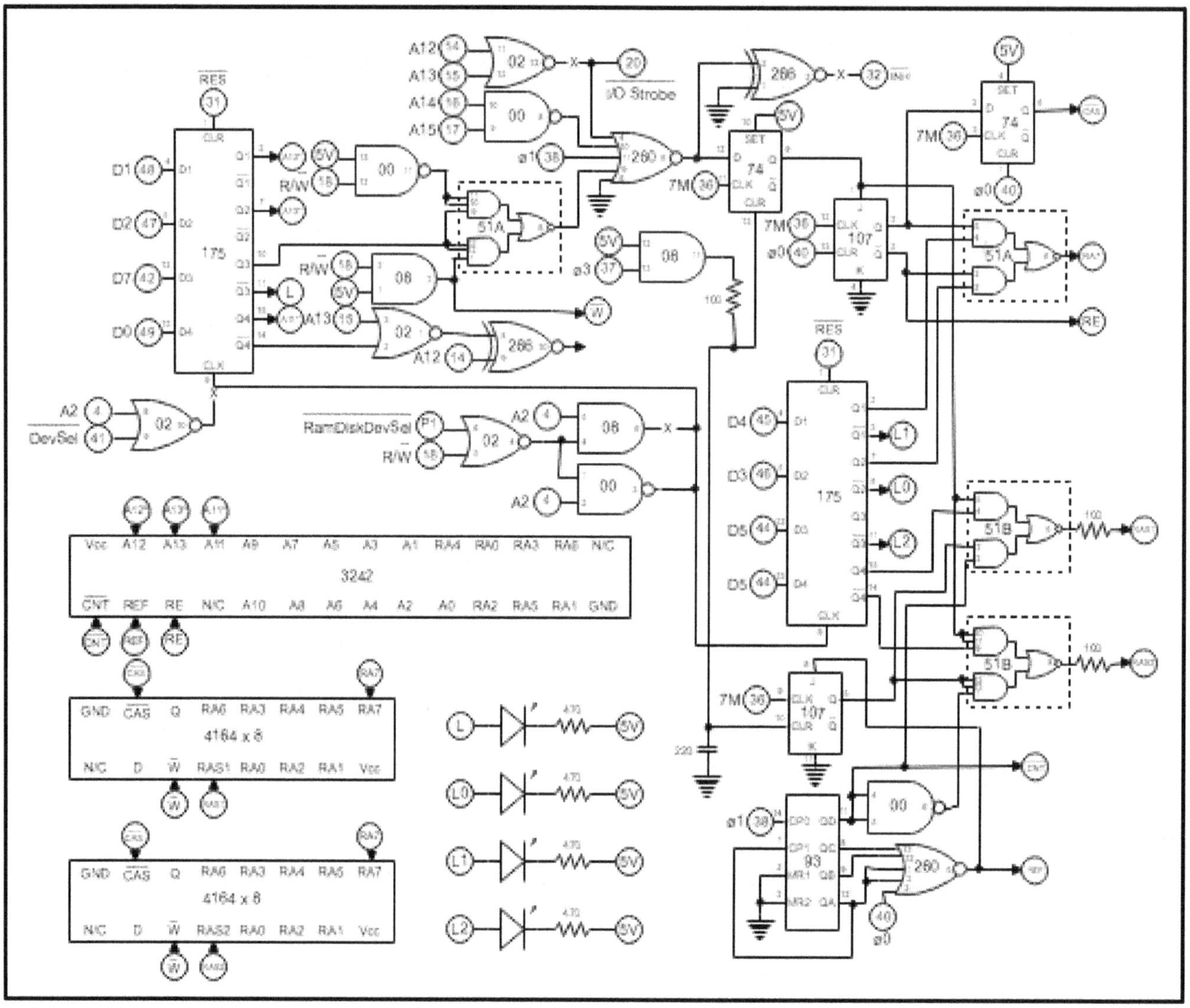

Figure V.11.2. Modified RAM Card Hardware Circuit Diagram

It was around 1992 when I figured out a procedure to physically modify the RAM Card in order to allow the firmware of the RAM Disk to control it, and to access it as if it was a RAM disk drive having thirty-two tracks. However, this modification required me to connect the RAM Card to the RAM Disk using a single control wire. I found that Slot 3 was the perfect slot for the RAM Card because the RAM Card no longer needs to respond to its own *DEVICE SELECT* signal, but rather respond to the simulated control *DEVICE SELECT* signal generated by the RAM Disk firmware. When the RAM Disk connects to DOS 4.5, it calls the `MNGDISK` routine on behalf of the RAM Disk **and** the RAM Card to add the addresses of its disk handlers to the disk address table `DISKADRS`, one address for the RAM Disk residing in slot 7 and one address for the RAM Card residing in slot 3. To be sure, the RAM Disk firmware is handling all of the `RWTS IOCB` traffic for the RAM Disk as well as the `RWTS IOCB` traffic for the RAM Card.

254

Regardless which slot the RAM Card occupies, the RAM Disk firmware saves the track and sector from the `RWTS IOCB` to the `0xC0n4` (where **n** is equal the slot number of the RAM Disk plus eight) peripheral-card I/O memory location on behalf of the RAM Card. Formatting either the RAM Disk drives for forty tracks or the RAM Card for thirty-two tracks is fundamentally easy in DOS 4.5 because the DOS `INIT` command can set the `ENDTRK` variable to those specific values using the `A` keyword.

Figure V.11.2 shows the modified RAM Card hardware circuit diagram. The 74LS175 quad D flip-flops latch the data bus bits except for Data Bit `D6`. Data Bits `D0` to `D5` contain the desired sector/track number and Data Bit `D7` is used to enable the RAM Card. The desired 6-bit sector/track Window and sector Page are calculated as follows:

```
W = ( track number * 2) + ( sector number / 8)
P = sector number ^ 7
```

The selected window `W` within the total memory of the RAM Card is determined by doubling the track number and adding in the sector number divided by eight. The selected page `P` within that window `W` that is mapped to the RAM Card peripheral-card expansion ROM memory is determined from the first three bits of the sector number, and that window is either the first eight sectors or the last eight sectors of the specified track. These calculations show that the 128K RAM Card provides sixty-four windows and each window provides eight pages of data. Now, the modified RAM Card circuit does not need to bring the *INH* line low anymore because it is **not** necessary to disable the Apple][ROMs. Figure V.11.3 shows the actual modifications that must be made to Figure V.11.1 in order to obtain Figure V.11.2. Fortunately, one 74LS00 gate was available in order to clock the 74LS175 control registers.

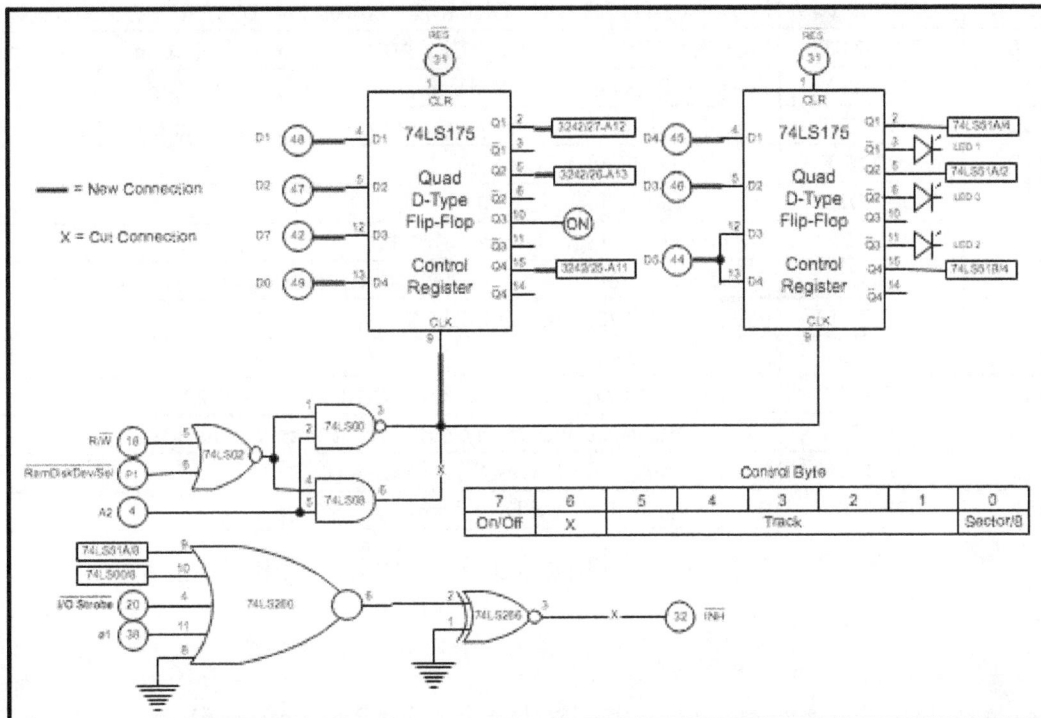

Figure V.11.3. RAM Card Hardware Modifications

In Figure V.11.3 the Control Byte is latched into the two control registers on the RAM Card only when Address Bit A02 is high as in STA 0xC084,X where the X-register contains the slot number of the RAM Disk times sixteen. The RAM Disk hardware does not respond to any value written to its peripheral-card I/O memory location when Address Bit A02 is high, but it does generate a suitable *DEVICE SELECT* signal that can be used by the RAM Card. Before the RAM Card is enabled the CLRROM address is read in order to disable the peripheral-card expansion ROM memory from 0xC800 to 0xCFFF. The moment the RAM Card is enabled the peripheral-card expansion ROM memory is instantly mapped to eight selected pages of RAM Card memory. Bit 0 of the Control Byte contains bit 3 of the desired sector number. Therefore, the peripheral-card expansion ROM memory displays sectors 0x00 to 0x07 when Control Byte bit 0 is low and sectors 0x08 to 0x0F when Control Byte bit 0 is high. Bits 1 to 5 of the Control Byte contain the desired track number. Bit 6 of the Control Byte is not used and bit 7 is used to enable or disable the RAM Card. The RAM Card can no longer function as a set of eight Language Cards after having had these hardware modifications.

Table V.11.2 shows the DOS RWTS entry points for the RAM Disk and for the RAM Card in the firmware that is mapped to the peripheral-card ROM memory residing in the EEPROM of the RAM Disk. The RAM Card hardware does not contain an EPROM or an EEPROM and, therefore, does not contain any firmware. The RAM Card depends entirely on the RAM Disk for its complete operation and for its connectivity to DOS RWTS.

Offset	Name	Description
0x00	RDBOOT	Entry point for DOS PR# command to boot DOS in drive 1
0x10	ROMHOOK	Entry point to attach the RAM Disk/RAM Card to the DOS in memory
0x18	ROMUHOOK	Entry point to detach the RAM Disk/RAM Card from the DOS in memory
0x20	RDENTRY3	Entry for DOS 3.3 RAM Disk RWTS processing, IOCB in Y-/A-registers
0x40	RDENTRY	Entry for DOS 4.1-4.5 RAM Disk RWTS processing, IOCB in Y-/A-registers
0x50	RCENTRY	Entry for RAM Card RWTS processing, IOCB in Y-/A-registers
0x5C	ROMBOOT	Disk][firmware-like entry point for Boot Stage 1 code at 0x0801
0x70	MODOS3	Patch DOS 3.3 after Boot Stage 2
0x80	BOOTEXIT	Issue CLRROM, jump to 0x0801
0x87	RCEXIT	Turn RAM Card off, fall into RDEXIT
0x90	RDEXIT	Save RWTS error code, issue CLRROM, return to caller
0x9E	HOOKEXIT	Exit for ROMHOOK and ROMUHOOK
0xA5	EXIT3	Exit for MODOS3
0xAC	RCRDWRT	Enable RAM Card, read/write RAM Card, exit to RCEXIT
0xD4	RCFORMT	Issue CLRROM, enable RAM Card, clear sectors, exit to RCEXIT
0xFE	VERSION	Version number for RAM Disk firmware (0x05)
0xFF	BUILD	Build number for RAM Disk firmware (0x05)

Table V.11.2. RAM Disk 320 Firmware Entry Points

According to manufacturing documentation the 28C16A is a fast, low power, 5V-only CMOS Parallel EEPROM organized as 2K x 8-bits. It requires a simple interface for in-system programming. On-chip address and data latches, Vcc power up/down write protection, and self-timed write cycle with auto-clear eliminates the need for additional timing and protection hardware. This chip is designed to endure a minimum of 10,000 program/erase cycles and this chip has a data retention of ten years. Fast read access time is 200 nanoseconds and fast write cycle time is 10 milliseconds maximum. The algorithm I developed to program this chip writes a byte of data to the EEPROM, reads the EEPROM, and then compares the byte that was read to the byte that was written until they are the same. The continuous read loop for this EEPROM is 300 μsec, and the loop is enabled for a maximum of 48 retries. This algorithm provides a generous 14.4 milliseconds for the write cycle time for each byte written, though data is typically written in far less time. If, for some reason, a data byte cannot be written within 14.4 milliseconds, programming is terminated and an error routine is called. Once each byte of the EEPROM is programmed, a verification routine is called to confirm the accuracy of the entire EEPROM data image. The complete programming process does take several minutes to fully program an EEPROM of this size, but the EEPROM only needs to be programmed once rather than having to program a static RAM chip every time the RAM Disk is powered ON. Figure V.11.4 shows the Connect Program main screen that copies a 35-track diskette to the RAM Disk in only seven seconds.

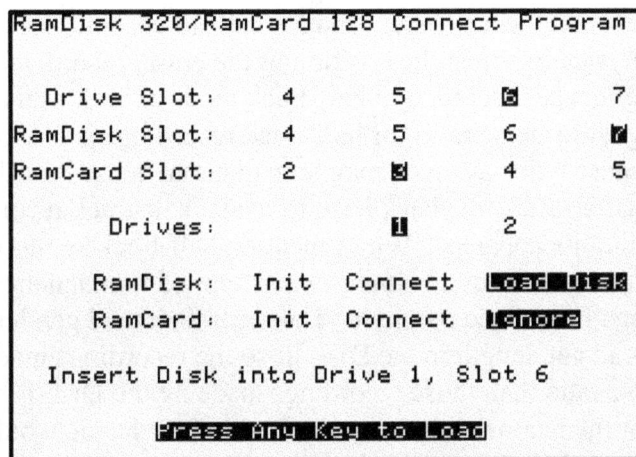

Figure V.11.4. RAM Disk/Card Connect Program

12. RanaSystems EliteThree

I met a very knowledgeable engineer at Hughes Aircraft Company a year or so after I was hired into the Digital Simulation and Integration Laboratory in 1986. Kathryn provided private consulting services to small companies and she designed proprietary databases for her customers. In order to document and track her services, she used a database system of her own design hosted on an Apple][computer connected to a single Disk][drive and a RanaSystems EliteThree drive as her massive database data storage container. She preferred the large storage capacity of the Rana and she thought the access time was a bit faster than the Disk][. When she sold her consulting business, she offered to sell me the Rana drive for $100 on November 14, 1988. I recently found her dated invoice in a folder along with the Rana manual she gave me. Obviously, the Rana is used, but certainly not dead, and I jumped at the offer. My early investigations into the Rana and its installation software revealed to me how tightly coupled it was to DOS 3.3. I didn't much care for all of the modifications the installation software had to make to DOS 3.3 in order to provide the various configurations the hardware was capable of supporting. These modifications were provided by Rana Enhancement Utilities and they were designed to modify DOS and *FID* on a Master DOS diskette. The Rana can read and write either side of a diskette, it can create tracks half the size of Disk][tracks, that is, it can create eighty tracks on each side of a diskette, and the Rana Elite Controller card is capable of hosting up to four disk drives of any manufacture. I basically left it at that, and put the Rana away for another time to explore its capabilities.

Well, that time has arrived to have another look at the RanaSystems EliteThree vis-à-vis DOS 4.5. Any configuration utilizing the hardware capabilities of the Rana needs to address the current VTOC structure, and how the VTOC can possibly be expanded to provide resources for more than fifty tracks in a disk volume. The Rana can seek up to eighty tracks on a double-sided, double-density diskette. The Rana can also access both sides of a diskette without having to manually flip the diskette over in order to access its backside, thereby providing direct access to a total of one hundred sixty tracks.

I recall fondly the time in 1968 when I sat in the Audio Music Library in Schoenberg Hall at UCLA listening to magnetic tape recordings for my class on Johann Sebastian Bach. The library used an array of four Viking 80 magnetic tape recorders to playback audio assignments for students enrolled in various music classes. I happened to own a Viking 880 which used vacuum tubes for its audio recording and playback circuits. The only difference the Viking 880 had with the Viking 80 is that the 880 came installed in a suitcase with two 2x6 inch speakers and a small stereo, solid state audio amplifier. This recorder has the ability to physically adjust the position of the erase, record, and playback heads in order to record or playback magnetic tapes recorded in half-track mode as well as magnetic tapes recorded in quarter-track mode. The signal-to-noise ratio for half-track recordings is obviously far superior to quarter-track recordings because twice as much magnetic material is used for the recorded signals. Even though the Viking used a quarter-track playback head to read a half-track recording, the increased signal-to-noise ratio was still quite apparent. Why I mention half-track versus quarter-track magnetic audio recording is that the concepts are quite similar when applied to magnetic disk recording using a Disk][recorder versus a Rana EliteThree recorder. The recording head gap length, or track size in the Rana is half the recording head gap length in the Disk][, so the recordings made by the Rana would have a smaller signal-to-noise ratio than those recordings made by the Disk][because half as much magnetic material is used for the recorded signal in the Rana. Pure havoc would occur if the Disk][tried to read a Rana disk recorded in 80 track mode.

Information is recorded in a magnetic material when that material is brought close to an electromagnet that contains a small gap where changing magnetic flux can easily flow across that gap. The width of that physical gap, its spacing, is critical and it is an important design component of the recording and playback circuitry. The required magnetic flux to impose changes in the magnetic material is determined by the current flowing in, the voltage across, and the impedance of the magnetic coil within the read/write disk head, and the width of the gap of the electromagnet that is formed by the magnetic coil. I simply point this out so that there is no confusion between the gap width and the gap length of a read/write disk head because the gap width and the gap length specifications are easily confused and thought to be synonymous when referring to the read/write disk head gap.

It would be possible to differentiate between diskettes recorded using the standard prologue bytes in the Address Field and in the Data Field headers, and those diskettes using other prologue header bytes. This simply makes this diskette readable by one RWTS and not by another RWTS. The Rana could certainly use such a protocol but I believe there is simply not enough code space in its peripheral-card expansion ROM memory to make this doable for more than one or two configurations regarding the number of tracks in the volume, the number of sectors per track, and the expansion of any of its VTOC bitmap data. Whatever configuration that uses the full capabilities of the Rana is most likely not going to be compatible with the Disk][. The DOS 4.5 VTOC structure is the only place where any compatibility argument can be derived for the Rana and for the Disk][. I believe that whatever is defined in the DOS 4.5 VTOC is what should be used to decide how best to utilize the Rana, though whatever configuration that turns out to be will most likely leave the Rana somewhat under-utilized.

Considering the lessons learned from half-track and quarter-track magnetic audio recording, and in view of the rather limited availability of double-sided, double-density magnetic media, I chose to implement full-track recording for the Rana, thus providing forty tracks on each side of the diskette knowing full well that the physical length of the recording head gap in the Rana is half the length of the recording head gap in the Disk][. I also chose to implement recording all track sectors 0x00 to 0x0F on the notched side of the diskette and recording all track sectors 0x10 to 0x1F on the un-notched side of the diskette. The VTOC can fully accommodate this configuration. The Rana EPROM can also accommodate this configuration within its available code space and implement all of the same RWTS commands for DOS 4.5L and for DOS 4.5H. This configuration provides forty tracks, each track having thirty-two sectors, to comprise a volume having a total of 1280 sectors. If the VTOC and Catalog use twelve of those sectors, a Data disk would potentially provide 1268 sectors for data storage, a rather massive amount of disk space accessible on a single diskette. This is precisely the configuration I chose to implement. Table V.12.1 shows the firmware entry points for the firmware that is mapped to the peripheral-card ROM memory in the Rana EliteThree Elite Controller card.

Offset	Name	Description
0x00	RANABOOT	Entry point for PR# DOS command to boot DOS in drive 1
0x10	ROMHOOK	Entry point to attach the Rana to the DOS in memory
0x18	ROMUHOOK	Entry point to detach the Rana from the DOS in memory
0x20	RANARWTS	Issue CLRROM; enter RWTS processing
0x5C	BOOTFW	Disk][firmware-like entry point for Boot Stage 1 code at 0x0801
0x83	FNDADDR	Read address field header for volume, track, and sector; checksum ignored
0xA6	FNDDATA	Read 342 disk nibbles, post-nibblize to memory, jump to 0x0801
0xFE	VERSION	Version number for Rana firmware (0x05)
0xFF	BUILD	Build number for Rana firmware (0x05)

Table V.12.1. Rana Disk Firmware Entry Points

The signal-to-noise ratio for the Rana drive is still very much a concern of mine because the Rana RWTS FORMAT algorithm rejects many of the double-sided/double-density diskettes I recently purchased. The FORMAT algorithm marks these diskettes as not safely recordable, but they are perfectly recordable using the Disk][hardware. Diskettes having been previously recorded by a Disk][will still contain residual and problematic magnetic information even after the Rana overwrites such a diskette using its FORMAT algorithm due to its smaller head gap length. Even after formatting, the bleed-through residual information between tracks still remains. It was after the successful formatting of several virgin diskettes that allowed me to finally test the Rana firmware that I designed. Designing this firmware gave me the opportunity to learn more about how the volume format was originally conceived to use a free sector bitmap that supports up to fifty tracks, where each track can have thirty-two sectors. These bitmap findings are thoroughly discussed in Sections I.5 and I.6. Needless to say, a CFFA volume having forty-eight tracks, where each track can have thirty-two sectors is just a minor extension to what

I designed and implemented for a Rana volume. Truth be said, the education I received from exploring the Rana and its capabilities proved to be absolutely invaluable in the design of DOS 4.5 and the CFFA software. Perhaps a future enhancement to DOS 4.5 would be an extension to the VTOC bitmap area?

VTOC bytes 0xF8 through 0xFF are normally used for the bitmaps for tracks 0x30 and 0x31 (i.e. tracks 48 and 49), but these bytes are currently unused even by the CFFA. I believe these eight bytes could easily serve as some sort of VTOC bridge to another available or designated sector in order to extend the free sector Bitmap of a Rana volume. Perhaps the Rana firmware could carry the burden of expanding the free sector Bitmap rather than DOS 4.5, since it is the Rana that is able to read and write far more tracks than most, if not all other disk hardware. I believe it is possible to modify the Rana Elite Controller card to access a larger EPROM that could possibly bank switch the peripheral-card expansion ROM memory area. Having substantially more expansion ROM memory could easily support the additional software necessary to extend the free sector Bitmap of the Rana VTOC. The calculation of Free Space on a volume would have to ignore these last eight bytes, and perhaps utilize those bytes to address the expanded Bitmap and process the additional sector Bitmap bytes on another sector.

DOS 4.5 uses a new, and unique algorithm to move the read/write disk head from one track to an adjacent track. Section I.10 describes the DOS 4.5 RWTS interface and the spacing of adjacent tracks in terms of half-phases. I have replaced the Rana firmware that I designed that supports DOS 4.1L and DOS 4.1H with new firmware that supports DOS 4.5L and DOS 4.5H. This new firmware includes all of the algorithms from DOS 4.5 for stepping the read/write disk head in half-phase increments. Whether the Rana interface firmware attaches to the DOS 4.5 DISKADRS table makes no difference because the same algorithms are used in both the Rana firmware and in the DOS 4.5 RWTS. Even the FORMAT routines are identical in both software. However, if the Rana firmware does attach to the DOS 4.5 DISKADRS table, the Rana firmware will be able to utilize its ability to access four disk drives as it was designed to handle. Because the Rana can access forty four-half-phase spaced tracks, it would be reasonable to expect the Rana to easily access forty-eight three-half-phase spaced tracks, too. Not only is this expectation reasonable, it is absolutely possible and factual.

13. First Class Peripherals Sider

Around 1985 my mother asked me to put together a computer system in order to store all of her genealogy records and data. She was becoming overwhelmed with family ancestry documentation, and she knew and understood how invaluable a computer would be that could store and link all of her data and information. I knew of a software product called *Family Roots* by Stephen C. Vorenberg and marketed by Quinsept, Inc., that would give my mother the power and the flexibility she needed in order to contain and organize all of her ancestry information. Her *Family Roots* database initially filled four data diskettes besides the three program diskettes when she asked me if there was a better alternative than swapping these diskettes in order to generate a family report. In its documentation *Family Roots* suggested using the Sider from First Class Peripherals, a fixed disk drive subsystem featuring a 10 MB hard disk drive having its data storage partitioned mostly as DOS 3.3 volumes. And, to tell the truth, I had been very interested in the Sider when I first heard about the drive, but I just didn't have the reason or the bankroll to afford such a luxury. Mom had both. When I inherited her Apple //e computer system, she had filled more than sixteen DOS 3.3 volumes on her Sider with genealogy data. The Sider proved to be the perfect data storage system for all of my mother's genealogy data.

The Sider consists of a Host Adapter peripheral slot card connected to an external housing by means of an IDE cable. The housing contains a Xebec 1410A controller board and a 10 MB Winchester hard drive. The Host adapter card contains a 2716 EPROM and it uses only two of its sixteen peripheral-card I/O memory locations in order to communicate with the Xebec controller. Essentially, the firmware transfers the first six bytes of an eight-byte Data Context Block, or DCB to the Host adapter card. The firmware uses the last two bytes of the DCB, or buffer address to transfer 256-bytes of data to or from the Xebec controller. The DCB contains the command, a 24-bit Logical Block Address (LBA), a block count, a step option, and a buffer address. The LBA buffer address specifies one 256-byte page of memory. A DOS 3.3 volume is configured to contain 560 pages, or Sider blocks of data. Even though a Sider may be configured not to use CP/M or ProDOS or Pascal formatted volumes, some Sider blocks are still set aside for those partitions. The Sider is partitioned only once to configure the sizes of the DOS 3.3, CP/M, ProDOS, or Pascal partitions. In the case of my mother's Sider, we partitioned her Sider for the maximum number of DOS 3.3 volumes and the minimum number of CP/M, ProDOS, and Pascal volumes. After partitioning, her 10 MB Sider contained 69 DOS 3.3 volumes beginning with Volume 0. *Family Roots* utilizes volume number exclusively in order to locate all system programs and all genealogy data. Of course, I was fascinated to learn how the Sider modified DOS 3.3 in order to *tame* volume number such that a program like *Family Roots* could utilize this invaluable parameter.

Table V.13.1 shows the original logical block structure of the Sider based on LBA number. The Xebec controller determines how this LBA number, or Sider block number is mapped to the hard drive. It is important to note that a volume is a contiguous group of blocks and that each volume follows the previous volume, or group of blocks. Table V.13.2 shows the modifications I made to the Sider Logical Block Structure in order to support DOS 4.1, DOS 4.3, and DOS 4.5. The new Sider peripheral-card ROM firmware I designed boots the DOS 4.5H image starting at block 184. Alternately, the DOS 4.5L image can be booted by calling 0xCs20, where **s** is the slot number of the Sider Host Adapter card, typically slot 7. The DOS 4.5H image can also be booted by calling 0xCs28. When a Sider DOS image boots, the DOS inserts the RWTS handler address for the Sider, 0xCs80, into the Disk Address Table. Table V.13.3 shows all of the Sider firmware entry points for the firmware that is mapped to the Sider peripheral-card ROM memory. There is a mathematical relationship between LBA and volume, track, and sector that are found in the RWTS IOCB. The first volume is Volume 0 and it is defined to begin at LBA address 464, or 0x01D0. A Sider volume is configured with thirty-five tracks and each track contains sixteen blocks, one block for each sector, or 560 (i.e. 0x0230) blocks for each volume.

$$LBA = (\ volume * 0x230\ ) + (\ track * 0x10\ ) + sector + 0x01D0$$

In order to calculate the LBA efficiently and with great speed, lookup tables are used that essentially perform all of the multiplication by using simple addition. There is sufficient room in the 2716 EPROM for the four lookup tables that are required to perform this calculation. The RWTS IOCB volume, track, and sector values are range-checked before the track and volume values are used as indices into a pair of tables, one pair of tables each for track and volume, and the extracted values are added to the sector value. The offset 0x01D0 is already incorporated within the data of the volume tables. I added the address of the DOS 4.5L image at index 69, the address of the DOS 4.5H image at index 70, the address of the DOS 4.1L image at index 71, the address of the DOS 4.1H image at index 72, the address of the DOS 4.3H image at index 73, and the address of the DOS Spare image at index 74 to the volume tables. Any of these DOS images or a selected Sider volume having a bootable DOS image can be booted using the BOOTVOL entry point from Table V.13.3 at 0xCs40, and a regular boot sequence is initiated.

LBA Range		Description
Start	End	
0	0	Sider boot block
1	1	Sider parameter block
2	36	DOS 3.3 boot image (35 blocks)
37	84	RAM card image (DOS) (48 blocks)
85	135	CP/M boot image point #1 (51 blocks)
136	255	Reserved for future use (120 blocks)
256	258	CP/M boot image point #2 (3 blocks)
259	463	Free area for any application (205 blocks)
464	1023	DOS 3.3 volume 0xFD (BU volume)
1024	????	User data area
????	????	12 alternate tracks

Table V.13.1. Sider Logical Block Structure

LBA Range		Description
Start	End	
0	0	Sider boot block
1	1	Sider parameter block
2	36	DOS 3.3 boot image (35 blocks)
37	84	RAM card image (DOS) (48 blocks)
85	135	CP/M boot image point #1 (51 blocks)
136	183	DOS 4.5L boot image (48 blocks)
184	231	DOS 4.5H boot image (48 blocks)
232	255	reserved for future use (24 blocks)
256	258	CP/M boot image point #2 (3 blocks)
259	263	Free blocks (5 blocks)
264	311	DOS 4.1L boot image (48 blocks)
312	359	DOS 4.1H boot image (48 blocks)
360	407	DOS 4.3H boot image (48 blocks)
408	455	DOS SPR1 boot image (48 blocks)
456	463	Free blocks (8 blocks)
464	1023	Volume 0 (560 blocks)
1024	39103	Volumes 1 to 68 (38080 blocks)
39136	39136	Park heads block

Table V.13.2. Modified Sider Logical Block Structure

If the Sider boot image is a DOS 3.3 image, the SDRWTS3 address is used to replace the RWTS address found at 0xB7B8 and 0xB7B9 in DOS 3.3. Otherwise, if the Sider boot image is a DOS 4.1, DOS 4.3, or a DOS 4.5 image, the SDRWTS4 address is added into their respective DOS Disk Address Table.

Offset	Name	Description
0x00	BOOTHR	Entry point for PR# DOS command to boot DOS 4.5H
0x10	ROMHOOK	Entry point to attach the Sider to the DOS Disk Address Table
0x18	ROMUHOOK	Entry point to detach the Sider from the DOS Disk Address Table
0x20	SDOS4.5L	Entry point to boot DOS 4.5L
0x28	SDOS4.5H	Entry point to boot DOS 4.5H
0x40	BOOTVOL	Entry point to boot any bootable volume on the Sider
0x50	PARK	Entry point to call ROMUHOOK and park the disk heads
0x5C	ROMBOOT	Simulate Disk][entry point for Boot Stage 1 code at 0x0801
0x70	SDRWTS3	RWTS handler for DOS 3.3
0x80	SDRWTS4	RWTS handler for DOS 4.1 or DOS 4.5
0xA0	DRIVER	Read/write a Sider LBA using an eight-byte DCB in regs Y/A
0xC0	GETSTAT	Get Sider status in Carry flag
0xD0	READSTAT	Read Sider status into a four-byte user buffer
0xF0	MODOS3	Patch DOS 3.3 after Boot Stage 2
0xFE	VERSION	Version number of Sider firmware (0x05)
0xFF	BUILD	Build number for Sider firmware (0x05)

Table V.13.3. Sider Firmware Entry Points

Family Roots utilizes Diversi-DOS in order to accelerate the loading of its humungous Applesoft programs, and it also utilizes DDMOVER by Diversi-DOS to relocate most of DOS 3.3 into the Language Card partition. Still, *Family Roots* requires four file buffers, and even after DDMOVER has moved DOS 3.3, these file buffers remain in lower memory. *Family Roots* chains from program to program keeping all of its global values in memory. This technique certainly makes *Family Roots* appear to seamlessly transfer control from one program to the next program particularly with the acceleration routines in Diversi-DOS for disk access. I have to say that I derived some of my inspiration from Diversi-DOS to incorporate disk acceleration routines to be native in DOS 4.1, and to move an early version of DOS 4.1, perhaps Build 32 or Build 33, into the Language Card partition. DOS 4.5H is based upon that early Language Card version of DOS 4.1H. Diversi-DOS moves bits and pieces of DOS 3.3 into the Language Card and it has to modify the addresses of all JMP and JSR instructions. Diversi-DOS creates a software interface between the routines it leaves in lower memory and the routines it moves into the Language Card partition in order to perform all necessary Bank switching protocol for the Language Card partition. Designing DDMOVER must have been a momentous effort to be sure, and having most of DOS 3.3 in the Language Card partition certainly gives *Family Roots* the *breathing room* it needs in view of the size of its Applesoft programs and the size of its variable and ASCII data arrays. And yet, the memory in the Language Card partition is actually less than fully utilized by Diversi-DOS.

I certainly understand how Diversi-DOS by Bill Basham at Diversified Soft Research is able to accelerate the I/O routines in the File Manager, and I understand how SPEEDOS from Applied Engineering accelerated its RamWorks products as well. I also looked at David DOS by David Weston and TurboDOS that is used with the original *Lisa*. I am sure there are others who have forsaken the DOS INIT command and utilize that code space for their particular ingenious acceleration algorithm. Even Don Worth and Pieter Lechner went so far as to suggest modifying the DOS sector interleave table in order to speed up the reading of large Applesoft and Binary program. None of these algorithms seemed to be the very best solution for managing disk I/O in DOS 3.3. At Sierra On-Line a software engineer colleague of mine (a gentleman from the United Kingdom, actually) did provide an additional `BLOAD` keyword that provided a Page parameter. This keyword parameter provided an additional and new *read pages* subcode for the File Manager. His `BLOAD` implementation was certainly fast and, if I recall correctly, it was used on the first version of King's Quest.

I decided that my goal to accelerate DOS I/O was not to rewrite the File Manager, but to add some additional logic to the File Manager. This logic would read pages of a file only when it was appropriate to do so. For example, the first two bytes of an Applesoft file must be read in order to calculate its program end address before the rest of the file is read into memory. The remaining `0xFE` bytes in its file buffer are copied to the target address, one byte at a time. However, the remaining sectors of the file, except for the last sector most likely, can be read directly into memory one page at a time. If there is a last sector that contains some bytes, the sector can be read into its file buffer and the remaining few bytes copied to the target address, again one byte at a time. Binary files are handled in the same way except that the first four bytes are copied into the DOS parameter area from its file buffer; that is, the target memory address and the size of the file in bytes. The remaining `0xFC` bytes in its file buffer are copied to memory one byte at a time. The remaining sectors of the file can be read directly to memory one page at a time.

I am quite sure that if DSR, Inc., had access to the source code for Apple DOS 3.3, it could have generated a native version of DOS 3.3 that would be resident in the Language Card partition and not require software like `DDMOVER`. My vision of DOS 4.5H is that it must boot directly into the Language Card partition and be wholly resident in the Language Card partition for the most part. It is one thing to cobble together a system from bits and pieces of a previous system, but it is quite another thing when a complete system is fully designed from the ground up specifically to reside in the Language Card partition. Initially, I designed DOS 4.1H to occupy the Language Card partition in Main memory natively. It has all of the functionality found in DOS 4.1L and more. All file buffers, up to five, are fully contained in the Language Card partition as well. There is even enough code space to provide a DOS `HELP` command that provides the basic syntax for all DOS commands. It is this version of DOS that became DOS 4.5H initially. Therefore, regardless of the number of file buffers in use, `HIMEM` is always set to `0xBE00`, the highest possible address in order to provide an Applesoft environment that can support monster programs like those found in *Family Roots*.

Furthermore, DOS 4.5 contains the same `CHAIN` algorithm that is found in DOS 4.1 with a few minor enhancements. Preliminary tests have shown that DOS 4.5 and `CHAIN` function beautifully with *Family Roots*. There are empty volumes on the Sider that can be used to conduct further tests with DOS 4.5 and *Family Roots*. Also, the *Family Roots* programs and Data volumes can be moved to a drive on the CFFA and tested there. Either hardware location would certainly verify the migration of *Family Roots* to DOS 4.5. I believe my mother would have certainly been very impressed, and she would have certainly provided me with hours of hands-on verification testing.

I replaced the Xebec 2716 EPROM with a 6116 static RAM chip and connected its R/W pin to finger 18 of the Host Adapter card. This allows me to experiment with my own firmware for the Sider in order to test its ability to boot different DOS images. Early versions of this firmware utilized some memory in the static RAM to save variables such as slot number, slot number times sixteen, and the version of DOS that is currently in memory. Using the static RAM for certain variables was the easiest path in order to implement communication with the Xebec controller. I simply ported over the RAM Disk Connect Program since the RAM Disk interface card also has used a 6116 static RAM. Figures V.13.1 and V.13.2 show the Sider Connect Program that I use to load the static RAM with the Sider firmware. Now that I have established a strong confidence level in the operation of this firmware, I have re-engineered the firmware to utilize the public and private memory bytes on the TEXT screen reserved for interface slot cards. This allows me to either utilize a 2716 EPROM or a 28C16A EEPROM for the Sider firmware.

```
┌─────────────────────────────────┐  ┌─────────────────────────────────┐
│      Sider Connect Program      │  │       Useful Entry Points       │
│                                 │  │                                 │
│                                 │  │                    Type From Type From│
│                                 │  │                    Applesoft  Monitor │
│ Sider Slot:    4    5    6    7 │  │ DOS 4.5H Boot:     CALL -14592  C700G │
│                                 │  │ DOS Connect:       CALL -14576  C710G │
│                                 │  │ DOS Disconnect:    CALL -14568  C718G │
│                                 │  │ DOS 4.5L Boot:     CALL -14560  C720G │
│     Sider:   Reconnect  Init  Abort │ DOS 4.5H Boot:     CALL -14552  C728G │
│                                 │  │ DOS Volume Boot:   CALL -14528  C740G │
│                                 │  │                                 │
│                                 │  │ Park Heads:        CALL -14512  C750G │
│                                 │  │                                 │
│                                 │  │ DOS 3.3 RWTS:      CALL -14480  C770G │
│                                 │  │ DOS 4.5 RWTS:      CALL -14464  C780G │
│                                 │  │                                 │
│                                 │  │ Sider DCB Driver:  CALL -14432  C7A0G │
│                                 │  │ Request Status:    CALL -14400  C7C0G │
│                                 │  │ Receive Status:    CALL -14384  C7D0G │
│                                 │  │                                 │
│                                 │  │    Press Any Key to Continue    │
└─────────────────────────────────┘  └─────────────────────────────────┘
```

Figure V.13.1. Sider Connect Program   Figure V.13.2. Sider Entry Points

It is interesting to note that the hardware logic on the Sider Host Adapter card maps the first seven pages of its EPROM data to the peripheral-card expansion ROM address range 0xC800 to 0xCEFF. The last page of its EPROM data is mapped to its peripheral-card ROM address range 0xCs00 to 0xCsFF, where s is the slot number of the Sider Host Adapter card. With the Sider peripheral-card expansion ROM enabled, the 0xCF00 to 0xCFFF data is the same as the 0xCs00 to 0xCsFF data. The hardware engineers at RanaSystems designed their Elite Controller card for the EliteThree disk drive using the very same EPROM to memory mapping. There really isn't a better EPROM to memory mapping scheme when a 2716 EPROM is selected. I believe a 2732 EPROM would be a far better choice, however! The first eight pages of the 2732 would be mapped to the peripheral-card ROM memory, one page for each slot after skipping the first page. The bytes in the first page would be programmed to 0xFF and left unused. Absolute addressing instructions could be used for the software routines used by each slot like the software I designed for *EOS* where the software is identical for each slot except for their absolute addressing instructions that enable or disable the quikLoader. The last eight pages of the 2732 would be mapped to the entire peripheral-card expansion ROM memory. This memory would contain the generic routines used by each slot no matter which slot the Sider Host Adapter card resides in. More importantly, the hardware logic design of the Host Adapter card would be greatly simplified. I wonder if the availability of 2716 verses 2732 EPROMs drove the design of the Sider and the RanaSystems Elite Controller cards. Perhaps cost was chosen over simplicity. An additional page of peripheral-card expansion ROM memory would have been rather nice to have. Perhaps this would be an interesting hardware upgrade project for these two peripheral interface cards?

14. Sourceror

I first *sourced Sourceror* so that I could modify its source code in order to create a more pleasing display of its available commands using a mixture of uppercase and lowercase ASCII before processing other object code files. *Sourceror*, like *Big Mac*, was written by Glen Bredon. *Sourceror* is a Binary program that originally executed at `0x8900` after `MAXFILES` is set to 1. This placed *Sourceror* just below the first file buffer in DOS 3.3 and in DOS 4.1L. I found only one coding error in *Sourceror*, a missing `CLC` instruction where the software handles 65C02 instructions. Occasionally, not always, the program counter was incremented one byte too many because a *Sourceror* routine assumed that the `Carry` flag would always be clear upon the return from a call to `GETNUM` at `0xFFA7`. Obviously, the `Carry` flag was not always clear after calling `GETNUM`. After I developed DOS 4.1H, I was able to relocate *Sourceror* to `0xAC00` thus allowing the sourcing of far larger object code files. DOS 4.1H provides more memory space for the input object code and more memory space for the output source code. A few more changes to its source code allowed *Sourceror* to function beautifully in concert with DOS 4.5.

```
Press RETURN to accept default Source
Code address 0x4000, or enter 0x

If the present location of the code
to be disassembled is at its original
location, press RETURN.  If not,
enter PRESENT location 0x900

In disassembling, use the ORIGINAL
location 0xAC00
```

Figure V.14.1. Sourceror Initialization

```
SOURCEROR - 65C02 - DOS4.5.05
           by Glen Bredon

A HEX byte nn after commands T or H
limits the output to nn bytes.

Commands (alone or after HEX address):

L - Disassemble (current mode)
N - Normal (next mode)
S - Sweet 16 (next mode)
T - Text (TT defeats DCI)
W - Address (W-: Address-1, WW: DDB)
H - HEX data (1 byte default)

R - Read (does not create source)
/ - Retrieve last default address
I - Instructions
Q - Quit

$
```

Figure V.14.2. Sourceror Startup/Help Display

```
$AC00L

                    ORG  $AC00
AC00-  78           SEI
AC01-  20 58 FF     JSR  $FF58
AC04-  BA           TSX
AC05-  BD 00 01     LDA  $0100,X
AC08-  58           CLI
AC09-  C9 AC        CMP  #$AC
AC0B-  F0 03        BEQ  $AC10
AC0D-  4C D3 03     JMP  $03D3
AC10-  4C 07 B0     JMP  $B007
AC13-  8D 8D 3C     STA  $3C8D
AC16-  09 0E        ORA  #$0E
AC18-  16 05        ASL  $05,X
AC1A-  12 13        ORA  ($13)
AC1C-  05 3D        ORA  $3D
AC1E-  03           ???
AC1F-  0E 14 12     ASL  $1214
AC22-  2E 20 03     ROL  $0320
AC25-  08           PHP
AC26-  2E 3E 20     ROL  $203E
AC29-  7C 46 4C     JMP  ($4C46,X)
$※
```

Figure V.14.3. Sourceror Source Listing 1

```
AC29-  7C 46 4C     JMP  ($4C46,X)
$AC13H2
AC13-               HEX  8D8D
$T
AC15-  ASC '<'
$T
AC16-  INV 'INVERSE=CNTR. CH.> '
$T
AC29-  FLS '<FLASH=LOWER CASE>'
$T
AC3B-
$AC3BH
AC3B-               HEX  8D
$T
AC3C-  ASC "^ IS BELOW BYTES WITH HIGH
       BIT SET."
$※
```

Figure V.14.4. Sourceror Source Listing 2

Sourceror already contains the text of a number of symbols in order for it to generate a symbol listing at the end of its generated source code file as per the convention that *Big Mac* follows for its output object code file. I added a number of additional symbols to the *Sourceror* source code that includes CLRROM, RAM2WP, ROM2WE, ROM2WP, RAM2WE, RAM1WP, ROM1WE, ROM1WP, RAM1WE, STROBE, LATCH, DATAIN, and DATAOUT.

Figure V.14.1 shows the initialization display after launching *Sourceror*. A loader program such as *Loadsrcrr* is no longer necessary because the HELLO file simply loads *Sourceror* at 0xAC00 and jumps to that address. Figure V.14.2 shows the startup, or Help display *Sourceror* displays with its command-line PROMPT $. Figure V.14.3 shows the Monitor source listing of *Sourceror* after the first L command is issued. Figure V.14.4 continues the sourcing of *Sourceror* using the H command followed by multiple T commands. Of course, these figures and the commands shown are for demonstration only.

Many years ago I used *Sourceror* to provide visibility and complete insight into DOS 3.3, and recently, insight into the CFFA firmware, and every other program and its generated object code that came in between, before, and after those two major projects in the last thirty-five years. Because of *Sourceror* I understand a fair amount of what there is to know about Apple][hardware architecture and about the design of Apple][software that is used to manage and exploit that hardware architecture. I have a tremendous debt of gratitude to Glen Bredon, his software utilities, and his brilliant insight into Apple][hardware and software architecture. Thank you Mr. Bredon for allowing me a peek into your world!

15. Applesoft Formatter

After about six months of writing test and demonstration Applesoft programs on my new Apple][+, I began thinking about writing a serious Applesoft program. Binary File Installation was that program, but it became a hybrid program because it included many attached assembly language routines as described next in section V.16. I also thought I was now capable of writing a standalone assembly language program. How an Applesoft program appeared on the display when it was listed or how an Applesoft program appeared when it was printed by my printer appalled me, and I was determined to use assembly language in order to design and write an *Applesoft Formatter* program. I wanted *Applesoft Formatter* to align program line numbers and consistently space all parentheses the way I liked them spaced. (The spacing of parentheses carried over to how I formatted and wrote all of my future C language software during my professional career.) One feature of this program is to optionally split multiple Applesoft commands that are contained within one line having a line number such that the two Applesoft commands would appear on separate display or print lines. Another feature is to optionally indent Applesoft commands within a FOR/NEXT loop no matter how nested the loops become. Since I owned an Epson MX100 printer, I could easily print up to 120 characters on each line if I used wide paper. Basically, this program became an exercise in parsing Applesoft tokens, keeping track of FOR/NEXT loops, and counting ASCII quote characters. As an interesting aside, I wrote this software so that it could execute at any memory address. It was certainly an intriguing exercise in order to develop and practice my skills at writing relocatable object code for the Apple][machine.

A very simple, unimaginative Applesoft test program is shown in Figure V.15.1 along with some results when that program is RUN. I have purposefully combined several Applesoft commands having the same line number and I have embedded a FOR/NEXT loop within several commands where the loop spans multiple line numbers. Even when this program is listed to a printer, it appears just as awkward and difficult to read. Needless to say, a program many times this size would be exceedingly difficult to read, to debug, and to analyze. I am sure there must have been at least one utility if not more that was available in the early 1980's like the Apple-Doc program by Roger Wagner, that could format and document Applesoft programs using multiple formatting options. And, I am sure those programs did their task work magnificently, too. But that was not my intention, to purchase the labor and product of someone else. I wanted to perform the labor of writing my own program and I wanted to own the results, or the product of that labor. Someone else may indeed choose differently.

```
]LOAD TEST
]LIST

 10 MN = 1:MX = 10: PRINT
 20 I = 0: FOR I = MN TO MX: IF I
    = 5 THEN  GOSUB 100
 30 S$ = "Entry #" +  STR$ (I):J =
    I + 7
 40 T$ = S$ +  STR$ (J): NEXT
 50 END
 100  PRINT "I = ",;I,," J = ";J;"
    , S$ = ";S$: RETURN
]

]RUN

I = 5, J = 11, S$ = Entry #4
]
```

Figure V.15.1. Applesoft Test Program Listing

```
Maximum Characters/Line (<161):  31
Split Line (Y,N):  Y
Indent (Y,N):  Y
Echo to Screen (Y,N):  Y
 10    MN = 1
       MX = 10
       PRINT
 20    I = 0
       FOR I = MN TO MX
         IF I = 5 THEN GOSUB 100
 30      S$ = "Entry #" + STR$( I )
         J = I + 7
 40      T$ = S$ + STR$( J )
       NEXT
 50    END
 100   PRINT "I = "; I; ", J = "; J;
       "  S$ = "; S$
       RETURN
]※
```

Figure V.15.2. Applesoft Formatted Program

I wanted to understand the organization of an Applesoft program as it is found in memory. Therefore, I needed to know about all of the rules in how an Applesoft program is constructed from the very first line of Applesoft statements having a line number to the very last line of Applesoft statements having a line number. I learned about the triple-NULL bytes that terminate an Applesoft program. The very first line of Applesoft statements having a line number in an Applesoft program begins at memory address 0x0801. At memory address 0x0801 there is a two-byte pointer that contains the address of the beginning of the second line of Applesoft statements having a line number in low/high byte order, such as 0x13, 0x08. These bytes, when reversed, point to the next line of Applesoft code in memory at 0x0813. This 16-bit pointer is followed by a two-byte line number, again expressed in low/high byte order. So, if the first line of Applesoft code is 10, then the two-byte line number would be found as 0x0A, 0x00 in memory. To reiterate, address pointers as well as line numbers are expressed in low/high byte order in Applesoft programs. All text data contained in an Applesoft program is always expressed in lower ASCII, that is, with the MSB turned OFF for each character byte. On the other hand, all Applesoft commands (i.e. tokens) are always given in upper ASCII, that is, with the MSB turned ON. For example, the first token in the list of BASIC statements in the ROM source code for Applesoft is for the END command, and its token value is 0x80. The last token in this source code is for the MID$ command, and its token value is 0xEA. The token values for all of the other Applesoft commands are within these two values. At the end of each Applesoft line of code having a line number is found a single byte NULL character. That NULL character terminates an Applesoft line of code having a line number. In other words, if the pointer to the next line of Applesoft code having a line number is found to be 0x0813, there will be a NULL character at memory address 0x0812.

Applesoft does not provide the ability to return to a previous line of Applesoft code having a line number. So lines of Applesoft code having a line number are organized in a single direction, left to right, linked list. To find line number 1000 when parsing for the command GOTO 1000, the Applesoft interpreter must start at the beginning of the Applesoft program at memory address 0x0801, and follow the linked list of pointers until the line number 0xE8, 0x03 (in low/high byte order) is found in memory. This organization of lines of Applesoft code having a line number suggests that highly utilized subroutines or functions should be placed early in an Applesoft program. I still find this surprisingly counter-intuitive even though I routinely place all of my subroutines and functions at the beginning of my C language programs where the program Main always comes last.

Now that I have a basic understanding of the organization of an Applesoft program as it is found in memory, I understand how to parse an Applesoft program in assembly language, and I understand how to separate Applesoft command tokens from variable names and embedded ASCII text. This exercise required me to do a little research, a little data and memory analysis, and a little hard work. Figure V.15.2 displays the output of *Applesoft Formatter* when the Split Line and the Indent options are both enabled. Seriously, the generated listing is totally easier to read, easier to debug, and far easier to analyze now that the Applesoft test program is formatted into an appealing and precise composition. I also gained an exceptional understanding of assembly language programming for the 6502-microprocessor, how best to use an assembler, and how to create relocatable object code so that *Applesoft Formatter* can execute at any memory address. Obviously, the lessons learned in designing and writing *Applesoft Formatter* early in the ownership of my Apple][+ are forever invaluable to me, and the effort I put into developing this program has paid off handsomely throughout my entire professional software career. I am still thankful today in having the experience in designing and in writing *Applesoft Formatter*.

16. Binary File Installation (BFI)

Binary File Installation (*BFI*) was the first totally useful Applesoft program I wrote for my Apple][+. I began writing Applesoft programs initially, but I soon started to explore assembly language for various data sort algorithms and disk I/O routines that fascinated me. If I wrote the data sort algorithms and disk I/O routines such that they could execute at any memory address, then I could attach their binary code to the end of an Applesoft program, modify some page-zero pointers, and save the composite, albeit hybrid program. Later, whenever I ran the Applesoft program, its initial program logic was designed to obtain its program size from certain page-zero locations and then calculate the locations in memory for the attached binary code routines knowing their length in bytes and the address for the end of the Applesoft program. A CALL could then be made directly to the start address of a data sort algorithm or to a disk I/O routine from any location within the Applesoft program. This capability of being able to CALL any of my own relocatable assembly language routines within an Applesoft program was exhilarating to me. I talked about this Applesoft programming capability to all of my co-workers who would listen, or to those who were patient with my *Apple computer* programming excitement.

I learned I could even pass parameters to an assembly language routine and also have resultant values returned to the Applesoft program. Any number of relocatable routines could be attached to the end of an Applesoft program and CALLed as long as their start location in memory could be precisely determined. I thought a utility could more easily handle this attachment process, so I created *BFI* to programmatically perform the Binary file attachment to an Applesoft program. The user tells *BFI* which

Applesoft program to target, that is, the program that is to receive all of the Binary file attachment(s), and then the user is offered a selection of all of the relocatable Binary files that can be attached. *BFI* modifies the size of the Applesoft program on disk (i.e. its first two bytes in the file data) and calls the File Manager to append the Binary files directly to the end of the Applesoft program on disk just after its last three NULL bytes: simple, clean, and efficient. Once the attachment is done, *BFI* prints the order and the size of all of the Binary files it attached. The Applesoft program can still be edited or changed at any time using the Apple Command Line and cursor move routines. Unfortunately, if a tool such as *GPLE* or *PGE* is used to edit the Applesoft program, any attached Binary files are stripped from the Applesoft program when the edited file is saved back to disk. I have yet to explore how to disable this feature in both *GPLE* and *PGE*. Figures V.16.1, V.16.2, and V.16.3 show the *BFI* initial Splash Screen, the Main Menu, and how the user selects the external devices for *BFI*. *BFI* only utilizes the disk drive or disk drives that are located in slot 6. When the Install icon is selected as shown in Figure V.16.2, the Applesoft program instructional screen as shown in Figure V.16.4 is displayed in order to allow the user time to locate and insert the desired diskette containing the target Applesoft program.

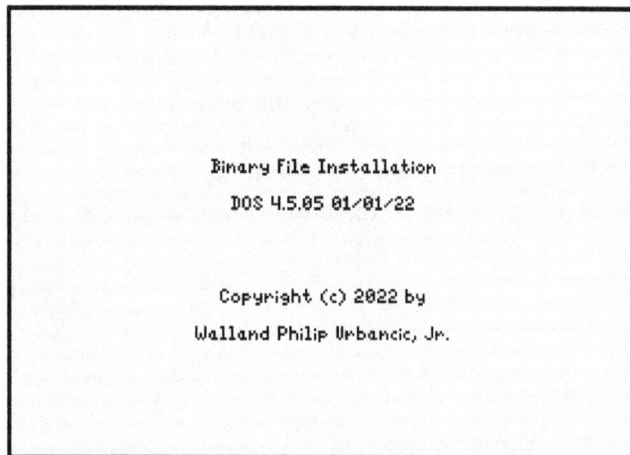

Figure V.16.1. BFI Splash Screen

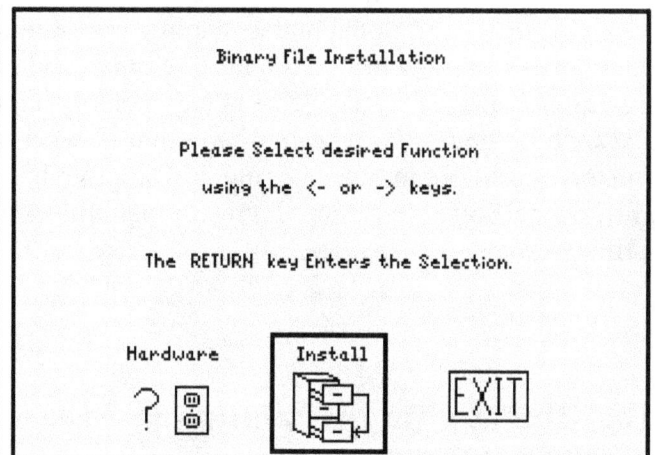

Figure V.16.2. BFI Main Menu

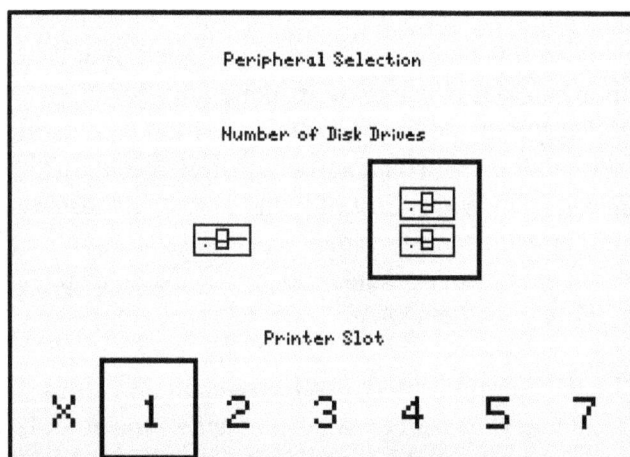

Figure V.16.3. BFI Peripheral Selection

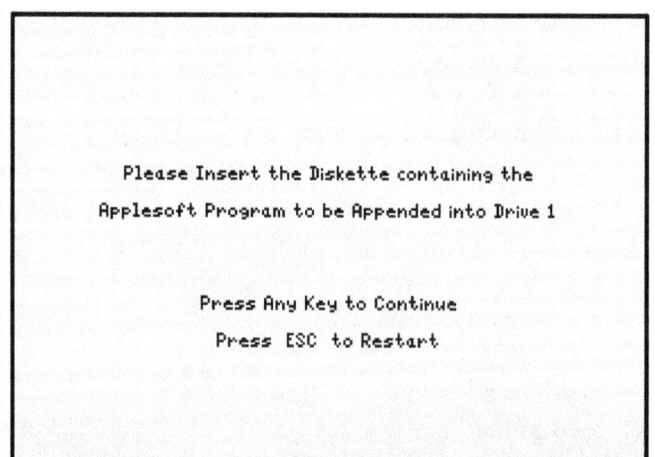

Figure V.16.4. Applesoft Program Directions

```
             File Selection

BFI                    BFI.RAW
HELLO                  NEW BFI
NEW BFI.RAW
```

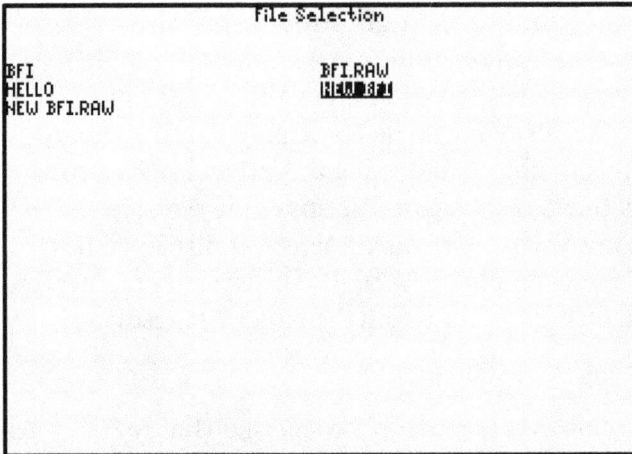

Figure V.16.5. Applesoft Program Selection

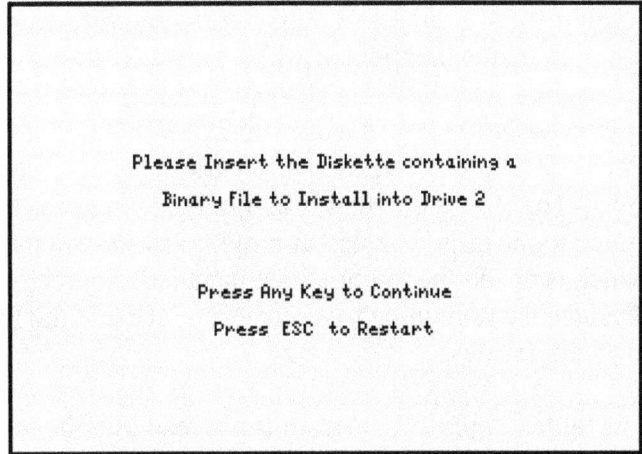

```
Please Insert the Diskette containing a
  Binary File to Install into Drive 2



      Press Any Key to Continue
      Press  ESC  to Restart
```

Figure V.16.6. Binary File Directions

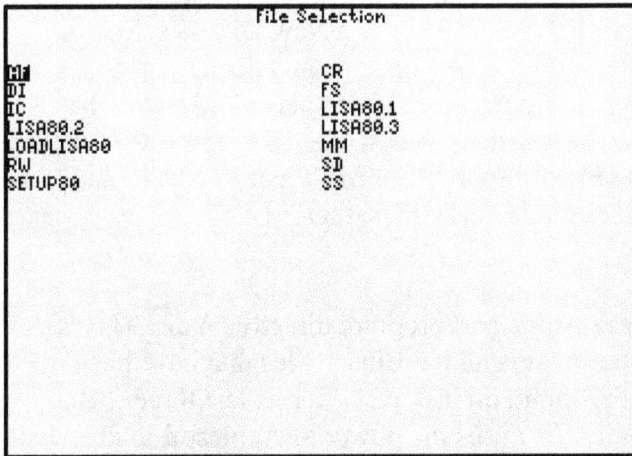

```
             File Selection

AF                     CR
DI                     FS
IC                     LISA80.1
LISA80.2               LISA80.3
LOADLISA80             MM
RW                     SD
SETUP80                SS
```

Figure V.16.7. Binary File Selection

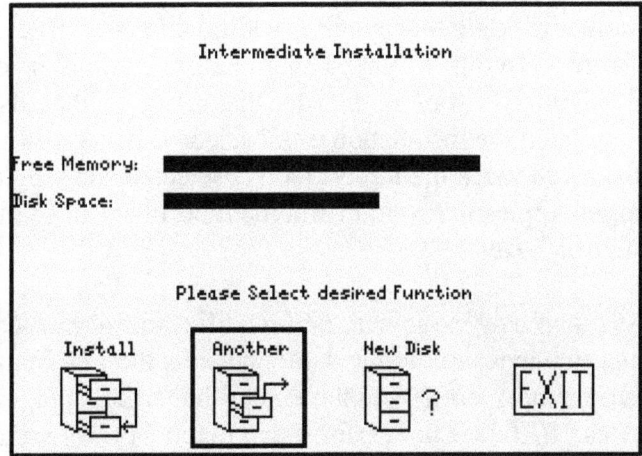

```
          Intermediate Installation

Free Memory: ████████████████████████

Disk Space:  ███████████████████


        Please Select desired Function

  Install      Another      New Disk
                                ?        EXIT
```

Figure V.16.8. Intermediate Installation Screen

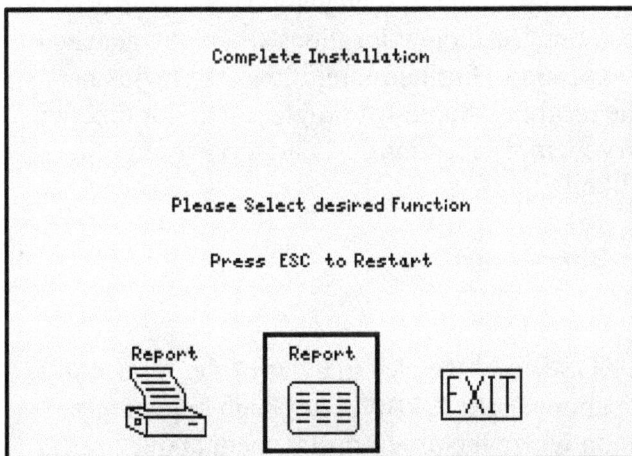

```
          Complete Installation




        Please Select desired Function

          Press  ESC  to Restart


  Report        Report
                            EXIT
```

Figure V.16.9. BFI Complete

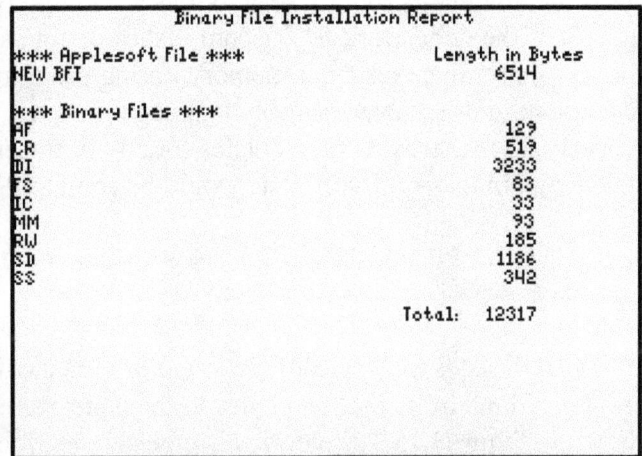

```
         Binary File Installation Report

*** Applesoft File ***        Length in Bytes
NEW BFI                            6514

*** Binary Files ***
AF                                 129
CR                                 519
DI                                3233
FS                                  83
IC                                  33
MM                                  93
RW                                 185
SD                                1186
SS                                 342

                       Total:    12317
```

Figure V.16.10. BFI Final Report

Applesoft Program selection is fairly straightforward using the left and right arrow keys. The Applesoft program that is highlighted when the RETURN key is pressed becomes the target Applesoft program as shown in Figure V.16.5. The Binary file instructional screen as shown in Figure V.16.6 is displayed next in order to allow the user time to locate and insert the desired diskette containing the first Binary file to install. Once again, Binary file selection is fairly straightforward using the left and right arrow keys. The Binary file that is highlighted when the RETURN key is pressed becomes the selected file to attach to the target Applesoft program as shown in Figure V.16.7. A graphic screen is displayed next which is called the Intermediate Installation screen as shown in Figure V.16.8. This screen graphically displays the remaining free memory space and the free disk space on which the target Applesoft program resides.

The target Applesoft program is not read into memory, however, but all of the selected Binary files must be read into memory. Using DOS 4.5H will provide the greater memory reservoir for selecting Binary files. Those selected Binary files must be appended to the target Applesoft program, therefore the diskette containing the target Applesoft program must contain sufficient disk space for that additional program code. The Intermediate Installation screen also provides the option to perform the Binary File Installation using all presently selected files, select another Binary file from the same diskette, change to another diskette that contains additional Binary files, or give up and exit. If a New Disk is selected, Figure V.16.6 is displayed again before reading the catalog of the new diskette and displaying an alphabetized list of all the files that reside on that diskette. Figure V.16.9 is displayed **after** *BFI* has completed the installation of all selected Binary files to the target Applesoft file, and Figure V.16.10 is displayed when the Report icon is selected showing the Final Report. The BFI Final Report includes the target Applesoft program and the report lists all of the selected Binary files, their installation order, and their file size.

As previously explained, *BFI* modifies the size of a target Applesoft program directly on disk (i.e. its first two bytes in the file data) and calls the File Manager to append the Binary files that have been read into memory directly to the end of the target Applesoft program on disk just after its last three NULL bytes. *BFI* does not perform that much work. Essentially, *BFI* uses the power of Applesoft to keep lists of filenames, file sizes, and the memory locations of various assembly language tools that help *BFI* to conduct its task in reading selected Binary files into memory from one or more diskettes and writing the content of those selected Binary files to another diskette at a precise file location that amounts to simply appending a target Applesoft program. Thus, *BFI* orchestrates a number of activities that can be performed manually, but those activities are highly prone to error and miscalculation. Still, the user can ruin all of the good work *BFI* accomplishes in not calculating the correct locations where the attached Binary file routines reside in memory during program execution. Furthermore, if the attached Binary files are not relocatable assembly language routines, the resulting Applesoft program will not function properly no matter what it calculates for any of the entry memory locations. Clearly, one of the first statements in the Applesoft code would be something like:

```
10    PE = PEEK( 175 ) + PEEK( 176 ) * 256
```

When DOS reads an Applesoft program into memory, DOS copies the size in bytes of the Applesoft program found in its first two bytes to the page-zero locations 0xAF/0xB0 in low/high byte order as shown in Figure I.15.1. And, this is precisely the location where the program statement above uses in order to calculate the value for PE, or Program End. According to the Final Report that *BFI* produces, an example shown in Figure V.16.10, the precise memory location for each of the attached Binary file routines may be determined as follows, starting with the last attached routine and going forward:

```
15      SS = PE – 342
20      SD = SS – 1186
25      RW = SD – 185
30      MM = RW – 93
35      IC = MM – 33
40      FS = IC – 83
45      DI = FS – 3233
50      CR = DI – 519
55      AF = CR – 129
```

As I increased my knowledge of the VTOC and RWTS as well as the HIRES screen and HIRES drawing routines, I have modified *BFI* a number of times. The experience I gained from assisting in porting the Sierra On-Line *ScreenWriter* product from the Apple][+ to the Apple //e allowed me the opportunity to study the HIRES screen font that was used in the Apple][+ *ScreenWriter* product. I adapted that HIRES screen font for *BFI* and developed the *CHAR Editor* and *LENGTH* tools. *BFI* also uses an adaptation of the HIRES icon drawing routines that I developed for Sierra On-Line's HomeWord Speller product. I even wrote the icon development and editing tool *ICON Maker* that I use to generate the *shape table* data for all of the screen icons that I use in *BFI*. I probably learned more about the design of my Apple][hardware and firmware from this single Applesoft hybrid program. Essentially, *BFI* became the development tool where I combined all of the talents that I had learned from working on a number of very interesting and successful programs that were in the Sierra On-Line catalog.

Notably, the String Draw or SD and Draw ICON or DI programs are large in size and it would be impractical to write those programs as relocatable assembly language routines. SD resides at 0x6000 and DI resides at 0x6500. *BFI* uses the second HIRES graphics page that resides at 0x4000 to 0x5FFF. Either *BFI* can BLOAD SD and/or DI to their operational memory address or *BFI* can move either one of them from their attachment memory address to their operational memory address. I did not favor having to carry around additional routines with *BFI*, so attaching SD and DI to *BFI* and moving them both to their operational memory address appealed to me. That necessitated me in having to develop a Memory Move or MM routine.

The raw version of *BFI*, that is, the version without any Binary file attachments is not the typical file type that can be manipulated like a Text file. Access to the File Manager is absolutely necessary in order to treat an Applesoft file as if it was a Text file and using its three NULL byte ending as simply a file location having a byte offset. Therefore, I created the little relocatable assembly language routine Append File or AF that performs the Binary file attachment to an Applesoft program. Another useful relocatable assembly language routine is Catalog Read or CR that reads the diskette catalog into an Applesoft filename character string array along with the file type, TSL track and sector, and file size into their respective integer number arrays. The descriptors for character string arrays and integer number arrays are well defined in Table I.15.2 along with a discussion of the DOS 4.5 CHAIN command. Assembly language provides easy access to Applesoft variables and arrays simply by passing the name of the variable or array in the CALL statement.

It is important to *BFI* for it to know if there is and if there will be sufficient disk space for *BFI* to attach all of the selected Binary files to the target Applesoft program. The relocatable assembly language routine Free Space or FS calculates the free sector space of a diskette by processing the default INPUT page at 0x0200. This routine and many other functions within *BFI* depend heavily on the relocatable assembly language routine Read/Write RWTS or RW. This routine will read or write any sector on any track of any drive on any slot using any memory page. It returns the error number generated by RWTS. I found that Applesoft does not have an unformatted input character command in its command repertoire. Therefore, I created a relocatable assembly language routine called Input Character or IC for that purpose in *BFI*. In my discussion of the Applesoft Garbage Collector I made it quite clear that all Applesoft character string variables and character string arrays are composed of ASCII characters having their MSB turned OFF. Therefore, IC is designed specifically for Applesoft programs in that IC returns the ASCII of any keypress with its MSB turned OFF.

How I cherish my memories of the time early in owning an Apple][+ when I started looking at various algorithms that sorted character strings. I am not entirely sure why sort algorithms caught my attention, but these algorithms certainly provided a wonderful vehicle for me to learn what an algorithm was and how one can convert an algorithm into lines of code that will capitalize on the intellectual concepts employed by that algorithm. Alphabetical sorting of the filenames in a diskette catalog is certainly not a fundamental requirement of *BFI*, but I found it to be a rather nice feature in order to display the filenames of a diskette in alphabetical order. My relocatable assembly language routine String Sort or SS can sort the entries of an Applesoft character string array in either direction, that is, from A to Z or Z to A. The entries of the character string array are not actually moved in memory. Instead, I return an integer array whose entries are the sorted index to the character string array. Doing so prevents unnecessarily filling the Character String Pool if, indeed, the entries to the character string array are swapped during the sorting process. Admittedly, the algorithm I chose to implement for sorting character strings is the classic Bubble Sort. As a general rule of thumb, when there are less than fifty character string items to sort, the Bubble Sort algorithm is a practical design choice. A thirty-five or thirty-six track diskette catalog will probably never exceed fifty filenames. Furthermore, *BFI* dimensions its filename, track, sector, and index arrays to fifty. In SS processing, only when two character strings do not differ in length does the algorithm start comparing the bytes of the two strings.

Hopefully, this general overview of *BFI* and its Binary file components will give you some idea on how powerful a hybrid program such as *BFI* can become. *BFI* takes advantage of the numerical and character string arrays and program organization that is inherent in a high level language such as Applesoft and the processing speed of assembly language for sorting and drawing icons and a character font on the HIRES graphics screen in the Apple][. Each routine has been specifically designed to exact the most productivity in the least amount of code space. Certainly, the memory space of an Apple][is a significant aspect in all program designs and its proper management must be considered at all times. The speed of Applesoft can be daunting in certain applications, thus using assembly language where appropriate can definitely relieve Applesoft of many of its potential bottlenecks. I believe *BFI* demonstrates how effective the Applesoft language is when it is paired with assembly language routines in order to create a useful and powerful hybrid tool that can be used to create even more useful and more powerful hybrid tools for the Apple][computer.

17. SCRG PROmGRAMER

The quikLoader marketed by the Southern California Research Group (i.e. SCRG) is of little value without a means to easily program EPROMs. So, SCRG also marketed the PROmGRAMER, designed by Bob Brice, which can program, or write EPROMs for the quikLoader, the Apple //e character generator ROM, and the Apple //e firmware ROM(s). The PROmGRAMER is designed to be configurable using DIP switches in order to access 2716, 2716A, 2732, 2732A, 2764, 27128, 27128A,

27256, and 27512 type EPROMs. The PROmGRAMER software by Bob Sander-Cederlof resides in memory beginning at `0x0803`, and the program cannot extend beyond `0x0FFF` because the desirable EPROM image start address is set at `0x1000`. This is necessary particularly in order to program a 27256 or a 27512 EPROM. For a 27256 EPROM its entire `0x8000` byte image must reside in memory for convenience, and if `0x1000` is its start address, then `0x8FFF` will be its end address, and that is very close to the beginning of the third DOS 3.3 file buffer. When `MAXFILES` is set to `3` in DOS 3.3, `HIMEM` is set to `0x9600`. To program a 27512 EPROM a `0x10000` byte image must be divided into two or more parts, so the EPROM must be programed in two or more sessions. It is for this reason that I highly recommend finding the midpoint for the contents of a 27512 EPROM so that it can be programmed in only two sessions where each session programs `0x8000` bytes. DOS 4.5L provides a useable memory workarea from `0x0800` to `0x95FF` and DOS 4.5H from `0x0800` to `0xBDFF`.

As shown in Figures V.8.10 and V.8.11, the 27512 EPROM image for *EOS* needs to be split at the `0x8000` byte halfway point. The source code is designed to have the *Lisa* assembler do all of the work in splitting the image at the correct location. Therefore, only two EPROM programming sessions are required to write the image of *EOS* into EPROM. The software Mr. Sander-Cederlof provided for the PROmGRAMER allows the user to enter a command, such as F (for Fast program), and the default parameters needed to program a 27256 or the first half of a 27512 EPROM image would be automatically entered on the command line. There was no command available with default parameters to program the second half of a 27512 EPROM, so those parameters had to be entered manually onto the command line. I found this to be rather unfortunate after I ruined one too many 27512 EPROM programming sessions where I had mistakenly entered the wrong parameters. So, I sourced the PROmGRAMER object code software and I added all the additional commands that I thought would be necessary in order to support the programming of a 27512 EPROM. Figure V.17.1 shows the new and enhanced configuration screen for PROmGRAMER and Figure V.17.2 shows all of the commands that are now available to the user. The commands that I added that support the programming of the 27512 EPROM are S, T, G, and A. I had to heavily modify the original source code in order to have enough code space that is required to support all of the new commands, and to have the entire program fit into memory from `0x803` to `0x0FFF`. The new code works incredibly well and it programs all EPROMs perfectly. To say that I am happy would be an understatement.

```
        S.C.R.G.  PROmGRAMER

Enter  Slot number (1-7):   5


              EPROM  Selection

      1 -- 2716        5 -- 27128
      2 -- 2732        6 -- 27128A
      3 -- 2732A       7 -- 27256
      4 -- 2764        8 -- 27512

Enter  selection:   ※
```

```
Working with a 27512 in Slot 5

                    Command Menu

        Start End  Offset
  R     1000  8FFF   0000    Read EPROM
  B     1000  8FFF   0000    Burn EPROM
  F     1000  8FFF   0000    Fast Burn & Compare
  C     1000  8FFF   0000    Compare RAM/EPROM
  S     1000  8FFF   8000    Read EPROM
  T     1000  8FFF   8000    Burn EPROM
  G     1000  8FFF   8000    Fast Burn & Compare
  A     1000  8FFF   8000    Compare RAM/EPROM
  D     1000  8FFF          Display RAM
  E     0000  FFFF          Erase Check EPROM
  H                          Help (Command Menu)
  Z                          Restart PROmGRAMER
  M                          Exit to Monitor
  Q                          Exit to DOS

Enter  command:
```

Figure V.17.1. PROmGRAMER Configuration   Figure V.17.2. PROmGRAMER Command Menu

18. Real Time Clock

The experience I gained in building the memory upgrade for my Apple][+ described in Section V.25 encouraged me to design and build my own *Real Time Clock* peripheral interface card. I had to learn some new skills in order to build a peripheral interface card that would fit within the dimensions allowed for such a card in the Apple][+ computer. I had never etched a double-sided copper clad board that large nor had I thought about how to place TTL components in terms of organization, data and control signal flow, wire length, and clean power. I also had to include and manage additional circuitry to recharge the onboard rechargeable batteries. All of these ideas mattered one way or another I am sure, but honestly, I didn't have much of a clue. In hindsight I should have taken a class in TTL circuit board design and layout before I was graduated with my degree in Electrical Engineering. My garage was my ultimate laboratory and workshop! But most importantly I wanted the hardware design of my *Real Time Clock* card to provide a simple, elegant, and thoroughly elementary interface to the onboard firmware that communicates with external software routines.

I wanted to design my *Real Time Clock* card around the SaRonix RTC58321 Real Time Clock module, which I probably obtained from Jameco Electronics in the mid 1980's. The pinout of the RTC58321 is shown in Table V.18.1 and this clock module incorporates an internal quartz crystal in a single 16-pin DIP package thereby eliminating the need for an external crystal and timing circuit. This clock module provided me with everything I needed in order to read and to write the date and time values and an external *BUSY* signal. I wanted the firmware interface to be as simple as possible so I put a lot of effort into the design of the interface card hardware logic so that the hardware would negotiate the data and address setup time requirements of the RTC58321. Unfortunately, the 6502-clock read/write period happens to be far too short for the data and the address setup time that the RTC58321 requires.

Pin	Name	Function
1	CS2	chip select #2, active high, low to disable
2	WRITE	write port, active high to write data, 2.0 μsec minimum
3	READ	read port, active high to read data, 1.0 μsec minimum
4	D3	read and write data bit 3
5	D2	read and write data bit 2
6	D1	read and write data bit 1
7	D0	read and write data bit 0
8	Vss	ground connection
9	ADRWRT	address write port, active high to latch address, hold time 0.1 μsec, pulse time 0.5 μsec
10	*BUSY*	active low, wait until high to continue
11	STOP	stop enable port, active high, low to run
12	TEST	test enable port, active high, low to test
13	CS1	chip select #1, active high, low to disable
14	NC	no connection
15	NC	no connection
16	Vdd	+5 volt connection

Table V.18.1. SaRonix RTC58321 Real Time Clock Pinout

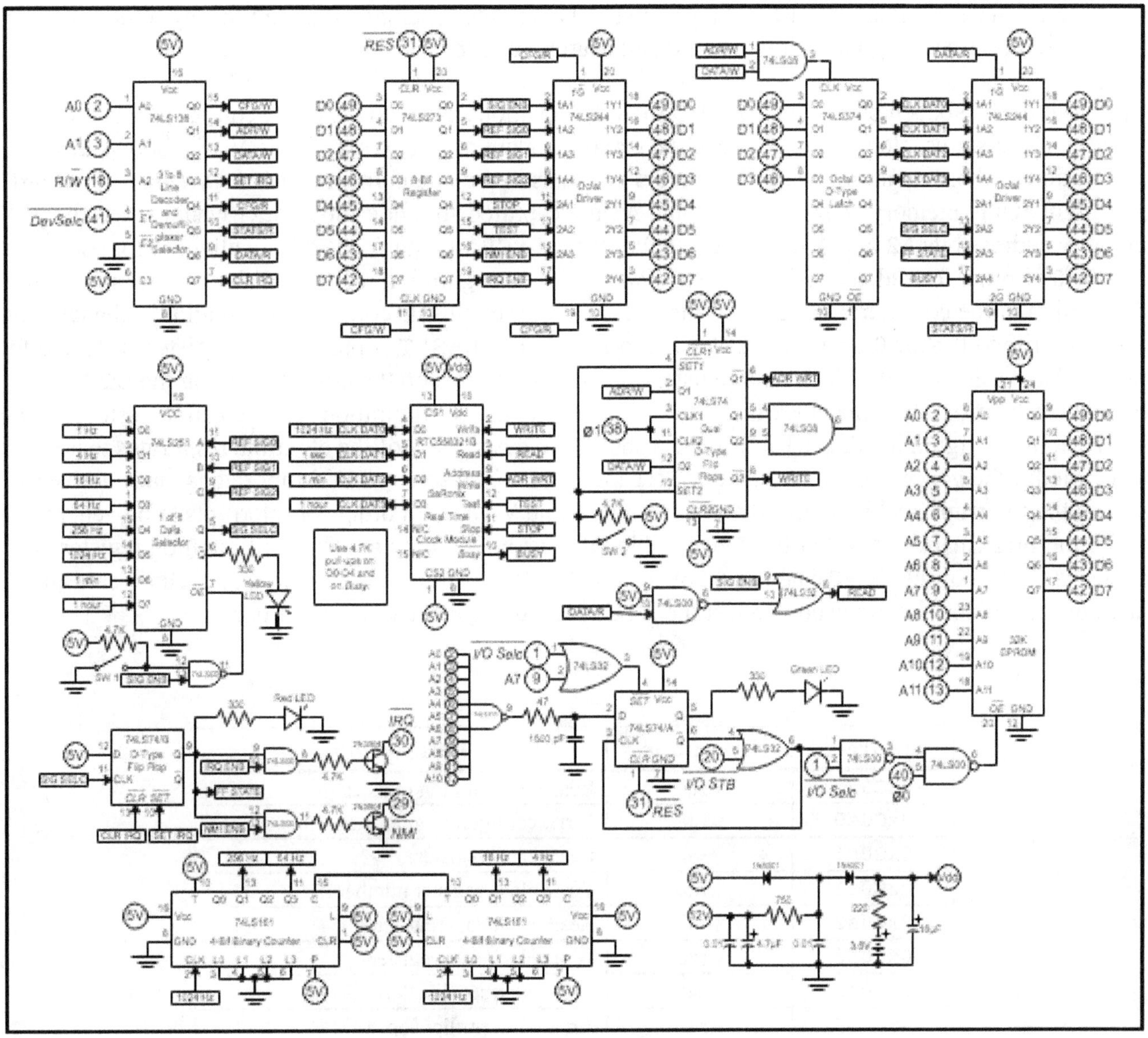

Figure V.18.1. Real Time Clock Circuit Diagram

I used a breadboard for the TTL logic components in order to figure out how to best negotiate with the RTC58321 using a full 6502-clock period and utilizing a flip-flop to increase the time of that clock period. Then I wrote the slot interface firmware for the onboard 2732 EPROM. I modeled my general user Applesoft interface after the Applied Engineering TimeMaster II Applesoft interface. Whatever commands the TimeMaster could handle, I made sure my clock card could handle in addition to all of the other commands and capabilities I could devise and had room for in the EPROM space. And I figured out how to make use of the standard signals that are generated by the RTC58321 to pull the IRQ and/or NMI line low in order to initiate a hardware interrupt. Once I had the schematic diagram drawn and the components nicely organized, I drilled all the necessary holes for chip sockets and components, and etched the copper for the power, ground, and a few of the basic logic lines. I hand-wired and soldered the remaining connections for the interface board slot finger, chip sockets, transistors, batteries, LEDs, configuration block, resistors, and capacitors. *Whew*! My *Real Time Clock* card is fully operational even today as it was over thirty-three years ago. I've only had to replace the rechargeable batteries a couple of times! Figure V.18.1 shows the complete schematic diagram for my *Real Time Clock* card that I had originally drawn and dated March 20, 1988.

Only four of the sixteen peripheral-card I/O memory locations are used for clock configuration, clock address, clock status, clock register, clock data, and interrupt clear and set. Table V.18.2 shows the description of those memory locations where **s** is equals to the slot number of the *Real Time Clock* card plus eight. Only memory address bits `A0` and `A1` are captured so it does not matter what is used for memory address bits `A2` and `A3`. Addresses `0xC0s4`, `0xC0s8`, and `0xC0sC` are all valid for address `0xC0s0` in order to read and write the *Real Time Clock* configuration register. Table V.18.3 shows the description of the configuration register bits. This register retains its configuration until it is changed by another write to `0xC0s0` or when `RESET` is pressed. When `RESET` is pressed this register is cleared to `zero`. Before loading the clock data registers it is important to stop the clock by setting the `STOP` Enable bit to `one`. Once the clock is loaded with its data, the configuration register can be restored with its previous configuration data. Table V.18.4 shows the description of the eight interrupt rates that are available for the generation of `IRQ` and/or `NMI` interrupts. The selected interrupt rate is made active by setting the Interrupt Enable bit to `one` as shown in Table V.18.3. In order for interrupts to be generated either the `NMI` Enable bit and/or the `IRQ` Enable bit must be set to `one`. The configuration register also provides control of the `TEST` enable port of the RTC58321. Unfortunately, I no longer can locate any documentation that describes how to test the RTC58321 using the `TEST` enable port.

Address	Operation	Description
`0xC0s0`	read	Read configuration register
`0xC0s0`	write	Write configuration register
`0xC0s1`	read	Read status register
`0xC0s1`	write	Write clock register number
`0xC0s2`	read	Read clock data register
`0xC0s2`	write	Write clock data register
`0xC0s3`	read	Clear interrupt flip-flop
`0xC0s3`	write	Arm interrupt flip-flop

Table V.18.2. Real Time Clock Peripheral Interface Card I/O Addresses

Bit	Description
0	Interrupt enable, 0 = OFF
1	Interrupt rate select A
2	Interrupt rate select B
3	Interrupt rate select C
4	STOP enable, 0 = RUN
5	TEST enable, 0 = normal operation
6	NMI enable, 0 = OFF
7	IRQ enable, 0 = OFF

Table V.18.3. Real Time Clock Configuration Register

C	B	A	Description
0	0	0	1 Hz interrupt rate
0	0	1	4 Hz interrupt rate
0	1	0	16 Hz interrupt rate
0	1	1	64 Hz interrupt rate
1	0	0	256 Hz interrupt rate
1	0	1	1024 Hz interrupt rate
1	1	0	1 minute interrupt rate
1	1	1	1 hour interrupt rate

Table V.18.4. Interrupt Rate Selection

Table V.18.5 lists the sixteen registers available in the RTC58321. Any time when an 0x0E or a 0x0F register number is latched, the clock module is put into its Idle state and the standard clock signals shown in Table V.18.5 are available at its data port when the READ port of the RTC58321 is set to one. Setting the READ port of the RTC58321 to one is accomplished by setting the Interrupt Enable bit in the configuration register to one as shown in Table V.18.3. The 1024 Hz signal coming out of D0 is divided by two 74LS161 binary counters to obtain the remaining interrupt rates that can be selected by the configuration register that are shown in Table V.18.4. Even though the *Real Time Clock* card can also generate an NMI interrupt, the EPROM firmware only has provisions to generate and handle an IRQ interrupt. Nevertheless, software can easily be written to utilize an NMI interrupt if there is an occasion for such an interrupt to be generated.

Reg	D3	D2	D1	D0	Name	D3	D2	D1	D0	Count	Notes
00	0	0	0	0	S1	s8	s4	s2	s1	0 to 9	1-second digit
01	0	0	0	1	S10	-	s40	s20	s10	0 to 5	10-second digit
02	0	0	1	0	MI1	mi8	mi4	mi2	mi1	0 to 9	1-minute digit
03	0	0	1	1	MI10	-	mi40	mi20	mi10	0 to 5	10-minute digit
04	0	1	0	0	H1	h8	h4	h2	h1	0 to 9	1-hour digit
05	0	1	0	1	H10	24/12	PM/AM	h20	h10	0 to 2 / 0 to 1	10-hour digit
06	0	1	1	0	W	-	w4	w2	w1	0 to 6	week digit
07	0	1	1	1	D1	d8	d4	d2	d1	0 to 9	1-day digit
08	1	0	0	0	D10	leap year		d20	d10	0 to 3	10-day digit
09	1	0	0	1	MO1	mo8	mo4	mo2	mo1	0 to 9	1-month digit
0A	1	0	1	0	MO10	-	-	-	mo10	0 to 1	10-month digit
0B	1	0	1	1	Y1	y8	y4	y2	y1	0 to 9	1-year digit
0C	1	1	0	0	Y10	y80	y40	y20	y10	0 to 9	10-year digit
0D	1	1	0	1	Reset	-	-	-	-		reset register
0E	1	1	1	0	Idle	1 hour	1 min.	1 sec.	1024 Hz		standard signal register
0F	1	1	1	1	Idle						

Table V.18.5. Real Time Clock Registers

Setting data bit D3 in register 0x05 of the RTC58321 to one selects 24-hour mode. Setting data bit D3 clears data bit D2 of the same register to zero. If 12-hour mode is selected by means of data bit D3, then data bit D2 selects PM if data bit D2 is set to one or AM if data bit D2 is cleared to zero. The RTC58321 divides the 10-year digit Y10 in register 0x0C by 4 in order to determine leap year. The remainder of this division is saved to data bits D2 and D3 of register 0x08. If the remainder is zero then leap year is selected. The RTC58321 may be reset by latching register 0x0D and writing any data to that register. This sets the WRITE port of the RTC58321 to one as shown in Table V.18.1. The EPROM firmware does not RESET the RTC58321.

The *Real Time Clock* card utilizes two switches to control its function. Closing Switch 1 disables the frequency data selector module and blocks the output of the selected interrupt rate. Therefore, the clock card cannot generate an interrupt even if the NMI enable bit or the IRQ enable bit is set to one in the configuration register. Closing Switch 2 disables the Address Write and Data Write flip-flops. Therefore, the data in the clock module cannot be changed, thus rendering the RTC58321 write protected. The clock card utilizes three LEDs to indicate what function the clock card is performing at that moment. The Green LED lights whenever the 2732 EPROM is accessed. The Yellow LED lights at the same frequency as the selected interrupt rate if the frequency data selector module is enabled by the Interrupt Enable bit in the configuration register and if Switch 1 is open. The Red LED lights whenever the output of the Interrupt Flip-Flop is set to one (i.e. armed) regardless whether the NMI enable bit or the IRQ enable bit is set to one in the configuration register. If either bit is set to one, the base of a 2N3904 general purpose transistor is pulled high thereby allowing its collector-emitter junction to conduct and pull the respective interrupt line safely to ground. I placed an R/C network between the output of the 74LS133 and the data input to the EPROM enable flip-flop in order to slightly extend the derived CLRROM signal because of the slight delay inherent in the clock pulse to that flip-flop.

The first half of the 2732 EPROM is used for eight copies of the same interface firmware for the peripheral-card ROM memory, one copy for each possible slot in which the Clock card could reside. The second half of the EPROM maps into the peripheral-card expansion ROM memory. Whenever the 6502-microprocessor fetches an instruction only in the first half of the peripheral-card ROM memory, 0xCs00 to 0xCs7F, where s is the slot number of the Clock card, the peripheral-card expansion ROM memory, 0xC800 to 0xCFFF, is enabled. The peripheral-card expansion ROM memory is **not** re-enabled when CLRROM is used in the second half of the peripheral-card ROM memory, a hardware design trick I learned from the hardware design of the RAM Disk 320 peripheral interface card. Table V.18.6 shows all of the entry points in the EPROM slot firmware for the *Real Time Clock* card. This firmware conforms to the clock card protocol where the first two instructions are PHP and SEI, and the last byte, the clock ID, is set to 0x03. Clock ID 0x07 can also be used. DOS 4.5 accepts either value as valid.

The program *Set Clock* utilizes some of the special features I designed into the *Real Time Clock* card hardware. Its primary purpose is to set the clock card with the current date and time, of course. The program also displays the current date and time that is stored in the clock registers, and those values may be automatically selected or new values may be entered for each of the data registers. The surprising feature of this program is that it utilizes an interrupt handler. The clock card is configured to generate an IRQ interrupt every second. Every time the IRQ interrupt occurs, its interrupt handler reads the clock card and displays the date and time data. Once the desired date and time data is selected, that data can be written to the clock card. The interrupt handler continues to display the current date and time data contained in the clock registers while the *Real Time Clock* continues to update its internal registers. Before the *Set Clock* program exits, it restores the data that it originally found at MASKIRQ (i.e. 0x3FE) as shown in Table I.9.3 and sets the clock card configuration register as shown in Table V.18.3 to zero.

Offset	Name	Description
0x00	MAINSELC	PHP instruction, DOS PR# and IN# command handler
0x01		SEI instruction
0x02		Issues CLRROM, branches to INITCLK
0x08	WRITSELC	Issues CLRROM, branches to LOADCLK
0x10	READSELC	Issues CLRROM, branches to READCLK
0x18	MODESELC	Issues CLRROM, branches to SETMODE
0x20	IRQSELC	Issues CLRROM, branches to SETIRQ
0x28	STRTSELC	Issues CLRROM, branches to STRTCLK
0x30	STOPSELC	Issues CLRROM, branches to STOPCLK
0x38	INITCLK	Saves registers, branches to HNDLINIT
0x3F	LOADCLK	Saves registers, branches to HNDLLOAD
0x46	READCLK	Saves registers, branches to HNDLREAD
0x4D	SETMODE	Saves registers, branches to HNDLMODE
0x54	SETIRQ	Saves registers, branches to HNDLIRQ
0x5B	STRTCLK	Saves registers, branches to HNDLSTRT
0x62	STOPCLK	Saves registers, branches to HNDLSTOP
0x69	WRITCLK	Issues CLRROM, branches to HNDLWRIT
0x71	SETRTN	Issues CLRROM, branches to HNDLRTN
0x79	IRQHNDLR	Issues CLRROM, branches to EXECIRQ
0x80	EXIT	Restores registers, issues CLRROM, returns to caller
0x8A	HNDLINIT	Gets slot, processes input command
0x93	HNDLLOAD	Gets slot, writes clock buffer at 0x2F0-0x2FC to clock
0x9C	HNDLREAD	Gets slot, reads clock to clock buffer at 0x2F0-0x2FC
0xA5	HNDLMODE	Gets slot, stores mode value 0x21-0x3E to MODE, 0x478
0xAE	HNDLIRQ	Gets slot, sets IRQ 0-7, clears IRQBUF, 0x2FD-0x2FF
0xB7	HNDLSTRT	Gets slot, updates clock config, puts SETRTN address in KSWL
0xC0	HNDLSTOP	Gets slot, stops clock, puts SETRTN address in KSWL
0xC9	HNDLWRIT	Saves registers, gets slot, stop CLK, write CLK register, start CLK
0xD7	HNDLRTN	Saves registers, gets slot, puts "RTN" at 0x200-0x201
0xE5	EXECIRQ	Saves registers, gets slot, updates IRQBUF, restores registers, issues CLRROM, returns with RTI instruction
0xFA	VERSION	upper ASCII "45"
0xFC	CLKNAME	upper ASCII "RTC"
0xFF	CLKID	0x03

Table V.18.6. Clock Firmware Entry Points

The *Set Clock* program first issues the SEI instruction to the 6502-microprocessor in order to inhibit all interrupts. During its initialization, it copies the address found at MASKIRQ to a safe location and then sets MASKIRQ to the address of the interrupt handler in *Set Clock*. *Set Clock* then sets the clock card configuration register to 0b10000001 in order to enable interrupts and to specifically enable the IRQ interrupt. See Section IV.17 for a thorough discussion on using MASKIRQ. Once the initialization routine issues the CLI instruction to the 6502-microprocessor, the interrupt handler in *Set Clock* is able to field all incoming IRQ interrupts while the user is setting the data registers in the RTC58321 with various values for the current date and time. When the interrupt handler is invoked, it first issues the

`CLD` instruction to the 6502-microprocessor, pushes the X- and Y-registers onto the stack, clears the `IRQ` interrupt on the *Real Time Clock* card, reads the *Real Time Clock* card date and time registers, displays the date and time data the handler just obtained, restores the X- and Y-registers from the stack, restores the A-register from the page-zero location `0x45`, and issues the `RTI` instruction to the 6502-microprocessor. It is amazing to me how simple it is to utilize interrupts in this assembly language program. Of course, the well-thought-out hardware design of the *Real Time Clock* card makes utilizing interrupts on the Apple][computer so easy and so much fun!

19. JFD Parallel Printer Buffer

When I saw the advertisement in one of my 1985 Apple magazines for the JFD Parallel Printer Buffer, I just had to have one. As I recall there were two, perhaps more Buffer configurations. One could choose a configuration having a single set of parallel input/output ports, two sets of parallel input/output ports, or perhaps a combination of these two configurations. Always budget minded I chose the Buffer with one set of parallel input/output ports. If I had more than one computer or more than one printer I may have chosen differently.

I spent so much time waiting for my computer and my printer to print hundreds of pages of code that I was more than ready to put this Buffer to work. This Buffer would allow me to work on the computer while the Buffer is supplying data to the printer, especially data from large graphic files. The Buffer comes with 256 KB of dynamic RAM, and once an ASCII listing or a page of graphics is printed, the Buffer provides a Copy pushbutton to select the number of additional copies (up to 255) to print if they are desired.

The Buffer connects to the Grappler+ Printer Interface peripheral slot card (inside of the computer) and to my Epson MX100 printer by means of parallel interface flat-ribbon cables. A large wall transformer powers the Buffer supplying it with nine volts DC. Besides the Copy pushbutton there is a Reset pushbutton. The Reset pushbutton causes the Buffer software to initialize. This initialization forces the input data of the next print job to be stored at the beginning of Buffer memory. This feature is useful particularly if I need multiple copies of only that print listing. Otherwise, if I use the Copy pushbutton after printing multiple items, the Buffer would print everything in its memory again.

The manual that comes with the Buffer did not discuss what happens when input data overflows memory. I had already seen some bizarre behavior like not printing some paragraphs when I use the Buffer to print many listings, especially when I forgot to press the Reset pushbutton prior to printing the next print job. Momentarily pressing the Copy pushbutton puts the Buffer into Pause Mode such that the Buffer can still accept input data; it just does not send any further data to the printer. Momentarily pressing the Copy pushbutton a second time takes the Buffer out of Pause Mode and data is again output to the printer. I took advantage of Pause Mode and sent a known, and very large amount of data to the Buffer. Then I took the Buffer out of Pause Mode and sent another known, and very large amount of data to the Buffer. When Buffer memory was filled it appeared to me that the Buffer was accepting 256-byte chunks of data after it printed approximately 256 bytes of data, but for only a certain period of time. Then the Buffer started to drop chunks of data, perhaps 256 bytes in size, but I wasn't absolutely sure. I could force this bizarre behavior every time I forced the Buffer memory to overflow. It appeared to me that the firmware contained some sort of software bug. I saw a challenge waiting for me.

I opened the Buffer and found a voltage regulator, an 8035-microprocessor, a 2716 EPROM, eight 1257-15 NMOS dynamic RAM chips, and an assortment of eight-bit latches and logic chips. There is a PCB location for an additional input parallel connector and a location for an additional output parallel connector. The Ready LED is inconveniently located on the rear apron of the Buffer. I moved this LED to the front apron since there is only one input parallel connector and plenty of blank space next to it. Ideally, I would have liked to have moved that input parallel connector to the rear apron alongside the output parallel connector. I worked at Hughes Aircraft at that time, so I had access to virtually any data book available, and I was able to obtain data sheets on the microprocessor and the RAM chips.

Being able to source and compile the MCS-8048 Instruction Set was certainly going to be a challenge, but I had already had some experience doing something similar for an external keyboard that used a 6802 microprocessor on its interface board. My technique is to set up a series of equates within *Lisa*, one equate for each MCS-8048 instruction. I have to keep in mind which instructions require additional parameters. Actual coding within *Lisa* only requires the BYT directive followed by an MCS-8048 instruction equate, and then followed by any required parameter when it is needed. I put a comment on each line documenting what the BYT directive and the instruction equate are actually doing. The next step is to reverse engineer the software contained in the EPROM located on the Buffer PCB.

Obtaining the data that is contained in the 2716 Buffer EPROM is easy using the PROmGRAMER. Sourcing that data is also easy because I wrote an Applesoft program that translated the MCS-8048 instructions into a Text file that uses the BYT directive that *Lisa* can easily EXEC into its memory. Analyzing that sourced code takes the most time and effort because I have to fully understand the architecture of the 8035-microprocessor, the operation of the 1257-15 dynamic RAM for data access and refresh requirements, and the hardware function of all of the eight-bit latches and supporting logic chips. The Grappler+ and the Epson printer also have handshake and data acknowledgement requirements as well. Slowly, I plowed my way through the code finding all the necessary logic that performs RAM refresh, access to RAM data, read Input data and write Output data, as well as logic that performs data initialization, printing diagnostic status information, reading the Reset and Copy pushbuttons, and LED ON/OFF control.

Unfortunately, I could not locate an error in the software logic that would cause the bizarre behavior that I could manufacture. I did locate the general logic where the Buffer would wait for a free page (256 bytes) of memory whenever the write pointer address approaches the read pointer address. I thought dropping or skipping a page of memory was occurring somewhere in this area of logic when the data pointers are near the end of memory or they are close to each other somewhere past the end of memory, but I could not find any strange logic or instructions. I'm sure it is some silly addition error, probably involving the Carry flag, or maybe when the pointers transition from the 0x3FFxx page to the 0x000xx page in order to access the continuum of data in the 256 KB buffer as the data overflows and wraps around memory.

I decided to scrape the original code and write my own version of this firmware. Of course, I had to borrow some of the original logic in order to access and refresh RAM, but I thought I could do a better job at controlling the data pointers and handling the memory overflow situation. I set up hardware on a breadboard to emulate a 2716 EPROM so that I could compile and test my new software strategies without having to program, or burn an actual EPROM. This hardware setup made it extremely easy to develop MCS-8048 software for the 8035-microprocessor. In May, 1989, I was successful in developing new firmware for this Buffer that did **not** fail any of my previous Buffer overflow tests. This new firmware also behaved exactly like the original firmware for the Pause Mode and for the Copy function. The Reset function also behaved exactly like in the original firmware. I programmed a 2716 EPROM, installed it, and used the Buffer with this firmware configuration thereafter.

I performed timing tests and documented the results for the original firmware and for my new Buffer firmware. I had calculated the time it **should** take the firmware to test all 256 KB of RAM with a minimum of a write followed by a read and a compare. The initialization routine for the original firmware did not take nearly the required amount of time that I thought it should have. My initialization routine took precisely the amount of time to complete in the time that I had predicted. I also timed how long each firmware version took to fill memory with the Pause Mode enabled and disabled. With Pause Mode enabled the original firmware took about 2.5 times longer to fill memory, that is, 2.91 KB/sec versus 7.28 KB/sec for my firmware. With the Pause Mode disabled the results were 2.91 KB/sec versus 6.90 KB/sec for my firmware. I sent a letter to JFD explaining what I had observed when memory overflow occurs, my timing test predictions and results, and a printed copy of my new Buffer firmware. I did not receive even an acknowledgement to my letter from JFD. I was terribly hurt and thoroughly disappointed. Whatever.

Recently, I took some time to look over and review the Buffer firmware I had designed back in 1989. I have had a lot of time over the last forty years to increase my knowledge and to mature my programming skills vis-à-vis hardware architecture. I noticed that I had used the built-in 8035-microprocessor Interval Timer as the Timer was used in the original Buffer firmware for timing events such as pushbutton debounce. I immediately thought, what a waste of a perfectly good Interval Timer! To waste an Interval Timer in order to time pushbutton debounce was idiocy. What became especially clear to me was how to use the Interval Timer in order to provide the basic timing interval for dynamic RAM refresh without having to guess and to hope that the RAM refresh routine was called often enough. In my version of the firmware, like that in the original JFD firmware, the MAIN loop calls the REFRESH routine, the CHECKT0 routine, and, if the printer is ready to accept another data character, the SENDMEM routine in that order in an infinite loop. The CHECKT0 routine checks if the Copy pushbutton is being pressed, and if so, the routine would flash the LED ON and OFF at a 0.5 Hz rate in order to set the number of desired copies. CHECKT0 can take huge amounts of time away from the REFRESH routine which left me pondering why memory never became corrupted. Or, did it? The REFRESH routine is totally ignored during any CHECKT0 processing no matter how long it occurs. I wondered if this logic design contributed to the actual cause of the bizarre behavior I had observed so many years ago? Or, did this Buffer RAM have built-in refresh capabilities? I didn't think so.

Byte Offset	Size	Name	Description
0x00	8 bytes	SELRB0	Primary registers, Bank 0
0x08	16 bytes	PSW	12-bit program counter and 4-bit status bits (PSW) in an 8 level stack
0x18	8 bytes	SELRB1	Secondary register, Bank 1
0x20	32 bytes	USERRAM	User RAM for indexed word locations

Table V.19.1. 8035-Microprocessor Memory Map

I have heavily documented the Printer Buffer source code as I developed the routines that utilize the Interval Timer for the timing of **all** functions. The MCS-48 8035-microprocessor utilizes sixty-four bytes of internal memory for its complete operation. The configuration of this memory is shown in Table V.19.1. There are two banks of eight 8-bit registers, an eight level stack for subroutine return addresses and status bits, and thirty-two bytes of indexed User RAM. When designing software for this microprocessor, one must be mindful that the stack only provides eight levels of subroutine return addresses. And, it is this indexed User RAM that is only slightly clumsy to access. My Buffer firmware does use four bytes in the indexed user RAM. The definition of User Flag 1, or F1, is shown in Table V.19.2. F1 is not part of the Program Status Word, or PSW. Table V.19.3 shows Port 1 and Port 2 utilization, that is, how each of the bits are used for both of these ports.

Bit	Name	Description
0	S0	Bit 0 of stack pointer
1	S1	Bit 1 of stack pointer
2	S2	Bit 2 of stack pointer
3	–	not used, set to 1
4	BS	Register bank select
5	F0	User flag 0
6	AC	Auxiliary carry flag
7	CY	Carry flag

Table V.19.2. User Flag 1 F1

Port:Bit	Name	Description
1:0	n/a	not used, set to 1
1:1	PDATENBL	Processor data enable, 1=disable
1:2	OLATENBL	Outport latch enable, 1=disable
1:3	n/a	not used, set to 1
1:4	ODATRDY	Outport data ready, 1=ready
1:5	n/a	not used, set to 1
1:6	n/a	not used, set to 1
1:7	PMEMENBL	PPB memory enable, 1=disable
2:0	ADR08ON	Address bit ADR08, 1=ON
2:1	LED1TGL	Test LED 1, 1=ON
2:2	LED2TGL	Test LED 2, 1=ON
2:3	RDLEDON	Ready LED, 1=ON
2:4	IDATENBL	In port data strobe, 1=disable
2:5	n/a	not used, set to 1
2:6	n/a	not used, set to 1
2:7	OCTLENBL	Octal latch enable, 1=disable

Table V.19.3. Port Utilization

The utilization of `SELRB0` is shown in Table V.19.4 and the utilization of `SELRB1` is shown in Table V.19.5. The R/W Block Number Bits in Primary Register `R3` is shown in Table V.19.6. The System Flag Bits in Secondary Register `R3` are shown in Table V.19.7.

Register	Description
R0	Input/output working
R1	`EXTIRQ` reg-A save
R2	Temporary data byte
R3	R/W block number for address bits `0x08` and `0x11`
R4	Address bits `0x00-0x07`, read data RAS
R5	Address bits `0x09-0x10`, read data CAS
R6	Address bits `0x00-0x07`, write data RAS
R7	Address bits `0x09-0x10`, write data CAS

Table V.19.4. SELRB0 Utilization

Register	Description
R0	Input/output working
R1	`REFRESH` reg-A save
R2	Temporary data byte
R3	System flag bits
R4	Copy number
R5	Refresh counter, LSB
R6	Timer counter, LSB
R7	Timer Counter, MSB

Table V.19.5. SELRB1 Utilization

Bit	Description
0	Read block number LSB
1	Read block number MSB
2	`zero`
3	`zero`
4	Write block number LSB
5	Write block number MSB
6	`zero`
7	`zero`

Table V.19.6. Primary R3 R/W Block Number Bits

Bit	Description
0	Refresh counter, ADR08
1	zero
2	zero
3	Overflow state flag, 0=OFF
4	Message state flag, 0=OFF
5	Copy state flag, 0=OFF
6	Pause state flag, 0=OFF
7	EXTIRQ state flag, 0=OFF

Table V.19.7. Secondary R3 System Flag Bits

If I followed the 1257-15 dynamic RAM data sheet requirement to perform a RAS-only refresh every 4.0 milliseconds or less, I could easily use the Interval Timer to schedule a dynamic RAM refresh at that interval rate. The Interval Timer could also serve as the basis for all other timing requirements like pushbutton debounce and LED flash rate. Central to the 8035-microprocessor is the RESET interrupt, the EXTIRQ interrupt, and the TIMRIRQ interrupt. The Reset pushbutton is connected to the RESET Interrupt pin, the Input connector from the computer is connected to the External Interrupt pin, and the Interval Timer is connected to the Timer Interrupt pin of the 8035-microprocessor. Each of these interrupt events is handled by a unique vector to an interrupt handler routine that resides at a hard-wired offset in page-zero of EPROM memory, that is, at offsets 0x00, 0x03, and 0x07. And, there are thirty-two bytes of indexed User RAM in internal microprocessor memory that is only slightly clumsy to access, but nevertheless available for use to store program variables, vectors, pointers, and data.

The 8035-microprocessor is clocked using a 6.0 MHz external crystal. This frequency is divided by fifteen, which is internal to the microprocessor, so the cycle time (i.e. Tcy for instructions) is 2.5 microseconds. Most instructions require one cycle, and all other instructions require only two cycles. The Interval Timer prescaler divides Tcy by thirty-two so that it becomes 80 microseconds in duration. Thus, loading the timer counter with a value of 0xFF causes a TIMRIRQ interrupt in only 80 microseconds when the timer counter overflows to zero after one count. Loading the timer with a value of 0xCF causes a TIMRIRQ interrupt in 3.920 milliseconds. However, the instructions to reset the Interval Timer require eight Tcy cycles, so the total timer interval for the load value of 0xCF is actually 3.940 milliseconds. This time is certainly within the specifications to refresh the 1257-15 dynamic RAM chips.

Part of the Interval Timer handler routine is to increment a 2-byte counter. Whatever value is pre-loaded into this counter is incremented every 3.94 milliseconds. Naturally, a number representing the negative of a value would be ideal to use in this application such that when the most significant byte becomes zero, the desired time is reached. For example, if a 63-millisecond debounce time is desired, then -16 must be pre-loaded into the 2-byte counter, or 0xFFF0. Also, an approximate 1.0 second wait period time can be achieved by loading 0xFF00 into the 2-byte counter; that is, 3.940 milliseconds * 255 = 1.0047 seconds.

Using the Interval Timer as the primary method to refresh the dynamic RAM of the Buffer changed the code only in the MAIN routine. Now, MAIN simply calls the CHECKT0 routine and the SENDMEM routine if the printer is ready to accept another data character, in an infinite loop. The CHECKT0 can take all the time it requires in order to count the number of LED flashes representing the desired number of copies. I added another bit-flag to the System Flag byte called the Overflow State Flag. If the write memory pointer should ever reach `0x00000` and overflow memory, the Overflow State Flag is turned ON. The Buffer software will bypass the copy counting logic in the `CHECKT0` routine and, as a protection, not allow whatever there is currently in memory to be sent to the printer as another copy if the Overflow State Flag is ON. Of course, pressing the Reset pushbutton resets all of the State Flag bits including the Overflow State Flag bit, and it re-enables the ability of the Buffer to make copies of whatever there will be in memory again. If copies is selected using the Copy pushbutton immediately after pressing the Reset pushbutton, nothing is printed as expected. I programmed a 2716 EPROM with this version of the firmware, installed it, and this is the firmware I have been using in the Buffer. Again, I have seen no further bizarre behavior even when the Buffer memory has reached memory overflow.

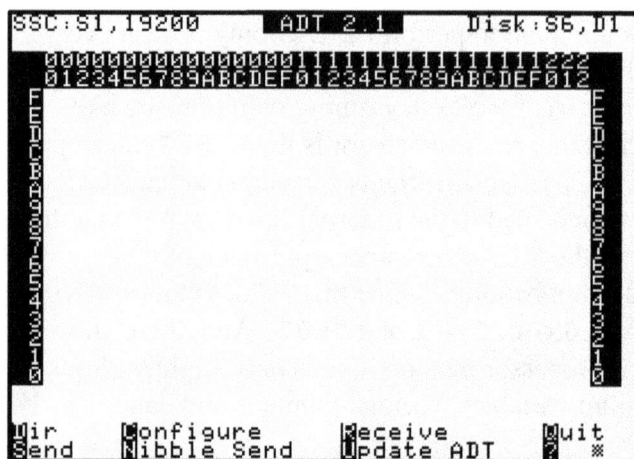

Figure V.20.1. ADT Window

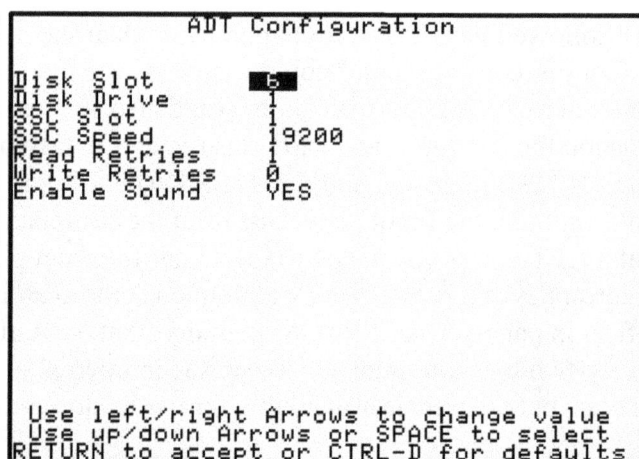

Figure V.20.2. ADT Configuration

20. Asynchronous Data Transfer (ADT)

I have developed a serious amount of software development for the Apple][computer using a MacBook Pro running the Virtual][emulation program by Gerard Putter. Virtual][can launch a utility called *A2V2* that is designed to transfer the image of a 140 KB volume to and from a real Apple][computer that is concurrently running a program called Asynchronous Data Transfer, or *ADT* by Paul Guertin. *ADT* was further enhanced by Gerard Putter. My Apple //e uses a Super Serial peripheral slot card connected to a Keyspan serial to USB adapter using a serial cable. The Keyspan is connected to the MacBook Pro using a USB cable. Only a 140 KB volume image is currently allowed to be transferred. Because the RAM Disk 320 supports up to forty tracks for its volumes and I typically utilize the RAM Disk to receive disk images, I would like to see the 140 KB restriction removed from *A2V2* and from *ADT*. I would even like to have Virtual][support up to forty-eight track diskettes, too, but Mr. Putter has already rejected that request.

I did source *ADT* so that I could add an `Update ADT` command to its command repertoire as shown in Figure V.20.1. After configuring *ADT*, `Update ADT` saves the *ADT* program with its new configuration set as its new default when *ADT* is launched again in the future. The *ADT* Configuration screen is shown in Figure V.20.2, which uses lowercase characters to assist in making the Apple screen text far easier for me to read in my opinion. If and when 160 KB and 200 KB volume images are supported, I will be ready. But let's not stop there! My RanaSystems EliteThree drive can support volumes having forty tracks where each track contains thirty-two sectors, so 320 KB volume images are possible, too. In order to process 320 KB volume images, *ADT* may need to utilize an 80-column display. Finally, a CFFA volume can support up to forty-eight 32-sector tracks that would require a 400 KB volume image. Now, that would be a seriously fun project to utilize an 80-colum display in order to show the image transfer of volumes having up to forty-eight tracks where each track can support either sixteen or thirty-two sectors. The `?` command shown in Figure V.20.1 displays credits to Paul Guertin, Gerard Putter, and myself for adding enhancements to *ADT*. These credits are displayed at the bottom of the screen in place of the *ADT* command repertoire as shown in Figure V.20.3.

Both the `Send` and the `Receive` *ADT* commands require a file name as shown in Figure V.20.4. The file name is for a file that is found in the `~/Documents/Virtual ][/`*A2V2* directory on the MacBook Pro computer. For example, if the hard drive is named `MacOS 10.12.6` for the MacBook Pro computer and the Username is `mozart`, the diacritical mark tilde used in the above pathname would be replaced such that now the fully qualified pathname would be as follows:

`MacOS 10.12.6/Users/mozart/Documents/Virtual ][/`*A2V2*

However, there is a far easier way to specify the volume that is currently in focus within Virtual][rather than a filename for a 140 KB volume image. As shown in Figure V.20.4, entering the @ symbol tells *A2V2* to process and send or receive the contents of the current volume that is in focus within Virtual][. This happens to be the exact procedure I have always used for *A2V2* and *ADT* communication.

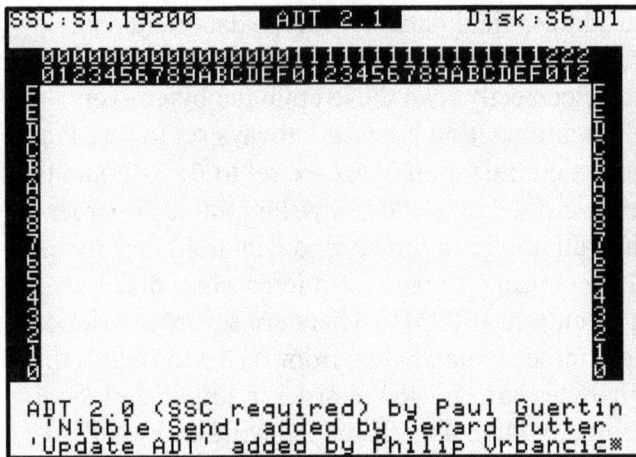

Figure V.20.3. ADT Software Credits

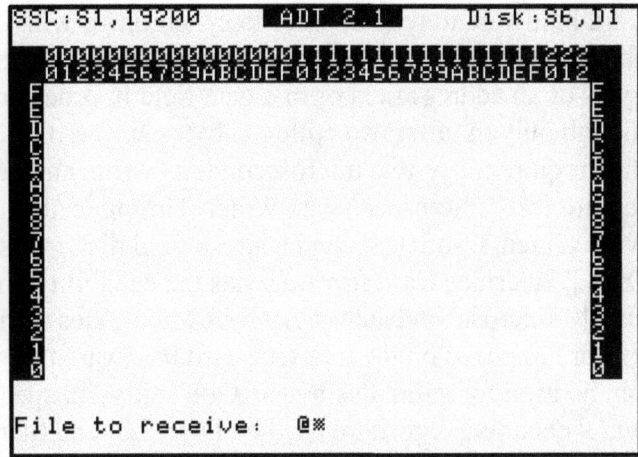

Figure V.20.4. ADT Receive File Name Entry

21. TrackScan

I found that the process of developing an algorithm to control the movement of the read/write disk head in a Disk][drive using half-phase increments to be extremely exciting, if not down-right challenging. There are so many physical parameters to consider while designing such an algorithm. In order to verify whether an algorithm is even working or coming close to providing the desired results, good tools are absolutely essential. Visual inspection that the Cam Table is being controlled appropriately is also invaluable information. As shown in Figures I.10.2 and I.10.3 I used a very fine liquid-ink pen to mark where the Cam Rider stopped along the Cam Channel as I positioned the read/write disk head over tracks `0x00`, `0x01`, `0x02`, and `0x03` before I started testing various half-phase-stepping algorithms. I already knew that tracks on a Master DOS diskette were separated by four half-phases, so those ink marks indicated where the first four tracks were located that have a separation of four half-phases along the Cam Channel. I also noticed that track `0x00` was not precisely at the Cam Stop, but very, very close to the Cam Stop. That indicated to me that Electromagnet `0` must be held in the `ON` state to ensure that Phase `0` coincides precisely with track `0x00`. No matter how many half-phases the Cam Table is turned in order to return the read/write disk head once again to track `0x00`, Electromagnet `0` is the last electromagnet to be de-energized and track `0x00` always coincides with Phase `0`.

During the development of DOS 4.1, I spent a considerable amount of time and energy mapping the processing steps of `RWTS`. I needed to include additional logic processing at the entry point of `RWTS` in order to obtain the correct Disk Address Table entry for the disk peripheral interface card based on the specified slot number that is used to index into the Disk Address Table. If a non-Disk][disk peripheral interface card handler is ever entered into the Disk Address Table, I have to include provisions to ensure that its peripheral-card expansion ROM memory is fully detached after its `RWTS` processing. After determining an even better set of processing steps for `RWTS` in DOS 4.5, I attacked the disk formatting routine again with gusto. I was already well acquainted with the read and write address field routines as well as the read and write data field routines. I also knew the lead-in and lead-out requirements for those fields so that the disk peripheral interface card firmware could always synchronize with the data about to be read. It is critical that the write address field and write data field routines incorporate these additional requirements in their processing.

A minimum of **five** 40-microsecond auto-synchronization bytes are necessary for the Disk][Interface Card hardware to read in order to synchronize with the address field data or with the data field data about to be read. At least one 32-microsecond synchronization byte must follow the final three epilogue bytes of an address field or of a data field in order to have correctly read those epilogue bytes even though only the first two epilogue bytes are verified. Synchronization bytes are always set to `0xFF` and they require thirty-two microseconds to write, and auto-synchronization bytes are set to `0x3FF` and they require forty microseconds to write. Timing is absolutely critical in the `RWTS` write routines in order to write all ten 32-microsecond address field disk bytes and all 350 32-microsecond data field disk bytes. Disk][Interface Card firmware has the capability and the capacity to read 32-microsecond disk bytes and 40-microsecond auto-synchronization bytes using its current PROMs. There are severe restrictions that are imposed on the interface card hardware that determines which bytes, from `0x80` to `0xFF`, that can be used for valid disk bytes. Only sixty-six specific bytes can be used in order to implement the *6 and 2* encoding algorithm used by DOS 3.3, and therefore, by DOS 4.5. Thus, the write address field routine and the write data field routine can only write 32-microsecond disk bytes from the *6 and 2* Write Translate Table and 40-microsecond auto-synchronization bytes having the form of `0x3FF`.

The copy protection algorithm used on many of the software products from Sierra On-Line such as *ScreenWriter* can only be implemented by using specialized diskette duplicating hardware. Even though Sierra On-Line owned the Form Master duplicating hardware, Sierra On-Line had to create the Form Master software that utilizes the duplicating capabilities of the machine in order to implement all of the features of the Apple][disk format and any other specific byte patterns and features that only this hardware could create. Sierra On-Line hired Mark Duchaineau to write this particular software, but his copy-protection scheme required the end user of this software to utilize a well maintained disk drive that is adjusted to always operate at the factory specified disk rotational speed. Any deviation from that factory specified rotational speed caused major problems for the copy protection scheme that was also designed by Duchaineau. The rendering algorithm as it is implemented within *ScreenWriter* that Duchaineau developed, stops reading disk data for a specific period of time and then reads the next available disk byte. That raw disk byte has to be a unique value for the rendering algorithm to accept and pass the diskette as a valid product produced by the Form Master. If the Sierra On-Line diskette is copied, even by *Locksmith*, the special region that the rendering algorithm skips reading cannot be precisely duplicated because the Form Master writes a series of invalid disk bytes that the Disk][Interface Card PROMs cannot physically read. That is, the Form Master manufactures specific disk bytes that it can write, but these bytes cannot be read by the Disk][because these bytes do not reside in the *6 and 2* Write Translate Table. Once I became acquainted with Duchaineau's rendering algorithm, I could easily spot its presence simply by viewing the sectors of any copy protected Sierra On-Line diskette using *Disk Window*. And, I could use *Disk Window* to *adjust*, that is, modify the rendering algorithm code on the diskette so that it would *pass* any value read for that special raw disk byte when the rendering algorithm starts reading disk bytes again.

A year or so later while I was self-employed and assigned to a Sierra On-Line project, I was challenged by the remaining software programmers who had not yet been laid off from Sierra On-Line with an assigned task. That challenge was to break the copy protection of a new product Sierra On-Line had recently received for its evaluation. Armed with my personal arsenal of disk tools and utilities, most of which I had authored, I rendered the new product free of copy protection within ninety-five seconds. To be sure, the copy protection scheme used by this new product revealed itself early in my investigation and I was able to defeat its implementation by using NOP and CLC instructions strategically placed. Of course, *Disk Window* made the task of rendering this new product free of copy protection in short order. There are hundreds of stories about other people who were very much like Mark Duchaineau, how his achievements became interwoven in the fascinating history of the personal computer, and how those achievements fueled the computer revolution. I happened to be working for Sierra On-Line as an employee when Steven Levy came to Sierra On-Line in order to research a few primary subjects for his future book *hackers*. Ken Williams was but one of many hundreds of subjects Mr. Levy found interesting and compelling to include in *hackers*. I have to admit that it is a fascinating book to read.

When I was analyzing the volume formatting routines in RWTS, I started to develop software tools that could read and store the raw disk bytes into memory for an entire track. I knew that a sector requires 359 (i.e. 10 + 349) 32-microsecond bytes for the address field, data field, and the prologue and epilogue bytes for those fields, and a bare minimum of ten 40-microsecond auto-synchronization bytes in total. However, the routine WRITADR writes SYNCNT auto-synchronization bytes before an address field and the routine WRITSCTR writes **six** auto-synchronization bytes before a data field. A track comprised of sixteen sectors would require 5744 32-microsecond bytes and 96 40-microsecond auto-synchronization bytes. The Disk][Interface Card firmware would take a minimum of 187,648 (i.e. 5744 * 32 + 96 * 40) microseconds to read all of those disk bytes. A diskette spinning at 300 revolutions per minute would make five revolutions per second, or take 200,000 microseconds to make one revolution. This would leave 12,352 microseconds available for all of the auto-synchronization bytes before the address field of each sector on a track assuming perfect speed control of the Disk][hardware.

The DISKFMT routine initializes SYNCNT to thirty-two, the number of auto-synchronization bytes that are written before an address field. Before the TRACKFMT routine begins writing the address field for sector 0x00 on track 0x00, it writes 128 auto-synchronization bytes. Before each address field for the sectors that follow sector 0x00, the TRACKFMT routine writes SYNCNT auto-synchronization bytes. The TRACKFMT routine then analyzes the track it just wrote to determine if it can read the address field

291

for sector 0x00. Obviously, an initial 608 (128 + 32 * 15) auto-synchronization bytes are about 325 auto-synchronization bytes too many, but this exercise provides a good start to determine the optimal value for SYNCNT. TRACKFMT then reduces SYNCNT and tries to format track 0x00 again. As soon as TRACKFMT can discover the address field for sector 0x00, TRACKFMT reduces SYNCNT a final time and uses that stored value for the number of auto-synchronization bytes it writes before the address field of all sectors on all tracks other than sector 0x00 on every track because TRACKFMT always begins the format of a track with 128 auto-synchronization bytes. Typically, the epilogue bytes that are written after the data field for the last sector, or sector 0x0F, are written somewhere within those initial 128 auto-synchronization bytes. In order to verify that TRACKFMT, as I designed it, performs its function correctly and as intended, I wrote a utility that reads and stores the raw disk data into memory for an entire track, and the utility analyzes that data so that the track properties can be properly displayed. That utility is *TrackScan*, and its Main Menu is shown in Figure V.21.1. I developed *TrackScan* using the *VMGR* program as its structural model. However, instead of specifying VOLUME as in *VMGR*, *TrackScan* uses PHASE in order to format a diskette using that parameter before *TrackScan* displays the properties of any selected track or track range. *TrackScan* can format a diskette with 35, 36, 40, or 48 tracks which is selected by the user as shown in Figure V.21.2.

TrackScan can scan and process any track on any volume, and *TrackScan* does not have to format a volume before it scans that volume. After *TrackScan* has scanned a selected track, it analyzes the raw track data after it locates the address field for sector 0x00 and verifies that it can locate the next instance of the address field for sector 0x00. *TrackScan* uses a total of eight processing steps in order to analyze the raw track data for each sector. It decodes the address field data and it displays that information first along with the number of synchronization bytes that come prior to the address field and the number of data bytes that comprise the address field. Recall that a synchronization byte is 0xFF in value and that it takes thirty-two microseconds to write that byte. It is not possible to distinguish synchronization bytes and auto-synchronization bytes except indirectly. *TrackScan* processing continues by locating the data field that follows the address field, and *TrackScan* analyzes its data structure and content. The number of synchronization bytes prior to the data field, the number of data bytes that comprise the data field, and the error status are displayed next for that sector. The error status shows the number of successful processing steps *TrackScan* completed during its analysis of that sector and a final error value for that processing step or zero for no errors. *TrackScan* continues its processing for each of the sectors contained in the raw track data.

```
     Apple ][ Track Scan
     DOS 4.5.05H 01/01/21

        Option Menu

  1 - Set Slot/Drive/Phase (6/01/04)
  2 - Set Track Start/End (00/00)
  3 - Scan Tracks
  4 - Format Volume (35 tracks)
  5 - Quit



Select Option:
```

```
     Apple ][ Track Scan
     DOS 4.5.05H 01/01/21

        Option Menu

  1 - Set Slot/Drive/Phase (6/02/04)
  2 - Set Track Start/End (00/00)
  3 - Scan Tracks
  4 - Format Volume (35 tracks)
  5 - Quit



Enter LAST Track (35/36/40/48):   35█
```

Figure V.21.1. TrackScan Main Menu   Figure V.21.2. TrackScan Format Volume

TrackScan displays the final value it determines for SYNCNT when *TrackScan* is used to format a volume as shown in Figure V.21.3. SYNCNT is used for the number of auto-synchronization bytes written prior to the address field for a sector after track 0x00 has been successfully formatted. HDRSYNC, or six auto-synchronization bytes are always written prior to the data field for a sector. Figure V.21.4 shows that *TrackScan* is prepared to scan tracks 0x00 to 0x22. The results of the scan for track 0x00 is shown in Figure V.21.5 and the results of the scan for track 0x11 is shown in Figure V.21.6. These scans were obtained from scanning a volume that was formatted by *TrackScan* with thirty-five tracks and a PHASE of four as previously shown in Figure V.21.2. *TrackScan* reported obtaining a value of 0x13 for SYNCNT in Figure V.21.3. This information and the data shown in Figures V.21.5 and V.21.6 can be used to determine if the actual number of auto-synchronization bytes written can be verified indirectly. Once the disk data latch has been loaded with a synchronization byte, data one's are clocked out by the interface card firmware to be recorded onto a volume.

```
         Apple ][ Track Scan
         DOS 4.5.05H 01/01/21

            Option Menu

  1 - Set Slot/Drive/Phase (6/02/04)

  2 - Set Track Start/End (00/00)

  3 - Scan Tracks

  4 - Format Volume (35 tracks)

  5 - Quit
                        SYNCNT=0x13
                        RETRYCNT=0x20
Return code from Format:  0x00.
```

Figure V.21.3. TrackScan Format Results

```
         Apple ][ Track Scan
         DOS 4.5.05H 01/01/21

            Option Menu

  1 - Set Slot/Drive/Phase (6/02/04)

  2 - Set Track Start/End (00/34)

  3 - Scan Tracks

  4 - Format Volume (35 tracks)

  5 - Quit


Select Option:  3
```

Figure V.21.4. TrackScan Scan Tracks

```
              Apple ][ Track Scan

Vol  Trk  Sec  Gap  Hdr  Gap  Data  Err
---  ---  ---  ---  ---  ---  ----  ---
000   00   00  068   4   10   343   8-0
000   00   01  024   4   10   343   8-0
000   00   02  024   4   10   343   8-0
000   00   03  024   4   10   343   8-0
000   00   04  024   4   10   343   8-0
000   00   05  024   4   10   343   8-0
000   00   06  024   4   10   343   8-0
000   00   07  024   4   10   343   8-0
000   00   08  024   4   10   343   8-0
000   00   09  024   4   10   343   8-0
000   00   10  024   4   10   343   8-0
000   00   11  024   4   10   343   8-0
000   00   12  024   4   10   343   8-0
000   00   13  024   4   10   343   8-0
000   00   14  024   4   10   343   8-0
000   00   15  024   4   10   343   8-0
Avg Header Gap = 24,  Remainder = 00/15
```

Figure V.21.5. TrackScan for Track 0x00

```
              Apple ][ Track Scan

Vol  Trk  Sec  Gap  Hdr  Gap  Data  Err
---  ---  ---  ---  ---  ---  ----  ---
000   17   00  058   4   10   343   8-0
000   17   01  024   4   10   343   8-0
000   17   02  024   4   10   343   8-0
000   17   03  024   4   10   343   8-0
000   17   04  024   4   10   343   8-0
000   17   05  024   4   10   343   8-0
000   17   06  024   4   10   343   8-0
000   17   07  024   4   10   343   8-0
000   17   08  024   4   10   343   8-0
000   17   09  024   4   10   343   8-0
000   17   10  024   4   10   343   8-0
000   17   11  024   4   10   343   8-0
000   17   12  024   4   10   343   8-0
000   17   13  023   4   10   343   8-0
000   17   14  024   4   10   343   8-0
000   17   15  024   4   10   343   8-0
Avg Header Gap = 23,  Remainder = 14/15
```

Figure V.21.6. TrackScan for Track 0x17

When WRITADR finishes writing an address field, it exits via WRITEXIT and leaves a synchronization byte stored in the data latch before returning the latch configuration to read-mode. By the time WRITSCTR begins its processing and enables the data latch for write-mode again, already 92 microseconds has elapsed. After WRITSCTR has written six auto-synchronization bytes, the total time from the end of the address field to the start of the data field is given by 92 + 6*40 = 332 microseconds. Figures V.21.5 and V.21.6 show that the second Gap column of numbers was observed to be ten 32-μsec bytes. The DOS 4.5 TRACKFMT routines predict that 332 / 32 = 10.38 bytes should be observed. Assuming only minor fluctuations in drive speed, the predicted and observed results through raw track data analysis are very much in agreement for the gap size between the address field and the data field.

Previously, it was determined that 12,352 microseconds should be available for additional auto-synchronization bytes before an address field assuming perfect speed control of the diskette. The total number of synchronization bytes observed before all address fields for track 0x00 is 428 from Figure V.21.5. The total number of synchronization bytes observed before all address fields for track 0x11 is 418 from Figure V.21.6. Strategically reducing SYNCNT from 0x15 to 0x13 for all tracks ensures that sector 0x00 is found, even on the very last track of the volume. The summation of all observed synchronization bytes found through raw track data analysis before an address field for track 0x00 would be (68 + 24*15) * 32 = 13,696 microseconds. This is only 1344 microseconds more than the predicted value of 12,352 microseconds. The summation of all observed synchronization bytes found through raw track data analysis before an address field for track 0x11 would be (58 + 24*14 + 23) * 32 = 13,344 μsec. This is only 992 microseconds more than the predicted value of 12,352 microseconds.

Another way to demonstrate how closely the raw track data analysis results compare with reality is to sum all of the data results shown separately in Figures V.21.5 and V.21.6.

From raw track data analysis for track 0x00, the sum of values for all sectors would be:

$$\{ (68 + 24 * 15) + (3 + 4 + 3 + 10 + 3 + 343 + 3) * 16 \} * 32 = 202{,}624 \text{ microseconds}$$

This is only 2624 microseconds more than the time it takes to rotate the diskette once.

From raw track data analysis for track 0x11, the sum of values for all sectors would be:

$$\{ (58 + 24 * 14 + 23) + (3 + 4 + 3 + 10 + 3 + 343 + 3) * 16 \} * 32 = 202{,}272 \text{ μsec}$$

This is only 2272 microseconds more than the time it takes to rotate the diskette once.

It is obvious that *TrackScan* is a very important tool that can be used to verify the efficacy of the DOS 4.5 TRACKFMT routines. Being able to initialize a volume with precision and being able to scan and analyze each track on that volume for correctness provides the necessary insight that confirms the validity of the TRACKFMT routines that comprise this algorithm. Now that a suitable volume formatting algorithm can be certified using *TrackScan*, a new algorithm to control the movement of the read/write disk head in a Disk][drive that is any multiple of a single half-phase can be rationally developed. *TrackScan* was instrumental in developing such an algorithm for it absolutely demonstrates the ability to read, analyze, and display every sector on every track after a volume has been initialized utilizing useful values for track PHASE separation.

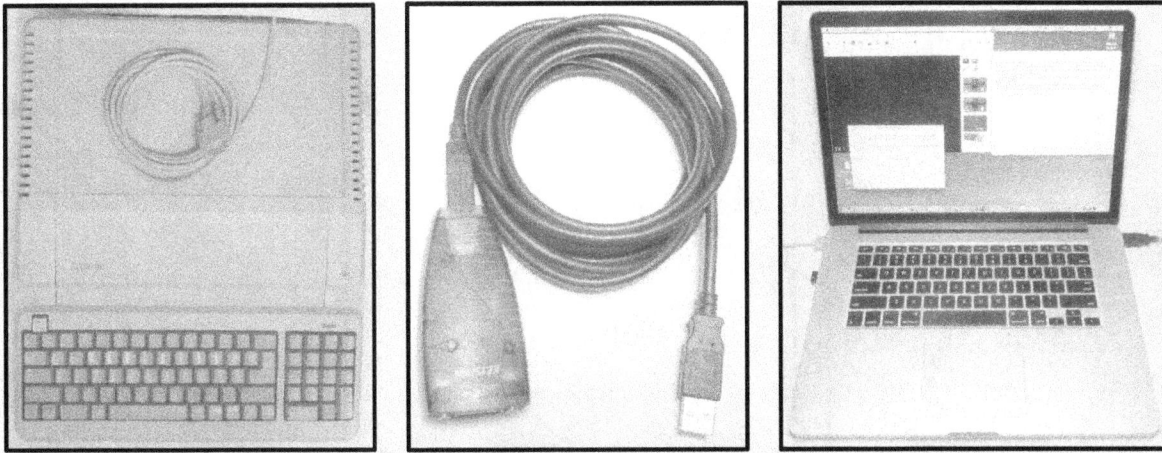

Figure V.22.1. Apple][Computer, Keyspan Adapter, MacBook Pro Computer

22. ClientServer

As my previous publications on Disk Operating Systems for the Apple][computer have substantially shown, I have certainly demonstrated that I have done a serious amount of software development for this computer. I typically develop Apple][computer software using a MacBook Pro computer running the Virtual][emulation program by Gerard Putter. Virtual][can launch a utility called *A2V2* that can transfer a 140 KB disk volume image to and from a real Apple][computer. The Apple][computer must be concurrently running a program called Asynchronous Data Transfer, or *ADT* by Paul Guertin and enhanced by Gerard Putter. My Apple //e computer uses a Super Serial peripheral slot card that is connected to a Keyspan serial to USB adapter using a serial cable. The USB port of the Keyspan adapter is connected to my MacBook Pro computer using a USB cable. These three components are shown in Figure V.22.1.

About a year after Apple introduced the Disk][floppy disk drive, probably around 1979, the Disk][Cam Table and supporting hardware were slightly modified in order to access thirty-six tracks rather than thirty-five tracks. For one reason or another this information never found its way into the Apple user community. Regardless, *ADT* only supports volumes having thirty-five tracks, so it only allows 140 KB volume images to be transferred to and from an Apple][computer and a MacBook Pro computer, or other similar personal computer device. Certainly, there are advantages in using a program like *A2V2* on the MacBook Pro:

1. *A2V2* does not depend on the Virtual][emulation of the Apple][computer
2. *A2V2* has full access to the MacBook Pro file system
3. *A2V2* allows the user to archive `~.dsk` images of diskettes in the MacBook Pro file system

On the other hand there are a few disadvantages in using *A2V2*:

1. *A2V2* only supports 35-track volumes
2. *A2V2* requires a USB to serial communication adapter (i.e. the Keyspan adapter)
3. There is no Keyspan driver available for an operating system beyond MacOS 10.12.6

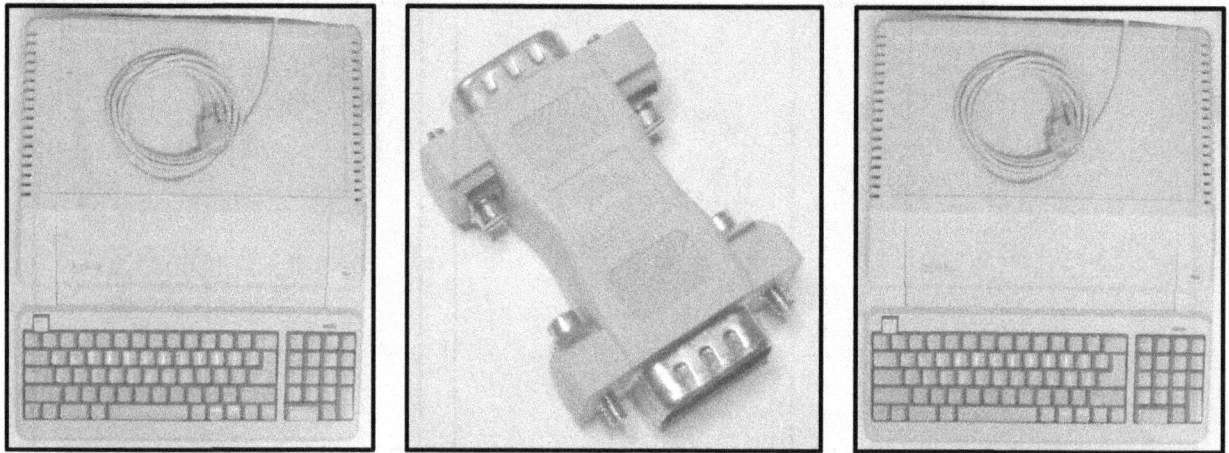

Figure V.22.2. Apple][Computer, Null Modem Adapter, Apple][Computer

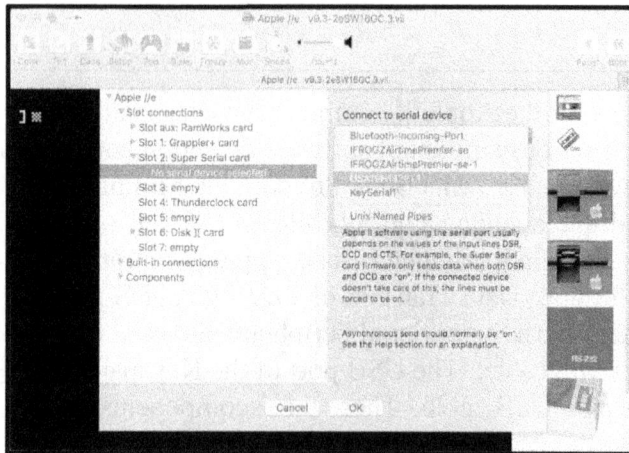

Figure V.22.3. Selecting the USA19H142P1.1

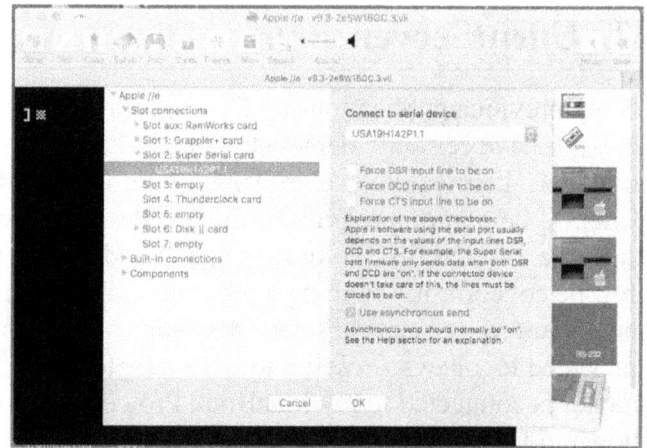

Figure V.22.4. Keyspan Connection Complete

In order for two Apple][computers to communicate with each other, a Super Serial peripheral slot card (or equivalent RS232 communication serial card) must reside in each Apple][computer and their external serial cables must be connected using a Null Modem adapter like the DB9 male to male adapter. These three components are shown in Figure V.22.2. The DB9 adapter may be obtained for around $1.58 from www.sfcable.com, for example. Figure V.22.3 shows how to connect the Keyspan driver USA19H142P1.1 to the Super Serial card that is emulated in Virtual][. Figure V.22.4 shows that the connection of the Keyspan serial to USB adapter to Virtual][is complete.

As presented in this book, I have developed specific firmware for the RanaSystems EliteThree disk drive interface slot card, the CFFA slot card, and the Axlon RAM Disk 320 interface slot card. My Rana firmware can access forty four-half-phase spaced tracks, where each track has thirty-two sectors, sixteen sectors on the front side of the diskette and sixteen sectors on the back side of the diskette. My CFFA firmware can access up to eighty-one drives, where each drive holds 256 volumes, and each volume may contain up to forty-eight tracks, where each track may have either sixteen or thirty-two sectors. Many Disk][compatible drives became available in the early 1980's that could access up to forty four-half-phase spaced tracks, where each track has sixteen sectors. Even the Axlon 320 can access its memory which is equivalent to a volume having forty tracks, where each track has sixteen sectors. Mr. Putter even provides the capability for his Virtual][software to read and to write a ~.woz version 2 diskette that may be initialized with forty-eight three-half-phase spaced tracks, where each track has sixteen sectors. In other words, my CFFA volumes, regardless of their size in tracks, may be archived on a MacBook Pro as a ~.woz version 2 file as long as the CFFA volume contain tracks that only have sixteen sectors. Unfortunately, the *A2V2/ADT* data transfer protocol cannot be used to archive any diskette images other than 140 KB sized volumes. This somewhat limits the usefulness of the Rana, CFFA, and Axlon data storage containers in being able to archive their contents using the *A2V2/ADT* data transfer protocol onto a MacBook Pro computer.

My analysis of the *ADT* software that executes on an Apple][computer was primarily focused to incorporate changes so that lowercase characters could be utilized in all menus in order to assist in making the Apple screen text easier for me to read in my opinion. My analysis also enabled me to incorporate an Update feature to the software that would allow me to save the *ADT* program back onto the disk volume when its slot/drive configuration has been modified. This feature alone has saved me much time when I have had to transfer a volume image a number of times during the testing phase of software development. The testing phase can be a very lengthy, iterative process, and it is quite helpful when changes to the configuration of a program can easily be saved and restored for the next test iteration. The documentation I found for the Super Serial slot card did not include the information I required for me to design serial communication software using this card. The *ADT* program provided me at least one example in how to transmit and to receive serial data using the various configurations available on the Super Serial slot card. These configurations include baud rate, data format, and parity.

Super Serial slot card documentation is absolutely necessary in order to understand the software *environment* that is required by its firmware. That is, its page-zero utilization, its addressing and control logic, how the ROM/RAM memory space is utilized in the computer, the operation of its Asynchronous Communications Interface Adapter (ACIA), and its Input/Output routine entry points all contribute to the software *environment* of the Super Serial slot card. Analyzing and understanding how others have utilized the various configurations and registers that are supported by the Super Serial slot card certainly help to coordinate and assimilate the written documentation to practical realizations for the design of serial communication software on the Apple][computer. My goal was to design serial communication software that would utilize a Super Serial slot card in one Apple][computer and another Super Serial slot card in a second Apple][computer in order to transfer the contents of a diskette volume from one Apple][computer to a second Apple][computer. Whether the Apple][computer was, in fact, a Virtual][emulation of an Apple][computer should not matter. If a Virtual][emulation of an Apple][computer is utilized, it is important to remember to always configure the virtual machine to the normal clock speed of an Apple][computer, which is 1.0 MHz. The emulated Super Serial slot card will not operate correctly if the virtual machine is configured to any of the higher processing clock speeds.

As indicated above, two Apple][computers are connected by means of two serial cables, each connected to their Super Serial Card (SSC), and the two serial cables are in turn connected to each other using a special serial cable connector. That special serial cable connector is called a Null Modem adapter and it connects the RX data line of one serial cable to the TX data line of the other serial cable. The serial communication software package I developed is comprised of two separate software programs, a Client Serial communication program and a Server Serial communication program. The Client Serial program executes on one Apple][computer and the Server Serial program executes on the other Apple][computer. It is critical that the Client and Server programs synchronize to each other so that the transfer of data can begin as efficiently as possible. In earlier versions of *A2V2* and *ADT*, program synchronization was problematic, and I could never find a reliable strategy to achieve immediate and repeatable, initial program synchronization. That is, I could not ascertain whether it was preferable to start *A2V2* first, and then start *ADT*, or if it was better to start *ADT* first, and then start *A2V2*. I tabulated conflicting results every time I changed the start order or the amount of time one program had been started before the other program, and I could never resolve my collected data to prefer one start order over another. However, the current version of *A2V2* that operates under MacOS 10.12.6 is Version 2.4, and in this version of *A2V2*, *A2V2* appears to have solved its problematic and timely synchronization with *ADT*. Of course, my design of Client and Server serial communication software must auto-synchronize immediately irrespective of start order or the amount of time one program is started before the other program.

```
  Client Serial Communication

                           Client   Server
                           ------   ------
Number of Retries      -      3        3
Volume Slot   Number   -      6        6
Volume Drive  Number   -     01       01
Volume Volume Number   -    000      000
Volume Phase  Number   -     04       04

Transfer Direction       - Client->Server
Server Volume Verify   - Write Check
Volume Tracks/Sectors -     35       16

Volume Transfer State - Ready to Run
Communication    State - Client Waiting

       0123456789ABCDEF0123456789ABCDEF
Track

Sector
```

Figure V.22.5. Waiting for Auto-Synchronization

```
  Server Serial Communication

                           Client   Server
                           ------   ------
Number of Retries      -      3        3
Volume Slot   Number   -      6        6
Volume Drive  Number   -     01       01
Volume Volume Number   -    000      000
Volume Phase  Number   -     04       04

Transfer Direction       - Client->Server
Server Volume Verify   - Write Check
Volume Tracks/Sectors -     35       16

Volume Transfer State - Ready to Run
Communication    State - Server Waiting

       0123456789ABCDEF0123456789ABCDEF
Track

Sector
```

Figure V.22.6. Waiting for Auto-Synchronization

```
  Client Serial Communication

                           Client   Server
                           ------   ------
Number of Retries      -      3        3
Volume Slot   Number   -      6        6
Volume Drive  Number   -     01       01
Volume Volume Number   -    000      000
Volume Phase  Number   -     04       04

Transfer Direction       - Client->Server
Server Volume Verify   - Write Check
Volume Tracks/Sectors -     35       16

Volume Transfer State ->Ready to Run
Communication    State - Synchronized

       0123456789ABCDEF0123456789ABCDEF
Track

Sector
```

Figure V.22.7. Auto-Synchronized to Server

```
  Server Serial Communication

                           Client   Server
                           ------   ------
Number of Retries      -      3        3
Volume Slot   Number   -      6        6
Volume Drive  Number   -     01       01
Volume Volume Number   -    000      000
Volume Phase  Number   -     04       04

Transfer Direction       - Client->Server
Server Volume Verify   - Write Check
Volume Tracks/Sectors -     35       16

Volume Transfer State - Ready to Run
Communication    State - Synchronized

       0123456789ABCDEF0123456789ABCDEF
Track

Sector
```

Figure V.22.8. Auto-Synchronized to Client

The Client program handles the complete operation of configuring and of transferring a volume image from one Apple][computer to another Apple][computer. A volume image may be transferred from the Client to the Server computer or from the Server to the Client computer. The Server program displays the same ongoing operation menu details for the volume image transfer as that shown by the Client program for its menu details, but the Server program is not utilized in order to configure the data transfer setup; the Server is utilized to show its real time processing of the data that is being transferred. However, both programs at startup automatically locate the slot number of their respective Super Serial peripheral slot card, perform its firmware initialization for baud rate in order to set the maximum data transfer rate, and to initiate its auto-synchronization to the serial communication program that is executing on the other Apple][computer. Figures V.22.5 and V.22.6 show the text screens of the Client and Server programs before auto-synchronization has occurred. Figures V.22.7 and V.22.8 show the text screens of the Client and Server programs after auto-synchronization has been achieved.

Command	Sent By	Description
A	Client	Command to Server to initiate auto-synchronization.
B	Server	Response to Client that the auto-synchronization command was received.
C	Client	Command to Server followed by CFDCB (configuration data).
D	Server	Response to Client that CFDCB data was correctly received.
E	Server	Response to Client that CFDCB data was not correctly received.
F	Client	Command to finish data transfer to calculate data transfer time duration. No response needed from Server.
H	Reader or Writer	Command to halt further data transfer and exit program.
L	Reader	Command to Writer followed by TSDCB (track/sector data).
M	Writer	Response to Reader that TSDCB data was correctly received.
N	Writer	Response to Reader that TSDCB data was not correctly received.
O	Reader	Command to Writer followed by RWDCB to tell Writer that Reader is Pausing to read disk.
P	Writer	Response to tell Reader that RWDCB data was correctly received.
Q	Writer	Response to tell Reader that RWDCB data was not correctly received.
R	Client	Command to tell Server to read/write/format verify its data disk.
S	Server	Response to tell Client that Server is ready for data transfer.
T	Reader	Command to Writer followed by TXDCB (sector data).
U	Writer	Response to Reader that TXDCB data was correctly received.
V	Writer	Response to Reader that TXDCB data was not correctly received.

Table V.22.1. Client/Server Commands and Responses

The Client program communicates to the Server program using specific commands and, in some instances, with specific Data Control Blocks, or DCBs. The complete list of Client/Server commands is shown in Table V.22.1. During auto-synchronization, the Client continuously transmits an A command every 250 milliseconds and waits for a B response from the Server. The Server must ignore any extra A commands it may receive after it responds with a B command response. It must be understood that prior to auto-synchronization, the Client and Server programs are executing their software asynchronously to each other, that is, each program is independent of the other. Once the Client and Server programs have auto-synchronized, their commands, DCBs, and sectors of data are transferred totally synchronously.

As noted earlier, a volume image may be transferred from the Client to the Server computer or from the Server to the Client computer. Once the user has configured the serial communication system using the Client program, both Client and Server programs transfer their control to either a Reader function or to a Writer function. That is, if the Client configures the system as a Client→Server volume image transfer, the Client will function as the Reader and the Server will function as the Writer. Alternatively, if the Client configures the system as a Server→Client volume image transfer, the Client will function as the Writer and the Server will function as the Reader. The Reader and Writer functions simply refer to which function reads data from a disk volume and which function writes data to a disk volume, respectively. Once the Reader/Writer functions have been established, all further commands will be initiated by the Reader and all command responses will be initiated by the Writer. After a volume image has been transferred, the Reader/Writer functions are complete and the Client/Server roles can resume so that data throughput calculations can be completed and displayed by the Client. The Server re-initializes its display and it retains the previous data transfer menu selections in order to initialize itself so that the Server can receive its next command from the Client. For example, the next command the Server may likely receive would be the Quit command.

Entry	Index	Size	Value Range	Description
VOLXFER	0x00	0x01	R=0, W=1	Volume transfer direction
INITFLAG	0x01	0x01	NO=0, YES=1	Volume initialization flag
VOLTRKS	0x02	0x01	18 to 48	Volume number of tracks
VOLSECS	0x03	0x01	16 or 32	Volume number of sectors
CLNTRTRY	0x04	0x01	1 to 9	Client number of retries
CLNTSLOT	0x05	0x01	1 to 7	Client drive slot number
CLNTDRV	0x06	0x01	1 to 81	Client drive number
CLNTVOL	0x07	0x01	0 to 255	Client volume number
CLNTPHAS	0x08	0x01	1 to 16	Client phase number
SRVRRTRY	0x09	0x01	1 to 9	Server number of retries
SRVRSLOT	0x0A	0x01	1 to 7	Server drive slot number
SRVRDRV	0x0B	0x01	1 to 81	Server drive number
SRVRVOL	0x0C	0x01	0 to 255	Server volume number
SRVRPHAS	0x0D	0x01	1 to 16	Server phase number
CLSRSTAT	0x0E	0x01	WAIT=0, SYNC=1	Client/Server Status
CLSRRUN	0x0F	0x01	WAIT=0, RUN=1, QUIT=2	Client/Server RUN state
CFDCBXOR	0x10	0x01	0 to 255	Checksum XOR
CFDCBSUM	0x11	0x01	0 to 255	Checksum ADC

Table V.22.2. CFDCBTBL Configuration Data Control Block Table Contents

Initialization data that is displayed on both the Client and the Server text screens is transmitted by the Client to the Server using the C command followed by the transmission of the contents of the Configuration Data Control Block CFDCB. This data block contains all of the information necessary to configure both the Reader and the Writer functions that perform the task of transmitting a Data volume image from one Apple][computer to another Apple][computer. The size in bytes of the CFDCB data block is given by CFDCBLEN, which is equal to eighteen bytes. Every time the user makes any change on the Client menu, the CFDCB data block is transmitted to the Server program. Once the Server program receives the CFDCB data block it calculates its own values for CFCDBXOR and CFDCBSUM. CFCDBXOR and CFDCBSUM are the two checksum variables that are found at the end of the CFDCB data block. If the calculated values for these checksum variables performed by the Server are equal to their respective values in the CFDCB data block, the Server returns the D command response, otherwise the Server returns the E command response indicating a checksum mismatch error. If the Client receives an E command response, the Client will attempt to re-transmit the C command followed by the transmission of the CFDCB data block. The Client will attempt this re-transmission of command and data block up to CLNTRTRY times, or the number of retries that are assigned to the Client. The CFDCB data block contents are shown in Table V.22.2 with a brief description for each entry. Both the Client and the Server programs will terminate with an error number when the number of retries is exceeded.

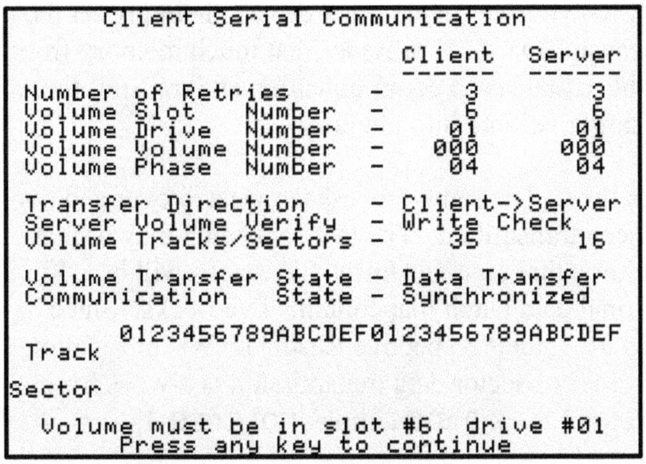

Figure V.22.9. Client Volume-Verify Message 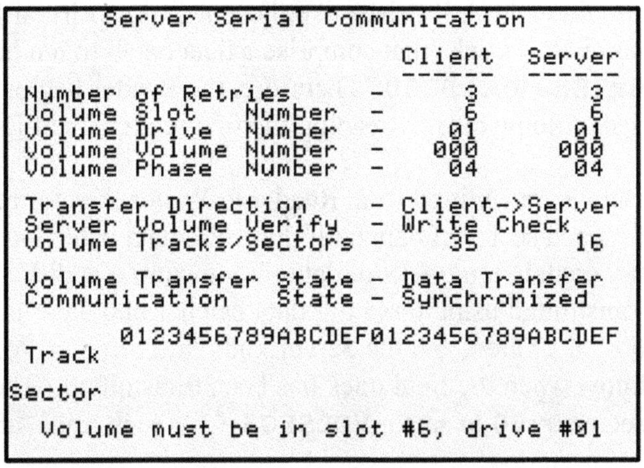   Figure V.22.10. Server Volume-Verify Message

When the CFDCB variable CLSRRUN is set to RUN (i.e. CLSRRUN = 1), the Client program and the Server program will both extract variables from their CFDCB data block in order to initialize either their Reader function or their Writer function based on the value of VOLXFER. Both programs will display a message at the bottom of their text screen as shown in Figures V.22.9 and V.22.10. As soon as the RETURN key is pressed on the Client computer, the Client program will issue the R command to the Server program to read-verify or to write-verify or to initialize-verify its target disk volume while the Client program performs the appropriate task for its target disk volume. For example, if VOLXFER is zero, then the Client becomes the Reader and it will read-verify its volume; the Server becomes the Writer and it will write-verify its volume if INITFLAG is zero or initialize-verify its volume if INITFLAG is one. On the other hand, if VOLXFER is one, then the Client becomes the Writer and it will write-verify its volume if INITFLAG is zero and initialize-verify its volume if INITFLAG is one; the Server becomes the Reader and it will read-verify its volume. VOLTRKS, VOLSECS, CLNTVOL or SRVRVOL, and CLNTPHAS or SRVRPHAS are used as input initialization parameters to RWTS in order to create a Data-type volume in the DOS 4.5 environment if a volume is selected to be initialized for its verification. All disk access, whether a volume is read from or written to, is handled exclusively by the DOS 4.5 external RWTS interface using an RWTS IOCB that is internal to the Client software and internal to the Server software. Once the Server program completes its target disk volume verification, it will issue the S command response to the Client program. If either program receives a return error value in their RWTS IOCB, the appropriate error message will be displayed at the bottom of the text screen and the program will wait for appropriate, corrective action to be made. If no errors are reported during the disk volume verification check process, the Client and Server software will transition into their role as a Reader or as a Writer function at this time.

The Client/Server serial communication programs are designed to process and transmit data batches comprised of ten tracks of data if those tracks contain sixteen sectors. If those tracks contain thirty-two sectors then a data batch will be comprised of five tracks of data. I conducted a plethora of timing tests to determine the optimum number of tracks that would comprise a data batch. Initially, the Reader must read a data batch into memory before any data can be transmitted to the Writer. During the data read/write process, as the Reader is reading the next data batch, the Writer is writing the previous data batch. After the Reader has transmitted the final data batch to the Writer, the Writer is left to finish the volume transfer by writing the final data batch. To my surprise it did not matter how many tracks of data comprise a data batch irrespective of disk drive type. My tests included real Disk][drives, simulated Disk][drives like those found in Virtual][, RAM drives, and CFFA drives. I simply set the number of tracks that comprise a data batch to ten because DOS 4.5H provides that much memory from 0x1E00 to 0xBE00. Therefore, the Reader begins the actual serial communication and transmission of disk volume data by reading the first ten tracks of its target volume into memory.

Data is transmitted from Reader to Writer a sector at a time. The same process is repeated over and over for each sector of data until the entire data batch has been transmitted. The last data batch may or may not contain ten tracks of data. For example, a disk volume that contains thirty-five tracks will be transmitted using three full data batches and a partial final data batch that contains five tracks. Since both the Client and the Server know the value of VOLTRKS, their respective Reader or Writer function know when the final track has been transmitted. The order of sector data transmission is always from sector 0x00 to sector VOLSECS-1 for each track, and from track 0x00 to track VOLTRKS-1.

As the Reader program reads each track into computer memory it records its activity by writing an ASCII R under its appropriate track number for the first 0x20 tracks. For track numbers beyond 0x20, an ASCII R is written on the next line under its appropriate track number modulo 0x20. This scheme does support a value for VOLTRKS up to sixty-four, but VOLTRKS is capped at forty-eight. As the Reader prepares and processes each sector for transmission, it records its activity by writing an ASCII R under its appropriate sector number up to a maximum of sixteen or thirty-two sectors. During the time the Reader is transmitting each sector of a given track, it records its track activity by writing an ASCII * in place of the previous ASCII R until the entire track has been transmitted. When all sectors have been transmitted, an ASCII + is used to replace the ASCII * in order to indicate that the entire track was transmitted successfully, otherwise a hexadecimal value from 0x01 to 0x0F is written in place of the ASCII * to indicated how many sectors were successfully transmitted for that track.

The preparation and processing of a sector before the sector data can be transmitted to the Writer program occurs in two steps. Certainly, there exists two major counters: TSTRACK and TSSECTOR. Both counters are initialized to zero by the Reader program. After the data for a sector is transmitted, the value of TSSECTOR is incremented until it reaches the value of VOLSECS. When that happens, TSSECTOR is reset to zero and TSTRACK is incremented until it reaches the value of VOLTRKS. When TSTRACK reaches VOLTRKS, the Reader program commands the Writer program to write the final data batch to its disk volume. In addition to these two counters, there is a third counter TRACKCNT that is initialized to BUFRTRKS, the number of tracks that comprise a data batch. The Reader program prepares the transmission of sector data by using the L command followed by the transmission of the contents of the TSDCB data block. The size in bytes of the TSDCB data block is given by TSDCBLEN, which is equal to four bytes. Once the Writer program receives the TSDCB data block, it calculates its own values for TSCDBXOR and TSDCBSUM which are the two checksum variables found at the end of the TSDCB data block. If the calculated values for these variables by the Writer equal the respective values in the TSDCB, the Writer returns the M command response, otherwise the Writer returns the N command response indicating a checksum mismatch error. If the Reader receives an N command response, the Reader will attempt to re-transmit the L command followed by the transmission of the contents of the TSDCB data block. The Reader will attempt this re-transmission of command and data block contents up to the number of retries that are assigned to the Reader (i.e. the number of retries of whichever program is hosting the Reader, either CLNTRTRY or SRVRRTRY). The TSDCB data block contents are shown in Table V.22.3 with a brief description for each entry. The Reader program will terminate with an error number when the number of retries is exceeded.

Entry	Index	Size	Value Range	Description
TSTRACK	0x00	0x01	0 to 47	Transfer track
TSSECTOR	0x01	0x01	0 to 31	Transfer sector
TSDCBXOR	0x02	0x01	0 to 255	Transfer checksum XOR
TSDCBSUM	0x03	0x01	0 to 255	Transfer checksum ADC

Table V.22.3. TSDCBTBL Track/Sector Data Control Block Table Contents

Entry	Index	Size	Value Range	Description
TXDCBBYT	0x00	0x02	0<n+2<512	Transfer bytes
TXDCBXOR	0x02	0x01	0 to 255	Transfer checksum XOR
TXDCBSUM	0x03	0x01	0 to 255	Transfer checksum ADC

Table V.22.4. TXDCBTBL Transfer Data Control Block Table Contents

Once the Reader has communicated the information of which sector onto which track the sector data belongs, the Reader begins the second step in the data transmission of sector data to the Writer program. The Reader program begins the transmission of sector data by sending the T command followed by the transmission of sector data that is compressed in real time followed by the TXDCB data block. The size in bytes of the TXDCB data block is given by TXDCBLEN, which is equal to four bytes. Once the Writer program receives the TXDCB data block, it calculates its own values for TXDCBBYT, TXCDBXOR, and TSDCBSUM which are the sector data contents in bytes and the checksum variables found in the TXDCB data block. Because the contents of the sector data is compressed in real time to an unknown total number of bytes, the value in TXDCBBYT is not a constant value. If the calculated values for these variables by the Writer equal the respective values in the TXDCB data block, the Writer returns the U command response, otherwise the Writer returns the V command response indicating a data size error or a checksum mismatch error. If the Reader receives a V command response, the Reader will attempt to re-transmit the T command followed by the transmission of the compressed sector data and the TXDCB data block. The Reader will attempt this re-transmission of command, compressed sector data, and data block up to the number of retries that are assigned to the Reader (i.e. the number of retries of whichever program is hosting the Reader, either CLNTRTRY or SRVRRTRY). The TXDCB data control block contents are shown in Table V.22.4 with a brief description for each entry. The Reader program will terminate with an error number when the number of retries is exceeded.

I developed the compression algorithm used to process a sector of data in real time exclusively for serial data transmission. There is no pre-processing required to determine the value for TXDCBBYT. TXDCBBYT, as well as TXDCBXOR and TXDCBSUM are continuously being calculated while the sector data is processed, compressed, and transmitted in real time. Obviously, the Writer is reverse processing and decompressing the sector data in parallel, and also in real time. Hopefully, the compression algorithm does not, in fact, cause more than 256 bytes of data to be transmitted, but there can exist certain data sets where this may occur, unfortunately. It is always a matter of weighing the benefits and the advantages of such an algorithm over the possible disadvantages that the algorithm might cause more data to be transmitted when the sector data contains a few groups of identical byte pairs.

The Client and Server programs initialize their Super Serial slot card to transmit serial data at the highest possible baud rate, which is 19,200 baud. That is, the Super Serial slot card is capable of transmitting one bit of information in a little over 52 microseconds. To transmit a full byte of information a Super Serial slot card requires nearly 417 microseconds. A 6502-microprocessor operating at 1.0 MHz can certainly perform a great deal of work within 417 microseconds, the time the Super Serial slot card is transmitting the previous sector data byte. So, it is completely reasonable to be able to design a data compression algorithm as well as a data decompression algorithm that iterates through sector data that looks for sequential data bytes that are equal to each other. As long as sector data bytes change in value from byte to byte, the sector data will be transmitted without modification. However, when two or more sequential bytes are the same in value, that group of bytes will be transmitted uniquely as a sequence of three bytes: two bytes of the same value (i.e. sequential duplicate bytes) and a third byte equal to the index of the next different byte. For example, if the first four bytes of sector data are equal to 0x0A (i.e. the ASL instruction four times), the transmitted data will be 0x0A, 0x0A, 0x04. When the Writer encounters sequential duplicate bytes, it understands that it is being directed to start filling its sector data buffer with the duplicate byte value up until it reaches the index given by the byte immediately following the duplicate bytes. If these same four duplicate bytes come at the end of the sector data stream, the transmitted data will be 0x0A, 0x0A, 0x00. Obviously, the index value of 0x00 would be the index of the next sector data buffer, which really does not exist, but it is a value that also concludes the transmission of the compressed data for that sector. The next four bytes received by the Writer would be those bytes of the TXDCB.

One may reach the erroneous conclusion that the real time sector data compression algorithm will require the transmission of only three data bytes when all of the data in a sector is the same value. Many times a disk volume will contain a few sectors that have not been utilized, and the data in those sectors will be set to 0x00 from the original initialization of that disk volume. Unfortunately, it is not possible for the Writer to set all bytes in a sector to the same value within 417 microseconds so that the Writer will still be able to receive the four TXDCB bytes that follow. What happens, regrettably, is a hardware disconnect between Reader and Writer, so synchronization is lost, and no further data can be correctly transmitted and/or received. I found this situation to be rather interesting and I studied it quite closely. The test programs I developed to monitor all data transmission and data receive transactions essentially filled specific buffers with data that I could analyze when the compression algorithm loses synchronization and starts to go awry. I did not know what I was looking for initially, but as I started to accumulate more and more data transactions, the better I could refine my test programs and capture the specific data they collected. As with all remedies I did not want the cure to be worse than the problem at hand, and I certainly wanted no impact, or at least minimal impact on the Writer decompression algorithm. In fact, the cure should not even affect the Writer, therefore leaving the entire management of the compression algorithm fully on the shoulders of the Reader.

My analysis of all the test program data I collected demonstrated that the Reader and the Writer programs will not lose synchronization as long as the Writer is not required to fill its sector data buffer with more than 0x40 consecutive data bytes having the same value. This was very good news indeed, and it was a very easy modification to implement within the compression algorithm for the Reader program. All 256 bytes of a disk sector that are identical in value, any value, can be transmitted using only twelve bytes. Those twelve bytes can be generated, transmitted, and expanded to completely fill the memory buffer of a specific volume sector in real time. Assuming an initialized sector is zero-filled, the twelve bytes that would be transmitted to the Writer program would be: 0x00, 0x00, 0x40, 0x00, 0x00, 0x80, 0x00, 0x00, 0xC0, 0x00, 0x00, 0x00. The time to transmit these twelve bytes would be approximately 5.0 milliseconds rather than 106.7 milliseconds in order to transmit the entire sector of 256 bytes that are the same value. Accumulatively, this would amount to a very substantial time savings if many such sectors comprised the bulk of a disk volume. What is most incredible about my sector data compression algorithm is that it is applied continuously, in real time, to all consecutive bytes of sector data that are identical in value without requiring any pre-processing whatsoever.

I know that *A2V2* and *ADT* both assume that when the sector data of one sector is fully transmitted, the sector number whose data will be transmitted next will be one less than the previous sector number. That is, sector number is decremented in descending order in these two programs. Sector number is first initialized to 0x0F, decremented until it becomes negative, and re-initialized to 0x0F while track number is incremented. When track number becomes equal to 0x23, *A2V2* and *ADT* are both finished transmitting and receiving sector data. My solution in communicating both sector and track number using the TSDCB ensures that both the Reader and the Writer programs are addressing the same relative page of data in memory. The variables TSSECTOR and TSTRACK are used to calculate the memory page number from where the sector data is read or to where the sector data is written using a very simple look-up table which could actually be generated programmatically. The code that calculates GETPAGE is shown in Figure V.22.11. If the disk volumes contain tracks that have sixteen sectors, BUFRTRKS contains the value of 0x0A and BUFRFLAG contains the value of 0x00. On the other hand, if these tracks contain thirty-two sectors, BUFRTRKS contains the value of 0x05 and BUFRFLAG contains the value of 0xFF. The target page number is returned in the A-register and saved to a page-zero pointer.

When the Reader program begins its processing, the very first call it makes is to GETRACKS in order to fill its memory with the contents of the first ten tracks (or five tracks if the volume has tracks containing thirty-two sectors) of its target disk volume. Later in its processing when the TRACKCNT variable becomes zero, the Reader program calls the SNDRWDCB routine to inform the Writer program that it is time to write its accumulated memory contents, or data batch to its target disk volume. The RWDCB provides the Writer with the information it requires to write a data batch to its target disk volume. The Reader program prefaces the transmission of the RWDCB by using the O command followed by the transmission of the contents of the RWDCB data block. The size in bytes of the RWDCB data block is given by RWDCBLEN, which is equal to four bytes. Once the Writer program receives the RWDCB data block it calculates its own values for RWDCBXOR and RWDCBSUM which are the two checksum variables found at the end of the RWDCB data block. If the calculated values for these variables by the Writer equal the respective values in the RWDCB, the Writer returns the P command response, otherwise the

Writer returns the Q command response indicating a checksum mismatch error. If the Reader receives a Q command response, the Reader will attempt to re-transmit the O command followed by the transmission of the contents of the RWDCB data block. The Reader will attempt this re-transmission of command and data block up to the number of retries that are assigned for the Reader (i.e. the number of retries of whichever program is hosting the Reader, either CLNTRTRY or SRVRRTRY). The RWDCB data block contents are shown in Table V.22.5 with a brief description for each entry. The Reader program will terminate with an error number when the number of retries is exceeded.

```
   :            :          :
15F5           459   ; Calculate the memory page for the sector and track values
15F5           460   ; contained in the Y-register and A-register, respectively.
15F5           461   ;
15F5           462   GETPAGE:
15F5 CD 34 19  463   ^1        cmp BUFRTRKS
15F8 90 05     464             bcc >2
15FA           465   ;
15FA ED 34 19  466             sbc BUFRTRKS
15FD 10 F6     467             bpl <1              ; always taken
15FF           468   ;
15FF 2C 35 19  469   ^2        bit BUFRFLAG
1602 10 01     470             bpl >3
1604           471   ;
1604 0A        472             asl
1605           473   ;
1605 AA        474   ^3        tax
1606           475   ;
1606 98        476             tya
1607 7D 57 19  477             adc TRACKTBL,X
160A           478   ;
160A 60        479             rts
   :            :          :
1934           22    BUFRTRKS dfs 1,ZERO
1935           23    BUFRFLAG dfs 1,ZERO
   :            :          :
1957 1E 2E 3E  44    TRACKTBL hex 1E2E3E4E5E
195A 4E 5E
195C 6E 7E 83  45             hex 6E7E8E9EAE
195F 9E AE
   :            :          :
```

Figure V.22.11. Calculation of GETPAGE

Once the Writer program receives the O command from the Reader program, it calls the RCVRWDCB routine to receive the RWDCB data block in order to have the parameters necessary before the PUTRACKS routine can be called. Working in parallel with the Writer, the Reader program calls GETRACKS to fill its memory with the next data batch unless TSTRACK in the Reader program has reached the value found in LASTTRK which was originally initialized to the value found in VOLTRKS (found in the DFDCB data control block). After the Reader completes its work in preparation to transmit the next data batch, the Reader waits for the S command response from the Writer before it can continue any further processing. Essentially, this gives the Writer all the time it requires in order to transfer the data batch saved in its memory to its target disk volume. After the Writer completes its transfer of data to its disk volume, it sends the S command response to the Reader. If the Reader takes longer to fill its memory with the next data batch read from its disk volume, the S command response will already be available for the Reader to read from its Super Serial card input data register.

Entry	Index	Size	Value Range	Description
RWTRACK	0x00	0x01	0 to 47	Start track
NTRACKS	0x01	0x01	0 to BUFRTRKS	Number of tracks to R/W
RWDCBXOR	0x02	0x01	0 to 255	Transfer checksum XOR
RWDCBSUM	0x03	0x01	0 to 255	Transfer checksum ADC

Table V.22.5. RWDCBTBL Read/Write Data Control Block Table Contents

One may rightfully reach the conclusion that many bytes of control data are transmitted to the Writer program and many bytes of response data are transmitted to the Reader program. I happen to strongly agree with that assessment. I could have followed more closely the design method used by the *A2V2/ADT* software programs, but I was more intrigued with the absolute control used in my design method. The transmission of the various ASCII commands and their associated DCB data blocks is rather minimal overhead, in my opinion, and they provide extraordinary control over the transmission of the contents of a disk volume from one Apple computer to another Apple computer. One needs to realize that the Client and Server programs, like all other programs, are designed with a certain underlying strategy such that they can be developed quickly, effortlessly, and flawlessly. I have always designed software with parallel *unit testing* in mind. When all the individual pieces of a software program have been *unit tested*, or tested individually outside of the scope of a program, there is a very strong likelihood that when these individual pieces of software are combined, the resulting program will more than likely function as designed. Other software engineers may utilize another strategy to design their software. I would always consider another approach to software design if I thought its strategies would provide me with a better end product and/or with less effort.

The Client and Server software programs contain many potential locations where failure of one kind or another can cause the transmission of sector data to terminate. Of course, the user may terminate data transmission at any time by pressing the ESCAPE key on either computer. And, the user may pause data transmission at any time by pressing any other key on either computer. Why one would want to pause data transmission is questionable, but nevertheless available. Pausing data transmission will simply increase the time data transmission is active, and that will factor into the calculation of its transmission rate. I could have factored out the time data transmission is paused, but it seemed like too much work for a rarely used, if at all, feature. Because of the high volatility of potential transmission errors beyond what can easily be accommodated, I designed a very large set of error codes that would indicate precisely where a transmission error occurred in the software. Because there is so much time available between the transmission of one data byte and the next data byte, pre-loading a register with an error code that would point to a transmission error at that precise location in the software would not affect the overall transmission rate whatsoever. And this is precisely the technique I employed to assist me in performing Client/Server program unit and verification testing and Client/Server program functional testing with real time error reporting.

A very comprehensive list of routines found in the Client program and in the Server program that can generate an error code is shown in Tables V.22.6 and V.22.7. The Client/Server functional design allocates a group of error codes to a specific routine function rather than assigning error codes sequentially. Either method would be acceptable, but I considered this approach to have more organization as well as more ease in adding an additional error to a routine function if it became necessary.

The SSC00 routines for transmit (TX) and for receive (RX) do not wait indefinitely for an empty ACIA transmit or receive register, respectively. These two routines will wait until the X-register has counted no more than 256 iterations of a sixteen microsecond loop that tests for DCD (Data Carrier Detect) and DSR (Data Set Ready) both to be TRUE. If this loop counter should expire the routine will simply return with the carry flag set, otherwise the carry flag is returned clear after writing data to the transmit register or reading data from the receive register. The transmit register and the receive register are actually the same ACIA register, and the function of this register is determined simply by how it is utilized. The SSC80 routines for transmit and for receive wait indefinitely for an empty ACIA transmit or receive register, respectively. There is no way to interrupt the eleven microsecond loop that tests for DCD and DSR both to be TRUE. Inspection of Tables V.22.6 and V.22.7 show that if the Client program or the Server program appears to be hanged, more than likely it is due to a call to the RXSSC80 routine. Throughout all of my testing I have yet to document a failure in reading the ACIA data register. It would be terribly inconvenient to have to differentiate the press of the ESCAPE key if it should be captured in a call to the RXSSC80 routine rather than from the GETKEY routine which is far more desirable. Again, the RXSSC80 routine cannot be interrupted.

Several of the Client and Server routines require calls to the GETKEY routine in order to obtain input direction from the user. It is during these functions where the user may immediately terminate the Client and Server programs. Less immediate are the functions that utilize the GETKEY routine that simply looks for any press of a key. If the ESCAPE key should be pressed then responsible action will be taken when it is most appropriate to do so. For example, if the ESCAPE key is pressed while sector data is being transmitted, it would not be appropriate to interrupt that function until it has completed. Delaying the response to the ESCAPE keypress until after the transmission of sector data has completed would leave the Super Serial card registers in a far better state. Furthermore, if the key press is not the ESCAPE key and sector data is being transmitted, that key press would be interpreted as a command to pause further transmission of sector data once the current transmission of data has completed. That is the implementation that is used for the Reader routine. Before the Reader sends the TSDCB data block, the keyboard is checked for any keypress. This would be the most appropriate time to pause sector data transmission. On the other hand, the Writer checks the keyboard for any keypress after receiving the TSDCB but before responding with the M response after it has successfully verified the TSDCB checksum bytes. That would be the most appropriate time to pause sector data transmission because the Reader can wait forever for the M response without losing synchronization with the other computer.

Tables V.22.8 and V.22.9 transform the information found in Tables V.22.6 and V.22.7 as well as provide additional information about each error code, the routine that issues that error code, and the calling routines. Of course, the user would be required to have a copy of the Client software and the Server software source code listing to fully appreciate the precise reason why any particular error code is generated. Considering all of the data that is transmitted to and from the Reader and Writer functions, approximately 268 bytes of data are transmitted for every sector of data assuming the data transmission of all bytes, and that every sector is filled with data that contains no sequential duplicate bytes. For a volume of thirty-five tracks, this amounts to transmitting around 150,080 bytes of data without error. This is quite a significant benchmark to achieve, and to repeat this performance every single time.

Routine	SSC00 TX	SSC00 RX	SSC80 TX	SSC80 RX	GETKEY	Error Number	Description
MAIN	F					01–02	
FINDSSC						10	C-flag set if SSC not found
INITSSC						[14–17]	resets, enables SSC registers; sets baud rate
AUTOSYNC	A^	(B)			18	[19–1F]	AUTOSYNC terminated by ESC keypress
EDITMENU					21	20	CLSRRUN=2 or ESC causes H to be sent
SHOWMENU						[28–2F]	no error handling; returns C-flag clear
CHK4DISK	R			(H, S)	36,37	30,34	extract CFDCB, CALLRWTS/RWTSREAD
DOREADER				(S)	47	40,41	SNDTSDCB, SNDTXDCB, SNDRWDCB, GETRACKS
DOWRITER	S			(H, O, S, T)		50,54–55	RCVRWDCB, PUTRACKS, RCVTXDCB, RCVTSDCB
SNDCFDCB*	C, CFDCB			(D, E)		60–65	send C, CFDCB; get D, E; return CLC, ESC
SNDTSDCB*	L, TSDCB			(M, N)		70–73	send L, TSDCB; get M, N; return CLC, ESC
RCVTSDCB	M, N	TSDCB				78–79	get TSDCB; send M, N; return CLC, ESC
SNDRWDCB*	O, RWDCB			(P, Q)		80–82	send O, RWDCB; get P, Q; return CLC, ESC
RCVRWDCB	P, Q	RWDCB				88–89	get RWDCB; send P, Q; return CLC, ESC
SNDTXDCB*	T, TXDCB			(U, V)		90–92	send T, TXDCB; get U, V; return CLC, ESC
RCVTXDCB	U, V	TXDCB				98–99	get TXDCB; send U, V; return CLC, ESC
PUTDATA	DATA					A0–A4	TX loop timeout
GETDATA		DATA				B0–B2	RX loop timeout
GETRACKS						C0–C1	calls CALLRWTS with RWTSREAD
PUTRACKS						D0	calls CALLRWTS with RWTSWRIT
EXITPGM			H				jumps to DOSCOLD

* = uses NRETRIES   ^ = no timeout   (*,*) = looking for   [*-*] = available, not used

Table V.22.6. Error Handling Error Codes for Client Routines

Routine	SSC00 TX	SSC00 RX	SSC80 TX	SSC80 RX	GETKEY	Error Number	Description
FINDSSC						10	C-flag set if SSC not found
AUTOSYNC	B			(H, A)		18–19	look for H, A
SHOWMENU						[28–2F]	no error handling; returns C-flag clear
CHK4DISK	R			(H, S)	37	30,34	extract CFDCB, CALLRWTS/RWTSREAD
DOREADER				(S)	47	40–41	SNDTSDCB, SNDTXDCB, SNDRWDCB, GETRACKS
DOWRITER	S			(H, O, S, T)		50,54–55	RCVRWDCB, PUTRACKS, RCVTXDCB, RCVTSDCB
RCVCFDCB	D, E	CFDCB		(H, C)		68–69	get CFDCB; send D, E; return CLC, ESC
SNDTSDCB*	L, TSDCB			(M, N)		70–73	send L, TSDCB; get M, N; return CLC, ESC
RCVTSDCB	M, N	TSDCB				78–79	get TSDCB; send M, N; return CLC, ESC
SNDRWDCB*	O, RWDCB			(P, Q)		80–82	send O, RWDCB; get P, Q; return CLC, ESC
RCVRWDCB	P, Q	RWDCB				88–89	get RWDCB; send P, Q; return CLC, ESC
SNDTXDCB*	T, DXDCB			(U, V)		90–92	send T, TXDCB; get U, V; return CLC, ESC
RCVTXDCB	U, V	TXDCB				98–99	get TXDCB; send U, V; return CLC, ESC
PUTDATA	DATA					A0–A4	TX loop timeout
GETDATA		DATA				B0–B2	RX loop timeout
GETRACKS						C0–C1	calls CALLRWTS with RWTSREAD
PUTRACKS						D0	calls CALLRWTS with RWTSWRIT
EXITPGM			H				jumps to DOSCOLD

* = uses NRETRIES   ^ = no timeout   (*,*) = looking for   [*-*] = available, not used

Table V.22.7. Error Handling Error Codes for Server Routines

Error	Error Name	Set in Routine	Called by Routine	Description
01	MAIN1.E	START	CLIENT	received carry set from call to PRESNCLR
02	MAIN2.E	START	CLIENT	received carry set from call to TXSSC00
10	FSSC.E	FINDSSC	INITPGM	unable to find a Super Serial Card in a slot
18	ASYNC.E	AUTOSYNC	CLIENT	received carry set from call to GETKEY
20	EMENU1.E	EDITMENU	START	when value of CLSRRUN becomes 2 (QUIT)
21	EMENU2.E	EDITMENU	START	received carry set from call to EDIT subprogram
30	CHK4D1.E	CHK4DISK	START	received carry set from call to TXSSC00
34	CHK4D2.E	CHK4DISK	START	received "H" from call to RXSSC80
36	CHK4D3.E	CHK4DISK	START	received carry set from call to PRESNCLR
37	CHK4D4.E	CHK4DISK	START	received carry set from call to PRESNCLR
40	READ1.E	DOREADER	START	did not receive "S" from call to RXSSC80
41	READ2.E	DOREADER	START	did not receive "S" from call to RXSSC80
47	READ3.E	DOREADER	START	received carry set from call to GETKEY
50	WRIT1.E	DOWRITER	START	received carry set from call to TXSSC00
54	WRIT2.E	DOWRITER	START	received "H" from call to RXSSC80
55	WRIT3.E	DOWRITER	START	received "H" from call to RXSSC80
60	SNDCF1.E	SNDCFDCB	START	received carry set from call to TXSSC00
61	SNDCF1.E+1	SNDCFDCB	EDITMENU	received carry set from call to TXSSC00
62	SNDCF2.E	SNDCFDCB	START	received carry set from call to TXSSC00
63	SNDCF2.E+1	SNDCFDCB	EDITMENU	received carry set from call to TXSSC00
64	SNDCF3.E	SNDCFDCB	START	RETRYCNT is zero or did not receive "D" or "E"
65	SNDCF3.E+1	SNDCFDCB	EDITMENU	RETRYCNT is zero or did not receive "D" or "E"
70	SNDTS1.E	SNDTSDCB	DOREADER	received carry set from call to TXSSC00
71	SNDTS2.E	SNDTSDCB	DOREADER	received carry set from call to TXSSC00
72	SNDTS3.E	SNDTSDCB	DOREADER	received "H" from call to RXSSC80
73	SNDTS4.E	SNDTSDCB	DOREADER	RETRYCNT is zero or did not receive "M" or "N"
78	RCVTS1.E	RCVTSDCB	DOWRITER	received carry set from call to RXSSC00
79	RCVTS2.E	RCVTSDCB	DOWRITER	received carry set from call to TXSSC00
80	SNDRW1.E	SNDRWDCB	DOREADER	received carry set from call to TXSSC00
81	SNDRW2.E	SNDRWDCB	DOREADER	received carry set from call to TXSSC00
82	SNDRW3.E	SNDRWDCB	DOREADER	RETRYCNT is zero or did not receive "P" or "Q"
88	RCVRW1.E	RCVRWDCB	DOWRITER	received carry set from call to RXSSC00
89	RCVRW2.E	RCVRWDCB	DOWRITER	received carry set from call to TXSSC00
90	SNDTX1.E	SNDTXDCB	DOREADER	received carry set from call to TXSSC00
91	SNDTX2.E	SNDTXDCB	DOREADER	received carry set from call to TXSSC00
92	SNDTX3.E	SNDTXDCB	DOREADER	RETRYCNT is zero or did not receive "U" or "V"
98	RCVTX1.E	RCVTXDCB	DOWRITER	received carry set from call to RXSSC00
99	RCVTX2.E	RCVTXDCB	DOWRITER	received carry set from call to TXSSC00
A0	PDATA1.E	PUTDATA	SNDTXDCB	received carry set from call to TXDATA4
A1	PDATA2.E	TXDATA4	PUTDATA	received carry set from call to TXSSC00
A2	PDATA2.E+1	PUTDATA	SNDTXDCB	received carry set from call to TXDATA2
A3	PDATA3.E	TXDATA2	PUTDATA	received carry set from call to TXSSC00
A4	PDATA3.E+1	PUTDATA	SNDTXDCB	received carry set from call to TXDATA2
B0	GDATA1.E	GETDATA	RCVTXDCB	received carry set from call to RXDATA2
B1	GDATA2.E	GETDATA	RCVTXDCB	received carry set from call to RXDATA2
B2	GDATA3.E	GETDATA	RCVTXDCB	received carry set from call to RXDATA2
C0	GTRACK.E	GETRACKS	DOREADER	received carry set from call to PRTRWERR
C1	GTRACK.E+1	GETRACKS	DOREADER	received carry set from call to PRTRWERR
D0	PTRACK.E	PUTRACKS	DOWRITER	received carry set from call to PRTRWERR

Table V.22.8. Client Source Routines for Error Codes

Error	Error Name	Set in Routine	Called by Routine	Description
10	FSSC.E	FINDSSC	INITPGM	unable to find a Super Serial Card in a slot
18	ASYNC1.E	AUTOSYNC	SERVER	received "H" from call to RXSSC80
19	ASYNC2.E	AUTOSYNC	SERVER	received carry set from call to TXSSC00
30	CHK4C1.E	CHK4DISK	START	received carry set from call to TXSSC00
34	CHK4C2.E	CHK4DISK	START	received "H" from call to RXSSC80
37	CHK4C3.E	CHK4DISK	START	received carry set from call to PRESNCLR
40	READ1.E	DOREADER	START	did not receive "S" from call to RXSSC80
41	READ2.E	DOREADER	START	did not receive "S" from call to RXSSC80
47	READ3.E	DOREADER	START	received carry set from call to GETKEY
50	WRIT1.E	DOWRITER	START	received carry set from call to TXSSC00
54	WRIT2.E	DOWRITER	START	received "H" from call to RXSSC80
55	WRIT3.E	DOWRITER	START	received "H" from call to RXSSC80
68	RCVCF1.E	RCVCFDCB	START	received carry set from call to RXSSC00
69	RCVCF2.E	RCVCFDCB	START	received carry set from call to TXSSC00
70	SNDTS1.E	SNDTSDCB	DOREADER	received carry set from call to TXSSC00
71	SNDTS2.E	SNDTSDCB	DOREADER	received carry set from call to TXSSC00
72	SNDTS3.E	SNDTSDCB	DOREADER	received "H" from call to RXSSC80
73	SNDTS4.E	SNDTSDCB	DOREADER	RETRYCNT is zero or did not receive "M" or "N"
78	RCVTS1.E	RCVTSDCB	DOWRITER	received carry set from call to RXSSC00
79	RCVTS2.E	RCVTSDCB	DOWRITER	received carry set from call to TXSSC00
80	SNDRW1.E	SNDRWDCB	DOREADER	received carry set from call to TXSSC00
81	SNDRW2.E	SNDRWDCB	DOREADER	received carry set from call to TXSSC00
82	SNDRW3.E	SNDRWDCB	DOREADER	RETRYCNT is zero or did not receive "P" or "Q"
88	RCVRW1.E	RCVRWDCB	DOWRITER	received carry set from call to RXSSC00
89	RCVRW2.E	RCVRWDCB	DOWRITER	received carry set from call to TXSSC00
90	SNDTX1.E	SNDTXDCB	DOREADER	received carry set from call to TXSSC00
91	SNDTX2.E	SNDTXDCB	DOREADER	received carry set from call to TXSSC00
92	SNDTX3.E	SNDTXDCB	DOREADER	RETRYCNT is zero or did not receive "U" or "V"
98	RCVTX1.E	RCVTXDCB	DOWRITER	received carry set from call to RXSSC00
99	RCVTX2.E	RCVTXDCB	DOWRITER	received carry set from call to TXSSC00
A0	PDATA1.E	PUTDATA	SNDTXDCB	received carry set from call to TXDATA4
A1	PDATA2.E	TXDATA4	PUTDATA	received carry set from call to TXSSC00
A2	PDATA2.E+1	PUTDATA	SNDTXDCB	received carry set from call to TXDATA2
A3	PDATA3.E	TXDATA2	PUTDATA	received carry set from call to TXSSC00
A4	PDATA3.E+1	PUTDATA	SNDTXDCB	received carry set from call to TXDATA2
B0	GDATA1.E	GETDATA	RCVTXDCB	received carry set from call to RXDATA2
B1	GDATA2.E	GETDATA	RCVTXDCB	received carry set from call to RXDATA2
B2	GDATA3.E	GETDATA	RCVTXDCB	received carry set from call to RXDATA2
C0	GTRACK.E	GETRACKS	DOREADER	received carry set from call to PRTRWERR
C1	GTRACK.E+1	GETRACKS	DOREADER	received carry set from call to PRTRWERR
D0	PTRACK.E	PUTRACKS	DOWRITER	received carry set from call to PRTRWERR

Table V.22.9. Server Source Routines for Error Codes

I am often amazed how easy this benchmark can be achieved with the Apple][computer, with its accessory vintage hardware, and with such an ancient (though exceedingly reliable) communication protocol such as RS232. But, indeed, the Client and Server programs perform this function flawlessly. Voltage spikes, noise, lost data bits, skewed timing, and a host of many other problems can cause failure during the transmission of a sector of data. When such intermittent failures occur, there is sufficient logic in the Client and in the Server programs to handle a modest level of failure. However, when there are serious communication problems, no level of error handling will ever be adequate.

The Client program obtains the current time of day and date by indirectly jumping to the RDCLKVSN vector at 0x03E1 with the carry flag clear, which is the protocol in DOS 4.5 to obtain the date and time data. DOS 4.5 fills the supplied 6-byte CLKBUFR, whose address is in the Y- and A-registers, with three bytes of time data and three bytes of date data. This data is supplied in Binary-Coded Decimal (BCD) format. In order to calculate elapsed transmission time, a call is made to RDCLKVSN before transitioning to the Reader/Writer functions and after returning from the Reader/Writer functions only in the Client program. The 6502-microprocessor can perform BCD arithmetic after it has processed the SED (set decimal) instruction. Once the BCD arithmetic is complete, the 6502-microprocessor must be returned to the hexadecimal mode by processing the CLD (clear decimal) instruction. The two BCD time buffers must be subtracted in order to obtain elapsed time in seconds. The math is trivial knowing there are 3600 seconds in one delta hour and 60 seconds in one delta minute. The total amount of data in bytes that is transferred from one Apple][computer to another Apple][computer is calculated by the successive addition of 0x4096 or 0x8192 (when VOLSECS is thirty-two) in a processing loop that is iterated VOLTRKS times using BCD arithmetic. The Client program displays how many bytes are transferred and the number of elapsed seconds for that transfer to take place, both as decimal values using hexadecimal display routines found in the Monitor. These calculations demonstrate the power of using the BCD format for integer values and the 6502-microprocessor set in decimal mode. This is the first opportunity I have had to utilize BCD arithmetic for time and date values that I chose to represent in BCD format in the design of DOS 4.5. I believe the simplicity of these calculations demonstrate that I made the correct design choice in choosing the BCD format to represent time and date in DOS 4.5.

23. CHAR Editor and LENGTH

I was thrilled when I obtained my copy of Sierra On-Line's *ScreenWriter* product years before I finally invested in a Videx UltraTerm video display card. *ScreenWriter*, copyrighted by David Kidwell in 1982, was able to draw up to seventy various graphic characters on a HIRES mixed graphics screen line whose character font was designed to be only as wide as the graphic character needed to be. Upper case characters were compressed in width, but were still seven pixels high, so combined with the lower case compressed characters that extended below the line, the font used the full eight pixels in height like that required in a normal mixed-case Text line. *ScreenWriter* did not provide a blank line one pixel high between lines of text in order to help assist in drawing its font so that it was more readable on my Amdek color monitor. It was not until several years later did I discover that the embedded RUNOFF commands used by *ScreenWriter* were modeled after an IBM mainframe word processor that I used extensively to document my Preliminary Design Reviews (PDR) and my Critical Design Reviews (CDR) for software I developed while I was employed at Hughes Aircraft company. And, it didn't take me long to find the code in *ScreenWriter* that was used to draw its graphic characters onto the HIRES screen in the Apple][+. When I was first employed by Sierra, I assisted in converting *ScreenWriter* to utilize the Apple //e 80-Column text card. My Videx UltraTerm video display card would never support *ScreenWriter*.

ScreenWriter utilizes a size table that contains the width in pixels for each of its graphic characters and graphic symbols. This table is used extensively to determine if the next word and the space between words could be displayed on the current line without overflowing the HIRES screen to the right.

ScreenWriter did a fantastic job in moving words from one line to another as characters were added to the current line while in Insert Mode or as characters were deleted from the current line while in Change Mode. The size table was also consulted anytime a group of words needed to appear centered on a line. Centering calculations are easy to execute simply by subtracting the sum of all character and symbol widths and pixel space between characters from two hundred eighty (i.e. 40 columns * 7 pixels/column) and logically shifting that difference once to the right. Thus, words could be drawn starting at a calculated number of pixels from the left side of the screen. This pixel number can be converted to a byte index number (or window) that ranged from `0x00` to `0x27` and a bit index number (or cell) that ranged from `0x00` to `0x06`. Using these two indices enables any character string to be drawn anywhere on the current line or on any other line knowing that each byte index contains seven pixels.

I adapted the **concept** of the *ScreenWriter* `HIRES` graphic characters for *BFI* and I developed the *CHAR Editor* and *LENGTH* tools to support that effort. And, I modeled *CHAR Editor* from my previous tool called *EDITROM* as described in Section II.6 that uses `LORES` graphics in order to create the *BFI* `HIRES` screen font. I only had to create the graphic characters for the ASCII characters from `0x20` to `0x7F` and not the graphic symbols that are used in *ScreenWriter* since I had no use for those symbols. Unlike the *ScreenWriter* graphic characters, the *BFI* upper case graphic characters are only six pixels high so they do not appear as tall and thin. The entire *BFI* font is only seven pixels high. These ninety-six characters provide ninety-six bytes of data for each of seven tables, one table for each scan line, and there is an additional table that has forty-eight entries called the character size table. The goal in designing a `HIRES` screen font is to use the smallest width practical for each of the font characters without making the character unreadable. The brain does an admirable job in filling in what the eyes do not necessarily see, and typically a person will recognize a word when, at the minimum, only the first two and/or the last two characters of the word are clearly recognized. Certain symbols like "$" and "&" can only be created when their widths are five pixels, but their usage is not that frequent. Similarly, letters like "M" and "W" can only be recognized when their widths are also five pixels. Even though the graphic representation of a character using `LORES` graphics appears boxy in *CHAR Editor*, when the graphic characters are displayed on the `HIRES` screen, their edges do not appear as sharp because the brain tends to smooth out all of those sharp corners and transitions.

To begin a graphic character font editing session with *CHAR Editor*, a suitable filename for CHAR data may be entered as shown in Figure V.23.1. Simply press `RETURN` if there is no new CHAR data file to read. The complete CHAR data file is `0x02D0` (or 720) bytes in size and it is read into memory at memory address `0x0E80`. There is no particular rationale for that load address: it simply is where the program *CHAR Editor* ends in memory. Figure V.23.2 shows the `LORES` display of the "@" character entry in the CHAR data file and four lines of Text at the bottom of the display. Line twenty-two in this display shows the HEX offset of the "@" character data in the CHAR data file, the seven bytes of that character data (one byte from each table), the value for each byte of data, and how the character is currently displayed by the Apple][hardware for normal text as well as its width in pixels. There are two modes of operation used in *CHAR Editor*: Show Mode and Edit Mode. Show Mode simply duplicates the `LORES` character that is displayed on the left side and displays it on the right side of the screen, and duplicates the data that is currently in memory at the bottom of the screen on line twenty-four. As in *EDITROM*, there are only four commands that are used in Show Mode: `B` goes back one character, `E` enters Edit Mode, `RETURN` displays the next character, and `ESCAPE` exits the program.

There are only three commands along with the arrow key movements that are used in Edit Mode: `SPACE` toggles a character pixel `ON` and `OFF`, `RETURN` exits Edit Mode and saves all changes to memory, `ESCAPE` exits Edit Mode and discards all changes, and the arrow keys move the pixel cursor up and down or left and right. As shown in Figure V.23.3 Edit Mode displays the new character data on line twenty-four that corresponds to the LORES character that is displayed on the right side of the screen. Pressing RETURN will accept these changes and pressing ESCAPE will discard these changes. Once all changes have been made to the CHAR data, pressing ESCAPE will exit the editor and the *CHAR Editor* program will ask for a filename in order to save the 0x02D0 bytes of CHAR data that is currently in memory as shown in Figure V.23.4. If a filename is not entered when *CHAR Editor* begins or when *CHAR Editor* exits, no file is read or saved, respectively. The DOS 4.5 DIFF command can be used to compare both the input and the output CHAR files to *CHAR Editor* in order to ensure that the output CHAR file contains no changes or contains the desired changes that were made to the CHAR file.

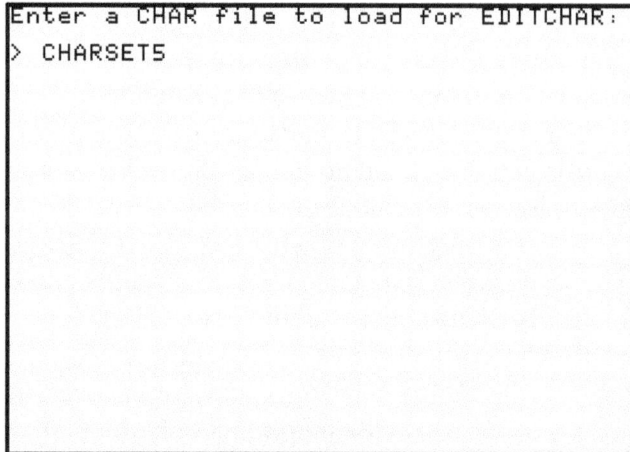

Figure V.23.1. Load CHAR File for EDITCHAR

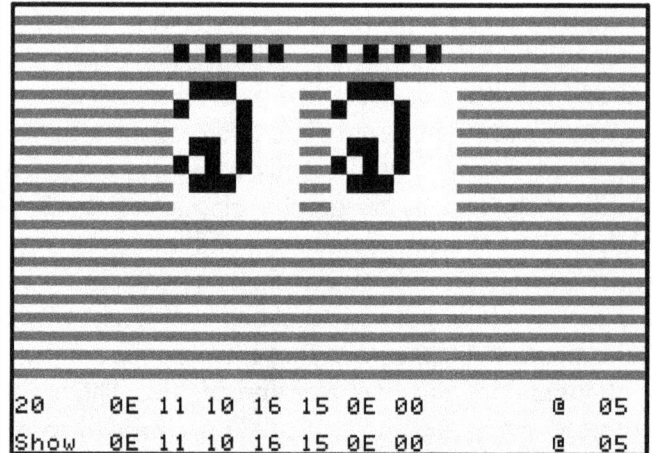

Figure V.23.2. CHAR Data Show Mode

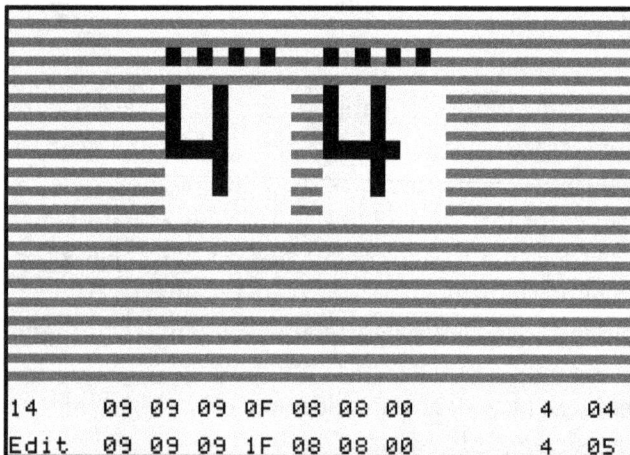

Figure V.23.3. CHAR Data Edit Mode

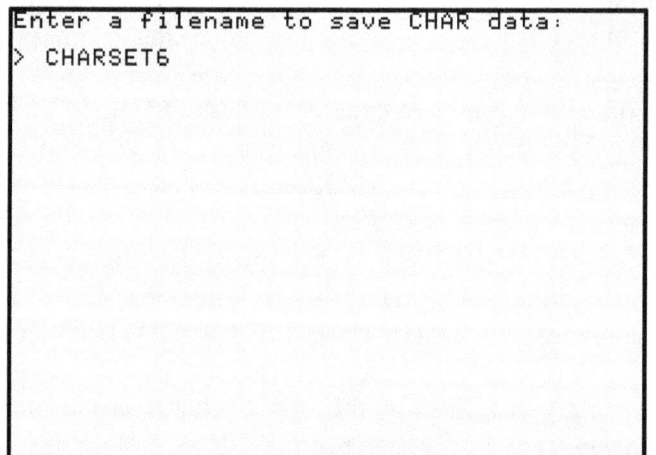

Figure V.23.4. Save CHAR Data for EDITCHAR

For those who are interested in understanding the correspondence with CHAR data and the display of that data by the Apple][hardware, a few data samples will easily illustrate their relationship by using the HIRES graphics screen. On the Apple Command Line enter HGR and then CALL-151. Assuming MIXEDON or 0xC053 is enabled, enter 2000:1 and 2400:40 on the Monitor Command Line. Now you will see that the least significant bit, or LSB (or bit 0) of the first data sample is displayed to the far left of the screen and bit 6 of the second data sample is displayed seven pixels to the right of the far left of the screen. Therefore, the Apple][hardware processes data starting with the LSB and shifts to the MSB and displays that data from left to right. The same hardware logic displays the CHAR data in the same fashion. Looking at Figure V.23.3, the first three data bytes for the edited character "4" on the right of the screen is `0x09`. In this data, the LSB or bit 0 is ON and the far left pixel is also ON. The next two bits in the data (shifting left towards the MSB) are OFF, thus keeping the next two pixels also OFF moving to the right on the screen. Since bit 3 is ON in the data, the top pixel of the right column of the character "4" is ON. The fourth data byte, or `0x1F` turns all five pixels ON, which is the new width of the edited character. All of the CHAR characters from `0x20` to `0x7F` are designed to begin its character pixels on the far left column and utilize the smallest pixel width practical without leaving the character unreadable. The edited version of the character "4" as shown in Figure V.23.3 would not be considered practical. Figure V.23.5 shows all of the graphic characters in the CHAR font file that is used in *BFI*.

The String Draw or `SD` program mentioned in Section V.16 that discusses Binary File Installation is used to draw any character string variable on a `HIRES` screen at any location on that screen. The interface to `SD` is defined by its `CALL` statement: `CALL SD,S$[,H%,L%,W%,C%,I%]`. In other words, at a minimum `SD` only requires a string variable `S$` in its `CALL` statement and the other parameters in the `CALL` statement are optional. As previously discussed, the `SD` routine begins at `0x6000` in memory. The `H%` parameter sets the MSB `HIRES` page to `0x20` or `0x40`, otherwise the parameter is ignored if it is set to `0x00`. The `L%` parameter tells `SD` on which screen line to draw `S$`, and its valid values range from 0 to 23. The `W%` parameter defines the window to begin drawing in, and its valid values range from 0 to 39. This parameter corresponds to the character byte number on a normal Text screen line. The `C%` parameter defines the cell within the current window in which to begin drawing, and its valid values range from 0 to 6. This parameter corresponds to the bit number within a character byte. Both the `W%` and `C%` parameter values are returned to the caller once `SD` processing has completed and `S$` has been drawn only if one or both of these parameters are included in the `CALL` statement. The `I%` parameter enables the drawing of `S$` in `INVERSE` anytime `I%` is not `zero`. Once `SD` processing has completed and `S$` has been drawn, `I%` is automatically reset to `zero`.

None of the characters in the CHAR font shown in Figure V.23.5 include a pre- or a post-character pixel providing some pixel space after the previous character or before the next character. Pixel space between all characters is automatically inserted by `SD`. Even the `SPACE` character `0x20` that is used between words is given an additional pixel insertion. After a cursory inspection of the figures shown in Section V.16 for *BFI*, nearly all of the character strings appear centered on the `HIRES` screen. It would be a significant challenge to manually process even one of these character strings in order to calculate how many pixels to the right the character string must be moved in order for that character string to appear centered on the `HIRES` screen. Not only must the size of each character be considered, but also consideration for that single pixel space that is inserted between each character and, of course, discounting the single pixel space after drawing the last character in the character string. What better time it is to develop a tool that can provide this critical information in the form that is useable by `SD`.

BFI is introduced by Figure V.16.1 where the character string "`Binary File Installation`" appears centered on the `HIRES` screen. The parameters that are used to display this particular character string include `L% = 8`, `W% = 12`, and `C% = 5` according to my Applesoft source code. When this same character string is entered into the *LENGTH* program as shown in Figure V.23.6, the entire character string is found to be 102 pixels in length if it is drawn on the `HIRES` screen by `SD`. Knowing that there are two hundred eighty pixels on each HIRES scan line, the character string would need to be moved to the right eighty-nine pixels for the character string to appear centered on the HIRES screen. For SD to accomplish this, the parameters W% and C% in the CALL statement would need to be set to 12 and 5, respectively. I processed all of the character strings that appear centered in *BFI* using the program *LENGTH*. It is fairly obvious that I saved more time in creating and utilizing the program *LENGTH* than the time it would have taken to determine the values manually for the parameters W% and C% manually for all of the character strings that appear centered in *BFI*, let alone guarantee the accuracy of these values if they were determined manually. What an utter illogical use of time that would have been. Furthermore, I now own a valuable and useful program, a tool that I can utilize at any time if I should develop another Applesoft program that uses SD to draw character strings that appear centered on a HIRES screen. This alone should be sufficient inducement to anyone who considers spending their time pursuing a repetitive task manually rather than using their time to write a valuable and useful program, a tool to perform that repetitive task.

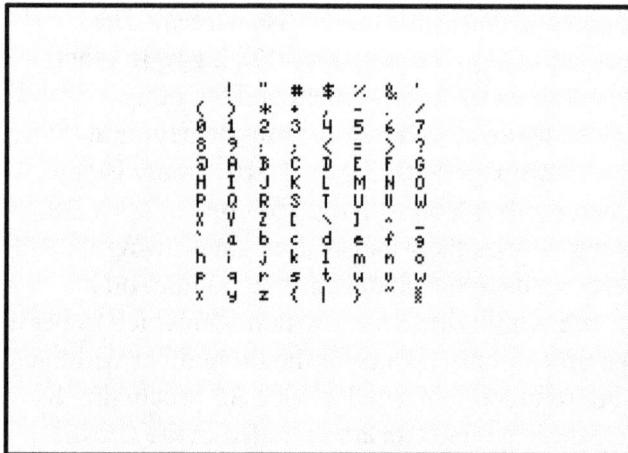

Figure V.23.5. Complete BFI CHAR Font

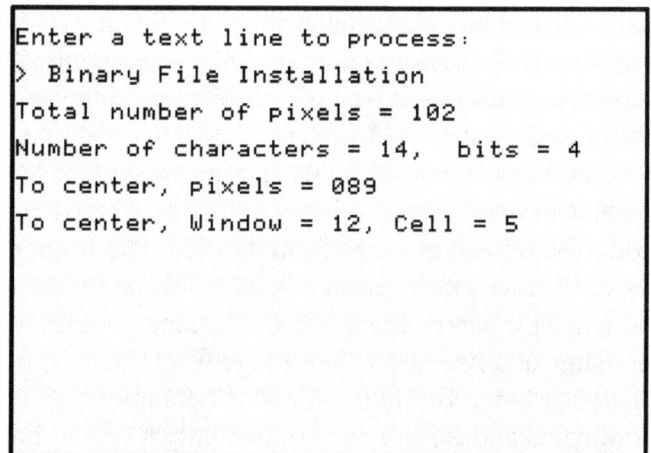

Figure V.23.6. Using LENGTH for String Draw

24. ICON Maker

During my discussion of the Applesoft hybrid program *BFI* in Section V.16, I introduced the subject of *ICON Maker*, the HIRES editing tool that I developed for Sierra On-Line in order to generate the *shape table* data for the screen icons that I use in *BFI*. I wrote the original *ICON Maker* tool in Applesoft and utilized ROM routines to draw lines on the HIRES graphics screen. I knew that the same ROM routines would be utilized by Sierra On-Line's customers in displaying the icons I had designed for its products. Actually, I never completed the Applesoft *ICON Maker* tool and there were several features that were still not yet complete. These incomplete features, however, were not important nor were they critical in delivering the icons and the icon display routines for the Sierra products. My present day *ICON Maker* tool is complete and it is written entirely in assembly language, and this version incorporates the same very high speed HIRES line drawing routines that are used in Draw ICON. Draw ICON, or DI is also introduced in Section V.16 for *BFI*. *ICON Maker* and Draw ICON do **not** utilize any ROM routines.

The icon window defines an area on the HIRES graphics screen where the *shape table* objects are drawn. The location of the first pixel in the upper left-hand corner of the icon window defines the start location for the entire icon. The icon is drawn relative to this start location which occurs within some index byte in some index bit from the left side of the screen on some index scan line from the top of the screen. In other words, the icon start location is some number of pixels to the left from the left side of the HIRES screen and some number of pixels (or scan lines) down from the top of the HIRES screen. When the icon window is defined, its location is specified by its X- and Y-coordinates in pixels. These coordinates are used additively to the *shape table* data when drawing each component of the icon.

In order to speed up and accelerate the drawing of lines and shapes in *ICON Maker* and in Draw ICON or in any other utility or game that utilizes HIRES graphics and animation, lookup tables are used for maximum calculation speed. Given an X-location on a scan line that is some number of pixels from the left side of the screen, that location must be converted into a byte index and a bit index that is within that index byte. Across each scan line, forty bytes of memory contain the data for the two hundred eighty pixels that are displayed, or seven pixels for each byte of data. Obviously, converting pixel number to byte index and bit index requires the division by seven with a remainder. This is a terrible division to implement without using lookup tables. The first set of lookup tables called XBASEL and XBASEH accomplishes this division easily at the expense of 0x118 bytes of data. XBASE simply determines the byte index from the base screen location that is found in GBAS, a page-zero pointer at 0x26/0x27. Pixel number is also used to index into a MASKNDX table in order to determine which index bit will be turned ON or OFF within the index byte, so this table provides the value for the remainder in the division by seven operation. The MASKNDX table is 0x100 bytes in size. In order to support color on the HIRES graphics screen, *ICON Maker* uses a COLORNDX table that is 0x100 bytes in size and this table is also indexed by pixel number. COLORNDX determines which color byte is selected from the 8-byte COLORBYT table. Specific bytes are copied from the COLORTBL table to form the COLORBYT table that supports a selected color for the icon component that is currently being drawn. The COLORTBL is 0x20 bytes in size. At this point, 0x340 bytes of table data are required just to support the X-location in pixels in order to accelerate the calculations for drawing lines and shapes in *ICON Maker*.

The Y-location in pixels (or scan lines) is used to initialize the base screen location or address for the page-zero pointer GBAS. Steven Wozniak constructed the Apple][HIRES graphics screen in three sections where each section consists of eight Text lines, and each Text line consists of eight scan lines. Therefore, there are a total of one hundred ninety-two scan lines that are used for the entire HIRES graphics screen. Within each of the three screen sections, the address of one Text line to the next Text line (or group of eight scan lines to the next group of eight scan lines) is incremented by 0x80 and each screen section is incremented by 0x28. Within one Text line, its eight scan lines are each incremented by 0x400. Wozniak's design of the hardware that displays the data in memory to the HIRES graphics screen requires the least number of hardware components when the data in memory is addressed and displayed using the above specifications. It is quite understandable and in view of the above specifications that using a lookup table to initialize GBAS using scan line as the index into the YBASE tables would definitely accelerate the calculations for drawing lines and shapes in *ICON Maker*. YBASE consists of two tables called YBASEL and YBASEH that define the full 16-bit base screen address for the start of each scan line. Obviously, these two tables are each 0xC0 (or 192) bytes in size.

Thus, the total number of bytes that are found in the lookup tables used to accelerate the calculations for drawing lines and shapes in *ICON Maker* and in Draw ICON is 0x4C0 bytes. Is using this much memory for lookup tables worth it? You bet it is! When lookup tables are utilized, an icon can be drawn nearly instantaneously. If the HPLOT ROM routine at 0xF457 and the HLIN ROM routine at

`0xF53A` are used instead, the icon would be drawn comparatively at a snail's pace. There is no faster way to accelerate the calculations for drawing dots and lines on the `HIRES` graphics screen than using these lookup tables for initializing the base screen address, the index byte, the index bit within that index byte, and the desired color mask. Another advantage for not using the `HPLOT` and `HLIN` ROM routines is that the `HLIN` ROM routine is flawed as I discussed in Section II.1. My analysis of the code for the `HLIN` ROM routine shows that the algorithm does not correctly calculate the delta difference of the horizontal and the vertical start to end points before drawing a line. This calculation error severely affects the appearance of all diagonally drawn lines in my opinion. The `HLIN` routine in *ICON Maker* and in Draw ICON does not contain this flaw. All diagonal lines are drawn precisely and diagonal lines are segmented equally in all instances and the results will always be the same without regard to the direction in which the lines are drawn. The `HLIN` ROM routine cannot make these same guarantees.

Command Name	Value	Command Size	Description
COLORCMD	0xF0	2 bytes	set COLOR index command
HORZCMD	0xF1	4 + n bytes	draw HORZ shape command
VERTCMD	0xF2	4 + n bytes	draw VERT shape command
DIAGCMD	0xF3	4 + n bytes	draw DIAG shape command
CURVECMD	0xF4	4 + n bytes	draw CURVE shape command
BOXCMD	0xF5	5 bytes	draw BOX shape command
PARLLCMD	0xF6	7 bytes	draw PARALLEL shape command
DOTCMD	0xF7	3 + 2n bytes	draw DOT shape command
CHAINCMD	0xF8	1 byte	exit ICONPROC with C-flag set command
GRPAGCMD	0xF9	2 bytes	set HIRES graphics page command
GROFFCMD	0xFA	4 bytes	set ICON window coordinates command
GRSIZCMD	0xFB	3 bytes	set ICON window size command
GRWIDCMD	0xFC	2 bytes	set ICON window frame thickness command
FRCLRCMD	0xFD	1 byte	clear ICON window frame command
FRSETCMD	0xFE	1 byte	draw ICON window frame command
EXITCMD	0xFF	1 byte	exit ICONPROC with C-flag clear command

Table V.24.1. Drawing Commands Available in ICONPROC

Color Name	Index	Color Value	Description
Black1	0x00	0x00000000	turn all graphic data bits OFF, MSB OFF
Green	0x01	0x2A552A55	set odd bit in even byte, even bit in odd byte, MSB OFF
Purple	0x02	0x552A552A	set even bit in even byte, odd bit in odd byte, MSB OFF
White1	0x03	0x7F7F7F7F	turn all graphic data bits ON, MSB OFF
Black2	0x04	0x80808080	turn all graphic data bits OFF, MSB ON
Orange	0x05	0xAAD5AAD5	set odd bit in even byte, even bit in odd byte, MSB ON
Blue	0x06	0xD5AAD5AA	set even bit in even byte, odd bit in odd byte, MSB ON
White2	0x07	0xFFFFFFFF	turn all graphic data bits ON, MSB ON

Table V.24.2. Simple Colors Available in ICONPROC

Graphic tools such as *ICON Maker* are not particularly suited for building colorful icons. Typically, this tool initializes the color of a new icon to `White1`, that is, with all bits `ON` except for the MSB, or color-group bit. It is only necessary to set color once, at the beginning of a *shape table*, and that color will be remembered and used to draw the rest of the icon. If color is used in some shapes and white in all other shapes, then every shape will be required to initialize its color space with its first entry command. Of course it is possible to use color in some of the shapes contained in an icon and white in the remaining shapes, or multiple colors within an icon. The subject of Apple][`HIRES` color is complicated, and very interesting. Color pairs are best used on the same scan line in a group of bytes, and the color pair may remain the same or change on the previous or next scan line. Color pairs are `Green` and `Purple` because the MSB is `OFF` in both colors, and `Orange` and `Blue` because the MSB is `ON` in both colors. `Black1` and `White1` are compatible with `Green` and `Purple` and `Black2` and `White2` are compatible with `Orange` and `Blue`. Any of the four colors may be used from byte to byte as long as the color bits begin on a byte boundary. If the icon is shifted, even by one bit left or right, its colors will shift, perhaps making the icon difficult to interpret. If the icon is shifted up or down, the colors will remain constant. Creating a colorful icon in *ICON Maker* does not guarantee that that icon will even look like the same icon or have the same color palette when it is drawn *in situ* by its target program. However, for those willing to develop strategies that can properly place a colorful icon as it is designed on the correct byte boundary, then *ICON Maker* will provide the necessary color commands that can be used to create an icon that will meet your needs.

The routine `ICONPROC` in *ICON Maker* utilizes a total of sixteen commands, five of which are for initialization, two of which draw or clear an ICON window frame, seven of which actually draw lines and shapes, and two of which chain to another *shape table* or exit the current *shape table*. These commands begin with the value of `0xF0` and they end with the value of `0xFF`. The data in the *shape table* is specifically designed to never equate to a command value, particularly the data in the `CURVE` and the `PARALLEL` commands as will soon become apparent. The `ICONPROC` commands are shown in Table V.24.1 with their command name, their value, and a brief description of their function. Table V.24.2 lists all of the simple colors that are available in `ICONPROC`. These colors, as well as the complex colors that are shown in Table V.24.3, are referenced by their Index number which is the number that is used in conjunction with the `COLORCMD`, `0xF0`. As previously explained above, the Index number for a color is used to copy specific bytes from the `COLORTBL` table to form the `COLORBYT` table. The complex colors are included in the *ICON Maker* and in the Draw ICON source code, but the color values are not included in the assembly. Additional changes to the source code for `ICONPROC` would be necessary in order to include all of the complex colors, though these changes would probably be trivial. Presently, the `COLORBYT` table is set to eight bytes in size and it will only support the complex colors that are six bytes or less in length because only six bytes can be indexed when using the `COLORNDX` table in its present form. The `COLORNDX` table would need to be expanded in order to index all ten color bytes that are associated with the last four complex colors shown in Table V.24.3.

When I designed *ICON Maker* originally, I had already created a number of icons using graph paper. I knew the range of sizes I needed for the ICON window. The ICON window must be large enough to accommodate the largest icon I needed to create, but not so large as to limit the number of icons I wanted to display at the bottom of a `HIRES` screen. And, the ICON window could not be so small as to prevent the display of an icon that could not represent the concept that I needed to convey. For example, an icon showing a standard dot-matrix printer of the day had to contain enough features of a typical printer to make it recognizable, but not so large and complex as to limit the number of other icons that needed to be displayed as well. During the process of creating a number of icons on graph paper, I kept in mind what I needed to distill from these icons: the icon was simply a collection of fundamental, basic, and easy-to-define shapes. The purpose of using a collection of fundamental and basic shapes to create a complete icon was to generate an icon *shape table* whose data set was reasonably small in size yet powerful enough to create a complete icon quickly and easily.

Color Name	Index	Color Value
Green/Black1	0x08	0x22440811
Purple/Black1	0x09	0x11224408
Orange/Black2	0x0A	0xA2C48891
Blue/Black2	0x0B	0x91A2C488
Green/White1	0x0C	0x3A5D2E57 6B75
Purple/White1	0x0D	0x5D2E576B 753A
Orange/White2	0x0E	0xBADDAED7 EBF5
Blue/White2	0x0F	0xDDAED7EB F5BA
White1/Green/Black1	0x10	0x3A746851 23470E1D
White1/Purple/Black1	0x11	0x74685123 470E1D3A
White2/Orange/Black2	0x12	0xBAF4E8D1 A3C78E9D
White2/Blue/Black2	0x13	0xF4E8D1A3 C78E9DBA
White1/Green/Black1/Green	0x14	0x3A510B5D 68452E74 2217
White1/Purple/Black1/Purple	0x15	0x510B5D68 452E7422 173A
White2/Orange/Black2/Orange	0x16	0xBAD18BDD E8C5AEF4 A297
White2/Blue/Black2/Blue	0x17	0xD18BDDE8 C5AEF4A2 97BA

Table V.24.3. Complex Colors Not Available in ICONPROC

Command	Usage	Example
0xF0	F0nn	F003
0xF1	F1xxyyXxYyXxYy ...	F10B1808210310
0xF2	F2xxyyYyXxYyXx ...	F20C1909220411
0xF3	F3xxyyXxYyXxYy ...	F30B18200E1128
0xF4	F4xxyyXYXYXY ...	F40C1929229299
0xF5	F5xxyyXxYy	F50B182824
0xF6	F6xxyyXxYyXYnn	F60C191B189203
0xF7	F7xxyyXXYYxxyyXXYY ...	F70B181D100D1B1B13
0xF8	F8	F8
0xF9	F9nn	F940
0xFA	FAxxXXyy	FA640032
0xFB	FBxXyY	FB2828
0xFC	FCnn	FC02
0xFD	FD	FD
0xFE	FE	FE
0xFF	FF	FF

Table V.24.4. Using ICONPROC Drawing Commands

Table V.24.4 defines the usage of each Drawing command including an example containing actual data. This example data is for demonstration purposes only. The HORZCMD command, or 0xF1 first establishes a fully qualified starting coordinate relative to the upper left-hand corner which is defined as the pixel location where the X-coordinate equals zero and the Y-coordinate equals zero. In the example data given for this command, the fully qualified starting coordinate is X = 11 and Y = 24. The remaining bytes of data following the fully qualified starting coordinate toggle between changing the horizontal coordinate and then changing the vertical coordinate, starting with the horizontal coordinate in this command. The HORZCMD as well as the VERTCMD only draw straight lines either horizontally or vertically. From the example data of seven bytes in Table V.24.4, the first byte of data changes the X-coordinate so that X = 8 while leaving the Y-coordinate unchanged, or Y = 24. A straight is drawn from 11,24 to 8,24. The next data byte changes the Y-coordinate so that Y = 33 while leaving the X-coordinate unchanged, or X = 8. A straight line is drawn from 8,24 to 8,33; then a line is drawn from 8,33 to 3,33; and finally a line is drawn from 3,33 to 3,16. With this command, seven bytes of data will draw four lines, eight bytes of data will draw five lines, *et cetera*.

The VERTCMD command, or 0xF2, functions exactly like the HORZCMD except the Y-coordinate is changed first with the first byte of data that comes after the fully qualified starting coordinate. From the example data of seven bytes in Table V.24.4, four lines are drawn: a line is drawn from 12,25 to 12,9; then a line is drawn from 12,9 to 34,9; then a line is drawn from 34,9 to 34,4; and finally a line is drawn from 34,4 to 17,4.

The DIAGCMD command, or 0xF3, draws diagonal lines from fully qualified coordinate data. This is a far more expensive command in terms of data utilization because fully qualified coordinate data must specify both the X- and the Y-coordinates for every point to which a line is drawn. Therefore, seven bytes of data will draw two lines, nine bytes of data will draw three lines, *et cetera*. From the example data of seven bytes in Table V.24.4, two diagonal lines are drawn: a line is drawn from 11,24 to 32,14; and finally a line is drawn from 32,14 to 17,40.

The CURVECMD command, or 0xF4, draws diagonal lines from a fully qualified start coordinate to any direction that has a ±7 pixel displacement. Each byte of data that follows the fully qualified start coordinate contains a ±7 pixel displacement for the X-coordinate in the upper nibble and a ±7 pixel displacement for the Y-coordinate in the lower nibble. The extraction of the coordinate displacements is performed by the DELTA routine. The A-register must contain the *shape table* data value for the input to this routine, and the DELTA routine exits with the displacement of the X-coordinate in the A-register and the displacement of the Y-coordinate in the Y-register and the C-flag clear. The code for the DELTA routine is shown in Figure V.24.1. Any negative displacement of a coordinate produces a two's compliment value that will provide the desired displacement when that value is added to the current coordinate value with the C-flag clear. In other words, a negative displacement of -1 is affected when the upper or lower nibble contains 0x8, a negative displacement of -2 is affected when the upper or lower nibble contains 0x9, *et cetera*. Therefore, the upper negative limit for any delta displacement data would be 0xEE which would affect a -7 displacement to both coordinates. This upper negative limit would ensure that the values for the Drawing commands in ICONPROC are protected. From the example data of seven bytes in Table V.24.4, four diagonal lines are drawn: a line is drawn from 12,25 to 14,23; then a line is drawn from 14,23 to 16,25; then a line is drawn from 16,25 to 14,27; and finally a line is drawn from 14,27 to 12,25. This results in a perfectly drawn diamond shape.

The BOXCMD command, or 0xF5, draws a square or rectangular box given the fully qualified coordinate values for its upper left-hand corner and its lower right-hand corner. With only five bytes of data, a box having four sides is perfectly drawn anywhere within the ICON window. From the example data of five bytes in Table V.24.4, a rectangular box is drawn: a line is drawn from 11,24 to 40,24; then a line is drawn from 40,24 to 40,36; then a line is drawn from 40,36 to 11,36; and finally a line is drawn from 11,36 to 11,24. This is certainly one of the more powerful Drawing commands in ICONPROC.

```
  :              :            :
4F59 48        152   DELTA   pha
4F5A           153   ;
4F5A 29 0F     154           and #CMDMASK
4F5C C9 08     155           cmp #$08
4F5E 90 02     156           bcc >1
4F60           157   ;
4F60 49 F7     158           eor #DLTACOMP
4F62           159   ;
4F62 A8        160   ^1      tay
4F63           161   ;
4F63 68        162           pla
4F64           163   ;
4F64 4A        164           lsr
4F65 4A        165           lsr
4F66 4A        166           lsr
4F67 4A        167           lsr
4F68           168   ;
4F68 C9 08     169           cmp #$08
4F6A 90 03     170           bcc >2
4F6C           171   ;
4F6C 49 F7     172           eor #DLTACOMP
4F6E           173   ;
4F6E 18        174           clc
4F6F           175   ;
4F6F 60        176   ^2      rts
  :              :            :
```

Figure V.24.1. DELTA Calculation in ICONPROC

The PARRLCMD command, or 0xF6, draws multiple, equally positioned, and equally offset parallel lines within the ICON window. To be sure, this command is the more complex of all the Drawing commands, but it provides so many unique features that make it a highly desirable command to use often. The PARRLCMD command requires seven bytes of data to draw at least two parallel lines, but it is capable of drawing up to two-hundred fifty-five additional parallel lines however impractical that may be. *ICON Maker* does not limit the additional parallel line count for this command. What *ICON Maker* does is limit the number of additional parallel lines that can be **drawn** within the ICON window given the specifications of the first line, the offsets to the second and remaining lines, and the line count for the additional parallel lines. From the example data of seven bytes in Table V.24.4, the initial diagonal line is drawn from two fully qualified coordinates, that is, from 12,25 to 27,24. The next byte of data provides the delta value for the second and remaining additional lines that will be drawn parallel to the initial diagonal line. The number of additional diagonal lines that are drawn is provided by the last byte of data which is the line count. The delta value, as in the CURVECMD command, can provide up to a ±7 pixel displacement to the initial fully qualified coordinates. In this example data, the delta value is 0x92 giving a -2 displacement to the X-coordinate and a +2 displacement to the Y-coordinate to **both** initial coordinates. Thus, the first additional parallel line, or second diagonal line is drawn from 10,27 to 25,26. The same delta values are applied to these coordinates two more times in order to draw a total of

322

three additional lines. The last two lines are drawn from 8,29 to 23,28 and from 6,31 to 21,30. It is absolutely exquisite how the parallel lines appear after they have been drawn so quickly and so easily!

The DOTCMD command, or 0xF7, draws one or more single dot pixels within the ICON window given the fully qualified coordinate that provides the X- and the Y-coordinate values for each pixel drawn. Multiple pixels may be specified with a single DOTCMD command. With this command, three bytes of data will draw one pixel, five bytes will draw two pixels, *et cetera*. From the example data of nine bytes in Table V.24.4, four pixels are drawn at 11,24; at 29,16; at 13,27; and at 27,19. A colorful icon would be the most difficult of all icons to create if a single pixel of a particular color is necessary at a required ICON window location. The difficulty would be compounded if multiple colored pixels were necessary at required locations since a color will only appear when its pixel is ON in even bits of even bytes or in even bits of odd bytes or in odd bits of even bytes or in odd bits of odd bytes throughout a scan line. The DOTCMD command is the most costly in terms of its shape size to its data size for all of the Drawing commands in ICONPROC. However, this command, with only two bytes of data for the fully qualified coordinate for a single pixel, is still the better option than wastefully using any of the other commands to implement turning ON a single pixel.

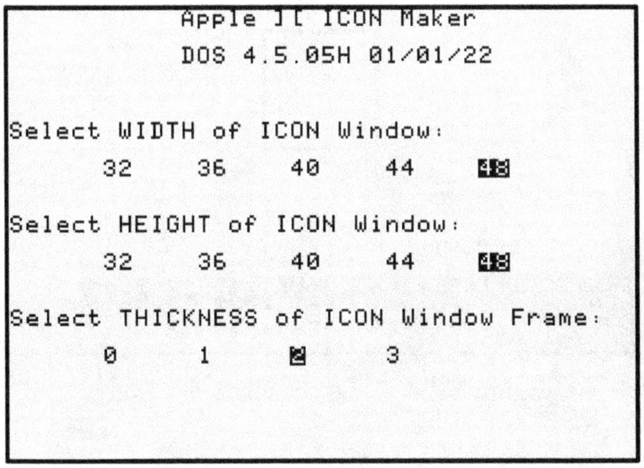

Figure V.24.2. Initialization of ICON Maker

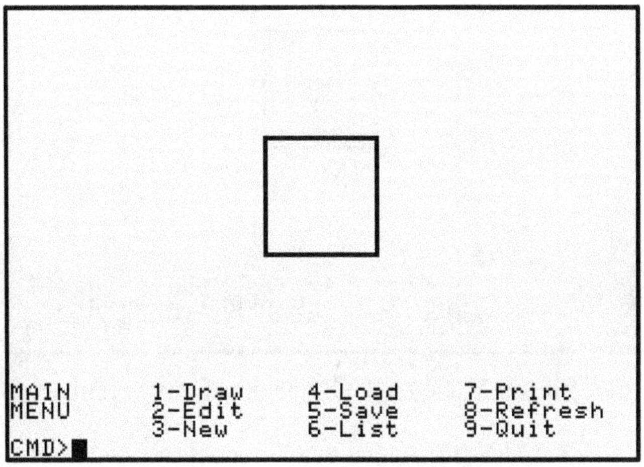

Figure V.24.3. ICON Maker Main Menu

BFI uses two sizes for its ICON windows: 0x28 x 0x28 and 0x30 x 0x30. *BFI* only uses ICON window frames that are two pixels in thickness. These parameters are the first values that *ICON Maker* requests, so when *ICON Maker* first starts up as shown in Figure V.24.2, the WIDTH and HEIGHT of the ICON window and the THICKNESS of the ICON window frame can be easily selected. I believe that values smaller and/or larger than those offered would be excessive or not within the purview of *ICON Maker*. The Main Menu for *ICON Maker* is shown in Figure V.24.3 with an ICON window frame that is drawn based on the selected values for WIDTH, HEIGHT, and THICKNESS. The ICON window is placed on the HIRES screen at calculated coordinates in order to center the window and set it at a pleasing height to the user's point of view. The X- and Y-coordinates are calculated as follows:

```
X = 140 — WIDTH / 2
Y =  80 — HEIGHT / 2
```

The ICON window and the ICON window frame are drawn by `ICONPROC` after *ICON Maker* has initialized an ICON Shape Structure using the Drawing commands `0xF0`, `0xF9`, `0xFA`, `0xFB`, and `0xFC` and the values selected from Figure V.24.2. For example, if the ICON window is 48x48, the coordinates for the window will be X = 116 and Y = 56. The ICON window frame is always drawn exterior to the ICON window such that all *shape table* values will be added to the upper left-hand coordinate that is equal to 116,56 for the window shown in Figure V.24.3. All calculations involving the X-coordinate will automatically set the most significant byte to `zero`. In this example, the ICON window frame will be drawn from 115,55 to 164,55 to 164,104 to 115,104 and to 115,55 and from 114,54 to 165,54 to 165,105 to 114,105 and to 114,54 because the `THICKNESS` of the ICON window frame is equal to two. *ICON Maker* initializes a number of objects such as `ERRORNDX`, `ASONERR`, `PROMPT`, `ASRUN`, and the configuration of the `HIRES` screen. The `ICONBUFR` is initialized with the color command and the color `WHITE1`. When building an icon in `ICONBUFR`, if the color command is chosen first with a different color, that color replaces `WHITE1`.

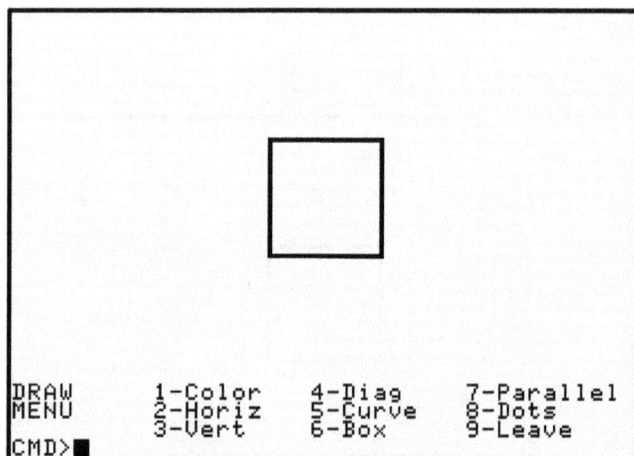	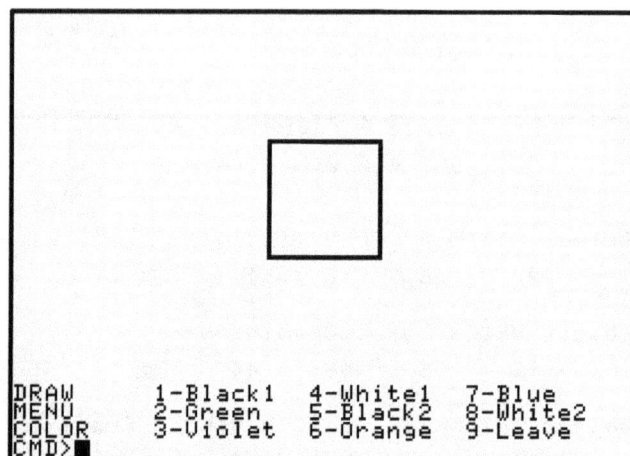
Figure V.24.4. ICON Maker Draw Menu	Figure V.24.5. Draw Menu for Color

The first option available in the Main Menu is the `Draw` option, and the `Draw` option displays the Draw Menu as shown in Figure V.24.4. `Color` is the first option available in the Draw Menu, and the `Color` option displays the Draw Menu Color as shown in Figure V.24.5. This menu allows one to select any of the simple colors that are available in `ICONPROC` as shown previously in Table.V.24.2. Once a complete icon has been created or any time during its creation, the `Edit` option in the Main Menu enables an entire icon to be shifted left or right or up or down within the ICON window. The complete icon can never be shifted out of the ICON window. Perhaps an icon is first designed within a large ICON window; the complete icon can be shifted towards the upper left-hand corner using `Edit`, then `Saved`, and finally `Loaded` into a smaller ICON window for display. An example in using `Edit` to move a complete icon within an ICON window is shown in Figures V.24.6 and V.24.7. This icon can presumably be placed within a smaller ICON window. Selecting the `New` option in the Main Menu simply clears `ICONBUFR` except for the initial color command and the color `WHITE1`. Selecting the `Load` option in the Main Menu provides the ability to enter a filename as shown in Figure V.24.8. Any DOS disk error is reported immediately as shown in Figure V.24.9. When a DOS disk error does occur, the appropriate error message is displayed without causing an interruption to the *ICON Maker* program.

Figure V.24.6. Main Menu for Edit

Figure V.24.7. Moving an Icon in Edit

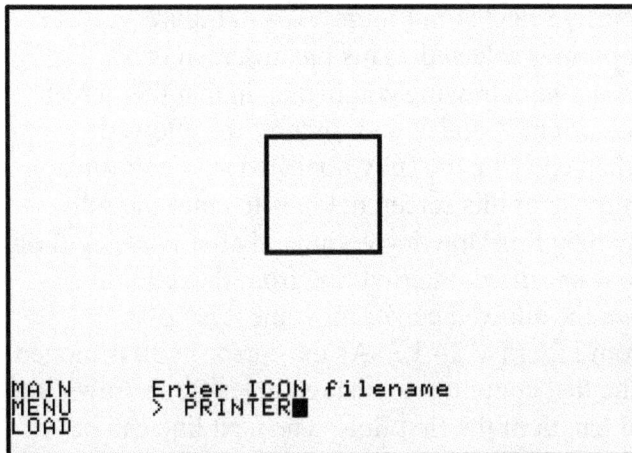

Figure V.24.8. Main Menu for Load

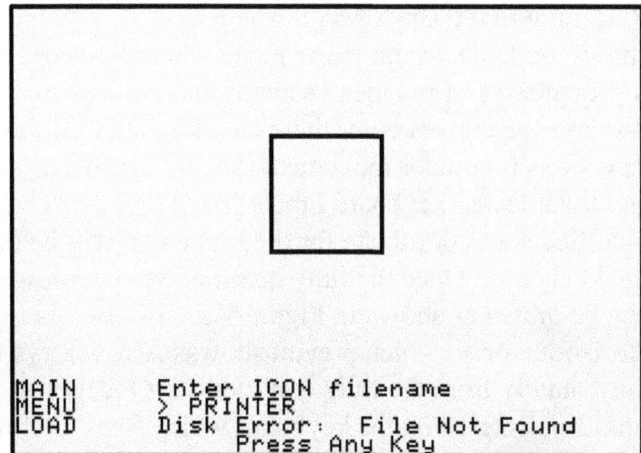

Figure V.24.9. Disk Errors in ICON Maker

Selecting the `Save` option in the Main Menu provides the ability to save the data that is currently in memory in `ICONBUFR` into a binary file or into a Text file as shown in Figure V.24.10. The actual filename that is used to save the binary data or the Text data is entered next as shown in Figure V.24.11. Example Text data for an icon in memory whose binary data is currently in `ICONBUFR` is shown in Figure V.24.12. This is the same Text data that would be written into a Text file after selecting the `Save` option in the Main Menu or displayed by the `List` option in the Main Menu or sent to the printer by the `Print` option in the Main Menu. *ICON Maker* formats the binary data in memory such that each Text line begins with a Drawing command followed by the data that is utilized to draw the shape that is specified by that command. All Drawing commands and their data are expressed in Hexadecimal. The last option in the Main Menu is the `Refresh` option. `Refresh` clears the `HIRES` screen of the ICON window contents and the ICON window frame, and redraws the ICON window frame and sends the contents of `ICONBUFR` to `ICONPROC` in order for that data to be drawn as a complete icon. `Refresh` ensures that the data currently in `ICONBUFR` is correct and it verifies that all of the Drawing commands and their data components draw the shapes that are specified in `ICONBUFR` without error.

Figure V.24.10. Main Menu for Save

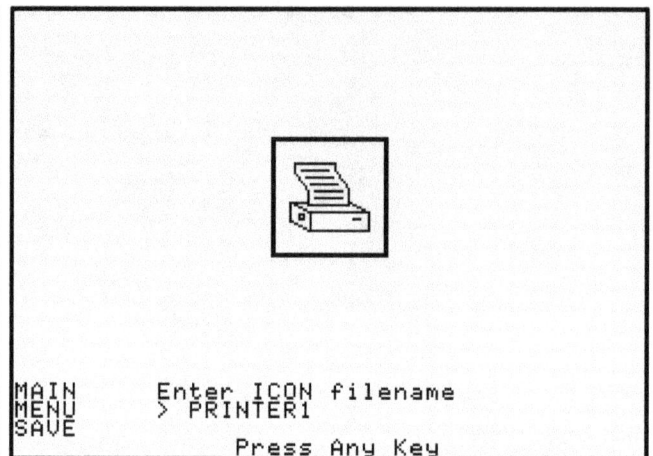

Figure V.24.11. Entering Filename in Save

Returning to the Draw Menu where `Color` was previously selected in Figure V.24.4, Figure V.24.13 shows the Draw Menu Horiz menu when the `Horiz` option is selected. This menu screen is representative of the menu screens that are shown for the other Drawing commands in that this screen displays the current color that is in effect as well as the current X and Y coordinates, the allowed directions for cursor movement (i.e. all Arrow Keys when entering the fully qualified start coordinate), and the allowed keyboard inputs (i.e. `S` and `Q`). The purpose of this screen menu is to enter the fully qualified start coordinate for the shape that will be drawn by this Drawing command after pressing `S` on the keyboard. Once the fully qualified start coordinate is specified, the first line from that coordinate can be drawn as shown in Figure V.24.14. In this figure the allowed cursor movement is now Horizontal only, which previously was Arrow Keys from Figure V.24.13. As the cursor point is moved horizontally from the fully qualified start location, a line that continues to change in length is drawn until `D` is entered on the keyboard which fixes the final length of the first line. The next line can be drawn only in the Vertical direction, followed by the third line in the Horizontal direction, and followed by the fourth line in the Vertical direction as shown in Figure V.24.15 that ends at X = 3 and Y = 25.

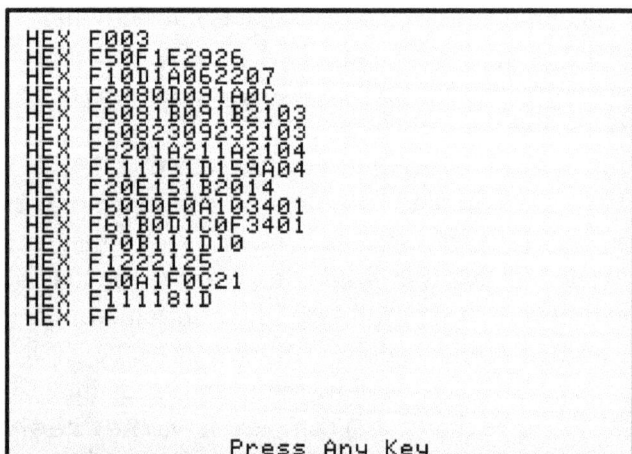

Figure V.24.12. ICON Maker Text Data for Icon

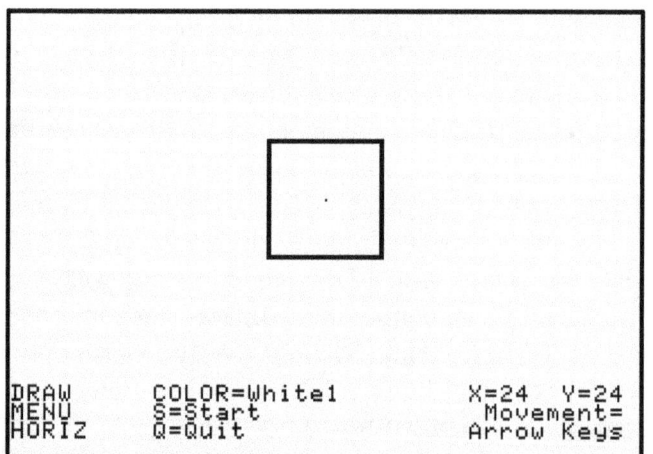

Figure V.24.13. Draw Menu for Horiz

326

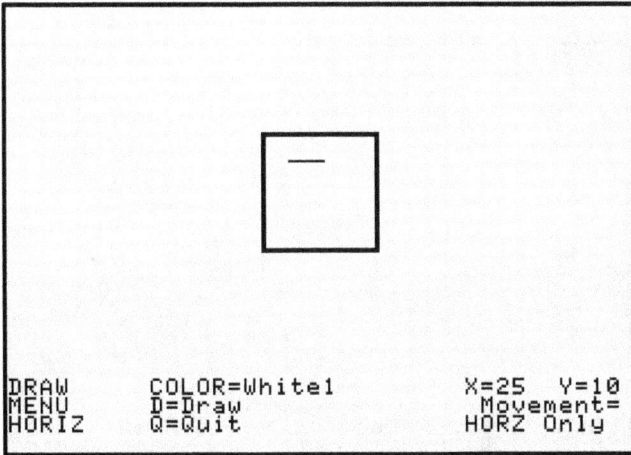

Figure V.24.14. Drawing Lines in Horiz

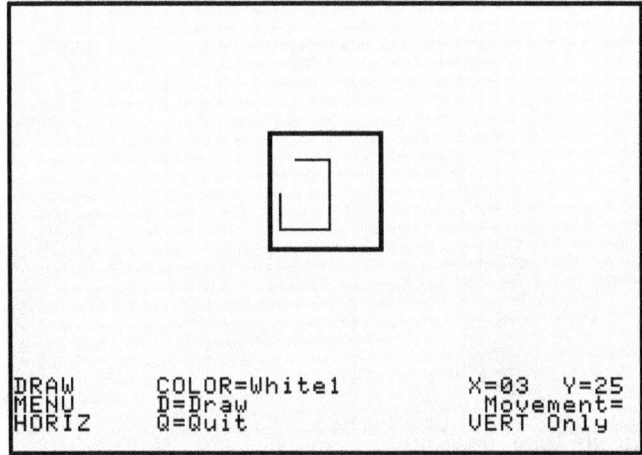

Figure V.24.15. Drawing More Lines in Horiz

After selecting the `Vert` option in Figure V.24.4 and entering the fully qualified start coordinate as in the example for the `Horiz` option shown in Figure V.24.13, the first Vertical line can be drawn as shown in Figure V.24.16 where the allowed cursor movement is Vertical only. As the cursor point is moved vertically from the fully qualified start location, a line that continues to change in length is drawn until `D` is entered on the keyboard which fixes the final length of the first line. The next line can be drawn only in the Horizontal direction, followed by the third line in the Vertical direction, and followed by the fourth line in the Horizontal direction as shown in Figure V.24.17 that ends at X = 22 and Y = 7.

The `Diagonal` option in Figure V.24.4 allows the drawing of a diagonal line in any direction from the fully qualified start coordinate after that coordinate has been specified. This diagonal line may be drawn having any length, and when `D` is pressed on the keyboard, its final fully qualified end coordinate is recorded into `ICONBUFR` as shown in Figure V.24.18. Any number of diagonal lines may be drawn from end to end where each time `D` is pressed on the keyboard, the current fully qualified coordinate is recorded into `ICONBUFR` as shown in Figure V.24.19. As noted earlier, `DIAGCMD` is a far more expensive command in terms of data utilization because every line ends at a fully qualified coordinate.

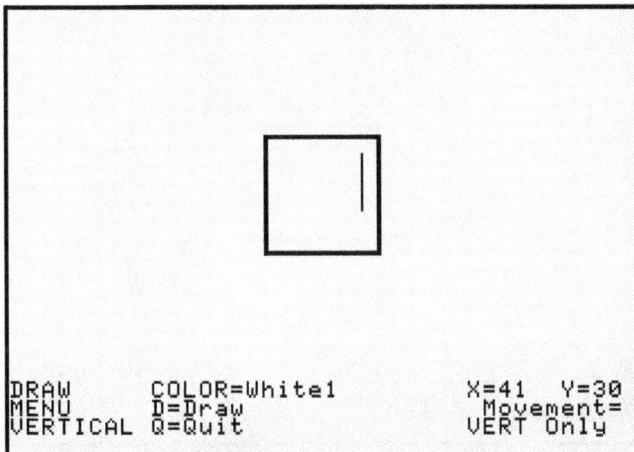

Figure V.24.16. Draw Menu for Vertical

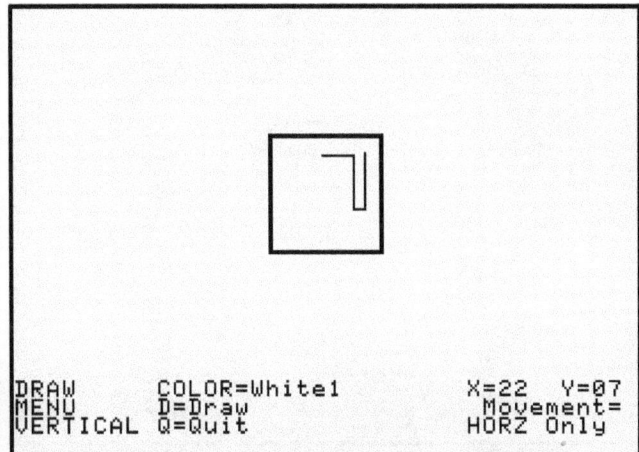

Figure V.24.17. Drawing Lines in Vertical

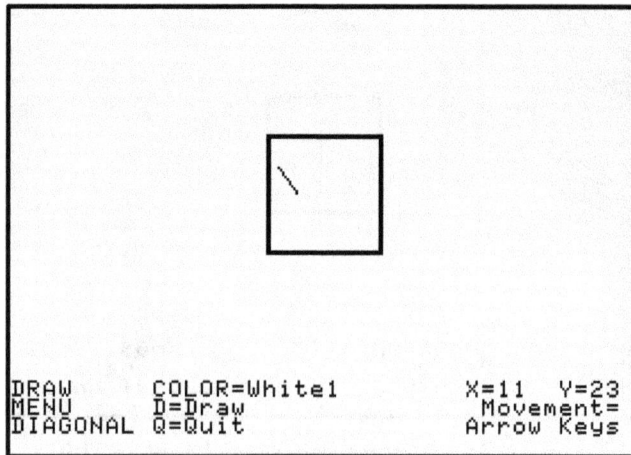
Figure V.24.18. Draw Menu for Diagonal

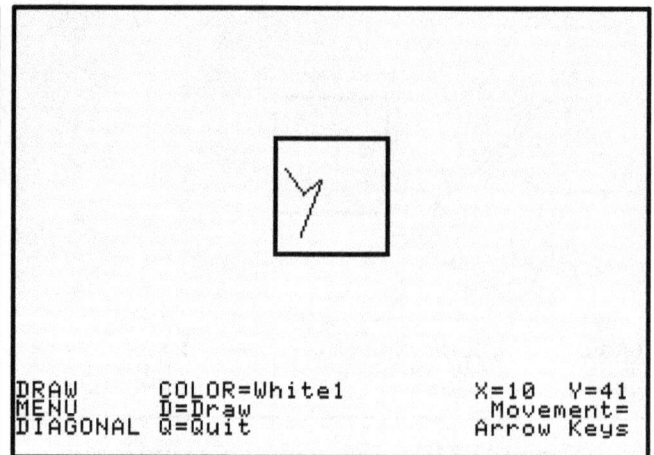
Figure V.24.19. Drawing Lines in Diagonal

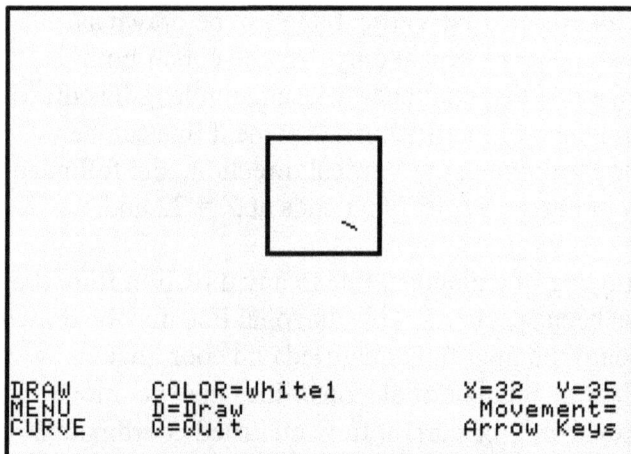
Figure V.24.20. Draw Menu for Curve

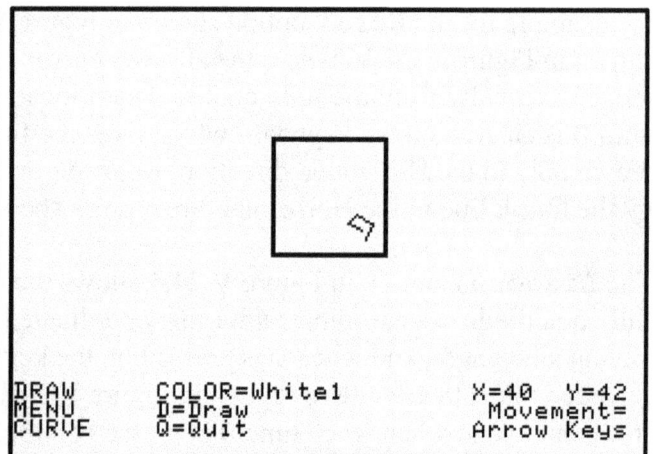
Figure V.24.21. Drawing Lines in Curve

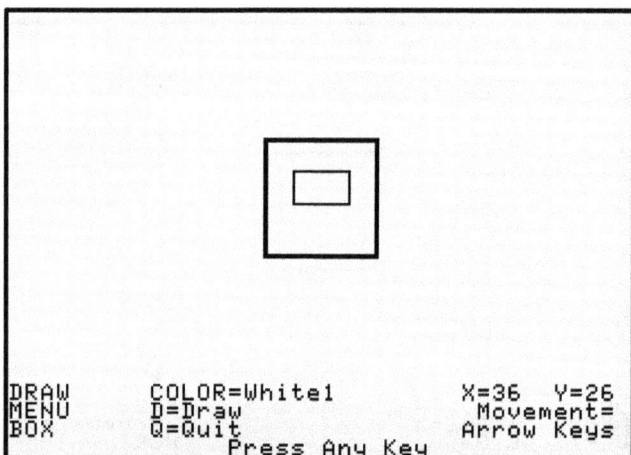
Figure V.24.22. Draw Menu for Box

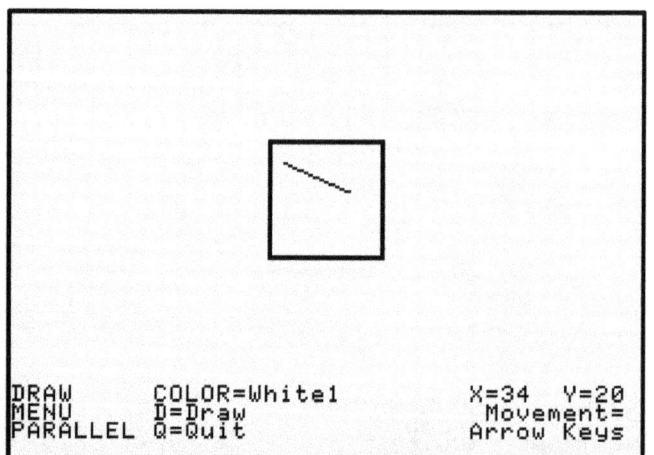
Figure V.24.23. Draw Menu for Parallel

The `Curve` option in Figure V.24.4 allows the drawing of a diagonal line in any direction from the fully qualified start coordinate after that coordinate has been specified. This diagonal line is limited to be drawn having up to a ±7 pixel displacement from the fully qualified start coordinate as shown in Figure V.24.20. This displacement is recorded into `ICONBUFR` as a single byte containing both the X and the Y displacements with the X displacement in the upper nibble and the Y displacement in the lower nibble. Any number of diagonal lines may be drawn from end to end having up to a ±7 pixel displacement, and each time `D` is pressed on the keyboard a single byte displacement value is recorded into `ICONBUFR` as shown in Figure V.24.21.

The `Box` option in Figure V.24.4 is one of the most entertaining Drawing commands to draw. After the fully qualified start coordinate has been specified for the upper left-hand corner of a box, the lower right-hand corner of the box can then be specified. A new box is continuously drawn as the cursor is moved either vertically or horizontally until `D` is pressed on the keyboard. Of course, if `Q` or `ESCAPE` is pressed the `Box` option is immediately terminated and the Draw Menu of Figure V.24.4 is displayed. As soon as `D` is pressed on the keyboard, the current fully qualified coordinate of the lower right-hand corner of the box is recorded into `ICONBUFR` as shown in Figure V.24.22.

The `Parallel` option in Figure V.24.4 is used to create one of the more complex of all the Drawing commands. This option begins by first creating a diagonal line similarly in how a diagonal line is initially created for the `Diagonal` option shown in Figure V.24.18. This diagonal line may be drawn in any direction having any length from the fully qualified start coordinate, and when `D` is pressed on the keyboard, its fully qualified end coordinate is recorded into `ICONBUFR` as shown in Figure V.24.23. The diagonal lines that will be drawn parallel to this initial diagonal line will be drawn having up to a ±7 pixel displacement from the start and end coordinates that were established by the initial diagonal line. When `D` is pressed on the keyboard, that displacement byte from the start coordinate is recorded into `ICONBUFR` and the Arrow Keys are used to increment or decrement the number of additional parallel lines that are drawn in addition to the diagonal line that was drawn initially as shown in Figure V.24.24. When `D` is pressed on the keyboard a final time for `Done`, the line count for the additional parallel lines that are drawn is recorded into `ICONBUFR`. Of all the Drawing commands and for only seven bytes of data this command requires, the `PARRLCMD` command provides so many unique features that makes this command a highly desirable command to use often.

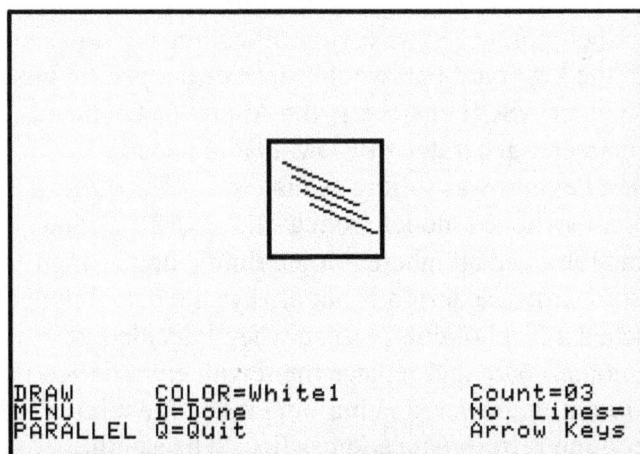

Figure V.24.24. Drawing Lines in Parallel

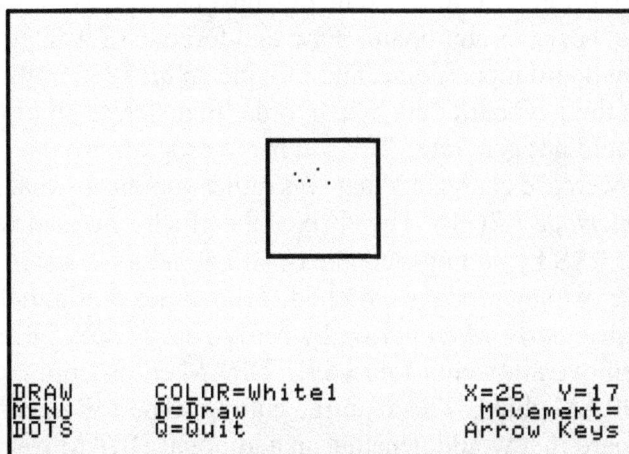

Figure V.24.25. Drawing Single Points in Dots

329

The `Dots` option is the last drawing option shown in Figure V.24.4, and this option is used to create one or more shapes that are a single dot pixel in size. When `D` is pressed on the keyboard, the fully qualified coordinate is recorded into `ICONBUFR` which is for the X- and the Y-coordinate values of the drawn pixel as shown in Figure V.24.25. The Arrow Keys are used to select the coordinate values for each desired dot pixel.

Draw ICON is designed to draw a specific set of icons on a `HIRES` screen. *BFI* utilizes five sets of icons for all of its `HIRES` pages. In two of these sets of icons is the icon of a file cabinet having different drawers open and closed. In order to reduce the amount of data used for each *shape table*, the common portion of the file cabinet is drawn followed by its unique portion in two sets of icons for their particular `HIRES` screen. However, to prevent Draw ICON from moving to the next icon to draw in the "draw icon loop" before the unique portion of the file cabinet can be drawn in the current icon, the `CHAINCMD` command is utilized. The `CHAINCMD` command terminates the *shape table* of an icon leaving the C-flag set instead leaving the C-flag clear as in the `EXITCMD`. This allows the "draw icon loop" to operate on the C-flag state and "chain" to another *shape table* in order to complete the icon that was started by the previous *shape table*. The `CHAINCMD` command cannot be added as the terminator of a *shape table* by *ICON Maker*; this command must be added manually. For example, when a Text file containing a *shape table* is read into a Lisa file using `EXEC`, the source code for that *shape table* can be modified at that time and the `EXITCMD` command can be changed to the `CHAINCMD` command. *BFI* only uses the `CHAINCMD` command once in order to draw one particular icon several different ways. It is quite extraordinary how nicely it works and how much *shape table* data is saved.

ICON Maker is a unique `HIRES` drawing and editing tool I developed and wrote, a tool which I used to design and generate the *shape table* data for *BFI* screen icons. *ICON Maker* does not depend on any of the `HIRES` ROM routines that are used by the Applesoft drawing command repertoire such as the `HPLOT` and `HLIN` statements. On the other hand, *ICON Maker* uses its own very high speed `HIRES` line drawing routines.

25. Apple][+ Memory Upgrade

As an Electrical Engineering graduate student in the early 1980's, I wanted to utilize my Apple][+ as an opportunity to make some practical hardware modifications to the Apple][+ motherboard and to the keyboard circuit board. First and foremost I wanted to incorporate a shift key modification, add in keyboard repeat logic, and provide an *alt* key circuit to the keyboard that would set or clear specific bits in the keyboard data byte in order to generate all of the other ASCII characters the Apple][+ keyboard could not generate. This led me to program my own character generator EPROM that included lowercase characters that was rather similar to what Dan Paymar was selling as his *Lowercase Adaptor Interface PROM*. Then I fixed the glitch I noticed when I switched modes from `TEXT`, `LOWRES`, and `HIRES` by adding a couple of additional logic gates that removed an inherent logic timing delay when the display mode is switched. Sometimes a minimalistic hardware design is not always the better choice particularly when video glitches are easily seen. I reached a level of competence when I decided to remove all twenty-four 16 Kb DRAM chips from the motherboard and replace them with eight 64 Kb DRAM chips. This required cutting some foil traces, rerouting power, and building a satellite circuit board that would generate an additional DRAM row/column refresh/data address line. The satellite circuit even includes logic to model the memory of the Language Card partition in order to emulate the action of certain addresses that acted like Soft Switches. In theory it all worked perfectly in my head, of course. The satellite circuit I developed is shown in Figure V.25.1. I paused a very, very long moment before applying power to my modified motherboard the very first time. I was pleased, if not absolutely delighted to find that my 48 KB Apple][+ was now fully 64 KB functional as if a Language Card resides in Slot 0. There was no blue smoke that went *Puff*. Wow! Even today I marvel at how gutsy I was to implement this drastic modification to the motherboard of my beloved Apple][+.

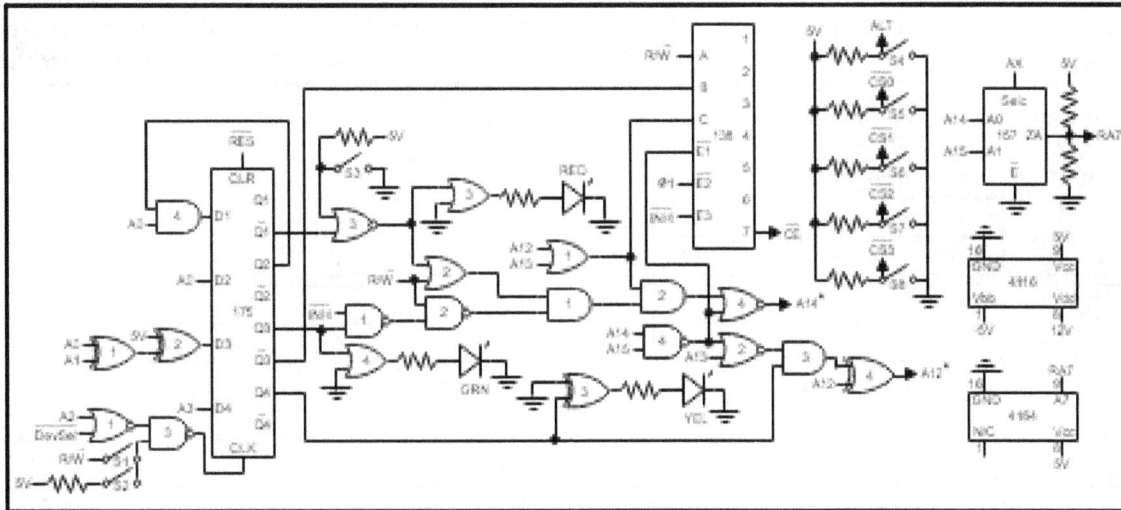

Figure V.25.1. Apple][+ Satellite Circuit Diagram

Signal	Location	Signal	Location
ø1	B1,6 (74LS175)	A12	H4,3 (8T97)
AX	C2,14 (74LS195)	A13	H5,3 (8T97)
DevSel	H2,15 (74LS138, Slot 0)	A14	J1,9 (74LS257)
INH	F3,18 (ROM-E8)	A15	J1,12 (74LS257)
RES	A7,3 (keyboard socket)	A12*	to C1,3 (74LS157)
R/W	H5,5 (8T97)	A14*	to F2,14 (74LS139)
A0	H5,11 (8T97)	RA7	to all 4164,9
A1	H4,5 (8T97)	CE	to all EPROM's CE
A2	H5,7 (8T97)	ALT	to all EPROM's A14
A3	H5,9 (8T97)	CS0–CS3	to each EPROM CS

Table V.25.1. Apple][+ Satellite Circuit Board Connections

As shown in Figure V.25.1, the satellite circuit board contains eight logic chips, three LEDs, eight DIP switches, and a 26-pin connector for all of the signals shown in Table V.25.1, along with power and ground. Either DIP switch 1 or 2 must be closed, but not both. If DIP switch 1 is closed then the 74LS175 configuration register is clocked only with a read to 0xC08n, where **n** can be 0x0 to 0xF. If DIP switch 2 is closed then the configuration register is clocked with either a read or a write to 0xC08n. RAM memory in the Language Card partition is enabled if 0xC080, 0xC083, 0xC088, or 0xC08B is read, and the green LED glows. If RAM Bank 1 is enabled (i.e. `0xC088` to `0xC08F` is read) the yellow LED glows. RAM is write-enabled if `0xC081`, `0xC083`, `0xC089`, or `0xC08B` is read twice, and when DIP switch 3 is closed, the red LED glows. Opening DIP switch 3 will absolutely electrically write-protect RAM memory in the Language Card partition.

Input to 74LS175 Latch	Input Address Bus	Red LED State	Grn LED State	Yel LED State	Final A12* State	RAM Enabled		ROM Read Enable	Output Address Bus RAM/ROM
						R	W		
0xC080 RAM2 WP 0b0100	<0xC000	0	1	0	A12	1	1	0	<0xC000
	0xCnnn	0	1	0	0	0	0	0	0xCnnn
	0xDnnn	0	1	0	1	1	0	0	0xDnnn
	0xEnnn	0	1	0	0	1	0	0	0xEnnn
	0xFnnn	0	1	0	1	1	0	0	0xFnnn
0xC081 ROM2 WP 0b0010	<0xC000	0	0	0	A12	1	1	0	<0xC000
	0xCnnn	0	0	0	0	0	0	0	0xCnnn
	0xDnnn	0	0	0	1	0	0	1	0xDnnn
	0xEnnn	0	0	0	0	0	0	1	0xEnnn
	0xFnnn	0	0	0	1	0	0	1	0xFnnn
0xC081 0xC081 ROM2 WE 0b0011	<0xC000	1	0	0	A12	1	1	0	<0xC000
	0xCnnn	1	0	0	0	0	0	0	0xCnnn
	0xDnnn	1	0	0	1	0	1	1	0xDnnn
	0xEnnn	1	0	0	0	0	1	1	0xEnnn
	0xFnnn	1	0	0	1	0	1	1	0xFnnn
0xC082 ROM2 WP 0b0000	<0xC000	0	0	0	A12	1	1	0	<0xC000
	0xCnnn	0	0	0	0	0	0	0	0xCnnn
	0xDnnn	0	0	0	1	0	0	1	0xDnnn
	0xEnnn	0	0	0	0	0	0	1	0xEnnn
	0xFnnn	0	0	0	1	0	0	1	0xFnnn
0xC083 RAM2 WP 0b0110	<0xC000	0	1	0	A12	1	1	0	<0xC000
	0xCnnn	0	1	0	0	0	0	0	0xCnnn
	0xDnnn	0	1	0	1	1	0	0	0xDnnn
	0xEnnn	0	1	0	0	1	0	0	0xEnnn
	0xFnnn	0	1	0	1	1	0	0	0xFnnn
0xC083 0xC083 RAM2 WE 0b0111	<0xC000	1	1	0	A12	1	1	0	<0xC000
	0xCnnn	1	1	0	0	0	0	0	0xCnnn
	0xDnnn	1	1	0	1	1	1	0	0xDnnn
	0xEnnn	1	1	0	0	1	1	0	0xEnnn
	0xFnnn	1	1	0	1	1	1	0	0xFnnn
0b0001	This configuration is not possible to select, so it is not valid.								
0b0101	This configuration is not possible to select, so it is not valid.								

Table V.25.2. Apple][+ Satellite Circuit Board Operation, Part 1

Input to 74LS175 Latch	Input Address Bus	Red LED State	Grn LED State	Yel LED State	Final A12* State	RAM Enabled		ROM Read Enable	Output Address Bus RAM/ROM
						R	W		
0xC088 RAM1 WP 0b1100	<0xC000	0	1	1	A12	1	1	0	<0xC000
	0xCnnn	0	1	1	1	0	0	0	0xDnnn
	0xDnnn	0	1	1	0	1	0	0	0xCnnn
	0xEnnn	0	1	1	0	1	0	0	0xEnnn
	0xFnnn	0	1	1	1	1	0	0	0xFnnn
0xC089 ROM1 WP 0b1010	<0xC000	0	0	1	A12	1	1	0	<0xC000
	0xCnnn	0	0	1	1	0	0	0	0xDnnn
	0xDnnn	0	0	1	0	0	0	1	0xCnnn
	0xEnnn	0	0	1	0	0	0	1	0xEnnn
	0xFnnn	0	0	1	1	0	0	1	0xFnnn
0xC089 0xC089 ROM1 WE 0b1011	<0xC000	1	0	1	A12	1	1	0	<0xC000
	0xCnnn	1	0	1	1	0	0	0	0xDnnn
	0xDnnn	1	0	1	0	0	1	1	0xCnnn
	0xEnnn	1	0	1	0	0	1	1	0xEnnn
	0xFnnn	1	0	1	1	0	1	1	0xFnnn
0xC08A ROM1 WP 0b1000	<0xC000	0	0	1	A12	1	1	0	<0xC000
	0xCnnn	0	0	1	1	0	0	0	0xDnnn
	0xDnnn	0	0	1	0	0	0	1	0xCnnn
	0xEnnn	0	0	1	0	0	0	1	0xEnnn
	0xFnnn	0	0	1	1	0	0	1	0xFnnn
0xC08B RAM1 WP 0b1110	<0xC000	0	1	1	A12	1	1	0	<0xC000
	0xCnnn	0	1	1	1	0	0	0	0xDnnn
	0xDnnn	0	1	1	0	1	0	0	0xCnnn
	0xEnnn	0	1	1	0	1	0	0	0xEnnn
	0xFnnn	0	1	1	1	1	0	0	0xFnnn
0xC08B 0xC08B RAM1 WE 0b1111	<0xC000	1	1	1	A12	1	1	0	<0xC000
	0xCnnn	1	1	1	1	0	0	0	0xDnnn
	0xDnnn	1	1	1	0	1	1	0	0xCnnn
	0xEnnn	1	1	1	0	1	1	0	0xEnnn
	0xFnnn	1	1	1	1	1	1	0	0xFnnn
0b1001	This configuration is not possible to select, so it is not valid.								
0b1101	This configuration is not possible to select, so it is not valid.								

Table V.25.3. Apple][+ Satellite Circuit Board Operation, Part 2

Table V.25.1 lists all of the signals that I required and the location on the Apple][+ motherboard where I obtained that signal. In order to provide two banks of RAM memory in the Language Card partition for the 0xD000 to 0xDFFF address range, address lines A12* and A14* must be derived from the outputs of the 74LS175 configuration register on the satellite circuit board, and from the real A12, A13, A14, and A15 address lines. The A14 and A15 address line are from a 74LS257 at motherboard location J1, and they also support memory data access and memory data refresh. These two derived address lines are connected directly to the pins of C1,3 and F2,14. Memory refresh for the 4164 chips is accomplished using the current RA0 through RA6 signals on the motherboard without regard to the derived RA7 signal. The RA7 signal simply provides the eighth row and eighth column address in order to access the full 64 Kb of each 4164 DRAM chip. Tables V.25.2 and V.25.3 provide the details of the operation of the Apple][+ Satellite Circuit Board vis-á-vis the input address bus, the state of each LED, whether RAM is read-enabled or write-enabled, whether ROM is read-enabled, and the effective memory address generated for all other motherboard logic.

A 27128 EPROM is the minimum size that can hold the ROM firmware from 0xD000 to 0xFFFF, although the first 4 KB of this EPROM is not addressed. When a 27256 EPROM is used to contain two ROM firmware images, DIP switch 4 (to pin 27, A14) can be used to select the desired image. If DIP switch 4 is closed, the lower image is selected. DIP switches 5, 6, 7, and 8 select one of four possible EPROMs on the Apple][+ motherboard. I removed all six 24-pin ROM sockets and installed four 28-pin EPROM sockets ensuring that pins 1, 2, 27, and 28 were electrically isolated from the motherboard. Only one of these four DIP switches should be closed, otherwise multiple EPROMs would be enabled simultaneously. Honestly, I ended up preparing and programming only a single 27256 EPROM containing two ROM images. Providing access to three more similar EPROMs never became necessary and the design was slightly over-kill. Better to have too much than too little EPROM expansion capabilities!

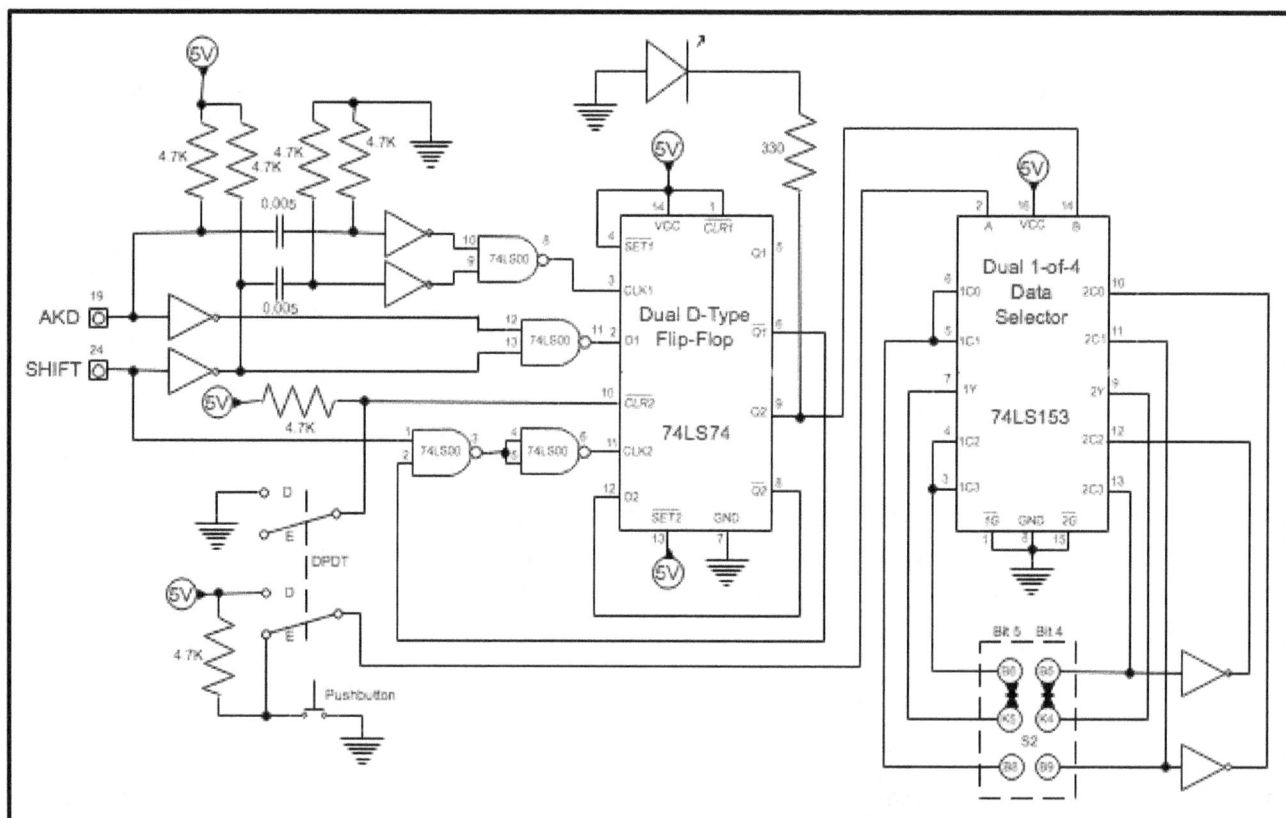

Figure V.26.1. Apple][+ Keyboard Modification Circuit

26. Apple][+ Keyboard Modification

After I started programming on my new Apple][+ computer, my coworker Randy at Rockwell let me borrow a few of his computer magazines. I wanted to read all about the latest enhancements that were available for my computer. The Dan Paymar *Lowercase Adaptor Interface PROM* fascinated me and that adaptor was instrumental in encouraging me to invest in an EPROM programmer so that I could design my own lowercase character set. I was also very interested in adding some digital logic to the piggy-back circuit board of my Apple][+ keyboard in order to provide a CapLock function, and I thought that adding a tiny LED to the inside of the cap over the SHIFT key would be totally awesome to visually show the state of the SHIFT key. I also wanted to add a pushbutton to the left of the left SHIFT key. That small pushbutton would set or clear a specific bit in the keyboard data byte in order to generate all the other ASCII characters that the Apple][+ keyboard could not generate.

When I started to design the keyboard modification circuit, I had just accepted employment in the Digital Simulation Laboratory at Hughes Aircraft and I had access to virtually any data book available. Also, I was not hesitant at all in opening up my Apple][+ and doing some initial testing on the piggy-back circuit board of the keyboard using a few logic chips from my growing toolbox. I had a Heathkit oscilloscope so I could actually view some of the signals on this circuit board. *The Apple][Circuit Description* by Winston D. Gayler helped me to understand the function of S2 and a 6-pad connector on the piggy-back circuit board that contains two electrical bowties that have to be cut in order to modify bits 4 and 5 of the keyboard data byte. If I recall correctly, my testing was more trial and error rather than from experience when I began designing the keyboard modification circuit shown in Figure V.26.1.

Select Input		Data Inputs				Strobe	Output
B	A	C0	C1	C2	C3	G	Y
X	X	X	X	X	X	H	L
L	L	L	X	X	X	L	L
L	L	H	X	X	X	L	H
L	H	X	L	X	X	L	L
L	H	X	H	X	X	L	H
H	L	X	X	L	X	L	L
H	L	X	X	H	X	L	H
H	H	X	X	X	L	L	L
H	H	X	X	X	H	L	H

Table V.26.1. 74LS153 Truth Table

The 74LS153 dual 1-of-4 data selector device is the perfect logic chip that can be used in order to generate all of the ASCII characters that are unavailable on the Apple][+ keyboard. The truth table for the 74LS153 data selector device is shown in Table V.26.1. Select Input A is controlled by the Pushbutton switch I placed to the left of the left SHIFT key and Select Input B is controlled by the state of the CapLock flip-flop as shown in Figure V.26.1. Both of these signals are enabled by a Double-Pole Double-Throw (DPDT) switch that I added to my keyboard modification circuit. The 74LS153 along with S2 and the 6-pad connector pass bit 5 of the generated keyboard data byte back into the keyboard logic in order to derive the lowercase characters. On the other hand, bit 4 must be inverted in order to derive the ASCII characters that are not available on the keyboard from those characters that are available on the keyboard.

Push Button	SHIFT Key	CTRL Key	Input Character	Input ASCII	Output ASCII	Output Character
ON	ON	ON	L	0x0C	0x1C	fs
ON	ON	ON	O	0x0F	0x1F	us
ON	ON	OFF	K	0x4B	0x5B	[
ON	ON	OFF	L	0x4C	0x5C	\
ON	ON	OFF	M	0x4D	0x5D	]
ON	ON	OFF	O	0x4F	0x5F	_
ON	OFF	OFF	k	0x6B	0x7B	{
ON	OFF	OFF	l	0x6C	0x7C	|
ON	OFF	OFF	m	0x6D	0x7D	}
ON	OFF	OFF	n	0x6E	0x7E	~
ON	OFF	OFF	o	0x6F	0x7F	rub
ON	OFF	OFF	p	0x70	0x60	`

Table V.26.2. Generation of Unavailable Characters

Bit 5 is properly handled by means of S2 connectivity in order to create lowercase and uppercase ASCII characters. Of course, this assumes that the character generator EPROM contains the bit images (or pixels) for the characters normally in the 0x60 to 0x7F ASCII range and not for a repeat of the characters from the 0x40 to 0x5F ASCII range. The inversion of bit 4 is accomplished by using the Pushbutton switch to the left of the left SHIFT key in combination with an available character which is very much like deriving a control character using the CTRL key. Table V.26.2 shows how to derive the unavailable characters from the available keyboard characters, the SHIFT key, and the Pushbutton. The Pushbutton is a normally open switch so that it does not modify normal keyboard logic when it is not being pressed.

The piggy-back circuit board contains a 555 timer circuit for the REPEAT key that is connected to a signal called Any Key Down (AKD). The REPEAT key in combination with any keyboard key generates multiple instances of that pressed key. My keyboard modification circuit uses the AKD signal along with an inverted SHIFT key signal to provide automatic toggling of CapLock when the SHIFT key is held a bit longer than normal typing. This is accomplished by generating a digital pulse using a half-monostable circuit made up of a capacitor, a resister, and an inverter for both of these signals. When CapLock is ON, an LED mounted in the cap of the left SHIFT key glows. The DPDT switch disables CapLock simply by pulling the CLR input of the CapLock flip-flop to ground in order to force its output low. The DPDT switch also disables the Pushbutton by connecting Select Input A to +5 volts.

There is sufficient room to mount the keyboard modification circuit board to the left side of the piggy-back circuit board which in turn is connected to the keyboard using a 40-pin dual incline connector. I use a short length of 10-connector ribbon cable between the keyboard modification circuit board and the piggy-back circuit board. The ten signals include +5 volts, ground, SHIFT, AKD, and the 6-pad connector. Also, the LED and the Pushbutton each require two leads to the keyboard modification circuit board and the DPDT slide switch is mounted directly onto the keyboard modification circuit board. I have no idea why anyone would choose to disable the CapLock function or the ability to generate those ASCII characters that are unavailable on the Apple][+ keyboard. Regardless, the keyboard modification circuitry can be selectively disabled when desired.

27. Last Concluding Thoughts

There have been many books and articles published telling the story about the history, the evolution, and the people, some of whom are definitely characters, who have been involved in the Computer Revolution. I must say that I was part of that revolution, though perhaps more realistically on the periphery of that revolution. Ken Williams did attract a host of other entrepreneurs to Oakhurst, California, where Sierra On-Line was located. Like these other entrepreneurs, he was involved in developing certain programs and software products that were targeted for the soon-to-be-released Apple //c. The Apple //c was very hush hush, and indeed, access was strictly *on a need to know* basis. It was fascinating to be living in Oakhurst in that period of time and witness those events personally, and to know that Wozniak and Jobs were among those who occasionally visited Williams. I know that there are many others like me who look back upon those years with a high degree of nostalgia. It was a glorious time to be writing software for the Apple][family of computers!

Even today I must admit that the Apple][computer holds a unique charm for me, and that charm continuously draws me into its technical and software environment. People like Gerard Putter and Richard Dreher certainly must also experience this Apple][charm as well. They have created invaluable tools, one software and the other hardware, that keep Apple][enthusiasts like me motivated and excited about creating more useful software and hardware products for this computer today. I believe that in creating DOS 4.5 it is my way of acknowledging and demonstrating the level of my understanding and my proficiency for the Apple][computer solely in terms of its hardware. It was fortunate that I studied Electrical Engineering at University rather than Computer Science. I certainly absorbed enough Computer Science during my professional career designing and building very, very high speed radar and sensor data collection systems.

DOS 4.5 is also the culmination of all of my ideas that are derived from my original DOS 4.1 Wish List and from the *parameter needs* of a large number of commercial software programs. Understanding those commercial software programs was vital in focusing my attention in order to design and to provide an interface between DOS 4.5 internals and DOS 4.5 users. I suppose that studying Control Systems and viewing DOS similarly as a system having inputs, outputs, and feedback loops all contributed in how I wanted to design DOS 4.5 as the proverbial *black box* not to have its internals recklessly poked and prodded. At least for the most part I believe that I have succeeded in designing an Apple][disk operating system and file and volume management system that fulfills all of my software needs. I certainly think that DOS 4.5 is capable of fulfilling the needs of others, particularly the owners of the CFFA card and the users of commercial programs like *Family Roots* who do not utilize ProDOS. This has been an incredible journey for me and I have enjoyed solving every problem and every issue that has come my way while I was developing, designing, and writing DOS 4.5.

I still believe that there is a huge potential use for the 6502-microprocesser IRQ and NMI interrupts in some sort of hardware/software product. What that product is, is yet another mystery to me. But I still keep thinking about potential uses of interrupts in view of how much fun I had in implementing interrupts on my clock card. And that is part of the charm that the Apple][generates because of its open architecture. It allows people to build their own peripheral interface cards and to seat them into a real computer slot! I was so fortunate to have the opportunity to experiment and to design and to tryout my ideas that significantly increased my knowledge and my understanding of digital electronics and software design. There is no better classroom than an engineer's laboratory, and my laboratory happened to be my garage. Others may have a basement or a spare room for their laboratory. The point is, book knowledge is essential for understanding theory, but the real learning happens when you apply that theory and build something that is your own design, be it something intellectual or something tangible, for both are meaningful and both stimulate creativity. At least that is the case for me especially when I recall that the original Apple and Apple I computer were first designed and built in a garage.

I have yet to explore integrating my love for the Apple][hardware and software and my love for model railroading, specifically S-gauge that is used by the American Flyer model trains. I have boxes and boxes of these trains and many accessories stored in my garage. Perhaps it is time I introduce Mr. American Flyer to Mr. Apple. The relationship could be rather exciting if not downright explosive. Oh, not in the sense of Addams Family explosive, but in the sense of opening up a whole new world of awesome challenges, struggles, creativity, and a whole lot of downright fun.

Today's generation of young engineers have the opportunity to explore computer-assisted or computer-associated projects particularly with the affordable Raspberry Pi computer. The Raspberry Pi is the size of a credit card having four USB ports, an Ethernet port, HDMI video and audio, raw video, and stereo sound outputs, and it only requires an input of five volts at 2.4 amps for full operation and control. The Pi computer uses a micro Secure Digital (SD) memory card that hosts its UNIX-like operating system and its C language compiler and linker. It provides twenty-six General Purpose Input/Output (i.e. GPIO) pin connections, or ports to the outside world. The GPIOs are software configurable to be an input or an output port that accept or provide a 3.3-volt digital signal, respectively. That is totally genius.

I designed my Sunrise/Sunset computer assisted controller around the Raspberry Pi to control all of my outside decorative lightening. My control software considers my location on planet Earth in terms of longitude, latitude, and azimuth in order to calculate precisely when sunrise and sunset occurs each day of the year. The software refers to an input configuration file having selectable offsets in order to adjust program timing so that my decorative lights turn ON thirty minutes after sunset and turn OFF forty-five minutes before sunrise. One GPIO pin is used as a 3.3-volt output port in order to illuminate the LED of a TRIAC controller. When the TRIAC is turned ON, 120 volts of Alternating Current (AC) is gated to a medium-duty 120 volt AC electromagnetic relay. This relay can control an AC load of up to fifteen amps at 240 volts AC. The AC transformer that provides the twelve volts AC to my decorative lights draws no more than eight amps at 120 volts AC through the relay. As the days become longer and the nights shorter my decorative lights turn ON and turn OFF according to sunset and sunrise, respectively. And, as the days become shorter and the nights longer my decorative lights are appropriately turned ON and turned OFF.

There is absolutely no need to make any further adjustments to this decorative light controller throughout the year. The Raspberry Pi assisted controller is totally maintenance free because it receives its time-of-day from the Internet by means of a USB wireless adapter that communicates with my wireless Internet Router. There must be an interesting project or two that could tie Mr. Apple to Mr. Raspberry Pi. I already use a Keyspan serial to USB adapter with my Apple //e and my Apple MacBook Pro. And, I already have the programming tools on the Raspberry Pi to write even more C language programs. The best part is that the Raspberry Pi only costs around $45.00. It has massive programming power and agility for just pennies in investment cost. The only thing remaining is applying a little knowledge, a little enthusiasm, and a little creativity.

Would I trade those early years in learning how to program on an Apple][for present day years to learn how to program on the Raspberry Pi or other similar UNIX computer? I am very fond of all those past memories, and software and hardware versions in those years did not change quite so often. It is surprising how many years DOS 3.3 survived. Today, it seems like my iPad or my iPhone receives a new iOS update every other month or so. Software development occurs at a frenzied pace now, and considerations for size of application and available memory are totally unimportant. Of course, I could not last even ten minutes in today's aerospace industry because I do not have the understanding or the experience of the tools that today's young engineers have access to nor do I have their current intellectual growth processes as a foundation. My intellectual foundation was the slide rule where the knowledge of concepts was tested rather than having to reach a particular numerical result. So I am satisfied with my memories and the fascinating experiences that I had, and the interesting characters that I happened to meet along the way. It is comforting to know that through my travels in time I may have touched someone else's curiosity.

Curiosity in and of itself is the driving force for all intellectual achievements. Without curiosity nothing would have been created. There would simply be no interest in building the world of today without curiosity. Furthermore, curiosity paired with mankind's fundamental and stubborn laziness would never have prompt the design and development of the Industrial Revolution. The Industrial Revolution was sparked by the great mathematician, physicist, astronomer, theologian, and author Isaac Newton. It was Isaac Newton's *Philosophiae Naturalis Principia Mathematica* that directly paved the way to our modern world. Laziness, the fundamental human character is what drives mankind to create a world of comfort, pleasure, and safety. Laziness is the star ingredient in the First Postulate that formulates the Theory of Volitional Science.

It was pure laziness that prompt me to create the theoretical design equations for a multiple input operational amplifier summer while I was an Electrical Engineering student. My paper detailing the process in how I arrived at these theoretical design equations was published by IEEE and my paper is the reason why my Electrical Engineering professors submitted me for the Alton B. Zerby Outstanding Student Award. Furthermore, it was my curiosity that continuously drove all of my electrical engineering pursuits. Here is the full story of how laziness, paired with my curiosity, drove me to write my paper on the design of multiple-input operational amplifier summers.

Back in 1981 I registered for Professor Gene H. Hostetter's course in Operational Amplifiers (op amps), which was about seven years before his untimely death in 1988. Dr. Hostetter, still a young man, presented the course materials in syllabus format because this syllabus would eventually become the basis of an electrical engineering textbook. He believed that for learning to be successful it was necessary and important to apply the new theory and concepts he presented in lecture format to real-life design problems. Dr. Hostetter created a huge array of design problems that were generic to the design of multiple input op amp summers. He also wanted his current students to filter out those problems that best helped them to learn the course material, and those particular design problems would be included in his forthcoming textbook. I recall Dr. Hostetter assigning fifty design problems on a beautiful Friday afternoon and expecting their solutions by Monday afternoon. The assignment was given in two parts: solve all fifty problems using the techniques he had discussed in class and then solve all fifty problems again to remove all Direct Current (DC) voltage imbalances at the input connections of the op amp. A total of one hundred homework problems due Monday would surely prevent any other weekend plans, and I did have plans to party that weekend.

I solved the first two design problems Friday evening. They each took about thirty minutes to complete before and after considering all DC voltage imbalances. I could not believe that this weekend was going to be spent doing nothing but this homework, and only this homework. Being incredibly lazy by nature drove my initial curiosity to apply Kirchhoff's Voltage Law for a closed loop circuit and Ohm's Law for parallel resistance vis-à-vis what Dr. Hostetter presented in class for general op amp theory. It seemed as though the more I manipulated those op amp equations with these two fundamental laws, the more I started to see interesting and new relationships begin to develop between the variables on the positive side of the op amp and the variables on the negative side of the op amp along with some feedback from the output of the op amp. By the end of the evening I had developed a set of equations that I called the *front door equations* and a set of equations that I called the *back door equations*. Incredible as it seems, these two independent sets of equations actually reduced to a shared commonality. I now had a tremendously powerful set of theoretical design equations that I could use in order to solve any multiple input op amp summer design problem. By Saturday afternoon I had solved all one hundred of Dr. Hostetter's homework problems mostly by visual inspection! That is, I performed little if any calculations to solve these problems. To be sure, I spent the rest of the weekend at a well-deserved party totally enjoying myself.

Early Monday morning I met with Dr. Hostetter in his office and presented to him the process I used to develop my op amp design equations. Understand, he had been teaching this subject for nearly twenty years. He was amazed, flabbergasted, excited, and could not wait for class that afternoon. I declined his offer to present my design equations to my classmates because Dr. Hostetter used a brilliant lecture technique that made any topic he discussed easy to follow and easy to understand. In summary, all of my classmates scored 100% on their midterm exam. A year or two later my professor Clement J. Savant, Jr., asked if he could publish my design equations in his forthcoming textbook *Electronic Circuit Design An Engineering Approach.* I gave him a resounding **YES!**

Whatever your particular talents might be or whatever your personal aspirations are, your innate curiosity of perhaps building a star ship, or a star gate, or growing a garden of flowers, will always be realized when you utilize the power of your inbred laziness. It is this wonderful human characteristic from which we can all benefit and for which we can all utilize. Use your curiosity to unlock your full potential and let your desire for more leisure, more down-time, and more pleasure reward you with a better understanding of Mother Nature. She is the ultimate judge on what is good, what works, and what will always survive!

VI. Autobiographical Information

Grandfather Vrbančić was born in Trg, Croatia, once a province of Yugoslavia, and he was named Vid. Vid decided to immigrate to the United States around 1907, and he joined his older brother in Rankin, Pennsylvania. There, he and Marko worked in the coal mines. This work did not appeal to him, so he moved to Cleveland, Ohio, to work in the steel mill industry. Vid did not have a profession and he had no desire to learn a trade, so he became one of the many immigrant laborers living in the Cleveland area. There were many other Croatian and Slovenian immigrant laborers living in the same suburbs, and they tended to retain their European style of living and speak their native languages. Vid had lived in America for nearly ten years when he met Veronika Sneperger. Veronika had not been in America as long as Vid, but she became far more fluent in English than he. She was also fluent in six other languages. Vid and Veronika were married on June 25, 1917, in Saint Paul's Church and they moved into a lovely, but small apartment on the east side.

Veronika's mother Tvka (Eva) Stefančić had already died in 1910 and the steel mill industry was no longer manufacturing wartime supplies by the 1920's. Vid was finally laid off in 1921 and he could not find any other work in the Cleveland area. He did not want to move his wife, daughter Josephine, and son Andrew to Rankin where his younger brother Franjo was now living and working as a policeman. Veronika's father Jure, a widower for over ten years now, wrote many letters to Vid and Veronika and pleaded with them to return to Croatia. He even promised to give them his home in Maklen and all of his farm land if they would agree to care for him in his old age. Vid finally relented and he and his family set sail back to Croatia. Unfortunately, Jure had blatantly lied to both Vid and Veronika as he never intended to give them his home or any of his farm land. He also did not want Vid working his farm land using the methods Vid had learned while he was growing up in Trg. Regardless of their near hopelessness, Mathew was born in February, 1922, in Maklen.

By 1923 the steel mill industry in Cleveland had converted back to manufacturing household and industrial supplies, and they sent pleas to European countries for mill workers. The industry even offered to pay the man's passage and assist him in finding an apartment. Even though Josephine and Andrew were American citizens, Vid, Veronika, and Mathew were not. When Vid inquired about bringing his family to America, he was told he would need to become an American citizen, have $2000 in a savings account, provide an adequate place for his family to live, and have the required fare for their passage from Maklen to Cleveland. So, if Vid took the job offer, he would have to leave his family behind. After much soul searching and in view of being duped and lied to by Jure, Vid did accept the job offer to return to Cleveland. But, to make financial matters even worse, Vid left Croatia six months before the birth of his fourth child in February, 1924. Grandmother named him Valentin because Father was born on Saint Valentine's Day.

Jure's property would have rightfully gone to his son George (Jure in Croatian) before it would go to Veronika if Jure should die. But George had left for America in 1899 and was never heard from again. Jure never trusted banks or a hiding place at home for his money, so he carried all of his cash with him and made this fact known to all. In 1925 Jure's cousin shot him through the heart and decapitated him while he was taking a shortcut through the woods. To this day there is tree with a four foot cross carved into its bark marking the crime spot. It is believed that teenage boys in the neighborhood keep that cross scrapped clean of bark and retell the killing of Jure. No one was officially charged with the crime, but Jure's cousin admitted to the crime on his deathbed. Even though Veronika inherited her father's home in Maklen and all of his farm lands, life was still very hard for Grandmother raising and feeding her four growing children without her husband there.

341

Josephine and Andrew both attended a one-room school in Brod Moravice; Mathew and Valentin were still too young to attend school. They explored the surrounding villages and farms, but were afraid to venture into the woods where their grandfather had been murdered. They did explore several of the caves in the area only when an older boy accompanied them. Grandmother's farm had many fruit trees they could climb and they would feast on the fruit. Vid wrote to his family often and told them he was progressing well with all of the requirements needed to bring everyone to Cleveland. He sent Veronika sufficient funds for her to obtain passport photos, visas, clothes, and luggage necessary for the long journey to America. Many government officials had to stamp their passport papers. These included officials in Brod Moravice, officials in the municipality of Delnice, officials in the district of Rijeka, officials in the city of Zagreb (the capital of Croatia), and finally officials in the city of Belgrade (the capital of Yugoslavia). In each case there were fees to be paid to the official for each paper and visa they stamped, and for every outstretched hand (otherwise the papers and visas would be confiscated). In 1930 Veronika and her four children left Maklen, Croatia, forever and boarded the USS Paris in Le Havre, France, for their voyage to the United States of America.

Father says he remembers when the Statue of Liberty first became visible because all of the passengers crowded to that side of the ship to get a good look at the Lady who promised so much to the newly arriving immigrants. When he gazed upon the statue, he was puzzled why everyone seemed so excited at the sight, but he was only six years old. The ship docked at Ellis Island and everyone had to file through the various designated checkpoints. Father remembers having his hair and body examined, and he was given a mental aptitude test which he thought was some sort of game. Once everyone was examined and tested, Veronika gathered up her children and luggage and boarded a train to Cleveland. When they arrived in Cleveland, Father met his father Vid for the first time. I can only imagine what that stern-faced man had to say, if anything, to his youngest son? Everyone was ushered up to a second floor apartment that had three bedrooms. No one seems to remember when Father's name was changed from Valentin to Walland. Since Father did not speak English, it is believed that a teacher at East Madison Grade School misunderstood the name Valentin when Father pronounced it for her, and she changed it to Walland. Father has been called Wally ever since.

I was named after Father so I was given the Junior designation. Over the years the name Walland coupled with the last name Vrbančić has given many of my teachers and counselors tremendous pause in how to address me and how to pronounce my name. The diacritic marks over the two "c's" of my last name provided even more confusion except to another Eastern European raised speaking any of the Serbo-Croatian dialects. I have always been called Philip to differentiate me from Father. That part of my journey through time has always been very interesting to me. The fact that I was born with a moderately severe speech impediment, a stutter, has not been so interesting, and only those who also have a stutter know precisely why.

We lived in California and I still have very vivid memories when I was very young, lying on a throw rug in our living room listening to Mother practice her violin. She produced the most wonderful music to my ears and it was then that I became very much attracted to that instrument. Mr. Joe Burger came to my fourth grade classroom looking for potential music students. When he played *The Flight of the Bumblebee* by Nikolai Rimsky-Korsakov, I was forever charmed. I immediately requested a permission slip for my parents to sign so that I could study the violin under Mr. Burger. Mother rented a student-sized violin to see how well I would progress before considering buying a decent instrument. She must have been very happy with my progress that year because she convinced Father to invest in a "very nice" instrument. Mother took me to meet Mr. Lewis Main in central Long Beach to select my violin. Mr. Main took me alone into his studio at the back of his home where I saw hundreds of instruments, some still wet with varnish, hanging from wires stretched high across the room. He wanted to talk to me privately in order to evaluate what sort of personality I had. He said he could match the violin to the student, much like in the Harry Potter book where Mr. Ollivander matched the wand to the student wizard. I had to wait some months before Mother received a call from Mr. Main. She was so excited and told me Mr. Main had found my violin.

Apparently, many appraisers traveled about England to attend estate sales, and the appraiser who worked with Mr. Main only purchased instruments at those particular sort of sales. My violin, a *Gemünder Art* Violin (A266), was handcrafted in 1930 by Oscar A. Gemünder of August Gemünder & Sons, New York, New York. It was purchased new, originally for a young English girl who was beginning her studies on the violin. So, this instrument has traveled across the Atlantic Ocean twice before I became its second owner. Not only did Mr. Main match the instrument to me perfectly, he matched an 1801 French violin to my younger sister a year later. Many years passed when I discovered that the American violinist Camilla Wicks was a close friend to the Main family, and when she and Mr. Main's son were teenagers, they would spar endlessly to see who was the better violinist! When my parents purchased my violin, Mr. Main's son was already a professional violinist and he performed primarily in Las Vegas, Nevada. Camilla Wicks performed as an international soloist. As for my study of the instrument after Mr. Burger, my private violin teachers included Carol Higley (Lakewood, California) in elementary and junior high school, Professor Frank Bellino (Denison University, Granville, Ohio) in high school, Professor Stanley Plummer (University of California, Los Angeles, California) while at University, and Mr. Allan Carter (Long Beach, California) when I wanted to study and perform chamber music in my mid-forties. Plummer and Carter were both students of Vera Barstow (Pasadena, California), though perhaps nearly a generation apart.

I always excelled in mathematics and science classes during high school, so I decided to study Zoology at UCLA as an undergraduate in the mid-sixties after I was graduated from high school. At that time Mother, a registered nurse, was managing the department of surgery at a local hospital and her vision was to send me to medical school after graduation from University. Father, on the other hand, thought my talents were more inclined towards engineering. He was a graduate of the University of Southern California, school of Industrial Engineering, and he was a licensed Professional Engineer. My secret dream or illusion was to become a concert violinist, or at least a professional orchestral musician. Honestly, I was too immature when I attended UCLA, let alone live on campus at Sproul Hall. I was not passionate enough about any of my studies and, unfortunately, I did not have sufficient time nor talent to adequately prepare my lessons for Professor Plummer. It was a dynamic, historical time to attend University during the mid-sixties. The political arena was in an uproar with President Reagan in office. The war in Vietnam was still being waged. Communists like Angela Davis (a student of Herbert Marcuse) were teaching and giving lectures down the hall from my required Political Science (clearly, an oxymoron) class. She and others were permitted to corrupt the minds of children with their lectures of political fantasy, socialism, and the destruction of God-given values and rights. In hindsight, I should have stepped back, attended a community college for a year or two, so I could mature a bit more emotionally.

One particularly horrifying experience I had while I was a student at UCLA was when I walked into my second quarter German class and saw the instructor's name written on the blackboard: Frau Milovanović. She pronounced my name perfectly and clearly, rolling the "r" in my last name majestically, when she took attendance, and she ordered me to stay after class. I knew she was Serbian, or, at least her husband was Serbian, but that did not matter to me. When the other students left the classroom and were out of earshot, she told me I was a "dirty, filthy Croatian" and she wanted to know if I was going to give her any "trouble" (she used other colorful language as well). Literally, shaking in my boots, I told her I was born an American and I did not have any resentment towards any ethnic group of people. I worked my tail off in that class and I managed to squeak by with a "C" grade. She found fault in most everything I wrote. After the final exam I thanked her for all of the "special" attention she gave me! At least I did not have a "melt down" entirely, but finished my studies, and was graduated with a Bachelor's of Science degree in Zoology.

Father suggested I enroll in a two-year program through USC Medical Center for training as an Orthopedic Physician's Assistant. I thoroughly enjoyed every aspect of that program, I completed all of the requirements, and I earned my certificate to work as an OPA. I was quickly hired by a local hospital where I worked for over nine years. By the mid-seventies I had already worked as an OPA for about four years when I experienced some sort of intellectual "awakening" and decided Father was right after all, and I should have studied engineering, particularly Electrical Engineering. My epiphany to return to another tour of undergraduate studies was perhaps precipitated by the lectures I was attending at that time. The lectures were given by the renowned Astrophysicist Andrew J. Galambos, PhD. Professor Galambos was now an entrepreneur giving lectures on Volitional Science. I had already enrolled in his V-201 course which continued for over a year, one three-hour lecture once a week with a few weekend sessions as well. Previous to the V-201 course, I had enrolled in Professor Galambos's V-50 course which was now being presented by J. S. Snelson. It would not be possible for me to summarize here the knowledge I gained from the V-50 and the V-201 courses, and from several other lectures I attended to celebrate unique and historical events.

Before I enrolled in the OPA program at USC Medical Center, I did work as a phlebotomist in a doctor's office for nearly two years. Both doctors treated obese patients using diet and an array of medications they prescribed and provided onsite. In the early 1970's it was common practice to prescribe either Dextroamphetamine Sulfate or Levoamphetamine Sulfate (the enantiomer of amphetamine), or any of the combinations of these powerful and addicting drugs with other ingredients to help promote weight loss. More importantly, I had a lot of spare time during working hours, and my manager allowed me to read. In fact, she encouraged me to read the works of Ayn Rand. I even attended a few meetings where I was introduced to laissez-faire capitalism. Years later I suppose that when I heard Snelson's presentation of V-50 I was entirely comfortable with the subject of capitalism, and I was amazed at how far the concepts of Galambos had surpassed those of Rand. After attending the V-201 course, it was very difficult for me to manage the "blab forth syndrome", and I was guilty of trying to explain some of the concepts from V-201 to my colleagues for many, many years. Once again, it is something that is difficult to explain in short order.

It was completely normal for me to take apart, dismantle, and study the innards of every toy, train, erector set, chemistry set, or electrical set Santa brought me when I was young, and reconstruct that toy to working order, without inflicting any significant internal damage. Countless times Father would see a radio or tape recorder completely disassembled on the floor of my room and ask me, laughingly, "How long until it works again?" This sense of curiosity even when I was very young should have given me a clue as to what I should have initially studied at University. I have felt some degree of regret that it took me nearly ten years after high school to realize my mistake. Electrical Engineering became my absolute passion. I worked full time on second shift at the hospital and during the morning hours I attended at least three lecture classes and I included one laboratory class each semester for the next five years. IEEE published my original paper that detailed my theoretical design equations for multiple input operational amplifier summers, and my professors submitted me for the Alton B. Zerby Outstanding Student Award. I won first place in the Region Six IEEE Student Paper contest and placed third nationally that same year during WESCON in 1982. My operational amplifier design equations were also published in a textbook written by one of my professors on that subject. All of these accomplishments coupled with a 4.0 GPA gave me many choices for my next employer. Father worked for Rockwell International, though it was originally known as North American Aviation. I did interview at TRW and I received a very lucrative job offer, but I decided to join the team at Rockwell, in the Space Shuttle Simulation Laboratory. I was hired about five months before the launch of STS-1, thus changing my hospital scrubs for a coat and tie, and a whole lot more money!

About three months after Rockwell hired me, the Simulation Laboratory manager hired a Computer Science Engineer to join the ranks of Initialization Engineers. He and I had the daunting task of learning how to initialize the computers and electronics that comprised the total simulation of a Space Shuttle trajectory from Main Engine Cutoff (MECO) to landing at a few selected sites within the United States. The computers that were initialized with flight and target parameters included a PDP-11 and two Xerox mainframes. The mainframes were initially programmed using front-panel rocker switches: the Sigma 5 had 16 KB of magnetic core memory and the Sigma 9 had 64 KB of magnetic core memory. We used Hollerith cards to insert faults into the General Purpose Computers (GPCs) like those aboard the shuttle. We used a color Eidophor projector to project visual images of our landing site runways into a shuttle cockpit simulator in which the astronauts trained. Finally, we used Nova computers by DEC and DEC word processing software to generate all required customer documentation and, I might add, to play Adventure.

My system initialization colleague was an early Apple][owner when Integer Basic was first available in ROM. The following year Rockwell offered a home computer purchase program and provided us the choice between an IBM PC or the Apple][+ which had the Autostart ROM. My colleague strongly encouraged me to request the Apple computer, and he assisted me in selecting the monitor, the disk drive, and the printer accessories. The total cost was a lot of money for me, but Rockwell loaned me the money and paid the total cost. I repaid the interest-free loan through weekly payroll deductions making the purchase relatively painless. Thus, my dream of having my own personal computer was fullfilled. My ever-constant V-50 and V-201 "blab forth syndrome" did interest another colleague of mine who actually enrolled in the V-50T (i.e. "T" for Tape) course. Later, he enrolled in the V-201 and many other "V" courses after completing V-50T. In fact, he became the personal assistant to Professor Galambos during the last and final trip Galambos made to Budapest, Hungary, his native country. Mrs. Galambos stayed behind to manage the curriculum of their Free Enterprise Institute (FEI). Professor Galambos recognized that he was beginning to display the symptoms of Alzheimer's disease and he entrusted my colleague with handling more and more of the private living affairs for both he and his wife. Andrew J. Galambos and Suzanne J. Galambos established their Natural Estates Trust that was to manage all of their Intellectual Property. From my vantage point it appeared to me that my colleague participated in and contributed to what I considered to be dishonorable activities not in the favorable interests of this Natural Estates Trust. My colleague's activities primarily involved the convoluted publishing of *Sic Itur Ad Astra* by Andrew J. Galambos after his death on April 10, 1997.

I became fascinated with all aspects of the Apple][+ computer, and I wanted to incorporate it into my studies for my Master's degree. My assigned advisor was analyzing tomographic reconstructions of the human spinal column, and he thought perhaps I could assist him. He wanted to be able to make measurements between any two points within the computer image of a spinal column, even after rotating or enlarging the image. I was tasked to develop the Fortran programs that could be launched on a Microsoft Z80 Softcard in an Apple][+ that would provide him with these capabilities. I found an ingenious way to reduce the size of the three-dimensional rotational matrix in order to accelerate data image processing and the remapping of the resulting HIRES image to the computer display. My professor was very pleased with my progress. However, I was becoming increasingly interested in high-speed graphics animation, and the only way I thought I could learn that technology was to work for Ken

Williams at Sierra On-Line. I terminated my work on my Master's degree, I gave notice to Rockwell, I packed my bags, and I moved to Oakhurst, California.

At Sierra On-Line I was tasked to assist a colleague in migrating *ScreenWriter* to the new Apple //e which was recently available for purchase. On another project I wrote all of the I/O routines and ICON drawing routines for HomeWord Speller. When I started working as a self-employed contractor, I was given the *Goofy's Word Factory* project which was a children's computer game to teach English grammar. Williams had a license to display certain Disney characters on a bit-mapped computer display per approval by Disney for visual likeness, color, and movement. I would have finished *Goofy's Word Factory* if John (Williams's brother), the assigned designer of the game, could have developed the third game feature (and strategy) in a timely fashion. He apparently could not do so before I secured a position at Hughes Aircraft Company back in Los Angeles. I did utilize Williams's high-speed graphics animation algorithms in *Goofy's Word Factory*, which I had to redesign in order to include collision detection on a dithered background. No other computer game could detect collisions on a dithered background at that time. Williams was impressed, and it was really hard to impress Williams. I stayed all of 18 months at Sierra On-Line.

The major observation I made after I was hired by Hughes Aircraft was how different their culture was to the culture I had experienced at Rockwell. At Rockwell I found it exceedingly difficult to have anyone who had written a software tool or program to explain to me how that tool or that program worked, and the algorithms the software utilized or exploited. When I was tasked to migrate a software tool from Fortran to C language at Rockwell, I found some incorrect logic that eventually affected the final output data. Given certain input parameters, this tool could calculate a three-dimensional corridor in space and either interpolate points within or extrapolate points outside of that corridor. I presented my findings to its original Fortran author showing how I could insert the same incorrect logic into the C code and generate the same wrong output data. He told me to keep the incorrect logic and not disclose my findings to management. I refused. This was totally unthinkable to me, and this would never have happened at Hughes. In fact, CIP awards were presented to engineers who found such errors in software and who reported those errors to management. The Hughes culture encouraged the aggressive sharing of knowledge, and it gave rewards to those who made software improvements. The Rockwell culture cultivated self-preservation tactics where knowledge was thought to be job security and not to be shared, but to be kept undisclosed. Hughes certainly provided me with a great opportunity in the Digital Simulation Laboratory where I learned about real time executive software that was hosted on Gould SEL mainframe computers (2750, 6750, 8780, and 9780). I also learned about MIL-STD-1553 protocol communication software and real time software interface drivers to a host of various external data processors. Our purpose was to create a digital time frame in order to simulate in real time the environment for a tactical Radar Digital Processor (RDP) flying above the surface of the earth.

Due to the general slowdown in the engineering industry, I returned to Rockwell in 1990. I believed that my knowledge in real time executive software hosted on SEL mainframe computers would be my passport to a nice software engineering career closer to where I wanted to live. How I regret that major blunder in judgment because my employment at Rockwell was terminated just a few years later. I had co-authored a *White Paper* outlining the risks associated with using off-the-shelf RISC processors in certain applications, and the response from my colleagues was very unfavorable. This and my disclosure of software errors I uncovered during a Fortran-to-C language conversion eventually led to my dismissal. Fortunately, my former Hughes management was able to reinstate my position, and I was tasked to gain expertise in real time data collection software for tactical radar systems.

Hughes tactical radar systems are programmed to operate in many different modes depending upon various situations and the immediate needs that are faced by the pilot of a military aircraft. During the development of a radar mode, its processing is heavily instrumented which generates a large amount of output data as the mode progresses through its various processing stages. It is critical to capture all this generated data, primary and incidental in nature, in order to ensure and verify that the mode is behaving as expected and is generating its data according to pre-established boundaries, much like comparing the data to some gold standard. My task was to capture all of the In-phase and Quadrature (I/Q) components of radar data in real time, process certain other data components, package the data according to generated source and timestamp, and save the resulting files using some recording device. It is important to understand that there are many independent generating sources of data in a radar system whose timestamps are totally asynchronous. At a later time the data that is packaged in those files would be analyzed to determine if, in fact, the processing modes operated as expected. Physically collecting this I/Q data during real time tactical maneuvers was quite a challenge, and recorders designed to operate in this environment were costly. Preparing for a data collection session involved securing a military aircraft, a flight crew, a ground crew, and people to securely bring the recorded data back to my tempested lab. This certainly added to my responsibilities, and my mantra was to neither add, subtract, nor modify any data word or data bit while that data was in my immediate possession and while my software algorithms extracted and processed that data into prescribed data formats. Those data formats would allow the data analysis tools to function more efficiently for the mode builders.

I was thoroughly vetted and held maximum-security clearances that allowed me to process data from many different and independent classified programs not only in Los Angeles, but also in other locations, and even out of state. The general data collection software engines I began designing in the unclassified world served as my software library for every classified program to which I was assigned. Perhaps I was simply in the right place at the right time that steered my career to become the sole resident expert in Transcription Software Engines. That is, to process, encrypt, and store in real time at least a terabyte of data every second. Or, perhaps I was in the right place at the right time that allowed me to develop a task beyond its envisioned potential. There is a direct ancestral linkage between my unclassified software library of tools, routines, and transcription engines and every single classified program with which I was associated that required my tools, routines, engines, and expertise. I was practicing *code reuse* light-years before it became a topic that some managers thought could reduce software development costs. "How insightful!" I jokingly thought of management, silently, and very highly disrespectfully in my private thoughts. "How insightful."

Initially, I was given the opportunity to host my current Transcription Software engine on a newly acquired SGI Origin 300 having four bricks, or sixteen CPUs. *Code reuse* made this task fairly straightforward, thus demonstrating the Origin's practicality for this feasibility study. After a fact-finding tour to the SGI facilities at Mountain View, California, I was assigned the momentous task of designing a Transcription Software engine for an SGI Origin 3000 having eight bricks (i.e. thirty-two CPUs) running IRIX, and using Big Endian memory management. This turned out to be one of my greatest solo achievements. Even at this time, little did my management understand how effortlessly I could build my Transcription Software engines primarily using *code reuse*. I was extremely fortunate to have had one very intelligent manager who casually asked me to think about the possibility of building a digital playback system. Such a system did not yet exist. Some highly respected engineers with Ph.D. degrees had tried building an analog playback system a few years earlier with absolutely no success. Instead of analyzing the collected instrumented data, one could observe how the simulated RDP behaved when the recorded high-speed I/Q data and the slow-speed environment data were injected back into its system using a playback system. A few months later I presented my first digital playback recorder and pre-processing system, my last and greatest achievement at Raytheon (former Hughes). I was assigned the unique privilege to design and build a second digital playback recorder and pre-processing system for another classified program. That program, like the previous program which used my first digital playback recorder and pre-processing system, saved countless hours of analysis time and mission costs before I scheduled my overdue retirement.

A few years after I retired, I was presented with an astonishing diagnosis by my partner that seemed to explain some, if not all of the idiosyncrasies I have displayed my entire life as far back as elementary school: I may have been living with Asperger's. Indeed, how does one know what is truly normal; that which falls under the umbrella of a Gaussian curve? We are all volitional beings and our behavior is internal to each of us. Our brain is composed of carbon-based synapses whose billions of inter-connections and cross-connections compose the very person and personality we have become or have allowed ourselves to become. It is simply miraculous that any of our species reach total fulfillment of their dreams. I would like to believe I have come closer than most in reaching many of my major dreams and aspirations.

Now I have the time and the continuing curiosity to delve into the Disk Operating System, that is, the File and Volume Disk Management System of the Apple][computer. I now have the opportunity to create my own version of a File and Volume Disk Management System that contains the power and the flexibility I always believed an Apple][Disk Operating System ought to and could have.

I called my previous versions of Apple][DOS, DOS 4.1 and DOS 4.3. DOS 4.1 was complete with its 46th build in 2019. DOS 4.3 was complete with its eight build in 2020. What a ride I have been on! Why? To see what I could do for this wonderful machine and its magnificent architecture!

I completed DOS 4.1 in March, 2019, after I agreed to have the Build 45 Manual published by *Call-A.P.P.L.E.* I requested no fees, no incentives, nor any royalties. But I continued to innovate DOS 4.1 and Build 46 contains the final modifications I wanted to make to this DOS. I felt that I could not take DOS 4.1 any further due to the memory constraints of DOS 4.1L, and I did not want to increase its size nor add additional sectors to its volume image. However, I could continue to develop Apple][DOS if I concentrated only on the version that resides in the memory of the Language Card partition. I naïvely thought perhaps I could utilize Auxiliary Memory and move DOS there. To that end, I copied my source code for DOS 4.1H into a new directory and gave it a new name, and that was the birth of DOS 4.3. In the same fashion, from DOS 4.3 came the birth of DOS 4.5. I continued to develop DOS 4.5 for the remainder of 2020 and through 2021. As in the development of DOS 4.1 and in DOS 4.3, I have reached a point with the fifth build where I do not wish to continue any further development of DOS 4.5. And it is now time to complete the DOS 4.5 documentation as well. The End (for now?).

After all that I have seen and all that I have done during my life and in my travels through time, I am always comforted when I recall the following beautiful thought:

The diversity in the human family should be the cause of love and harmony, as it is in music where many different notes blend together in the making of a perfect chord.

~~~ Abdu'l-Bahá ~~~

Index

www.ingramcontent.com/pod-product-compliance
Lightning Source LLC
Chambersburg PA
CBHW081436190326
41458CB00020B/6222